LEADING AND MANAGING IN NURSING

LEADING AND MANAGING IN NURSING

Patricia S. Yoder Wise, R.N., C., Ed.D., C.N.A.A., F.A.A.N.

Texas Tech University Health Sciences Center
Lubbock, Texas, and Odessa, Texas

 Mosby

St. Louis Baltimore Boston Carlsbad Chicago Naples New York Philadelphia Portland
London Madrid Mexico City Singapore Sydney Tokyo Toronto Wiesbaden

Publisher: Nancy L. Coon
Executive Editor: Darlene Como
Developmental Editor: Dana Knighten
Project Manager: Chris Baumle
Production Editor: Stacy M. Guarracino
Designer: Nancy McDonald
Manufacturing Supervisor: Karen Lewis
See page 582 for photo credits.

FIRST EDITION

Printed in the United States of America

Mosby–Year Book, Inc.
11830 Westline Industrial Drive
St. Louis, Missouri 63146

Library of Congress Cataloging–in–Publication Data

Leading and managing in nursing / (edited by) Patricia S. Yoder Wise.
    p. cm.
    Includes bibliographical references and index.
    ISBN 0-8151-9244-4 (alk. paper)
    1. Nursing services--Administration. 2. Leadership. I. Yoder Wise, Pat S.
    [DNLM: 1. Nurse Administrators. 2. Leadership. 3. Personnel
Management. WY 105 L4325 1994]
RT89.L43 1995
362. 1'73'068--dc20
DNLM/DLC
for Library of Congress   94-36948
                                                                 CIP

Contributors

Nancy Beardslee, R.N., Ed.D.
Associate Professor
School of Nursing
University of Northern Colorado
Greeley, Colorado

Michael R. Bleich, R.N., M.P.H., C.N.A.A.
Vice President for Patient Care Services
Bryan Memorial Hospital
Lincoln, Nebraska;
Adjunct Assistant Professor
College of Nursing
University of Nebraska
Omaha, Nebraska

Carol Alvater Brooks, R.N., D.N.Sc., C.N.A.A.
Associate Professor, Nursing Administration
College of Nursing
Syracuse University
Syracuse, New York

Joyce N. Faris, R.N., M.S.N.
Associate Professor
Nursing and Healthcare Management
Metropolitan State College of Denver
Denver, Colorado

Jennifer Jackson Gray, R.N., M.S.N.
Specialist
School of Nursing
University of Texas
Arlington, Texas

Ginny Wacker Guido, R.N., J.D., M.S.N.
Professor and Chair
Department of Nursing
Eastern New Mexico University
Portales, New Mexico

Joseph B. Hurst, Ph.D., Ed.D.
Professor
College of Education and Allied Professions
University of Toledo
Toledo, Ohio

Mary J. Keenan, R.N., Ph.D.
Associate Professor
School of Nursing
Medical College of Ohio
Toledo, Ohio

Jacquelyn Komplin, R.N., M.S.N.
Ed.D. student
University of San Francisco

Karren Kowalski, R.N., Ph.D., F.A.A.N.
Associate Professor and Chairperson
Maternal Child Nursing Department
Rush University College of Nursing;
Director, Patient Care Services
Women's and Children's Hospital
Rush-Presbyterian-St. Luke's Medical Center
Chicago, Illinois

Mary N. McAlindon, R.N., Ed.D., C.N.A.A.
Assistant to the Vice President
Nursing Informatics
McLaren Medical Center
Flint, Michigan

Kristi D. Menix, R.N., M.S.N., C.N.A.A.
Assistant Professor
School of Nursing
Texas Tech University Health Sciences Center
Lubbock, Texas

Dorothy A. Otto, R.N., Ed.D.
Associate Professor
University of Texas-Houston Health Science Center
School of Nursing
Houston, Texas

Mary Ellen Rauner, R.N., M.A.
Vice President for Nursing
The General Hospital Center at Passaic
Passaic, New Jersey

Cindy Whittig Roach, R.N., D.S.N.
Chairperson
Adult Health Department
Beth El College of Nursing
Colorado Springs, Colorado

Lori Rodriguez, R.N., C., M.A., M.S.N.
Director of Education
El Camino Hospital
Mountain View, California

Karen Kelly Schutzenhofer, R.N., Ed.D., C.N.A.A.
Director, Critical Care Services
St. Elizabeth's Hospital
Belleville, Illinois

Arlene P. Stein, R.N., C., Ph.D.
Clinical Manager
Surgical Unit
Memorial Hospital
Colorado Springs, Colorado

Darlene Steven, R.N., M.H.S.A., Ph.D.
Associate Professor
School of Nursing
Lakehead University
Thunder Bay, Ontario, Canada

Ana M. Valadez, R.N., Ed.D., C.N.A.A., F.A.A.N.
Associate Professor
School of Nursing
Texas Tech University Health Sciences Center
Lubbock, Texas

Darla J. Vale, R.N., M.S.N., C.C.R.N.
Assistant Professor
Department of Nursing
College of Mount St. Joseph
Cincinnati, Ohio

Rose Aguilar Welch, R.N., M.S.N., Ed.D.
Assistant Professor
California State University at Dominguez Hills
Carson, California

Deborah Wendt, R.N., M.S., C.S.
Assistant Professor
Department of Nursing
College of Mount St. Joseph
Cincinnati, Ohio

Donna Westmoreland, R.N., Ph.D.
Assistant Professor
University of Nebraska Medical Center
College of Nursing
Omaha, Nebraska

Elizabeth Wywialowski, R.N., C., Ed.D., C.C.R.N.
Clinical Nurse Specialist, Spinal Cord Injury
Veterans Administration Hospital
Milwaukee, Wisconsin

DEDICATION

This book is dedicated to the families who supported all of us who created it, to the faculty who use it to develop nursing's new leaders and managers, and to the learners who have the vision and insight to grasp today's reality and mold it into the future of dynamic nursing leadership.

Instructor Preface

Leading and managing are two essential expectations of all professional nurses, and they are more important than ever in today's rapidly changing healthcare system. To lead and manage successfully, nurses must possess not only knowledge and skills but also a caring and compassionate attitude. After all, nursing management is about *people*.

Volumes of information on leadership and management principles can be found in the nursing, healthcare administration, business, and forecasting literature. The numerous journals in each of these fields offer research and opinion articles focused on improving leaders' and managers' abilities. However, in the past, many instructors who taught nursing management courses found that most of the available texts were out of touch with the realities of contemporary nursing management and with today's nursing students. Finding resources to help teach practical application of nursing management concepts and skills was even more difficult. Unlike clinical nursing texts, which offer exercises and assignments designed to provide opportunities for students to apply theory to practice, nursing leadership and management texts traditionally have offered limited opportunities of this kind. We are changing that tradition in an exciting new way by incorporating application exercises within the text and offering a companion skills workbook for students.

This book results from our strong belief in the need for a text that focuses on the nursing leadership and management issues of today and tomorrow in a totally new way. We also found that we were not alone in this belief. Before the writing of this book began, the Mosby–Year Book Company, primarily through the efforts of Darlene Como, solicited faculty members' and administrators' ideas to find out what they thought professional nurses most needed to know about leading and managing, and what kind of text would best help them obtain the necessary knowledge and skills. From their comprehensive list of suggestions, we began planning and developing this text.

CONCEPT AND PRACTICE COMBINED

Innovative in both content and presentation, *Leading and Managing in Nursing* merges theory, research, and practical application in key leadership and management areas. Our overriding concern throughout the writing of this book has been to create a text that, while well grounded in theory and concept, presents the content in a way that is *real*. Wherever possible, we have used real-world examples from the continuum of today's healthcare settings to illustrate the concepts. Because each chapter contributor has focused on synthesizing his or her assigned content, you will find no lengthy quotations in these chapters. Instead, we have made every effort to make the content as engaging, inviting, and interesting as possible. Reflecting our view of the real world of nursing management today, the following themes pervade the text:

■ The focus of healthcare is shifting from the hospital to the community.

■ Healthcare clients and the healthcare work force are becoming increasingly culturally diverse.

■ Today, virtually every professional nurse leads and manages regardless of his or her position.

■ Consumer relationships now play a central role in the delivery of nursing and healthcare.

■ Communication, collaboration, team building, and other interpersonal skills form the foundation of effective nursing leadership and management.

DIVERSITY OF PERSPECTIVES

Among this book's strengths is that the contributors themselves have been recruited from diverse settings and diverse geographical areas, enabling them to offer a broad perspective on the critical elements of nursing leadership and management roles. To help bridge the gap often found between nursing education and nursing practice, some contributors were recruited from academia; others, from practice settings. Some contributors were so enthusiastic about this project that they also volunteered to contribute to the Instructor's Resource Manual and the Nursing Leadership and Management Skills Workbook.

AUDIENCE

This book is designed for undergraduate students in nursing leadership and management courses, particularly those in BSN and BSN-completion courses. Because today's students tend to be more visually oriented than students a decade ago, we have incorporated illustrations, boxes, and a functional full-color design to stimulate their interest and maximize their learning. In addition, we have included numerous examples and "A Manager's Viewpoint" in each chapter in response to common student complaints that most nursing management texts lack relevance to the real world of nursing.

ORGANIZATION

We have organized this text around issues that are key to the success of professional nurses in today's constantly changing healthcare environment:

Part I, Managing and Leading Presents basic concepts of managing and leading, with emphasis on their application to today's changing healthcare system. It includes coverage of legal and ethical issues, strategic planning, leading change in an evolving healthcare environment, and problem solving and decision making.

Part II, Managing the Organization Discusses healthcare organizations, cultural diversity in healthcare, and various organizational structures.

Part III, Managing Resources Explains the principles and practice of quality, risk, time, information, and financial management.

Part IV, Leading and Managing People Includes discussions on team building, staff development, communication, and conflict management.

Part V, Managing Consumer Care Focuses on consumer relationships, care delivery systems, and patient-related issues.

Part VI, Managing Personal Resources Offers career management and guidance via discussion of roles, power and politics, stress management, and career management.

Since repetition plays a crucial role in how well students learn and retain new content, some topics appear in more than one chapter, and in more than one section. We have also made an effort to express a variety of different views on some topics, as in the real world of nursing.

DESIGN

A functional full-color design distinguishes this text from any other nursing management text ever published. As described in the sections below, the design is used to emphasize and identify the text's many teaching/learning strategies features to enhance learning. Full color photographs provide visual reinforcement of concepts such as body language and the changes occurring in contemporary healthcare settings, while adding visual interest. Figures elucidate and graphically depict concepts and activities described in the text.

TEACHING/LEARNING STRATEGIES

The numerous teaching/learning strategies features in this text are designed both to stimulate student interest and to provide constant reinforcement throughout the learning process. In addition, the visually appealing, full-color design itself serves a pedagogical purpose. Color is used consistently throughout the text to help the reader identify many of the various chapter elements described below:

CHAPTER OPENER ELEMENTS

Preview briefly describes the purpose and scope of the chapter.

Objectives articulate the chapter's learning goals at the application level or higher.

Questions to Consider stimulate students to think about their personal viewpoint or experience of the topics and issues discussed in the chapter.

A Manager's Viewpoint presents a contemporary nurse manager's real-world view of the aspect of managing addressed in the chapter.

ELEMENTS WITHIN THE CHAPTERS

Margin Annotations serve as quick locators for topics in the chapter and a convenient study/review aid. Margin annotations always appear in bold italic type in the margins of every chapter.

Glossary Terms appear in bold type in every chapter. They are also listed in the "Terms to Know" at the end of the "Chapter Checklist." Definitions appear in the Glossary at the end of the text.

Exercises stimulate students to think critically about how to apply chapter content to the workplace and other "real world" situations. They provide experiential reinforcement of key leading and managing skills. Exercises always appear in yellow boxes within the margins of every chapter and are numbered sequentially to facilitate using them as assignments or activities.

Research, Theory, and Literature Perspectives illustrate the relevance and applicability of current scholarship to practice. Perspectives always appear in green boxes with an "open book" logo.

Boxes contain lists, tools such as forms and worksheets, and other information relevant to chapter content that students would find useful and interesting. Boxes appear on a pale orange background in every chapter.

END OF CHAPTER ELEMENTS

Chapter Checklists summarize key concepts from the chapter in both paragraph and itemized list form. A list of glossary "Terms to Know" is included as an additional study/review aid.

References and Suggested Readings provide the student with a list of key sources for further reading on topics found in the chapter.

OTHER TEACHING/LEARNING STRATEGIES

End-of-text Glossary contains a comprehensive list of definitions of all boldfaced terms used in the chapters. As a further study aid, each definition ends with a cross-reference indicating the page number(s) in which that term is discussed.

COMPLETE TEACHING AND LEARNING PACKAGE

Together with *Leading and Managing in Nursing,* the companion workbook, the accompanying video series, and the instructor's resource manual comprise a complete teaching and learning package. Because students learn most successfully when information is presented in a variety of ways, the workbook and video series are designed to give students the opportunity to reinforce their learning both experientially and visually.

NURSING LEADERSHIP AND MANAGEMENT SKILLS to accompany Yoder Wise, LEADING AND MANAGING IN NURSING

Prepared by Mary J. Keenan, R.N., Ph.D. and Joseph B. Hurst, Ph.D., Ed.D. (who are also contributors to the text), as well as other professionals from business, academia, and healthcare, the companion workbook corresponds chapter by chapter with the text, reinforcing text content via objectives and numbered learning activities. Using detailed scenarios, case studies, role plays, and follow-up questions, the workbook provides students with ample opportunity to practice essential leading and managing skills in the classroom. Other activities include interviews with healthcare professionals, self-assessments and worksheets, and discussion questions to stimulate critical thinking about workplace situations a nurse manager would be likely to encounter. Activities are designed for individuals and small and large groups.

MOSBY'S NURSING LEADERSHIP AND MANAGEMENT VIDEO SERIES

Produced by David Wallace, Ph.D., Studio Three Productions, with Patricia Yoder Wise, R.N., C., Ed.D., C.N.A.A., F.A.A.N., as consultant, this series addresses the increasing demand for nursing graduates who can exercise leadership and management skills in today's varied healthcare settings. The series emphasizes application of essential leadership and management principles to concrete practice situations. The video medium's ability to capture and convey both verbal nuance and body language with immediacy and clarity is particularly well-suited to a series illustrating interpersonal skills. Realistic case scenarios interspersed with narrative focus on key nursing leadership and management concepts and skills, while interviews demonstrate how real-life nurse managers successfully employ these concepts and skills in their practice. A survey of academic and staff development faculty was undertaken to identify the topics for which videos were most needed. The eight titles in the series are:

Video 1: Problem Solving and Decision Making: Critical Thinking in Action
Video 2: Dealing with Difficult People
Video 3: Effective Communication
Video 4: Managing Change
Video 5: Building Teams
Video 6: Delegating Effectively and Appropriately
Video 7: Managing Conflict
Video 8: Leadership

Each video is approximately 25 minutes long and is available either individually or as part of the set. An Instructor's Resource Booklet accompanies each video.

INSTRUCTOR'S RESOURCE MANUAL with Transparency Masters and Test Bank Prepared by Ginny Wacker Guido, R.N., J.D., M.S.N. (also a contributor to the text), the Instructor's Resource Manual is a compendium of teaching suggestions prepared by contributors to the text. This manual offers practical suggestions and resources for presenting material in the text, making the most effective use of the companion workbook and video series in conjunction with the text, and testing. The chapter-by-chapter test bank includes a total of 229 multiple choice questions, with answer keys at the end of each set of chapter questions. The manual also includes 36 transparency masters of key illustrations from the text and other materials of interest.

Acknowledgments

REVIEWERS

We are indebted to our reviewers, whose insightful comments and suggestions were invaluable in helping shape the final manuscript. The end result of their efforts, as in any peer review process, is a stronger presentation. We are deeply grateful to the following people for their assistance:

Mary Ann Brandt, R.N., M.N.
Assistant Professor
Kent State University
School of Nursing
Kent, Ohio

Karen Grigsby, R.N., Ph.D.
Assistant Professor
University of Nebraska Medical Center
College of Nursing
Omaha, Nebraska

Marlene Jenkins, R.N., M.S.N., C.N.A.
Associate Faculty Coordinator
School of Health, Division of Nursing
California State University at Dominguez Hills
Carson, California

Barbara Mandleco, R.N., Ph.D.
Associate Professor
College of Nursing
Brigham Young University
Provo, Utah

Sue Wajert, R.N., M.B.A.
Program Director
Management of Healthcare Services
College of Mount St. Joseph
Cincinnati, Ohio

We also thank the numerous nurse educators and managers who participated in the surveys undertaken to plan the text and its ancillaries.

SPECIAL ACKNOWLEDGMENTS

Many people helped to make this book a reality. First, I would like to acknowledge and thank the School of Nursing at Texas Tech University Health Sciences Center in Lubbock for allowing us to use its facilities in shooting many of the photographs that appear in this book. Kathy Quilliam Gregory and Sharon Decker worked with the Texas Tech University Health Sciences Center chapter of the Texas Nursing Students Association and the

Ambassadors (a service entity) to secure volunteer models. Kathy also secured contacts and specific agency involvement. Thanks also go to the Hospice of Lubbock, Lubbock City Health Department, Total Home Health, the Veterans Administration Outpatient Clinic, and Texas Tech University Health Sciences Center Healthnet. Bob Gentry, R.N., B.S.N., and Mary Strange, R.N., B.S.N., were incredibly resourceful in securing volunteers.

Many of the Texas Tech University Health Sciences Center faculty and staff also agreed to pose for photographs. Many received calls, helped track me down, and offered encouragement, especially during the numerous deadline times. Thanks to all who make Texas Tech University Health Sciences Center School of Nursing the special place it is.

All of the contributing authors to this book worked within very tight time frames to accomplish their work. To them I extend my deepest appreciation for being responsive, making the necessary revisions, and sounding eager to hear from me whenever I called. AT&T, Federal Express, fax, and Kinko's became household words!

Special thanks go to our editor, Darlene Como, for having great insight, commitment and humor; to our developmental editor, Dana Knighten (and her predecessor), for answering questions, providing the "latest" version of whatever we were talking about, and doing all sorts of tasks that kept us on track (while keeping her sense of humor); to Patrick Watson for his creative photography; to those who exceeded our wildest expectations of involvement (you know who you are); and to Robert Thomas Wise, my husband and best friend, for being such a great sounding board and consistent supporter.

One final note: no learner can remain stagnant. The context in which nurses manage and lead is constantly changing, sometimes for the better, sometimes for the worse. The key to success is to keep learning, keep caring, and maintain our passion for nursing. That, if nothing else, must be instilled in our leaders of tomorrow.

Patricia S. Yoder Wise, R.N., C., Ed.D., C.N.A.A., F.A.A.N.
Texas Tech University Health Sciences Center
Lubbock, Texas, and Odessa, Texas

Preface to the Student

As a professional nurse in today's changing healthcare system, you will need strong leadership and management skills more than ever, regardless of your specific role. *Leading and Managing in Nursing* not only provides the conceptual knowledge you will need but also offers practical strategies to help you hone the various skills that are so vital to your success as a leader and manager.

This book is divided into six parts that reflect the key issues in nursing leadership and management. Part I helps you gain insight into the concepts that underlie contemporary leading and managing practices. Parts II and III help you apply those concepts to the organization and its resources. Part IV focuses on managing the people who make up the nursing team, while Part V focuses on the healthcare consumer. Part VI offers information and practical strategies to help strengthen your ability to manage your professional and personal self. Because repetition is a key strategy in learning and retaining new information, you'll find many topics discussed in more than one chapter. And, as in the real world of nursing, you'll often find several different views expressed on a single topic.

To help you make the most of your learning experience, try the following strategy after you complete each chapter: Stop and think about what the chapter conveyed. What does it mean for you as a leader and manager? How does the chapter's content, and your interaction with it, relate to the other chapters you have already completed? How might you briefly synthesize the content for a non-nurse friend? Reading the chapter, restating its key points in your own words, and completing the text exercises and skills workbook activities will go far to help you make the content truly your own.

We think you'll find leading and managing to be an exciting, challenging field of study, and we've made every attempt to reflect that belief in the design and approach of this book.

LEARNING AIDS

Leading and Managing in Nursing incorporates some important tools to help you learn about leading and managing and apply your new knowledge to the real world. The next few pages graphically point out how to use these study aids to your best advantage.

The vivid full-color chapter opener **photographs** and other photographs throughout the text help convey each chapter's key message while providing a glimpse into the real world of leading and managing in nursing.

Each chapter opener includes these features:

The **Preview** tells you what you can expect to find in the chapter. To help set the stage for your study of the chapter, read it first and then summarize in your own words what you expect to gain from the chapter.

The list of **Objectives** helps you focus on the key information you should be able to apply after having studied the chapter.

The **Questions to Consider** challenge you to think critically about issues in the chapter. You might want to write down your answers both before and after reading the chapter, and then compare them.

In **A Manager's Viewpoint,** practicing nurse managers offer their real-world views on how concepts presented in the chapter apply in the workplace. Has a nurse manager you know made similar or dissimilar statements?

Team Building   275

PREVIEW

This chapter explains major concepts and presents tools with which to create and maintain a smoothly functioning team. Many areas of our lives require that we work together in a smooth and efficient manner; not the least of these is the team in the work setting. Such teams often include members with a variety of backgrounds and educational preparation. A healthcare team often includes physicians, nurses, administrators, allied health professionals, and support staff such as housekeeping and dietary. Each team member has something valuable to contribute and deserves to be treated honorably and with respect. When teams are not working, all team members must change how they interact within the team.

OBJECTIVES

- Distinguish between a group and a team.
- Identify four key concepts of teams.
- Discuss the three personal questions each team member struggles to answer.
- Apply the guidelines for acknowledgment to a situation in your clinical setting.
- Compare a setting that uses the rules of the game with your current clinical setting.
- Develop an example of a team that functions synergistically, including the results such a team would produce.

QUESTIONS TO CONSIDER

- What differentiates a team from a group?
- How does one create a team?
- What are key aspects of a well-functioning team?
- What are the key issues or questions team members want to know?
- What role do agreements or guidelines play in a well-functioning team?
- How do some teams function like well-oiled machines and achieve extraordinary results?
- What are the behaviors and attitudes that destroy teams?
- Do teams go through stages of development?

A Manager's Viewpoint

Working as a team is crucial in getting the work of the unit completed. In the neonatal intensive care unit, the medical staff and nursing staff are thrown together and expected to function smoothly and effectively. Often they are told they are a team even though they may have no understanding or preparation to function as a team. Consequently, they proceed to display several ineffective team behaviors. It's important to reinforce active participation at each meeting and to remove judgments and personal dislikes of other team members. If team members validate ineffective or destruction behavior, it guarantees future ineffectiveness in the team. There needs to be agreement among team members that each must focus on the agreed-upon outcomes and support a positive, supportive process that enables achieving the outcomes. Such team behaviors are the key to keeping the true team spirit vital and alive. This approach creates the work environment that people want.

Diane Gallagher, R.N., M.S.
Unit Leader, Neonatal ICU
Women's and Children's Hospital
Rush-Presbyterian-St. Luke's Medical Center
Chicago, Illinois

affiliated teaching hospitals that provide only the clinical portion of a health education institution's teaching program. Traditionally these programs have received government reimbursement to cover the costs to the institution of the educational program that are not covered by typical fees for patient care. Costs include financial coverage for salaries of physicians who supervise students' care delivery and participate in educational programs such as teaching rounds and seminars. Currently these expenses are reimbursed based on a formula that takes into consideration the cost of caring for low-income and uninsured patients who populate academic teaching programs. Revisions in this reimbursement will need to be adjusted if the concept of universal coverage of costs is adopted.

EXERCISE 7-3
Return to the data started in the first exercise and add financial and teaching status information.

CONSOLIDATED SYSTEMS

Healthcare organizations are being organized into **consolidated systems** both through formation of multihospital systems that are for profit or not for profit and through development of networks of independently owned and operated healthcare organizations.

national hospital companies

voluntary affiliated systems

Consolidated systems tend to be organized along five levels. The first includes the large national hospital companies, most of which are investor owned; they include Hospital Corporation of America and Humana. The second level involves large voluntary affiliated systems such as Voluntary Hospitals of America, an organization that represents over 500 hospitals in the country, providing them with access to capital, political power, management expertise, joint venture opportunities, and linkages with health insurance services. The third level involves regional hospital systems such as Southwest Health Care System in New Mexico and Intermountain Health Care System in the Salt Lake area. The fourth level involves metropolitan-based systems such as Henry Ford in Detroit and the New York Health and Hospital Corporation. The fifth level is composed of the special interest groups that own and operate units organized along religious lines, teaching interests, or related special interests that drive their activities. This level often crosses over the regional, metropolitan, and national levels described above. An example of the fifth level is the Sisters of Mercy Health Corporations, which has its headquarters in Farmington Hills, Michigan and has hospitals in Michigan, Iowa, and Indiana. Some reasons for creating multiunit systems are to increase the power of the units in competing for clients, influencing public policy, and obtaining funding in an increasingly competitive and complex marketplace (Shortell, Kaluzny, et al., 1988).

regional systems

metropolitan systems

special interests

AMBULATORY BASED ORGANIZATIONS

Many health services are provided on an amb[ulatory basis ...]
tional setting for much of this care has been the [physician's] office. A growing form of group practice is prep[aid, re]ferred to as **managed care** systems, which combi[ne fund-]ing and provide comprehensive services for a fixed [fee. ...]
services is to reduce the cost of expensive acute ho[spital ...]
on out-of-hospital preventive care and illness foll[ow-up. These]
plans take a variety of forms. One form has a cen[tral agency that]
directs and salaries physician practice, such as HM[Os...]

managed care systems

HMOs

The HMO is a configuration of health agen[cies...]

The margins of each chapter contain italicized **annotations** that help you locate topics quickly. They are also a convenient study/review aid. The wide margins also provide room for you to add your own annotations and notes.

Key Terms appear in boldface type throughout the chapter. (A list of all "Terms to Know" used in the chapter appears in the "Chapter Checklists" at the end of the chapter, and the Glossary at the end of the text contains a list of their definitions.)

EXERCISE 5-4
Recall a work or personal situation where a particular individual tried to get you or a group to do something but did not succeed. Why did you/they decide not to cooperate? Think about the following factors: Was the idea silly, inappropriate, unsafe? Was the person making the suggestion not known, understood, or trusted? Was the person making the suggestion unaware of the real situation, not part of carrying out the idea, or had he/she not received permission to influence activities? Can you see that change agents and innovators need specific qualities and abilities to be effective?

EXERCISE 5-5
Plan an actual or hypothetical change that is meaningful to you in your personal, work, or school life. Select a change that allows you an opportunity to apply the principles of planned change, yet that will not overwhelm you. Using the guidelines and worksheet included in the appendix to this chapter, draft a hypothetical or actual plan for change, drawing on the chapter content and paying particular attention to the array of change principles discussed. Share your plan and the rationale used with peers or a small group of other healthcare providers. Ask for their comments and suggestions. (If you need a hypothetical change to work with, consider this one: You are the assistant manager for a home health agency. The agency administrator just informed you by memorandum that in one month, because of new reimbursement rules, the agency will begin caring for patients receiving chemotherapy. How will you prepare for this change?)

Self-Assessment: How Receptive to Change and Innovation Are You?

Read the following items. Circle the answer that most closely matches your attitude toward creating and accepting new or different ways.

1. I enjoy learning about new ideas and approaches.	YES	DEPENDS	NO
2. Once I learn about a new idea or approach, I begin to try it right away.	YES	DEPENDS	NO
3. I like to discuss different ways of accomplishing a goal or end result.	YES	DEPENDS	NO
4. I continually seek better ways to improve what I do.	YES	DEPENDS	NO
5. I frequently recognize improved ways of doing things.	YES	DEPENDS	NO
6. I talk over my ideas for change with my peers.	YES	DEPENDS	NO
7. I communicate my ideas for change with my manager.	YES	DEPENDS	NO
8. I discuss my ideas for change with my family.	YES	DEPENDS	NO
9. I volunteer to be at meetings when changes are being discussed.	YES	DEPENDS	NO
10. I encourage others to try new ideas and approaches.	YES	DEPENDS	NO

If you answered "yes" to eight to ten of the items, you are probably receptive to creating and experiencing new and different ways of doing things. If you answered "depends" to five to ten of the items, you are probably receptive to change conditionally based on the fit of the change with your preferred ways of doing things. If you answered "no" to four to ten of the items, you are probably not receptive, at least initially, to new ways of doing things. If you answered "yes," "no," and "depends," an equal number of times, you are probably mixed in your receptivity to change based on individual situations.

CHAPTER CHECKLIST

Change is an unavoidable constant in the rapidly changing healthcare delivery system. As a result, uncertainty is an element in most healthcare institutions. Anticipating and preparing for change can facilitate a more stable work environment. Creating and leading change and innovation rather than merely reacting can promote overall organizational effectiveness.

■ Change occurs in sequential stages:
  • awareness of need for change
  • experience of change
  • integration of change

■ The appropriate use of the basic managerial functions of planning, organizing, implementing, and evaluating to lead an ongoing process involved in creating and facilitating change and innovation:

Every chapter contains numbered **Exercises** that challenge you to think critically about concepts in the text and apply them to real-life situations.

Research Perspective

Burner, O., Cunningham, P., & Hattar, H. (1990). Managing a multicultural staff in a multicultural environment. Journal of Nursing Administration, 20(6), 30–34.

More a norm than an exception is the fact that numerous healthcare facilities have a large number of multiculturally diverse groups in their work force, as well as an equally diverse patient population. These authors focused on a multiculturally diverse work force by doing an in-depth study of one medical center adjacent to the Los Angeles area. The demographics of this center clearly depicted a diverse work force: 63 percent of the staff (680 employees) belong to minority groups; 77 percent are females; 64 percent of the total professional and ancillary staff belong to minority groups; 45 percent of the medical staff are either foreign born or of a minority group; and 70 percent of the registered nurses and licensed vocational nurses are either foreign born or of a minority group. The problems found in this medical center include language problems, lack of awareness by non-Asian groups; lack of understanding of different cultural values when delivering healthcare and lack of experience by supervisory personnel on how to manage a culturally diverse work force.

Implications for Practice

Top management in this medical center took a strong proactive approach to address the identified work force problems, the principles of which can be widely applied. The following major changes were undertaken:
- A top priority included building a cohesive work force by emphasizing through educational programs team building among U.S.-educated black, caucasian, and hispanic nurses from Great Britain and the Philippines.
- Staff awareness of multicultural value systems for personnel as well as patients is emphasized during orientation.
- The manager acts as a facilitator when cultural clashes among employees occur and a reasonable solution to the differences is an expected outcome.
- Each new staff nurse is assigned a preceptor with the nurse recruiter taking the lead for coordinating and supervising preceptee/preceptor activities.
- Top-level management and nurse managers continue to work together in designing ways to develop and maintain a cohesive work force that respects each other's specific ethnic culture values.

Actions such as these can support team building and promote mutual understanding wherever cultural diversity in the workplace is an issue.

EXERCISE 8-7
On a periodic basis, plan an international birthday party. Have each group member bring a dish that represents a food preference. Have the members bring the recipe for their dish to share with others.

Although the literature has addressed multicultural needs of clients, it is sparse in identifying effective methods for nurse managers to use when dealing with multicultural staff. Differences in education and culture can impede client care, and uncomfortable situations may emerge from such differences. For example, staff members may be reluctant to admit language problems that hamper their written communication. They may also be reluctant to admit their lack of understanding when interpreting directions. Psychosocial skills may be troublesome as well, because non-Westernized countries encourage emotional restraint. Staff may have difficulty addressing issues that relate to private family matters. For example, non-Asian nurses may have difficulty accepting the intensified family involvement of Asian cultures. The lack of assertiveness in some cultures and the subservient physician–nurse relationships are other issues that provide challenges for nurse managers.

Every chapter contains at least one **Research, Theory, or Literature Perspective** box that you can identify by the "open book" logo. These boxes summarize articles of interest and point out their relevance and applicability to practice. Check the journal that the article came from to find a list of indexing terms to help you locate additional and even more recent articles on the same topic.

The **tables** that appear throughout the text provide convenient capsules of information for your reference.

TABLE 7-2	Continuum of Healthcare Organizations	
TYPE OF CARE	**PURPOSE**	**ORGANIZATION OR UNIT PROVIDING SERVICES**
Primary	Entry into system Health maintenance Long-term care Chronic care Treatment of temporary nonincapacitating malfunction	Ambulatory care centers Physician's offices Preferred provider organizations Nursing centers Independent provider organizations Health maintenance organizations School health clinics
Secondary	Prevent disease complications	Home health care Ambulatory care Nursing centers
Tertiary	Rehabilitation Long-term care	Home health care Long-term care Rehabilitation centers Skilled nursing facilities Assisted living programs

Courage Self-Assessment Checklist

How often do you do whatever it takes to get the job done?
How often do you say what is so, even if you know the result may not be pretty?
When was the last time you declared that something was not working? (A failure)
Are you comfortable with taking 100 percent responsibility when things go wrong?
When was the last time you refused to be stopped, pursuing a new but unpopular course?
How often is your communication inauthentic because it is easier to look good or not make waves?
Are you attached to your way of being and "the way we do things here"?
Would anyone use the word *persistence* to describe you?
Are you clear on what your commitment is and do you act out of that commitment?
Are you willing to take a stand for an unpopular idea because it is part of your larger commitment?
Do you have the courage to learn from your mistakes?
Can you be as good at follow-up as you are at leadership?

Steps to Support Motivation

Determine what the employee needs
Use achievable goals
Promote a positive environment
Have a positive attitude
Encourage participation in decision making
Acknowledge, acknowledge, acknowledge
Provide honest and direct communication
Look for the gold, interact with the gold
Remove game players and nonperformers from positions crucial to success

The **boxes** in every chapter highlight key information such as lists and contain forms, worksheets, and self-assessments to help reinforce chapter content.

The numerous full-color **illustrations** visually reinforce key concepts.

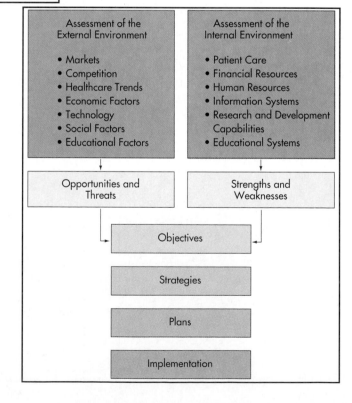

Assessment of the External Environment

- Markets
- Competition
- Healthcare Trends
- Economic Factors
- Technology
- Social Factors
- Educational Factors

Assessment of the Internal Environment

- Patient Care
- Financial Resources
- Human Resources
- Information Systems
- Research and Development Capabilities
- Educational Systems

Opportunities and Threats

Strengths and Weaknesses

Objectives

Strategies

Plans

Implementation

The Role of Nurse Manager   33

of nursing for a group of healthcare providers are inherent in the role of a manager.

CHAPTER CHECKLIST

The role of the nurse manager is complex. Integrating clinical concerns with management functions, synthesizing leadership abilities with management requirements, and addressing human concerns while maintaining efficiency are the challenges of a manager.

- There are five basic functions of a manager:
  - Establish objectives and goals and communicate them
  - Organize and analyze activities, decisions, and relations, and divide them into tasks
  - Motivate and communicate
  - Analyze, appraise, and interpret performance and communicate meaning
  - Develop people
- There are differences between leaders and managers. Managers do:
  - Planning
  - Budgeting
  - Setting of target goals
  - Organizing
  - Staffing
  - Controlling
  - Problem solving
- Nursing is influenced by the leadership style of women because of its gender makeup.
- Nurse leaders identify five descriptive competencies:
  - Managing the dream
  - Mastery of change
  - Organizational design
  - Anticipatory learning
  - Taking the initiative
- Covey's seven habits is an approach to view effectiveness.
- Nurse managers link technical, behavioral, and conceptual skills with the variables of motivation, abilities, and role clarity to form their own distinct style.
- Managing in healthcare settings focuses on managing resources from a perspective of total quality management (TQM).
- Nurse managers must set examples of professionalism and lead for the future.

TERMS TO KNOW

• leader	• TQM (total quality management)
• nurse manager	• trait
• role	• transformational leadership

EXERCISE 2-6

Sue B., a young nurse on a surgical orthopedic unit, has been asked several times during her eight-hour shift for some medication for pain by one of her patients, Mr. Jones, who had foot surgery three days ago. Sue B.'s assessment of Mr. Jones leads her to believe that he is not having that much pain. Although he does have a p.o. medication order for pain, Sue independently decides to administer a placebo by subcutaneous injection and documents her medication intervention. Mr. Jones did not receive any relief from this sub-q medication. When Sue B. was relieved by the night nurse, Sue B. gave the nurse a report of her intervention concerning Mr. Jones' pain. The following morning, the night nurse reports Sue B.'s medication intervention to you, the nurse manager. You will have to address Sue's behavior. What will you do? What resources will you use to handle Sue B.'s behavior? How will you demonstrate professionalism?

The **CHAPTER CHECKLIST** at the end of every chapter provides a quick summary of key points in the chapter. To help you keep in mind the broad themes of the chapter, read it immediately *before* you start reading the chapter.

The **Terms to Know** in every "Chapter Checklist" includes all the key terms used in that chapter. You might find it helpful to review this list before reading the chapter and to look up in the Glossary any definitions that are unfamiliar.

Glossary   541

GLOSSARY

Absenteeism	The rate at which an individual misses work on an unplanned basis. *(Chapter 19)*
Acceptance	The second phase of the change process when the change is willingly used. *(Chapter 5)*
Accommodating	An unassertive, cooperative approach to conflict in which the individual neglects own personal needs, goals, and concerns in favor of satisfying those of others. *(Chapter 17)*
Acculturation	The process of becoming familiar and comfortable with and able to function within a different culture or environment, while retaining one's own cultural identity (Simons et al., 1993). *(Chapter 8)*
Acknowledgment	Recognition that an employee is valued and respected for what he or she has to offer to the workplace, team, or group; acknowledgments may be verbal or written, public or private. *(Chapter 14)*
Active listening	Focusing completely on the speaker and listening without judgment to the essence of the conversation; an active listener should be able to repeat accurately at least 95 percent of the speaker's intended meaning. *(Chapter 14)*
Advocacy	Multidimensional concept that refers to acting on or in behalf of another who is unable to act for him/herself. *(Chapter 20)*
Agenda	A written list of items to be covered in a meeting and the related materials that meeting participants should read beforehand or bring along. Types of agendas include structured agendas, timed agendas, and action agendas. *(Chapter 11)*
Anxiety	An arousal state that is a reaction to stress as the individual attempts to identify and define the problem (Kozier et al., 1992). *(Chapter 25)*
Apparent agency	Doctrine whereby a principal becomes accountable for the actions of his/her agent; created when a person holds himself/herself out as acting in behalf of the principal; also known as apparent authority. *(Chapter 3)*
Arbitration	Process by which an impartial person, chosen by the parties to a dispute, attempts to resolve the dispute. *(Chapter 3)*

The **Glossary** at the end of the text lists alphabetically all the boldfaced terms from the chapters. To help you as you study, each definition also specifies which chapter number(s) contain that glossary term.

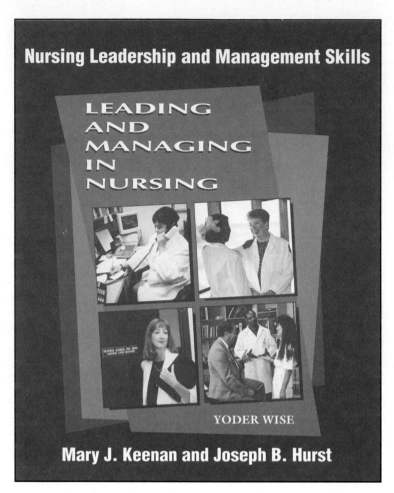

STUDENT SKILLS WORKBOOK

Developed by contributors to this textbook and other professionals, Keenan and Hurst's *NURSING LEADERSHIP AND MANAGEMENT SKILLS to accompany Yoder Wise, LEADING AND MANAGING IN NURSING* reinforces concepts presented in the text and integrates them with activities designed to help you apply essential leading and managing skills. It includes:

- Detailed scenarios, case studies, and role plays with follow-up questions
- Interviews with healthcare professionals
- Self-assessments, forms, and worksheets
- Discussion questions to stimulate critical thinking about workplace situations that you'll be likely to encounter as a nurse manager

VIDEO SERIES

MOSBY'S NURSING LEADERSHIP AND MANAGEMENT VIDEO SERIES is an excellent tool to reinforce your learning of key leadership and management skills both visually and experientially. Using realistic case scenarios interspersed with narrative, each video demonstrates the application of interpersonal skills for leaders and managers. Whether you have personal access to these videos or view them only in class, you will find them especially helpful because of their ability to convey subtleties of communication such as verbal nuance and body language with immediacy and clarity. The eight titles in the series are:

Video 1: Problem Solving and Decision Making: Critical Thinking in Action
Video 2: Dealing with Difficult People
Video 3: Effective Communication
Video 4: Managing Change
Video 5: Building Teams
Video 6: Delegating Effectively and Appropriately
Video 7: Managing Conflict
Video 8: Leadership

Contents

PART ONE

MANAGING AND LEADING

THE CONCEPTS

CHAPTER 1

MANAGING AND LEADING

Michael R. Bleich, R.N., M.P.H., C.N.A.A.

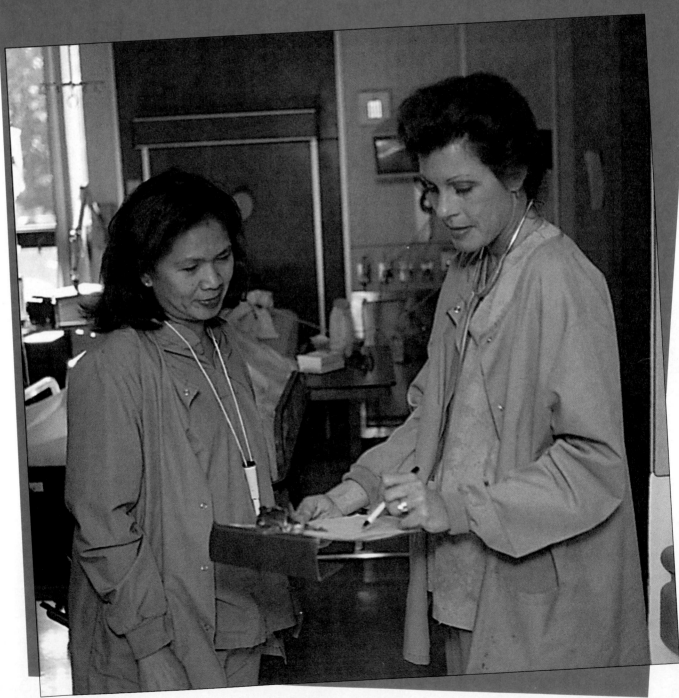

PREVIEW

This chapter explains the need to embrace leading and managing as an integral part of professional nursing practice, either at the bedside or in a management position. By examining leadership and management theories, personal attributes, and tasks, the student or nurse is able to reflect and assess leadership and management readiness to influence patient care and organizational outcomes.

OBJECTIVES

- Demonstrate leading and managing behaviors as important functions of professional nursing.
- Use leadership and management theories to guide self and others in managing patient care and carrying out organizational functions.
- Develop personal attributes to promote self as a leader and/or manager.
- Apply nine essential tasks performed by leaders and managers to clinical practice.
- Assess and implement the use of gender strengths to manage professional relationships.

QUESTIONS TO CONSIDER

- Have you considered leading and managing as a part of professional nursing practice? How has your upbringing influenced your ideas and skill development in leading and managing?
- What leading and managing skills do you possess and practice in your current role? What future leadership and management expectations will be placed on you as your roles change?
- What personal leading and managing skills are you most comfortable with? What skills should be further developed?

A Manager's Viewpoint

When I first became a nurse, I never really thought of myself as a leader, much less a manager. My real focus was on obtaining skills in patient assessment and in performing complex interventions to meet my patients' needs. I'm not sure when it really occurred to me but while working in oncology, a patient shared his fears with me about his diagnosis and the changes that he would have to face in his life. I thought to myself, Why would this patient, a distinguished older man, share this information with me? And then I realized that he trusted me—his nurse—to do something about his fears. I helped him clarify the hopes and dreams that he had for his future and helped him put his prognosis into focus. Then, together, we developed an action plan to help him reach his goals. I communicated, planned, and organized an approach to care, and secured the resources that would help him. I realized that I was leading and managing his care, referring information to other disciplines as needed so that they, too, could help this patient.

After this patient, I never saw myself in the same way; I didn't just *do* care for patients, I *managed* care. Eventually, I helped other nurses do the same thing. After several years of experience, some as a cancer resource nurse, I became a coordinated care manager for this unit. In this role I work closely with patients and families to perform specialized assessments, patient education, and discharge planning. I develop care maps for each of the patients in my caseload. Each day, I am able to assign staff to meet needs according to the developed plan or a population-specific standard of care. I am expected to be creative in my approach to patient care, solve problems, meet patient and staff demands, and control costs. In this position, I work closely with the medical staff and all other relevant disciplines needed as part of the care team.

Today my focus is not only on leading and managing patient care, but also on helping the organization enhance and expand its services, develop systems for monitoring resources and quality, and problem solve and create new patient care delivery options.

Mary Jo Tietjen, R.N., B.A., O.C.N.
Coordinated Care Manager
Bryan Memorial Hospital
Lincoln, Nebraska

INTRODUCTION

Too often, nurses think leading and managing are the responsibility of the nurse manager, or some other designated nursing leader. What they fail to realize is that *all* professional nurses must display characteristics of leadership and engage in leading and managing activities, either at the bedside or in positions of responsibility for other staff, for a unit within an organization, or for the function of nursing within an entire organization. Other activities, such as serving on committees and task forces, also require leadership and management skills. In healthcare organizations today, there are more opportunities for professional nurses to influence patient care through self-governance, quality-related activities, or participative opportunities, such as serving on committees and task forces. For these activities, as well as for improving professional nursing care to patients, leading and managing skills are important for all nurses to recognize and develop.

leadership   For the purpose of this chapter, **leadership** relates to the personal traits necessary to establish a vision for patient care consistent with the mission and purpose of an organization, to assess the current condition or status of the patient or organization, and to enter into relationships with others (patients, families, or peers) to motivate and inspire these individuals to

management   achieve the desired outcome. **Management** relates to the activities needed to plan, organize, motivate, and control the human and material resources needed to achieve these outcomes. Historically leadership traits were thought to be innate, or instinctually "embedded" in each individual. While there are qualities within each person that enhance leadership activities, current trends demonstrate that leadership attributes can be acquired and developed. Ideally, management activities are embedded within leadership tasks. It is possible, however, for management activities to be performed without the benefit of leadership.

All nurses must be leaders if they are to assess patient care needs, relate and influence the patient's vision for improved health, and apply interventions to meet the patient's objective for improved health. All nurses must manage the patient's clinical pathway by allocating resources such as time, materials, and expertise to achieve the patient's objective in the most cost-effective manner. Some nurses will hold special leadership and management roles in an organization and will work with both patient and organizational objectives. These roles include utilization management nurses, nurse managers, case managers, supervisors, and clinical nurse specialists.

PERSONAL ATTRIBUTES OF LEADERS/MANAGERS

Leading and managing require different skills from those associated with the technical aspects of nursing. Leading and managing require self-awareness of **personal motives,** those intangible driving factors that are influenced by our values and beliefs and that give meaning to our lives, both personally and professionally. Many nurses are motivated by the desire to help others, care for those who are unable to care for themselves, relieve social injustice, and the like. Still, the behaviors of nurses with these motives may vary greatly. One nurse who believes strongly in relieving social injustice may care for HIV/AIDS patients in an inner-city clinic, another may be an activist for so-

Many nurse leaders and managers are motivated by a strong desire to care for those who cannot care for themselves.

cial policy development, and another may engage in research. Being aware of one's motivations is not always an easy task; it is beyond the human condition to ever be totally self-aware. Leaders and managers must constantly seek self-awareness of their motives and values in order to inspire others.

The motives of the nurse influence the types of individuals who relate to that nurse as a leader and manager. These motives, coupled with other personal traits, shape the impact that the nurse as a leader/manager can have. The box on page 6 entitled "Attributes of Leaders/Managers" identifies some of the traits that attract other individuals to associate with a nurse leader.

DEVELOPMENT OF MANAGEMENT AND LEADERSHIP THEORY

The development of management and leadership theory expanded at the beginning of the twentieth century when industries were created to achieve mass production. Leadership theory development included attempts to describe the nature of leaders, that is, who they were, what they did, and the circumstances that required leadership intervention. Two major bodies of research, one focusing on leadership traits and the other on the situations where leaders were needed, resulted from the attempt to acquire insight into leadership.

In the research that focused on the traits of leaders, researchers identified individuals who were perceived as leaders and described the characteristics that created their success. Douglas McGregor (1960) believed that leaders held certain traits constant based on the characteristics of subordinates. Even though we know today that leadership traits are not always constant, the

EXERCISE 1-1
Imagine a clinical leader, manager, or teacher you admire and think of a specific situation in which this leader influenced positive change that affected you in some manner. Write down what you think the motivations were that made this leader want to facilitate change. Then describe the factors that made you feel drawn to work with this leader: Was it the leader's energy and stamina? His or her decision-making capabilities? Was it the leader's ability to make a decision without being paralyzed by too much data? Was it the leader's sincerity in dealing with people? Did the leader respect the confidence of those who shared information? Did you know where you stood at all times with the leader? Were you clear about the objective you were working toward? Was the leader competent in the issue being tackled? Did the leader act assertively? Did the leader have a plan for evaluating the impact of change? Share this assessment with the person that you identified as the leader and get feedback on your observations.

Attributes of Leaders/Managers

- Uses focused energy and stamina to accomplish a vision
- Uses critical thinking skills in decision making
- Trusts personal intuition, then backs up intuition with facts
- Willingly accepts responsibility and follows up on the consequences of actions taken
- Identifies the needs of others
- Skillfully deals with people: coaches, communicates, counsels
- Demonstrates ease in standard/boundary setting
- Flexibly examines multiple options to accomplish the objective at hand
- Is trustworthy; handles information from a variety of sources with respect for the source
- Assertively motivates others toward the objective at hand
- Demonstrates competence or is capable of rapid learning in the arena where change is desired

attributes of leaders and managers described by McGregor are considered a foundation for the leadership research that emerged.

theory X
McGregor describes leadership traits around two very divergent views of people responding to the leader. The **theory X** view of people suggests that managers must be directive, structured, and controlling because subordinates prefer the safety of supervisory direction over self-direction. A theory X staff is employed for the purpose of securing money and other benefits for survival and will respond to the fear associated with losing this security. Work is a

theory Y
means to secure a quality of life. In contrast, **theory Y** was developed to suggest that workers can contribute independently to organizational goals if the manager molds an environment where self-direction and creativity is permitted. Theory Y managers must be assured of the direction and purpose of the organization and communicate these objectives to staff. Staff must be trusted to achieve these objectives and the manager must support the enrichment and development of staff.

situational/contingency theory
Another body of research is known as situational, or contingency, theory. **Situational theory** suggests that leaders assume the characteristics needed based upon the situation they find themselves in; none of us holds a constant leadership "style" in all circumstances. In situational theory, the variables that influence leading and managing behaviors include the size and complexity of the organization or the work unit; the climate of the organization or work unit; its ability to adapt and react to change; the characteristics of the leader, such as the leader's capacity for influence and power; the characteristics of the staff members, including their skills, knowledge, and expertise; and the environment of the organization, whether stable and predictable, or hostile and subject to rapid change. Fiedler (1967) advanced the notion of situational leadership by examining two basic leadership "styles": task oriented and relationship oriented. Task-oriented leaders perform best when situations call for control. Relationship-oriented leaders perform best when there is no imminent issue or crisis to address.

Hersey and Blanchard (1988) advanced situational theory building on the work of Fiedler through the development of the tri-dimensional leader effectiveness model. This work expands on the notion of the importance of leader and follower interaction. They contend that the behavior of the leader, coupled with group maturity and leader effectiveness, has impact on the work performance of the group.

Through analysis of the leader and the group, leadership styles can be described in one of four ways:

- high directive, low supportive (where extensive direction and supervision of task completion is required);
- high directive, high supportive (where coaching and performance support is required);
- high supportive, low directive (where the leader promotes task achievement); and
- low supportive, low directive (where the leader can delegate to the group for group decision making).

Clearly, there is no one right school of thought. Rather, the exploration of managing and leading behaviors is ongoing, using the information obtained from each perspective to achieve the objectives at hand.

TASKS OF LEADING AND MANAGING

The list of attributes of leaders and managers shown earlier provides some insight into the personal qualities that make leading and managing possible. But for individuals who have or are developing these attributes, opportunities to carry out leadership tasks will strengthen leadership and management functioning. Gardner (1990) describes the tasks of leadership in his book *On Leadership* (see the box below).

Gardner's Tasks of Leadership

1. Envisioning goals
2. Affirming values
3. Motivating
4. Managing
   - planning and setting priorities
   - organizing and institution building
   - keeping the system functioning
   - setting agendas and making decisions
   - exercising political judgment
5. Achieving workable unity
6. Developing trust
7. Explaining
8. Serving as symbol
9. Representing the group
10. Renewing

Reprinted with permission from Gardner, J.W. (1990). On Leadership. New York: Free Press.

Nurses as leaders and managers have daily opportunities to carry out these nine tasks, whether the focus is on patient care management or on unit/organizational management.

ENVISIONING GOALS

relationships

Envisioning goals for purposes beyond personal goal setting and attainment requires the development of a relationship between the professional nurse and the patient, or in the case of a nurse manager, the manager and unit staff. Relationship building is a product of time, circumstances, and the personal attributes of the nurse and the client. In a clinical emergency situation, where the patient is in crisis, the time factor may be reduced to moments before information is shared and a relationship established. The patient may not even realize who the attending nurse is, so long as the patient's perception of the nursing profession is positive and the individual providing care is perceived as someone who can resolve the crisis. In other client-based situations, relationships are built over time, as the individual nurse or nurse manager proves to be competent and trustworthy, a good decision maker; able to prioritize the client's needs; and able to provide realistic options to solving problems. The point is this: being in a relationship with a client is essential for realistic goals to be established. The leader/manager respects all opportunities for interaction with clients—patients or staff—and establishes goals based on this information.

vision

Establishing vision is an important leadership concept. "Visioning" requires the leader to assess the current reality, determine what a desired state would be, and then manage the resultant tension between the two states in a positive manner. If the nurse manages the client positively, creative tension will result. Creative tension is positive tension that moves the client toward the desired goal. If the nurse fails to have a positive relationship with the client, or fails to recognize cues about the client's real circumstances, emotional tension results. Emotional tension drains the energy of the client and can cause even further distress. Visioning is an important function of leading and managing. Visioning goals give purpose to all leadership activities.

AFFIRMING VALUES

values

Values are the inner forces that give us purpose and character. Organizations have values that guide its purpose and character and are expressed in its mission and philosophy. Leaders have values that influence decision making, priority setting, and the like, and clients (either patients or peers being influenced by the leader) have values that drive their purposes and objectives and shape their visions. Values are deep-seated and are a persuasive force driving how we choose to act and respond to others.

The word *value* conjures up an image of something that has worth; our values have worth to us. A leader always seizes the opportunity to clarify and optimize the values that underlie the need to problem solve or create something new. This is because values are powerful forces that promote acceptance of change and achievement of a vision. In groups, awareness of the values that drive change helps those impacted relate to the importance of the change. Shared values build cohesiveness in a group. For example, the implementation of a new patient care delivery model will be enhanced if the persons affected by the change understand the values behind it, such as continuity of care, quality outcomes, and opportunities for demonstrating caring behaviors. If these values are known and important to the group, the change is more easily implemented and celebrated among all who share the values associated with it.

MOTIVATING

When we let our values drive our actions, we make meaningful commitments to enacting our vision. Values become a source of motivation. Motivation is tapping into what we value, personally and professionally, and reinforcing those factors to achieve growth and movement toward our vision. Motivators are the reinforcers that keep positive actions alive. Examples of motivators include positively influencing patient outcomes, creating work efficiencies that improve teamwork, and the like.

motivation

Theories of motivation identify and describe the forces that motivate people. Two examples of motivation theory are Maslow's need hierarchy theory (1943) and Herzberg's two-factor theory (1991). Maslow suggests that persons are motivated by a hierarchy of needs, beginning with physiologic needs, then progressing to safety, social, esteem, and self-actualizing needs. In this theory, when the need for food, water, air, and other life-sustaining elements are met, the human spirit reaches out to achieve affiliation with others and promotes the development of self-esteem, competence, achievement, and creativity. Lower-level needs will always drive behavior before higher-level needs will be addressed. This is not difficult for nurses to comprehend; every day we see evidence that patients who are physiologically unstable must achieve proper oxygenation and pain control before belonging to a social network becomes important. From Maslow's perspective, motivators can be predicted in a hierarchy, and once a lower level factor is secure, it will no longer be a "motivating force."

Maslow

Herzberg's theory describes two factors, *hygiene factors* and *motivator factors*. Hygiene factors motivate workers by meeting the safety and security needs and avoiding *job dissatisfaction*. Motivator factors promote job enrichment by creating *job satisfaction*. Hygiene factors include working conditions, salary, status, and security. Motivator factors include achievement, recognition, and the satisfaction of the work itself.

Herzberg

When motivating the diverse work force employed in healthcare agencies today, it is important for nurse managers to use both hygiene and motivator factors in recruiting and retaining staff. Innovation in employee benefit options and salary packages, as well as benefits that promote career development, are examples of hygiene factors. Patient-focused care initiatives that create "whole jobs," work diversification, and autonomous decision making are contemporary examples of motivator factors used to enhance employee job satisfaction. This chapter's "Research Perspective" highlights the importance of motivation and reward in recruiting and retaining nurse managers.

Motivating patients and staff as individuals is a challenging task. Leaders recognize that often they do not have the luxury of working with individuals. The nurse leader works to motivate not only the patient but also the patient's family and support system. Nurse managers often must lead whole groups of staff toward a common vision. Leaders managing groups soon discover that a variety of motivation strategies are necessary to move everyone toward the same vision. The box on page 11 provides suggestions for unlocking the motives of individuals and groups so that appropriate reward systems are in place to motivate behavior change. Chapter 15 in this text discusses motivation in more detail.

EXERCISE 1-2
Develop a vision statement with a patient with whom you have a positive and "knowing" relationship. What is the patient's *current reality,* that is, what are the factors the client is facing as a result of disease, disability, lack of endurance, and so on? Ascertain with the client what his/her *future state* could be like, adding your own professional knowledge and expertise to the client's perceptions. When you have finished your vision statement, ask the client, "If you could have your vision, would you take it?" Then, ask the client to make an affirmation statement: "I choose to _____" (fill in the blank). A vision is then set for your collective intervention (Adapted from Fritz, 1989).

Research Perspective

Boston, C., & Forman, H. (1994). A time to listen: Staff and manager views on education, practice, and management. Journal of Nursing Administration, 24, 16–18.

A group of researchers from *The Nursing Spectrum* and the American Organization of Nurse Executives (AONE) surveyed 185 nurses eligible for middle management positions in healthcare to find out what would motivate them to apply for such a position. After learning that the nurses agreed unanimously that money alone was not enough, and that recruitment and retention of nurse middle managers was a particular problem, the researchers asked the same group of nurses to participate in a series of focus groups to identify specific motivational and demotivational factors. The nurses chosen to participate were from major centers in the East, the Midwest, and the South.

The researchers distributed a demographic assessment instrument and questionnaires to the nurses, who had been divided into three groups: middle managers, manager-eligible nurses, and relatively new graduates. Responses were very similar regardless of the area of the country the nurse was from. Nearly all nurses agreed that the prime motivational factors for recruiting and retaining nurse managers were individual empowerment, recognition, respect, true autonomy, and participation in decision making—essentially the same factors identified earlier by Maslow and Herzberg.

The middle managers' responses to the survey indicated that their sense of job satisfaction came from having the power to effect change; enjoying a sense of personal accomplishment grounded in their ability to influence and develop staff to provide consistent, quality nursing care; receiving recognition from their patients, staff, colleagues in other disciplines, and upper management; and being afforded the dignity concomitant with their position. The most frequently noted difficulties were fiscal constraints, insufficient time to do everything, uncompensated time, and accountability without authority. The group identified key components of the middle management role as including both traditional and transformational concepts such as planning, directing, and controlling; motivating, facilitating, mentoring, problem solving, and advocating (both for staff and patients); and communicating effectively in all directions. All respondents agreed that good managers needed both strong fiscal skills and clinical competence.

Implications for Practice

Nurse executives at the organizational level can use the information gleaned from this survey to help ensure that the work environment is truly supportive for all nurses and that strategies essential for nurse manager effectiveness, such as empowerment, recognition, and compensation, are in place. AONE is also using the focus groups' results to plan educational strategies for its 5,700 members.

Vroom and Yetton (1973) suggest that *felt* needs cause the desire for behavior change. The *effort* extended and the *performance* achieved will ultimately sustain outcomes. The awareness and synchrony of leaders in facilitating awareness of patient/staff needs, streamlining effort, and reinforcing positive outcomes will promote ongoing change.

MANAGING

Ideally, managing is a subset of leading because leading reflects the importance of mutual relationships and vision setting between the leader and the clients. Managing is not void of relationship opportunities, but the tasks can

Suggestions for Unlocking Individual and Group Motives

- Know your staff and patients and the factors that are influencing them to seek healthcare, work, and so on. Do your "homework" in a respectful and courteous manner.
- Analyze individual and group responses to past rewards.
- Ask for information from the group on how they would choose to celebrate work accomplishments.
- Choose a variety of hygiene and motivator rewards to meet the variety of needs that may be present in a group.

be done in relative isolation of leading. The successful nursing leader today has both leadership and management skills.

Management skills require planning and priority setting. Once a vision has been established, planning requires the following (see also Chapter 4):

1. Deciding on a course of action.
2. Determining the chronology of events that must occur to achieve the vision.
3. Determining the talents and skills needed to accomplish the objective and assigning these tasks to individuals who can most effectively meet the needs.
4. Assessing the time requirements to accomplish the objectives and coordinate tasks around deadlines.
5. Considering the driving forces that will promote accomplishment of the objective. Driving forces are those political forces working in one's favor to promote transition to the established vision. Optimize the work that driving forces can achieve.   *driving forces*
6. Considering the restraining forces that will work against the desired accomplishments. Restraining forces are those political forces working *against* the desire to achieve the established vision. Decreasing these forces will help you achieve the vision. Use political skills to develop alliances to assist in minimizing restraining forces.   *restraining forces*
7. Developing methods to stabilize the desired state once it is reached. Reinforcement is an important function of leadership.
8. Evaluating the attainment and maintenance of the desired state. Too often, leaders lose their effectiveness because they fail to recognize what they have accomplished. Celebrate the accomplishment and reinforce the values and efforts that led to the success.

Other aspects of managing include using and promoting human resources to creatively develop new services or programs or extend existing services that help fulfill the mission and vision of the organization. By involving staff in service and program development, the leader promotes institution building through all levels of the organization.

Equally important is the leader's capacity to involve others in day-to-day problem solving. Keeping existing services and systems functioning is a challenging endeavor in healthcare organizations. Once a service or a system is designed it may be taxed by the volume and/or acuity of patients who may use the product. Realistically, all patient needs cannot always be met with existing services or rigid systems. The leader empowers staff to respect, use, and adapt systems of care to meet the needs of customers. (Chapter 5 contains more on problem solving)

The freedom that leaders give staff to meet customer needs is best evidenced in the quality of decision making that surrounds meeting customer needs. Staff who are free to make decisions without fear of repercussion can have positive impact on the organization's capacity to carry out its mission. The astute leader also examines the quality of the staff's decision making in order to become politically involved in developing the organization's agenda for improvement. When leaders are politically astute, they seek forums to continuously advance ways to enhance services, systems, and products.

This chapter has addressed the importance of establishing a vision and applying leadership skills to achieve a desired state. Leaders do not influence organizational or client-centered change by just focusing on problem solving. If this were the case, leaders would be satisfied solving the same problems over and over. Leadership is about creating new systems and methods to accomplish the desired vision.

ACHIEVING WORKABLE UNITY

Another challenge when leading and managing is to achieve workable unity and to avoid or diminish conflict so that the desired vision can be achieved. It is essential for leaders to acquire conflict-resolution skills.

When a dispute occurs, whether due to conflicting values or interests, it is useful to follow a defined set of principles for conflict resolution. Ury, Brett, and Goldberg (1988) describe a highly effective approach for restoring unity and movement toward the vision desired, as shown in the box below entitled "Principles of Conflict Resolution." Chapter 17 in this text discusses conflict resolution in more detail.

Principles of Conflict Resolution

1. Put the focus on interests
   - examine the real issues of all parties
   - be expedient in responding to the issues
   - use negotiation procedures and processes, such as ethics committees, and other "neutral" sources
2. Build in "loop-backs" to negotiation
   - if resolution fails, allow for a "cooling off" period before reconvening
   - review the likely consequences of not proceeding with all parties, so that they understand the full consequences of failure to resolve the issue
3. Build in consultation *before* and feedback *after* the negotiations
   - build consensus and use political skills to facilitate communication before confrontation, if anticipated, occurs
   - work with staff or patients after the conflict to learn from the situation and to avoid a similar conflict in the future
   - provide a forum for open discussion

EXERCISE 1-4

Examine the mechanisms available to you in your current capacity that are used for dispute resolution. How is the mechanism set up to accomplish the principles listed above? Has the system been used? What were the results? Were the disputants able to move on to achieve an outcome that was satisfactory to all parties? What was the role that the nurse leader or manager played in the resolution process?

> **Principles of Conflict Resolution—cont'd**
>
> 4. Provide the necessary motivation, skills, and resources
>   • make sure that the parties involved in conflict are motivated to use procedures and resources that have been developed; this requires ease of access and a nonthreatening mechanism
>   • assure that those working in the dispute have skills in problem solving and dispute resolution
>   • provide the necessary resources to those involved to offer support, information, and other technical assistance
>
> *Adapted from Ury, W., Brett, J., & Goldberg, S. (1988). Getting Disputes Resolved: Designing Systems to Cut the Costs of Conflict. San Francisco: Jossey-Bass.*

EXPLAINING

Leading and managing require a willingness to communicate and explain—again and again. The art of communication requires the leader to:

1. Know what information needs to be shared.
2. Know the parties who will receive the information. What will they "hear" in the process of the communication? Present information for the listener's self-interest.
3. Provide the opportunity for dialogue and feedback. Face-to-face communication is always preferable to written communication because of the immediacy of information feedback to the leader and the opportunity for clarification of information. Written feedback is useful for reinforcement of the message or to follow up on inquiries.
4. Know that it is possible to give too much information, which can temporarily paralyze the listener.
5. Be willing to repeat information in many different ways, at different times. The more diverse the group being addressed, the more important it is to avoid complex terms, concepts, or ideas. Keep information simple.
6. Always explain *why* something is being asked or is changing. Reinforce the values behind the communication.
7. Acknowledge loss, and provide the opportunity for honest communication about what will be missed, especially if change is involved.
8. Be sensitive to nonverbal communication. It may be necessary in complex situations to have someone reinterpret key points and provide you with feedback about the clarity of your message after the meeting. Use every opportunity for explaining as a vehicle to fine-tune your communication skills. (See Chapter 16 for more on communication.)

SERVING AS SYMBOL

Every leader has the opportunity to speak for others. Nurses speak to physicians on behalf of patients; managers speak to other departments on behalf of their staff. Serving as a symbol means that unity, collective identity, and continuity of service is represented.

REPRESENTING THE GROUP

While serving as a symbol of nursing, or of nursing management, there are many opportunities for leaders to represent the group. As mentioned in the

communication

> **EXERCISE 1-5**
> Examine a recent conversation in which you were in a leadership capacity. In one column write down what you said. In the next column, write down the response you received. In a third column, write down what you were thinking, but did *not* say. Analyze the conversation: Did you use language common to the listener? Did you share enough information to be clear, but not too much information to clutter the point of your communication? Were you honest in your communication? Did you allow time for feedback? Did you express main ideas in several different ways or summarize information for clarity? (Adapted from Chris Argyris as described in Senge, P.M. (1990). The leader's new work: Building learning organizations. *Sloan Management Review, 32*(3), 7–22.)

introductory remarks to this chapter, progressive organizations today are creating more vehicles for employee participation. Many organizations are decentralizing decision making and removing layers of management. In an environment that is rapidly changing, the high technology and skill level associated with healthcare professionals, and the need for rapid organizational change, has created the need for collective decision making. Leaders should treat these newfound opportunities with respect and honestly try to represent the group with an attitude of openness and integrity. During these representative opportunities, leaders are called on to demonstrate an understanding of the organization's objectives and to contribute to its mission and purpose.

Whether on- or off-duty, leaders must be cognizant that their public image is always being viewed by others. As both a symbol of the organization and a representative of the professional discipline, the leader behaves in ways that uphold the dignity and quality of the organization and professional discipline.

RENEWING

Leaders have the capacity for generating energy within and among others. A true leader does not just expend the energy of the group or allow the group to lose its focus. In organizations and nursing practice, there is a constant need to find a balance between problem solving (energy expending) and vision setting (energy producing). When changes are made based on vision, they can be met with renewed spirit and purpose if the leader uses Gardner's nine tasks of leadership as a base. This chapter's "Literature Perspective" highlights the importance of vision setting.

Further, leaders must take care of themselves—eat a balanced diet, get adequate sleep and exercise, and participate in other wellness-oriented activities—in order to maintain their perspective and the necessary energy level. Likewise, they must ensure that their constituents are given similar opportunities for renewal. Gardner (1990) states that, "The consideration leaders must never forget is that the key for renewal is the release of human energy and talent" (p. 136). This requires focused energy and personal well-being.

In Table 1-1 Gardner's leadership tasks are presented to provide a contrast between leaders who focus in the delivery of professional nursing and leaders who hold formal management positions representing the interests of the organization.

TABLE 1-1	Contrasting Leading/Managing Behaviors of Nurses in Clinical Positions and Those in Management Positions	
	BEHAVIORS	
GARDNER'S TASK	**CLINICAL POSITION**	**MANAGEMENT POSITION**
Envisioning goals	Visioning patient outcomes for single patients/families; assists patients in formulating their vision of future well-being.	Visioning patient outcomes for aggregates of patient populations and creating a vision of how systems support patient care objectives; assists staff in formulating their vision of enhanced clinical and organizational performance.

TABLE 1-1	Contrasting Leading/Managing Behaviors of Nurses in Clinical Positions and Those in Management Positions—cont'd

| GARDNER'S TASK | BEHAVIORS | |
	CLINICAL POSITION	MANAGEMENT POSITION
Affirming values	Assisting the patient/family to sort out and articulate their personal values in relation to health problems and the impact of these problems on lifestyle adjustments.	Assisting the staff in interpreting organizational values and strengthening staff members' personal values to more closely align with those of the organization. Interprets values during organizational change.
Motivating	Relating to and inspiring patients/families to achieve their vision.	Relating to and inspiring staff to achieve the mission of the organization and the vision associated with organizational enhancement.
Managing	Assisting the patient/family with planning, priority setting, and decision making. Makes sure that organizational systems work in the patient's behalf.	Assisting the staff with planning, priority setting, and decision making. Makes sure that systems work to enhance the staff's ability to meet patient care needs and the objectives of the organization.
Achieving workable unity	Assisting patients/families to achieve optimal functioning to benefit transition to enhanced health functions.	Assisting staff to achieve optimal functioning to benefit transition to enhanced organizational functions.
Explaining	Teaching and interpreting information to promote patient/family functioning and well-being.	Teaching and interpreting information to promote organizational functioning and enhanced services.
Serving as symbol	Representing the nursing profession and the values and beliefs of the organization to patients/families and other community groups.	Representing the nursing unit/service and the values and beliefs of the organization to staff, other departments, professional disciplines, and the community at large.
Representing the group	Representing nursing and the unit in task forces, total quality initiatives, shared governance councils, and other groups.	Representing nursing and the organization on assigned boards, councils, committees, and task forces, both internal and external to the organization.
Renewing	Providing self-care to enhance ability to care for patients, families, and the organization served.	Providing self-care to enhance ability to care for staff, patients, families and the organization served.

Literature Perspective

Davidhizar, R. (1993). Leading with Charisma. Journal of Advanced Nursing, 18, 675–679.

Traditional approaches to management include the use of authority, control, competition, and logic through management behaviors that are autocratic, directive, and task oriented. Today, organizations are changing to focus on human needs, and *transformational leadership* is emerging as a modern management style to accommodate workers who value working in organizations that are personally fulfilling. Organizations with transformational leadership are characterized by mutuality and affiliation, acknowledging complexity and ambiguity, cooperating versus competing, emphasizing human relations, defining processes versus tasks, accepting feelings, promoting networking versus hierarchy building, and recognizing the value of intuition.

Charismatic leaders are required to guide organizations into transformational cultures. The effect of charismatic leaders is based on the leader's appeal to followers, and the leader's ability to enter into the "psyche" of the followers in a manner that fosters the presence of loyalty or enthusiasm. "Charismatic effect" is created when there is a gifted leader, dependent followers, and situations for the leader to depict to followers.

To use charisma in leadership requires leaders to have positive self-regard/self-esteem, an orientation to people and a visible focus on the human needs of followers, a vision that gives individuals something to work for and be committed to, skill in promoting and selling the vision, and the ability to create structures and processes to attain the vision.

Implications for Practice

The organizational climate in healthcare is experiencing rapid change. Today's professional workers are characterized as individuals who relate more to their profession than to the organization that employs them; these attitudes are particularly prevalent given organizational mergers, department consolidation, and the addition of services extending beyond the traditional "walls" of the organization. These factors require charismatic leadership. Traditional leaders will either be reschooled in their approach to management, or will find themselves replaced by others who are able to generate focus, enthusiasm, and energy in their staff. Hypervigilant supervision must be replaced by open communication, personal mentoring, and creative problem solving.

DIVERSITY IN LEADERSHIP, DIVERSITY IN ORGANIZATIONS

The healthcare industry is spiraling through unparalleled change, often away from the traditional industrial models that reigned throughout the twentieth century. Today it is no longer acceptable for workers to understand only their singular part in how the work of the organization is achieved; rather, they must understand how their work fits in with the whole system of care delivery. It is the responsibility of leadership to acquire this "whole system" knowledge, imparting and reinforcing it to all staff. Healthcare organizations are being "retooled" to meet customer expectations and to achieve optimal clinical outcomes.

Traditional views of management and leadership are evolving in this chaotic environment. Work forces are now characterized by workers who require more flexibility and balance in their work and personal lives; they want to know that what they do is being valued and is contributing toward a common goal, in spite of abbreviated work hours. Organizations are becoming known for their flexibility rather than their bureaucracy.

These changes create the opportunity for the emergence of a new type of nursing leader, both at the bedside and in formal management positions. While hospital leadership historically has been provided largely by men, women are assuming key organizational positions that add depth and diversity to management decision making. Research on the role of women in leadership positions supports the many personal characteristics that are desirable for organizations to succeed in the marketplace and in understanding the workforce.

Furthermore, in providing care to patients, nursing has historically been close to the true mission of the healthcare enterprise, and is therefore in a strong position to recognize the impact that change can have on patient outcomes.

Helgeson (1990) described the characteristics of four women in top leadership and management positions:

traits of women as leaders/managers

1. Women worked at a steady pace, scheduling small breaks throughout the day to reduce the amount of "frantic" stress.
2. Women leaders were perceived as being more accessible. They did not view unscheduled tasks and encounters as interruptions and shared information with peers more readily.
3. Women were perceived as caring, involved, helpful, and responsible for their leading and managing functions.
4. Women were more likely to make time for functions not directly associated with their work. This enabled them to gain a broader perspective on the issues faced in the business environment.
5. Women successfully maintained a complex network of relationships with people outside of their organizations. Again, this added a broader perspective on issues faced in the business environment.
6. Women focused on the ecology of leadership, reducing the likelihood of being caught in the here and now and focusing on future-oriented long-range planning.

As female nurses embark on the functions of leading and managing, they should do so recognizing that the characteristics that they bring to the healthcare setting are very much needed in this environment of change. Not only are these the characteristics of excellent clinical providers, but also they are characteristics consistent with excellent leadership in healthcare organizations.

In contrast to women, men tend to be socialized with values of distance and autonomy rather than connection and intimacy. Historically, society has expected men to use logic, analysis, and abstract thinking, and to express their opinions (Belenky et al., 1986). Men who are in leadership positions must recognize that it may be difficult for women to merely "trust" this work of logic and fact-giving, particularly when their own experiences represent different truths. To capitalize fully on the potential of both genders, leaders must facilitate understanding of gender differences and, as mentioned earlier in this chapter, blend the use of intuition backed up by fact. Leaders must continue to grow in self-understanding so that they have the insight to appreciate the gifts of those they lead.

CHAPTER CHECKLIST

This chapter addresses the attributes and tasks of leadership as a significant function for professional nurses to fulfill, whether in clinical or management positions. Leadership requires understanding of self, commitment to the objectives of the organization and patient care, special skills and knowledge of organizations, human behavior, values, vision setting, problem solving and decision making, and the care of oneself. Organizations are going through major changes throughout our country, changes that require new attributes in their leaders. Many of these attributes are complementary to roles that women have not been fully recognized for in the past.

Traditional leaders must alter their styles to accommodate a changing work force, the need for rapid decision making void of all the necessary facts, and a patient-as-customer orientation. Professional nurses will make major contributions to healthcare if they develop their leadership potential. Leading and managing are professional functions of nurses, whether in clinical or management positions.

- The personal attributes needed for effective leading and managing include:

  - focused energy and stamina to accomplish the vision;
  - ability to make decisions in an intelligent manner;
  - willingness to use intuition, backed up with facts;
  - willingness to accept responsibility and to follow up;
  - sincerity in identifying the needs of others;
  - skill in dealing with people, for example, through coaching, communicating, counseling;
  - comfortable standard/boundary setting;
  - flexibility in examining multiple alternatives to accomplish the objective at hand;
  - trustworthiness, a good "steward of information";
  - assertiveness in motivating others toward the objective at hand;
  - demonstrable competence and quick learning in the arena where change is desired.

- The tasks of leading and managing include:

  - Envisioning goals
  - Affirming values
  - Motivating
  - Managing
    - planning and priority setting
    - organizing and institution building
    - keeping the system functioning
    - setting agendas and making decisions
    - exercising political judgment
  - Achieving workable unity
  - Explaining
  - Serving as symbol
  - Representing the group
  - Renewing

- Traditional bureaucracies are changing due to the global changes in economy and health care. Organizations require new leadership skills and diversity in managing and leading.
- The attributes of women are desirable for the new environments that are being created. Specifically, women are suited for leadership positions because they:
  - work at a steady pace, with less frantic stress;
  - do not view unscheduled tasks and encounters as interruptions and are more likely to share information;
  - are more likely to be perceived as caring, involved, helping, and being responsible;
  - are more likely to make time for functions not associated with their work and maintain a complex network of relationships that serve to offer a broader perspective in problem solving in a business environment;
  - focus on the ecology of leadership, not losing sight of long range objectives because of short-term pressures.

TERMS TO KNOW

- **leadership**
- **management**
- **personal motives**
- **situational theory**
- **theory X**
- **theory Y**
- **values**

REFERENCES

Belenky, M.F., Clinchy, B.M., Goldberger, N.R., & Tarule, J.M. (1986). *Women's Ways of Knowing: The Development of Self, Voice, and Mind*. New York: Basic Books.

Boston, C., & Forman, H. (1994). A time to listen: Staff and manager views on education, practice, and management. *Journal of Nursing Administration, 24,* 16–18.

Davidhizar, R. (1993). Leading with charisma. *Journal of Advanced Nursing, 18,* 675–679.

Fiedler, F.A. (1967). *A Theory of Leadership Effectiveness*. New York: McGraw-Hill.

Fritz, R. (1989). *The Path of Least Resistance: Learning to Become the Creative Force in Your Own Life*. New York: Fawcett Columbine.

Gardner, J.W. (1990). *On Leadership*. New York: Free Press.

Helgeson, S. (1990). *The Female Advantage: Women's Ways of Leadership*. New York: Bantam Doubleday.

Hersey, P., & Blanchard, K. (1988). *Management of Organizational Behavior Utilizing Human Resources,* 5th ed. Englewood Cliffs, NJ: Prentice-Hall.

Herzberg, F. (1991). One more time: How do you motivate employees? In Ward, M.J., & Price, S.A. *Issues in Nursing Administration: Selected Readings*. St. Louis: Mosby–Year Book.

Maslow, A. (1943). A theory of human motivation. *Psychological Reviews, 50,* 370–396.

McGregor, D. (1960). *The Human Side of Enterprise*. New York: McGraw-Hill.

Senge, P.M. (1990). The leader's new work: Building learning organizations. *Sloan Management Review, 32*(3), 7–22.

Ury, W., Brett, J., & Goldberg, S. (1988). *Getting Disputes Resolved: Designing Systems to Cut the Costs of Conflict*. San Francisco: Jossey-Bass.

Vroom, V.H., & Yetton, P. (1973). *Leadership and Decision-Making*. Pittsburgh, PA: University of Pittsburgh Press.

SUGGESTED READINGS

Belenky, M.F., Clinchy, B.M., Goldberger, N.R., & Tarule, J.M. (1986). *Women's Ways of Knowing: The Development of Self, Voice, and Mind.* New York: Basic Books.

Bridges, W. (1991). *Managing Transitions: Making the Most of Change.* Reading, MA: Addison-Wesley.

Covey, S. (1991). *Principle-Centered Leadership.* New York: Summit.

Fisher, R., & Ury, W. (1991). *Getting to Yes: Negotiating Agreement Without Giving In.* New York: Penguin.

Leebov, W., & Scott, G. (1990). *Health Care Managers in Transition.* San Francisco: Jossey-Bass.

Marriner-Tomey, A. (1993). *Transformational Leadership in Nursing.* St. Louis: Mosby–Year Book.

CHAPTER 2

THE ROLE OF NURSE MANAGER

Ana M. Valadez, R.N., Ed.D., C.N.A.A., F.A.A.N.

Dorothy A. Otto, R.N., Ed.D.

PREVIEW

This chapter identifies key concepts related to the role of nurse manager. It describes basic manager functions, explains differences between leaders and managers, illustrates management principles that are inherent in the role of professional practice, and identifies descriptive competencies for the nurse manager. Theory is crucial to forming the right questions to ask in a management or clinical situation, helping the practitioner identify problems and anticipate needs. This chapter provides the theoretical backdrop for further development of practical skills.

OBJECTIVES

- Analyze the relationship of the nurse manager and nurse leader.
- Evaluate behaviors of professionalism of the nurse manager.
- Analyze roles and functions of a nurse manager.
- Evaluate management resource allocation/distribution.
- Explain quality/outcomes of delivery systems.

QUESTIONS TO CONSIDER

- Why do you want to be a nurse manager?
- What type of setting would you like as a nurse manager?
- How do you manage current resources?
- Do you yearn for increased involvement in key decisions, changing systems, working with people, improving client care?
- How will your clinical expertise be used in the setting?

A Manager's Viewpoint

When I took this job, I did not know that top management also wanted me to be a change agent, fiscal manager, communicator, and collaborator. I paused to reflect on what I had learned about the contemporary nurse manager . . . one who carries out multiple roles and has effective client and personnel outcomes. I reviewed the characteristics of a good leader: the ability to inspire commitment and team spirit, to envision new directions for the organization, to take risks, to communicate plans for change, and to motivate. And I rediscovered the impact of a total quality management workshop I had taken on my management practice. The workshop helped me renew my commitment to team building, customer satisfaction, and planning to prevent errors. I became energized when I worked with all disciplines for the improvement of patient services. I know I possess the qualities of a good manager.

Loretta Tumengan, R.N.
Head Nurse, Coronary Care Unit
Veterans Affairs Medical Center
Houston, Texas

INTRODUCTION

roles What is involved in management? What is the **role** of the nurse manager? Practicing **nurse managers** illustrate role perceptions. Some nurse managers would cite decision making and problem solving as major roles, for which maintaining objectivity is sometimes a special challenge.

Another additional element is being a collaborator. Throughout educational programs, students have multiple opportunities to collaborate with other nurses. **Leaders** must also be involved in collaboration with other departments to enhance quality patient outcomes. Truly effective care is the result of efforts by the total healthcare team. Effective collaboration includes honesty, directness, and listening to other points of view.

Styles (1982) says that significant self-examination should be requisite for one who desires to become a nurse manager through the process of career development. A prerequisite for self-actualization is a bonding between the nurse and the community, for a nurse manager's clients and staff make up the community.

MANAGEMENT VERSUS LEADERSHIP ROLES

Management is a generic function that includes similar basic tasks in every discipline and in every society. However, before the nurse manager can be effective, she/he must be well grounded in nursing practice. Drucker (1974)

five basic functions identifies five basic functions for a manager:
- Establishes objectives and goals for each area and communicates them to the persons who are responsible for attaining them.
- Organizes and analyzes the activities, decisions, and relations needed and divides them into manageable tasks.
- Motivates and communicates with the people responsible for various jobs through teamwork.
- Analyzes, appraises, and interprets performance and communicates the meaning of measurement tools and their results to staff and superiors.
- Develops people, including self.

Table 2-1 shows how these basic management functions apply to the nurse manager.

TABLE 2-1	Basic Manager Functions and Nurse Manager Functions
BASIC MANAGER FUNCTION[A]	**NURSE MANAGER FUNCTION**
Establishes and communicates goals and objectives	Delineates objectives and goals for assigned area Communicates them effectively to staff members who will help attain goals
Organizes, analyzes, and divides work into tasks	Assesses and evaluates activities on assigned area Makes sound decisions about dividing up daily work activities for staff

TABLE 2-1	Basic Manager Functions and Nurse Manager Functions—cont'd	

BASIC MANAGER FUNCTION[a]	NURSE MANAGER FUNCTION
Motivates and communicates	Stresses the importance of being a good team player Provides positive reinforcement
Analyzes, appraises, and interprets performance and measurements	Completes performance appraisals of individual staff members Communicates results to staff and management
Develops people, including self	Addresses staff development continuously through mentoring and preceptorships Furthers self-development by attending educational programs and seeking specialty certification credentialing

[a]Drucker, P.F. (1974). *Management: Tasks, Responsibilities, Practices.* New York: Harper & Row.

individual focus

A manager's development efforts focus on the individual. Their aim is to enable the person to develop his/her abilities and strengths to the fullest and to achieve excellence. According to Hershey and Blanchard (1977), "People differ not only in their ability to do, but also in their will to do or their motivation. . . . Commitment to a goal increases when people are involved in their own goal setting" (pp. 16, 25). Thus, goals must be realistic before a person makes a real effort to achieve them. Goals should be set high enough, yet be attainable. Active participation, encouragement, and guidance from a director and from the organization are needed for the manager's development efforts to be fully productive. Nurse managers who are successful in motivating staff are often providing an environment in which appropriate goals can be attained through personal satisfaction.

Employees on all levels from lowest to highest need to be given responsibility for the affairs of the institution and their community (Drucker, 1989). The manager's staff must be held responsible for setting goals for their own work and for managing themselves by objectives and self-control.

manager qualities

The nurse manager must possess qualities similar to those of a good leader: knowledge, integrity, ambition, judgment, courage, stamina, communication skills, planning, and administrative abilities. The arena of management versus leadership has been addressed by numerous authors, and while there are differences in points of view, there are some similarities between managers and leaders.

manager functions

Managers address complex issues by planning, budgeting, and setting target goals. They meet their goals by organizing, staffing, controlling, and problem solving. By contrast, leaders set a direction, develop a vision, and communicate the new direction to the staff. Managers address complexity while leaders address change. The accompanying box compares the characteristics of a leader with those of a manager.

According to Drucker (1989), the most probable assumption today is the unique event, which cannot be predicted. However, unique events can be

EXERCISE 2-1
In a small group, discuss how clients pay for services of hospitals, clinics, hospices, or private provider offices. Hypothesize about what portion of those costs represents nursing care. How does a manager contribute to cost effectiveness?

Leader Versus Manager Traits

Leader traits
- Values commitment, relationships with others, and esprit de corps in the organization.

- Provides a vision that can be communicated and has a long-term effect on the organization.
- Takes risks; shuns the status quo and moves the organization into new directions.
- Communicates the rationale for changing paths; new paths lead to progress.
- Endorses and thrives on taking risks that bring about change.
- Demonstrates a positive feeling in work and relates the importance of workers.

Manager traits
- Emphasizes organizing, coordinating, and controlling resources (for example, space, supplies, equipment, and people).
- Attends to short-term objectives/goals.

- Maximizes results from existing resources.

- Interprets established policy, procedure, and mandates.

- Moves cautiously; dislikes uncertainty.

- Enforces policy mandates, contracts, etc. (gatekeepers).

foreseen and one can take advantage of them. Nurse managers can have strategies for the future that anticipate the area in which the greatest changes are likely to occur; strategies that enable the unit, department, or institution to take advantage of the unforeseeable. Strategic planning aims to exploit the new and different opportunities of tomorrow. The nurse manager can assist the staff to think strategically about what it is doing and what it should be doing for its clients, for example, in today's world of cost containment, examining what clients pay for the care they receive from the healthcare professionals.

influence of women

Because the nursing profession is predominantly a woman's profession, it is important to acknowledge leadership styles attributed to women. Rosner (1990) reports that early women leaders tended to use commanding, controlling styles generally associated with men. Ames (1989) depicts the commanding, controlling, no-nonsense style of a male chief executive officer (CEO). Most of this leader's messages are not open for discussion, but rather are mandates for action. If outcomes do not meet expectations, the CEO does not hesitate to use punitive negative reinforcement. Rosner also reports that as women leaders became more comfortable with themselves they began to successfully use their own leadership style. This style often is called **transformational leadership.** Leadership of this type encourages subordinates to transform their own interests into group interests, with concern for a broader goal. Transformational leaders are interactive people who try diligently to make their interactions positive for everyone. They are not afraid to share their power in order to enhance their staff's self-worth.

transformational leadership

Murphy and DeBack (1991) believe that the profession has a cadre of nursing leaders who are in influential positions and are providing the impetus for reshaping nursing practice to meet the challenges of the twenty-first century. They conducted research through in-depth interviews of thirteen nurses considered to be leaders in this era of change. The data reveal many similar characteristics and competencies. Table 2-2 depicts these nurses' descriptive competencies.

TABLE 2-2	Nurses' Descriptive Competencies

COMPETENCIES	DESCRIPTION
Managing the dream	Sensing windows of opportunities; articulating the vision
Mastery of change	Providing life to the vision; taking risks; accepting error; managing change
Organizational design	Tailoring the organizational design to the vision; using pilot projects; retooling nurses to think differently
Anticipatory learning	Preparing futuristically, including preparing others; energizing the vision through learning with co-workers
Taking the initiative	Making things happen; beginning the idea and seeing it to completion; not allowing everyday distractions to blur their goals; using corporate strategies; presenting the "idea" for the organization, not for nursing

EXERCISE 2-2
Select a nurse manager in one of your clinical facilities. Observe the manager over a period of time (e.g., two to three hours). What style does this manager exhibit? Is power shared or centralized? Are interactions positive or negative? Would your summation of this observation relate more to managerial characteristics or leadership characteristics, or both?

These leaders also exhibited other similarities. For example, their own leadership style denoted a commitment to decentralization, optimism, and a belief in the vision. They expected nothing but the best from the people around them and they continuously maintained a telescopic view of the vision. Bennis (1992) describes leadership **traits** that also are found in the leaders in Murphy and DeBack's study. The traits include being expert articulators, admitting failures, and capitalizing on their strengths. They know the world they live in and what they want out of it. They are integrated selves, who are working on the new healthcare frontier and shaping the future for tomorrow's nurse leaders.

traits

Nurse managers should use a leadership style that is comfortable for them and can bring about win-win situations. By ascribing to a particular leadership style a manager supports the belief that there is strength in diversity of leadership style.

As Covey (1989) writes: "Our character, basically, is a composite of our habits. . . . Because they are consistent, often unconscious patterns, they constantly, daily, express our character and produce our effectiveness . . . or ineffectiveness" (p. 46). Nurse managers also must be credible clinicians in the areas they manage. A critical factor in being an excellent nurse manager is how to manage clients and families and allocate resources and technology in the ever-changing healthcare environment. The nurse manager–clinician is confronted with complex and ambiguous client care situations. Sometimes decisions are made to meet one important client care need at the expense of another. Benner (1984) writes that not even expertise can rid the clinician of the uncertainty inherent in clinical practice. Despite this uncertainty, though, some of the behaviors and qualities that enhance the nurse leader's effectiveness remain constant. The box on page 28 lists key abilities and skills that nurse leaders and managers most need.

credible clinician

Joiner and Corkrean (1986) refer to three types of skills needed by a nurse manager: technical, behavioral, and conceptual. However, the key to success in the nurse manager role includes linking three variables to these skills. These variables are motivation, ability, and role clarity. Figure 2-1 depicts these necessary elements for a successful nurse manager. The "Research Perspective" identifies several other issues that managers in healthcare will need to address in the decade to come.

unique role per

Key Abilities and Skills for New Nurse Leaders/Managers

- Critically analyze nursing care requirements
- Influence others in their enactment of nursing
- Create a desire in others to continue self-development
- Synthesize data from multiple sources
- Develop staff, considering their abilities and the organization's needs
- Translate the organization's vision into work reality
- Make informed decisions readily
- Solve problems fairly and effectively, using staff input
- Mentor, coach, acknowledge, empower, and challenge staff
- Communicate clearly and accurately
- Exhibit flexibility, creativity, commitment, enthusiasm, caring, and cultural sensitivity
- Demonstrate clinical competence
- Evaluate others and their work in light of standards
- Predict, control, and evaluate needed resources
- Have "long-short" vision (balance today's demands without losing sight of tomorrow's needs)
- Build teams and their commitment
- Choose your own management style
- Assess, plan, implement, and evaluate
- Embrace change and quality
- Resolve "unending" disputes creatively
- Live a positive life
- Manage your career and facilitate others' careers
- Enjoy your work
- Value people
- Facilitate goal attainment
- Enrich the environment
- Maintain humor
- Have faith

Adapted from T.M. Marrelli, RN, MA, The Nurse Manager's Survival Guide: Practical Answers to Everyday Problems, copyright © 1993 Mosby Year-Book, Inc.

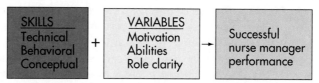

FIGURE 2-1 Skills and qualities of the successful nurse manager.

MANAGING HEALTHCARE SETTINGS

Current and emerging issues and the forces shaping them are the kinds of information that may be helpful for nurse managers to know in order to meet the challenges that arise in managing healthcare settings. Some of the current and emerging issues are the organization of health services, cost, quality, and

Research Perspective

Chase, L. (1994). Nurse manager competencies. Journal of Nursing Administration. 24(4S)56-64.

This descriptive study dealt with research conducted on in-hospital first line managers through the use of a mailed questionnaire. A sample of 300 nurse managers was obtained from the American Organization of Nurse Executives Nurse Manager Council members. What makes this study so pertinent to the nurse manager's role is that unlike other similar studies that addressed characteristics and responsibilities of nurse managers, this study attempted to answer three key questions: a) what competencies are necessary to be an effective nurse manager?, b) what competencies are more important?, and c) is there a direct relationship between competencies and agency size, nurse's age, education, tenure and management experience?

The nurse managers identified knowledge of and the use of effective communication and decision making as the most significant skills necessary for their functioning. Other competencies that ranked high as necessary and important included problem solving, effective counseling, staffing methodologies, team building, performance evaluations, delegation, use of effective disciplinary outcomes and the change process. The demographic findings of the study revealed that agency size, nurse's age, education and tenure significantly impacted the competency ratings; whereas, clinical practice did not.

Implications for Practice

As emerging models of health care delivery systems become a reality, in-hospital agencies need to heed close attention to the cadre of competencies necessary to be an effective nurse manager. While fiscal restraints in agencies have prevailed for some time; education, on site as well as formal systems, need to provide nurse managers with the knowledge they need to function in the key pivotal role that is being mapped out for them.

EXERCISE 2-3
Make a quick list that need not be all-inclusive, but reflects a fairly accurate count of your "bag of skills" in each of the three categories: technical, behavioral, conceptual. Describe yourself in terms of motivation. How can your skills assist in linking the three additional variables of motivation, ability, and role clarity in a position as a nurse manager? (For example, if you hold a high value for clinical expertise then coordination of resources may be easier for you. Clinical expertise gives you insight about follow-up care of clients and delegation potential to selected staff.)

ethics; all are shaped significantly in some way by the forces of demand for greater fiscal and clinical accountability, technological growth and innovation, changing supply of labor, changing composition of the health industry and the population itself, and growing numbers of uninsured people (Crane, Hersh, and Shortell, 1992).

Healthcare settings are rapidly changing. They are an exciting, "full of opportunity" experience, yet there is flux in relation to where and how nurses will practice. Nurse managers may be redefining their role as case managers. The paradigm of client care is shifting from in-hospital settings to client-directed outpatient and community settings. Nurse managers are in a position to promote disease prevention and good health practices. High technology will continue to modify the nurse managers' roles. For example, because of the ability to perform more complex surgery through surgi-centers, nurse managers will find themselves practicing with short-term or ambulatory care admissions. While there are no blueprints to help nurses practice in these new settings, old principles of management are not necessarily inapplicable.

With some modification, however, the basic principles of management still work. For instance, a key to successful management is interdependence. Covey (1989) makes a salient point when he addresses interdependence

dynamic role

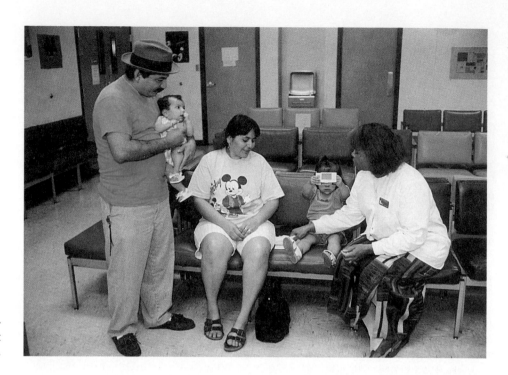

Client care is shifting from in-hospital settings to outpatient and community settings.

collaboration

as a necessity to achieve life goals, whether family or organizational. A critical component of interdependence is collaboration, which uses the different strengths of each person. Collaboration requires one to be flexible and broadminded, and to have a strong self concept. Vestal (1987) views collaboration as having key elements such as open communication, role clarification, and a trusting relationship in the performance of others. In the healthcare arena interdisciplinary collaboration should be the framework for effective client outcomes.

The practice settings of tomorrow will no doubt continue to include in-hospital care; however, numerous innovative practice models operating from a community-based framework may be found also. Predictors of effective outcomes to insure quality client care include rationed and multi-tiered distribution of healthcare services, such as health maintenance organizations (HMOs), Preferred Provider Organizations (PPOs), or independent private payment plans; very precise outcome-oriented quality assurance measures, such as critical pathways or care MAPs; and concerted efforts to control the spiraling health costs by increasing productivity and efficiency of healthcare providers. The nurse of the year 2005 may be a proprietor of a nurse-managed HMO. Other practice models, differentiated practice, shared governance, and restructured work environments make use of all levels of healthcare personnel.

MANAGING RESOURCES

The manager is responsible for managing all resources designated to the unit of care. The wise manager quickly determines that a unit must function economically, and in so doing, realizes that there are many opportunities to reshape how nursing is delivered. Budget and people have always been considered to be critical resources. However, as technology grows, informatics must be integrated with budget and people as a critical resource element.

INFORMATICS

Informatics is in a stage of constant change and it highlights for nurse managers two roles that have prevailed: educator and research translator. Both of them have become easier to accomplish because informatics has given quick and ready access to current and retrospective clinical client data. Similarly, educating staff, clients, and families is facilitated through the array of informatic tools available. Because of informatics, nurse managers have quick assess to patient classification systems that denote acuity of care and to personnel hours that directly relate to client acuity. A manager must ensure that the staff's data input is accurate and demonstrate leadership in synthesizing how the data are used to deliver care.

BUDGETS

Budgetary allocations, whether they are related to the number of dollars available to manage a unit or in full-time equivalent employee formulas, may be the direct responsibility of nurse managers in the future. Budgets should be:
* outcome oriented
* understandable and based on informational data bases
* flexible, prompt, and contingency based
* rudimented on controllable factors
* fair and objective (Joiner and Corkrean, 1985).

Perhaps, the most important aspect of a budget is the provision for a mechanism that allows some self-control and does not require advance approval or constant rationale for budgetary spending.

PEOPLE AND WORKPLACE VIOLENCE

Human resources pose new challenges for nurse managers in today's society. One such challenge is violence in the workplace. Lipscomb (1993) addresses violence in the workplace as a recent addition to workplace hazards facing healthcare workers. It is not only prevalent but also on the increase. Two issues complicate the existing research on violence: underreporting and the perception that assaults on healthcare workers are part of the job. Definitions of what is considered violence in the workplace are open to many interpretations and biases. The Occupational Safety and Health Administration (OSHA) has the most encompassing and often-used definition. OSHA defines an occupational injury as one that results in death or in "lost work days, loss of consciousness, restrictions of work or motion, termination of employment, transfer to another job, or medical treatment (other than first aid)" (Carmel and Hunter, 1989).

Beginning or aspiring nurse managers need to consider workplace violence as a serious threat to the workforce and to the clients. Perhaps the most important issues to consider when addressing workplace violence include education of the staff so that they can assess adequately and intervene appropriately. The Joint Commission on Accreditation of Healthcare Organizations (JCAHO), the accrediting agency for most healthcare facilities, has included in the survey since 1989 criteria development and evaluation of programs to address workplace violence.

critical resources

informatics

budgetary allocations

human resources

EXERCISE 2-5
Visit a city health department or an adult day-care facility. What type of information system is used? Are both paper (hard copy) and computer sources used? What can you assume about the budget based on the physical appearance of the setting? Does any equipment appear dated? How do the employees (and perhaps volunteers) function? Do they seem motivated? Ask two or three to tell you, in a sentence or two, what the purpose (vision or mission) of the organization is. Can you readily identify the nurse manager? What does the manager do to manage the three critical resources?

TOTAL QUALITY MANAGEMENT

Most corporations, whether small or large, have wholeheartedly embraced the concept of **total quality management** (TQM) for customer satisfaction. Healthcare facilities are no different; they, too, want satisfied customers/clients and TQM seems to be the answer. The emerging nurse manager will need to fully understand and support TQM.

culture
What is TQM? Who are the field players? What can the nurse manager expect as a result of TQM? Total quality management means that the organization ascribes to a culture that supports the continuous attainment of customer/client satisfaction through the use of integrated tools, techniques, and training. Sashkin and Kiser (1993) rely heavily on W. Edward Deming's work addressing measurable customer satisfaction. Deming (often viewed as the creator of TQM) called TQM a philosophy of management. Although Deming initially emphasized achieving quality through tools, techniques, and training, in later years he focused on the philosophy aspect of management.

perspective
TQM team composition is dependent on who can best solve the dissatisfied customer/client complaint. As one nurse manager stated, "If I had been told that to solve a dietary complaint I would be sitting in a group with an informatics expert, an engineer, and a medical administrator, I would have said, you are kidding, of course! While I was prepared to work with the dietary department and nursing, I never realized that some very important components of customer/client satisfaction involved the utilization of other customer-related services." In essence, what the nurse manager learned was that the philosophy of all those that affect customer/client satisfaction must be thoroughly blended and focused on satisfactory outcomes. Nurse managers may be faced with the challenge of being excellent communicators who can articulate their points of view to the TQM team. Total quality management requires establishing a common healthcare language that allows all team members to share their expertise.

PROFESSIONALISM

Nurse managers must set examples of professionalism, which include academic preparation, roles and function, and increasing autonomy. The American Nurses' Association's classic, *Nursing: A Social Policy Statement* (1980), provides significant ideals for all nurses, specifically, that nurses are guided by a humanistic philosophy that includes the highest regard for self-determination, independence, and choice in decision making, whether for personnel or for clients. A nurse manager's professional philosophy also should include the client's rights. These rights have traditionally identified such basic elements as human dignity, confidentiality, privacy, and informed consent. Additional basic rights now include self-determination through advance directives (living wills and durable power of attorney for healthcare) and the right to healthcare accessibility.

client rights

Professionalism is all-encompassing; the way a manager interacts with personnel, other disciplines, and patients/clients and families reflects a professional philosophy. Professional nurses are ethically and legally accountable for the standards of practice as well as nursing actions delegated to others. Conveying high standards, holding others accountable, and shaping the future of nursing for a group of healthcare providers are inherent in the role of a manager.

CHAPTER CHECKLIST

The role of the nurse manager is complex. Integrating clinical concerns with management functions, synthesizing leadership abilities with management requirements, and addressing human concerns while maintaining efficiency are the challenges of a manager.

■ There are five basic functions of a manager:
- Establish objectives and goals and communicate them
- Organize and analyze activities, decisions, and relations, and divide them into tasks
- Motivate and communicate
- Analyze, appraise, and interpret performance and communicate meaning
- Develop people

■ There are differences between leaders and managers. Managers do:
- Planning
- Budgeting
- Setting of target goals
- Organizing
- Staffing
- Controlling
- Problem solving

■ Nursing is influenced by the leadership style of women because of its gender makeup.

■ Nurse leaders identify five descriptive competencies:
- Managing the dream
- Mastery of change
- Organizational design
- Anticipatory learning
- Taking the initiative

■ Nurse managers link technical, behavioral, and conceptual skills with the variables of motivation, abilities, and role clarity to form their own distinct style.

■ Managing in healthcare settings focuses on managing resources from a perspective of total quality management (TQM).

■ Nurse managers must set examples of professionalism and lead for the future.

TERMS TO KNOW

- leader
- nurse manager
- role
- TQM (total quality management)
- trait
- transformational leadership

EXERCISE 2-6

Sue B., a young nurse on a surgical orthopedic unit, has been asked several times during her eight-hour shift for some medication for pain by one of her patients, Mr. Jones, who had foot surgery three days ago. Sue B.'s assessment of Mr. Jones leads her to believe that he is not having that much pain. Although he does have a p.o. medication order for pain, Sue independently decides to administer a placebo by subcutaneous injection and documents her medication intervention. Mr. Jones did not receive any relief from this sub-q medication. When Sue B. was relieved by the night nurse, Sue B. gave the nurse a report of her intervention concerning Mr. Jones' pain. The following morning, the night nurse reports Sue B.'s medication intervention to you, the nurse manager. You will have to address Sue's behavior. What will you do? What resources will you use to handle Sue B.'s behavior? How will you demonstrate professionalism?

REFERENCES

American Nurses' Association. (1980). *Nursing: A Social Policy Statement.*

Ames, C.B. (November-December 1989). Straight talk from the CEO. *Harvard Business Review.*

Benner, P. (1984). *From Novice to Expert.* Menlo Park, CA: Addison-Wesley.

Bennis, W. (1992). *On Becoming a Leader.* Menlo Park, CA: Addison-Wesley.

Carmel, H., & Hunter, M. (1989). Staff injuries from inpatient violence. *Hospital and Community Psychiatry, 40*(1), 41–46.

Chase, L. (1994), Nurse manager competencies. *Journal of Nursing Administration.* 24(4S), 56–64.

Covey, S.R. (1989). *The 7 Habits of Highly Effective People.* New York: Simon & Schuster.

Crane, S.C., Hersh, A.S., & Shortell, S.M. (1992). Challenges for Health Services Research in the 1990s. In Shortell, S.M. & Reinhart, U.E. *Improving Health Policy and Management: Nine Critical Research Issues for the 1990s.* Ann Arbor MI: Health Administration Press.

Drucker, P.F. (1974). *Management: Tasks, Responsibilities, Practices.* New York: Harper & Row.

_____ (1989). *Managing in Turbulent Times.* New York: Harper & Row.

Hershey, P., & Blanchard, K.H. (1977). *Management of Organizational Behavior,* 3rd ed. Englewood Cliff, NJ: Prentice-Hall.

Joiner, C., & Corkrean, M. (1986). *Critical Incidents in Nursing Management.* Norwalk, CT: Appleton-Century-Crofts.

Lipscomb, J. (1993). Violence in the health care industry: An overview of the problem with policy recommendations regarding research. Presentation to the American Academy of Nursing.

Murphy, M.M., & DeBack, V. (1991). Today's nursing leaders: Creating the vision. *Nursing Administration Quarterly, 16*(1), 71–80.

Rosner, J.B. (November-December, 1990). Ways women lead. *Harvard Business Review,* 119–125.

Sashkin, M., & Kiser, K. (1993). *Putting Total Quality Management to Work.* San Francisco: Berrett-Koehler.

Styles, M.M. (1982). *On Nursing Toward a New Endowment.* St. Louis: C.V. Mosby.

Vestal, K.W. (1987). *Management Concepts for the New Nurse.* Philadelphia: J.B. Lippincott.

SUGGESTED READINGS

Chez, N. (1994). Helping the victim of domestic violence. *American Journal of Nursing.* 94(7), 32–37.

Decker, P.J., & Sullivan, E.J. (1992). *Nursing Administration: A Micro/Macro Approach for Effective Nurse Executives.* Norwalk, CT: Appleton & Lange.

Kouzes, J.M., & Posner, B.Z. (1987). *The Leadership Challenge: How to Get Ordinary Things Done in Organizations.* San Francisco, CA: Jossey-Bass.

Maddux, R.B. (1988). *Successful Negotiation: Effective "Win-Win" Strategies and Tactics,* revised ed. Los Altos, CA: Crisp Publications.

Manning, M., & Haddock, P. (1989). *Leadership Skills for Women: Achieving Impact as a Manager.* Los Altos, CA: Crisp Publications.

Martin, W.B. (1989). *Managing Quality Customer Service: A Practical Guide for Establishing a Service Operation.* Los Altos, CA: Crisp Publications.

Nothstine, W.L. (1989). *Influencing Others: A Handbook of Persuasive Strategies.* Los Altos, CA: Crisp Publications.

Valadez, A.M. (1991–1992). *Independent Study Module: Differences Between Leaders and Managers.* Austin: Texas Nurses' Association.

Walton, M. (1986). *The Deming Management Method.* New York. Putnam.

CHAPTER 3

LEGAL AND ETHICAL ISSUES

Ginny Wacker Guido, R.N., J.D., M.S.N.

PREVIEW

This chapter highlights and explains key legal and ethical issues as they pertain to managing and leading. It discusses malpractice, types of liability, and federal and state employment laws that pertain to legal and ethical issues. In addition to explaining basic ethical theories and principles, it also provides specific guidelines for avoiding legal liability. All of the issues as described are applicable to everyday professional practice.

OBJECTIVES

- Examine nurse practice acts, including the legal difference between licensed registered nurses and licensed practical (vocational) nurses.
- Apply various legal principles, including malpractice, privacy, confidentiality, reporting statutes, and doctrines that minimize one's liability to leading and managing roles in professional nursing.
- Analyze ethical theories and principles, including autonomy, beneficence, non-maleficence, veracity, justice, paternalism, fidelity, and respect for others.
- Apply an ethical decision-making model to an ethical dilemma.
- Apply manager's rights and responsibilities from a legal and an ethical perspective to selected examples.
- Examine legal implications of resource availability versus service demand from a manager's perspective.
- Analyze key aspects of employment law, including the collective bargaining process, and give examples of how these laws benefit professional nursing practice.
- Apply five guidelines that a nurse manager can implement to encourage a professional, satisfied work setting.

QUESTIONS TO CONSIDER

- What are the most common potential legal liabilities for nurse managers and how can they be avoided or minimized?
- How can nurse managers incorporate ethical principles in their everyday relationships with employees?
- What federal employment laws impact the nurse managers' work setting?
- How does the nurse manager determine which course of action to implement when a legal and/or ethical dilemma arises?

A Manager's Viewpoint

"Why should I, as a nurse manager, be concerned with legal and ethical principles? Surely, there are already enough concerns for nurse managers, such as staffing, power issues, budgets, and the like, to make legal and ethical issues background issues. And surely my time is better spent learning about the organizational structure, creating a motivational climate, and preventing conflict." I often hear questions like this, especially just as I have requested both time and financial resources to attend a workshop for nurse managers about either legal or ethical concerns. I gently remind the questioner that legal and ethical principles are equally important in today's world. By understanding and applying the principles of ethics, I have become a better manager and have developed a staff that also understands and applies ethical principles in everyday clinical situations. I have also learned to apply legal principles and have seen dramatic changes in both the quality of nursing care as delivered to patients as well as in the staff members themselves, who no longer fear that their practice is not legally sound but know that they are functioning within the legal aspects of their professional practice. Documentation has improved, we have fewer incident reports, and patient privacy and confidentiality rights are being met by all members of the nursing staff.

I know that I have improved as a nurse manager by being knowledgeable about all aspects of management that affect my role. Legal and ethical issues are just as vital to my effective role performance as are understanding staffing, lines of authority, handling conflicts, and effective communications. I also know that legal and ethical issues are important for staff nurses to understand and apply in everyday practice. Thus, I encourage staff members to attend such conferences and continuing education programs. I have included ethical grand rounds as part of the education opportunities offered to staff nurses and am including more legal programs as part of the continuing education programs offered by my department. Once nurse managers learn these principles, I am confident that they will also see dramatic changes within their institution.

Judy Trevor, R.N., M.S.N., C.C.R.N.
Nurse Manager, Critical Care
University Medical Center
San Francisco, California

INTRODUCTION

The role of professional nursing has expanded rapidly within the past few years to include increased expertise, specialization, autonomy, and accountability, both from a legal and an ethical perspective. This expansion has forced new concerns among nurse managers and a heightened awareness of the interaction of legal and ethical principles. Areas of concern include professional nursing practice, legal issues, ethical principles, labor-management, and employment. Each of these areas is individually addressed in this chapter.

PROFESSIONAL NURSING PRACTICE

NURSE PRACTICE ACTS

The **scope of nursing practice,** those actions and duties that are allowable by a profession, is defined and guided individually by each state in the **nurse practice act** and by common law. **Common law,** is "derived from principles rather than rules and regulations and consists of broad and comprehensive principles based on justice, reason, and common sense" (*Bishop v. United States,* 1971, p. 418). Common law principles govern most interactions affecting nursing; they are based on a traditional justice perspective rather than a caring relationship. The state nurse practice act is the single most important piece of legislation for nursing because the practice act affects all facets of nursing practice. Further, the act is the **law** within the state and state boards of nursing cannot grant exceptions, waive the act's provisions, or expand practice outside the act's specific provisions.

common law

Nurse practice acts and common law essentially define three categories of nurses: licensed practical or vocational nurses, licensed registered nurses, and advanced practice nurses. The acts, along with common law, set educational and examination requirements, provide for licensing by individuals who have met these requirements, and define the functions of each category of nurse, both in general and specific terminology. The nurse practice act must be read to ascertain what actions are allowable for the three categories of nurses. Some states have separate acts for licensed registered nurses (RNs) and licensed practical/vocational nurses (LPN/LVNs); if two acts exist, they must be reviewed at the same time to ensure that all allowable actions are included in one of the two acts and that there is not overlap between the acts. Some state acts do not have advanced nursing roles defined or delineated.

Each practice act also establishes a state board of nursing. The main purpose of the state board of nursing is to ensure enforcement of the act, regulating those who come under its provisions and preventing those not addressed within the act from practicing nursing.

Since each state has its own nurse practice act and state courts hold jurisdiction on the common law of the state, the nurse manager is well advised to know and understand the provisions of the state's nurse practice act. This is especially true in the area of diagnosis and treatment; states vary greatly on whether nurses can diagnose and treat or merely assess and evaluate. What may be an acceptable action in one state might be considered the practice of medicine in a bordering state. Thus, the nurse manager must know applicable state law and use the act for guidance and appropriate action. Remember, managers are responsible for applying these legal principles in their own practice, for monitoring the practice of employees under their charge, and for ensuring that personnel maintain current and valid **licensure.**

PROFESSIONAL MALPRACTICE

malpractice

Malpractice concerns professional actions and is the failure of a person with professional education and skills to act in a reasonable and prudent manner. Issues of malpractice have become increasingly more important to the nurse as nursing's authority, accountability, and autonomy have increased. There are essentially six elements that must be presented in a successful malpractice suit; all of these factors must be proven before the court will find liability against the nurse and/or institution. Table 3-1 outlines these elements.

TABLE 3-1	Elements of Malpractice

ELEMENTS	EXAMPLE
Duty owed the patient Nature of the duty Existence of the duty	Failure to monitor a client's response to treatment
Breach of the duty owed	Failure to communicate change in status to the primary healthcare provider
Foreseeability	Failure to insure minimum standards are met
Causation	Failure to provide patient education
Injury	The patient falls
Damages	Fractured hip

EXERCISE 3-1
Read your state nurse practice act, including rules and regulations that the state board of nursing has promulgated for the profession. You may need to read two acts if RNs and LPN/LVNs come under different licensing boards. Does your state address advanced practice? How do the definitions of nursing vary for the RN, LPN/LVN, and advanced practice nurses? Using these definitions, formulate three lists showing which tasks or assignments you would delegate to each category of nurses, referencing the nurse practice act as needed.

To understand how the law applies each element of malpractice to specific court cases, the following scenario is helpful. A nurse, employed by a state medical center, has been assigned to care for Mrs. J., a patient admitted for necessary elective surgery and has had that surgery two days ago. The patient is 69, is in relatively good health, and has no prior instances of mental confusion or forgetfulness. While caring for Mrs. J. on the night shift, the nurse failed to ensure that both side rails were raised and locked and Mrs. J., needing to use the bathroom, fell while attempting to get out of bed and use the bathroom by herself. Current institution policy requires that side rails will be raised on all patients over 65 from 10 P.M. to 8 A.M.. Mrs. J. broke her left hip and suffered a mild concussion when she fell. She will be hospitalized for several additional days as she undergoes hip replacement surgery and physical therapy.

Elements of Malpractice

duty owed

The first element is duty owed the patient and involves both the existence of the duty as well as the nature of the duty. That a nurse owes a duty of care to a patient is usually not hard to establish. Often this is established merely by showing the valid employment of the nurse within the institution. The more difficult part is the nature of the duty and this involves standards of care that represent the minimum requirements that define acceptable practice. In the above scenario, the applicable standard of care is taken from the institution

Nurses sometimes serve as expert witnesses whose testimony helps the judge and jury understand the applicable standards of nursing care.

policy and procedure manual and concerns the standard of care owed the elderly patient regarding his/her safety at night. Standards of care are established by reviewing the institution's policy and procedure manual, the individual's job description, and the practitioner's education and skills, as well as pertinent standards as established by professional organizations, journal articles, and standing orders and protocols.

Several sources may be used to determine the applicable **standard of care.** The American Nurses' Association (ANA) as well as a cadre of specialty organizations publish standards for nursing practice. The overall framework of these standards is the nursing process. In 1988, the ANA published *Standards for Nurse Administrators,* a series of nine standards incorporating responsibilities of nurse administrators across all practice settings. Accreditation standards, especially those published yearly by the Joint Commission on Accreditation of Healthcare Organizations (JCAHO), also assist in establishing the acceptable standard of care for healthcare facilities. In addition, many states have healthcare standards that affect the individual institution and its employees.

breach of care   The second element is breach of the duty of care owed the patient. Once the standard of care is established, the breach or falling below the standard of care is easy to show. Remember, though, that the standard of care may differ depending upon whether the injured party is trying to establish the standard of care or whether the hospital's attorney is establishing an acceptable standard of care for the given circumstances. The injured party will attempt to show that the acceptable standard of care is much higher than the acceptable standard of care shown by the defendant hospital and staff. Expert witnesses give testimony at court to determine the applicable and acceptable standard of care on a case-by-case basis and to assist the judge and jury in understanding nursing standards of care. In the scenario, the injured party's expert witness would quote the institution policy manual and the nurse's expert witness would note any viable exceptions to the stated policy.

The third element, **foreseeability,** involves the concept that certain events may reasonably be expected to cause specific results. The nurse must have prior knowledge or information that failure to meet a standard of care may result in harm. The challenge is to show what was foreseeable given the facts of the case at the time of the occurrence, not when the case finally comes to court. In the given scenario, it was foreseeable that the patient could fall and harm herself if the side rails were not raised.

foreseeability

The fourth element is causation, which means that the nurse's actions or lack of actions directly caused the patient's harm and not merely that the patient had some type of harm. There must be a direct relationship between the failure to meet the standard of care and the patient's injury. The resultant injury, the fifth element, must be physical, not merely psychological or transient. In other words, there must be some physical harm incurred by the patient before malpractice will be found against the healthcare provider. In the given scenario, Mrs. J came to harm as a direct result of the side rails not being raised and she incurred both a broken hip and a concussion.

causation

injury

Finally, the injured party must be able to prove damages, the sixth element of malpractice. Damages are vital as malpractice is non-intentional and unintended. Thus, the patient must show financial harm before the courts will allow a finding of **liability** against the defendant nurse and/or hospital. Mrs. J., in the given scenario, would be able to show additional hospital costs related to her hip replacement surgery, physical therapy needs, and home nursing care required once she was discharged from the hospital.

damages

As a nurse manager, one must know the applicable standards of care and ensure that all employees of the institution meet and/or exceed them. Review the standards periodically to ensure that they remain current and attuned to new technology and newer ways of performing tasks. If standards of care appear outdated or absent, notify the appropriate committee within the institution so that timely revisions can be made. Finally, ensure that all employees meet the standards of care by performing and/or reviewing all performance evaluations for evidence that standards of care are met, randomly reviewing patient charts for standards of care documentation, and inquiring of employees what constitutes standards of care and appropriate references for standards of care within the institution.

EXERCISE 3-2
Critically look at a policy and procedure manual at a community nursing service with which you are familiar. Are there policies that are outdated? Find out who is in charge of revising and writing policies and procedures for the agency. Take an outdated policy and revise it or use an issue that you determine should be included in the policy and procedure manual and write such a policy. Does your rewritten or new policy define standards of care? Where would you find criteria for ensuring that your policy and procedures fit a national standard?

LIABILITY: PERSONAL, VICARIOUS, AND CORPORATE

Personal liability defines each person's responsibility and accountability for individual actions or omissions. Even if others can be shown to be **liable** for a patient injury, each individual retains personal accountability for his/her own actions. The law sometimes allows other parties to be liable for certain causes of negligence. Known as **vicarious,** or substituted, **liability,** the doctrine of **respondeat superior** (let the master answer) makes employers accountable for the negligence of their employees. The rationale underlying the doctrine is that the employee would not have been in a position to have caused the wrongdoing unless hired by the employer and that the injured party will be allowed to suffer a double wrong merely because most

respondeat superior

employees are unable to pay damages for their wrongdoings. Nurse managers can best avoid these issues by ensuring that the staff members they supervise know and follow hospital policy and procedure and deliver competent nursing care.

Often nurses believe that the doctrine of vicarious liability shields them from personal liability; the institution may be sued, but not the individual nurse or nurses. Patients injured due to substandard care have the right to sue both the institution and the nurse. And the institution has the right under **indemnification** to sue the nurse for damages paid an injured patient. The principle of indemnification is applicable when the employer is held liable based solely on the actions of the staff member's **negligence** and the employer pays monetary damages because of the employee's negligent actions.

indemnification

negligence

Corporate liability is a newer trend in the law and essentially holds that the institution has the responsibility and accountability for maintaining an environment that ensures quality healthcare delivery for consumers. Corporate liability issues include negligent hiring and firing issues, a duty to maintain safety in the physical environment, and maintenance of a qualified, competent, and adequate staff. Nurse managers play a key role in assisting the institution to avoid corporate liability. For example, the nurse manager is normally delegated the duty to ensure that the staff remains competent and qualified, that personnel within their supervision have current licensure, and that incompetent, illegal, or unethical practices are reported to the proper persons or agencies.

CAUSES OF MALPRACTICE FOR NURSE MANAGERS

Nursing managers are charged with maintaining a standard of competent nursing care within the institution. Several potential sources of liability for malpractice among nurse managers may be identified. Once identified, guidelines to prevent or avoid these pitfalls can then be developed.

DELEGATION AND SUPERVISION

The field of nursing management involves supervision of a variety of personnel who directly provide nursing care to patients. The nurse manager remains personally liable for the reasonable exercise of delegation and supervision activities. The failure to delegate and supervise within acceptable standards of professional nursing practice may be seen as malpractice. Additionally, in a newer trend in the law, failure to delegate and supervise within acceptable standards may extend to direct corporate liability for the institution.

Note, though, that nurse managers are not liable merely because they have a supervisory function. The degree of knowledge concerning the skills and competencies of those one supervises is of paramount importance. The doctrine of "knew or should have known" becomes a legal standard in delegating tasks to the individuals whom one supervises. If it can be shown that the nurse manager delegated tasks appropriately and had no reason to believe that the assigned nurse was anything but competent to perform the task, then the nurse manager has no personal liability. But the converse is also true; if it can be shown that the nurse manager was aware of incompetencies in a given employee or that the assigned task is outside the employee's capabilities, then the nurse manager does become potentially liable for the subsequent injury to a patient.

Nurse managers have a duty to ensure that the staff members under their supervision are practicing in a competent manner. The nurse manager must be aware of staffs' knowledge, skills, and competencies and that they maintain their competencies. Knowingly allowing a staff member to function below the acceptable standard of care subjects both the nurse manager as well as the institution to potential liability. Some means of ensuring continued competency are continuing education programs and assigning the staff member to work with a second staff member to improve technical skills.

STAFFING ISSUES

Three different issues arise under the general term *staffing*. These include adequate numbers of staff members in a time of advancing patient acuity and limited resources, floating staff from one unit to another, and using temporary or "agency" staff to augment hospital staffing. Each area is addressed separately.

Accreditation standards, namely by the Joint Commission on the Accreditation of Healthcare Organizations (JCAHO), the Community Health Accreditation Program (CHAP), as well as other state and federal standards, mandate that healthcare institutions must provide adequate staffing with qualified personnel. This includes not only numbers of staff, but also the legal status of the staff member. For instance, some areas of an institution must have greater percentages of RNs than LPN/LVNs, such as critical care areas, post-anesthesia care areas, and emergency centers, while other areas may have equal or lower percentages of RNs to LPN/LVNs or nursing assistants, such as the general nursing areas and some long-term care areas. Whether short-staffing or understaffing does exist in a given situation depends on a careful, objective analysis of the number of patients, the amount of care required by each patient, and the number and classification/type of staff members (Fiesta, 1990). Courts will determine whether understaffing did indeed exist on an individual case (Guido, 1988).

While the institution is ultimately accountable for staffing issues, nurse managers may also incur some potential liability as they directly oversee numbers of personnel assigned to a unit on a given shift. For such nurse manager liability to incur, it must be shown that the resultant patient injury was directly due to the short-staffing and not due to the inappropriate or incompetent actions of an individual staff member, that is, sufficient numbers and competencies are available to meet nursing needs.

Guidelines for nurse managers in "short-staffing" issues include alerting hospital administrators and upper level managers of concerns. First, though, the nurse manager must have done whatever was under his/her control to have alleviated the circumstances, such as approving overtime for adequate coverage, reassigning personnel among those areas he/she supervises, and restricting new admissions to the area. Second, nurse managers have a legal duty to notify the chief operating officer, either directly or indirectly, when understaffing endangers patient welfare. One way of notifying the chief operating officer is through formal nursing channels, for example, by notifying the nurse manager's direct supervisor. Upper management must then decide how to alleviate the short-staffing, either on a short-term or long-term basis. Appropriate measures could be closing a certain unit or units, restricting elective surgeries, or hiring new staff members. Once the nurse manager can show that he or she acted appropriately, used sound judgment given the circumstances, and alerted his/her supervisors of the serious nature of the situation, then the institution becomes potentially liable for staffing issues.

Floating staff from unit to unit is the second issue that concerns overall staffing. Institutions have a duty to ensure that all areas of the institution are

accreditation standards

EXERCISE 3-3
Judy Jones, R.N., has worked in the emergency center for several years. She is currently ACLS (advanced cardiac life support) certified as are the other emergency care nurses; the hospital policy requires ACLS certification for employment in critical care areas. A new hospital policy expressly forbids the intubation of patients by nurses; only physicians may intubate patients. A crisis occurs in the emergency center one evening and Judy Jones intubated (successfully) a patient in full cardiac arrest. What do you do about this issue?

"short-staffing"

floating

adequately staffed; thus, units temporarily overstaffed either due to low patient census or a lower patient acuity ratio usually float staff to units less well staffed. Floating nurses to areas with which they have less familiarity and expertise can increase potential liability for the nurse manager, but to leave another area understaffed can also increase potential liability.

Before floating staff from one area to another, the nurse manager should consider staff expertise, patient care delivery systems, and patient care requirements. Nurses should be floated to units as comparable to their own unit as possible. This requires the nurse manager to match the nurse's home unit and float unit as much as is possible or to consider negotiating with another nurse manager to cross-float the nurse. For example, a manager might float a critical care nurse to an intermediate care unit and float an intermediate care unit nurse to a general unit. Or the manager might consider floating the general unit nurse to the postpartum unit and floating a postpartum nurse to labor and delivery. Open communications regarding staff limitations and concerns as well as creative solutions for staffing can alleviate some of the potential liability involved and create better morale among the float nurses. A positive option is to cross-train nurses within the institution so that nurses are familiar with two or three areas and can competently float to areas in which they have been cross-trained.

temporary personnel   The use of temporary or "agency" personnel has created increased liability concerns among nurse managers. Until recently, most jurisdictions held that such personnel were considered to be **independent contractors** and thus the institution was not liable for their actions, although their primary employment agency did retain potential liability. Today, courts have begun to hold the institution liable under the principle of **apparent agency.** Apparent authority or apparent agency refers to the doctrine whereby a principal becomes accountable for the actions of his agent. Apparent agency is created when a person (agent) holds himself/herself out as acting in behalf of the principal; in the instance of the agency nurse, the patient is unable to ascertain if the nurse works directly for the hospital (has a valid employment contract) or is working for a different employer. At law, lack of actual authority is no defense. This principle applies when it can be shown that the reasonable patient believed that the healthcare worker was an employee of the institution. If it appears to the reasonable patient that this worker is an employee of the institution, then the law will consider the worker as an employee for the purposes of corporate and vicarious liability.

This newer trend in the law makes it imperative that the nurse manager consider the temporary worker's skills, competencies, and knowledge when delegating tasks and supervising his/her actions. If there is reason to suspect that the temporary worker is incompetent, the nurse manager must convey this fact to the agency. The nurse manager must also either send the temporary worker home or reassign the worker to other duties and areas. Screening procedures, the same as those used with new institution employees, should also be performed with temporary workers.

Additional areas that nurse managers should stress when using agency or temporary personnel include assuring that the temporary staff member is given a brief but thorough orientation to institution policies and procedures, is made aware of resource materials within the institution, and is made aware of documentation procedures. It is also advisable that nurse managers assign a resource person to the temporary staff member. This resource person serves in the role of mentor for the agency nurse and serves to prevent potential problems that could arise merely because the agency staff member does not know the institution routine or is unaware of where to turn for assistance. This resource person also serves as a mentor for critical decision making for the agency nurse.

STRICT PRODUCT LIABILITY

When patient injury occurs because of equipment, the issue becomes one of whether the patient was injured due to a defect of the equipment (product) or whether the injury was due to the misusage or improper maintenance of the equipment. Product liability cases usually involve the manufacturer of the equipment, the institution, and the staff using the equipment. Nurse managers can lessen potential liability by ensuring that equipment is used in the proper manner, that equipment is maintained properly, and that any storage of the equipment follows the written manufacturer's guidelines. These are most often ensured by holding frequent and mandatory in-service classes on new equipment or on a new use of previously used equipment, recording necessary maintenance procedures, and quickly investigating any concern or problem with equipment. Remember, nurse managers may be found responsible along with staff members when equipment is misused or when maintenance procedures are not followed.

PROTECTIVE AND REPORTING LAWS

Protective and reporting laws ensure the safety or rights of specific classes of individuals. Most states have reporting laws for suspected child and elder abuse as well as laws for reporting certain categories of diseases and injuries. Examples of reporting laws include the reporting of venereal diseases, abuse of residents in nursing and convalescent homes, and organ donation. Nurse managers are frequently the individuals who are responsible for ensuring that the correct information is reported to the correct agencies, thus avoiding potential liability against the institution.

Many states now also have mandatory reporting of incompetent practice, especially through nurse practice acts, medical practice acts, and the National Practitioner Data Bank. Frequently, the reporting of incompetent practice is restricted to issues of chemical abuse and special provisions prevail if the affected nurse voluntarily undergoes drug diversion or chemical dependency rehabilitation. Mandatory reporting of incompetent practitioners is a complex process, involving both legal and ethical concerns. Nurse managers must know what the law requires, when reporting is mandated, to whom the report must be sent, and what the individual institution expects of its nurse managers. When in doubt, the nurse manager should seek clarification from the state board of nursing and hospital administration.

INFORMED CONSENT

Informed consent is the authorization by the patient or the patient's legal representative to do something to the patient and is based upon legal capacity, voluntary action, and comprehension. Legal capacity is usually the first requirement and is determined by age and competency. All states have a legal age

informed consent

requirements

for adult status defined by **statute;** competency involves the ability to understand the consequences of actions or the ability to handle personal affairs. In the instance that a minor or incompetent adult is involved, state statutes mandate who can serve as the patient's representative. In selected instances, the following types of minors may be able to give valid informed consent: **emancipated minors,** minors for treatment related to substance abuse or communicable diseases, and pregnant minors. Voluntary action, the second requirement, means that the patient was not coerced by fraud, duress, or deceit into allowing the procedure or treatment.

Comprehension is the third requirement and the most difficult to ascertain. The law states that the patient must be given sufficient information, in terms he/she can reasonably be expected to comprehend, to make an informed choice. Information that must be included appears in the box entitled "Required Information for Informed Consent."

Required Information for Informed Consent

- An explanation of the treatment/procedure to be performed and the expected results of the treatment/procedure
- Description of the risks involved
- Benefits that are likely to result because of the treatment/procedure
- Options to this course of action, including absence of treatment
- Name of the persons performing the procedure/treatment, and
- Statement that the patient may withdraw his/her consent at any time.

EXERCISE 3-4
A patient is admitted to your surgical center for minor surgery, specifically for a breast biopsy under local anesthesia. The surgeon has previously informed the patient of the surgery, risks, alternatives, desired outcomes, and possible complications. You give the surgery permit form to the patient for her signature. She readily states that she knows about the surgery and has no additional questions; she signs the form with no hesitation. Her husband, who is visiting with her, states he is worried as she will be awake during the procedure and he is afraid that something may be said to alarm her. What do you do at this point? Do you alert the surgeon that informed consent has not been obtained? Do you request that the surgeon revisit the patient and reinstruct her about the surgery? Or is there anything more that you should do as the patient has already signed the form?

Inherent in the doctrine of informed consent is the right of the patient to informed refusal. Patients must clearly understand the possible consequences of their refusal. In recent years, most states have enacted statutes to ensure that the competent adult has the right to refuse care and that the healthcare provider is protected should the adult validly refuse care.

Frequently, issues of informed consent among nurses concern the actual signing of the informed consent document, not the teaching and information that makes up informed consent. Many nurses serve as witnesses to the signing of the informed consent document and are attesting only to the voluntary nature of the patient's signature. There is no duty on the part of the nurse to insist that the patient repeat what has been said or what he/she remembers. Should the patient ask questions that alert the nurse to the inadequateness of true comprehension on the patient's part or express uncertainty while signing the document, then the nurse has an obligation to inform the primary healthcare provider and appropriate persons that informed consent has not been obtained.

PRIVACY AND CONFIDENTIALITY

privacy   **Privacy** is the patient's right to protection against unreasonable and unwarranted interference with the patient's solitude. This right extends to protection of personality as well as protection of one's right to be left alone. Within a medical context, the law recognizes the patient's right against (a) appropriation of the patient's name or picture for the institution's sole advantage, (b) intrusion by the institution upon the patient's seclusion or affairs, (c) publication of facts that place the patient in a false light, and (d) public disclosure of private facts about the patient by the hospital or staff. **Confidentiality** is the right to privacy of the medical record.

Institutions can reduce potential liability in this area by allowing access to patient data, either written or oral, only to those with a "need to know." Persons with a need to know include physicians and nurses caring for the patient, technicians, unit clerks, therapists, social service workers, and patient advocates. Usually, this need to know extends to the house staff and consultants. Others wishing to access patient data must first ask the patient for permission to review a chart. Administration of the institution can access the patient record for statistical analysis, staffing, and quality of care review.

The nurse manager is cautioned to ensure that staff members both understand and abide by rules regarding patient privacy and confidentiality. "Interesting" patients should not be discussed with others and all information concerning patients should only be given in private and secluded areas. Individual managers may need to review the current means of giving report to oncoming shifts and policies about telephone information. Many institutions have now added to the nursing care plan a reference to persons to whom the patient has allowed information to be given. If the caller identifies himself/herself as one of those listed persons, then the nurse can give patient information without violating the patient's privacy rights. Patients are becoming more knowledgeable about their rights in these areas and some have been willing to take offending staff members to court over such issues.

A concurrent issue in this area is the patient's right of access to his/her medical record. While the patient has a right of access, individual states mandate when this right attaches. Most states give the right of access only after the medical record is completed; thus, the patient has the right to review the chart after discharge. Some states do give the right of access while the patient is hospitalized, so individual state law governs individual nurses' actions. When supervising a patient's review of his/her record, explain only the entries that the patient questions or asks for further clarification about. Make a note in the record after the session indicating that the patient has viewed the record and what questions were answered.

Patients also have a right to copies of the chart, at their expense. The medical record belongs to the institution as a business record and patients never have the right to retain the original record. This is also true in instances where a subpoena is obtained to secure an individual's medical record for court purposes. A hospital representative will verify that the copy is a "true and valid" copy of the original record.

An issue that is closely related to the medical record is that of incident reports or unusual occurrence reports. These reports are mandated by JCAHO and serve to alert the institution concerning risk management and quality assurance within the setting. As such, incident reports are considered to be internal documents and thus not discoverable (open for review) by the injured party and/or attorneys representing the injured party. In most jurisdictions where this question has arisen, the courts have held that the incident report was discoverable and thus open to review by both sides of the suit.

It is therefore prudent for nurse managers to complete and to have staff members complete incident reports as though they will be open records. Omit any language of guilt such as "The patient would not have fallen if Jane Jones, R.N., had ensured that side rails were in their up and locked position." State only pertinent observations and all care that was given the patient, such as x-rays for a potential broken bone, medication that was given, and consultants who were called to examine the patient. It is also advisable not to note the occurrence of the incident report in the official record as that incorporates the incident report "by reference" and there is no way to keep the report from being seen by the injured party and/or attorneys for the injured party.

POLICIES AND PROCEDURES

risk management

Risk management is a process that identifies, analyzes, and treats potential hazards within a given setting. The object of risk management is to identify potential hazards and to eliminate them before anyone is harmed or disabled. Written policies and procedures fall within the scope of risk management activities. Written policies and procedures are a requirement of JCAHO. These documents set standards of care for the institution and direct practice. They must be clearly stated, well delineated, and based on current practice. Nurse managers should review the policies and procedures frequently for compliancy and timeliness. If policies are absent or outdated, request the appropriate person or committee to either initiate or update the policy.

EMPLOYMENT LAWS

The federal and individual state governments have enacted laws regulating employment. To be effective and legally correct, nurse managers must be familiar with these laws and how individual laws affect the institution and labor relations. Many nurse managers have come to fear the legal system because of personal experience or the experiences of colleagues. Much of this concern, though, may be directly attributable to uncertainty with the law or partial knowledge of the law. By understanding and correctly following federal employment laws, nurse managers may actually lessen their potential liability as they have complied with both federal and state laws. Table 3-2 gives an overview of key federal employment laws.

EQUAL EMPLOYMENT OPPORTUNITY LAWS

Several federal laws have been enacted to expand equal employment opportunities by prohibiting discrimination based upon gender, age, race, religion, handicap, pregnancy, and national origin. These laws are enforced by the Equal Employment Opportunity Commission (EEOC). Additionally, states have enacted statutes that address employment opportunities and the nurse manager should consider both when hiring and assigning nursing employees.

The most significant legislation affecting equal employment opportunities today is the amended 1964 Civil Rights Act (43 Fed. Reg. 1978). Section 703 (a) of Title VII makes it illegal for an employer "To refuse to hire, discharge an individual, or otherwise to discriminate against an individual, with respect to his compensation, terms, conditions, or privileges of employment because of the individual's race, color, religion, sex, or national origin." Title VII was also amended by the Equal Opportunities Act of 1972 so that it applies to private institutions with fifteen or more employees, state and local governments, **labor unions,** and employment agencies.

EXERCISE 3-5
You are assigned some risk management activities in the nursing facility where you work. In investigating incident reports that were filed by your staff, you discover that this is the third patient this week who has fallen while attempting to get out of bed and sit in a chair. How would you handle this issue? Decide where you would start a more complete investigation of this issue. For example, is it a nursing facility–wide issue or one that is confined to one unit? What safety issues are you going to discuss with your staff and how are you going to discuss these issues? Design a unit inservice class for the staff concerning incident reports and safety of patients.

TABLE 3-2	Selected Federal Labor Legislation

YEAR	LEGISLATION	PURPOSE AND EFFECT
1935	Wagner Act; National Labor Act	Established many rights in unionizations; National Labor Relations Board (NLRB) established
1947	Taft-Hartley Act	Resulted in more equal balance of power between unions and management
1962	Executive Order 10988	Permitted public employees to join unions
1963	Equal Pay Act	Made it illegal to pay lower wages to employees based solely on gender
1964	Civil Rights Act	Protected against discrimination due to race, color, creed, national origin, etc.
1967	Age Discrimination Act	Made it illegal for employers to discriminate against older men and women
1974	Wagner Amendments	Allowed nonprofit organizations to join unions; opened unionization in nursing
1990	Americans with Disabilities Act	Barred discrimination against disabled individuals in the workplace
1991	Civil Rights Act	Addressed specifically sexual harassment in the workplace; overrode and modified previous legislation in this area
1993	Family and Medical Leave Act	Addressed needs for leave based on family and medical needs

Adapted from Marquis and Huston, 1992, p. 319

In 1991, the Civil Rights Act was signed into law. This act further broadened the issue of sexual harassment in the workplace and supersedes many of the sections of Title VII. Sections of the new legislation define sexual harassment, its elements, and the employer's responsibilities regarding harassment in the workplace, especially prevention and corrective action. The Civil Rights Act is enforced by the EEOC as created in the 1964 act; its powers were broadened in the 1972 Equal Employment Opportunity Act. The primary activity of the EEOC is the processing of complaints of employment discrimination. There are three phases: investigation, conciliation, and litigation. Investigation focuses on determining whether or not Title VII has been violated by the employer. If the EEOC finds "probable cause," an attempt is made to reach an agreement or conciliation between the EEOC, the complainant, and the employer. If conciliation fails, the EEOC may file suit against the employer in federal court or issue to the complainant the right to sue for discrimination.

EEOC

The EEOC also promulgated written rules and regulations that reflect its interpretation of the laws under its auspices. Included in these written rules and regulations are those relating to staffing practices and those relating to sexual harassment in the work place. The EEOC defines sexual harassment broadly and this has generally been upheld in the courts. Nurse managers must realize that it is the duty of employers (management) to prevent employees from sexually harassing other employees. The EEOC issues policies and practices for employers to implement both to sensitize employees to this problem and to prevent its occurrence; nurse managers should be aware of these policies and practices and seek guidance in implementing them if sexual harassment occurs in their units.

There are a number of bases upon which employers may seek exceptions to Title VII. For example, it is lawful to make employment decisions on the basis of national origin, religion, and gender (never race or color) if such decisions are necessary for the normal operation of the business, though the courts have viewed this exception very narrowly. Promotions and layoffs based on bona fide seniority or merit systems are permissible (*Firefighters Local 1784 v. Scotts,* 1984) as are exceptions based upon business necessity.

AGE DISCRIMINATION IN EMPLOYMENT ACT OF 1967

This act made it illegal for employers, unions, and employment agencies to discriminate against older men and women. The law, in a 1986 amendment, prohibits discrimination over the age of 40. The practical outcome of this act has been that mandatory retirement is no longer seen in the American workplace.

As with Title VII, there are some exceptions to this act. Reasonable factors, other than age, may be used when terminations become necessary; such reasonable factors would be a performance evaluation system and some limited occupational qualifications, for example tedious physical demands of a specific job.

AMERICANS WITH DISABILITIES ACT OF 1990

The Americans with Disabilities Act (ADA) of 1990 provides protection to persons with disabilities and is the most significant civil rights legislation since the Civil Rights Act of 1964. The purpose of the ADA is to provide a clear and comprehensive national mandate for the elimination of discrimination against disabled individuals and to provide clear, strong, consistent, enforceable standards addressing discrimination in the workplace. The ADA is closely related to the Civil Rights Act and incorporates the antidiscrimination principles established in Section 504 of the Rehabilitation Act of 1973.

The act has five titles and Table 3-3 shows the pertinent issues about each title. The ADA has jurisdiction over employers, private and public, employment agencies, labor organizations, and joint labor-managed committees. It defines disability broadly: with respect to an individual a disability is (a) a physical or mental impairment that substantially limits one or more of the major *disability* life activities of such individual, (b) a record of such impairment, or (c) being regarded as having such an impairment [42 *USC* sec. 12102(2)]. The overall effect of the legislation is that persons with disabilities will not be excluded from job opportunities or adversely affected in any aspect of employment unless they are not qualified or are otherwise unable to perform the job. The ADA thus protects qualified and disabled individuals in regard to job application procedures, hiring, compensation, advancement, and all other employment matters.

TABLE 3-3	Americans With Disabilities Act of 1990

TITLE	PROVISIONS
I	Employment: defines purpose of the act and who is qualified under the act as disabled
II	Public services: concerns services, programs, and activities of public entities as well as public transportation
III	Public accommodations and services operated by private entities: prohibits discrimination against disabled in areas of public accommodations, commercial facilites, and public transportation services
IV	Telecommunications: intended to make telephone services accessible to individuals with hearing or speech impairments
V	Miscellaneous provisions: certain insurance matters; incorporation of this act with other federal and state laws

Adapted from 42 USC sec. 12101 et seq.

The act requires the employer or potential employer to make reasonable accommodations to employ the disabled. The law does not mandate that disabled individuals be hired before fully qualified, nondisabled persons; it does mandate that the disabled not be disqualified merely because of an easily accommodated disability. Also, the act specifically excludes from the definition of disability sexual behavioral disorders such as homosexuality and bisexuality, gamblers, kleptomaniacs, pyromaniacs, and those who currently use illegal drugs [42 USC sec. 12211(a) and (b)(1)]. Moreover, employers may hold alcoholics to the same job qualifications and job performance standards as other employees even if the unsatisfactory behavior or performance is related to the alcoholism [42 USC sec. 12114 (c)(4)]. As with other federal employment laws, the nurse manager should have a thorough understanding of the law as it applies to the institution and his/her specific job description, and know who to contact within the institution structure for clarification as needed.

AFFIRMATIVE ACTION

The policy of affirmative action (AA) differs from the policy of equal employment opportunity (EEOC). AA enhances employment opportunities of protected groups of people while EEO is concerned with utilizing employment practices that do not discriminate against or impair the employment opportunities of protected groups. Thus, AA can be seen in conjunction with several federal employment laws; for example, in conjunction with the Vietnam Era Veterans' Readjustment Act of 1974, the AA requires that employers with government contracts take steps to enhance the employment opportunities of disabled veterans and other veterans of the Vietnam era.

EQUAL PAY ACT OF 1963

The Equal Pay Act makes it illegal to pay lower wages to employees of one gender when the jobs (a) require equal skill in experience, training, education, and ability; (b) require equal effort in mental or physical exertion; (c) are of equal responsibility and accountability; and (d) are performed under similar working conditions. Courts have held that unequal pay may be legal if based upon seniority, merit, incentive systems, and a factor other than gender. The main cases filed under this law in the area of nursing have been by nonprofessionals.

OCCUPATIONAL SAFETY AND HEALTH ACT

The Occupational Safety and Health Administration (OSHA) Act of 1970 was enacted to assure that healthful and safe working conditions would exist in the workplace. Among other provisions, the law requires isolation procedures, the placarding of areas containing ionizing radiation, proper grounding of electrical equipment, protective storage of flammable and combustible liquids, and the gloving of all personnel when handling bodily fluids. The statute provides that if no federal standard has been established, state statutes prevail. Nurse managers should know the relevant OSHA laws for the institution and his/her specific area. Frequent review of new additions to the law must also be undertaken, especially in this era of AIDS and infectious diseases, and care must be taken to ensure that necessary gloves and equipment as specified are available on each unit.

EMPLOYMENT-AT-WILL AND WRONGFUL DISCHARGE

Historically, the employment relationship has been considered as a "free will" relationship. Employees were free to take or not take a job at will and employers were free to hire, retain, or discharge employees for any reason. Many laws, some federal but predominantly state, have been slowly eroding this at-will employment relationship. Evolving case law provides at least three exceptions to the broad doctrine of employment-at-will.

exceptions   The first exception is a public policy exception. This exception involves cases where an employee is discharged in direct conflict with established public policy (Twomey, 1986). Some examples would be discharging an employee for serving on a jury, for reporting an employers' illegal actions (better known as "whistle blowing"), and for filing a worker's compensation claim.

The second exception involves situations in which there is an implied contract. The courts have generally treated employee handbooks, company policies, and oral statements made at the time of employment as "framing the employment relationship" *(Toussaint v. Blue Cross and Blue Shield, 1980)*. In that case, the court held that a statement in the company's policy handbook that stated an employee would only be discharged for "good cause" provided an enforceable contract between the employer and employee.

The third exception is a "good faith and fair dealing" exception. The purpose of this exception is to prevent unfair or malicious terminations and the exception is used sparingly by the courts. In *Fortune v. National Cash Register* (1977), an employee was discharged just before a final contract was signed between his employer and another company for which the employee would have received a large commission. The court held that he was discharged in bad faith, solely to prevent paying his commission by National Cash Register.

Nurse managers are urged to know their respective state law concerning this growing area of the law. Managers should also review institution documents, especially employee handbooks and recruiting brochures, for unwanted statements implying job security or other unintentional promises. Managers are also cautioned not to say anything during the pre-employment negotiations and interviews that might be construed as implying job security or other unintentional promises to the potential employee.

COLLECTIVE BARGAINING

Collective bargaining, also called labor relations, is the joining together of employees for the purpose of increasing their ability to influence the employer and improve working conditions. Usually, the employer is referred to as management and the employees, even professionals, are labor. Those persons involved in the hiring, firing, scheduling, disciplining, or evaluating of employers are considered management and may not be included in a collective bargaining unit. Those in management could form their own group, but are not protected under these laws. Nurse managers may or may not be part of management; if they have hiring and firing authority, then they are part of management.

Collective bargaining is defined and protected by the National Labor Relations Act and its amendments; the National Labor Relations Board (NLRB) oversees the act and those who come under its auspices. The NLRB ensures that employees are able to choose freely whether they want to be represented by a particular bargaining unit and it serves to prevent or remedy any violation of the labor laws.

Collective bargaining may be new to some nurses. Executive Order 10988 in 1962 made it possible for public employees to join collective bargaining units and nonprofit healthcare organizations have been subject to these laws only since 1974 with an amendment to the Wagner Act. The American Nurses' Association has long supported the right of nurses to bargain collectively; since 1946, the American Nurses' Association through its state constituent associations has collectively represented the interests of nurses within the individual states. Two of the main reasons proposed for this support are (a) collective bargaining allows for achieving the basic elements of professional status, and (b) collective bargaining allows a mechanism for nurses to resolve conflicts within the workplace setting, thereby enhancing quality of care to patients.

Collective bargaining is a power strategy based on the premise that there is increased power in numbers. Collective bargaining assists in the following areas: (a) basic economic issues such as salary, shift differentials, overtime pay, length of the workday, vacation time, sick leave, lunch breaks, health insurance, and severance pay; (b) unfair or arbitrary treatment such as scheduling, staffing, rotating shifts, on-call, transfers, seniority rights, and posting of job openings; and (c) maintenance and promotion of professional practice such as acceptable standards of care, other quality of care issues, and adequate staffing ratios.

Issues against collective bargaining by professionals include the charges of unprofessionalism and unethical behavior, especially when faced with a strike situation, that it is divisive, and that job security is actually endangered because of the concept of a closed shop (everyone must join the union). Most healthcare unions are open shops, allowing nurses to either join the union or not. All of these issues have many sides that can be argued; many nurses now acknowledge that they have progressed because of collective bargaining and unionization.

The process of unionization is a complex one. The accompanying box highlights some of the terms used in unionization and collective bargaining. Organizing is the first phase in which a labor organization is formed, called an

EXERCISE 3-6
A staff member in a collective bargaining group approaches you requesting to be scheduled for vacation for the next two weekends. She explains that there is a family wedding out of state one weekend and that her mother is having surgery on the Friday of the second week and that she has promised to help take care of her that weekend. How do you proceed in this instance? What if the contract is silent as to how many weekends a worker can work during a four-week period?

unionization process

Collective Bargaining Terms

Arbitration: the terminal step in the grievance process during which an impartial third party attempts to come to a reasonable solution taking into consideration both management and labor issues; may be either a voluntary or a government-enforced compulsory process; this person has the final power of decision making in the dispute

Closed shop: synonymous with union shop

Collective bargaining: the relations between employers and labor; employers act through their management representatives and labor acts through its union representatives

Conciliation and mediation: these are synonymous terms describing the activity of a third party to assist the disputants reach an acceptable agreement; unlike the arbitrator, this individual has no final power of decision making

Free speech: under Public Law 101, Section 8, the "expression of any views, argument, or dissemination thereof, whether in written, printed, graphic, or visual form, shall not constitute or be evident of unfair labor practice under any provision of this Act, if such expression contains no threat of reprisal or force or promise of benefit"

Grievance: process undertaken when the perception exists on the part of a union member that management has failed in some way to meet the terms of the labor agreement

Lockout: consists of closing a place of business by management in the course of a labor dispute for the purpose of forcing employees to accept management terms

National Labor Relations Board: formed to implement the Wagner Act and serves to (a) determine who should be the official bargaining unit when a new unit is formed and who should be in the unit, and (b) adjudicate unfair labor changes

Open shop: also known as an agency shop; employees are not required to join a union, although they may if they so desire and one exists within the workplace

Professionals: have the right to be represented by a labor union; cannot belong to a union that also represents nonprofessionals unless a majority of the professionals vote for inclusion into the nonprofessional unit

Strike: a concerted withholding of labor supply in order to bring economic pressure upon management and force management to grant employee demands

Supervisor: someone who has the authority to hire, fire, transfer, and promote employees; supervisors are excluded from protection under the Taft-Hartley Act and cannot be represented by a union

Union shop: also known as a closed shop; all employees are required to join the union and to pay dues

organizing council. This proceeds to NLRB supervised elections when enough written interest has been expressed to warrant the formulation of a recognized union. This election period is normally tense and both management and union officials attempt to influence the vote in their favor.

If the election is successful for the union and the bargaining agent is certified by the NLRB, a contract negotiation period is begun. Each side appoints a spokesperson and good-faith bargaining is mandated by law for both sides. During this phase, there may be stalemates, mediation, and binding **arbitration.** The arbitrator is a neutral party whose purpose is to be fair to both sides; the arbitrator's solution and recommendations are binding to both sides, so often the two sides are more likely to negotiate for small favors.

If the two sides cannot agree and are unwilling to call for arbitration, work stoppages by employees and lockouts by management can occur. With ten days' notice, the union can then proceed to a strike. Usually ratification of the agreement is reached as no side wants a strike and negotiations take on added fervor during work stoppages and lockouts.

Once ratified, collective bargaining does not end, but enters the enforcement stage. Grievances can be brought by either management or employees if there are disputes and complaints. Grievances typically can be solved without further steps being taken, but there are specific provisions for resolution, including arbitration.

From a management position, there are several things that nurse managers and upper-level management can do to prevent unionization. Since most unions form because of real or perceived disagreement with management, a well-rounded, high-quality, effective leadership team is needed to prevent dissatisfaction from becoming rampant. Some suggestions for management include:

1. Provide opportunity for participation in organization decision making; a participative approach may extend to unit self-governance.
2. Maintain salaries in relationship with the education required and the responsibility given.
3. Treat professionals as true professionals; this entails affording respect, trust, and value to all professionals in the organization.
4. Develop, implement, and refine a grievance procedure. This ensures that staff members have direction when they feel dissatisfied and prevents dissatisfaction from becoming so overwhelming that unionization is the only foreseeable answer.
5. Conduct timely and regular surveys and meetings to allow staff an opportunity to express their feelings and views. Open channels of communications are crucial in maintaining positive working relationships.

Once the contract has been accepted and the nurse manager is managing and leading within a union framework, there are some things that he/she must remember. First, know and understand the contract provisions. A thorough understanding and following of the contract can prevent most grievances. Second, treat all persons being supervised with equal respect and consideration, both union and nonunion members. This will prevent a charge of discrimination and should serve to maintain morale. Third, should an issue arise, perform as a professional, be nondefensive, and do not crumble under the pressure. Admit wrong statements or decisions and negotiate a better solution to the problem, assuring that the institution goals will be upheld. Fourth, if necessary, seek assistance from upper management, especially if the conflict cannot be immediately resolved. And, fifth, continue to expand personal knowledge of management principles through either formal education or continuing education and practice those principles.

PROFESSIONAL NURSING PRACTICE: ETHICS

ETHICAL THEORIES

ethics

Ethics is the science relating to moral actions and one's value system. Many nurses envision ethics as dealing with principles or morality and thus what is right or wrong. A broader conceptual definition of ethics is that ethics is concerned with motives and attitudes and the relationship of these attitudes to the good of the individual. "Ethics has to do with actions we wish people would take, not actions they must take" (Hall, 1990, p. 37). Thus, **values** are interwoven with ethics; values are personal beliefs about the truth and worth of thoughts, objects, and behavior.

Ethics may be distinguished from the law as ethics is internal to oneself, looks to the good of an individual rather than society as a whole, and concerns the "why" of one's actions. The law, comprised of rules and regulations pertinent to society as a whole, is external to oneself and concerns one's actions and conduct. What did the person do or fail to do as opposed to why did the person act as he/she did? Ethics concerns the good of an individual within society while law concerns society as a whole as opposed to the individual in society. Law can be enforced through the courts and statutes while ethics are enforced via ethics committees and professional codes. Table 3-4 shows the distinctions between law and ethics.

Today, ethics and legal issues often become entwined and it is difficult to separate ethics from legal concerns. Legal principles and doctrines assist the nurse manager in decision making, and ethical theories and principles are often involved in those decisions. Thus, the nurse manager must be cognizant of both areas in everyday management concerns.

TABLE 3-4	Distinctions Between Law and Ethics	
	LAW	**ETHICS**
Source	External to oneself; rules and regulations for society	Internal to oneself; values beliefs and individual interpretations
Concerns	Conduct and actions—what did the person do?	Motive and attitudes—why did the person act as he/she did?
Interests	Society as a whole	Individuals within a society
Enforcement	Courts and statutes	Ethics committees; professional organizations

Adapted from Guido, 1988, p. 264.

Many different ethical theories have evolved to justify existing moral principles; these theories are considered normative as they are universally applicable theories of right and wrong. Most normative approaches to ethics fall under two broad categories:

deontology

Deontological (from the Greek *deon,* or "duty") **theories** derive norms and rules from the duties human beings owe to one another by virtue of commitments made and roles assumed. Generally, deontologists hold that a sense of duty consists of rational respect for the fulfilling of one's obligations to other human beings. The greatest strength of this theory is its emphasis on the dignity of human beings. Deontological ethics look not to the end or consequences of an action, but to the intention of the action. It is one's good intentions, the intentions to do a moral duty, that ultimately determine the praiseworthiness of the action. Deontological ethics have sometimes been subdivided into situation ethics, wherein the decision making takes into account the unique characteristics of each individual, the caring relationship between the person and the caregiver, and the most humanistic course of action given the circumstances.

teleology

Teleological (from the Greek *telos*, for "end") **theories** derive norms or rules for conduct from the consequences of actions. Right consists of actions that have good consequences and wrong consists of actions that have bad consequences. Teleologists disagree, though, about how to determine the goodness or badness of the consequences of actions. This theory is frequently referred to as utilitarianism; what makes an action right or wrong is its utility and useful actions bring about the greatest amount of good into existence. An alternate way of viewing this theory is that the usefulness of an action is determined by the amount of happiness it brings. Utilitarian ethics can then be subdivided into rule and act utilitarianism. Rule utilitarianism seeks the greatest happiness for all; it appeals to public agreement as a basis for objective judgment about the nature of happiness. Act utilitarianism tries to determine in a particular situation which course of action will bring about the greatest happiness, or the least harm and suffering, to a single person. As such, act utilitarianism makes happiness subjective (Guido, 1989).

ETHICAL PRINCIPLES

Ethical principles actually control professionalism nursing practice much more than do ethical theories. Principles encompass basic premises from which rules are developed. Principles are the moral norms that nursing, as a profession, both demands and strives to implement in everyday clinical practice. Ethical principles that the nurse manager should consider when making decisions include the eight items listed in the accompanying box. Each of these principles can be used by itself, though it is much more common to see more than one ethical principle in practice.

autonomy

The **autonomy** principle addresses personal freedom and the right to choose what will happen to one's own person. The legal doctrine of informed consent is a direct reflection of this principle. This principle underlies the

---

Ethical Principles

- Autonomy
- Beneficence
- Non-maleficence
- Veracity
- Justice
- Paternalism
- Fidelity
- Respect for others

concept of progressive discipline as the employee has the option to meet delineated expectations or take full accountability for his/her actions. This principle also underlies the professional nurse's clinical practice as autonomy is reflected in individual decision making about patient care issues as well as in group decision making about unit operations decisions. The accompanying "Research Perspective" depicts how important autonomy is to both staff members and nurse managers.

Research Perspective

Blegen, M.A., Goode, C., Johnson, M., Maas, M., Chen, L., & Moorhead, S. (1993). Preference for decision-making autonomy. Image, 25(4), 339–344.

Autonomy is an ethical principle that affects both patients as well as nurses. Autonomy concerns the right of the individual to take independent action based upon his/her unique values and desires. Researchers have studied nurses' lack of autonomy for several decades and have concluded that a correlation of .42 exists between perceived autonomy and job satisfaction (Blegen, et al., 1993).

As changes have occurred within the mangement of nursing care settings there is now an increasing level of staff autonomy. This study was conducted to determine the amount of autonomy perceived by nurses in both patient care activities and unit operation activities. Autonomy was defined as "authority and accountability for patient care and unit operations, and referred to the right to make decisions and the responsibility for outcomes" (Blegen et al., 1993, p. 340). Five questions were developed for the research study and concerned the level of autonomy as perceived by nurses, a desire for increased autonomy, and whether nurses desired more autonomy in patient care decisions and/or unit operation decisions.

This was a descriptive study with a sample of 356 randomly selected staff nurses and 130 head nurses from sixteen hospitals in Iowa. All nurses were employed at least 50 percent of the time and the resultant sample had fairly even numbers of nurses from small, medium-sized, and large hospitals. Average years of employment was twelve for staff nurses and nineteen for head nurses. Each subject was given a Likert-styled questionnaire to complete that involved twenty-one patient care decisions and twenty-one unit operations decisions. Respondents were asked to "indicate whether they thought staff nurses should: 1) have no authority and accountability, 2) assume authority and accountability when asked, 3) share authority and accountability with others and participate in group decisions, 4) consult with others and then make the decision and assume accountability, or 5) have full independent authority and accountability" (Blegen et al., 1993, p. 341).

Conclusions of the study showed that staff nurses agreed on the desired level of autonomy and accountability for 60 percent of the decisions for which they were asked to respond. Nurses desired a more independent level of authority and accountability for patient care decisions and desired more group participation in unit operation decisions. Respondents indicated that they already had a higher degree of autonomy in patient care decisions and that they desired more involvement in unit operation decisions. Head nurse responses indicated that staff nurses already had a higher degree of involvement in all decisions than the staff nurses indicated that they should have. Perhaps this support for staff nurse involvement, especially at the unit operation level, has not been conveyed to staff nurses.

Research Perspective—cont'd

Implications for Practice

Implications for nurse managers include that a set of specific decisions be transferred to staff nurses. In patient care decisions, these decisions concern patient education, pain management, scheduling, and discussing the plan of care with the patient as well as consulting with other providers. Within unit operation management, these decisions include setting policies, unit goals, job descriptions, and standards for quality assurance and job performance. In decisions for which there was little agreement among the respondents, managers may have to work toward increasing staff nurse autonomy and involvement. Decisions will need to be made concerning what is critical to patient care and nurse satisfaction within individual institutions. The study implied that nurse managers should expect a greater desire for staff involvement in staff nurses who are prepared at the baccalaureate level and those staff nurses who are active members of professional organizations.

The **beneficence** principle states that the actions one takes should promote good. In caring for patients, good can be defined in many ways including allowing a person to die without advanced life support. Good can also prompt the nurse to encourage the patient to undergo extensive, painful treatment procedures as these procedures will incresae both the quality and quantity of life. This principle is used when nurse managers accentuate the employee's positive attributes and qualities rather than focusing on the negative and the employee's failures and shortcomings.

beneficence

The corollary of beneficence, the principle of **non-maleficence,** states that one should do no harm. Many nurses find it difficult to follow this principle when performing treatments and procedures that bring discomfort and pain to patients. Thus, the principle of beneficence may be chosen as even pain and suffering can bring about good for the patient. As a nurse manager following this principle, performance evaluation should emphasize the employee's good qualities and give positive direction for growth. Destroying the employee's self-esteem and self-worth would be considered doing harm under this principle.

non-maleficence

Veracity concerns truth telling and incorporates the concept that individuals should always tell the truth. The principle also compels that the truth be completely told. Nurse managers use this principle when they give all the facts of a situation, truthfully, and then assist employees to make decisions. For example, with low patient censuses, employees must be told all the options and then be allowed to make their own decisions about floating to other units, taking vacation time, or taking a day without pay if the institution has such a policy.

veracity

Justice concerns the issue that persons should be treated equally and fairly. This principle usually arises in times of short supplies or when there is competition for resources or benefits. This principle is considered with holiday and vacation time and paid attendance at national conferences; overall performance should be considered, rather than who is next on the list to attend a conference or to be allowed time off.

justice

This principle, **paternalism,** allows one to make decisions for another and often is seen as a negative or undesirable principle. Paternalism assists persons

paternalism

fidelity

respect for others

EXERCISE 3-7
The community has been suffering from a severe nursing shortage made worse by a particularly virulent flu that has affected many of the staff members. Upper management is aware of the severity of the shortage and has decreased bed census by 20 percent and only emergency surgery is being performed until the crisis abates. You are considering reassigning a portion of your critical care staff, including dialysis and emergency care nurses, to the general medical-surgical floors as the crisis is most severe on the general units. None of the staff has been cross-trained specifically to the general units. From an ethical standpoint, how would you begin to achieve this task? How would you select which nurses to reassign and which nurses to retain in the unit? Would you involve the nurses themselves in the decision-making process? Why or why not?

MORAL model

to make decisions when they do not have sufficient data or expertise. Staff members frequently use some degree of paternalism when they assist patients and their family members to decide if surgical procedures should be undertaken or if medical management is a better option. Paternalism becomes undesirable when the entire decision is taken from the patient or employee. Nurse managers use this principle in a positive manner by assisting employees in deciding major career moves and plans.

Fidelity is keeping one's promises or commitments. Staff members know not to promise to patients commitments that they may not be able to keep, such as assuring the patient that no code will be performed before consulting with the patient's physician for such an order. Nurse managers abide by this principle when they follow through on any promises they have previously made to employees, such as a promised leave, a certain shift to be worked, or a promotion to preceptor within the unit.

Many think the principle of **respect for others** is the highest principle and incorporates all other principles. Respect for others acknowledges the right of individuals to make decisions and to live by these decisions. Respect for others also transcends cultural differences, gender issues, and racial concerns to name some specific examples. Nurse mangers positively reinforce this principle daily in their actions with employees, patients, and peers for they serve as role models for staff members and others in the institution.

ETHICAL DECISION-MAKING FRAMEWORK

Ethical decision making involves reflection on the following: who should make the choice; possible options or courses of action; available options; consequences, both good and bad, of all possible options; rules, obligations, and values that should direct choices; and desired goals or outcomes. When making decisions, nurses need to combine all of these elements using an orderly, systematic, and objective method; ethical decision-making models assist in accomplishing this goal.

There are various models for ethical decision making. All of the models have five to eight ordered steps that start with fully comprehending the dilemma and conclude with evaluation of the implemented option. An example of a traditional model for ethical decision making might include the following steps:

1. Identify the problem
2. Gather data to analyze the causes and consequences of the problem
3. Explore optional solutions to the problem
4. Evaluate these optional solutions
5. Select the appropriate solution from all the options
6. Implement the selected solution
7. Evaluate the results

Perhaps the easiest ethical decision-making model to remember and to implement in practice is the MORAL model (see box) developed by Thiroux in 1977 and further developed for nursing by Halloran in 1982. Many nurses prefer this method as the letters of the acronym remind nurses of the subsequent steps to take.

Ethical decision making is always a process. To facilitate the process, use all available resources, including the institutional ethics committee, and communicate with and support all those involved in the process. Some decisions are easier to reach and support. It is important to allow sufficient time for the process so that a supportable option can be reached.

MORAL Model for Ethical Decision Making

M   Massage the dilemma. Identify and define the issues in the dilemma. Consider the opinions of all the major players in the dilemma as well as their value systems. This includes patients, family members, nurses, physicians, clergy, and any other interdisciplinary healthcare members.

O   Outline the options. Examine all the options, including those less realistic and conflicting. This stage is designed only for considering options and not for making a final decision.

R   Resolve the dilemma. Review the issues and options, applying the basic principles of ethics to each option. Decide the best option based upon the views of all those concerned in the dilemma.

A   Act by applying the chosen option. This step is usually the most difficult as it requires actual implementation while the previous steps had only allowed for dialogue and discussion.

L   Look back and evaluate the entire process, including the implementation. No process is complete without a thorough evaluation. Ensure that those involved are able to follow through on the final option. If not, a second decision may be required and the process must start again at the initial step.

Adapted from Thiroux (1977) and Halloran (1982).

CHAPTER CHECKLIST

This chapter addresses the issues of legal and ethical interaction with regard to nurse managers. Legislative and legal controls have been established to clarify the boundaries of professional practice and to protect consumers. Thus there are some definite answers and guidelines to assist practitioners from the legal and legislative areas. These controls are constantly evolving and the nurse manager must continually be aware of these changes as they affect the scope of the practice. Ethics has no such answers. Nor are there rules and guidelines that cover all aspects of human life. Thus nurse managers must explore value systems and become expert in using ethical models, incorporating both ethical theories and principles. The use of a systematic, humanistic approach reduces bias, facilitates decision making, and allows the best working conditions possible from an ethical standpoint.

- Understanding and using legal and ethical principles are key strategies to be integrated into the role of an effective nurse manager.
- Nurse practice acts define the scope of acceptable practice for licensed registered nurses as well as licensed practical (vocational) nurses.
- Legal principles, if effectively integrated into all aspects of nursing management, minimize one's potential legal liability.
  - Malpractice is the failure of a person with professional education and skills to act in a reasonable and prudent manner.
  - Causes of malpractice for nurse managers include:
    - Issues of delegation and supervision
    - Staffing issues

- Liability may be classified as personal, vicarious, corporate, or strict product.
- Protective and reporting laws ensure the safety or rights of specific groups of people.
- Informed consent is the authorization by the patient or the patient's legal representative to do something to the patient.
- Privacy and confidentiality rights protect the patient from unreasonable and unwanted interference and secure the privacy of the patient's medical record.
- Federal and state governments have enacted a number of employment laws that nurses need to understand and follow when dealing with managerial issues. These include:
  - Taft-Hartley Act
  - Equal Pay Act
  - Civil Rights Act
  - Age Discrimination Act
  - Americans with Disabilities Act

■ Managers can implement five guidelines to help ensure that the work setting is professional and satisfying:
- Take a participative approach to decision making
- Maintain fair, competitive salaries
- Treat professionals as professionals
- Develop, implement, and refine a grievance procedure
- Conduct regular meetings to open communication channels

■ Ethical theories and principles relate to moral actions and value systems and apply both to patient situations and management situations.
- Ethical theories justify existing moral principles and are considered universally applicable.
- Ethical principles exert direct control over professional nursing practice and encompass basic premises from which rules are developed.
- The "MORAL" model is an easy acronym to remember in ethical decision making.

TERMS TO KNOW

- apparent agency
- arbitration
- autonomy
- beneficence
- collective bargaining
- common law
- confidentiality
- consent
- defendant
- deontological theory
- emancipated minor
- ethics
- expert witness
- fidelity
- forseeability
- indemnification
- independent contractor
- informed consent
- jurisprudence
- justice
- labor union
- law
- lay witness
- liability
- liable
- licensure
- malpractice
- negligence
- nonmaleficence
- Nurse Practice Act
- paternalism
- personal liability
- plaintiff
- privacy
- reporting statutes
- respect for others
- respondeat superior
- scope of practice
- standards of care
- statutes
- teleological theory
- testimony
- values
- veracity
- vicarious liability

REFERENCES

American Nurses' Association. (1988). *Standards for Nurse Administrators.* Kansas City: American Nurses' Association.

Bishop v United States, 334 F. Supp. 415 (D.C. Tex.), 1971.

Blegen, M.A., Goode, C., Johnson, M., Maas, M., Chen, L., & Moorhead, S. (1993). Preference for decision-making autonomy. *Image, 25*(4), 339–344.

Civil Rights Act, 43 Fed. Reg. 1978, Sec. 703 et. seq, 1964.

Executive Order 10988, 1962.

Fiesta, J. (1990). The nursing shortage; whose liability problem? Part II. *Nursing Management, 21*(2), 22–23.

Firefighters Local 1784 v Scotts, 467 US 561, 34 FEP Cases 1702, 1984.

Fortune v National Cash Register Company, 272 Mass. 96, 264 NE 2d 1251, 1977.

42 *USC* sec. 12101 et. seq., 1990.

Guido, G.W. (1988). *Legal Issues in Nursing: A Source Book for Practice.* Norwalk, CT: Appleton and Lange.

_____ (1989). Ethical and legal principles affecting decision-making in critical care nursing. In Dolan, J. *Critcal Care Nursing: Clinical Management through the Nursing Process.* Philadelphia: F.A. Davis.

Hall, J.K. (1990). Understanding the fine line between law and ethics. *Nursing 90, 20*(10), 37.

Halloran, M.C. (1982). Rational ethical judgments utilizing a decision-making tool. *Heart and Lung, 11*(6), 566–570.

Marquis, B.L., & Huston, C.J. (1992). *Leadership Roles and Management Functions for Nurses.* Philadelphia: J.B. Lippincott.

Thiroux, J. (1977). *Ethics: Theory and Practice.* Philadelphia: Macmillan.

Toussaint v Blue Cross and Blue Shield, 408 Mich. 579, 292 NW 2d 880, 1980.

Twomey, D.P. (1986). *A Concise Guide to Employment Laws: EEO and OSHA.* Cincinnati: South-Western.

SUGGESTED READINGS

Goldstein, A.S., Perdew, S., & Pruitt, S. (1989). *The Nurses Legal Advisor.* Philadelphia: J.B. Lippincott.

Sullivan, P.A., & Brown, T. (1991). Common sense ethics in administrative decision making: part II. *Journal of Nursing Administration, 21*(11), 57–61.

Veatch, R.M., & Fry, S.T. (1987). *Case Studies in Nursing Ethics.* Philadelphia: J.B. Lippincott.

CHAPTER 4
STRATEGIC PLANNING, GOAL SETTING & MARKETING

Darlene Steven, R.N., M.H.S.A., Ph.D.

PREVIEW

This chapter discusses the application of several organizational elements to planning for the future, such as the strategic planning process, goal setting and management by objectives, and marketing. Where appropriate, examples of planning and marketing strategies used in the healthcare field are presented.

OBJECTIVES

- Describe the importance of environment assessment.
- Explain the planning process.
- Analyze the purpose of mission statement, philosophy, goals, and objectives.
- Analyze goal setting in relation to strategic planning.
- Analyze strategies for implementing shared governance, continuous quality improvement, and peer review in an organization.
- Explain the importance of marketing plans in the healthcare field.
- Forecast planning and marketing activities for the year 2000.

QUESTIONS

- How is the strategic plan used to implement change in an organization?
- How do the mission statement, philosophy, goals, and objectives merge with the strategic plan of the organization?
- How can you influence the direction of your organization by effective planning?
- If you had a "vision" of where your facility should be directed in the future, how would you go about making your vision a reality?

A Manager's Viewpoint

Strategic planning helps us function more effectively in today's turbulent healthcare environment. Budgetary restraints and changes are occurring in our practice settings every day. I also have to keep up with reading and responding to documents, as well as deal with crises with patients, staff, and other administrators. Planning helps us all remain more calm and collected. Everyone in the organization is involved in the planning process and is accountable and responsible for his or her area. This doesn't mean that we don't have crises—for example, the Social Contract enacted in Ontario, giving staff an additional thirteen days off. You can imagine the complexities in staffing and scheduling, especially in the critical care areas, where nurses are trained for high-tech procedures and staff are not always available because of cost constraints. We always develop a major strategic plan, but we also attempt to be innovative and flexible. If plan A is not appropriate, then we move to plan B. One of the keys to success with this approach is to have other alternatives and be willing to implement them in light of uncertainty.

Shirley La Forme, R.N.
Vice President, Patient Services
McKellar General Hospital
Thunder Bay, Ontario, Canada

INTRODUCTION

The healthcare system is in a state of change. The "perception that additional funding of the healthcare system will not necessarily result in improved health, combined with government debt levels that have not been seen since the early 1950s, has resulted in strategies that call for a restructuring of our healthcare system" (Roche 1991, p. 8). Restructuring of our healthcare system includes:

- patient empowerment
- comprehensive and coordinated service delivery
- efficient and effective use of resources, manpower, and technology
- emphasis on health promotion and prevention

The demographics of our society are also in a state of change and include a dramatic increase in the elderly population.

The importance of thoughtful, deliberate planning in the face of uncertainties cannot be overstated. Wilkinson (1988) offers this insight:

> An employee in an organization—manager, supervisor, or an [employee]—who has no clearly defined, benefit oriented, attainable, measurable objectives is like a ship without a compass or a chart. Such people do not know where they are going, where they should be going, at what rate, at what cost, in what control. They are not managing their working lives or helping others to manage theirs (p. 6).

Nurses have the opportunity to make a difference in planning new strategies for the future and for influencing the direction of healthcare. Nurses are active voters—we can and will influence the delivery of health services if we are prepared to stand united and speak to government in a unified voice by our lobbying efforts. To achieve this we must be proactive in our stance and efforts. "Proactive" means "aggressive planning, which provides direction for one's efforts towards which others then must react. Thus greater control is possible so that one's preferred future becomes a probability, not just a possibility" (Hersey and Duldt, 1989, pp. 140–141). Thus, strategic planning is one way to help achieve this control.

STRATEGIC PLANNING

strategic planning

Strategic planning is a process that is "designed to achieve goals in dynamic, competitive environments through the allocation of resources" (Andrews, 1990, p. 103).

The strategic planning process as shown in Figure 4-1 consists of a series of steps:

- Search of the environment to determine those forces or changes that may affect the work of the organization or that may be crucial to its survival.
- Appraisal of the organization's strengths and weaknesses—its potential for dealing with change.
- Identification of the major opportunities and threats.
- Identification and evaluation of the various strategies available to the organization to meet these opportunities and threats.
- Selection of the best option that balances the organization's potential with the challenges of changing conditions, taking into account the values of its management and its social responsibilities.

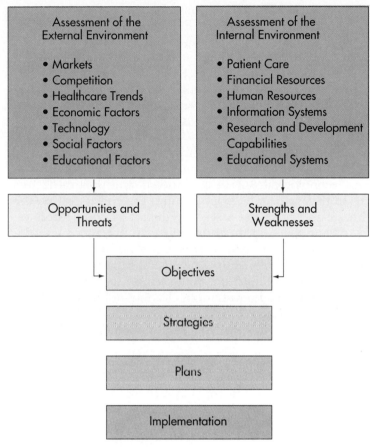

FIGURE 4-1
Key steps in strategic planning.

- Preparation of the strategy.
- Implementation and evaluation of the strategy.

REASONS FOR PLANNING

To survive constant change and restructuring of the healthcare system, the importance of thoughtful and deliberate planning becomes a necessity. This process leads to success in achievement of goals and objectives, gives meaning to work life, and provides direction for operational activities of the organization. Further, planning may result in efficient and effective use of resources and assist in the formulation of visionary activities and the future direction of the agency. There are numerous reasons why nursing administrators do not plan in a systematic manner: lack of knowledge regarding philosophy, goals, and external and internal operations of the organization; lack of understanding of the planning process; and focus on day-to-day operations rather than on short- and long-range plans.

PHASES OF THE STRATEGIC PLANNING PROCESS

Strategic planning is an "open systems approach to steering an enterprise over time through uncertain environmental circumstances" (Andrews, 1990, p. 103). The strategic planning process is proactive, vision directed, action oriented, creative, innovative and oriented toward change.

assumptions

Strategic planning is based on the assumptions that "planning is an inherently desirable activity in which administrators should engage; strategic planning has yielded desirable results in education, business, and other disciplines; and strategic planning concepts borrowed from other disciplines apply to nursing" (Andrews, 1990, p. 103).

The term *strategic planning process* usually entails the development of a plan of action for three to five years, although some agencies are now working toward seven to ten years. The initial phase is the most difficult.

Phase 1: Assessment of the External and Internal Environment

External environmental assessment   Assessment of the external environment is the initial phase in the strategic planning process. The social, economic, demographic, technological, social, educational, and political factors are assessed in terms of their impact on opportunities and threats within the

impact

environment. Healthcare managers can assess the impact of competitors on their environment and thus plan and monitor their own operations and develop other creative and visionary programs. For example, if the government introduces a non-licensed community support worker whose role will be to provide complete care for the individual in a home setting (e.g., total patient care, dressing change, medication administration, cleaning of house including windows, banking, and even specialized care including dialysis) this will have tremendous impact on the present roles and responsibilities of registered nurses.

Internal environmental assessment   The internal assessment of the environment includes a review of the effectiveness of the structure, size, programs, financial resources, human resources, information systems, and research and development capabilities of the organization. The management team involves all levels of staff in this process and focuses on the purpose of the organization; the missions of management and clinical staff; the capabilities, skills, and relationships of professional and nonprofessional staff; and the weaknesses and strengths of staff in such areas as leadership, planning, coordination, research, and staff development.

Phase 2: Review of Mission Statement, Philosophy, Goals, and Objectives

Mission statement   A mission statement reflects the purpose and direction of the healthcare agency or a department within it. The importance of the mission statement cannot be overstated, yet it is questionable how many individuals in an organization when questioned directly could enunciate the key points in the mission statement or the philosophy of a healthcare setting.

Covey (1990) relates that the mission statement is vital to the success of an organization. He believes that everyone should participate in the development of the mission statement: "The involvement process is as important as the written product and is the key to its use" (p. 139). Covey relates the belief system of IBM: individual excellence and service—everyone in this organization is committed to these values. This illustration of a mission statement is worthy of further consideration by healthcare agencies. It is often the most simplistic of statements and the involvement of individuals in the development of the mission statement that truly makes a difference. "An organizational mission statement—one that truly reflects the deep shared vision and values of everyone within that organization—creates a unity and tremendous commitment" (p. 143).

strengths and weaknesses

mission process

EXERCISE 4-1

What is your opinion about the economic situation in the city in which you live? What are the demographics of the area? What are the educational resources?

EXERCISE 4-2

Select a clinical organization with which you have been affiliated. How effective is the structure? (Does the organization operate effectively and efficiently?) What overall human resources are present (e.g., various titles and numbers of people)? What information systems are used? Now apply those same questions to the nursing component only.

Covey cites the example of a hotel where all staff—housekeepers, waitresses, desk clerks, and kitchen staff—participated in the development of the mission statement "Uncompromising personalized service." Each one carried out the mission statement with no supervision—offering at any time to assist patrons who had any difficulties. Contrast this to a simple request clients might make regarding dietary practices that may not be met in an institutional setting.

Philosophy   Similarly a statement of philosophy which is a series of belief statements, guides an organization. The philosophy, too, should be visible in employee beliefs and behaviors.

Goals   Goal setting is the process of developing, negotiating, and formalizing the targets or objectives that an employee is responsible for accomplishing.

targets

Locke, a leading authority on goal setting, and his colleagues (1981) expand on this concept:

> The concept is similar in meaning to the concepts of purpose and intent. . . . Other frequently used concepts that are also similar in meaning to that of goal include performance standard (a measuring rod for evaluating performance) quota (a minimum amount of work or production), work norm (a standard of acceptable behaviour defined by a work group), task (a piece of work to be accomplished), objective (the ultimate aim of an action or series of actions), deadline (a time limit), and budget (Locke et al., cited in Kreitner and Kinicki, 1992, p. 219).

Goals assist nurse administrators and other members of the healthcare team to focus attention on what is relevant and important and to develop strategies and actions to achieve the goals. Goal setting tends to work differently in various cultures (Locke et al., 1981).

Practically, specific goals are more likely to lead to higher performance than vague or very general goals such as "do your best." Feedback, or knowledge of results, is likely to motivate individuals toward higher performance levels and commitment to the achievement of goals.

There are three key steps in implementing a goal-setting program: (1) set goals that are specific and adhere to a deadline, (2) promote goal commitment by providing instructions and support to employees and managers, and (3) support the achievement of goals with appropriate feedback as soon as possible.

key steps

Objectives   The ability to write clear and concise objectives is an important aspect of nursing administration. Characteristics of well-written objectives include:

characteristics

1. The objective statement is properly constructed:
   - it begins with an action verb
   - it specifies a single result to be achieved
   - it specifies a target date for its attainment.
2. The objective is measurable.
3. The objective can be easily understood by those required to achieve its attainment.
4. The objective conforms to the following criteria: achievable, attainable, measurable, ends oriented, and specific.

Phase 3: Identification of Strategies

The third phase of the strategic planning process involves the identification of major issues, establishment of goals, and development of strategies to meet the goals. All departmental managers are involved in this process and are responsible for preparing a detailed plan of action, which may include the following: review of mission statement, philosophy, and objectives;

EXERCISE 4-3
Review a healthcare organization's mission statement. Tell a colleague in your own words what that statement means in general, then give specific examples of how it translates to nursing.

development of short- and long-term objectives; formulation of annual department objectives; allocation of resources; and preparation of the budget.

Phase 4: Implementation

priorities

In the fourth phase of the strategic plan, the specific plans for action are implemented in order of priority. This entails open communication with staff about priorities for the next year and subsequent periods, formulation of revised policies and procedures about the changes, and formulation of area and individual objectives related to the plan. The specific plans to be focused upon include market, program, operating plans and budget, and human resource plans.

Phase 5: Evaluation

At set periods, the strategic plan is reviewed at all levels to determine if the goals, objectives, and activities are on target. As stated previously, it is important to consider that objectives may change as a result of legislation, budget cutbacks, change in structure, or other environmental factors. Therefore optional activities may need to be adapted to the situation. For example, one agency was informed that there had to be a decrease in the budget of $500,000 in the next six months. The savings were realized, and the staff was involved in the development of creative methods for ensuring the necessary changes occurred. Savings were realized with organizational restructuring and the elimination of nursing supervisors during the evening, night, and weekend shifts; overtime was curtailed; and changes occurred in medication administration. Case Study 1 in the appendix to this chapter describes how one nurse manager developed a strategic plan of action to implement and evaluate changes within her organization (see pages 79–81).

IMPLEMENTING THE STRATEGIC PLAN

Once the general directions of a strategic plan are known, it is critical to develop four additional plans. These are program plans, marketing plans, operating plans, and human resource plans. The latter two topics are addressed elsewhere in this book.

PROGRAM PLANS

The purpose of program plans is to translate the strategic plan into usable services or products. The program plan identifies the objectives of the new (or revised) program, the activities needed to produce and maintain the product line, the designated responsibility and accountability, and the time frame to keep product development on target. The program plan is based on meeting a need of a specific market, for example, an incontinence clinic for women. The actual plan may be presented to the nursing personnel who will implement it, or members of the organizational unit, especially those recognized as leaders and managers, may develop the plan.

Equally important in assuring the success of new **product lines** is the marketing plan. When these two plans are combined, with the requisite operating and human resource plans, efforts toward portraying the strategic plan as real are possible.

MARKETING PLAN

marketing

To "sell" the targets and desired outcomes noted in a strategic planning process requires creating a marketing plan. **Marketing** may be defined as the

---

EXERCISE 4-4

You are a staff nurse at a public health department in a small rural town. The director of nursing has assigned you to work on a planning committee. The purpose of the committee is to devise long- and short-term departmental goals.

The population of the town is 25,000 and the chief industry is agriculture. It is estimated that 8,000 more people will move there in the next five years; a majority will be immigrants from Asia and Mexico.

The health department currently has four full-time baccalaureate nurses and the state has not approved additional funding for this year.

Considering the concepts of strategic planning you have just read, what would be a specific strategic plan for your department? How will you determine between long-term and short-term plans? What additional information will your committee need to realistically plan for the next five months and the next five years?

Research Perspective

Colangelo, R., & Goldrick, B. (1991). Needs assessment as a marketing strategy: An experience for baccalaureate nursing students. Journal of Nursing Education, 30(4), 168–170.

The objective of the project was to conduct a needs assessment utilizing the concepts of marketing and to identify health needs of a community. The sample consisted of 200 adults ($N = 200$) over the age of 20.

A community needs assessment questionnaire was developed using focus groups to brainstorm ideas. A demographic data sheet was utilized to assess age, marital status, educational level, number of dependent children, and town of residence.

A total of 149 questionnaires were completed (a response rate of 50 percent). A total of 41 percent of the respondents were not familiar with the agency and the services provided. Of those who responded to the survey, the services utilized were health screening and counseling, transportation to appointments, health education, meals-on-wheels, ill-child day care for working parents, and adult day care.

Implications for Practice

A marketing orientation holds that the main task of community health nurses is to determine the needs of the community and provide services with regard to design of programs, pricing, and provision of competitively viable products and services. Practitioners and students need to develop a knowledge base in planning and marketing and must strive to access opportunities for community involvement at various levels.

"analysis, planning, implementation, and control of carefully formulated programs designed to bring about voluntary exchanges of values with target markets for the purpose of achieving organizational objectives" (Harvey, 1990, pp. 186–187). One example of a marketing strategy is a needs assessment for a community health nursing organization. This chapter's "Research Perspective" focuses on such an assessment.

STRATEGIC MARKETING PLANNING PROCESS

The strategic marketing planning process is similar in nature to the strategic planning process and the nursing process. A comparative chart outlining the steps in the process appears in Figure 4-2.

The steps include:
- Assessment
- Planning
- Implementation
- Evaluation

STEP 1: ASSESSMENT

In the marketing process, an environmental assessment is conducted to identify and research the target market. An example of this is conducting a needs assessment of the services presently provided by an agency to develop new services or promotional activities to meet the needs of the population being served.

target market

NURSING PROCESS	MARKETING PROCESS	STRATEGIC PLANNING
Assessment	Environmental Assessment	Environmental Assessment
	Identify Target Market	• External • Internal
	Research Target Market	Opportunities & Threats
Planning	Marketing Plan	Strategic Plan
	• Service/Program • Cost •Promotional Activities	Goal Setting
		Objectives
		Plans
Implementation	Market/Service Program Implementation	Implementation
Evaluation	Evaluation	Evaluation
	FEEDBACK	

FIGURE 4-2

Marketing framework as compared with the nursing process and strategic planning.

EXERCISE 4-5

Select a clinical agency where you have affiliated. Recall what their "special" services/products are. Recall who their target populations are. Make a summary statement of your recollections. Now go to that organization and peruse the literature in the lobby. Does the literature reaffirm your statements? What is different? After you have read the literature, determine what the mission is, how the organization has positioned itself in the community, and how the mission and targets have impact on nursing.

programs and promotion

STEP 2: PLANNING

The environmental assessment is followed by the development of a marketing plan. This plan outlines the service/program to be provided, a detailed budget/cost analysis, and the promotional activities designed to promote the program.

STEP 3: IMPLEMENTATION

The implementation phase includes establishing the program and promotional activities designed to communicate benefits of the service/program to clients. Forms of promotion may include media releases, brochures, pamphlets, newsletters, and "word of mouth" advertising.

STEP 4: EVALUATION

The evaluation may incorporate satisfaction surveys, interviews with clients, and further research studies designed to assess reasons why clients are using or not using the service/program or product. Feedback is an essential component of the marketing process.

Case Study 2 in the appendix to this chapter is an example of how the steps in the strategic marketing planning process were followed to plan for delivery of breast cancer screening services to women in a widespread rural area of Ontario, Canada.

Pamphlets and brochures are promotional materials that inform clients about the benefits of a healthcare agency's programs and services.

CHAPTER CHECKLIST

Strategic planning is critical to the effectiveness of any organization. Nurse leaders and managers must be sufficiently aware of the critical elements to facilitate the process. Setting goals and defining marketing strategies for product lines are part of the role professional nurses must perform to achieve effective organizational results in creating a niche in healthcare services.

- The planning process leads to success in achievement of goals and objectives, gives meaning to work life, and provides direction for organizational activities of the organization.
- Strategic planning is similar in nature to the nursing process and involves:
  - assessment of the environment (internal and external);
  - appraisal of the organization's strengths and weaknesses;
  - identification of the major opportunities and threats;
  - development of strategies to meet these opportunities; and
  - implementation and evaluation of the strategy.
- Implementing the strategic plan requires the creation of program plans and marketing plans.
- Marketing strategies will play a vital role in healthcare settings in the year 2000 as competition increases to provide services and programs to the public.
- Steps in the strategic marketing planning process are:
  - Assessment
  - Planning
  - Implementation
  - Evaluation

■ Nurses can play a pivotal role in development of visionary programs and services that meet the needs of the population.

TERMS TO KNOW

- continuous quality improvement
- demographics
- marketing
- peer review
- product line
- program management
- shared governance
- strategic planning

REFERENCES

Andrews, M. (1990). Strategic planning: Preparing for the twenty-first century. *Journal of Professional Nursing, 6*(2), 103–112.

Colangelo, R., & Godrick, B. (1991). Needs assessment as a marketing strategy: An experience for baccalaureate nursing students. *Journal of Nursing Education, 30*(4), 168–170.

Covey, S. (1990). *The Seven Habits of Highly Effective People.* Toronto: Simon & Schuster.

Harvey, J. (1990). Integrating marketing into health care organizations. In J. Dienemann. *Nursing Administration: Strategic Perspectives and Applications.* Norwalk: Appleton & Lange.

Hersey, P., & Duldt, W. (1989). *Situational Leadership in Nursing.* Norwalk: Appleton & Lange.

Kreitner, R., & Kinicki, A. (1992). *Organizational Behavior.* Boston: Irwin.

Locke, E., Shaw, K., Saari, L., & Latham, G. (1981). Goal setting and task performance: 1969–1980. *Psychological Bulletin, 90*(1), 125–152.

Roche, P. (1991). Promotional health screening as a marketing tool. *Medical Laboratory Observer, 23*(7), 63–68.

Wilkinson, R. (1988). Whether your face fits or not…it's the results that matter. *Supervision, 49*(12), 6–8.

SUGGESTED READINGS

Bolton, L., Aydin, C., Popolow, G., & Ramseyer, J. (1992). Ten steps for managing organizational change. *Journal of Nursing Administration, 22*(6), 14–20.

Britton, P. (1991). Marketing forces. *Nursing Times, 87*(32), 68, 70.

Bryant, L., Dobal, M., & Johnson, E. (1990). Strategic planning: Collaboration and empowerment. *Nursing Connections, 3*(3), 31–36.

Chenoy, N., & Carlow, D. (1993). Changing perspectives on hospital governance. *Healthcare Management Forum, 6*(1), 4–10.

Christie, H. (1991). Never mind the quality, feel the marketing. *Senior Nurse, 11*(1), 7–10.

Curtin, L. (1991). Strategic planning: Asking the right questions. *Nursing Management, 22*(1), 7–8.

Davis, D., & Salmen, K. (1991). Nursing, planning, and marketing: From theory to practice. *Nursing Administration Quarterly, 15*(3), 66–71.

Dienemann, J., & Wintz, L. (1992). Designing a marketing plan that works. *Journal of Nursing Administration, 22*(1), 23–28.

Dubuque, S., & Neathawk, R. (1993). Applying a marketing framework to staff recruitment and retention. *Journal of Home Health Care Practice, 5*(2), 1–8.

Fairhead, N. (1992). Competitive marketing: Here's how. *Business Quarterly, 57,* 75–82.

Gill, J., & Whittle, S. (1992). Management by panacea: Accounting for transience. *Journal of Management Studies, 30*(2), 281–295.

Halpern, D., & Osofsky, S. (1990). A dissenting view of MBO. *Public Personnel Management, 19*(3), 321–330.

Hardy, K. (1992, Spring). The three crimes of strategic planning. *Business Quarterly, 57,* 71–74.

Ireson, C., & Weaver, D. (1992). Marketing nursing beyond the walls. *Journal of Nursing Administration, 22*(1), 57–60.

Johnson, L. (1992). Interactive planning: A model for staff empowerment. *Nursing Administration Quarterly, 16*(3), 47–57.

Kolatch, A. (1991). Marketing home health care. *Journal of Nursing Administration, 21*(11), 52–56.

Koska, M. (1990, July 5). Adopting Deming's quality improvement ideas: A case study. *Hospitals, 64,* 58–64.

Lee, H., & Papadopoulos, I. (1992). Survival of strategic planning. *Senior Nurse, 12*(2), 17–20.

Levinson, H. (1991). Management by whose objectives? *Harvard Business Review, 69*(2), 176.

MacDonald, S., Beange, J., & Blachford, P. (1992). Planning for strategic change? A participative planning approach for community hospitals. *Healthcare Management Forum, 5*(3), 31–37.

McCarthy, E., Shapiro, S., & Perreault, W. (1989). *Basic marketing: A Managerial Approach.* Boston: Richard D. Irwin.

Miles, C. (1993, August 12). Market values. *Health Service Journal,* 34–35.

Naisbitt, J., & Aburdene, P. (1990). *Megatrends 2000.* New York: William Morrow.

Pattan, J. (1991). Nurse recruitment: From selling to marketing. *Journal of Nursing Administration, 21*(9), 16–20.

Philbin, P. (1993, March 5). Transition to a new future: An expert lays our strategies for a redesigned system. *Hospitals,* 20–23.

Porter O'Grady, T. (1986). *Creative nursing administration: Participative management into the 21st Century.* Rockville, MD: Aspen.

Reeves, P. (1993). Issues management: The other side of strategic planning. *Hospital and Health Services Administration, 38*(2), 229–241.

Schmidt, C., Gillies, D., Biordi, D., & Child, D. (1990). Marketing the home healthcare agency. *Journal of Nursing Administration, 20*(11), 9–17.

Schuler, H. (1991). The strategic management of quality. *Nursing Administration Quarterly, 15*(2), 53–58.

Selder, F., & Wassem, R. (1990). Nursing and marketing: Collaborative teaching. *Nurse Educator, 15*(4), 8–11.

Skafel, J. (1993). Change or business as usual. *Healthcare Management Forum, 6*(2), 45–48.

Skelton-Green, J. (1993). Planning: A cyclical and participative approach. *Canadian Journal of Nursing Administration, 6*(1), 16–19.

Smeltzer, C., & Hinshaw, A. (1993). Integrating research in a strategic plan. *Nursing Management, 24*(2), 42–44.

Stonerock, C. (1991). Maximizing market potential in home care. *Journal of Nursing Administration, 21*(12), 49–53.

Syre, T., & Wilson, R. (1990). Health care marketing: Role evolution of the community health educator. *Health Education, 21*(1), 6–8.

Taft, S., Jones, P., & Minch, E. (1992). Strengthening hospital nursing part 2: Characteristics of effective planning processes. *Journal of Nursing Administration, 22*(6), 36–46.

——— (1992). Strengthening hospital nursing part 3: Differences among professional groups in the hospital planning process. *Journal of Nursing Administration, 22*(7), 41–50.

Taft, S., Minch, E., & Jones, P. (1992). Strengthening hospital nursing part 1: The planning process. *Journal of Nursing Administration, 22*(5), 51–63.

Thomas, A. (1993). Strategic planning: A practical approach. *Nursing Management, 24*(2), 34–35, 38.

Totten, N., & Scott, V. (1993). Who's on first? Shared governance in the role of the nurse executive. *Journal of Nursing Administration, 23*(5), 28–32.

Tubbs, M. (1993). Commitment as a moderator of the goal-performance relation: A case for clearer construct definition. *Journal of Applied Psychology, 78*(1), 86–97.

Valentine, K. (1992). Strategic planning for professional practice. *Journal of Nursing Care Quality, 6*(3), 1–12.

Walton, M. (1991). Deming management at work. *Small Business Reports, 16*(6), 59–62.

Wright, K. (1992). A marketing plan for the nineties. *Journal of ET Nursing, 19*, 1–4.

Chapter 4 Appendix

CASE STUDY 1: EDUCATIONAL PROGRAM AND STRATEGIC PLAN OF ACTION FOR ROYAL ONTARIO HOSPITAL

Mrs. Bright, the Assistant Executive Director for Patient Services of Royal Ontario Hospital, recently attended a national meeting of nursing administrators and was convinced that there was a need for the following changes within the organization:

- Shared governance
- Program management
- Continuous quality improvement
- Peer review

Mrs. Bright anticipates that the changes will occur in the next six-month period. As a member of the administrative team, she has been requested to develop an educational program and a strategic plan of action for the implementation and evaluation of the above concepts for presentation to the management team. The following format is to be used for the presentation:

1. Learning objectives
2. Definitions for shared governance, program management, continuous quality improvement, and peer review
3. Principles inherent in shared governance, program management, continuous quality improvement, and peer review
4. Strategic plan of action outline

In response to this request, Mrs. Bright develops the following materials to use in her presentation.

Learning Objectives

At the conclusion of this educational program, the Administrative Council participants will be able to:

- Define the concepts of shared governance, program management, continuous quality improvement, and peer review.
- Determine the interrelationships between shared governance, program management, continuous quality improvement, and peer review.
- Relate the principles inherent in these concepts.
- Outline strategies for implementation.

Definitions

Shared governance "is a method of placing professional accountability, direction and self-determination in the hands of each professional" (Perry and Code, 1991, p. 27).

Program management organizes care in a distinct unit for planning, budgeting, and service delivery.

Continuous quality improvement refers to "a structured system for creating organization-wide participation in planning and implementing a continuous improvement process to meet and exceed customer demands" (Wilson, 1992, p. 277).

Definitions—cont'd

Peer review is a process whereby a group of practicing nurses evaluate the quality of another's performance.

Principles Inherent in the Concepts

SHARED GOVERNANCE

- Autonomy of nursing practice with empowerment
- Development of a councillor (departmental/divisional) structure: nursing administration, nursing education, nursing practice, nursing continuous quality improvement and risk management, and nursing research to guide the organization (Thrasher, et al., 1992, p. 15)
- Election of staff by peers to leadership roles
- Staff roles are based on accountability, direction, and self-determination
- Communication in this model is open and matrix oriented
- Staff have direct input into all aspects of decision making including planning, staffing, organizing, budgeting, and quality of life issues

PROGRAM MANAGEMENT

- Enhanced decentralization of decision making
- Less formalized rules and regulations
- Increased personal satisfaction and achievement
- Enhanced communication and coordination of services

CONTINUOUS QUALITY IMPROVEMENT

- Create constancy of purpose for the improvement of product and service
- Adopt a new philosophy
- Cease dependence on mass inspection
- Improve constantly and forever the system of production and service
- Institute leadership; the concept of manager must change to that of facilitator
- Drive out fear
- Break down barriers between departments—a common organizational vision is required
- Eliminate slogans and numerical quotas
- Remove barriers to pride of workmanship
- Institute a vigorous program of education and retraining
- Take action to accomplish the transformation (Butterfield, 1991)

PEER REVIEW

- The quality of one's work performance is evaluated by colleagues with same expertise
- It may enhance self-esteem to be judged by peers
- It may decrease potential managerial errors in performance appraisal as one is judged according to preestablished standards by peers.

Strategic Plan of Action Developed by the Administrative Council, Royal Ontario Hospital

Objective	Activities	Responsible Council	Time Frame
1. To implement shared governance, program management, continuous quality improvement (CQI), and peer review in the agency.	1.1 To conduct a literature review related to each of these topics: • Shared governance • Program management • CQI • Peer review	• Admin • Admin • CQI • CQI	Jan–Feb 94
	1.2 To review the organizational structure, mission statement, philosophy, and objectives, and revise accordingly.	• Admin • All units	Feb 94
	1.3 To develop an advisory committee of the Administration Council to oversee the implementation of these concepts.	• Ad hoc	Feb 94
	1.4 To develop and implement educational sessions for staff on these concepts utilizing video presentations and written teaching packages.	• Education	Feb–April 94
	2.1 To develop questionnaires related to satisfaction reshared governance, program management, CQI, and peer review.	Research	Jan–Sept 94
2. To evaluate the effectiveness and efficiency of these programs.	2.2 To distribute questionnaires to staff.	Research	Oct 94
	2.3 Data collection/analysis of results.	Research	Jan 95
	2.4 To distribute results of questionnaire and revise strategic plan accordingly.	Research	Jan–Mar 95
	2.5 To collect and collate data related to: • occupancy • length of stay • admissions • discharge • clinical and nonclinical service utilization • test utilization • preoperative waiting times • incident reports • staff/patient injuries • clinical product evaluation • staff/patient complaints • insurance claims	Research CQI	Apr–Dec 94

CASE STUDY 2: STRATEGIC MARKETING PLANNING PROCESS FOR DELIVERY OF BREAST CANCER SCREENING SERVICES IN RURAL ONTARIO, CANADA

Breast cancer is the leading cause of morbidity and premature death. More than 4,000 women develop breast cancer in the province of Ontario and 1,700 die annually. (It is estimated that one in eight women are affected.) The incidence of breast cancer is increasing with the subsequent increase in the age and size of the population. If prevention of this disease is not realized, the number of deaths will continue to rise.

It is important to note that Northwestern Ontario encompasses a vast area of land, the land is rugged, and during the winter months some areas may only be reached by icy roads. The multicultural community with a large native population has approximately 21,000 women aged 50 to 69.

In 1989, the ministry announced that $15 million would be dedicated to the Ontario Breast Screening Program. The overall purpose of the program was to deliver high-quality comprehensive and coordinated services to the women aged 50 to 69 in Northwestern Ontario. The mission statement, overall goal, and objectives for the program are shown below. A description of the four steps in the strategic marketing plan follows.

Mission Statement, Goals, and Objectives of the Northwestern Ontario Breast Screening Program

MISSION STATEMENT

To reduce the leading cause of cancer deaths in women by delivering a comprehensive, organized, and evaluated breast screening program for women between 50 and 69 years of age. In accordance with Ontario's health goals, the Ontario Cancer Treatment and Research Foundation is committed to deliver a program that is sensitive to women's needs, building on health promoting behaviors, and fostering partnerships with interest groups in the community.

OVERALL GOAL

To integrate health promotion strategies and health practices in order to reduce mortality from breast cancer by 40 percent using breast screening of women aged 50 to 69 years.

OBJECTIVES

- To detect breast cancer earlier than would occur if organized screening was not available.
- To develop and implement a community mobilization plan for the program.
- To develop and implement a social marketing plan, including a health education component for the program.
- To establish protocols and standards for healthcare professionals associated with the program.

Mission Statement, Goals, and Objectives of the Northwestern Ontario Breast Screening Program—cont'd

OBJECTIVES—cont'd

- To establish protocols for the interaction of the target population with the program.
- To develop and implement training and technical assistance for those associated with the delivery of the program.
- To develop a partnership with healthcare professionals that will facilitate program delivery.
- To establish a regional breast screening service such that all women in the target population have equal access to breast screening.
- To ensure that a minimum of 70 percent of women in the target population participate in screening every two years.
- To document the follow-up of all women in whom an abnormality has been detected.
- To provide screening that is sensitive and acceptable to the target population.
- To evaluate the program on a continual basis, including needs assessment, and measurement of process, economic, and outcome variables.

STRATEGIC MARKETING PLANS
Step 1: Situational Assessment

One of the first activities was to establish an advisory committee comprised of representatives from the medical community—oncologists, nurses, radiologists—and relevant community agencies to oversee the assessment, development, implementation, and evaluation of the program.

As this was a new program, the external resources in the community were evaluated. Thunder Bay, a regional center, has four mammogram machines; two mammogram machines were located in other cities, but residents of this area would have to travel 10 to 12 hours to get there.

A proposal was written for funding purposes outlining the overall goal of the program, objectives, background information related to the area and other programs available, and a potential description of the proposed breast screening program.

The most appropriate mode of delivery for this program was a mobile van. But, many obstacles were encountered. First, the committee was instructed to buy a special van and then place a $150,000 mammogram machine in the back. The committee countered with a request for a forty six-foot mobile van containing a reception area, an examination room, and the mammogram machine. The van needed to be designed in such a manner as to withstand extreme cold weather and the mammogram machine needed to be portable so it could be transported by plane, if necessary, to remote northern communities.

Lobbying efforts on behalf of the committee ensued. The minister of this region was invited to a meeting of the advisory committee, and the need was so apparent that the van (approximately $350,000) and the mammogram machine ($150,000) were funded within two days.

Step 2: Marketing Plan

The overall goal of the program was to integrate health promotion strategies and clinical practices in order to reduce mortality from breast cancer by 40 percent using breast screening of women aged 50 to 69 years. The advisory committee developed a strategic plan of action for the development, implementation, and evaluation of the project including specific timelines for hiring personnel. Costs for each activity were clearly delineated. In addition, a detailed promotional campaign was designed.

Step 3: Implementation

A health promotion coordinator was hired to relate activities of the program, initiate media coverage, develop pamphlets (a number of the pamphlets have been translated to Ojibwa, Oji-Cree, and other languages), and promote groups in the area to utilize the service.

The coordinator organized a promotional campaign in each community, prior to the van's arrival. Flyers, brochures, and newsletters describing the service were delivered to each household by volunteers. Posters were on exhibit in each of the community agencies. Staff visited each of the communities to promote the service and answer any questions posed by health professionals and members of the community.

A grand opening of the program was held in the community auditorium in Thunder Bay and there was extensive media coverage throughout Northwestern Ontario. The benefits of the program were outlined to the women in the area. The response to the program was overwhelming.

Step 4: Evaluation

Each year the medical director, the administrative coordinator and the health promotion coordinator prepare a business plan that is presented to the advisory committee for review. The plan is reviewed every three months. Research is needed to determine why recruitment in certain areas is under 70 percent.

In summary, the success of this program depended on the vision, commitment to high-quality service, consumer orientation, marketing, and dedication of advisory committee members, the community, the public, and the staff of the breast screening program.

REFERENCES

Butterfield, R. (1991). Deming's 14 points applied to service. *Training, 28*(3), 50–59.

Perry, F., & Code, S. (1991). Shared governance: A Canadian experience. *Canadian Journal of Nursing Administration, 4*(2), 27–28, 30.

Thrasher, T., Bossman, V., Carroll, S., Cook, B., Cherry K., Kopras, S., Daniels, S., & Schaffer, P. (1992). Empowering the clinical nurse through quality assurance in a shared governance setting. *Journal of Nursing Care Quality, 6*(2), 15–19.

Wilson, S. (1992). Market research techniques. A synopsis for CE providers. *Journal of Continuing Education in Nursing, 23*(4), 182–183.

CHAPTER 5

LEADING CHANGE: NURSE MANAGER AS INNOVATOR

Kristi D. Menix, R.N., M.S.N., C.N.A.A.

PREVIEW

This chapter describes the general nature of change and innovation and the processes, responses, principles, and strategies typically involved in creating and leading change. The leader-manager's role of change agent and innovator entails anticipating and creating change, then leading effective implementation processes. This involves the purposeful use of specific behaviors and strategies. The constant need for the leader/manager to create and facilitate change, not just react to imposed change, and to promote staff involvement in order to achieve change goals is emphasized throughout. The terms *leader* and *manager* are used interchangeably to mean the nurse responsible and accountable for integrating a defined set of work goals through the efforts of an employee group for a 24-hour period. The terms *change* and *innovation* are also used synonymously to refer to an alteration in the work environment that is new or different from what existed previously.

OBJECTIVES

- Analyze the general characteristics of change.
- Relate the stages of change and principles to the process of planned change.
- Evaluate select strategies to common responses to change.
- Relate the desirable qualities of effective change agents to the leader/manager role.

QUESTIONS TO CONSIDER

- What is your view of change? What is your usual response to unexpected change? What is your usual response to deliberate, planned change?
- Do you actively seek and propose better ways of achieving practice and management goals?
- What kinds of activities and behaviors do you possess that could be applied to promote change through staff participation and involvement?
- What do you do to recognize and reinforce positive responses to change? How do you identify and handle responses that challenge the change idea or its implementation process?
- What can you do as an effective change agent to create and facilitate change that fosters continuity in the work environment?

A Manager's Viewpoint

Healthcare is changing so rapidly. We've got to be able to look ahead to see what is coming and be prepared for it. As a nurse manager, I have to anticipate how changes are going to affect me and my staff and be proactive rather than reactive. The biggest challenge I face is how to present change to staff in such a way that they will buy into it and own it. One way to do that is to say, "Here's the problem," and let them solve it. Then, they're invested in both the problem and the solution. For example, we recently had a bad month financially. I believe that staff members need to know the financial information I get at my department directors' meetings—How is the hospital doing? What changes are coming? So I called a staff meeting. I wrote the word *challenge* on the blackboard and said to the staff, "We can look at this a lot of different ways, but I'm challenging you to look at how we do business. We're not facing layoffs at this point. How can we make sure that we don't?" They started brainstorming and came up with a long list of suggestions. I think they felt a lot better because they were part of deciding the changes to make in their work lives.

I also meet with my charge nurses monthly to explain the problems and situations and the goals we have to accomplish within guidelines. The two assistant nurse managers and I work at maintaining open communication, so that we have the same ideas about where we're going and what goals we want to accomplish. We've also created "standards of practice" committees comprised of both RNs and LVNs from all three shifts on each of the two units. These nurses experience a lot of the problems firsthand. It's easy for me to sit in the "ivory tower" and make decisions, but until I've had to work a week on each shift and see the problems up front, I don't really know what they are.

As healthcare changes, it's crucial that we make sure our staff members understand what is going on and participate in the decision-making process. I think the biggest secret strategy to leading change is to always be up front with the staff, to let them know what's coming down the pike, and to discuss how it's going to affect them.

Linda Taliaferro, R.N., C., B.S.N.
Nurse Manager, 4 West and 4 East
University Medical Center
Lubbock, Texas

INTRODUCTION

Constant **change** is an inevitable result of the evolution of a rapidly changing healthcare delivery system. Forces outside healthcare organizations compel adaptations within healthcare settings. Organizational adaptations to external influences mix, and sometimes collide, with changes and influences occurring inside already dynamic organizations. The uncertainty and unpredictability of internal healthcare environments combine with the haphazard and sudden demands of the external environment to forge potentially chaotic work environments. For example, when state and federal governments change reimbursement policies for services provided by various healthcare organizations to various consumer groups, the organization must respond internally from the top to the bottom to assure continued financial stability.

challenge   The challenge for nurse managers is to establish effective systems that embrace both deliberate and unexpected change as unavoidable and routinize approaches for anticipating and preparing for new demands. A unit's communication system, for example, can be structured in a way that the staff receives information and guidance quickly and accurately to promote the creation and/or timely integration of a change into work processes. Likewise, prearranged orientation programs for new staff can facilitate integration into the unit.

Change may occur for multiple reasons. Change may be imposed at random by other external entities or by the deliberate efforts of the involved unit. Change can also result due to the natural process of organizational development and maturation. Many healthcare organizations either expand or eliminate services based on changes in the economy. Change may involve structure and people elements such as personnel policies that revise health benefits or staff determinations that add new nursing assistive personnel. Change may affect the technology and values of organizations such as improved computerization that includes nurse documentation capability or leadership philosophy that emphasizes client *and* staff welfare.

source   Change may originate at the top or bottom of the organization. An administrative committee may approve a physician's use of a new medical device for orthopedic clients that stimulates a need for education for nursing staff. A change or innovation may have a short or long duration. Merging two client services into one is a **change process** that generally has a clear end goal achievable in a relatively short period of time. Implementing a new delivery system like case management is usually an ongoing and lengthy process spanning several years. Importantly, one change has the potential to have an impact on the immediate work environment as well as on adjacent environments.

Regardless of the source or character of change and **innovation,** effective manager–**change agents** proactively create and lead change processes by thoughtfully blending applicable research findings; selectively planning, organizing, implementing, and evaluating activities; and by utilizing interpersonal competencies to facilitate staff involvement and **integration** of the change. The ultimate goal is to achieve stability in the work environment while the agents, implementors, and recipients of new expectations gradually experience and integrate the change.

FACILITATING THE CHANGE PROCESS

Because of the uncertainty of change, the effective manager proactively anticipates and prepares to handle the simultaneous influences and consequences of multiple, interactive change situations. Without data gathered from appropriate forecasting, considerable energy and time is expended dealing with the confusion potentially resulting from misguided change. Facilitating deliberate as well as unanticipated change with staff participation and team approaches is important in order to maintain work flow and positive relationships even when making multiple changes simultaneously.

Managers at any given time are usually juggling the tasks of hiring and orienting staff, assuring the proper functioning of equipment, attending to client and family concerns, overseeing the coordination of interunit responsibilities, and communicating new information to staff. The goal is to keep confusion to a minimum. Understanding the change process and knowing when and how to use **strategies,** the stages of change, the planning process, and other principles of change can promote successful change.

The process used for preparing in advance to make or facilitate change is dynamic and ongoing. Change in any of the three phases requires the selection and application, in no particular order, of one or more elements of the process. Sometimes all elements are in use at the same time! The elements of this process represent the primary functions of management. Planning, organizing, implementing, and evaluating activities, when used purposefully and effectively within a specific change situation, can move resources toward an identified goal.

PHASES OF CHANGE

Whether planning a new change or managing one in progress, it is important to remember that change occurs in three generally sequential phases. Knowing the characteristics of each stage not only helps to explain change processes and varied responses to them but also assists in choosing particular actions/strategies to effectively plan a change. It is important to integrate the essence of each phase into plans for change.

Lewin (1947) describes the three stages of change as *unfreezing, experiencing the change,* and *refreezing.* "Unfreezing" refers to the awareness of an opportunity, need, or problem and perception that some action is necessary. This phase may occur naturally due to progressive development or it may result from a deliberate activity as a first step in planning a change. When the current way of giving report is ineffective and errors occur in delivering care, the staff's **awareness** brings to light the need for a change. As in the case of the manager interviewed in the section A Manager's Viewpoint, (p. 87), a shift report problem could go to a standards of practice committee for resolution. But a managerial survey conducted to measure attitudes toward a current shift report method may point out the need for a different approach for communicating patient information. Further awareness may develop with active participation by staff in devising a better method.

"Experiencing" the change leads to incorporation of what is new or different into work and interpersonal processes (Lewin, 1947). Again, deciding to begin use of the change or being thrust into the change can result in potential **acceptance** of the new way. In the case of the shift report, staff will implement another way to deliver patient information that is perceived as improved. Managers and committees will try to facilitate acceptance. Likewise, a new staff nurse will learn to provide the shift report using the new method without benefit of knowing the problems of the prior method.

"Refreezing" occurs when the participants in the **change situation** accept and use the new attitude or behavior like a new habit (Lewin, 1947).

EXERCISE 5-1
Facilitators and barriers either support or hinder the achievement of change goals and may be associated with people, technology, structure, or values. (See the Research Perspective on page 90.)
Identify these factors and rate their potential effect on the attainment of the change in the following situation: Administration wants the pediatric neurology unit to merge with the pediatric cardiac unit for improved cost-effectiveness. Staff nurses and managers from both units reluctantly compose the merger planning committee along with the appointed chair, the organization's powerful personnel director. Administration says that a new facility will be provided to house the merged units.

Lewin
unfreezing

experiencing

refreezing

Acceptance is assumed once most staff integrate the change into work processes. After a period of time, most staff will complete the shift report using the new method without noticing it is different. Surveys conducted at various points after implementation of a designated change can assess the level of acceptance by the recipients of change.

FUNCTIONS AND TECHNIQUES

The primary functions that typify management work in a work setting can easily be applied to a personal situation as demonstrated in later exercises. Use of these same functions and their associated techniques compose a series of actions instrumental to creating and facilitating change. Planning, organizing, implementing, and evaluating provide a framework through which a change can be created and implemented to reach a specific **change goal.** Various techniques are essential options to choose when carrying out the functions of planning, organizing, implementing, and evaluating. This chapter shows an example of a change plan designed to guide a change process.

planning

Planning is simply looking ahead to decide how to achieve some result, goal, or outcome. Planning is a critical function ideally completed prior to implementation. Putting plans for change in writing establishes a visual method to communicate ideas, decisions, and responsibilities to a group or an individual staff member or those who will be affected by the process or the outcome of the process. A written plan is a tool, if used as such, to communicate the

assessing

change process. Assessing the current and desired situation is part of the initial and ongoing planning activity and also provides the data that clarify the conditions and direction of the advancing plan. It is important to carefully assess factors in the change situation that predictably will support or interfere with the development or implementation of a change. This chapter's "Research Perspective" illustrates the use of research methods to identify the reasons (**facilitators** and **barriers**) why nurses did or did not document care appropriately.

Research Perspective

Tapp, R.A. (1990). Inhibitors and facilitators to documentation of nursing practice. Western Journal of Nursing Research, 12, 229–240.

This study describes the reasons given by fourteen randomly selected nurse subjects working in a 357-bed, acute-care hospital during one-on-one interviews for their documenting or not documenting nursing care according to professional and institutional standards. Initial findings show that the subjects' philosophies of nursing differed when comparing their educational preparation and workplace values. Some nurses believed that documenting care is not an act of nursing like providing actual care to patients. Specific facilitators that improved the nurses' documentation activities include flow sheets, occurrence of unusual patient behavior or status change, use of a theoretical framework built into documentation forms, and receipt of positive reinforcement from supervisors. Inhibitors that interfered with completion of documentation are lack of time, busyness with care, rating patient care more important than documentation, repetitious forms, lack of confidence in using appropriated terminology, and negative views of some forms (such as medication error forms).

Research Perspective—cont'd

Implications for Practice

Before determining specific strategies to use in creating or implementing change and innovation, it is helpful to identify the forces operating in the change situation. Techniques such as one-on-one interviews, written surveys, or roundtable discussions can help the change agent identify whether certain factors will support (facilitators) or hinder (inhibitors) achievement of the overall change goal. Some related questions to ask are these:

1. Are the inhibitors and facilitators identified by the small sample representative of the overall nurse population of the hospital?
2. Based on the data collected, what system alterations could reduce the strength of the inhibitors identified by the sample? Likewise, what system alterations could increase the strength of the facilitators identified by the sample?
3. What strategies could actively empower nurses to devise acceptable solutions to the expectation of documenting nursing care appropriately, regardless of the healthcare setting?

Organizing entails making decisions about reaching the goal in terms of time, personnel, materials, communication, or other activities and resources. For reasons of efficiency it is important to weigh the costs and benefits of options to reach the change goal. Organizing builds clarity into the plan by formalizing the desired sequence and means of accomplishing the change. *organizing*

Implementing ideally occurs *after* a plan is established. However, unexpected change may sometimes require immediate action. Plans made quickly after the change can facilitate handling the effects of the change. Successful implementation, or putting the plan into action, depends on the appropriateness of the change and the participation of the change recipients. It is important to remember that a change in one part of a system can affect the function in other related systems. *implementing*

Evaluating entails judging the degree to which the change goal or objective meets some preset criteria. Establishing criteria instills quality into the change process. Monitoring is the ongoing observation of the aspects of the change process by which problems can be recognized and corrected early. Deciding whether or not a goal has been fully or partially met occurs in the final stage of the change process. *evaluating*

RESPONSES TO CHANGE

Because change ultimately has impact on people and their environment, various responses are possible. System responses may emerge in work processes as evidenced by more or less efficiency or effectiveness. These reactions may result from the unanticipated consequences of a change or the uncoordinated efforts of integrating several ongoing, interactive changes. Changes in the pharmacy's operation, for example, may result in misunderstandings by the nursing staff that may affect patient care concerns. Analysis of the systems for breakdowns can lead to corrective revisions that restore effective and efficient functioning. *system responses*

The responses of individuals and groups in the change situation may be inconsistent and unpredictable. Responses may vary from acceptance and willing *individual and group response*

creative solutions

participation/involvement in creating and achieving change to open rejection of all or part of the change and the process employed to achieve the change goal. The initial receptivity to change and innovation may be, but is not always, reluctance and resistance. It is important to have differing views rather than passive acceptance of changes that may not fit the identified problem or need. Controversy and conflict can lead to creative solutions. Initially, staff may voice disapproval with the introduction of new pharmacy policies. However, if the consequence of the policies is improved service to patient care areas, acceptance of the policies may increase.

Individuals react in a variety of ways to change particularly if they perceive that it threatens personal security derived from working or interacting in preferred ways. Responses may be hidden or may be visible to the observer. Some nurses may verbalize their dissatisfaction with new pharmacy policies; others may quietly accept the task of adjusting. Experiencing a change affects both cognitive and emotional dimensions of individuals. Changing positions from clinic nurse to critical care nurse can cause the nurse to feel temporarily incompetent and isolated, both cognitive and emotional responses to change.

response patterns

Generally, the responses of individuals in change situations may fall into particular **patterns of behavior.** It is possible with observation and interaction to identify to what degree a change recipient or participant is willing and able to be involved in or accept a change. Rogers (1983) describes these behaviors in terms of ideal and common patterns: innovators, early adopters, early majority, late majority, laggards, and rejectors.

Innovators enjoy change and at times may be involved in change that has opposing sides. Their behavior typically disrupts attempts to achieve a smooth implementation. *Early adopters* usually have respect from their peers and tend to support and facilitate change (Rogers, 1983).

As expected, others accept the new or different way of doing things later than most individuals. The *early majority* adopt the change eventually but only after careful thought. Their desire is to maintain stability. To the *late majority* acceptance of change is a matter of submission and occurs only after most others accept it. They express their resistance to the change and may not support peers who adopt the change (Rogers, 1983).

Those who threaten the success of a change pose a special challenge to the manager–change agent. *Laggards,* for example, are the last individuals to adopt the desired change. Though quite capable in their performance, they show their distrust by sidestepping situations associated with the change process. *Rejectors* may conceal their attempts to undermine all aspects of a change process including the change agent (Rogers, 1983).

The insightful manager recognizes most patterns of behavior exhibited by various individuals in the change process. Effective managers capitalize on the willingness of early adopters and early majority to readily accept and support change by facilitating their roles as additional change agents.

Just as important is the manager's early recognition of individuals who may interfere, even prevent, the success of the change process. A difficult challenge is dealing with those who do not verbalize their resistance to the change. Initially, attempts to use specific communication strategies may reduce disruption or increase interaction. If these methods are unsuccessful, manipulation and coercion may be tried. Further unrest may result, however. The manager usually continues to encourage participation and acceptance of the change. The manager enlists these and other strategies to address the multiple responses that can occur in change situations.

EXERCISE 5-2

Think about the last time you prepared to take a course you needed in order to graduate. You reviewed your overall degree program and decided that this particular course would fit into that semester's schedule along with your other courses, work obligations, and personal activities. At one point you may have realized that you would need to either request a different work schedule or rearrange your personal time in order to take the course at the time it was offered. You registered, then bought the syllabus and textbooks. You decided to pay with a check instead of cash. What were you trying to accomplish as an end result of your activities? What management functions (planning, organizing, implementing, evaluating) did you use? Did you use all or just some of them? Did you use them in any particular order or more than once? What is the significance of your schedule, books, and use of check to the process you used to prepare for taking the course?

STRATEGIES

The manager–change agent uses various strategies to facilitate the planned change process. Human responses to deliberate and unanticipated change can be attitudinal, cognitive, and/or behavioral in nature. Strategies are approaches designed to achieve a particular purpose based on consideration of the character of these responses. Strategies such as education and communication, participation and involvement, facilitation and support, negotiation and agreement, manipulation and co-optation and coercion can be used individually or in combination with each other (Kotter and Schlesinger, 1979). The intent of the change agent and those supporting the change is to promote the continued acceptance of change and slow down and eliminate, if possible, any harmful resistance to the change. The key to using the various strategies effectively is to learn to match the appropriate strategies with the demonstrated behavior as it relates to the circumstances of the change situation.

Communication and education refer to interchanges among the manager, the change participants, and others for the purpose of integrating the elements of the change process. It involves interacting in various ways. Staff meetings and informal discussions are ways to keep people informed and clarify change activities. *communication and education*

It is critical to involve the individuals who want and support the change and those who will be most affected by the change. Participation and involvement promote ownership of both the process and the decisions made during the process. In A Manager's Viewpoint, (p. 87), the nurse manager cited this strategy to be the most effective way to garner support and acceptance for a change. *participation and involvement*

Facilitation and support strategies are typically used to reassure and assist those in the change situation who do not accept a change because of anxiety and fear. When personal security is threatened, people tend to want to keep on doing what they have always done. A staff member with financial problems may believe that a new benefit plan will leave less take-home pay. The nurse manager–change agent can reassure by providing the actual calculations to show the fear is unfounded. *facilitation and support*

When individuals or groups in the change situation have the power or resources to adversely affect the success of a particular change, negotiation and agreement strategies can revise the terms of the change to accommodate the involved parties. The nursing department could negotiate an agreement with the pharmacy department to modify some of the new pharmacy policies that are causing an increase in medication errors. *negotiation and agreement*

Co-optation usually entails manipulated involvement through an appointed or assigned role. An example of this strategy is appointing this type of individual to a change task force. Typically, this strategy necessitates a reluctant or resistive individual to get more actively involved in creating or facilitating change. Manipulation appeals to motivational needs of others and influences them to participate in change when they might not do so on their own initiative. Expecting staff to be cooperative by participating in a new shift reporting method on a three-month trial basis can reduce barriers of resistance. *co-optation and manipulation*

Coercion involves the use of power to force others to make a change, particularly when time is critical to implementation. For example, offering to retain a staff member's position during staff reductions if that individual accepts certain conditions could be viewed as coercion. *coercion*

The strategies discussed are useful when used appropriately. It is important to recognize cognitive responses or concerns, for example, which may be met

TABLE 5-1   **Matching Strategies to Situations**

SITUATION	EDU-CATION	SUPPORT	FACILI-TATION	COMMUNI-CATION	PARTICI-PATION	NEGOTI-ATION	MANIPU-LATION	CO-OPTA-TION	COER-CION
Staff not sure of next best step in change process			✓	✓					
Two staff members reluctantly try change		✓			✓				
Staff has heard rumors about new program	✓			✓					
Several staff members propose a different method		✓	✓		✓				
One nurse consistently lags behind in accepting a change			✓		✓				
A group of staff expresses discouragement with new peer	✓			✓	✓		✓		
Three staff members challenge the need for a change	✓			✓		✓			
Staff member avoids change task force membership						✓			✓
Four staff members have become change agents with manager		✓	✓	✓	✓				
A group of staff verbalizes satisfaction with status quo	✓			✓	✓		✓	✓	
One nurse disrupts the change process with other ideas							✓	✓	
Two nurses try to get others to oppose change				✓		✓	✓		✓

with education, information, or other forms of communication. When the issue is motivational, the more effective strategies to use may be manipulation or coercion. Participation, facilitation, and support can be choices to address the emotional components of accepting change, such as fear or anxiety. Typically, combinations of strategies are applied simultaneously, rather than one strategy singularly. Table 5-1 captures the challenge of selecting appropriate strategies to fit the ongoing needs and responses associated with creating and facilitating change.

ROLE OF CHANGE AGENT AND INNOVATOR

One of the manager's key roles is creating and facilitating change. Understanding the appropriate application of associated functions, processes, and principles can assist in meeting the challenges of both deliberate and unexpected changes yet maintain continuity in the work environment. For a future change agent and innovator or the facilitator and creator of change, it is helpful to evaluate current personal and developing professional and managerial qualities against generally accepted desirable change agent characteristics. The accompanying box highlights these characteristics.

creator/facilitator

General Characteristics of Effective Change Agents

- Is a respected member of organization (insider) or community (outsider)
- Possesses excellent communication skills
- Understands change process
- Knows how the groups function
- Is trusted by others
- Participates actively in change process
- Possesses expert and legitimate power

(Adapted from Langford, 1990)

CHANGE AGENT FUNCTIONS

Change agents and innovators, usually members within the healthcare organization, use their personal, professional, and managerial knowledge and skills to implement change. Their commitment to the institution and desire to follow through the implementation of a change is a prerequisite to their effectiveness. Typically, these established members of organizations are called insiders. Respected members of the community, sometimes termed outsiders, may also play effective roles in facilitating change satisfactorily in organizations.

Being an effective change agent requires the use of excellent communication skills (Langford, 1990). Knowing how to interact with others in order to plan and facilitate movement toward a change goal is critical. Assertiveness projects self-confidence. Giving and receiving information appropriately promotes involvement and acceptance by others. Simple, easily understood explanations of the change goal and process can encourage receptivity to the change. Because the effects of change are unpredictable, the change agent's flexibility and immediate action is necessary to anticipate and handle staff and environmental responses. It is important to deal with potential or real conflict in effective ways. Persistence and persuasion communicate the change agent's commitment to the change goal. The effective change agent uses established channels of communication to promote mutual understanding of the ongoing change process. Meeting with change participants as needed can reduce misunderstandings.

communication

Understanding the interrelatedness of a change process and group dynamics (Langford, 1990) assists in selecting appropriate strategies. Change recipients who share the creation and implementation of a change or innovation that affects them directly will usually integrate change more fully. The unique culture of each work group particularly necessitates the use of well-fitting approaches. Group culture can be described as the dominant values, beliefs, and

group

Being an effective change agent requires excellent communication skills.

attitudes that determine how members interact and get work done. A group's acceptance of change varies according to the influence of individual members on other members to conform to the group's prevailing culture. Planning or revising a change to fit the teamwork preferences of a group shows sensitivity to specific group preferences.

Generating trust with individual members and particular groups can decrease the time needed to develop and initiate a change successfully. Change participants tend to be more receptive to new or different ideas when they originate from someone they trust (Langford, 1990). Consequently, change agents who have earned the confidence and support of the change participants can make some decisions independent of the change participants, usually without negative response. Deciding to hire an available experienced nurse to work with cardiac clients and their families may be more readily accepted by staff because confidence exists in the manager's past decisions.

role modeling   Actively participating in the change situation creates role-model opportunities to assess progress and take appropriate actions to encourage involvement or reinforce acceptance (Langford, 1990). Change recipients and participants translate the behavior of the manager into what is expected of them. The ultimate goal is a coordinated movement of manager, staff, and other participants toward the mutual achievement and adoption of something new or different. A manager who experiences the use of a new computerized medication dispensing system may be more likely to earn the respect of change participants. Problems with the new system can be identified firsthand and corrected appropriately.

Change occurs more readily when the change agent possesses expert power, the base of which is the specific knowledge and skill required by the change situation. Change participants depend on the change agent's advice and expertise to competently facilitate a smooth change process. Expert power coupled with the legitimate power of authority and responsibility bestowed by the organization enhances the change agent's opportunity for creating and leading a change process successfully (Langford, 1990).

PRINCIPLES

Principles are assumptions and general rules that guide behavior and processes. Principles useful to creating and leading change successfully form the substance of this section. Principles that further explain or reinforce previously mentioned principles are provided in the box below.

Principles Characterizing Effective Change Implementation

- The recipients of change feel they own the change.
- Administrators and other key personnel support the proposed change.
- The recipients of change anticipate benefit from the change.
- The recipients of change participate in identifying the problem warranting a change.
- The change holds interest for the change recipients and other participants.
- Agreement exists within the work group about the benefit of the change.
- The change agent(s) and recipients of change perceive compatibility of values.
- Trust and empathy exist among the participants of the change process.
- Revision of the change goal and process is negotiable.
- The change process is designed to provide regular feedback to its participants.

(Adapted from Harper, Exploring Social Change, 2nd ed., © 1993. Reprinted by permission of Prentice-Hall, Inc., Englewood Cliffs, N.J.)

EFFECTIVENESS

Creating innovation and leading change is one of the vital roles of the nurse leader-manager. The keys to effectiveness in this role are several. Effectiveness revolves around understanding the constant nature and effects of a rapidly changing healthcare delivery system. Effectiveness depends on having a working knowledge of the multiple and complex intricacies of change as a major and dynamic element of the work environment. Effectiveness rests on the manager–change agent's personal, professional, and managerial qualities and abilities as recognized by the recipients and participants of change. Effectiveness hinges on adhering to a philosophy of planned change rather than reactive change. Effectiveness involves using a repertoire of skills to facilitate both deliberate and unexpected change promoted by responsive systems and empowered change participants. Effectiveness improves with the increased use of new knowledge to develop superior services for clients and first-rate environments for employees. Perhaps the greatest challenge of managers in healthcare, regardless of setting, is leading change effectively.

EXERCISE 5-3

From the perspective of a manager applying these same functions to a change process, consider the manager's responsibility to orient a new staffing coordinator. Ideally, the manager, new staffing coordinator, and the assistant nurse manager will map out in writing (plan) the goals of the orientation, the activities (organize) for meeting the goals, and a schedule (organize) for accomplishing them. The assistant nurse manager and staffing coordinator agree to meet (organize) as needed as well as weekly to review progress (evaluate) and address informational or confidence need (implement). Part of this plan includes the option to alter the plan based on unexpected changes (plan and organize). The staffing coordinator will begin the position in two weeks (plan) and put the prearranged outline of activities (plan) into action (implementation). The assistant nurse manager's responsibility will be to guide and support (plan and organize) the education of the new staffing coordinator. Unexpected occurrences, such as the staff coordinator being absent for a few days, will create the need to modify (evaluate) the goal, activities, or time frame of the orientation plan (dynamic quality of process).

EXERCISE 5-4

Recall a work or personal situation where a particular individual tried to get you or a group to do something but did not succeed. Why did you/they decide not to cooperate? Think about the following factors: Was the idea silly, inappropriate, unsafe? Was the person making the suggestion not known, understood, or trusted? Was the person making the suggestion unaware of the real situation, not part of carrying out the idea, or had he/she not received permission to influence activities? Can you see that change agents and innovators need specific qualities and abilities to be effective?

EXERCISE 5-5

Plan an actual or hypothetical change that is meaningful to you in your personal, work, or school life. Select a change that allows you an opportunity to apply the principles of planned change, yet that will not overwhelm you. Using the guidelines and worksheet included in the appendix to this chapter, draft a hypothetical or actual plan for change, drawing on the chapter content and paying particular attention to the array of change principles discussed. Share your plan and the rationale used with peers or a small group of other healthcare providers. Ask for their comments and suggestions. (If you need a hypothetical change to work with, consider this one: You are the assistant manager for a home health agency. The agency administrator just informed you by memorandum that in one month, because of new reimbursement rules, the agency will begin caring for patients receiving chemotherapy. How will you prepare for this change?)

Self-Assessment: How Receptive to Change and Innovation Are You?

Read the following items. Circle the answer that most closely matches your attitude toward creating and accepting new or different ways.

1. I enjoy learning about new ideas and approaches.	YES	DEPENDS	NO
2. Once I learn about a new idea or approach, I begin to try it right away.	YES	DEPENDS	NO
3. I like to discuss different ways of accomplishing a goal or end result.	YES	DEPENDS	NO
4. I continually seek better ways to improve what I do.	YES	DEPENDS	NO
5. I frequently recognize improved ways of doing things.	YES	DEPENDS	NO
6. I talk over my ideas for change with my peers.	YES	DEPENDS	NO
7. I communicate my ideas for change with my manager.	YES	DEPENDS	NO
8. I discuss my ideas for change with my family.	YES	DEPENDS	NO
9. I volunteer to be at meetings when changes are being discussed.	YES	DEPENDS	NO
10. I encourage others to try new ideas and approaches.	YES	DEPENDS	NO

If you answered "yes" to eight to ten of the items, you are probably receptive to creating and experiencing new and different ways of doing things. If you answered "depends" to five to ten of the items, you are probably receptive to change conditionally based on the fit of the change with your preferred ways of doing things. If you answered "no" to four to ten of the items, you are probably not receptive, at least initially, to new ways of doing things. If you answered "yes," "no," and "depends," an equal number of times, you are probably mixed in your receptivity to change based on individual situations.

CHAPTER CHECKLIST

Change is an unavoidable constant in the rapidly changing healthcare delivery system. As a result, uncertainty is an element in most healthcare institutions. Anticipating and preparing for change can facilitate a more stable work environment. Creating and leading change and innovation rather than merely reacting can promote overall organizational effectiveness.

- Change occurs in sequential stages:
  - awareness of need for change
  - experience of change
  - integration of change
- The appropriate use of the basic managerial functions of planning, organizing, implementing, and evaluating to lead an ongoing process involved in creating and facilitating change and innovation:

- Define clearly the identified problem, need, or discrepancy requiring change
- Describe specifically the change goal
- Identify and rate the strength of facilitators and barriers in the change situation
- Select specific strategies to manage forces
- Decide on use of specific strategies
- Develop implementation plan:
  - State change goal in terms of criteria to meet
  - State objectives in terms of steps to achieving goal
  - Develop actions to use to deal with unexpected
  - Design evaluation methods
- Evaluate and revise the change process and achieved outcomes

- The human responses to change manifest in various behavior patterns that may help or hinder movement toward achievement of the change goal:
  - innovators
  - early adopters
  - early majority
  - late majority
  - laggards
  - rejectors

- Multiple strategies are used selectively to promote involvement by the recipients of change and to facilitate the overall change process:
  - education and communication
  - participation and involvement
  - facilitation and support
  - negotiation and agreement
  - manipulation and co-optation
  - coercion

- The effective nurse manager-leader displays these characteristics in the change situation:
  - Is a respected member of organization or community
  - Possesses excellent communication skills
  - Understands change process
  - Knows how groups work
  - Is trusted by others
  - Participates actively in change
  - Possesses expert and legitimate power

TERMS TO KNOW

- acceptance
- awareness
- barrier
- change
- change agent
- change goal
- change process
- change situation
- facilitator
- innovation
- innovator
- integration
- patterns of behavior
- strategy

REFERENCES

Harper, C.L. (1993). *Exploring Social Change,* 2nd ed. Englewood Cliffs, NJ: Prentice Hall.

Kotter, J., & Schlesinger, L. (1979, March-April). Choosing strategies for change. *Harvard Business Review, 57,* 106–114.

Langford, T.L. (1990). *Managing and Being Managed: Preparation for Reintegrated Professional Nursing Practice,* 2nd ed. Lubbock: Landover.

Lewin, K. (1947, June). Frontiers in group dynamics: Concept, method, and reality in social science; social equilibria and social change. *Human Relations,* 1(1), 5–41.

Rogers, E.M. (1983). *Diffusion of Innovations,* 3rd ed. New York: Free Press.

Tapp, R.A. (1990). Inhibitors and facilitators to documentation of nursing practice. *Western Journal of Nursing Research, 12*(2), 229–240.

SUGGESTED READINGS

Babington, L. (1993). Cautionary notes on innovation in nursing practice. *Nursing Administration Quarterly, 17*(3), 22–26.

Baronas, A.M. (1991). Achieving lasting organizational improvements through employee involvement. *Nursing Economics, 9*(4), 277–280.

Bennis, W.G., Benne, K.D., & Chin, R. (1984). *The Planning of Change,* 4th ed. Fort Worth: Holt, Rinehart and Winston.

Bolton, L.B., Aydin, C., Popolow, G., & Ramseyer, J. (1992). Ten steps for managing organizational change. *Journal of Nursing Administration, 22*(6), 14–20.

Bushy, A., & Kamphuis, J. (1993). Response to innovation: Behavioral patterns. *Nursing Management, 24*(3), 62–64.

Clark, P.C., & Hall, H.S. (1990). Innovations Probability Chart: A valuable tool for change. *Nursing Management, 21*(8), 128V–128X.

Coeling, H.V., & Simms, L.M. (1993). Facilitating innovation at the nursing unit level through cultural assessment, part 1: How to keep management ideas from falling on deaf ears. *Journal of Nursing Administration, 23*(4), 46–53.

———(1993). Facilitating innovation at the unit level through cultural assessment, part 2. Adapting managerial ideas to the work group. *Journal of Nursing Administration, 23*(5), 13–20.

Coyle, L.A., & Sokop, A.G. (1990). Innovation adoption among nurses. *Nursing Research, 39*(3), 176–180.

Evans, S.A. (1990). The NOAH principle: Change, challenge and creativity. *Heart & Lung, 19*(4), 23A–27A.

Everson-Bates, S. (1992). First line managers in the expanded role. *Journal of Nursing Administration, 22*(3), 32–37.

Funk, S.G., Champagne, M.T., Wiese, R.A., & Tornquist, E.M. (1991). BARRIERS: The barriers to research utilization scale. *Applied Nursing Research, 4*(1), 39–45.

Goodroe, J.H., & Beres, M.E. (1991). Network leadership and today's nurse. *Nursing Management, 22*(6), 56–57, 60, 62.

Hersey, P., & Blanchard, K.H. (1988). *Management of Organizational Behavior,* 5th ed. Englewood Cliffs, NJ: Prentice Hall.

Manion, J. (1990). *Change From Within: Nurse Intrapreneurs as Health Care Innovators* (Publ. No. G-178). Kansas City, MO: American Nurses Association.

———(1993). Chaos or transformation? *Journal of Nursing Administration, 23*(5), 41–48.

———(1994). The nurse intrapreneur: How to innovate from within. *American Journal of Nursing, 94*, 38–42.

Marriner-Tomey, A. (1993). *Transformational Leadership in Nursing.* St. Louis: Mosby–Year Book.

Perlman, D., & Takacs, G.J. (1990). The 10 stages of change. *Nursing Management, 21*(4), 33–38.

Romano, C.A. (1990). Innovation: The promise and perils for nursing and information technology. *Computers in Nursing,* 8(3), 99–104.

Chapter 5 Appendix

USING A PLANNING WORKSHEET

INTRODUCTION

This worksheet provides a general framework for planning simple or more complex change. The worksheet headings and sections outline essential points to consider when preparing to implement a change. The guidelines explain the completion of the worksheet section by section. A completed sample worksheet is included as a model to follow in doing Exercise 5-5 in this chapter.

GUIDELINES

SECTION I: SITUATIONAL ASSESSMENT AND ANALYSIS

Developing an appropriate plan requires an accurate understanding of the situation prior to the implementation. Effective assessment results in accurate identification of the discrepancy, not to be confused with symptoms of the discrepancy. The discrepancy may be a problem needing resolution, a need requiring innovative action, or a measure improving quality.

Parts A and B

Describe the current situation and the situation needing change in concrete detail addressing the who, what, when, where, why, and how elements.

Part C

Using your initial assessment data in parts A and B, identify facilitators and barriers currently operating in the change situation. Using a numerical weighting system, rate each factor's strength or potential to either promote or hinder the change process (1 is low and 5 is high). Choose strategies that have the most potential to increase the influences of facilitating factors and reduce or eliminate the effects of interfering factors.

SECTION II: IMPLEMENTATION PLAN

Clearly writing the intended change goal, objectives, and evaluation methods as well as predicting potential interruptions with predetermined corrections gives a visual reference and map that directs activities of change agents and participants.

Part A

Describe the goal in terms of the desired outcome using specific, concrete language. Though broad in nature, the goal contains the criteria against which progress is measured throughout and at the end of change implementation.

Part B

Objectives are specific descriptions of the step-by-step process needed to achieve the change goal. State objectives in specific terms of needed resources (materials, space, finances, staff) and desired time lines. List objectives according to the approximate order in which they will occur.

Part C

It is probable that unexpected occurrences and circumstances will have impact on the change process. Predict these potential occurrences and designate actions to respond to them if they do happen.

Part D

Various methods exist for collecting information throughout and at the end of the change process. Choose appropriate methods as needed to measure attitude, behavior, or knowledge prior to or after the change, the influences or concerns hampering the implementation process, or the degree to which goals and objectives are being or have been met.

SECTION III: EVALUATION AND REVISION

It is important to judge the effectiveness of the plan for change and its implementation. Both the processes and outcomes of the change should be evaluated for what worked and what could be improved or avoided in future endeavors.

Worksheet for Planning a Change

SECTION I: Situational Assessment and Analysis
A. Describe current situation in terms of who, what, when, where, how, why:

B. Describe desired change in terms of who, what, when, where, how, why:

C. Identify facilitating and interfering factors in the change situation, numerically rate their potential strength, then indicate strategies appropriate to managing the influences of the factors:

Facilitators	Strength	Strategies	Barriers	Strength	Strategies

SECTION II: Implementation Plan
A. State goal for proposed change in terms of specific, measureable outcomes:

B. State and sequence objectives in terms of specific resources, timelines, staff:

1.

2.

3.

4.

5.

Worksheet for Planning a Change—cont'd

C. Identify potential unexpected occurrences and actions to handle:

1.

2.

D. State methods for measuring the initial status, progress, and outcome of the change process:

1.

2.

3.

SECTION III: Evaluation and Revision
A. State to what degree initial or revised goal was met:

B. Indicate ways to improve the change process or goal quality:

Sample Worksheet

SECTION I: Situational Assessment
A. Describe current situation in terms of who, what, when, where, how, and why.
RNs/LVNs hear patient information only on assigned patients at shift change due to unit's 15-month-old policy of nurse-to-nurse shift reports. Frequent complaints exist due to nursing staff's inability to knowledgeably assist other patients, families, and healthcare providers. Miscommunications increase the risk for errors.

B. Describe desired change in terms of who, what, when, where, how, and why.
All RNs/LVNs will receive information on all unit patients at each shift change. The patient care Kardexes will provide a standardized format to ensure that information is as comprehensive as possible for the reports. The standards of practice (S.O.P.) committee will assume responsibility for achieving the desired change.

C. Identify facilitating and interfering factors in the change situation, numerically rate their potential strength, and then indicate strategies appropriate to managing the influences of the factors:

Sample Worksheet—cont'd

FACILITATORS	STRENGTH	STRATEGIES	BARRIERS	STRENGTH	STRATEGIES
Nurse manager supportive	+4	Communication Facilitation	Two nurse rejectors	+4	Coercion Co-optation
Staff's desire for patient information	+3	Communication Support	Perceived late start to do patient care	+2	Communication Facilitation
Effectiveness of S.O.P. committee	+3	Involvement Support	Increased accountability for all patients	+2	Negotiation Support
Staff's desire to reduce frustrations	+2	Participation Encouragement	Change in usual reporting routing	+2	Education Support Participation

Section II: Implementation Plan

A. State goal for proposed change in terms of specific, measurable outcomes.
  By June 25, all RNs/LVNs will be knowledgeable about all patients on unit due to comprehensive shift report using the patient care Kardex as tool for standardization of information reported.

B. State and sequence objectives in terms of specific resources, timelines, and staff.
  1. *By May 1, S.O.P. committee representatives meet with all nursing staff (on all three shifts) to define problem, identify solutions, and seek staff involvement.*
  2. *By May 15, staff will complete short survey to determine overall willingness to adopt specific options for change in report method.*
  3. *By June 1, S.O.P. committee will communicate most popular option with rationale and then field staff comments (survey results).*
  4. *By June 7, S.O.P. committee and nurse manager will produce new written policy and conduct short educational sessions at staff meetings.*
  5. *On June 10, begin new shift report method for the transition between each shift change.*

C. Identify potential unexpected occurrences and actions to handle.
  1. *Lack of general agreement on new shift report method: Reidentify problems and associated legal-ethical issues with staff.*
  2. *Reluctance/harmful resistance of staff members: Identify at beginning of change process and use appropriate strategies to prevent sabotage of change process (communication ⟶ manipulation ⟶ coercion).*

D. State methods for measuring the initial status, progress, and outcome of the change process.

Sample Worksheet—cont'd

1. *Survey of six to ten questions to poll attitudes and abilities to support one or more options for new shift report method early in change process.*
2. *Informal interviews of RNs/LVNs during implementation process that include random attendance/discussion at shift reports.*
3. *Conduct discussions with individual RNs/LVNs on all three shifts at random to assess knowledge of all patients on unit after change has been implemented for one to five weeks.*

Section III: Evaluation and Revision

A. State to what degree initial or revised goal was met.

After six weeks of full implementation, random discussion with staff and attendance at all three shift report times show almost all staff knowledgeable about all unit patients. Patient, family, and provider information needs met more quickly and accurately.

B. Indicate ways to improve the change process or goal quality.

Conduct quality assurance study at monthly intervals to attain threshold of 95% consistently for 6 months at minimum. Build in more frequent points of feedback to staff (each shift initially, then weekly) related to movement toward goal, with recognition provided for compliance and effort and redirection facilitated for inability and unwillingness.

CHAPTER 6

PROBLEM SOLVING AND DECISION MAKING

Rose Aguilar Welch, R.N., M.S.N., Ed.D.

PREVIEW

This chapter describes the key concepts related to problem solving and decision making. It explains the primary steps of the problem-solving and decision-making processes and offers analytical tools that are helpful in planning and visualizing decision-making activities. It also presents strategies for individual or group problem solving and decision making. These strategies may be applied to both personal and professional situations.

OBJECTIVES

- Identify the steps in the problem-solving process.
- Utilize a decision-making format to list options to solve a problem, identify the pros and cons of each option, rank the options, and select the best option.
- Evaluate the effect of faulty information gathering on a decision-making experience.
- Investigate the decision-making style of a nurse leader/manager.
- Design a flowchart for a personal or professional project.

A Manager's Viewpoint

In my experience, effective problem solvers and decision makers are good listeners, have good observation skills, and use assertive communication. Some of my staff members have a "necessity is the mother of invention" attitude because they perceive problems as opportunities to take a new look at the world.

A common barrier to effective problem solving I have observed occurs when a manager is confronted with a problem that is beyond the range of his or her experience or ability at the time. My advice is to talk to others about the problem. Include those most affected by the problem in your effort to resolve it. Dialogue generates ideas.

Effective problem solvers believe that fairness and honesty are virtues. In trying to make decisions fairly I always ask myself, "If I were the other person(s) involved, what would I want?" By identifying the needs and expectations of all parties involved, I can enhance my own sensitivity and empathy toward others.

Vickie Lemmon, R.N., M.S.N.
Director of Nursing
St. Johns Regional Medical Center
Oxnard, California

INTRODUCTION

Problem solving and **decision making** are vital abilities for nursing practice. Not only are these processes involved in managing and delivering care, but also they are essential for engaging in planned change. Myriad technological, social, political, and economic changes have had a dramatic effect on healthcare and nursing. Increased patient acuity, shorter hospital stays, and the rise of ambulatory and home healthcare are some of the changes that require nurses to make rational and valid decisions that achieve results. In addition to the focus on achieving results, more emphasis is now placed on making decisions that are people oriented.

Nurses at all levels must possess the basic knowledge and skills required for effective problem solving and decision making. These competencies are especially important for nurses with leadership and management responsibilities.

Problem solving and decision making are not synonymous terms. However, the processes for engaging in both behaviors are similar. Both skills require **critical thinking,** which is a higher cognitive process, and both can be improved upon with practice.

decision making
Decision making is a purposeful and goal-directed effort using a systematic process to choose among options. Not all decision making begins with a problem situation. Instead, the hallmark of decision making is the identification and selection of options. For example, the nurse manager of a home health agency is strategizing ways to empower her staff nurses. The options she is considering include allowing the staff to make out the schedule, perform self-evaluations, or have more input in the formulation of agency policy.

problem solving
Problem solving, which includes a decision-making step, is focused on trying to solve an immediate problem. A problem can be viewed as a gap between "what is" and "what should be." In addition, there is the dissatisfaction that the problem creates for individuals and/or groups. For example, a nurse educator complains to a unit manager that her staff nurses rarely attend the in-service classes or continuing education programs that are offered. In attempting to address this issue, the parties will gather and examine information in order to define the problem and identify possible solutions.

critical thinking
As previously mentioned, effective problem solving and decision making are predicated on an individual's ability to think critically. Although critical thinking has been defined in numerous ways, the National Council for Excellence in Critical Thinking Instruction defines it as the "intellectually disciplined process of actively and skillfully conceptualizing, applying, analyzing, synthesizing, or evaluating information gathered from, or generated by, observation, experience, reflection, reasoning or communication, as a guide to belief and action" (Paul, 1993, p. 110). Critical thinking is a composite of knowledge, attitudes, and skills (Watson and Glaser, 1980).

It is important for managers to assess their staff members' ability to think critically and enhance their knowledge and skills through staff development programs, coaching, and role modeling. Attitudes, or the disposition to think critically, can be enhanced by establishing a positive and motivating work environment.

Creativity is essential for the generation of options or solutions. Creative individuals are able to conceptualize new and innovative approaches to a problem or issue, by being more flexible and independent in their thinking.

The model depicted in Figure 6-1 demonstrates the relationship among decision making, problem solving, creativity, and critical thinking. Critical thinking is the concept that interweaves and links the others. An individual, through the application of critical-thinking skills, engages in problem solving and decision making in an environment that can promote or inhibit these skills. It is the manager's task to model these skills and promote them in others.

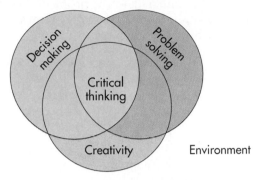

FIGURE 6-1
Problem-solving and decision-making model. [Adapted from Sullivan, E.J., & Decker, P.J. (1992). *Effective Management in Nursing.* 3rd ed. Redwood City, CA: Addison-Wesley]

PROBLEM SOLVING

Before attempting to solve a problem a manager needs to ask certain key questions:
1. Is it important?
2. Do I want to do something about it?
3. Am I qualified to handle it?
4. Do I have the authority to do anything?
5. Do I have the knowledge, interest, time, and resources to deal with it?
6. Can I delegate it to someone else?
7. What benefits will be derived from solving it?

If the answer to questions one through five is "no," why waste time, resources, and personal energy? At this juncture a conscious decision is made to ignore the problem, refer or delegate it to others, or consult or collaborate with others to solve it. On the other hand, if the answers are "yes," the decision maker chooses to accept the problem and thus assume responsibility for it.

METHODS OF PROBLEM SOLVING
The main principles for diagnosing a problem are know the facts, separate the facts from interpretation, be objective and descriptive, and determine the scope of the problem. Managers also need to determine how to establish priorities for solving problems. For example, does a manager tend to work first on problems that are encountered first, on problems that appear to be the easiest or take the shortest amount of time to solve, or on urgent problems?

Common methods for problem solving include trial and error, experimentation, and purposeful inaction ("do nothing") approaches. Often, inexperienced managers use trial and error by trying one intervention after another until one method seems to address the problem. For example, patients' visitors have been complaining about the restrictive visiting hours in nursing units.

trial and error

experimentation

Without an in-depth analysis of the problem, an inexperienced manager institutes different visiting policies until one seems to generate the least amount of complaints. Trial and error is the simplest technique, but is often time-consuming and may not be effective, especially if the problem is complex.

Scientific experimentation involves studying the situation under controlled conditions often using trial periods or pilot projects. It is useful when additional information is needed to understand the problem further. Although the likelihood of achieving positive outcomes is greater, sufficient time is required for the experimental approach to be effective.

To utilize an experimentation approach in the above example, after gathering data on the specific nature of the visitors' complaints, the manager might institute one visiting policy in one unit and a different visiting policy in another unit. After a designated period of time, visitor satisfaction might be assessed through a survey, questionnaire, or interviews, and the results compared.

After identifying the problem, the decision maker must decide whether it is significant enough to require intervention and whether it is even within his/her control to do anything about it. Sometimes new managers feel they need to "solve" every problem brought to their attention. There are situations such as some interpersonal conflicts that are best resolved by the individuals who "own" the problem. Known as purposeful inaction, a "do nothing" approach might be indicated when problems should be resolved by other persons or if the problem is beyond the manager's control. Consider the following *scenario:*

> Mary complains to her nurse manager that Sam, a fellow nurse, was rude and abrupt with her during a hallway interchange. How should the nurse manager handle Mary's complaint? Should she discuss the problem with Sam? Should Mary be present during the discussion? What are the possible risks or benefits of such an approach? Alternatively, should the manager assist Mary in developing her communication skills so that Mary can solve the problem herself?

Some decisions are "givens" as they are based on firmly established criteria in the institution, which may be based on the traditions, values, doctrines, culture, or policy of the organization. Every manager has to live with mandates from persons higher in the organizational structure. Although a manager may not have the authority to control certain situations, he/she still may be able to influence the outcome. For example, due to losses in revenue, administration has decided to lay off the clinical educators for the nursing units and place the responsibility for clinical education on the senior staff nurses. It is beyond the manager's control to reverse this decision. Nevertheless, the manager can explore the staff nurses' fear and concerns regarding this change and facilitate the transition by preparing them for the new role.

In these examples, it is a misnomer to refer to the approach as "do nothing" since there is deliberate action on the part of the manager. This approach should not be confused with the laissez-faire (hands-off) approach taken by a manager who chooses to do nothing when intervention is indicated.

purposeful inaction

EXERCISE 6-1
Using the decision-making format presented in the box on page 115, list these and other options for this scenario and the advantages and disadvantages of each approach. Rank the options in order of most desirable to least desirable and select the best option.

PROBLEM-SOLVING PROCESS

The traditional process for problem solving is illustrated in Figure 6-2. This figure gives the appearance of a sequential and linear process, like the nursng process. But, like the nursing process, the problem-solving process is a dynamic one. These steps are described in more detail in the following section.

Define the Problem, Issue, or Situation

The most common cause for failure to resolve problems is the improper identification of the problem; therefore, problem recognition and identification is considered the most vital step. The quality of the outcome is dependent on the accurate identification of the problem. Problem identification is influenced by the information available, by the values, attitudes, and experiences of the decision makers, and by time. Sufficient time should be allowed for the collection and organization of data. All too often, an inadequate amount of time is allocated for this essential step, resulting in unsatisfactory outcomes.

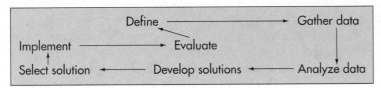

FIGURE 6-2
The problem-solving process.

Gather Data

Assessment, through the collection of data and information, is done continuously throughout this dynamic process. The data gathered consist of objective (facts) and subjective (feelings) information. Information gathered should be valid, accurate, relevant to the issue, and timely. Moreover, individuals involved in the process must have access to information and adequate resources in order to make cogent decisions.

Analyze Data

Data are analyzed to further refine the problem statement and identify possible solutions or options. It is important to differentiate a problem from the symptoms of a problem. For example, a nurse manager is dismayed by the latest continuous quality improvement (CQI) report indicating nurses are not documenting patient teaching. Is this evidence that patient teaching is not being done? Is lack of documentation the actual problem? Perhaps it is the symptom of the actual problem. Upon further analysis the manager may discover that the lack of a specific form for documentation of patient teaching is the problem. By distinguishing the problem from the symptoms of the problem, a more appropriate solution can be identified and implemented.

Develop Solutions

The goal of generating options is to identify as many choices as possible. Occasionally the quality of outcomes is hampered by rigid "black and white" thinking. A nurse, unhappy with her job, but who can only think of two options—stay or quit—is displaying this type of thinking.

Being flexible, open-minded, and creative is critical to being able to consider a range of possible options. Everyone has preconceived notions and ideas when confronted with certain situations. Putting these notions on hold and considering other ideas is beneficial, although it is difficult to do. However, asking questions such as the following can allow a person to consider other viewpoints:

- Am I jumping to conclusions?
- If I were (insert name of role model), how would I approach it?
- How are my beliefs and values affecting my decision?

Select Solution

The decision maker should then objectively weigh each option according to its possible risks and consequences, as well as positive outcomes that may be derived. Criteria for evaluation might include variables such as cost,

EXERCISE 6-2
Consider a situation in which an unsatisfactory outcome or decision was made based upon inaccurate or incomplete information. How could this have been avoided and what would you recommend to prevent this from occurring in the future?

cost-effectiveness, time, and legal or ethical considerations. The options should be ranked in the order in which they are likely to result in the desired goals or objectives. The solution selected should be the one that is most feasible and satisfactory and have the least undesirable consequences. Managers need to consider whether they are picking the solution because it is the best solution or because it is the most expedient. Being able to make cogent decisions based upon thorough assessment of a situation is an important yardstick of a manager's effectiveness.

Implement

The implementation phase should include a contingency plan to deal with negative consequences, should they appear. In essence, the decision maker should be prepared to institute "plan B" should the need arise.

Evaluate

Considerable time and energy is usually spent on identifying the problem or issue, generating possible solutions, selecting the best solution, and implementing the solution. However, not enough time is allocated for evaluation and follow-up. It is important to establish early in the process how evaluation and monitoring will take place, who will be responsible for it, and when it will take place.

Take the previous example of the manager who instituted new visiting policies in response to visitor complaints. To ensure that this action was effective in solving the problem, an evaluation and monitoring plan should be developed in advance. In collaboration with the nursing staff, the manager would determine when follow-up surveys should be distributed, who will be responsible for their distribution, collection, and analysis, and how the findings will be communicated to appropriate personnel.

DECISION MAKING

The primary steps of the decision-making process are similar to those of the problem-solving process. The phases include defining the objectives, generating options, identifying the advantages and disadvantages of each option, ranking the options, selecting the option most likely to achieve the predefined objectives, implementing, and evaluating. The accompanying box below contains a form that can be used to complete these steps.

A poor-quality decision is likely if the objectives are not clearly identified or if they are inconsistent with the values of the individual or organization. The essential step of defining the goal, purpose, or objectives is illustrated in the following excerpt from *Alice's Adventures in Wonderland* by Lewis Carroll.

> One day Alice came to a fork in the road and saw a Cheshire cat in a tree. "Which road do I take?," she asked. His response was a question: "Where do you want to go?" "I don't know," Alice answered. "Then," said the cat, "it doesn't matter."

Decision-Making Format

Issue/problem: _____

Objective: _____
_____

Options:
_____
_____
_____
_____

Evaluation of options:

Option	Advantages	Disadvantages

Rank priority of options (1 being most preferred)

Select the best option

DECISION MODELS

The traditional decision-making process discussed above has been described as a **normative or prescriptive model** that is most appropriately used when the information is objective, when routine decisions are involved, and when the problem is structured. Another way to look at this issue is to consider the degree of certainty that exists. If options are known and each option has a predictable outcome that is likely to occur should the option be selected, a condition of certainty exists and an optimizing approach is appropriate.

This approach involves comparing the solutions to the objective and selecting solutions that will best meet the objective, taking into account the

optimizing

descriptive/behavioral model

satisficing

costs against the benefits and the positive and negative consequences for each option. Although this type of decision making may not be the easiest to implement, it may yield the highest probability of achieving the desired outcome.

However, in many circumstances it is more realistic to utilize a **descriptive or behavioral model.** With this approach, it is acknowledged that not all options, outcomes, or consequences are known. Therefore, uncertainty exists and instead of seeking the maximal option, the goal is to select an acceptable option. This has been referred to as a **satisficing decision,** one in which the decision makers select the solutions that minimally meet the objectives or standards for a decision. This conservative method has been described as selecting the solution that is just "good enough" as it is generally the easiest choice. However, it may not be the best decision to make. The conservative nurse manager who wishes to avoid "rocking the boat" or "making waves" may select this type of decision strategy. Further, managers do not always have unlimited time and resources to conduct an exhaustive search and analysis of options. When time is a factor, the manager might have to pick the most expedient choice.

To illustrate, consider the following scenario: Staff nurses on a medical-surgical unit have complained that excessive time is spent documenting on numerous flowcharts and forms, often charting the same information in several places. Their frustration over charting is exacerbated by the inaccessibility of the medical records on the unit.

An **optimizing** decision might involve creating a task force to investigate the feasibility of streamlining or eliminating forms, hence reducing redundant charting. A satisficing decision might involve separating the nursing forms from the medical record and placing them on a clipboard for easy access.

Managers use both approaches depending on the circumstances. Both involve comparing solutions to predefined goals. The main difference is that the optimizing approach involves selecting the most ideal solution. Table 6-1 illustrates the characteristics, approaches, advantages, and disadvantages of these approaches.

TABLE 6-1 Decision-Making Models

MODEL	CHARACTERISTICS	APPROACHES	ADVANTAGES	DISADVANTAGES
Normative prescriptive	Certainty exists Objective Rational Structured Routine Quantifiable	Standard operating Procedures Delegate Optimize Use analytical tools	Efficient Predictable	Not realistic for all situations
Behavioral descriptive	Uncertainty exists Subjective Ill-structured Non-routine	Group process Satisfice Use past experience Gather more data Use creative approaches	More creative	May not result in best decision

| TABLE 6-2 | Vroom and Yetton's Leadership Methods |

METHOD	CHARACTERISTICS
Autocratic I (AI)	Manager independently solves problems and makes decisions based upon information at hand
Autocratic II (AII)	Manager obtains information from others prior to solving problems and making decisions; only information is sought from others, not opinions
Consultive I (CI)	Manager discusses the problem with others *individually* to obtain information and recommendations; the decision made may or may not reflect their suggestions
Consultive II (CII)	Manager discusses the problem with others as a *group* prior to making decisions that may or may not reflect their suggestions
Group II (GII)	Manager functioning as a discussion leader discusses the problem with the group; the group decides the action to be taken

Reprinted from *LEADERSHIP AND DECISION-MAKING*, by Victor H. Vroom and Philip W. Yetton, by permission of the University of Pittsburgh Press. © 1973 by University of Pittsburgh Press.

DECISION-MAKING STYLES

The decision-making style of a nurse manager is similar to the leadership style that the manager is likely to utilize. A manager who leans toward an autocratic style may choose to make decisions independent of the input or participation of others. This has been referred to as the "decide and announce" approach. On the other hand, a manager who utilizes a democratic or participative approach to management involves the appropriate personnel in the decision-making process. Participative management has been shown to increase work performance and productivity, decrease employee turnover, and enhance employee satisfaction.

autocratic

democratic

Any decision style can be used appropriately or inappropriately. Like the tenets of situational leadership theory, the situation and circumstances should dictate which decision-making style is most appropriate.

In their classic book, *Leadership and Decision Making*, Vroom and Yetton (1973) provide a useful model for defining the most appropriate leadership style based upon the characteristics of the problem. Although it is beyond the scope of this chapter to describe the model in detail, the salient points are presented.

Vroom and Yetton identified and defined five primary leadership methods. These are described in Table 6-2.

What variables determine the method to utilize? Vroom and Yetton established seven variables or decision rules to assist the decision maker in selecting the most appropriate style:
1. the importance of the decision quality to institutional success
2. the degree to which the manager possesses the information and skills to make the decision
3. the degree to which the problem is structured
4. the importance of subordinate commitment
5. the likelihood that an autocratic decision would be accepted

EXERCISE 6-3

Interview a nurse manager about his/her decision-making style. What decision-making process does he/she utilize? What barriers or obstacles to effective decision making has he/she encountered? What strategies does he/she use to increase the effectiveness of the decisions made?

6. the strength of subordinate commitment to institutional goals
7. the likelihood of subordinate conflict over the final decision (Vroom & Yetton, 1973, pp. 21-30).

The autocratic method results in more rapid decision making and is appropriate in crisis situations or when groups are likely to accept this type of decision style. However, staff members are generally more supportive of consultive and group approaches. Although these approaches take more time, they are more appropriate when conflict is likely to occur, when the problem is unstructured, or when the manager does not have the knowledge or skills to solve the problem.

FACTORS AFFECTING DECISION MAKING

internal factors

external factors

effective characteristics

There are numerous factors affecting individuals and groups in the decision-making process. The perception of the problem can be influenced by internal and external factors. Internal factors include variables such as the decision maker's physical and emotional state; personal characteristics; cultural, social, and philosophical background; past experiences; interests, knowledge, and attitudes. External factors include environmental conditions and time.

One's values affect all aspects of decision making from the statement of the problem to how evaluation will be carried out. Values are determined by one's cultural, social, and philosophical background.

Certain personality factors such as self-esteem and self-confidence affect whether one is willing to take risks in solving problems or making decisions. Characteristics of an effective decision maker reported in the literature include courage, a willingness to take risks, self-awareness, energy, creativity, sensitivity, and flexibility.

Vickie Lemmon, Director of Nurses at St. Johns Regional Medical Center in Oxnard, California identified other characteristics of effective problem solvers and decision makers. These are presented in A Manager's Perspective that appears at the beginning of the chapter.

In addition to relying on your own knowledge and experience, listed in the accompanying box are tips for increasing your effectiveness as a problem solver and decision maker.

Tips for Problem Solving and Decision Making

- Seek additional information from other sources even if it doesn't support the preferred action.
- Learn how other people approach problem situations.
- Talk to colleagues and superiors who you believe are effective problem solvers and decision makers. Observe these positive role models in action.
- Read journal articles and relevant sections of textbooks to increase your knowledge base.
- Risk using new approaches to problem resolution through experimentation.

EXERCISE 6-4
Reflect on your own strengths and weaknesses as a problem solver and decision maker. List them in two columns and identify strategies for working on the weaknesses.

GROUP PROBLEM SOLVING AND DECISION MAKING

There are two primary criteria for effective decision making. First, the decision must be of a high quality; that is, it achieves the predefined goals or objectives. Second, the decision must be accepted by those who are responsible for its implementation.

Variables that influence the quality of decisions include the following:

- Was the information used factual, complete, and relevant to the situation?
- What were the behavioral characteristics of the decision makers?
- Were they able to process the data?
- Is the decision defensible in that the solution generated can be justified?
- Did the benefits of the decision outweigh the risks that were involved?
- How well did the decision solve the problem or meet the identified need?

variables

Higher-quality decisions are more likely to result if groups are involved in the problem-solving and decision-making process. When individuals are allowed input into the process, they tend to function more productively and the quality of the decision is generally superior. Unfortunately, some evidence suggests that nurse managers do not include staff in problem solving. Consider the research conducted by Schmieding (1990) in this chapter's "Research Perspective."

group effectiveness

Research findings suggest the characteristics of effective groups include the following: all members are involved, the group is moderately cohesive, there is equal participation and communication among members, active verbal

Research Perspective

Schmieding, N.J. (1990). Do head nurses include staff nurses in problem solving? *Nursing Management, 21*(3), 58–60.

Previous research suggests that the majority of nurse managers do not involve their staff in problem solving. Head nurses generally take care of problems alone or tell staff nurses what to do. This finding served as the impetus for Schmieding's study, which sought to determine the actions head nurses take and how these actions compare to the actions desired by staff nurses.

Questionnaires consisting of six nursing scenarios were distributed to head nurses and staff nurses employed in ten general hospitals in Massachusetts. The responses provided by the respondents were coded according to whether or not the response was exploratory (involved the staff nurse) or nonexploratory (staff not involved).

Of the thirty-seven head nurses who returned the survey, 41 percent indicated they would tell the staff nurse what to do, while 27 percent indicated they would handle the situation alone. Only 31 percent indicated responses that would involve the staff nurse in the problem-solving process. An even more startling finding was that 52 percent of the staff nurses ($n = 35$) preferred the head nurse to handle the situation alone and 39 percent wanted the head nurses to tell them what to do. Only 9 percent of the responses indicated staff preference for involvement in the problem-solving process.

Implications for Practice

Conclusions must be made cautiously, as this study was limited by its small sample size and nonrandom sample selection. The authors recommended further research to determine if head nurses use the noninvolvement approach as a learned response based upon the approach their own superiors use. Further, the relationship between one's decision-making process and previous exposure to decision-making theory is not known. Additional research in these areas is needed. Nevertheless, this study illustrates the need for education and training for both management and staff on the various approaches to problem solving and decision making. How can staff be a part of the solution if they are not a part of the problem-solving process?

participation from members is encouraged, minimal self-oriented behavior is observed, and members are trained in group process (Pankowski, 1984).

group construct

In deciding to utilize the group process for decision making, it is important to consider group size and composition. If the group is too small, there will be a limited number of options generated and fewer points of view will be expressed. Conversely, if the group is too large, it may lack structure and consensus becomes more difficult. Homogeneous groups may be more compatible; however, heterogeneous groups may be more successful in problem solving. Research has demonstrated that the most productive groups are those that are moderately cohesive. If groups are too cohesive, excessive time may be spent on socialization and camaraderie. If they are not cohesive enough, goals may not be achieved (Pankowski, 1984).

For groups to be able to work effectively, the group facilitator or leader should carefully select members on the basis of their knowledge and skills in problem solving. Individuals who are aggressive, authoritarian, or manifest self-oriented behaviors tend to decrease the effectiveness of groups. Further, the leader should provide a nonthreatening and positive environment in which group members are encouraged to actively participate. Using tact and diplomacy, the facilitator can control aggressive individuals who tend to monopolize the discussion and can encourage the more passive individuals to contribute by asking direct, open-ended questions. Providing positive feedback such as "You raised a good point," protecting members and their suggestions from attack, and keeping the group focused on the task creates an environment conducive to problem solving.

advantages

The advantages of group decision making are numerous. The adage "two heads are better than one" illustrates that when individuals with different knowledge, skills, and resources collaborate to solve a problem or make a decision, the likelihood of a quality outcome is increased. More ideas can be generated by groups than by individuals functioning alone. Additionally, when individuals are directly involved in this process they are more apt to accept the decision due to an increased sense of ownership or commitment to the decision. Implementing solutions becomes easier when individuals have been actively involved in the decision-making process. Involvement can be enhanced by making information readily available to the appropriate personnel, requesting input, establishing committees and task forces with broad representation, and utilizing group decision-making techniques.

The group leader needs to establish with the participants what decision rule will be followed. Will the group strive to achieve consensus (100 percent agreement) or will the majority rule? In determining which decision rule to use, the group leader should consider the necessity for quality and acceptance of the decision. Although achieving both a high-quality and acceptable decision is possible, to do so requires more involvement and approval from individuals affected by the decision.

consensus

Groups will be more committed to an idea if it is derived by consensus rather than as an outcome of individual decision making or majority rule. Consensus requires that all participants agree to go along with the solution. Individuals may not necessarily agree with the option selected as their first choice but may commit to go along with the group. Although achieving consensus requires considerable time, it results in both high-quality and high-acceptance decisions.

majority rule

Majority rule can be used to compromise when 100 percent agreement cannot be achieved. This method saves time, but the solution may only partially

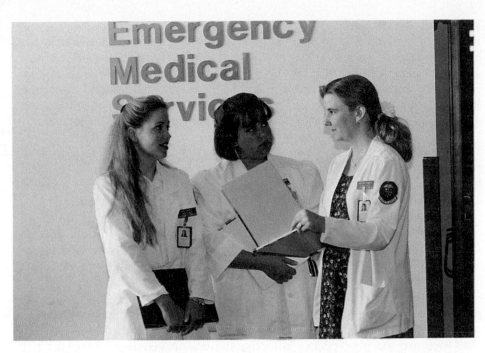

To be part of the solution, staff members must be part of the problem solving process.

achieve the goals of quality and acceptance. In addition, majority rule carries certain risks. First, if the informal group leaders happen to fall in the minority opinion, they may not support the decision of the majority. Certain members may go so far as to build coalitions to gain support for their position and block the majority choice. After all, the majority may represent only 51 percent of the group. In addition, group members may support the position of the leader even though they don't agree with the decision because they fear reprisal or wish to obtain the leader's approval. *In general, as the importance of the decision increases, so does the percentage of group members required to approve it.* Decisions made by individuals acting alone take the least amount of time but also result in decisions low in both quality and acceptance (McFarland, Leonard, and Morris, 1984).

To secure the support of the group, the leader should maintain open communication with those affected by the decision and be honest about the advantages and disadvantages of the decision. The leader also should demonstrate how the advantages outweigh the disadvantages, suggest ways the unwanted outcomes can be minimized, and be available to assist when necessary.

Although group problem solving and decision making have distinct advantages, involving groups also carries certain disadvantages and may not be appropriate in all situations. As previously stated, group decision making requires more time. In some situations this may not be appropriate, especially in a crisis situation requiring prompt decisions.

Another disadvantage of group decision making relates to unequal power among group members. Dominant personality types may influence the more passive or powerless group members to conform to their points of view. Further, individuals may expend considerable time and energy defending their positions such that the primary objective of the group effort is lost.

Groups may be more concerned with maintaining group harmony than engaging in active discussion on the issue and generating creative ideas to

disadvantages

groupthink address it. Group members who manifest a "groupthink" mentality are so concerned with avoiding conflict and supporting their leader and other members that important issues or concerns are not raised. The term *groupthink* was originally introduced by Janis in 1973 based upon research of high-level government decision-making groups (Sampson and Marthas, 1981). Failure to bring up options, explore conflict, or challenge the status quo results in ineffective group functioning and decision outcomes.

STRATEGIES

Strategies exist to minimize the problems encountered with group problem solving and decision making. These strategies include brainstorming, nominal group techniques, total quality management, and the Delphi technique.

brainstorming Brainstorming can be an effective method for generating a large volume of creative options. Often, creativity and idea generation is stifled by the premature critique of ideas. When members use inflammatory statements, euphemistically referred to as "killer phrases," the usual response is for members to stop contributing.

The hallmark of brainstorming, a right-brain activity, is to list all ideas as stated without critique or discussion. The group leader or facilitator should encourage people to tag on to or spin off ideas from those already suggested. One idea may be piggybacked off others. Ideas should not be judged nor should the relative merits or disadvantages of the ideas be discussed at this time. The goal is to generate ideas, no matter how seemingly unrealistic or absurd. It is important for the group leader or facilitator to cut off criticism and be alert for nonverbal behaviors signaling disapproval.

Since the emphasis is on the volume of ideas generated, not necessarily the quality, solutions may be superficial and fail to solve the problem. Group brainstorming also takes longer and the logistics of getting people together may pose a problem.

nominal group The nominal group technique, a method designed by Delbecq Van de Ven and Gustafson in 1971, allows every group member the opportunity for input into the decision-making process (Sullivan & Decker, 1988). Although the group is physically present, participants are asked not to talk to each other as they write down their ideas to solve a predefined problem or issue. After a period of silent generation of ideas, generally no more than ten minutes, each member is asked to share an idea that is displayed on a chalkboard or flip chart. Comments and elaboration are not allowed during this phase. Each member takes a turn sharing an idea until all ideas are presented, after which discussion is allowed. Members may "pass" if they have exhausted their list of ideas. During the next step, ideas are clarified and the merits of each idea are discussed. In the third and final step, each member privately assigns a priority rank to each option. The solution chosen is the option that receives the highest ranking by the majority of participants. The advantage of this technique is that it allows equal participation among members and minimizes the influence of dominant personalities. The disadvantages of this method is that it is time-consuming and requires advance preparation. In addition, it requires that the group physically come together.

quality Total quality management (TQM), also referred to as continuous quality improvement (CQI), has replaced the outmoded quality assurance method that focuses on the symptoms of problems, establishes thresholds of performance, and utilizes inspection in an effort to achieve quality. TQM emphasizes making gradual and systematic changes that focus on achieving measurable, short-term goals. The hallmarks of TQM for achieving defined targets are brainstorming, problem-solving teams, on-going education and training, empowerment of staff, and qualified leadership that functions in roles such as team leaders, facilitators, and guides. All departments work together to transform the organization from one in which productivity is measured in quotas to one in which a vision for excellence is shared by all.

It can take up to five years to institute a TQM environment in an institution. Visionary leadership and the ability to communicate the vision throughout the organization is essential.

A method that avoids the problem of getting people together, yet retains the advantages of group decision making, is the Delphi technique. This technique was developed by the Rand Corporation in 1950 to forecast technological developments (Whitman, 1990). It involves systematically collecting and summarizing opinions and judgments from respondents on a particular issue by use of interviews, surveys, or questionnaires. Opinions of the respondents are repeatedly fed back to them with a request to provide more refined opinions and rationales on the issue or matter under consideration. Between rounds, the results are tabulated and analyzed in order to report the findings to the participants. This allows the participants to reconsider their responses. The goal is to achieve a consensus. An example of the Delphi technique appears in the box below.

Delphi

EXERCISE 6-5
Consider the last time you were involved with a group in a problem-solving or decision-making session. Did you suggest something only to hear people say, "It will never work," "Administration won't go for it," "What a dumb idea," "It's not in the budget," "If it ain't broke, don't fix it," "We tried that before"? Think of other "killer phrases" that stifled creativity and caused resentment. For example, if you are involved in groups that tend to stifle creativity and input through verbal and nonverbal behaviors, try this approach: Agree that when "killer phrases" are used, an individual assigned as a "killer phrase" monitor will ring a bell. This will raise individuals' levels of awareness and put a halt to behaviors that can stifle creativity and cause bruised egos.

The Delphi Technique

Prior to a strategic planning retreat for middle managers, a nurse administrator sought to obtain consensus on the future goals for the nursing department. The administrator distributed in advance the agency philosophy, mission statement, goals and objectives, long-range plans, trends, and future forecasts. The middle managers were asked to review the documents and develop up to three goals congruent with the agency's philosophy.

In the next step, the administrator compiled the list of goals preferred by the managers. For the second round, the administrator asked the managers to rate the goals in order of preference, number one being the most preferred. Further, they were asked to provide a brief rationale for their selection. The results of the second round were fed back to the managers with the narrative comments.

In a third round, the managers were asked to take the feedback into consideration and rank the goals in order of priority. This process was repeated until consensus or the predefined level of agreement was achieved.

With this process occurring before the strategic planning retreat, the participants came together already in agreement about the goals for the nursing department. This provided a sense of accomplishment before the retreat began and saved time.

There are different variations on the Delphi technique. Nevertheless, the procedure generally calls for anonymous feedback, multiple rounds, and statistical analyses.

One advantage of this technique is the ability to involve a large number of respondents because the participants don't need to assemble together. Indeed, participants may be located throughout the country or world. Also, the questionnaire or survey requires little time commitment on the part of the participant. This technique may actually save time as it eliminates the "off-the-subject" digressions typically encountered in committee meetings. In addition, the Delphi technique avoids the negative or unproductive verbal and nonverbal interactions that can occur when groups work together. Although the Delphi technique has its advantages, using the Delphi technique may result in a lower sense of accomplishment and involvement as the participants are detached from the overall process and do not communicate with each other.

DECISION-MAKING TOOLS

Several decision-making tools, sometimes referred to as models, exist to aid a nurse manager in planning a decision-making process or selecting the best decision among the available options. The most common quantitative tools include decision grids, payoff tables, and program evaluation and review technique (PERT) charts or critical pathways. These tools are most appropriately used when information is available and options are known.

decision grids
Decision grids facilitate the visualization of the options under consideration and allow comparison of options using common criteria. Criteria, which are determined by the decision makers, may include time required, ethical or legal considerations, equipment needs, and cost (see Figure 6-3). The relative advantages and disadvantages of the different options should be enumerated for each option.

Options Under Consideration	Time	Cost	Legal/ethical Considerations	Equipment Needed

FIGURE 6-3
Decision grid.

payoff tables
Payoff tables require the manager to establish the cost versus benefit relationships and the probabilities of certain outcomes using current information and historical data. To illustrate, the manager of a hospital education department is evaluating whether it is better to retain the services of an outside consultant to coordinate an advanced cardiac life support course in the hospital or pay the per-person fees to send the staff elsewhere. The type of information this manager might compile includes a breakdown of the costs for both options, equipment needs, benefits of each option, the number of nurses needing the course, future training needs, and the feasibility of training hospital staff to conduct the course.

PERT charts
The program evaluation and review technique (PERT) was designed by Lockheed Aircraft Corporation in 1959 to be used as a planning device for the development of the Polaris Weapons System (Marquis & Huston, 1992). Used primarily in industry, PERT charts can be highly complex diagrams computing mathematical probabilities for outcomes. However, the concept can be adapted to nursing application.

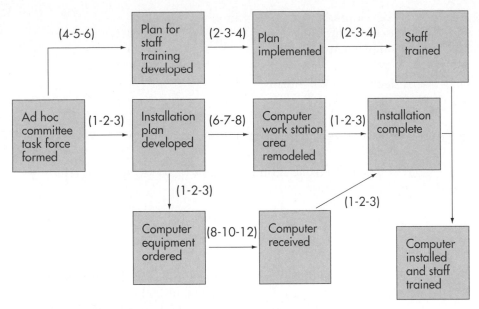

FIGURE 6-4
A PERT chart. [Adapted from Marquis, B.L., & Huston, C.J. (1992). *Leadership Roles and Management Functions in Nursing: Theory and Application.* Philadelphia: J.B. Lippincott, p. 35.]

First, the decision maker identifies the terminal event or desired outcome of the project and each key event that precedes it. Next, the specific activities or tasks that must be carried out to complete the event are identified. Time lines for completion of the activities are often included by identifying the proposed date of completion of the project and/or the number of weeks required to complete the component tasks.

Figure 6-4 is an example of a PERT chart used to track the implementation of a new computer system on a nursing unit. Key events are highlighted by boxes, while the sequence of events, sometimes referred to as the critical path, is illustrated by the arrows. Located in parentheses is the anticipated time required (in weeks) to complete each component task. The weeks are listed from left to right ranging in order from most optimistic, to most likely, to least optimistic. Some events and activities can occur simultaneously.

CHAPTER CHECKLIST

The ability to make good decisions and encourage effective decision making in others is a hallmark of nursing leadership and management. A nurse manager is in a good position to facilitate effective decision making by individuals and groups. This requires good communication skills, knowledge of the vagaries of groups dynamics, and the ability to foster an environment conducive to effective problem solving, decision making, and creative thinking.

   ■ The main steps of the traditional problem-solving process include:
   • define the problem, issue, or situation
   • gather data
   • analyze data

EXERCISE 6-6
Based upon information in the section entitled "Decision-Making Tools," design a PERT chart or decision grid for a personal or professional project.

- develop solutions and options
- select solution
- implement
- evaluate

■ A decision-making format involves:
- listing options
- identifying the pros and cons of each option
- ranking the options in order of preference
- selecting the best option

■ If you want to make sound decisions or solve problems effectively, information gathered must be:
- accurate
- relevant
- valid
- timely

■ The situation and circumstances should dictate the leadership style used by managers to solve problems and make decisions.

■ Analytical tools that are helpful in planning and illustrating decision-making activities include:
- decision grids
- PERT charts
- critical pathway.

TERMS TO KNOW

- **creativity**
- **critical thinking**
- **decision making**
- **descriptive/behavioral model**
- **normative/prescriptive model**
- **optimizing decision**
- **problem solving**
- **satisficing decision**

REFERENCES

Marquis, B.L, & Huston, C.J. (1992). *Leadership Roles and Management Functions in Nursing*. New York: J.B. Lippincott.

McFarland, G.K., Leonard, H.S., & Morris, M.M. (1984). *Nursing Leadership and Management*. New York: John Wiley, pp. 163–181.

Pankowski, M.L. (1984). Creating participatory, task-oriented learning environments. *New Directions for Continuing Education*, 11–24.

Paul, R.W. (1993). *Critical Thinking: How to Prepare Students for a Rapidly Changing World*. Santa Rosa, CA: Foundations for Critical Thinking.

Sampson, E.E., & Marthas, M. (1981). *Group Process for the Health Professionals*. New York: Delmar.

Schmieding, N.J. (1990). Do head nurses include staff nurses in problem solving? *Nursing Management, 21*(3), 58–60.

Sullivan, E.J., & Decker, P.J. (1988). *Effective Management in Nursing*. Menlo Park, CA: Addison-Wesley.

Vroom, V.H., & Yetton, P.W. (1973). *Leadership and Decision-Making*. Pittsburgh: University of Pittsburgh Press

Watson, G., & Glaser, E.M. (1980). *Critical Thinking Appraisal Manual*. The Psychological Corporation, Harcourt, Brace, and Jovanovich.

Whitman, N.I. (1990). The committee meeting alternative: Using the Delphi technique. *Journal of Nursing Administration, 20*(7/8), 30–36.

SUGGESTED READINGS

Bernhard, L.A., & Walsh, M. (1990). *Leadership: The Key to the Professionalization of Nursing.* St. Louis: C.V. Mosby.

Gould, D. (1992). A decision tree approach to sensible solutions. *Nursing Management, 23*(9), 70–71.

Grohar-Murray, M.E., & DiCroce, H.R. (1992). *Leadership and Management in Nursing.* Norwalk, CT: Appleton and Lange.

Holpp, L. (1992, May). Making choices: Self-directed teams or total quality management? *Training,* 69–76.

Lopresti, J., & Whetstone, W.R. (1993). Total quality management: Doing things right. *Nursing Management, 24*(1), 34–36.

Manthey, M. (1990). Three simple rules. *Nursing Management,* 21(12), 19–20.

PART TWO

MANAGING THE ORGANIZATION

CHAPTER 7
HEALTHCARE ORGANIZATIONS
Carol Alvater Brooks R.N., D.N.Sc., C.N.A.A.

PREVIEW

This chapter presents an overview of the various types of healthcare organizations and the characteristics that differentiate them. Its purpose is to provide a basic understanding of the types of organizations and their services. It also identifies the economic, social, and demographic factors that are the driving forces for change in healthcare organizations and the nursing leadership and management responses that healthcare organizations need to evolve.

OBJECTIVES

- Relate characteristics that are used to differentiate healthcare organizations.
- Classify healthcare organizations by major types.
- Analyze economic, social, and demographic forces that are driving the development of healthcare organizations.
- Explain implications for nursing leadership and management role functions of healthcare organization evolution.

QUESTIONS TO CONSIDER

- What are the types of healthcare organizations that make up the healthcare system in your community?
- What are the characteristics of ownership, service orientation, teaching status, and financing that differentiate the healthcare organizations in your community?
- What economic, social, and demographic factors are forces that are driving development of healthcare organizations in your community?
- What leadership and management functions are nurses performing in relationship to the evolution of healthcare organizations in your geographic region?

A Manager's Viewpoint

My position is that of nurse manager for a medicare certified hospice agency that provides services in a five-county rural area. The hospice agency is a member of a large integrated healthcare system that offers a full continuum of care in a forty-county area of New York and Pennsylvania.

The current healthcare climate poses the challenge for hospice and home care agencies to provide the highest quality services for a reduced rate of reimbursement. In the past, relationships with healthcare units, other professionals in the community, and provider coalitions offered networking and support advantages for this nurse manager. Increasingly I find that such relationships are crucial to the ongoing financial viability of the agency. The challenge for me is to enhance collaborative efforts within the healthcare system and to stimulate efforts to formalize relationships with other hospice providers and community groups in order to develop strategies that enhance cost-effectiveness of services.

The biggest challenge is to demonstrate combined proficiency of leadership, management, business and clinical skills, and knowledge. I believe that these combined skills are crucial in creating an environment that supports professional autonomy, maintains quality client care outcomes, and is financially viable. I have found this same combination of skills and knowledge necessary to maintain credibility in interaction with professionals of other disciplines across the larger healthcare system and the community at large. Understanding the full spectrum of healthcare services clarifies the relationships each of us must have with the whole.

Jocelyn O'Donnell, R.N., M.S.
Nurse Manager
Guthrie Hospice
Waverly, Pennsylvania

INTRODUCTION

Healthcare organizations make up the healthcare system, which provides the totality of services offered by all of the health disciplines. Economic, social, and demographic factors affect the purpose and structuring of the system, which in turn affect the mission, philosophy, and structure of healthcare organizations.

In the past, healthcare organizations provided two general types of services: illness care (restorative) and healthcare (preventive). Illness care services help the sick and injured. Healthcare services promote better health and illness and accident prevention. Although most organizations (such as hospitals, clinics, public health departments, community-based organizations and physicians' offices) have provided both illness and wellness services, the focus has been on illness. Recent economic, social, and demographic changes have placed emphasis on development of organizations that focus on health (wellness and prevention) in order to meet consumers' needs in more cost-effective ways. Emphasis is being placed on the role of the nurse as both a designer of these restructured organizations and as a healthcare leader and manager within the organizations.

Nurses practice in many different types of healthcare organizations. Nursing roles develop in response to the same social, economic, and demographic factors that shape the organizations in which they work. As the largest group of healthcare professionals providing direct and indirect care services to consumers, nurses have an obligation to present unified direction for development of healthcare, social, and economic policies that shape healthcare organizations.

CHARACTERISTICS AND TYPES OF ORGANIZATIONS

The healthcare industry is made up of many types of organizations. Since the process of healthcare system development is in a continual state of evolution, issues surround both the characteristics used to differentiate healthcare organizations and the types of organizations. Table 7-1 highlights the key factors influencing healthcare organizations and how they are classified.

INSTITUTIONAL PROVIDERS

Hospitals and long-term and rehabilitation facilities have traditionally been classified as institutional providers. Major characteristics that differentiate institutional and other types of healthcare organizations are (a) services offered, (b) ownership, (c) financial provisions, (d) teaching status, (e) length of direct service provision, (f) geographical location, and (g) accreditation and licensure status.

services offered   Services offered is a key characteristic used to differentiate institutional providers. They range from specialty institutions limited to providing services for a specific disease entity or population segment to those referred to as general, which provide a full range of services for all segments of the population. Examples of specialty hospitals are those limited to psychiatric care, burn care, children's care, women's and infant's care, and oncology care. Another aspect is the duration of services offered. Some services are short term, such as that provided in acute care institutions where patients are discharged as soon as their conditions are stabilized. Others are long term, such as that provided by

| TABLE 7-1 | Types, Characteristics, and Key Influences of Healthcare Organizations | | |

TYPES OF HEALTHCARE ORGANIZATIONS	CHARACTERISTICS	KEY INFLUENCES

Institutional
  Hospitals
  Long-term care facilities
  Rehabilitation centers
	General
	Specialty
	Multi-unit
		Networks
		Between points of service
		Regional and corporate

Consolidated systems	Not for profit For profit	Alliance-building
Healthcare networks	Acute	

Ambulatory based
  Physicians' offices
  Surgi-centers
	Long-term	

Urgent care center		
Managed care systems	Public Private	

Community based
  Public health
  School health programs
  Home care
  Hospice
  Self-help
	Teaching status
	
	Geographic location
		Restatement of missions
		
		Reengineering of organizational structures

Regulatory and planning		Patient focus
Accreditation Third-party payers	Accreditation status	
Medical, pharmaceutical, and other resource suppliers		

some geriatric organizations that provide care services from onset of impairments until death. Many institutions, however, are multi-unit and have components of both short-term and long-term services; they may provide acute care, home care, hospice care, ambulatory clinic care, day surgery, and an increasing number of other services such as day care for dependent children and adults or focused services such as Meals-on-Wheels. *Healthcare networks* is a term used to refer to units connected with institutions that are either owned by the institutions or have cooperative agreements with the institutions to provide a full spectrum of wellness and illness services ranging from **primary care** (first access care) to **secondary care** (disease restorative care) through **tertiary care** (rehabilitative or long-term care). Table 7-2 describes the continuum of care and the units of healthcare organizations that provide services in the three phases of the continuum.

healthcare networks

TABLE 7-2	Continuum of Healthcare Organizations	

TYPE OF CARE	PURPOSE	ORGANIZATION OR UNIT PROVIDING SERVICES
Primary	Entry into system Health maintenance Long-term care Chronic care Treatment of temporary nonin-capacitating malfunction	Ambulatory care centers Physician's offices Preferred provider organizations Nursing centers Independent provider organizations Health maintenance organizations School health clinics
Secondary	Prevent disease complications	Home health care Ambulatory care Nursing centers
Tertiary	Rehabilitation Long-term care	Home health care Long-term care Rehabilitation centers Skilled nursing facilities Assisted living programs

ownership

Ownership designated as either **private** or **public** is a second characteristic used to classify healthcare organizations. Private institutions are those directed and supported by private citizens. Multihospital systems, which are defined as two or more institutional providers having common owners, represent a significant development that has taken place in the last two decades. Public institutions are government-owned organizations providing health services to groups of people under the support and direction of the local, state, or federal government. Public institutions' services are often provided without cost to specially designated clients such as veterans and prisoners. They may also be offered at a reduced rate to the medically indigent. These organizations are directly answerable to the sponsoring government agency or boards and indirectly responsible to elected officials and taxpayers who support them. Examples of these at the federal level are Veterans, Army and Navy, Indian, Marine, and prisoner healthcare organizations. State-supported organizations may be health service teaching facilities, chronic care facilities, and prisoner facilities. Local supported facilities include county and city supported facilities. Table 7-3 shows how several common healthcare organizations are classified.

Financial provisions, referred to as operating either **for profit** or **not for profit,** is another characteristic that classifies organizations. Operating without profit means that funds are redirected into the organization for maintenance and growth rather than as dividends to stockholders. These organizations are required to serve people regardless of their ability to pay. Not-for-profit organizations located in impoverished urban and rural areas have frequently been economically disadvantaged by amounts of uncompensated care that they provide. Some states, such as New York, have created charity pools to which all not-for-profits in the state are required to contribute in order to offset financial problems of the disadvantaged institutions. Tax exempt not-for-profit or-

EXERCISE 7-1
Using the local telephone directory, determine the types and numbers of primary care, secondary care, and tertiary care services available. Table 7-3 is an example of a format for collecting data.

TABLE 7-3	Characteristics and Types of Healthcare Organizations

HEALTH CARE ORGANIZATION	CHARACTERISTICS					
	TYPE	SERVICES	OWN	FIN	TCHG	MULTI
Veterans Administration	Instit	General	Fed	NP	Y	Y
Upstate Medical Center	Instit	General	State	NP	Y	Y
Community General	Instit	General	Private	NP	N	Y
Shriners Burn Hospital	Instit	Specialty	Private	NP	N	N
Prepaid Health Plan	Ambu group HMO	General	Private	NP	N	N
Public Health Department	Commun	General	State	NP	N	N
Eastside Women's and Infants' Project	Commun	Specialty	State	NP	N	N
Brookdale Geriatric Corporation	Instit	Long term	Private	NP	N	Y

Key: Own = ownership   P = profit   Fed = federal
Fin = financing   NP = nonprofit   Ambu = ambulatory
Tchg = teaching status   N = No   Instit = institutional
Multi = multi - unit   Y = Yes

EXERCISE 7-2
Review the major healthcare organizations in your city. Is it possible to readily determine their ownership? How? Complete the data started in Exercise 7-1.

ganizations that meet health needs of the public may also be referred to as voluntary agencies. Although not-for-profit organizations have been tax-exempt, the continuation of this exemption is being debated (Theisen and Pelfrey, 1993). Ownership of these organizations includes churches, communities, industries, and special interest groups such as labor unions.

Organizations that operate for profit are also referred to as proprietary organizations. These investor-owned hospitals serve only people who can pay for their services either directly or indirectly through organizations such as private or public insurers, known as **third-party payers.** Owners may be individuals, partnerships, corporations or multisystems. Many for-profits, like the not-for-profits, receive supplementary funds through private and public sources for provision of special services and research. This funding provides a means for them to provide financial assistance to clients who can afford ordinary care, but are not in a position to finance catastrophic occurrences such as vital organ failure, birth of premature or sick infants, or bone marrow transplants for metastatic disease.

Investor-owned multihospital systems are becoming increasingly popular. Nursing homes, home care, psychiatric services, and health maintenance organizations (HMOs) are frequently units in such systems.

Teaching status is a fourth characteristic that is used to classify healthcare organizations. The **teaching institution** is applied to academic health centers such as the Massachusetts General Hospital in Boston, Massachusetts and to

teaching status

affiliated teaching hospitals that provide only the clinical portion of a health education institution's teaching program. Traditionally these programs have received government reimbursement to cover the costs to the institution of the educational program that are not covered by typical fees for patient care. Costs include financial coverage for salaries of physicians who supervise students' care delivery and participate in educational programs such as teaching rounds and seminars. Currently these expenses are reimbursed based on a formula that takes into consideration the cost of caring for low-income and uninsured patients who populate academic teaching programs. Revisions in this reimbursement will need to be adjusted if the concept of universal coverage of costs is adopted.

CONSOLIDATED SYSTEMS

Healthcare organizations are being organized into **consolidated systems** both through formation of multihospital systems that are for profit or not for profit and through development of networks of independently owned and operated healthcare organizations.

Consolidated systems tend to be organized along five levels. The first includes the large national hospital companies, most of which are investor owned; they include Hospital Corporation of America and Humana. The second level involves large voluntary affiliated systems such as Voluntary Hospitals of America, an organization that represents over 500 hospitals in the country, providing them with access to capital, political power, management expertise, joint venture opportunities, and linkages with health insurance services. The third level involves regional hospital systems such as Southwest Health Care System in New Mexico and Intermountain Health Care System in the Salt Lake area. The fourth level involves metropolitan-based systems such as Henry Ford in Detroit and the New York Health and Hospital Corporation. The fifth level is composed of the special interest groups that own and operate units organized along religious lines, teaching interests, or related special interests that drive their activities. This level often crosses over the regional, metropolitan, and national levels described above. An example of the fifth level is the Sisters of Mercy Health Corporations, which has its headquarters in Farmington Hills, Michigan and has hospitals in Michigan, Iowa, and Indiana. Some reasons for creating multiunit systems are to increase the power of the units in competing for clients, influencing public policy, and obtaining funding in an increasingly competitive and complex marketplace (Shortell, Kaluzny, et al., 1988).

AMBULATORY BASED ORGANIZATIONS

Many health services are provided on an ambulatory basis. The organizational setting for much of this care has been the group or private physician's office. A growing form of group practice is prepaid group practice plans, referred to as **managed care** systems, which combine care delivery and financing and provide comprehensive services for a fixed prepaid fee. A goal of these services is to reduce the cost of expensive acute hospital care through focusing on out-of-hospital preventive care and illness follow-up care. Group practice plans take a variety of forms. One form has a centralized administration that directs and salaries physician practice, such as HMOs.

The HMO is a configuration of health agencies that provide basic and

---

EXERCISE 7-3
Return to the data started in the first exercise and add financial and teaching status information.

national hospital companies

voluntary affiliated systems

regional systems

metropolitan systems

special interests

managed care systems

HMOs

supplemental health maintenance and treatment services to voluntary enrollees who prepay a fixed periodic fee without regard to the amount of services used. To be federally qualified, an HMO company must offer hospital and outpatient services, treatment and referral for drug and alcohol problems, laboratory and radiologic services, preventive dental services for children under 12, and preventive health services in addition to physician services.

Independent practice associations (IPAs) are a form of group practice in which physicians in private offices are paid on a **fee-for-service** basis by a prepaid plan to deliver care to enrolled members. Preferred provider organizations (PPOs) operate similarly to IPAs in that contracts are developed with private practice physicians, but here fees are discounted from their usual and customary charges. In return, physicians are guaranteed prompt payment.

Nurse practitioners' leadership in managing patients in these group practices has contributed greatly to their success. Examples of this can be found by reviewing literature related to nurses' activities at the Kaiser Permanente HMO in California and the Harvard Community Health Plan in Boston, Massachusetts.

A growing number of freestanding ambulatory centers are developing. These organizations include surgi-centers, urgent care centers, primary care centers, and imaging centers.

IPAs

PPOs

EXERCISE 7-4
Again return to the data started in the first exercise and add information about the status of multiunit systems being in place.

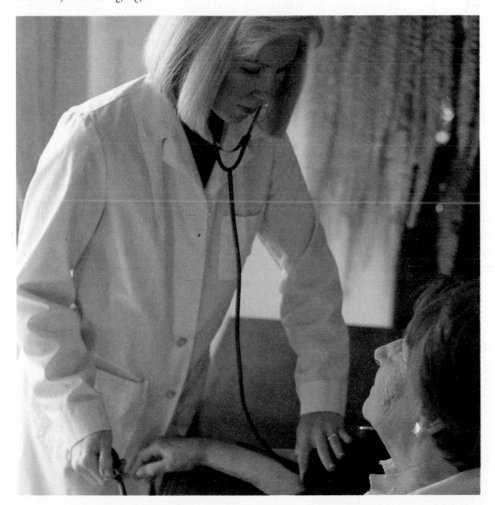

Visiting nurse associations provide follow up care at home for many patients.

COMMUNITY SERVICES

Community services, including public health departments, are focused on treatment of the community rather than the individual. The historical focus of these organizations has been on control of infectious agents and provision of preventive services under the auspices of public health departments. Funds are allocated to local health departments by local, state, and federal governments for personal health services that include maternal and child care, communicable diseases such as AIDS and tuberculosis, children with birth defects, and mental health. Monies are also allocated for environmental services such as ensuring that food services meet established standards and for health resources such as control of reproduction, promotion of safer sex, and breast cancer screening programs. Local health departments have been provided some autonomy in designating usage of funds that are not designated for categorical programs.

School health programs whose funds are also allocated to them by local, state, and federal governments have traditionally been organized to control infectious disease outbreaks, to detect and refer problems that interfere with learning, to treat on-site injuries and illnesses, and to provide basic health education programs. Increasingly, schools are being seen as primary care sites for children.

Visiting nurse associations, which are voluntary organizations, have provided a large amount of the follow-up care for patients following hospitalization and for newborns and their mothers. Some are organized by city and others serve regions.

OTHER SERVICES

Although hospitals, nursing homes, health departments, visiting nurse services, and private physician offices have made up the traditional primary service delivery organizations, it is important to recognize the increasing role that other organizations that may be freestanding or units of hospitals or other community organizations are playing within the community. These include home health agencies and hospices and they are proliferating. This rapid growth was spurred by the implementation of the prospective pricing system which resulted in early discharge of many patients from acute-care facilities. These early patients required highly technical continuing nursing care in order to maintain a stable status. The focus of these organizations is on care of individuals and their family and significant others in contrast to a focus on the community as a whole. Many of these organizations are functioning as PPOs and this is expected to be a continuing pattern in the future.

home health   Home health organizations may be hospital based, nursing home based, or free standing, and may be for profit or not for profit (Stulginsky, 1993). Hospices that provide care to the terminally ill are frequently linked to home care programs, but may be individual units of hospitals or visiting nurse associations or may be freestanding within the community. A Manager's Viewpoint, (p. 131), presents one nurse manager's description of the hospice organization that she directs.

nursing centers   Nursing centers, which are nurse owned and operated and where care is provided by nurses, are another rapidly developing community based organization (Barger and Rosenfeld, 1993). Many nursing centers are administered by schools of nursing and serve as a base for faculty practice and research and clinical experience for students. Others are owned and operated by groups of nurses. These centers have a wide variety of missions. Some focus on care for specific populations such as the homeless or on care for people with AIDS, such as the organization connected with the University of Colorado Health Sciences Center School of Nursing. Others, such as the one at Pace University in New York, have taken responsibility for university health services. Some have assumed responsibility for school health programs in the community; and others operate employee wellness programs, hospices, and home care services. Some are freestanding and others like St. Mary's Carondolet in Tucson, which is operated as an HMO, are units of hospitals. Church-affiliated organizations, sometimes operating as parish (shul) nursing, are another part of the growing movement of nursing-run organizations (King, Lakin, and Stepe, 1993).

Other organizations are the self-help/self-care organizations. These organizations also have a variety of forms. They are frequently composed of and directed by peers who are consumers of health services. Their purpose is most often to enable patients to provide support to each other and raise community consciousness about the nature of a specific physical or emotional disease. AIDS support groups and Alcoholics Anonymous are two examples.

self-help

SUPPORTIVE AND ANCILLARY ORGANIZATIONS

Organizations involved in the direct provision of healthcare are supported by a number of other organizations whose operations have a significant effect on provider organizations as well as on the overall performance of the health system. These organizations include regulatory and planning organizations, third-party financing organizations, pharmaceutical and medical equipment supply corporations, and various educational and training organizations.

> **EXERCISE 7-5**
> Identify supportive and ancillary organizations operating in your community. Can you determine if nurses are playing roles in those organizations and what functions are assigned to existing nursing roles? How?

REGULATORY AND PLANNING ORGANIZATIONS

A subset of supportive and ancillary organizations are the regulatory and planning organizations. These organizations set standards for healthcare organizations' operation, ensure compliance with federal and state regulations developed by governmental administrative agencies, and investigate and make judgments regarding complaints brought by consumers of service and the public. They are responsible for licensing organizations based on their ability to comply with all standards contained in health codes and for ensuring that the organizations and their personnel continue to meet those standards. Compliance with established standards is necessary for authorization to receive Medicare and Medicaid funding from both state and federal governments. Public agencies sometimes approve private organizations as surveyors for compliance based on their ability to meet certain criteria. Nursing leaders have played active roles in establishing standards and ensuring that organizations comply with standards in both their roles as members of healthcare organizations providing direct and indirect services to clients and as members of, or advisors to, regulatory agencies.

licensing approval

In addition to roles of approving organizations to function as providers of care and receive public funds for their services, regulatory and planning agencies influence decisions regarding capital construction, cost and charges for service, personnel standards, quality of services, and working conditions (among other things).

Two private organizations that have played significant roles in both establishing standards and ensuring care delivery compliance with standards are the Joint Commission on Accreditation of Healthcare Organizations (JCAHO)

JCAHO
CHAP
and the Community Health Assessment Program (CHAP) established by the National League for Nursing. Both organizations have met federal requirements for deemed status, which means that federal agencies will accept their inspection approvals as authorization for continuing payment of federal funds for services. Individual states, because of states rights provisions, make their own decisions as to whether to accept their approvals.

PROs
A third group of regulatory organizations are the peer review organizations (PROs) that are mandated by federal regulation to be organized in each state for the purpose of monitoring hospital service utilization and quality of care of Medicare patients. These organizations, like all others, are in a continuous state of evolutionary transformation brought about by the changing needs related to healthcare delivery. Nurses have played key roles in developing, implementing, and evaluating the review processes of these regulatory agencies.

THIRD-PARTY FINANCING ORGANIZATIONS

Organizations that provide for the financing of healthcare make up a second subset of supportive and ancillary organizations. The government, through financing mechanisms such as Medicare and Medicaid, represents the largest third-party organization involved in healthcare provision.

private health insurance
Private health insurance carriers who account for most of the remaining financing are composed of nonprofit and profit-making components. Blue Cross and Blue Shield represent the nonprofit components. The Blues have led the move of insurers from fee for service insurance to managed care. This has been both a cost reduction mechanism and a marketing response to the managed care concept introduced by health maintenance organizations and arrangements discussed previously in relation to physician practice agreements. Commercial insurance companies such as Metropolitan, Prudential, and Aetna represent the private sector.

health alliances
Roles of third-party financing organizations have major effects both on the actual delivery of healthcare and in shaping that delivery through political influence. Proposals of a single national payer system and of group insurance purchase by consumer-constituted health alliances are changes under consideration for these organizations. These proposals are generated by the constantly escalating percentage of the gross national product (GNP) that is devoted to healthcare costs and the increasing percentage of the population that is uninsured. Reconfiguration of the third-party payer system and its organizations will in turn bring about restructuring of healthcare organizations responsible for service delivery. Understanding of the interrelation of changes in healthcare organizations can be gained by examining the results of the 1982 enactment of the Tax Equity and Reimbursement Act (TEFRA) by Congress, introducing the prospective payment system for Medicare reimbursement. One of the results was the rapid development of home care organizations in response to the early discharges engendered by the system's financial incentives and the institution of financial penalties if clients had to be readmitted within certain time periods.

PHARMACEUTICAL AND MEDICAL EQUIPMENT SUPPLY SYSTEMS

A third subset of the supportive and ancillary organizations are the pharmaceutical and medical equipment supply organizations. About one-tenth of all healthcare expenditures are allocated to drugs and medical equipment. When other healthcare supply organizations, such as healthcare information system corporations, are considered, the estimated percentage may rapidly escalate toward the one-quarter mark. Nurses, as primary users of these products, play a significant role in healthcare organizations in setting standards for safe and efficient products that meet both consumers' and organizations' needs in a cost effective manner. Supply organizations frequently seek out nurses as customers and as participants in market surveys for design of new products, services, and marketing techniques. Nurses are employed by these organizations as designers of new products, marketing representatives, and members of the sales force. Examples of the roles played by nurses can be seen by studying the Hewlett Packard Company, which employs nurses to design new products and market them through production and distribution of a newsletter and ongoing continuing education presentations.

product development

PROFESSIONAL ORGANIZATIONS

Another subset of the supportive and ancillary organizations are the professional organizations whose primary purposes are to protect and enhance the interests of the service delivery organizations and their professional and nonprofessional workers. These organizations, because of their tremendous influence on the healthcare delivery system, must be considered in any discussion of healthcare organizations. Professional organizations operate at the local, state, and federal level and perform a number of functions including protection and support through political lobbying; education; and development and maintenance of standards for caregivers, resources, environment, and care. Examples of these are the American Nurses Association, the American Medical Association, and the American Hospital Association. In addition to the professional organizations, labor organizations representing healthcare organization employees are playing a significant and increasing role in healthcare organization development.

FORCES THAT INFLUENCE HEALTHCARE ORGANIZATION DEVELOPMENT

The radical restructuring of the healthcare system that is required to reduce the continuing escalation of economic resources into the system and to make healthcare accessible to all citizens will necessitate ongoing changes in healthcare organizations. Healthcare organizations, functioning as corporate actors, are a major repository of power within the healthcare system. As previously discussed, healthcare expenditures represent a significant percentage of the GNP and as federal and state governments continue to be major purchasers of care, the influence of healthcare corporate actors will increase. Healthcare organizations and their leaders can actively influence their environment and therefore can create and manage the future of the organizations. Demonstration of the professional nursing organizations' ability to influence their environment has been shown by the many points in Nursing's Agenda for Health Care Reform (1991) included in the President's Health Security Plan (1993). Economic, social, and demographic factors provide the input for future development, and act as the major forces driving the evolution of healthcare organizations.

Economic Factors

The complexity of controlling costs is and will remain a major issue driving development of the healthcare system. Perhaps the most immediate change will be in the increasing direct involvement of industrial corporations as

industry influence

healthcare costs rise and as the financing of mandated employee benefit programs remains a major concern. This involvement is presently taking the form of initiating audits of employee healthcare utilization and designing of benefits packages to control utilization. A form of benefit package, previously referred to under the section of the text on third-party insurers, is managed care, which uses specific standards for approving diagnostic testing, medical treatment, and technological interventions, and periods of time for use of inpatient and community service. Another form of control of healthcare organization services is the development of local coalitions composed of community health providers, consumers, and corporations, acting to unify business initiatives in healthcare cost containment and provide consumers' input into health planning and policy development. Wellness programs designed to modify consumers' use of and demand for services such as health promotion campaigns, ergonomic programs to reduce work-related injuries such as carpal tunnel syndrome, and fitness and exercise programs are other industrial corporate initiatives being introduced to reduce costs. Nurses are playing key roles in managed care and in organizing and directing wellness programs.

implications   There are many implications for the economy of nurses in healthcare organizations. Development of strategies that allow clients to become empowered controllers of their own health status is primary among these. Responsive structural changes in service delivery will be needed to maintain congruence with new missions and philosophies developed in response to changes. Continuous evaluation will be needed to access cost and quality outcomes related to change. Issues of quality care and access to care will require a continual focus in order that bottom line costs do not overshadow quality care provisions. Nurses have a major role to play in demonstrating that access to care and quality management are essential components of cost control. With increasing involvement of industry, business management techniques will assume increasingly greater emphasis in healthcare organizations. Nurse leaders and managers will need to go beyond obtaining education in business techniques to gaining skill in adapting the knowledge to meet the specific needs of delivery of cost-effective quality care. One example of an integrated community health system is described in this chapter's "Literature Perspective."

Social Factors

relationships   Increasing consumer attention to disease prevention and promotion of healthy lifestyles is redefining relationships of healthcare organizations and their clients. Clients are becoming increasingly active in their care planning, implementation, and evaluations, and are seeking increased participation with their providers. Nursing's history of work with development of interactive strategies with clients places nurses in a position to assume leadership roles in this area of organizational development.

Demands will be made of healthcare organizations for more personal, responsive, and coordinated care. Leadership will need to be taken by nurses to redesign roles and restructure nursing departments. Evidence of the leadership needed in changing roles to meet these needs through redesign of clinical specialist roles is illustrated by reports from the Brigham and Women's Hospital in Boston (Fay et al., 1993). The redesign involved placing clinical specialists in positions responsible for managing care of patients in their clinical specialties. An education program in leadership and management was designed to prepare the specialists for their new role and functions as case managers.

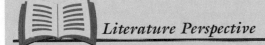

Literature Perspective

Cummings, K., & Abell, R. (1993). Losing sight of the shore: How a future integrated health care organization might look. Health Care Management Review, 18(2), 39–51.

This article presents a vision of the integration of a community healthcare system on a continuum of care that begins with birth and ends after death. Integration and accountability are presented as key elements of the future healthcare system. Elements to be integrated are administration, management, education programs, clinical services, and public health services. Accountability resides with both the care providers and the community. An array of services, connection of the services with events and understanding of community motivation are essential elements of the system.

Implications for Practice

An integrated system such as the one this article describes would be patient focused and sensitive to the patient's concerns and understanding. Central components of the system would include wellness through education, early diagnosis and treatment, and patient responsibilities. Nurses' work could be restructured from an inpatient care setting to a community-based system. Nursing can also take advantage of opportunities to demonstrate its value in integrated healthcare organizations. New paradigms will also be necessary as frameworks for developing nursing roles in new healthcare organizations in order to ensure that nursing value is recognized and rewarded.

Demographic Factors

Resources of geographic regions such as regional employment status and incomes of the populations and age of the country's population are chief among the demographic factors influencing design of healthcare organizations.

rural

Economic and demographic characteristics of many rural communities result in a larger number of uninsured and underinsured citizens in rural areas (President's Health Security Plan, 1993). Geographic isolation frequently limits access to necessary health services and impedes recruitment of health personnel. Community-based rural health networks that provide primary care linkages to urban health centers for teaching, consultation, sharing of personnel, and provision of high technological services are one solution to meeting needs in rural areas. Federal and state funding, which includes incentives for healthcare personnel to work in rural areas, is another approach. Strategic planning by nursing has provided means of economically responding to needs of rural communities in some institutions (Smith, Sat, and Piland, 1993).

aging population

The largest influence exerted on healthcare organizations comes from the aging of the population. By the year 2025, it is predicted that over 18 percent of the population will be over 65. Increasing numbers of the population are in the group classified as "the old old," over 80. Recent information shows that this segment of the population does not have the dependency needs society anticipated. Despite these findings, the aging of the population is creating a need for more long-term beds, supportive housing, and community programs. To meet these emerging needs of the elderly, new healthcare organizations will continue to evolve, be evaluated, and be restructured based on findings. New roles for nurses as leaders and managers of elderly care are evolving, such as the roles being played by advanced nurse practitioners in directing care of clients who have become members of geriatric corporations.

economically disadvantaged   Another major impact on the system will come from the increasing number of poor people who are able to afford care to meet only their most basic needs, if that. The need to create means to cover a broader array of basic healthcare expenses assumes increasing importance because of the increase in expenses caused by not treating a minor problem, such as a high blood pressure reading, until it results in a high-cost illness such as a cerebral vascular accident. This lack of healthcare provision is compounded by the number of people excluded from coverage due to preexisting health conditions and job loss. Means of financing care will change as partial solutions to these problems; those changes will affect existing healthcare organizations.

A SYSTEMS THEORETICAL PERSPECTIVE

Systems theory produces a model that explains the process of healthcare organization evolution (see Figure 7-1). Systems theory presents an explanation of organizational evolution that is similar to biological evolution. This theory sees organizations as sets of interdependent parts that together form a whole

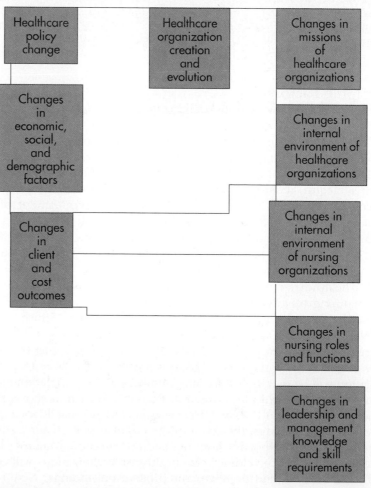

FIGURE 7-1
Healthcare organizations as open systems.

(Thompson, 1967). The survival of the organization, as portrayed throughout this chapter, is dependent on its evolutionary response to changing environmental forces; it is seen as an open system. The response to environmental changes brings about internal changes (see Chapter 9), which in turn produce changes that alter environmental conditions. The changes in the environment in turn act to bring about changes in the internal operating conditions of the organization.

A very simplified example of this can be seen by again studying the implementation of the prospective payment system that was caused by the economic driving force of healthcare cost escalation. Ambulatory surgery, same-day admissions, and hospital- and community-based home care organizations are some of the internal healthcare organization changes caused by this environmentally driven policy change, which put a cap on reimbursing expenses incurred by hospitalized patients. These internal organizational developments placed pressure on the external environment to create mechanisms to respond to increasing percentages of the population with self-care deficits who were returning to the community.

This open systems approach to organizational development and effectiveness emphasizes a continual process of adaptation of healthcare organizations to external driving forces and a response to the adaptations by the external environment, which generates continuing inputs for further healthcare organization development. This open system is in contrast to a closed system approach that views a system as being sufficient unto itself. The effects of external forces on internal structures of healthcare organizations are discussed in Chapter 9 of the text.

continual process

NURSING ROLE AND FUNCTION CHANGES

The implications for the increasing leadership and management skills and knowledge that nurses will need are clear in the evolving development of healthcare organizations. They are linked vertically in providing a continuum of individualized care based on client need and horizontally in making efforts to increase their economic viability and their influence in designing and implementing healthcare policy.

Leadership and management roles for nursing are proliferating in the changing healthcare organizations that are developing in response to environmental driving forces. Nurses are finding the proportion of jobs in the community increasing as jobs in acute care grow fewer. Nurses need new knowledge and skills to coordinate care of clients with the many disciplines and organizational units that are providing the continuum of care to clients. Nurses are needed who can engage in the political process of policy development, coordinate care across disciplines and settings, use conflict management techniques to create win-win situations for clients and providers in resolving the healthcare system's delivery problems, and use business savvy to market and prepare financial plans for delivery of cost-effective care.

The fact that healthcare organizations function as open systems requires that nurses be continuously alert to assessing both the internal and external environment for the forces that act as inputs to changes needed in healthcare organizations and for the effects of changes that are made. Awareness of the changing statuses of healthcare organizations and ability to play a leading role in creating and evaluating adaption in response to changing forces will be a central function of nurse leaders and managers in healthcare organizations. Nurses

EXERCISE 7-6
Think about the changes you can quickly identify in your community. How will they influence healthcare organizations?

will need to develop a foundation of leadership and management knowledge that they can build on through a planned program of continuing education.

CHAPTER CHECKLIST

Knowledge of types of healthcare organizations and characteristics used to differentiate healthcare organizations provides a foundation for examining the operation of the healthcare system. Understanding the economic, social, and demographic forces driving changes in healthcare organizations identifies needs that organizations must be designed to fit. A recognition that alterations in the environment and in healthcare organizations are mutually interactive is necessary to determine the effects of change and the next steps that need to be taken in response to the constant changes. Changes in focus of nursing roles and settings in which nurses provide service are changing the leadership and management knowledge and skills that nurses need. These changes are part of a continual evolution that demands a foundation in leadership and management knowledge that serves as a basis for future development.

- Key characteristics that differentiate types of healthcare organizations are:
  - profit or nonprofit status
  - public or private ownership
  - teaching status
  - geographic location
  - clinical services provided
  - number and types of units operated
  - relationship with a healthcare network.
- Major types of healthcare organizations are:
  - institutions
  - ambulatory based
  - community based
  - third-party payers
  - regulatory and planning agencies
  - pharmaceutical and medical equipment suppliers
  - professional organizations.
- Economic forces driving development of healthcare organizations are:
  - high and continuing escalating percentages of the gross national product composed of healthcare costs.
- Social forces driving development of healthcare organizations are:
  - a focus of society that is changing from illness to health
  - an increasing demand by individuals that they participate in designing their own customized care plans.
- Demographic forces driving development of healthcare organizations are:
  - increasing percentage of society that is composed of the elderly
  - increasing percentage of poor people who do not have the financial resources to have access to a car
  - inability of isolated rural areas to provide ready and economical access to needed health services.

■ Implication of healthcare organization evolution for leadership and management role functions of professional nurses:

- Increased ability to attune to the altered environmental driving forces that predict and direct changes necessitated in healthcare organizations
- Increased ability to attune to the healthcare organization's internal environment in order to predict and direct changes required in both the internal and external environment
- Knowledge and skill in both influencing the development of and in developing healthcare policy at the federal, state, local, and organizational level
- Knowledge and skill in coordinating and collaborating with peers and other disciplines providing services within a point of service and in networks created by interconnection of many points of service
- Skill in utilizing business knowledge in planning and evaluating delivery of healthcare in healthcare organizations that must market cost and outcome effectiveness in order to survive
- Knowledge and skill in planning and directing group work, which promotes optimal health statuses with minimal utilization of personnel and material resources.

TERMS TO KNOW

- consolidated systems
- corporate health alliance
- fee for service system
- not-for-profit
- managed care
- network
- point-of-service
- primary care
- private
- public
- regional healthcare alliance
- secondary care
- teaching institutions
- tertiary care
- third-party payers

REFERENCES

American Nurses' Association. (1991) *Nursing's Agenda for Health Care Reform.* Washington, DC: The Association.

Barger, S., & Rosenfeld, P. (1993). Models in community health care: Findings from a National Study of Community Nursing Centers. *Nursing and Health Care, 14*(8), 402–407.

Cummings, K., & Abell, R. (1993). Losing sight of the shore: How a future integrated health care organization might look. *Health Care Management Review, 18*(2), 39–51.

Fay, M., Higgins, J.M., James, J.R., Madden, M.J., & Ponte, P.R. (1993). Clinical specialist development needs before and after role revision. *Journal of Nursing Administration, 23*(8).

King, J., Lakin, J., & Strepe, J. (1993). Coalition building between public health nurses and parish nurses. *Journal of Nursing Administration, 23*(2), 27–31.

Montgomery, P. (1993). Starting a hospital based home health agency: Parts I, II, III. *Nursing Management, 24*(8, 9, 10).

President's Health Security Plan. (1993). New York: Random House.

Shortell, S.M., Kaluzny, A.D., et al. (1988). *Health Care Management: A Text in Organization Theory and Behavior,* 2nd ed. New York: John Wiley.

Smith, H.L., Sat, A.M., & Piland, N. (1993). Nursing department strategy, planning and performance in rural hospitals. *Journal of Nursing Administration, 23*(4), 23–33.

Stulginsky, M.M. (1993). Nurses' home health experiences. *Nursing and Health Care, 14*(8), 402–407.

Theisen, B.A., & Pelfrey, S. (1993). The advantage and risks of being a tax-exempt, non-profit organization, *Journal of Nursing Administration, 23*(2), 36–41.

Thompson, J.D. (1967). *Organizations in Action.* New York: McGraw-Hill.

SUGGESTED READINGS

Ghoshal, S., & Bartlett, C.A. (1990). The multinational corporation as an interorganization network. *Academy of Management Review, 15*(4), 603–625.

Harrington, C. (1992). The organization and financing of long-term care. In Aiken, L.A., & Fagin, C., eds. *Charting Nursing's Future: Agenda for the 1990's.* Philadelphia: J.B. Lippincott, pp. 181–197.

Hospitals. (1992, March 20). Managed care in the 1990's: Provider's new role for innovative health delivery. pp. 26–34.

Hospitals & Health Networks. (1994, February 5). Phoenix: Capitation drives the creation of a hospital alliance. pp. 64–66.

Igoe, J.B. (1992). Is health a school issue? School-based health services. In Aiken, L.A., & Fagin, C., eds. *Charting Nursing's Future: Agenda for the 1990's.* Philadelphia: J.B. Lippincott, pp. 270–286.

Kast, F.E., & Rosenzweiz, J.E. (1991). General systems theory: Applications for organization and management. In Ward, M.J., & Price, S.A., eds. *Issues in Nursing Administration: Selected Readings.* St. Louis: Mosby, pp. 60–73.

Lumsdon, K. (1993, December 5). Bridging the gap. *Hospitals and Health Networks,* pp. 44, 48.

Lundeen, S.P. (1994). Community nursing centers: Implications for health care reform. In McClosky, J.C., & Grace, H.K., eds. *Current Issues in Nursing,* 4th ed. St. Louis: Mosby, pp. 382–387.

Morrow, H. (1982). The fundamental influences of political, social and economic factors on health and health care. *International Nursing Review, 29*(6), 183–186.

Selby, T. (1990). Home health care finds new ways of caring. *The American Nurse, 22*(12).

Williams, C. (1992). Public health nursing: Does it have a future? In Aiken, L.A., & Fagin, C., eds. *Charting Nursing's Future: Agenda for the 1990's.* Philadelphia: J.B. Lippincott, pp. 255–269.

CHAPTER 8

CULTURAL DIVERSITY IN HEALTHCARE

Dorothy A. Otto, R.N., Ed.D.

Ana M. Valadez, R.N., Ed.D., C.N.A.A., F.A.A.N.

PREVIEW

This chapter focuses on the importance of cultural consideration for clients and staff. Although it does not address details about any specific culture, it does provide guidelines for actively incorporating cultural aspects into the roles of leading and managing. It presents concepts and principles of transculturalism, describes techniques for managing a culturally diverse work force, emphasizes the importance of respecting different lifestyles, and discusses the effects of diversity on staff performance. This chapter also contains exercises and scenarios to promote an appreciation of cultural richness.

OBJECTIVES

- Use concepts and principles of culture, cultural diversity, and cultural sensitivity in leading and managing situations.
- Analyze differences between cross-cultural, transcultural, multicultural, and intracultural.
- Describe common characteristics of any culture.
- Illustrate the richness of cultures as they relate to personnel and clients through storytelling.
- Evaluate individual and societal factors involved with cultural diversity.
- Compare and contrast values and beliefs about illness that affect management of nursing care interventions in clients from specific cultures.
- Use tools to address personnel and client cultural diversity.

QUESTIONS TO CONSIDER

- Why is it necessary to understand values, beliefs, and rituals held by culturally diverse personnel and clients?
- What implications would "cultural sensitivity" have for you as a nurse manager?
- In what ways do health-related or personal problems vary with the culture of patients and personnel?
- What specific tools could you use to incorporate cultural diversity into your practice setting?

A Manager's Viewpoint

When I first became a nurse manager, I continually felt perplexed with the nursing unit I had to lead. My staff consisted of a variety of ethnic groups and the patients also displayed various cultural diversities. It seemed to me that misunderstandings between staff, patients, and their families were constantly serving as irritants to one another. I would go home exhausted and wonder how I was ever going to work on my two top priorities, team building and quality care. One day, while sitting in the lounge eating lunch, I overheard a Hispanic patient trying his best to communicate his needs to a nurse from India. Neither one came out of the situation satisfied. The miscommunication encountered served as a "light bulb" for me. While I was working on my priorities, I had totally neglected what I had so diligently been taught in nursing school. I remember a management teacher who often said, "People have to understand and respect each other before they can have a therapeutic relationship."

Aha! What I had forgotten was the impact of social diversity on staff and patients. That evening at home, I quickly regrouped and began my long but enjoyable journey to making my unit the "model unit" where people from all ethnic groups not only work together but also espouse a philosophy of respect and love for each other.

Althea Edwards, R.N., C., B.S.N., Head Nurse
Veterans Affairs Medical Center
Houston, Texas

INTRODUCTION

The American Nurses' Association (ANA) has a long and shining history supporting human rights. As early as 1972 the profession supported numerous efforts to eliminate discriminatory practices against specific clients and nurses. In 1993 the ANA took further action that provided a giant step for assuring human rights for everyone. The House of Delegates in an action report agreed that ANA, along with state constituencies, ethnic minority organizations, and other influential groups such as NOLF (Nursing Organization Liaison Forum), should develop programs that will promote an effective diverse and multicultural nursing work force. The House of Delegates also requested ANA to sponsor a plenary session during the 1994 convention. The session was designed to address multiethnic and multicultural awareness, as well as sensitivity in the nursing work force.

American healthcare has consistently focused on individuals and their health problems. We have failed some people as a group in recognizing their cultural differences, beliefs, symbolism, and meaning of illness. Geissler's (1994) *Pocket Guide to Cultural Assessment* provides the nurse manager and staff with a concise resource of healthcare beliefs and practices. Frequently, the clients whom healthcare practitioners care for are newcomers to healthcare in the United States. This is true also for new staff. They are neither acculturated nor assimilated into the cultural values of the dominant culture. The knowledge base necessary for providers to recognize and manage cultural differences of clients and staff must be addressed.

Some areas of the United States may have a greater need than others to respond quickly to the cultural needs of different groups. The government statistics for 1988 report that, of the 1.9 million registered nurses, 73,500 were foreign graduates who were concentrated on the East and West Coasts and in the Sun Belt. These nurses and their families have definite cultural needs that should be addressed.

MEANING OF DIVERSITY IN THE ORGANIZATION

Leading and managing **cultural diversity** in an organization means managing one's own thinking and helping others to think in new ways. Managing problems that involve culture, whether institutional, ethnic, gender, religious, or any other kind, requires patience and persistence and much understanding. An organization's culture is significantly affected by the stories that circulate within it. Stories have symbolic power.

Staff who know what is valuable to the clients and to themselves can act accordingly and feel good about it. Having a clear mission, goals, rewards, and acknowledgment of efforts leads to a greater productivity and work effort from a culturally diverse staff that aspires to unity and uniqueness.

assessment   When assessing personnel diversity, the nurse manager can ask these three questions:
- What is the composition of the unit's work force?
- What is the cultural representation of the work force?
- What kind of team-building activities do they need to create a cohesive work force for effective healthcare delivery?

techniques   The following box lists some of the techniques that may be effective when managing a culturally diverse work force.

EXERCISE 8-1
Think of a recent event in your unit or in your institution, such as a project, task force, celebration, or the like. What meaning did people give the event? Was it viewed as being a symbol of some quality of the unit, such as its effectiveness, its values and beliefs, or its innovativeness?

Techniques for Managing a Culturally Diverse Workforce

- Have patience. Treat all questions as equally important even though they may be common everyday knowledge to you.
- Be cognizant that foreign or minority staff may not consider themselves deprived or of lesser socioeconomic status than the majority.
- Do not treat gender bias or those with different lifestyles as needing intervening techniques to change behaviors. Assume they are happy with their choice.
- Do not assume emotional outbursts represent anger. This may be a natural communication style for different groups.
- Treat compliments from your staff with respect. Avoid feeling that they are trying to request a special favor from you. In some cultures compliments are used quite often to demonstrate respect.
- Do not assume that physical features denote a specific race or ethnic identify. Some Hispanics demonstrate Asian features while some Puerto Ricans or Jamaicans may be mistaken for African blacks.
- Take the time to know your work force. Make time for conversational chats that will facilitate learning about each other.
- Always remember that the less you know about your staff, the more difficult your job will be as an effective manager.
- Be aware that people in your work force may at one time or another have felt or actually been part of an oppressed group. Give them a feeling of value and dignity.

CONCEPTS AND PRINCIPLES

transculturalism

Transculturalism sometimes has been considered in a narrow sense as a comparison of health beliefs and practices of people from different countries or geographic regions. However, culture can be construed more broadly to include differences in health beliefs and practices by gender, race, ethnicity, economic status, gender preference, age, and disability/physical challenge. Thus, when concepts of transcultural care are discussed, we should consider differences not just in health beliefs and practices between and among countries, but between genders, among races, among ethnic groups, among different economic strata, and so on. This requires us to consider multiple factors about any individual, whether client or employee.

For example, in the medical intensive care unit of the Veterans Affairs Medical Center in Houston, Texas, one of the staff nurses thought of an ingenious idea to help patients who faced temporary physical challenges because they were intubated and on ventilators. This young Filipino nurse developed a "talking board" that allowed patients to point to words that reflected their needs, such as "turn me," "I have pain," or "I am cold." As the patients became stronger and were able to write, they used part of the talking board to write their needs in their own words.

Leininger (1990) identified several major theoretical premises relating to transcultural nursing theory that nurse managers and staff can follow:

Culturally based care values, beliefs, and practices are essential to human growth, living and survival; health values, beliefs, and practices are derived from the culture, and vary between and within cultures; health and care concepts are identifiable by cultural groups and are linked together by cultural values and action patterns; features of social structure are powerful forces influencing health and care in any culture; and, folk and professional care and health values and action patterns are identifiable in a given culture.

communication

Perhaps *communication* is the most important factor that reflects who we are, how we react, and how we approach problems and interpret them. How close we stand to each other is a variable of culture. So are hand gestures, intonation and inflections, slang (see the accompanying box), patterns of exchange (your turn/my turn variations), use of adjectives (greater in women than in men), and facial expressions. As one nurse manager said, "When we address culture and its embracing parameters, we all bring our own baggage with us. That means that each of us views the world from an individual perspective." All of us have misunderstood or stereotyped people who are different from us, especially in communication styles. What we have done is to expect similar groups to exhibit the same behaviors or norms, thus grouping them into a special cultural "species." Nurse managers need to ensure that ineffective communication by staff with clients and other staff does not lead to misunderstandings and eventual alienation. The staff needs to be able to communicate with clients of various cultures. An understanding, cohesive work force avoids use of foreign language with clients when they do not verbally comprehend that language. For example, in terms of communication between staff and patients, many times it may be the difference in language or the heavy accent of the nurses. Patients may lack understanding or, depending on the way they were raised, they may have feelings about a certain group of individuals. Body language is also different. People living in the United States tend to use slang; people of other origins may think it means one thing when in reality it means something else. Also, their personalities are different. One person may see a warm greeting as shaking someone's hand, when this might be taboo in another person's country.

SLANG TERMS AND THEIR MEANINGS

TERM	MEANING
"lip lard"	lipstick
"low riders"	flat shoes
"barrilito"	overweight
"lengón"	talkative
"get a grip!"	take control
"don't have a clue"	confused

culture

What is culture? Does it exhibit certain characteristics? What is cultural diversity and what do we think of when we refer to cultural sensitivity? *Culture* is a way of life that is developed and communicated by a group of people and consists of their ideas, habits, attitudes, customs, and traditions (Simons, Vazquez, and Harris, 1993). Harris and Moran (1987) offered a varietyof characteristics that provide a convenient framework for *cultural understanding.* Some of the characteristics included "health," which addresses the way a cultural group prevents, cures, or inhibits the spread of disease; "work habits and practices," that is, a work ethic that expects all members to engage in worthwhile activities; "mental habits and practices," which address the unique way a culture defines reasoning processes, evaluating right or wrong and desirable or undesirable; "sense of self," the way a culture substantiates its unparalleled self; and "beliefs and attitudes," the group's influence on themselves and others. *Cultural diversity* is the term use currently to describe a vast range of cultural differences among people who are different from each other; *cultural sensitivity* describes the affective behaviors in individuals, the capacity to feel, convey, or react to ideas, habits, customs, or traditions unique to a group of people.

cultural diversity

The Institute on Black Chemical Abuse (1993) cited four inherent *characteristics of culture:*

characteristics of culture

1. it develops over time and is responsive to its members and their environment;
2. its members learn it and share it;
3. it is essential for survival and acceptance;
4. it changes with difficulty.

For the nurse manager these characteristics are important to keep in mind, because the underlying thread in all four of them is that staff and patients' cultures have been with them all of their lives. Their individual culture is viewed as normal and the challenge is for the nurse manager to view it also as normal and to assimilate it into her/his existing work force.

Nurse managers who ascribe to a positive view of culture and its characteristics acknowledge cultural diversity among clients and staff. Cultural competence includes providing culturally congruent care to clients while simultaneously balancing a culturally diverse staff. For example, cultural diversity might mean being sensitive or being able to embrace the emotions of a large multicultural group made up of staff and patients. Unless we know the differences we cannot come together and make decisions in the best interest of the patient.

INDIVIDUAL AND SOCIETAL FACTORS

Nurse managers must work with staff to foster respect of different lifestyles. To do this, nurse managers need to accept three key principles: **multiculturalism,** which refers to maintaining several different cultures; **cross-culturalism,** which means mediating and **transculturalism,** which denotes a bridging of significant differences in cultural practices.

According to Simons, Vazquez, and Harris (1993), some of the most difficult cultural differences to understand arise from gender. This is so because our concept of gender resides deep within our individual psyches and is similarly deeply embedded in our social context. However, a person's sexual orientation—heterosexuality, homosexuality, bisexuality, or celibacy—should not cause him or her to be treated unfairly or discriminated against in the workplace.

gender

There is a vast developing body of literature about homosexuality and bisexuality. Simons, Vazquez, and Harris (1993) offer the following suggestions to help guide the manager's practice:

Assume that these persons are already a part of your organization and that you and others are already dealing with them successfully; value the unique perspective that

**Respecting cultural diversity fosters
cooperation and supports sound
decision making.**

many people have gained by being homosexual, bisexual, or celibate, for example,
their increased sensitivity to oppressed groups. Dealing with the misunderstandings
and irritants that arise from gender differences is as important as dealing with overt
sexual harrassment. (p. 185)

Thus, the norm for gender recognition should be that males or females be
hired, promoted, rewarded, and respected for how successfully they do the
job, not because of who they are, where they come from, or who they know.

In today's workplace, female–male collaboration should provide powerful
models for the future. Gender does not determine response in any given situation. Yet men reportedly seem to be better at figuring out what needs to be
done, whereas women are best in collaborating and getting others to collaborate
in accomplishing a task. Men tend to take neutral, logical, and objective stands
on problems, while women become involved in how the problems affect people.
It is important to recognize that women and men bring separate perspectives to
resolving problems, which can help them function more effectively as a team on
the nursing unit. Men and women must learn to work together and value the
contributions of the other and the differences they bring to any situation.

Accessibility to healthcare in America is linked to specific social strata. This
challenges the nurse manager, who must strive for worth, recognition, and

individuality for clients and staff regardless of their ascribed economic and social standing. Beginning nurse managers may feel that the knowledge they bring to their job lacks "real life" experiences that provide the springboard to address staff/patient/client needs. In reality, although lack of experience may be a bit hampering, it is by no means an obstacle to addressing individualized attention to staff and patients. The key is that if the nurse manager respects people and their needs, economic and social standing become a moot point. Nurse managers need to be cognizant of divergent views about healthcare as a right for all people rather than a privilege for a few. Healthcare services are moving from a largely unicultural to a multicultural approach.

LEARNING THROUGH ROLE MODELING

Traditionally, beginning nurse managers have learned many aspects of clinical *role modeling* from faculty and later from expert practitioners. Roberson (1993) writes:

> Would it be realistic to hope to learn all the multitude of diverse cultural beliefs in the health arena? No, of course not. What is realistic, however, is for each and every nurse to incorporate principles of transcultural nursing into practice just as you do with other specialized knowledge, such as principles of psychiatric mental health nursing. Thus, nurses can avoid ethnocentric behaviors. (p. 6)

Ethnocentrism, believing one's own values are the best, most desired, or preferred, is the basis of "cultural imposition," according to Leininger (1990). Ethnocentrism is viewed as a major concern in nursing. Leininger defines cultural imposition as "the tendency of nurses to impose their values, beliefs, and practices on another culture" (p. 55). Such practice occurs from nurses' lack of awareness about the different cultures and nurses' ethnocentric tendencies. An example of ethnocentricity is found in how our values affect how we view our role as nurses in situations where abortions are performed.

ethnocentrism

EFFECTS OF DIVERSITY ON STAFF PERFORMANCE

Failure to address cultural diversity leads to negative effects on performance and staff interaction, as described in this chapter's "Research Perspective." Nurse managers can find many ways to address this issue. For example, in relation to performance, a nurse manager can make sure messages about patient care are received. This might be accomplished by sitting down with the staff nurse and analyzing the situation to make sure that understanding has occurred. In addition, the nurse manager might use a communication notebook that allows the nurse to slowly "digest" information by writing down communication areas that may be unclear. For effective staff interaction, the nurse manager can also make a special effort to pair mentors and mentees who are of different ethnic backgrounds. This strategy works because the mentor is able to pick up on mentee clues that allow her to draw out information that leads to a therapeutic interaction for both mentor and mentee.

EXERCISE 8-6
Consider doing a group exercise to enhance cultural sensitivity. Ask each group member to write down four to six cultural beliefs that he or she values. When everyone has finished writing, have the group members exchange their lists and discuss why these beliefs are valued. When everyone has had a chance to share their lists, have a volunteer compile a single all-encompassing list that reflects the values of your work force. (The key to this exercise is that many of the values are similar or perhaps even identical.)

RICHNESS OF CULTURES

In many health facilities the staff members, as well as the clients, have a variety of multiculturally diverse backgrounds. Nurse managers must understand and appreciate the richness of cultures. They should work toward consensus building that offers the staff a practice area that promotes quality care for clients.

Research Perspective

Burner, O., Cunningham, P., & Hattar, H. (1990). Managing a multicultural staff in a multicultural environment. Journal of Nursing Administration, 20(6), 30–34.

More a norm than an exception is the fact that numerous healthcare facilities have a large number of multiculturally diverse groups in their work force, as well as an equally diverse patient population. These authors focused on a multiculturally diverse work force by doing an in-depth study of one medical center adjacent to the Los Angeles area. The demographics of this center clearly depicted a diverse work force: 63 percent of the staff (680 employees) belong to minority groups; 77 percent are females; 64 percent of the total professional and ancillary staff belong to minority groups; 45 percent of the medical staff are either foreign born or of a minority group; and 70 percent of the registered nurses and licensed vocational nurses are either foreign born or of a minority group. The problems found in this medical center include language problems, lack of awareness by non-Asian groups; lack of understanding of different cultural values when delivering healthcare and lack of experience by supervisory personnel on how to manage a culturally diverse work force.

Implications for Practice

Top management in this medical center took a strong proactive approach to address the identified work force problems, the principles of which can be widely applied. The following major changes were undertaken:
- A top priority included building a cohesive work force by emphasizing through educational programs team building among U.S. educated black, caucasian, and hispanic nurses from Great Britain and the Philippines.
- Staff awareness of multicultural value systems for personnel as well as patients is emphasized during orientation.
- The manager acts as a facilitator when cultural clashes among employees occur and a reasonable solution to the differences is an expected outcome.
- Each new staff nurse is assigned a preceptor with the nurse recruiter taking the lead for coordinating and supervising preceptee/preceptor activities.
- Top-level management and nurse managers continue to work together in designing ways to develop and maintain a cohesive work force that respects each other's specific ethnic culture values.

Actions such as these can support team building and promote mutual understanding wherever cultural diversity in the workplace is an issue.

EXERCISE 8-7

On a periodic basis, plan an international birthday party. Have each group member bring a dish that represents a food preference. Have the members bring the recipe for their dish to share with others.

Although the literature has addressed multicultural needs of clients, it is sparse in identifying effective methods for nurse managers to use when dealing with multicultural staff. Differences in education and culture can impede client care, and uncomfortable situations may emerge from such differences. For example, staff members may be reluctant to admit language problems that hamper their written communication. They may also be reluctant to admit their lack of understanding when interpreting directions. Psychosocial skills may be troublesome as well, because non-Westernized countries encourage emotional restraint. Staff may have difficulty addressing issues that relate to private family matters. For example, non-Asian nurses may have difficulty accepting the intensified family involvement of Asian cultures. The lack of assertiveness in some cultures and the subservient physician–nurse relationships are other issues that provide challenges for nurse managers.

Kerfoot (1990) believes that nurses have much experience in cultural diversity because staff and clients always have been culturally diverse. As Kerfoot views it, perhaps our weakest link lies in the fact that we have not followed in the footsteps of industry—that is, establishing councils or formal programs to address the staff's diversity and making use of mentoring programs to understand cultural diversity. Nursing can learn much from business about how to recognize strengths in the work force that reflect multicultural diversity.

DEALING EFFECTIVELY WITH CULTURAL DIVERSITY

Nurse managers hold the key to making the best use of cultural diversity. Managers have positions of power to begin programs that enrich the diversity among staff. For example, it is possible to capitalize on the knowledge that all staff bring to the client for better quality care outcomes. One method that can be used is to allow staff to verbalize their feelings about particular cultures in relationship to personal beliefs.

MENTORING

The establishment of *mentoring programs* should be done so that all staff can expand their knowledge about cultural diversity. Programs that address the staff's cultural diversity should not try to make people of different cultures pattern their behavior on the prevailing culture. Nurse managers must select carefully those mentors that ascribe to transcultural, rather than ethnocentric, values and beliefs. A much richer staff exists when nurse managers build on the valuable culture of all staff and when diversity is rewarded. The pacesetter for the cultural norm of the unit is the nurse manager. For example, to demonstrate commitment to cultural diversity, a nurse manager could utilize whatever programs are sponsored by his/her institution. The nurse manager might make a special effort to ensure that programs such as African-American, Asian-American, and Hispanic days are recognized by the staff. Staff who are active participants in these programs can then be given positive reinforcement by the nurse manager. These activities promote a better understanding and appreciation of individuals' cultural heritage.

Generalizations can lead to *stereotypes* such as believing that all Hispanics are Roman Catholics, all Jewish people are orthodox in their dietary practices, all caucasians are WASPs (white, Anglo-Saxon Protestants), or all Asians eat rice. Nurse managers must develop synergism and high morale for a culturally diverse staff. An excellent way to do this is for the nurse manager to use group projects. For example, have two or three staff members present a patient care conference. The nurse manager can facilitate the presentation by providing coffee and a relaxed environment. Buttons that convey messages, such as "I'm on a winning team" or "Caring is my job," are high morale boosters for staff.

A program at the Veterans Affairs Medical Center, Houston, Texas called "Caught Caring" has been a tremendous morale booster for the staff. The unit "caught caring" is awarded a plaque and given a pizza party by top management. In addition, the staff's pictures are proudly displayed near the human resources service. If synergism and high morale are accomplished, they can lead to increased quality of care coupled with positive staff attitudes, thereby lessening cultural stereotyping. The valuing of cultural diversity is the key element of an effective manager.

mentoring programs

stereotypes

EXERCISE 8-8
Assess several clinical settings. Do these settings have programs related to cultural diversity? Why? What are the programs like? If there are no programs, why do you think they have not been implemented?

EXERCISE 8-9
When is Martin Luther King's birthday? What does it represent? What does Cinco de Mayo represent? Think about how you could help staff celebrate these events if the organization did not.

foreign nurse graduates

Challenges with *foreign nurse graduates* include demonstration of non-assertive compromising behavior with the medical staff and their lack of American **acculturation.** Two distinguished nurse leaders, Linda Burmes Bolton, president of the National Black Nurses' Association, and Sara Torres, president of the National Association of Hispanic Nurses, speak to the special needs of these two ethnic groups. Bolton (1992–1993) believes that different cultures require different approaches; therefore, the key is to become culturally competent in providing quality care. To become culturally competent, nurse managers need to conduct a cultural assessment and appreciate the value of it. For example, learn why an individual responds to a chronic illness in a certain manner. Knowing such details of a person's response to a situation provides the foundation to learn about the culture of the group over a period of time. Bolton also elaborates on the main point of patient-focused care, that is, looking at healthcare from the individual's perspective. Changing one's practice to make sure that it meets the client's needs ensures the needed treatment without creating undue problems for the correct care and treatment plan.

CONTINUING EDUCATION PROGRAMS

continuing education

Continuing education programs should assist nurses in learning about the care of different ethnic groups. Torres (Baye, 1992–1993) stated that continuing education and mentors are essential to the education of Hispanic nurses. She believed that there are not enough Hispanic role models for these nurses to emulate. Torres also strongly supports better educational preparation for Hispanic nurses so that they may be qualified for leadership positions and can have impact on healthcare policy and delivery.

A nurse manager may encounter a situation that requires choices or decisions. Kavanagh's and Kennedy's (1992) *Interactive Decision Model,* as adapted in Figure 8-1, provides a process for intervention. This model evolved from attempts to understand students and colleagues in their interactive situations in healthcare settings. According to Kavanagh and Kennedy, behavioral choices are a part of every situation. In making decisions from available behavioral choices, the two-way flow of problem-solving communication is best facilitated through positive encounter, dealing with the situation, and mutual communication. Opportunities will exist for reassessing a situation and its complementary decision. However, the two-way process of responding to a situation may lead to potential denial or coercion. A new situation is formed when new considerations and choices are made. Obviously, some decisions may lead to more productive outcomes than others. All decisions produce outcomes of some type (for example, rejection or acceptance). Kavanagh's and Kennedy's model shows that mutual communication is the most productive approach in situations involving diversity and cultural variables and, perhaps, will ultimately lead to maintenance or restoration of respect for individuals or groups of individuals.

problem-solving communication

The two scenarios described in the box below illustrate how problem-solving communication can promote mutual understanding and respect. The first senario involves a compromise between staff members and a patient's family, and the second involves a nurse manager and a staff member from a different culture.

EXERCISE 8-10

Identify a situation in which care to a culturally diverse client had positive or negative outcomes of care. If negative outcomes resulted, what could you do to make it a positive one?

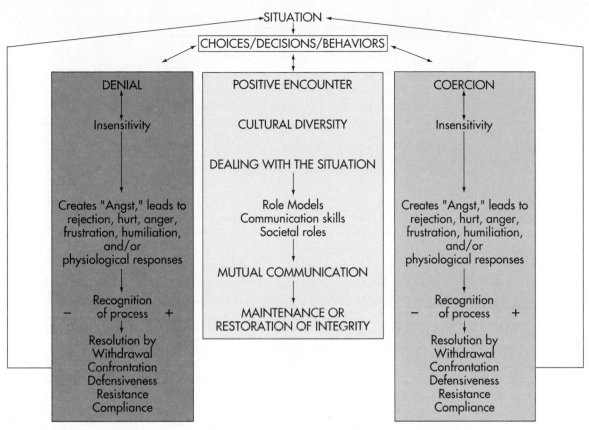

FIGURE 8-1 Interactive decision model. [Adapted with permission from Kavanagh, K.H., & Kennedy, P.H. (1992). Promoting Cultural Diversity. Newbury Park, CA: Sage Publications, p. 12.]

Problem-Solving Communication: Honoring Cultural Attitudes Toward Death and Dying

Scenario 1—Staff and a Patient's Family
What nurses often call interference with the care of a client frequently reflects family attitudes toward death and dying. Often, Hispanic families rush to the hospital as soon as they hear of a relative's illness. Since most Hispanics believe that death is the passing of oneself to a life that offers tranquillity and everlasting happiness, being at the bedside offering prayers and encouragement is the norm rather than the unusual. The nurse manager, herself a non–American-educated nurse manager, had worked extensively at helping her staff to understand different cultures. A consensus compromise was worked out between the staff and family. The family, consisting of three generations, was given the authority to decide who and for how long each family member could stay at the loved one's bedside. By doing this the family felt they had control of the environment and quickly developed a priority list of family members that could stay no more than five minutes at the patient's bedside. As the family member left the bedside his/her task was to report the condition of their loved one to other family members "camping" in the visitors lounge. Although their loved one did not survive a massive intracranial hemorrhage, all of the family felt a part of the "passage of life" by their loved one.

Problem-Solving Communication—cont'd

Scenario 2—A Nurse Manager and Another Staff Member
Eastern world cultures that profess Catholicism as their faith celebrate the death of a loved one 40 days after the death. The nurse manager needs to recognize that time off for the nurse involved in this celebration is imperative. Such an occurrence had to be addressed by a nurse manager of Asian descent. The nurse manager quickly realized that the nurse, whose mother died in India, did not ask for any time off to make the necessary burial arrangements, but rather waited 40 days to celebrate his mother's death. The celebration included formal invitations to a church service, as well as a dinner after the service. One day during early morning rounds the nurse explained how death is celebrated by Eastern world Catholics. The Bible's description of the Ascension of the Lord into heaven 40 days after his death served as the conceptual framework for the loved one's death. The grieving family believed their loved one's spirit stays on earth for 40 days. During these 40 days the family holds prayer sessions that will assist the "spirit" to prepare for its ascension into heaven. When the 40 days have passed, the celebration previously described marks the ascension of their loved one's spirit into heaven.

Because this particular unit truly espoused a multicultural concept, the nurses had no difficulty in allowing the Indian nurse two weeks of unplanned vacation so that his mother's "passage of life" could be accomplished in a respectful, dignified manner.

EXERCISE 8-11
Identify a situation involving a staff member in which a request was made that requires a "culturally sensitive" decision. What have you observed about religious or ethnic practices in regard to this decision?

Passages of life that culminate in happy events also can challenge the nurse manager—for example, the *quinceñera* observed by Hispanic families. This event is the celebration for 15-year-old girls to be introduced into society. The nurse whose daughter is celebrating this event must have time to make plans for this festive celebration. Because of the significance of the celebration and the pride that the parents take in their daughter, it is common practice to invite "key" staff personnel to the *quinceñera*. This is one more example of how culture influences nurses and nursing.

CHAPTER CHECKLIST

All potential or current nurse managers must acknowledge and address cultural diversity among staff and patients. Culture lives in each of us. It determines how we think, what we value, how we behave, and how we communicate with each other. In everyday work activities, the nurse manager must be able to:

- Assess personnel diversity and use techniques to manage a culturally diverse work force.
- Lead staff with a clear understanding of principles that embrace culture, cultural diversity, and cultural sensitivity.
- Be able to communicate effectively with staff and clients from diverse cultural backgrounds:

- Recognize slang terms that have different meanings in different cultures.
- Understand that nonverbal behaviors also carry different connotations depending on one's culture.
- Describe basic characteristics of any culture.
- Appraise factors, both individual and societal, inherent in cultural diversity:
  - Three key principles relate to respect for different lifestyles:
    - Multiculturalism refers to maintaining several different cultures simultaneously.
    - Cross-culturalism refers to mediating between two cultures (one's own and another).
    - Transculturalism denotes a bridging of significant differences in cultural practices.
  - Sexual orientation and gender recognition are important factors to consider in dealing fairly with all patients and staff members.
- Effectively use tools that clarify personnel and client cultural diversity:
  - Mentoring programs can help staff expand their knowledge of cultural diversity.
  - Continuing education programs can help nurses learn about caring for different ethnic groups in ways that honor their beliefs.
  - The interactive decision model is an intervention tool that can promote two-way communication, especially when conflict and confrontation are likely.
- Appreciate the cultural richness found among staff and patients/clients.

TERMS TO KNOW

- **acculturation**
- **cross-culturalism**
- **culture**
- **cultural diversity**
- **cultural sensitivity**
- **ethnocentrism**
- **multiculturalism**
- **subculture**
- **transculturalism**

REFERENCES

American Nurses' Association. (1993). *Summary of Proceedings of 1993 House of Delegates.* Washington, DC: American Nurses' Association.

Baye, A.L. (1992–93). Hispanic advancement. *Graduating Nurse,* 46–47, 53.

Bolton, L.B. (1992–1993). The changing faces of American health care. *Graduating Nurse,* 60–64.

Burner, O., Cunningham, P., & Hatter, H. (1990). Managing a multicultural staff in a multicultural environment. *Journal of Nursing Administration, 20*(6), 30–34.

Geissler, E.M. (1994). *Pocket Guide to Cultural Assessment.* St. Louis: Mosby–Year Book.

Harris, P.R., & Moran, R.T. (1987). *Managing Cultural Differences.* Houston: Gulf.

Institute on Black Chemical Abuse. (1993). Eighth Annual Summer Institute. Minneapolis.

Kavanagh, K.H., & Kennedy, P.H. (1992). *Promoting Cultural Diversity: Strategies for Health Care Professionals.* Newbury Park, CA: Sage Publications.

Kerfoot, K.M. (1990). Nursing management considerations. *Nursing Economics, 8*(5), 359–362.

Leininger, M. (1990). Culture: The conspicuous missing link to understanding ethical and moral dimensions of human care. In Leininger, M. *Ethical and Moral Dimensions of Care* editor. Detroit: Wayne State University, pp. 49–65.

Roberson, M. (1993, September). Defining cultural and ethnic differences to a changing patient population. *American Nurse, 25*(8), 6.

Simons, G., Vazquez, C., & Harris, P.R. (1993). *Transcultural Leadership: Empowering the Diverse Workforce.* Houston: Gulf.

SUGGESTED READINGS

AAN Expert Panel Report. (1992). Culturally competent health care. *Nursing Outlook, 40*(6), 277–283.

American Nurses' Association. (1986). *Cultural Diversity in the Nursing Curriculum: A Guide for Implementation.* G-171. Kansas City, MO: American Nurses' Association.

Arbiter, J.S. (1988, September). The facts about foreign nurses. *RN,* 56–63.

Eliason, M.J. (1993). Ethics and transcultural nursing care. *Nursing Outlook, 41*(5), 225–228.

Giger, J., & Davidhizar, R.E. (1991). *Transcultural Nursing: Assessment and Intervention.* St. Louis: Mosby–Year Book.

Million-Underwood, S. (1992, May-June). Educating for sensitivity to cultural diversity. *Nurse Educator, 17*(3), 7.

Spector, R.E. (1991). *Cultural Diversity in Health and Illness,* 3rd ed. Norwalk, CT: Appleton & Lange.

Spicer, J., Ripple, H.B., Louie, E., Boj, P., & Keating, S. (1994). Supporting ethnic and cultural diversity in nursing staff. *Nursing Management, 25*(1), 38–40.

Wenger, A.F. (1992, Winter). Transcultural nursing and health care issues in urban and rural contexts. *Journal of Transcultural Nursing, 4*(2), 4–10.

West, E.A. (1993). The cultural bridge model. *Nursing Outlook, 41*(5), 229–233.

CHAPTER 9

UNDERSTANDING AND DESIGNING ORGANIZATIONAL STRUCTURES

Carol Alvater Brooks, R.N., D.N.Sc., C.N.A.A.

PREVIEW

This chapter explains key concepts related to organizational structures and provides information on designing effective structures. This information can be used to help new managers function in an organization and to design structures that support work processes. An underlying theme is designing organizational structures that will respond to changes taking place in the current healthcare environment.

OBJECTIVES

- Analyze the relationship between vision statements, mission, philosophy, and organizational structure.
- Analyze six factors that influence the design of an organizational structure.
- Relate three types of organizational structures with three distinguishing characteristics of each.
- Evaluate the three forces that are necessitating reengineering of organizational systems.

QUESTIONS TO CONSIDER

- What is the nursing organization's reason for being?
- What are the beliefs and values regarding patients, patient care, and the workers?
- What characteristics of the nursing organization's structure would best serve patients' and workers' needs and support work processes?
- Who in the nursing organization makes decisions about staffing, work hours, and conditions of employment?
- Where are decisions regarding patient care issues made?

A Manager's Viewpoint

This private, non-profit facility has as its mission providing service to the elderly most in need of rehabilitation and/or long-term skilled nursing care. As a healthcare manager of a sixty-bed skilled nursing unit, I can see organizational ideals that are not necessarily reflected in the existing conditions. Characteristics of organizational structure that are essential to contemporary function of the nurse manager are discussed, but not necessarily in order of priority.

In addition to client advocacy, which is a basic component of staff functions, evidence of a client-centered philosophy in the day-to-day operation of the organization provides elemental support for effective care. This client-centered philosophy, in practice, would include responsiveness to the changing needs of clients and the staff who provide direct care. Other evidence of such a philosophy would be the provision of adequate material resources and prepared, educated staff in adequate numbers to meet client needs.

A nonhierarchical structure enabling employees to act, in carrying out responsibilities for client care at the point of intervention, is a critical component of effective function. The decentralized structure that provides for a free flow of interaction and consultation among staff across disciplines affords the essential flexibility that enhances care as well as employee satisfaction. Turning the organizational structure on its head (or flattening the structure) necessarily creates a new genre of direct care staff who tend to hold peers as well as central administration accountable. I believe structure must represent and facilitate the mission, and professional nurses need to understand the organizational context in which they function.

Kin Daner, R.N., M.S.
Nurse Manager
Loretto Geriatric Facility
Syracuse, New York

INTRODUCTION

Professional nurses work mostly in organizations. Learning to determine how an organization accomplishes its work, how to operate productively within an organization, and how to influence organizational processes is essential to survival.

"Organization" as it is used here refers to the structure that is designed to support organizational processes. The **mission** or reason for the organization's existence influences the design of the structure, for example, to meet healthcare information needs of a designated population, to prepare patients for a peaceful death, to provide supportive and stabilizing care to an acute-care population. Another key factor influencing structure is the philosophy, which expresses the values and beliefs that members of the organization hold about the nature of their work, about the people to whom they provide service, and about themselves and others providing the services.

VISION STATEMENTS

Vision statements are future-oriented, purposeful statements designed to identify the desired future of an organization. They serve to unify all subsequent statements toward the view of the future. Typically, vision statements are brief, consisting of only one or two statements. Within this context, mission and philosophy statements are crafted.

MISSION

mission statement

The first order of business is the statement of the organization's reason for being. This statement is the foundation statement from which subsequent ones flow. The mission identifies the organization's customers and the types of services offered, such as education, supportive nursing care, rehabilitation, acute care, and home care. It enacts the vision statement.

The mission statement sets the stage by defining the services to be offered, which identify the kinds of **technologies** and human resources to be employed. Hospital's missions are primarily treatment oriented; ambulatory care group practices combine treatment, prevention, and diagnosis-oriented services; long-term-care facilities are primarily maintenance and social support oriented; and nursing centers are oriented to promoting optimum health statuses for a defined group of clients. The definition of services to be provided with its implications for technologies and human resources greatly influences the design of the **organizational structure.**

Nursing, as a profession providing a service within a healthcare agency, formulates its own mission statement that describes its contributions to achieve the agency's mission. A purpose of the nursing profession is to provide nursing care to clients. The statement should define nursing based on theories that form the basis for the model of nursing to be used in guiding the process of nursing care delivery. Nursing's mission statement tells why nursing exists. It is written so that others within the organization can know and understand nursing's role in achieving the agency's mission. The mission should be reviewed for accuracy and updated routinely by professional nurses providing care. It should be known and understood by other healthcare professionals, by clients and their families, and by the community. It indicates the relationships between nursing and patients, agency personnel, the community, and health and illness. This statement provides direction for the evolving statement of philosophy and the organizational structure.

Units that provide specific services such as intensive care, cardiac services, or maternity services also formulate mission statements that detail their specific contributions to the overall mission.

PHILOSOPHY

Philosophy states the values and beliefs held about the nature of the work required to accomplish the mission and the nature and rights of both the people being served and those providing the service. It states the nurse managers' and nurse practitioners' vision of what they believe nursing management and practice are and sets the stage for developing goals to make that vision a reality. It states the beliefs of nurse managers and nurse practitioners as to how the mission or purpose will be achieved. For example, the mission statement may incorporate the provision of individualized care as a purpose and the philosophy would support this purpose through expression of a belief in the responsibility of nursing staff to act as patient advocates and provide quality care according to the wishes of the patient, family, and significant others. Philosophy both shapes and reflects the organizational culture.

philosophy

Organizational culture is exemplified by behaviors that illustrate values and beliefs. Examples include rituals and customary forms of practice, such as celebrations of promotions, publications, degree attainment, professional performance, weddings, retirements, etc. Another example is the characteristics of the people that the organizational members recognize as heroes.

organizational culture

Philosophies are evolutionary in that they are shaped both by the social environment and the stage of development of professionals delivering the service. The nursing staff reflects the values of the times and the values acquired through their education in their statements of philosophy. Technology development such as that of information systems also shapes the philosophy. For example, information systems can provide people with data that allow them greater control over their work; workers are consequently able to make more decisions and take more autonomous action. Philosophies require updating to reflect the extension of rights brought about by such changes.

technology

Developing a philosophy can be an activity used for **reengineering** a nursing care delivery system. A group process of development provides a method of stating a believed-in ideal and envisioning methods to make that ideal a reality. The box on pages 170–171 is an example of a philosophy developed for a neurological unit with the leadership of a nurse manager and clinical instructor.

EXERCISE 9-2
Obtain a copy of a philosophy of a nursing department and identify behaviors that you observe on a unit of the department that relate or do not relate to the beliefs and values expressed in the document.

FACTORS INFLUENCING ORGANIZATIONAL DEVELOPMENT

Organizational structure defines how work is organized, where decisions are made, and the authority and responsibility of workers. Structure is a map for communication and decision-making paths.

organizational structure

Alexander and Bauerschmidt (1987) use contingency theory to explain nursing organizational development. They hypothesize that the **fit** between organizational structure and the technologies employed to accomplish the mission determine the efficiency with which the organizational mission is accomplished. In units such as intensive care and emergency departments, work is characterized by uncertainty and the need for on-the-spot decision making, which necessitates that workers be given authority to make care decisions. Units providing long-term care and rehabilitation are characterized by similarity in care problems such as immobility, urinary and fecal incontinence, and mental confusion; these units may function more effectively with a structure that provides common direction for dealing with these problems.

Mission and Philosophy for a Neurosurgical Unit

MISSION STATEMENT

This unit's purpose is to provide quality nursing care for neurosurgical patients, during the acute phase of their illness, which facilitates their progression to the rehabilitation phase; to cultivate a multidisciplinary approach to the care of the neurosurgical patient and to provide multiple educational opportunities for professional development of neurosurgical nurses.

PHILOSOPHY

The philosophy is based on Roy's Adaptation Model and on the American Association of Neurosurgical Nursing Conceptual Framework.

Patients

We believe:

- It is the right of the patients to make informed choices concerning their treatment.

- Patients have a right to high-quality nursing care and to opportunities for improving their quality of life regardless of the potential outcomes of their illness.

- The patient/family/significant other has a right to exercise their options to participate in care to the extent of their abilities and needs.

Nursing

We believe:

- Neuroscience nursing is a unique area of nursing practice because neurosurgical interventions and/or neurological dysfunction impacts on all levels of human existence.

- The goal of the neuroscience nurse is to engage in a therapeutic relationship with her patients, to facilitate adaptation to changes in physiological, self-concept, role performance, and interdependent modes.

- The ultimate goal for the neuroscience nurse is to foster internal and external unity of their patients in order that they may achieve their optimal health potentials.

Nurse

We believe:

- The nurse is the integral element that coordinates nursing care for the neurosurgical patient utilizing valuable input from all members of the patient care team.

- The nurse has an obligation to assume accountability for maintaining excellence in practice.

- The nurse has three basic rights: human rights, legal rights and professional rights.

- The nurse has a right to autonomy in providing nursing care based on sound nursing judgment.

Mission and Philosophy for a Neurosurgical Unit—cont'd

Nursing Practice
We believe:
- Nursing practice must be supported by, and support, activities in practice, education, research, and management.

- Insofar as possible, patients must be assigned one nurse who is responsible and accountable for their individual care throughout their stay on the neurosurgical unit.

- The primary nurse is responsible for consulting and collaborating with other healthcare professionals in planning and delivering patient care.

- The contributions of all members of the nursing team are valuable and an environment must be created that allows each member to participate fully in the delivery of care in accord with his or her abilities and qualifications.

- The nursing process is the vehicle used by nurses to operationalize nursing practice.

- Data generated in nursing practices must be continually and consistently collected and analyzed for the purpose of managing the quality of nursing practice.

Courtesy of Neurosurgery 7B, State University of New York Health Science Center, Syracuse, New York; William Painter, Nurse Manager, and Jocelyne VanNest-Kinne, Teaching Assistant, Syracuse University College of Nursing.

EXERCISE 9-3
Arrange to interview a nurse employed in a healthcare agency or use your own experience to identify examples of changes taking place that necessitate reengineering, such as implementation of diagnosis-related groups, development of policies to carry out legislative regulations related to the right to die, or development of labor/delivery/recovery rooms for marketing. Identify examples of how previous systems of communication and decision making are inadequate to cope with these changes.

The issues in healthcare delivery with their concomitant changes such as reimbursement regulation and development of networks for delivery of healthcare have profound effects on organizational structure designs. Consumerism, the demand by consumers of care that the care be customized to meet their individual needs, necessitates that decision making be placed where the care is delivered. Change is ongoing as efforts are made to reduce cost and improve outcomes of healthcare. Increasing knowledge of consumers and greater responsibility for selecting healthcare providers and options have resulted in consumers who demand customized care. Competition for clients is another factor influencing structure design. These three factors—change, consumerism and competition—necessitate reengineering healthcare structures. Reengineering, as described by Hammer and Champy (1993), connotes a complete overhaul of an organizational structure, not merely a "tinkering" with one aspect. *change*

consumerism

competition

reengineering

Technological change, particularly in information services, provides a means of customizing care. Its potential of making all information concerning a client immediately accessible to direct caregivers has profound implications for altering decision-making points.

CHARACTERISTICS OF ORGANIZATIONAL STRUCTURES

Knowledge of characteristics of different types of organizational structures and the theories on which designs are based provide a catalog of options to consider in designing structures that fit specific situations. This knowledge also provides useful information to assist managers in understanding structures in current situations in which they function.

An organization is a group of people working together to achieve a purpose. Organizational theory is based largely on the systematic investigation of the effectiveness of specific organizational designs in achieving their purpose. Organizational theory development is a process of creating knowledge to understand the effect of identified factors, such as organizational culture; organizational technology, which is defined as all the work being carried out; and organizational structure or organizational development. A purpose of such

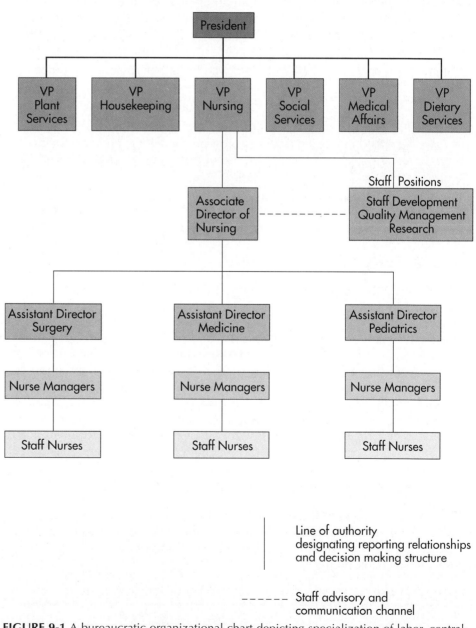

FIGURE 9-1 A bureaucratic organizational chart depicting specialization of labor, centralization, hierarchical authority, and line and staff responsibilities.

work is to determine how organizational effectiveness might be predicted or controlled through the design of the organizational structure. Although many relationships between the variables mentioned above have been hypothesized, there is a need for research studies that test these relationships. (See the following "Research Perspective" for an example of organizational research being carried out in healthcare organizations.)

Organizational designs are frequently classified by their characteristics of complexity, formalization, and centralization. Figure 9-1 illustrates specialization, centralization, authority and responsibility.

Complexity concerns the division of labor in an organization, the specialization of that labor, the number of hierarchical levels, and the geographical dispersion of organizational units. Division of labor and specialization refer to the separation of processes into tasks that are performed by designated people. The horizontal dimension of an organizational chart relates to the division and specialization of labor, functions attended by specialists.

Hierarchy connotes lines of authority and responsibility. *Chain of command* is a term used to refer to the hierarchy and is depicted in vertical dimensions of **organizational charts.** Hierarchy vests authority in positions on an ascending line away from where work is performed and allows for control of work.

complexity

Research Perspective

Anderson, R.A., & McDaniel, R.R. (1992). The implication of environmental turbulence for nursing unit design in effective nursing homes. Nursing Economics, 10, 117–125.

The purpose of this study was to examine the extent to which environmental turbulence (that is, rapidly changing and unpredictable customers, competitors, suppliers, regulatory agencies, and labor unions) is related to nursing unit design in effective nursing homes. The sample consisted of the skilled nursing unit in fourteen nursing homes rated superior by the Texas Department of Health. Instruments were used to measure environmental turbulence, decentralization, and participation in policy and resource decisions. Professionalization of the work force was measured by the proportion of registered nurses in the skilled nursing units. The results indicate that effective nursing homes use the strategy of decentralization when they perceive high environmental turbulence. The results also indicate that RNs' participation was highly correlated with environmental turbulence and negatively correlated for LVNs. RNs who have professional education appear to be the focus of information processing when the environmental turbulence is high. The proportion of RNs did not vary with environmental turbulence. Due to cost constraints and recruitment problems, the strategy of paying a more professional staff may not be available to nursing homes.

Implications for Practice

The key implication of this study is that when nurse managers perceive the environment to be turbulent, there should be an effort to decentralize decision making and to professionalize the decision making by increasing participation of RNs. Related issues to consider are (a) whether differences in services provided change the relationship of decentralization, participation, and professionalization of the nursing staff under the condition of environmental turbulence; and (b) how other components of organizational structure are related to environmental turbulence.

EXERCISE 9-4
Review nursing policies in a city health department, a school health office, a home health agency, and a hospital. Are there common policies? Does one of the organizations have more detailed policies than others? Is this formalization consistent with the structural complexity?

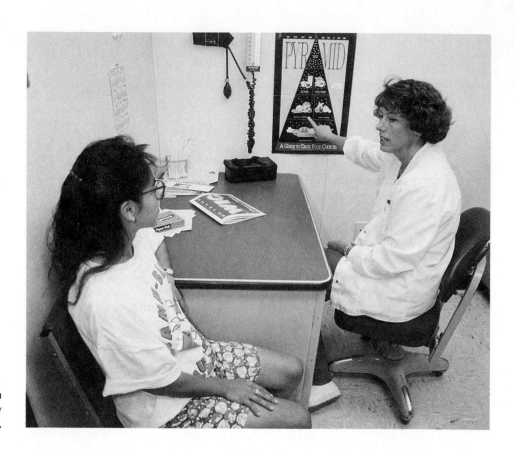

A school health clinic is an example of a geographically dispersed organization.

EXERCISE 9-5
Review a copy of a nursing department's organizational chart and identify the divisions of labor, the hierarchy of authority, and the degree of formalization.

Frequently workers are placed on a bottom line of the organization, and authority, which provides for control, is placed in higher levels.

Geographical dispersion refers to physical location of units. Units of work may be in one building, in several buildings in one location, spread throughout a city, or in different counties, states, or countries. An example of a geographically dispersed organization is Hospital Corporation of America, which owns healthcare facilities throughout the world. This aspect of complexity demands creative designs that place decision making related to client care close to the patient and consequently far from corporate headquarters. A similar type of complexity exists in organizations that deliver care at multiple sites in the community, such as school health programs in which care delivery sites are located in schools that usually are at great distances from the corporate office, which has overall responsibility for the school health program.

formalization

Formalization is the degree to which an organization has rules, stated in policy, that define a member's function. The amount of formalization varies among institutions.

centralization

Centralization refers to the location where a decision is made. In a centralized organization, decisions are made at the top of an organization. In a decentralized organization, decisions are made at or close to the patient-care level. Highly centralized organizations delegate responsibility without the authority necessary to carry out the responsibility. An example of this is illustrated by a story related to the writer by a staff nurse who was responsible for a unit that was at full capacity. A request was made to admit an additional patient. The director of nursing was called at home for the necessary permission and had to call the staff nurse for the information necessary for her to make the decision.

TYPES OF ORGANIZATIONAL STRUCTURES

There are three types of organizational structures: **bureaucratic, matrix, and flat.** Nursing organizations frequently combine characteristics from the three types, forming a structure that is a **hybrid. Shared governance** is a term frequently used to describe the flat types of structures presently being designed to meet the changing needs of nursing organizations.

BUREAUCRACY

Bureaucracy evolved from early theories on organizing work. It arose at a time of societal development when services were in short supply, workers' and clients' knowledge bases were limited, and technologies for sharing information were undeveloped. Characteristics of bureaucracy arose out of a need to control and were centered around division of processes into discrete tasks. Bureaucratic structures are formal, centralized and hierarchical and consist of divisions of labor and specialists. Rules, standards, and protocols ensure uniform actions and limit individualization of services and variance in workers' performance. As shown in Figure 9-1, communication and decisions flow from top to bottom, limiting workers' autonomy.

These characteristics at the time that they were developed promoted efficiency and production. As the general population's and workers' knowledge bases grew and technologies developed, the bureaucratic structure no longer fit the developing situation. Increasingly, workers and consumers functioning in bureaucratic situations complain of red tape, procedural delays, and general frustration.

Applying the characteristics of bureaucracy to an organization shows the characteristics present in varying degrees. An organization can demonstrate bureaucratic characteristics in some areas and not in others. For example, nursing staff in intensive care units may be granted autonomy in making and carrying out direct client care decisions, but may be granted no voice in determining work schedules or financial reimbursement systems for hours worked. A method of determining the extent to which bureaucratic tendencies exist in organizations is to assess the organizational characteristics of labor specialization (the degree to which client care is divided into highly specialized tasks), centralization (at what level of the organization decisions regarding the carrying out of work and remuneration for work are made), and formalization (what percentage of actions required to deliver patient care is governed by written policy and procedures).

Bureaucratic structures are commonly called line structures. Line structures usually have a staff component. Line structures have a vertical line, designating reporting and decision-making responsibility, that connects all positions to a centralized authority (see Figure 9-1).

Line functions are those that involve direct responsibility for accomplishing the objectives of a nursing department, service, or unit. Staff functions are those that assist the line in accomplishing the primary objectives. Line positions may include staff nurses, licensed practical/vocational nurses, and unlicensed assistive personnel who have the responsibility of carrying out all aspects of direct care. Staff positions may include staff development personnel,

characteristics of bureaucracy

EXERCISE 9-6
Develop a list of decisions that you as a staff nurse would like to make in order to optimize care for your patients. Determine where those decisions are made in a nursing organization with which you are familiar. Consider such issues as (a) deciding on visiting schedules that meet your own, your clients', and their significant others' needs; and (b) determining a personal work schedule that meets your personal needs and your clients' needs, for example talking to the children of an elderly confused client who work during the day shift, when you are on duty, and visit in the evening.

EXERCISE 9-7
Analyze the decisions identified in Exercise 9-6 from a manager perspective. Is that perspective similar to or different from the original perspective you identified?

researchers, and special clinical consultants who have the responsibility of supporting line positions through activities of consultation, education, role modeling, and knowledge development, with no authority for decision making. Line personnel have authority for decision making, while staff provide support, advice, and counsel. Organization charts usually indicate line positions through use of solid lines and staff positions through broken lines (see Figure 9-1).

To make line and staff functions effective, authority for decision making is clearly spelled out in position descriptions. Effectiveness is further ensured by spelling out competencies required for the responsibilities, providing methods of determining whether or not personnel possess the competencies, and providing means of maintaining and developing the competencies.

MATRIX STRUCTURES

function

Matrix structures are designed to focus on both product and function. Function is defined as all the tasks required to produce a product that is defined as the end result of the function. In an acute-care organization, the desired product may be defined as a satisfactory outcome to the client's problem that necessitated treatment while the function is defined as all the actions required to produce the product. In a matrix organization, the manager of a unit responsible for a service reports both to a functional manager and product manager. For example a director of pediatric nursing could report both to a

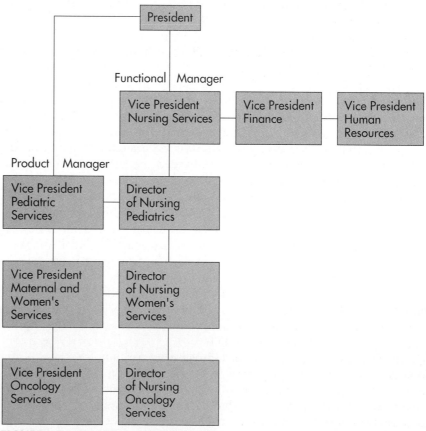

FIGURE 9-2 Matrix organizational structure.

chief executive officer (product manager) and a vice president of nursing (functional manager) (see Figure 9-2).

The matrix structure is usually centralized and hierarchical; product and functional decisions are made by the authorities ultimately responsible for product and function. A major problem has been the dual authority, which can produce frustration and confusion for workers. Decision making can be slow because of integrating mechanisms, such as meetings and information sharing sessions, which are required to maintain congruency between functional and product sides. The structure requires that both sides see the mission of the agency over that of their own area and understand and believe in the philosophy and mission of each other's area. Participants must be skilled in team building and conflict resolution. The primary advantage of centralizing expertise in both product and function close to the point of service has frequently been outweighed by the complexities created.

An approach to eliminating the need for matrix structures has been sought through preparing clinical nurse managers with the knowledge and skill needed to take responsibility for both product and function. An example of this is providing management and leadership education to clinical specialists so that they can use clinical, leadership, and management expertise in the roles of case managers who are responsible for function and product for specific cases. The education prepares nurse managers with knowledge and skills in areas such as finance, marketing, quality management, and conflict management. These educational efforts consist of organization- or nursing department–sponsored orientation and continuing education programs, incorporation of a management and leadership thread in undergraduate and graduate curricula, professional association–sponsored education programs and teaching tools, and graduate programs in nursing and management offering dual degrees (M.S.N./M.B.A.).

The development of matrix organizations was a sign of recognition that decisions regarding services needed to be made at the site of the service. Experience with the structure led many to believe that professionals performing the services needed to make the decisions. This recognition that nurses providing services must be involved in making clinical and managerial decisions is not only altering structures, but also mandating that professional nurses have basic and continuing preparation in management and leadership. Flattening structures has become a critical action.

FLAT STRUCTURES

Delegation of decision making to the professionals doing the work, referred to as participatory management, is the primary characteristic of flat organizational structures. The term *flat* signifies the removal of hierarchical layers granting authority to act and placing authority at the action level (see Figure 9-3). Decision making regarding work methods, individual patients' nursing care, and conditions under which workers' work are made in the place where the work is being carried out. Decentralization replaces the centralization of decision making at the top of the organization. A Manager's Viewpoint at the beginning of the chapter reflects the beliefs of a nurse manager in a long-term-care facility about benefits derived from flattening an organization. Providing staff with authority to make decisions at the place of interaction with clients is reflective of a flat structure.

flat

EXERCISE 9-8
Organizational structures vary in the extent to which they have bureaucratic characteristics. Using observations from your current situations, place a check mark (✓) in the "Present" column beside the bureaucratic characteristics that you believe apply to the agency. What does this analysis indicate about the bureaucratic tendency of the agency? Do the environment and technologies fit the identified bureaucratic tendency? (Consider the state of development of information systems, method of care delivery, clients' characteristics, workers' characteristics, regulatory status, and competition.)

Characteristic	Present
Hierarchy of authority	___
Division of labor	___
Written procedures for work	___
Written rules governing behaviors of workers	___
Limited authority for workers	___
Emphasis on written communication related to work performance and workers' behaviors	___
Impersonality of personal contact	___

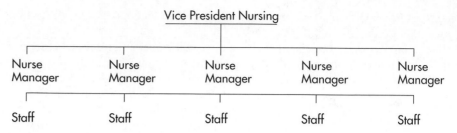

FIGURE 9-3 Flat organizational structure.

Flat organizational structures are less formalized than hierarchical organizations. A decrease in rules and policies allows for individualized decisions that fit specific situations and meet current needs created by consumerism, change, and competition.

The degree of flattening varies from organization to organization. Organizations that are decentralizing frequently retain bureaucratic characteristics. They may at the same time have units that are operating as matrix structures. *Hybrid* is a term applied to organizational structures that operate with characteristics of different types of structures.

hybrid

Problems with letting go of centralized control, and of top managers changing from boss roles to facilitator roles, are partially responsible for the development of hybrid structures. Managers are unsure of what needs to be controlled, how much control is needed, and which mechanisms can replace control. Fear of chaos without control predominates. Education that prepares managers to employ leadership techniques that empower nursing staff to take responsibility for their work is one method of eliminating managers' fears. These fears stem from loss of centralized control, as authority with its concomitant responsibilities moves to the place of interaction. The evolutionary development of self-governance structures in nursing departments demonstrates a type of flat structure being used to replace hierarchical control.

SELF-GOVERNANCE

Self-governance goes beyond participatory management through the creation of organizational structures that allow nursing staff to govern themselves. Accountability forms the foundation for designing self-governance models. To be accountable, authority to make decisions concerning all aspects of responsibilities is essential. This need for authority and accountability is particularly important for nurses who treat the wide range of human responses to wellness states and illnesses. The major cause of nurses' dissatisfaction with their work revolves around the absence of this accountability. The magnet hospital study (McClure et al., 1983), which identified characteristics of hospitals successful in recruiting and retaining nurses, found that nursing departments with structures that provided nurses the opportunity to be accountable for their own practice was the major contributing characteristic to success.

magnet hospitals

Shared governance or self-governance structure designs, sometimes referred to as professional practice models, go beyond decentralizing and diminishing hierarchies. Accountability is determined by needs arising from the services provided to clients. Authority, control, and autonomy are placed in specifically defined areas of accountability. For example, all issues related to nursing practices are dealt with by nursing staff.

Self-Governance Structure Evolution

PHASE ONE

Phase One: Representative staff nurses are members of clinical forums, which have authority for designated practice issues and some authority for determining roles, functions, and processes. Managers are members of the management forums, which are responsible for the facilitation of practice through resource management and allocation. Recommendations for action go to the *executive committee,* which has administrative and staff membership that may or may not be in equal proportion. The nurse executive retains final decision-making authority.

PHASE TWO

Phase Two: Representative staff nurses belong to nursing committees that are designated for specific management and/or clinical functions. These committees are chaired by staff nurses or administrators appointed by the vice president of nursing. The nursing committee chairs and nurse administrators make up the nursing cabinet, which makes the final decision on recommendations from the committees.

PHASE THREE

Phase Three: Representative staff nurses belong to councils with authority for specific functions. Council chairs make up a management committee charged with making all final operational organizational decisions.

All organizations require a foundation for operation. In a shared governance organization, the structure's foundation is the workplace rather than the hierarchy. Authority, responsibility, and accountability for all aspects of the work are vested in the nurses delivering care. The management/administrative level serves to coordinate and facilitate the work of the practicing nurses. Areas of accountability, such as quality management, are points of final authority for their designated accountability and are not subject to other sources for approval and mandated performance. Mechanisms are designed outside of the traditional hierarchy to provide for the functional areas needed to support professional practice. These functions include areas such as quality management, competency definition and evaluation, and continuing education. Structures of shared governance organizations vary. The box above shows three self-governance structures in progressive stages of evolution. As shown, evolution is moving structure beyond committees imposed on hierarchical structures to governance structures at the unit level. Minnen et al. (1993) provide an account of one such evolution. The authors describe one hospital's use of a multidisciplinary shared governance system to provide the structure and process support for the change initiated by work redesign.

Shared governance structures require new behaviors of all staff, not just new assignments of accountability. Behaviors required are in the areas of interpersonal relationship development, conflict resolution, and personal acceptance of responsibility for action. Education and experience in group work and conflict management are essential for successful transitions.

Changing nurses' positions from dependent employees to independent, accountable professionals is a prerequisite for (a) the required healthcare organization reengineering, (b) the radical redesign of healthcare organizations that is required to create value for clients and to abandon basic notions regarding the necessity of the diversion of labor, (c) the need for elaborate controls, and (d) the managerial hierarchy on which healthcare organizations have been founded. Structures providing nurses' accountability will meet needs for change, while also meeting consumers' demands and remaining competitive. Fitting nursing process and function with the governance process and determining that organizational structure characteristics fit the technology is an ongoing process.

CHAPTER CHECKLIST

Nursing care delivered in healthcare organizations is determined by the mission of the organization in which the care is delivered. Changes occurring in missions affect both the culture of the workplace and the philosophies regarding the work required to accomplish the mission. Actualizing new missions and philosophies requires reengineered organizational structures that place decision-making authority and responsibility where care is delivered. Decision-making responsibility requires staff to take responsibility for understanding the organization's mission and to participate in the development of mission and philosophy statements.

- Six factors influencing design of an organization structure are:
  - the types of service performed or the product produced;
  - the characteristics of the workers performing the service or producing the product;
  - the beliefs and values concerning the work, the people receiving the services, and the workers that are held by the people responsible for delivering the service;
  - the characteristics of people performing the service or producing the product;
  - the technologies used to perform the service and produce the product;
  - the needs, desires, and characteristics of the consumers using the product or service.
- Reengineering, complete overhaul of organizations' structures, is being driven by forces of:
  - change
  - consumerism
  - competition
- Bureaucratic structures are characterized by:
  - a high degree of formalization
  - centralization of decision making at the top of the organization
  - a hierarchy of authority
- Matrix structures are characterized by:
  - dual authority for product and function;
  - mechanisms such as committees to coordinate actions of product and function managers;
  - success is dependent on recognition and appreciation of each others' missions and philosophies and commitment to the organization's mission and philosophy.

■ Flat organizations are characterized by:

- decision making concerning work performed decentralized to the level where the work is performed;
- authority, accountability, and autonomy as well as responsibility for staff;
- low level of formalization in the way of rules with processes tailored to meet individual consumer's needs.

■ Mission and philosophy determine the characteristics of the organizational structure by:

- describing the consumers and services as a prescription for the technologies and human resources needed to accomplish the defined purpose (mission);
- citing values and beliefs which shape and are shaped by the nature of the work, the rights, and responsibilities of workers and consumers (philosophy);
- designing characteristics that support the service implementation to fulfill the mission and philosophy (structure).

TERMS TO KNOW

- **bureaucratic organization**
- **fit**
- **flat organization**
- **hierarchy**
- **hybrid organization**
- **matrix organization**
- **mission**

- **organizational chart**
- **organizational structure**
- **philosophy**
- **reengineering**
- **technology**
- **shared governance**

REFERENCES

Alexander, J.W., & Bauerschmidt, A. (1987). Implications for nursing administration of the relationship of technology and structure to quality of care. *Nursing Administration Quarterly, 11*(4), 1–10.

Anderson, R.A., & McDaniel, R.R. (1992). The implication of environmental turbulence for nursing unit design in effective nursing homes. *Nursing Economics, 10*(2), 117–125.

Hammer, M., and Champy, J. (1993). *Reengineering the Corporation: A Manifesto For Business Revolution*. New York: HarperCollins.

McClure, M.L., Poulin, M.A., Sovie, M.D., & Wandelt, M.A. (1983). *Magnet Hospitals, Attrition and Retention of Professional Nurses*. Kansas City, MO: American Nurses Association.

Minnen, T.G., Berger, E., Ames, A., Dubree, M., Baker, W.L., & Spinella, J. (1993). Sustaining work redesign innovations through shared governance. *Journal of Nursing Administration, 23*(7/8), 35–40.

SUGGESTED READINGS

Byham, W.C. (1988). *Zapp: The Lightening of Empowerment*. New York: Harmony Books.

Dumaine, B. (1988). The new non-manager managers. *Fortune, 127*(4), 80–84.

Graham, P., Constantine, S., Balik, B., Bedore, B., Hoake, M.C.M., Papin, D., Quamme, M., & Rivaid, R. (1987). Operationalizing a nursing philosophy. *Journal of Nursing Administration, 17*(3), 14–18.

Poteet, G., & Hill, A. (1988). Identifying the components of a nursing service philosophy. *Journal of Nursing Administration, 18*(10), 29–35.

Tonges, M.C. (1992). Work redesign: Sociotechnical systems for patient care delivery. *Nursing Management, 23*(1), 27–32.

Trexler, B. (1987). Nursing department purpose, philosophy, and objectives: Their use and effectiveness. *Journal of Nursing Administration, 17*(3), 8–12.

PART THREE

MANAGING RESOURCES

CHAPTER 10
MANAGING QUALITY AND RISK

Deborah Wendt, R.N., M.S., C.S.

Darla Vale, R.N., M.S.N., C.C.R.N.

PREVIEW

This chapter explains key concepts and strategies related to quality and risk management. It discusses the benefits of planning, the evolution of quality management, the quality improvement process, and methods of data collection. All healthcare professions need to be knowledgeable about, and involved in, continuous improvement of client care.

OBJECTIVES

- Apply quality management principles to clinical examples.
- Use the eight steps of the quality improvement process.
- Practice using selected quality improvement strategies to:
  a. Identify customer expectations
  b. Diagram clinical procedures
  c. Develop standards and outcomes
  d. Evaluate outcomes statistically
- Demonstrate the importance of planning in quality management.
- Differentiate between quality management and risk management.
- Employ the "five why" technique and triangulation method to obtain data about a situation or problem.

QUESTIONS TO CONSIDER

- How can a staff nurse make effective suggestions to improve nursing practice?
- If a colleague makes a mistake, what can you do to prevent future errors while protecting your colleague's self-esteem?
- How can clients' expectations be used to improve nursing care?

A Manager's Viewpoint

I personally welcome innovative ideas. Because of the bureaucracy in a public health department and the long time it takes to make changes, people probably get discouraged about the implementation of their ideas. What I like about total quality management is that you approach these ideas for improvement as a team. That allows more innovative ideas to rise from the bottom to the top.

We don't have actual quality circles. Within the department, we have what we call a "response team," which comes together to talk about issues. This is made up of people from community nursing, primary care, and health education. We meet once a week for about an hour and talk about current problems and make recommendations for change.

We recently had an outbreak of pertussis and this system allowed us to quickly provide more vaccines.

Barbara Gordon, R.N., M.S.N., C.N.M.
Nursing Director
Cincinnati Health Department
Cincinnati, Ohio

INTRODUCTION

Healthcare agencies and health professionals want to provide the highest-quality care with minimal risk to clients. But what is quality care? How can it be measured? As healthcare costs continue to rise, third-party payers, healthcare consumers, and health professionals increasingly ask these questions. The philosophy of **quality management** and the process of **quality improvement** strive to answer such questions by redesigning the corporate culture and teaching all employees specific skills for assessment, measurement, and evaluation of client care. Quality management stresses prevention of client care problems but, if problems occur, **risk management** activities focus on reducing the negative impact of such problems.

QUALITY MANAGEMENT IN HEALTHCARE

skepticism

Quality management is considered by some to be the current fad—a fast-moving bandwagon that healthcare is attempting to jump onto. The skeptics say, "It's okay for business, but not healthcare." The reality is that for healthcare systems to survive, they need to be run as businesses, producing quality, cost-efficient care for consumers.

Until recently, most healthcare agencies assigned quality monitoring activities primarily to a special person or department with the title of **quality assurance** (QA). Quality assurance specialists compare structure, process, and outcome measures to previously established criteria or standards. As a result of this process, nursing care errors or omissions are detected and corrections made.

evaluation of structure

The evaluation of structure targets the characteristics of healthcare providers and the work environment (Mitchell, 1993). Policies and procedures, job descriptions, and the physical facilities are some of the items that are evaluated under structure. To evaluate the process of nursing care, quality assurance personnel examine the interaction of nurses and clients. This may be done through direct observation or by interviewing nurses and clients. Outcome indicators relate to the results of nursing care. Were the client goals achieved? One of the methods frequently used to evaluate client outcomes is chart review or chart auditing (Marriner-Tomey, 1992).

chart audits

Chart audits may be conducted using the records of active and/or discharged clients. Charts are selected randomly and reviewed by qualified health professionals. In an internal audit, staff members from the same hospital or agency that generated the records examine the data. External auditors are qualified professionals from outside the organization who conduct the review. An audit tool containing specific criteria based on standards of care is applied to each chart under review. For example, auditors might compare the criterion, "Vital signs are documented every eight hours" to the documented vital signs in each record. If vital signs were documented every eight hours, the auditor checks off this criterion on the audit form. Auditors note compliance or lack of compliance with each audit criterion and report a summary of these findings to the appropriate manager or committee for corrective action (Humphrey and Milone-Nuzzo, 1991).

drawbacks

Quality assurance staff usually conduct or supervise the chart audits within an agency. Although these nurses are internal auditors, they may not be directly involved with the staff nurses whose charting is under review. Because the focus of the chart audit is on detecting errors and determining the person responsible for them, many staff members tend to view quality assurance as a nuisance or a threat.

Currently, many hospitals and community healthcare agencies are reducing the emphasis on quality assurance and instead are incorporating quality management and quality improvement concepts into their organizations. The popularity of the quality management philosophy, increasing competition among healthcare providers, and recent changes in the accreditation standards of the Joint Commission on Accreditation of Healthcare Organizations (JCAHO) and the Community Health Accreditation Program (CHAP) drive this trend.

popularity

The terms *quality management* and *quality improvement* have evolved from the business philosophy known as **total quality management,** which is discussed later in this chapter. Total quality management remains controversial. Many healthcare organizations prefer to use the term *quality management* because *total* quality management can never be achieved. Quality-related terminology or jargon changes rapidly. Table 10-1 lists past, present, and evolving quality abbreviations and terms. These terms are defined in the glossary.

controversy

Quality management and *quality improvement* are terms that are sometimes used interchangeably. However, quality management is a philosophy that defines a corporate culture that emphasizes customer satisfaction, innovation,

TABLE 10-1 **Past, Present, and Evolving Quality Terms**

PAST QUALITY TERMS	PRESENT QUALITY TERMS	EVOLVING QUALITY TERMS
Quality control	Total quality management	Quality management
Quality assurance	Continuous quality improvement	Quality improvement

and employee involvement. Quality improvement is an ongoing process of innovation, prevention of error, and staff development that is used by corporations and institutions who adopt the quality management philosophy. As healthcare adopts this new philosophy, quality assurance activities are gradually changing to quality improvement activities. Quality improvement describes a broader process than quality assurance. The similarities and differences between quality assurance and quality improvement are summarized in Table 10-2.

BENEFITS OF QUALITY MANAGEMENT

Healthcare systems can benefit in a number of ways from quality management. First, the financial environment with prospective payments has constrained budgets, which in turn caused a decrease in staff. Greater efficiency and proactive planning while maintaining quality may overcome some of the problems with prospective payments. Second, the abundance of legal malpractice suits emphasizes the need for quality of care. Quality management is based on the philosophy that we should do things right the first time and always strive for improvement. In America, this ideal notion is sometimes questioned, but in Japan, where quality management flourishes, people are committed to it. Third, quality management involves everyone on the improvement team and encourages everyone to make contributions. This style of participative

benefits

TABLE 10-2	Comparison of Quality Assurance and Quality Improvement Processes	
	QUALITY ASSURANCE PROCESS	**QUALITY IMPROVEMENT PROCESS**
Goal	To improve quality	To improve quality
Focus	Discovery and correction of errors	Prevention of errors
Major tasks	Inspection of nursing activities Chart audits	Review of nursing activities Innovation Staff development
Quality team	QA personnel or department personnel	Multidisciplinary team
Outcomes	Set by QA team with input from staff	Set by QI team with input from staff and clients/customers

management enhances job satisfaction. Employees feel valued as team members who can make a difference.

Because quality management and quality improvement were developed for industrial management, healthcare facilities must modify the basic concepts to fit into a healthcare environment. Some experts maintain that quality management is only effective if the philosophy is adopted by the entire hospital or agency. Arikian (1991) states that nurse managers can use quality management and quality improvement concepts on their units even if the larger system does not embrace the quality management philosophy.

need for commitment

To be successful, quality management and **continuous quality improvement** must be ideals accepted by everyone in the involved system. Emphasizing quality in slogans and posters is not enough. Each person must be committed to quality improvement. This commitment must be made one employee at a time. In a large organization, this change may take from six to ten years (Arikian, 1991). The number of potential interactions among workers and possible resistance to change increases dramatically with each additional employee (S. Wajert, Personal communication, September 10, 1993).

PLANNING FOR QUALITY IMPROVEMENT

costs of poor planning

Multidisciplinary planning using a systematic process is integral in the quest for quality. Planning takes time and money; however, quality managers say, "we don't have time *not* to plan." The price of poor planning can be very high in both human and dollar terms. Poor planning costs might involve redoing what was originally done poorly, increasing the risk of liability, making costly accidents and errors, risking a negative public image, and increasing employee frustration/turnover. For every dollar spent on prevention by an organization, ten to one thousand dollars may be saved by not having to correct a mistake (Labovitz and Chang, 1987).

The cost of errors and ineffective nursing actions are considered avoidable costs. These costs can be eliminated or reduced with quality improvement.

Unavoidable or necessary costs are those such as planning, implementing, and evaluating. After quality management has been implemented, the cost of planning/prevention increases slightly but the cost of problems and errors decreases significantly. This is demonstrated in Figure 10-1. Unfortunately, this cost-saving does not produce immediate bottom-line results, which is the focus of many American businesses. Initially, the planning time increases but the cost of errors may not change immediately because it is based on past practices. Over time, the financial benefits of quality management become apparent (Kirk, 1992).

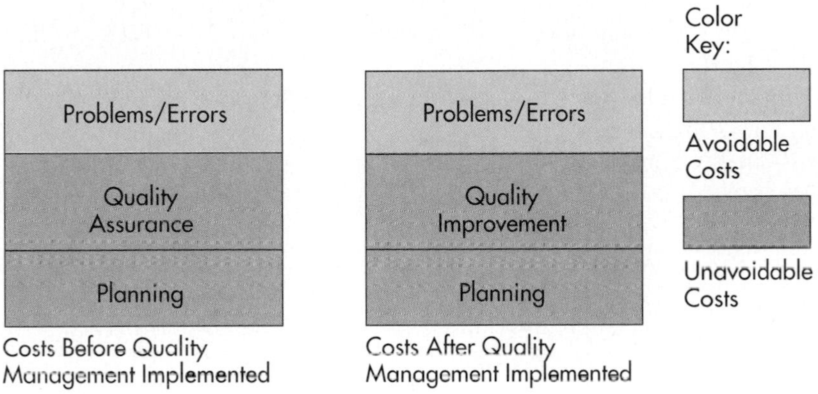

FIGURE 10-1
Necessary and avoidable costs of a system. [Adapted from Kirk, R. (1992). The big picture: Total quality management and continuous quality improvement. *Journal of Nursing Administration, 22*(4), 24–31.]

EVOLUTION OF QUALITY MANAGEMENT

W. Edwards Deming lectured about building quality into every product and service during a tour of postwar Japan. Using Deming's fourteen points of quality management as a guide, Japan recovered from the devastation of World War II and rapidly gained a reputation for efficient production and excellent products (Aguayo, 1990). A summary of Deming's fourteen management points appears in the accompanying box (p. 190). *Deming*

During the 1980s the United States faced increased competition for products in a global market. Deming's philosophy was rediscovered by Americans who enthusiastically began applying quality management to business, industrial, educational, and healthcare systems (Aguayo, 1990).

Deming's original management philosophy has been expanded and modified by various management theorists. Philip Crosby stressed conformance to standards and zero defects. According to Crosby, quality improvement is not a program but a permanent process of prevention. Joseph Juran developed a structured process for quality improvement. Although he advocated the use of self-directed quality improvement teams composed of workers, the responsibility for quality improvement always remains with upper management. Juran also emphasized the idea of creating a corporate culture that values quality improvement. The quality control circle, a team of workers who meet *Deming's philosophy expanded*

Deming's Fourteen Points of Quality Management

1. Create constancy of purpose for improvement of product and service.
2. Adopt the new philosophy.
3. Cease dependence upon inspection to achieve quality.
4. Minimize total cost by working with a single supplier.
5. Improve constantly and forever every process.
6. Institute training on the job.
7. Adopt and institute leadership.
8. Drive out fear.
9. Break down barriers between staff areas.
10. Eliminate slogans, exhortations, and targets for the work force.
11. Eliminate numerical quotas for the work force and numerical goals for management.
12. Remove barriers that rob people of pride of workmanship. Eliminate the annual rating system.
13. Institute a vigorous program of education and self-improvement for everyone.
14. Put everyone in the company to work to accomplish the transformation.

Brocka, B., & Brocka, M.S. (1992). Quality management: Implementing the best ideas of the masters. Homewood, IL: Richard D. Irwin, pp. 66–68. Fourteen points elaborated in Deming's work Out of Crisis, *Cambridge, MA: Center for Advanced Engineering Study. MIT Press. 1986.*

regularly to detect and correct quality problems, was the idea of Kaoru Ishikawa. He valued the use of statistical measurements and believed that all workers should be able to use basic statistics to improve the quality of products (Brocka and Brocka, 1992).

The combination of quality improvement ideas from these theorists is sometimes referred to as total quality management or, more simply, quality management. Whichever label is used, the basic tenets of quality management and quality improvement remain the same. These basic principles are summarized in the box on the next page and developed further in the next section of this chapter.

QUALITY MANAGEMENT AND QUALITY IMPROVEMENT

Managers need to be committed to quality management. Top-level managers retain the ultimate responsibility for quality management, but must involve the entire organization in the quality improvement process. Managers need to delegate properly, share decision making, and build effective teams. Healthcare agencies governed by the traditional bureaucratic hierarchy where most decisions are made by a small group of top-level executives are notoriously slow to change. In the current healthcare environment of changing technology and data systems and increased consumer expectations, organiza-

new corporate structure   tions are shifting to a new type of corporate structure. This new structure, flatter in style with decentralized authority, encourages teamwork and shared leadership among all levels of employees (Dixon, 1993). As the nursing director of the Cincinnati Health Department describes in "A Manager's Viewpoint" at the beginning of this chapter, teamwork facilitates innovation and change.

> **Principles of Quality Management and Quality Improvement**
>
> 1. Managers need to be committed to quality management.
> 2. All employees must be involved in quality improvement.
> 3. The goal of quality management is to provide a system in which workers can function effectively.
> 4. The focus of quality management is on improving the system, not on assigning blame.
> 5. Every agency has internal and external customers.
> 6. Customers define quality.
> 7. Decisions must be based on facts.
>
> *Adapted from Kirk, R. (1992). The big picture: Total quality management and continuous quality improvement. Journal of Nursing Administration, 22(4), 26.*

INVOLVEMENT

All employees must be involved in the quality process. To work in this new type of corporate environment, nurses must accept quality improvement as an integral part of their role. When a separate department controls quality activities, managers and nurses often relinquish responsibility and commitment for quality control to these quality specialists.

If all members of the healthcare team are to be actively involved in quality management, a nonthreatening environment must be established. Deming believed that fear was not an effective motivator of employees and even advocated eliminating annual performance reviews because they inhibit creativity (Aguayo, 1990). A nurse manager must create a work environment where employees feel free to make suggestions for improvement and innovation in client care. This requires a participative or democratic management style in which the nurse manager assumes the role of coach and facilitator (Dixon, 1993).

employee involvement

GOAL

The goal of quality management is to provide a system in which workers can function effectively. To encourage commitment to quality improvement, nurse managers must clearly articulate the organization's mission and future goals. Communication should flow freely within the organizational structure. All levels of employees, from nursing assistants to hospital administrators, must be educated about quality improvement strategies.

identifying goals and missions

FOCUS

The focus of quality management is on improving the system, not on assigning blame. Quality management's purpose is to change the system of healthcare delivery. It does not stress the detection of employees' errors. Approximately 85 percent of all mistakes in the workplace are caused by inefficient procedures, policies, or work processes. Only 15 percent of errors occur because of employee incompetence (Kirk and Hoesing, 1991). When problems occur, intervention should emphasize reeducation of staff rather than imposition of any punitive measures.

Since prevention, not correction, of mistakes is stressed in quality management, all employees must continuously try to improve patient care policies

EXERCISE 10-1
Think of a problem or potential problem that exists in the agency where you practice. Describe the problem using as many specific facts as possible. List the advantages to the staff, clients, and agency of correcting this problem. Describe several possible solutions to the problem. Decide who you would contact about this suggestion.

improving the system

internal and external customers

EXERCISE 10-2

For one week, list every person with whom you interact as a nurse. Which of these people work for the employing organization? These are the internal customers. Which of these people come from outside the employing agency? These are the external customers.

---

customer expectations

and procedures. Exercise 10-1 may be used to help make quality improvement suggestions.

Every agency has internal and external customers. Quality management involves not only managers and staff nurses but also the consumers or customers of nursing care. Nurses usually do not describe their clients as customers, but customers are an important part of the quality management philosophy. Customers are the reason any system exists. Internal customers are people or units within an organization who receive our products or services. A nurse working on a hospital unit could describe nurses on the other shifts, other hospital departments, and nursing supervisors as internal customers. For a nurse manager, the staff members working under him/her are internal customers. External customers are people or groups outside the organization who receive products or services. For nurses, these external customers may include clients, families, physicians, and the community at large. Exercise 10-2 will help you decide who your customers are.

Consumers of nursing care are important because they define quality care. Previously in healthcare systems, a nurse or group of health professionals devised standards for practice based on their own perceptions of quality care. Quality management requires that workers meet the expectations of customers to ensure their satisfaction. Workers must know what customer expectations are before improvements in care and service can be made. Therefore, nurse managers need to develop methods to determine what clients, physicians, and other departments expect and want. This can be done through surveys, meetings, and interviews. The accompanying box lists methods for obtaining input from clients about the quality of nursing care.

Techniques for Obtaining Quality of Care Information from Clients

1. Mail surveys to discharged clients.
2. Conduct telephone surveys of discharged clients.
3. Interview active clients.
4. Interview family members of active clients.
5. Conduct focus group discussions with inpatient or discharged clients.
6. Analyze unsolicited comments or letters from clients.
7. Systematically observe the behavior of clients and families on your unit or in your agency. Do they seem relaxed? Comfortable?

This chapter's "Research Perspective" describes a qualitative research study that utilized several methods to obtain client input. The data were then analyzed to determine hospitalized clients' perceptions of quality care.

unbiased data analysis

Decisions must be based on facts. The use of statistical tools enables nurse managers to make objective decisions about quality improvement. However, Ishikawa (1985) warned against collecting data merely to support a preconceived idea. In Japan, this was one of the most common reasons for poor decision making. Quality information must be gathered and analyzed without bias before improvement suggestions and recommendations are made.

THE QUALITY IMPROVEMENT PROCESS

Quality improvement involves continual analysis and evaluation of products and services to prevent errors and to achieve customer satisfaction. The work of continuous quality improvement never stops because products and services

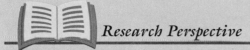

Research Perspective

Ludwig-Beymer, P., Ryan, C.J., Johnson, N.J., Hennessy, K.A., Gattuso, M.C., Epsom, R., & Czurylo, K.T. (1993). Using patient perceptions to improve quality care. Journal of Nursing Care Quality, 7(2), 42–51.

This qualitative research study investigated hospital patients' satisfaction with quality care and perceived caring of nursing. Three sources of data on patients' perceptions were examined and interpreted: unsolicited letters to hospital administrators, patient satisfaction surveys, and quality care surveys. Using a grounded theory approach, several prominent themes emerged. Patients described a global experience of quality care that included feeling attached to the hospital unit and experiencing a healing environment. Perceptions of quality nursing care involved the patient experiencing nurses as having a "calling of the head and the heart." These nurses were perceived as being very capable as well as caring and compassionate.

Implications for Practice

Perceptions of quality care in this client sample revealed that clients valued competent and caring nurses as well as a healing environment when hospitalized. Nursing competence is currently evaluated frequently using QA and QI techniques. This study implies that the caring quality of nurses and the environment of the unit also need to be assessed.

---

can always be improved. The old adage "If it ain't broke, don't fix it" conflicts with the main assumption of quality improvement. Improvement is always possible. Quality management and quality improvement are closely related. The quality improvement process thrives in a quality management environment. Quality management would be ineffective without the quality improvement process.

improvement always possible

The quality improvement process is a structured series of steps designed to plan, evaluate, and propose changes for healthcare activities. In most instances, a team of workers is involved in the process, but an individual can use the process to improve his/her own practice. Exercise 10-4 at the end of this section (p. 199) can be used to evaluate and improve individual nursing care.

Many models of the quality improvement process exist but all contain similar steps, as shown in the box below. These eight steps can easily be applied to clinical situations. The following example (p. 194) illustrates this process:

Steps in the Quality Improvement Process

1. Select a nursing activity for improvement.
2. Assemble a multidisciplinary team to review and revise the nursing activity.
3. Delineate all components of the activity using a flowchart.
4. Collect data to measure the current status of the activity.
5. Set a measurable standard for the activity.
6. Discuss various plans to meet the standard.
7. Select and implement one plan to meet the standard.
8. Collect data to evaluate the implementation of the plan and revise as needed.

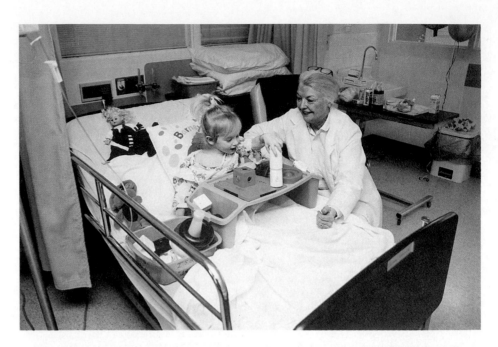

Quality nursing is both caring and compassionate.

A community clinic receives a number of complaints from clients about waiting up to two hours for scheduled appointments. The clinic manager assembles a multidisciplinary team to evaluate the process of scheduling clinic appointments. The team uses a flowchart to describe the scheduling process from the time a client calls to make an appointment until the client sees a physician or nurse practitioner in the examining room. Next, the team gathers and analyzes data about the important parts of the process: the number of calls for appointments, the number of clients seen in a day, the number of canceled or missed appointments, and the average time each client spends in the waiting room. The team discovers that too many appointments are scheduled because many clients miss appointments. This overbooking frequently results in long waiting times for the clients who do arrive on time. After a discussion of options, the team recommends that appointments be scheduled at more reasonable intervals, that clients receive notification of appointments by mail and by phone, and that all clinic clients be educated about the importance of keeping scheduled appointments. The team communicates its suggestions for improvement to the manager and staff and monitors the results of the implementation of their improvement suggestions. Within three months the average waiting room time per client had decreased by thirty minutes and the number of missed client appointments had decreased by 20 percent.

SELECT ACTIVITIES

The quality improvement process begins with the selection of a nursing activity for review. Theoretically, any and all aspects of nursing care could be improved through the quality improvement process. However, quality improvement efforts need to be concentrated on nursing care changes that will have *80/20 rule* the greatest impact. The 80/20 rule applies. Eighty percent of positive improvement in client care and customer satisfaction will come from changes in 20 percent of nursing activities (Kirk and Hoesing, 1991).

To determine which 20 percent of nursing activities are most important, hold discussions with staff nurses about what occupies most of their time. For example, if a hopsital unit handles many cardiovascular clients, improving nursing skills and procedures with this type of client will probably have the most impact.

ASSEMBLE A TEAM

Once an activity is selected for possible improvement, a team implements the quality improvement process. The team members should represent a cross section of workers who are involved with the problem. For example, if the activity under review is dinner tray delivery, representatives from the nursing units, nursing assistants, and dietary department should be on the team. When the activity under review involves medical treatment, physicians should be represented on the team (Lopresti and Whetstone, 1993).

Team members may need to be educated about their roles before starting the quality improvement process. Can they work effectively on a multidisciplinary team? The self-assessment exercise at the end of this chapter will help determine readiness to be a team player.

To develop effective quality improvement teams, the workplace environment must promote teamwork. Some healthcare facilities are more open to teamwork than others. Use Exercise 10-3 to decide if a clinical facility is ready for quality improvement teams.

CREATE A FLOWCHART

After the multidisciplinary team forms, the group sets boundaries for the identified activity and delineates all the activity components. A detailed flowchart helps to describe complex tasks and procedures. The flowchart is a tool that uses boxes and directional arrows to diagram a process or procedure (Longo and Bohr, 1991). Sometimes just diagramming a client care process in detail reveals opportunities for improvement. The flowchart in Figure 10-2 depicts the process of a home health agency receiving a new client referral.

COLLECT DATA

After the activity is described, the team collects data to determine the present status of the activity. A variety of statistical methods may be used to analyze and present this information. These methods include line graphs, histograms, Pareto charts, and fishbone diagrams. According to Ishikawa (1985), one of the reasons total quality management is so successful in Japan is because all high school graduates understand and use basic statistics. As healthcare agencies embrace the quality management philosophy, nurses as well as auxiliary workers will need to be well versed in statistics.

Line graphs present data by showing the connection between variables. The dependent variable is usually plotted on the vertical scale and the independent variable is usually plotted on the horizontal scale. In quality improvement, this technique is frequently used to show the trend of a particular activity over time and may be called a trend chart (Brocka and Brocka, 1992). The line graph in Figure 10-3 illustrates the number of referrals a home health agency receives over the course of a year.

The histogram in Figure 10-4 illustrates the number of home health referrals that come from five different referral sources during one year. A histogram is a bar chart that shows the frequency of events. A bar chart that identifies the major causes or components of a particular quality control problem is called a Pareto chart (Longo and Bohr, 1991). Used frequently in quality improvement, the Pareto chart helps the quality improvement team determine priorities. The Pareto chart in Figure 10-5 demonstrates that on a medical/surgical unit over a one-month period omission of vital signs is the most frequent type of documentation error.

multidisciplinary teams

EXERCISE 10-3
Ask yourself the following questions pertaining to your system:
1. Is communication between nurses and other disciplines promoted? If so, how?
2. Could the communication process be improved in any way?
3. Does your system encourage nurses to act as a team?
4. Are other disciplines/departments included in team activities?
5. Can the team focus be improved in any way?

flowcharts

statistics in data analysis

line graphs

histograms
bar charts

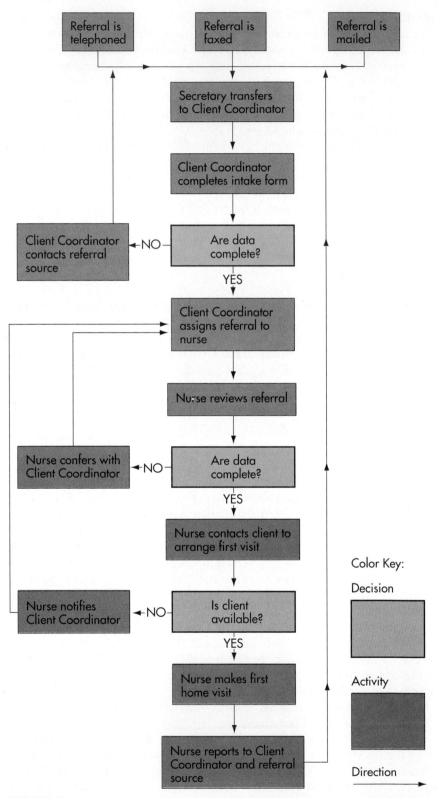

FIGURE 10-2
Steps in the flowchart diagramming process starting with the time a home health referral is made and ending with the first home visit.

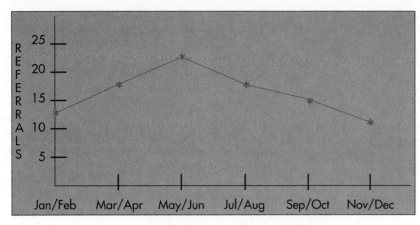

FIGURE 10-3
Line graph depicting the number of home health referrals received during one year.

The fishbone diagram, also called the cause-effect diagram, was developed by Ishikawa as a quality control tool. A specific problem or outcome is written on the horizontal line. All possible causes of the problem or strategies to meet the outcome are written in a fishbone pattern. This tool is an effective method of summarizing a brainstorming session (Brocka and Brocka, 1992). Figure 10-6 uses a fishbone diagram to present possible causes of clients' complaints about extended waits for clinic appointments.

fishbone diagrams

Although quality improvement teams should be able to use these basic statistical tools, more complex analysis is sometimes necessary. In this situation, a statistical expert could be included on the quality improvement team or the team may use a statistician as a consultant.

SET STANDARDS

After analyzing the data, the team next sets a goal for improvement. This goal can be established in a number of ways and always involves a standard of practice and a measurable client care outcome or indicator. The multidisciplinary team should utilize accepted standards of care and practice whenever possible. Sources that establish these standards include:

goal-setting

1. State Nurse Practice Act
2. Joint Commission on Accreditation of Healthcare Organizations and the Community Health Accreditation Program
3. Nationally recognized professional organizations
4. Nursing research
5. Internal policies and procedures
6. Agency for Healthcare Policy and Research (AHCPR).

Input from internal and external customers is also important for deciding the level of improvement needed. What do the customers expect? How do the customers define quality for this nursing activity? If another unit or agency is noted for excellence in this process or procedure, that system's standard may be adopted and becomes the benchmark of excellence. For example, a home health agency found it took an average of three days for the first home visit to be made after a referral was received. Through research, the home health agency staff discovered that most home health agencies in the area saw clients within two working days afer receiving a referral. Consequently, their new goal was to visit each new client within 48 hours after referral.

customer input

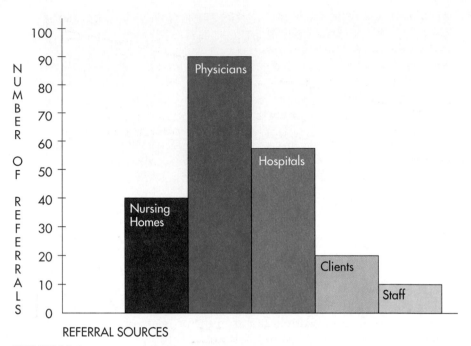

FIGURE 10-4
Histogram depicting the number of home health referrals from five sources during one year.

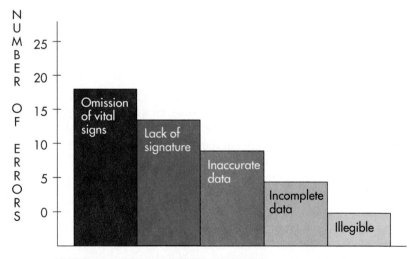

TYPES OF DOCUMENTATION ERRORS

FIGURE 10-5
Pareto chart presenting major types of documentation errors that occurred on a medical/surgical unit over a one-month period.

EXERCISE 10-4

Use the following steps to apply quality improvement principles to your own practice:

1. Identify a process or procedure that you perform routinely and wish to improve.
2. Using a flowchart, delineate each step of the procedure.
3. Collect data that show your present ability to do this process or procedure.
4. Set a measurable standard of excellence for this procedure. Use established standards if available, but remember to also determine what your customers value and expect.
5. Develop a plan to improve your practice to meet this standard. This could include further reading, education, or consultation with peers.
6. Collect data to document your improvement in this procedure.
7. When you successfully meet your performance standard, reward yourself.

DISCUSS PLANS

The team next discusses various strategies and plans to meet the new standard or outcome. The outcome should be a measurable result, such as 75 percent of all referrals will be seen within 48 hours. One plan is selected for implementation and the process of change begins. Since quality management stresses improving the system rather than assigning blame to employees, changing

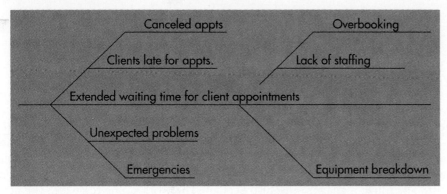

FIGURE 10-6
Fishbone diagram showing possible causes of extended waiting time for clinic clients.

strategies emphasize open communication and education of workers affected by the new standard and outcome. Quality improvement is not possible without continual education of all managers and workers. Even in a cost-conscious environment, staff education is not a luxury but a necessity (Arikian, 1991).

open communication and education

Policies and procedures may need to be written or rewritten during the quality improvement process. Policies should be frequently reviewed and updated so that they do not become barriers to innovation (Arikian, 1991). Communication about policy change or improvement to the team members at large is essential.

IMPLEMENT THE PLAN

As the plan is implemented, the team continues to gather and evaluate data to document that the new standard is being met. If the new standard is not met, revisions in the implementation plan are needed. Sometimes improvement in one part of a system presents new problems. For example, a school nurse wanted to improve the psychosocial assessment of children with possible family problems. A result of this improvement in care was a greatly increased number of referrals for counseling that overwhelmed the two school psychologists. The interdisciplinary team may need to reassemble periodically to handle the inevitable snags that develop with the implementation of any new process or procedure. The example that follows illustrates this idea:

continuous evaluation

A hospital is implementing a pneumatic tube system to dispense medications. A multidisciplinary team was assembled to discuss the process from a variety of viewpoints: pharmacy, nursing, pneumatic tube operation managers, aides who took the medications from the pneumatic tube to the client medication drawers, administrators, and physicians. The tube system is implemented. A nurse on one unit realizes that several clients do not have their morning medications in their medication boxes. The nurse borrows medications from other client's drawers and orders the rest stat from pharmacy. Other nurses on that unit and other units have the same problem and are doing the same or similar things. Several problems are occurring—some of the medications are being given late, the nurse wastes precious time by searching other medication boxes, the pharmacy charges extra for the stat medications and is overwhelmed with stat requests, and the situation increases the nurses' frustration level. Quality management principles would encourage the nurses to report the problems to the nurse manager or appropriate team member. The pneumatic tube team could compile data such as frequency of missing medications, timing of medication orders, and nursing units involved.

The problems are analyzed with a system perspective to effectively solve the late medication problem.

EVALUATE

outcome-focused evaluation

The focus of evaluation for quality improvement is on outcomes. The outcomes evaluated are clinical care outcomes of the clients, professional practice of the staff, and administrative governance of the system (Green and Katz, 1990).

celebrating success

When the change is successfully implemented, the quality improvement team disbands after celebrating its success. One of the crucial tasks of the nurse manager is to publicize and reward the success of each quality improvement team. The nurse manager must also evaluate the work of the team and the ability of individual team members to work together effectively.

RISK MANAGEMENT

quality management vs. risk management

origin of risk management

Although quality management and risk management are related concepts, quality management emphasizes the prevention of client care problems, while risk management attempts to analyze problems and minimize losses after a client care error occurs. These losses include financial loss due to malpractice or absorbing the cost of an extended length of stay for the client. They can also include negative public relations and employee dissatisfaction. If quality management was 100 percent effective, there would be no need for risk management. In the current healthcare environment, however, risk management departments are needed and utilized.

Risk management has blossomed since the malpractice crisis in the 1970s. Before that time, healthcare was assumed to be safe and of high quality except for a very few exceptions. Healthcare professionals were revered and medical treatment was not questioned. The abundance of liability suits in the 1970s had people doubting the validity of their faith in quality healthcare. The inclusion of risk management standards in the 1990 JCAHO guidelines further emphasized the importance of risk management (Green and Katz, 1990).

The risk management department has several functions. These include the following:
- define situations that place the system at some financial risk such as medication errors or client falls
- determine the frequency of those situations that occurred
- intervene and investigate identified events
- identify potential risks or opportunities to improve care.

incident reports

Each individual nurse is a risk manager. The nurse has the responsibility to identify and report unusual occurrences and potential risks to the proper authority. One method of communicating risks is through incident reporting. Incident reports should be a nonpunitive means of communicating an incident that did or could have caused harm to clients, family members, visitors, or employees. These reports should be used to improve quality care and decrease risk.

EVALUATING RISKS

five-why technique

Whenever a problem occurs, the question "why?" should be asked at least five times. This is referred to as the **"five-why" technique.** A client fall, one of the most frequent causes of nursing malpractice, demonstrates this technique:

EXAMPLE: An elderly client fell out of bed.

Risk manager: Why did this happen?

Nurse: The side rails on the bed were left down.

Risk manager: Why were the side rails left down?

Nurse: I was called out of the room suddenly and forgot to put them up.

Risk manager: Why were you called out of the room suddenly?

Nurse: Because the physician was on the phone.

Risk manager: Why was the physician calling on the phone?

Nurse: The physician was asking about lab reports from that morning that were not in the computer.

Risk manager: Why were the morning lab reports not in the computer?

Nurse: The morning labs never seem to be in the computer until 11:00 or after.

The scenario continues, as the risk manager attempts to get at the root of the problem instead of just treating the symptoms. In this instance, the physicians' attempt to obtain lab reports from the nurses, the delay of lab reports entered in the computer, as well as the nurse's behavior of leaving the side rails down could be addressed. The risk manager would look at the entire system to identify if this is an isolated event or a frequent problem.

The five-why technique is helpful in discovering the underlying problems that a cursory overview might miss. Risk managers also use a technique called **triangulation.** This technique involves utilizing multiple data sources and data collection techniques. Quantitative methods such as a yes/no questionnaire or chart records are merged with qualitative methods such as an open-ended question interview. This technique is also used in nursing research as a means to gain a broader perspective on nursing questions. Triangulation gives researchers, nurse managers, and risk managers additional information that might have been missed by only using one method. Triangulation takes more time to conduct and evaluate than just reading an incident report, so it should be used for significant issues.

triangulation

Self-Assessment: Are You An Effective Team Member?

Rate yourself from 1 to 5 on each of the following behaviors. 1—I never do this; 2—I rarely do this; 3—I occasionally do this; 4—I usually do this; 5—I always do this.

1. I listen actively during team meetings.   _____
2. I offer suggestions during team meetings.   _____
3. I communicate with team members before, during, and
   after the team meeting.   _____
4. I arrive on time for team meetings.   _____
5. I complete assignments on time.   _____
6. I attempt to resolve conflicts among team members.   _____
7. I speak positively about the team to other staff members.   _____
8. I place team goals above personal goals.   _____
                              Total score (40 points possible)   _____

Adapted from National Seminars Group. (1992). Total Quality Management. Overland Park, KS: Rockhurst College Continuing Education Center, p. 37.

CHAPTER CHECKLIST

Many healthcare organizations are in the process of transforming their system to quality management. Greater efficiency with improved quality is the goal of this approach. Effective quality improvement includes identifying consumer expectations, planning, involving a multidisciplinary approach, evaluating outcomes, and changing the system to provide an environment where employees can perform their best. Quality management is not just a buzz word of the present, it is the philosophy of healthcare in the future.

- The main principles of quality management are:
  - Managers need to be committed to quality management.
  - All employees must be involved in quality improvement.
  - The goal of quality management is to provide a system in which workers can function effectively.
  - The focus of quality management is on improving the system not on assigning blame.
  - Every organization has internal and external customers.
  - Customers define quality.
  - Decisions must be based on facts.
- The goal of quality management is to prevent errors. Quality management requires effective planning.
  - Initially, planning requires both time and money.
  - Quality management saves money in the long run.
- Quality management philosophy originated with Deming and is being modified by contemporary management theorists.
- The major steps in the continuous quality improvement process to evaluate and improve client care processes are these:
  - Select an activity for improvement
  - Assemble a multidisciplinary team
  - Create a flowchart of the activity's components
  - Collect data to measure current status
    - Line graphs
    - Histograms
    - Bar charts
    - Fishbone diagrams
  - Set a measurable standard for improvement
  - Discuss various plans to achieve the standard
  - Select and implement a plan
  - Collect data to evaluate the implementation
  - Revise plan as needed.
- Any process can be improved.
- Risk management focuses on minimizing loss after a client care error occurs. Techniques to obtain data include:
  - The "five-why" technique
  - Triangulation.

TERMS TO KNOW

- continuous quality improvement (CQI)
- "five why" technique
- quality assurance (QA)
- quality control
- quality improvement (QI)
- quality management (QM)
- risk management
- total quality management
- triangulation

REFERENCES

Aguayo, R. (1990). *Dr. Deming: The American who Taught the Japanese about Quality.* New York: Simon & Schuster.

Arikian, V.L. (1991). Total quality management: Applications to nursing service. *Journal of Nursing Administration, 21*(6), 46–50.

Brocka, B., & Brocka, M.S. (1992). *Quality Management: Implementing the Best Ideas of the Masters.* Homewood, IL: Richard D. Irwin.

Dixon, I. (1993). Continuous quality improvement in shared leadership. *Nursing Management, 24*(1), 40–45.

Green, E., & Katz, J. (1990). Blueprint of quality management: Three domains of nursing practice for standards development. *Journal of Nursing Quality Assurance, 4*(4), 75–85.

Humphrey, C.J., & Milone-Nuzzo, P. (1991). *Home Care Nursing: An Orientation to Practice.* Norwalk, CT: Appleton & Lange.

Ishikawa, K. (1985). *What is Total Quality Control? The Japanese Way.* Englewood Cliffs, NJ: Prentice-Hall.

Kirk, R. (1992). The big picture: Total quality management and continuous quality improvement. *Journal of Nursing Administration, 22*(4), 24–31.

Kirk, R., & Hoesing, H. (1991). *The Nurses' Guide to Common Sense Quality Management.* West Dundee, IL: S-N Publications.

Labovitz, G., & Chang, Y. (1987). *Tough Questions Senior Managers in Health Care should be Asking about Quality.* Washington, D.C.: Organizational Dynamics Inc.

Longo, D.R., & Bohr, D., eds. (1991). *Quantitative Methods in Quality Management: A Guide for Practitioners.* American Hospital Publishing.

Lopresti, J., & Whetstone, W.R. (1993). Total quality management: Doing things right. *Nursing Management, 24*(1), 34–36.

Ludwig-Beymer, P., Ryan, C.J., Johnson, N.J., Hennessey, K.A., Gattuso, M.C., Epsom, R., & Czurylo, K.T. (1993). Using patient perceptions to improve quality care. *Journal of Nursing Care Quality, 7*(2), 42–51.

Marriner-Tomey, A. (1992). *Guide to Nursing Management,* 4th ed. St. Louis: Mosby–Year Book.

Mitchell, P.H. (1993). Perspectives on outcome-oriented care systems. *Nursing Administration Quarterly, 17*(3), 1–7.

National Seminars Group. (1992). *Total Quality Management.* Overland, KS: Rockhurst College Continuing Education Center.

Wajert, S. (September 10, 1993). Personal communication.

SUGGESTED READINGS

Bechtel, G.A., Vertrees, J.L., & Swartzberg, B. (1993). A continuous quality improvement approach to medication administration. *Journal of Nursing Care Quality, 7*(3), 28–34.

Fairly, T., & Nance, D. (1992). Quality management in risk management and safety. In Koch, M., & Fairly, T., eds. *Integrated Quality Management: The Key to Improving Nursing Care Quality.* St. Louis: Mosby–Year Book, pp. 90–110.

Fannucci, D., Hammill, M., Johannson, P., Leggett, J., & Smith, M. (1993). Quantam leap into continuous quality improvement. *Nursing Management, 24*(6), 28–30.

Frost, M.H. (1992). Quality: A concept of importance to nursing. *Journal of Nursing Care Quality, 7*(1), 64–69.

Goldberg, A.M., & Pegels, C.C. (1985). *Quality Circles in Health Care Facilities: A Model for Excellence.* Rockville, MD: Aspen Systems.

Gugerty, B., Occhino, S., Ventura, M., & Haley, M. (1993). The interaction of information technology and nursing quality improvement: Important trends. *Journal of Nursing Care Quality, 7*(4), 19–25.

Kalunzy, A.D., McLaughlin, C.P., & Simpson, K. (1992). Applying total quality management concepts to public health organizations. *Public Health Reports, 107*(3), 257–264.

Koch, M., & Fairly, T. (1992). *Integrated Quality Management: The Key to Improving Nursing Care Quality.* St. Louis: Mosby.

Kralovec, O.J., Huttner, C.A., & Dixon, M.D. (1991). The application of total quality management concepts in a service-line cardiovascular program. *Nursing Administration Quarterly, 15*(2), 1–8.

Labovitz, G. (1990). *The Quality Advantage.* Burlington, MA: Organizational Dynamics Inc.

Luquire, R. (1989). Nursing risk management. *Nursing Management, 20*(10), 56–58.

Masters, F., & Schmele, J. (1991). Total quality management: An idea whose time has come. *Journal of Nursing Quality Assurance, 5*(4), 7–16.

Parisi, L.L., Johnson, T., & Keill, P. (1993). The nursing quality professional: A role in transition. *Journal of Nursing Care Quality, 7*(4), 1–5.

Patton, S., & Stanley, J. (1993). Bridging quality assurance and continuous quality improvement. *Journal of Nursing Care Quality, 7*(2), 15–23.

Peters, D.A. (1993). Improving quality requires consumer input: Using focus groups. *Journal of Nursing Care Quality, 7*(2), 34–41.

Poteet, G. (1983). Risk management and nursing. *Nursing Clinics of North America, 18*(3), 457–465.

Schmele, J.A., & Foss, S.J. (1989). The quality management maturity grid: A diagnostic method. *Journal of Nursing Administration, 19*(9), 29–34.

CHAPTER 11

MANAGING TIME

Patricia S. Yoder Wise, R.N., C., Ed.D., C.N.A.A., F.A.A.N.

PREVIEW

This chapter explains key concepts related to time management and provides practical, specific tips for managing time. Many of the strategies discussed can be used in personal as well as professional situations. Exercises throughout the chapter demonstrate techniques that can be applied to both personal and management situations. This chapter's appendix contains a tool to help identify and prioritize goals.

OBJECTIVES

- Define time management
- Incorporate one of six key principles for managing time in a typical management situation
- Analyze how time influences goals and priorities
- Analyze selected strategies to
  a. organize tasks
  b. get started with projects
  c. delegate
  d. manage meetings

QUESTIONS TO CONSIDER

- What do you spend your time doing?
- Are there things you want to do that currently don't fit in your schedule?
- How can you increase your productivity as a nurse?
- Does the way you spend your time reflect your priorities?
- How does a nurse manager use time to attain work goals?

A Manager's Viewpoint

When I heard that "everyone has the same amount of time available," I knew that I had to capitalize on time management. I found that flowcharts helped me organize my work. I thought I was through with an organizer when I finished school; but I bought one of those organizers so that I could record deadlines, management meetings, quality improvement time frames, and meetings I was expected to attend, even on my day off. I always prepare agendas if I'm in charge of a meeting. In addition to keeping me on track they provide a place for others to take their notes; and if someone can't attend a meeting or is reluctant to talk in the meeting, I tell them to use the agenda to give me their thoughts about a topic. That way everyone has the opportunity for input. Afterward I post the agenda with notes so everyone knows the gist of what happened. I think this approach also encourages interaction among the staff members and they know they have a part in where we're going. That's really important in meeting the goals of my work unit. I began to value the need to delegate. Knowing to whom I could delegate and how to maintain accountability has been critical for me. And, in terms of both my personal and professional life, I always try to keep my goals and priorities in mind, including the priorities of my work unit. Time management really works, even when more opportunities continue to emerge!

Yvonne Lovato, R.N., B.S.N.
Assistant Nurse Manager—Coronary Care Unit
St. Mary of the Plains Hospital and Rehabilitation Center
Lubbock, Texas

INTRODUCTION

When it comes to managing time, everyone has two choices: organize or agonize. Since everyone has the same number of hours available in a given day, it is clear some people use time more effectively than others. How people use time is what makes some people superstars and highly successful. As more demands are placed on people, following time management principles and strategies becomes more important to achieving personal and professional goals. **Time management** is the use of personal and professional management tools and strategies to assure that investment in activities leads toward achieving a desired, high-priority goal.

TIME MANAGEMENT CONCEPTS

principles

The key principles of time management are quite logical. They are designed to enhance effectiveness and increase productivity. The overriding theme is that every activity leads to the attainment of a goal, and that goal should be the number one priority at that time. The box below lists Alan Lakein's six critical time management principles. These principles are designed to help focus priorities and maximize the results of activities. These principles are equally applicable to personal and professional expectations. The first step is the most important: list goals and set priorities. Priorities and goals generally fall into one of three broad areas: Family/significant others, career and professional development, and personal development. To succeed in our careers, it is important to set goals and priorities with a group of people. Some goals may be givens, for example, providing cost-effective nursing care.

goals/priorities

Once goals are known, priorities are set. They may shift throughout a given period in terms of goal attainment. For example, working on a budget may take precedence at certain times of the year. Knowing what the goals and priorities are helps shape "to do" lists. On a nursing unit, or as we make community calls, we must know overall goals and current priorities. How we organize work may depend on geographic considerations, patient acuity, or some other schema. Exercise 11-1 is useful in prioritizing goals.

Although there are many routine tasks of any work, the tasks that have priority should be those related to the goals and priorities. In essence, the third point means starting with the most important (A's) and not being consumed with what may be easier but less important (C's). Asking the question, "What is the best use of my time right now?" keeps the important projects (A's) moving forward as opposed to doing several quick tasks of lower priority. Sometimes, however, the answer to the question is "Relax!" This response may

> **EXERCISE 11-1**
> Use the "Goal Setting" forms found in the appendix to this chapter to list and prioritize some of your career/professional, personal, and family goals. Complete the exercise by identifying specific activities that will help you achieve your top-priority goals.

Lakein's Principles

1. List goals and set priorities.
2. Make a daily "to do" list.
3. Start with the A's, not with the C's.
4. Ask: What is the best use of my time right now?
5. Handle each piece of paper only once.
6. Do it now!

Reprinted with permission from Lakein, 1973.

help reduce some tension that occurs on a particularly busy day and restore energy to resume more demanding activities later.

An example of an A is managing the quality of care; a B has a second-level importance, for example writing a report; a C is something that might not even need to be done, for example, rearranging a bulletin board display.

Handling each piece of paper only once is a great idea theoretically but may be difficult to implement. For example, if health records must be kept in a central office, some interim recording of data is necessary. Final recordings are duplicative, but necessary. In settings with state-of-the-art computerization, no paper is handled in relation to the health record because a computer or terminal is available at the point of delivery of service.

The last of Lakein's principles is to avoid delays in action. Maintaining the attitude of doing it now contributes to high achievement levels. The principle of "do it now" makes an important difference for highly productive people. As important tasks are delayed, they can take on crisis dimensions. For example, planning to finalize a report a week before it is due allows time to review and reorganize it. On the other hand, attending to the report until a few days before may be altered due to another work demand. Taking action can sometimes feel draining, especially at the end of a long day. Seldom does anyone need to decide to do something that's fun or stimulating. Our energy is restored by these tasks. Doing the mundane, even when we know it's critical, requires a personal commitment to "do it now."

Remember another critical strategy: Frequently ask yourself how you could apply what you are doing in one goal area or activity in another. For example, managers are expected to be skillful research consumers. Occasionally, to tackle a particular project or task, you may complete an extensive review of the literature. This is a time to think about other possible uses of this research, e.g., also gathering information for making a presentation, developing a manuscript for a professional journal, "translating" your synthesis for a general population publication, or working with a research colleague to develop a project proposal.

work synthesis

INTERRUPTIONS

A common distraction from priorities is interruptions. Some interruptions are integral to the position you hold. For example, if you are the only registered nurse on a small telemetry unit, being available to respond to a sudden cardiac arrest may be the primary reason you are assigned to a limited number of patients. More common, however, are the numerous interruptions precipitated by people who want "just a minute" of your time or seem to take forever to reach their main point. The box on page 210 identifies some specific strategies to prevent and control interruptions. Two keys to dealing with interruptions are to resume "doing it now" so an interruption doesn't destroy your schedule, and to maintain the attitude that whatever the interruption, it is a part of your responsibility. Every crisis is really an opportunity in disguise. When we make a conscious decision not to worry about the things we cannot control, we have more energy to maintain a positive perspective and to move projects ahead.

control

PROCRASTINATION AND PERFECTIONISM

Two big obstacles to success are procrastination and perfectionism. **Procrastination** is the tendency to put off to another time something that is important. **Perfectionism** is the tendency to never finish anything because it isn't quite perfect yet. Both of these tendencies interfere with efficiency and

definition

> **EXERCISE 11-2**
> Think of the last time you were in the clinical area. How often did you record the same piece of information (for example, a finding in your assessment of a client). Don't forget to include all steps—from your jotting down notes on a piece of paper to the final report of the day. Unless your most recent clinical experience was on a totally computerized unit (including bedside terminals), you may have recorded the same piece of information nearly a dozen times.

Specific Strategies to Prevent and Control Interruptions

Prevention Strategies/Examples

1. Provide a momentary delay—"I can talk with you in five minutes, unless it is an emergency."
2. Set appointments—"I know I have assigned you some difficult tasks. Let's check with each other at 0100 and 0230 unless something urgent comes up."
3. Set a psychological framework—"How long do you think this will take?"
4. Stand, if you have been sitting to encourage the interrupter to be brief.
5. Use better screening—(to unit secretary) "I am going down the hall for an important meeting; but I've put a call in to Dr. Anderson. If she calls, please page me. Meanwhile I have asked Mary Jones to cover my work group."
6. Set standing meetings with people for whom you are responsible—"I have set up meetings with each of you who will be working in one of the counties I am responsible for. Please plan to bring any non-urgent concerns to these meetings as well as a general update on the work you are responsible for."

Control Strategies

1. Keep interruptions short; set time limits.
2. Listen actively.
3. Focus on the problem and action to take, not on who's at fault or how something went wrong.
4. Reorganize your work area.
5. Meet regularly with people on your team.
6. Anticipate known deadlines and plan accordingly.
7. Set goals.
8. Acknowledge your frustration, don't let it take over.
9. Complete one task at a time or complete various task components in one geographic area.
10. Learn to say "No."
11. End conversations effectively. Say "Thank you," then stand and walk to the door.
12. Use resources, e.g., answering machines to record important messages when you don't want to be interrupted.

EXERCISE 11-3

Think about something that "nags" you. Perhaps you say to yourself, "I really should do ..." Ask yourself how important that activity is or to what goal it relates. Then ask yourself why, if this thing is important, you haven't done it. That answer may be, "There isn't enough time." Now think about how important that thing is in terms of other things you do. How can you make time to advance this goal? For example, if you value patient teaching but never seem to do it in an organized manner, you could reassess what you delegate to an assistant provider, or maybe streamlining data collection could create more time for education. Perhaps feeling more confident about teaching might increase your productivity in that area. If so, what can you do to increase your confidence in this area?

effectiveness because they are time-consuming (procrastination) and sometimes unattainable (perfectionism). Overcoming perfectionism takes a conscious effort. That doesn't mean people should not always try their best. Rather, being aware of perfectionism means people sometimes need to say it is okay to buy take-out rather than prepare dinner at home or to assess how much progress could be made on a task in a given situation at a given time.

There are some specific strategies for dealing with procrastination. These strategies may work for some people and not for others, and some strategies may be more useful in specific types of projects. The box below lists seven ideas from Edwin Bliss for moving difficult projects ahead, which, if used faithfully, prevent procrastination.

Getting Started with Difficult Tasks

Salami technique—Rather than "chewing off" more than you can manage, break a project into smaller tasks and do one slice at a time.

Leading task—Define what is the one thing to do to lead the whole project ahead.

Five-minute plan—Determine what you could do in the next five minutes to move your project forward.

Worst first—What's the least attractive element of your project? Do it first, the rest will seem easy.

Journal—Keep a journal of all your stress and progress related to the project so your notes are in one place.

Go public—Declare to others what you're doing so they can keep you on track.

Written reminder—Put a note in a conspicuous place to keep yourself on target.

Adapted from Bliss, 1976.

SETTING PRIORITIES

How is it possible to decide what the real priorities are? Stephen Covey identifies a particular strategy to become more productive. In his highly acclaimed book, *The Seven Habits of Highly Effective People,* he states that we typically *do* focus on those things that are important and urgent. By placing the elements of importance and urgency in Figure 11-1 in a grid, it is possible to classify all activities as shown. This chapter's "Literature Perspective" is an example of applying Covey's work in nursing.

Typically, we tend to focus on those items in cell A because they are both important and urgent and therefore command our attention. A management example of this might be making assignments. This task is both important to the work to be accomplished and frequently urgent because there is a time frame during which data about patients and the qualifications of staff can be matched. On the other hand, if something is neither important nor urgent (cell D), we might think of it as a waste of time, at least in terms of our goals. An example of a D might be reading junk mail. It still may contribute to our overall perspective of life, but it has relatively little value. Even if something is urgent but it is not important (cell C), it contributes minimally to our being productive and achieving our goals. An example of a C might be responding to a memo that has a specific time line but is not relevant to a particular work goal. So, the real key to increasing productivity is to attend to the Bs, that is, those items that are important but not urgent. Examples of these are sampling work behaviors, reviewing the strategic plan, and attending appropriate social and professional functions.

TIME TOOLS

Sometimes the real problem is that we let events of the day direct us. Our day may be so tightly scheduled that any small deviation becomes a crisis. Or perhaps we didn't actually plan the day and are consequently responding to any emerging event. Figure 11-2 on page 213 is a time log that can be used to list activities related to work. One reason we may not be able to plan well is that we

urgent/important

		IMPORTANT	
		yes	no
URGENT	yes	A	C
	no	B	D

FIGURE 11-1
Classification of priorities.

logging time

don't have a good estimate of what a particular activity involves or how many activities can be accomplished in a given time frame. Sometimes a whole work period is consumed with activities; only some of those activities may relate to goals to be accomplished. The time log also can incorporate family/significant others and personal development activities. This is a general tool that can be used to identify how you spend (or plan to spend) your time. It can be adapted to an eight-hour workday by using only common work activities and goals to be accomplished in a typical day. Activities such as patient education can be more realistically planned because estimates of specific time commitments are known from prior use of this tool.

flow sheet

Two other tools for planning the workday are the shift flow sheet that appears in Figure 11-3, and the charge nurse Kardex system that is shown in Figure 11-4 (pages 214 and 216 respectively). The Kardex provides a summary of information a manager typically needs to know about assigned patients. While this tool does not organize the time flow, it does organize overall care. For example, the section on laboratory studies and x-rays provides a check system to be sure this work is done. The results section provides a quick reference of findings. Tools such as this are especially helpful in reporting to subsequent care providers. Although it was designed for hospital use, this tool can be modified for a community or long-term care setting by creating appropriate headings. For example, geography might be an important factor when working in the community since travel time is costly. Using longer time frames to reflect conditions of clients in long-term settings would be more logical than the shorter time spans necessary in acute care settings.

client data organization

When an employment situation is stable, that is, a nurse manager works in the same area on a regular basis, it might be useful to keep client data cards in an organizer so the same information doesn't need to be recorded daily.

Literature Perspective

Carter, S. (1993). *Working harder and getting nowhere—No wonder you are stressed.* Nursing Administration Quarterly, 18(1), 51–56.

As work (and life) demands increase, the skill of effective time management becomes more critical to accomplish priorities. Using Covey's principles from *The Seven Habits of Highly Effective People*, it is possible to analyze goals and priorities to focus work efforts. The three principles are being proactive, beginning with the end in mind, and putting first things first.

One view of how nursing activities fit within the prioritization matrix in Figure 11-1 on page 211 is the thrust of this article. Examples of quadrant B activities (important, not urgent) are particularly helpful because Covey believes this is the quadrant to focus on to improve productivity. Elements in this quadrant include relationship building, recognizing new opportunities, planning, recreation, and prevention. To accomplish these tasks it is critical to delegate effectively. Delegation involves teaching and coaching. Leaders who focus in this quadrant are troubleshooters. The article also explains quadrants A, C, and D.

Implications for Practice

Because elements of care require delegation and other strategies to manage time, using Covey's approach to analyzing all activities can increase productivity toward goals.

Total	Activity										Goals									Notes
7:00-7:15																				
7:15-7:30																				
7:30-7:45																				
7:45-8:00																				
8:00-8:15																				
8:15-8:30																				
8:30-8:45																				
8:45-9:00																				
9:00-9:15																				
9:15-9:30																				
9:30-9:45																				
9:45-10:00																				
10:00-10:15																				
10:15-10:30																				
10:30-10:45																				
10:45-11:00																				
11:00-11:15																				
11:15-11:30																				
11:30-11:45																				
11:45-12:00																				
12:00-12:15																				
12:15-12:30																				
12:30-1:00																				
1:00-1:15																				
1:15-1:30																				
1:30-1:45																				
1:45-2:00																				
2:00-2:15																				
2:15-2:30																				
2:30-2:45																				
2:45-3:00																				
3:00-3:15																				
3:15-3:30																				
3:30-3:45																				
3:45-4:00																				
4:00-4:15																				
4:15-4:30																				
4:30-4:45																				
4:45-5:00																				

FIGURE 11-2

Time log. Repetitive or key activities are entered in the first section, "Activity." Primary goals are entered in the second section, "Goals." When this log is used for a workday only, all goals may relate to career and professional development but could include those from family/significant others and personal development. The third section, "Notes," could be used to describe feelings and observations about events or ideas for making an activity more productive.

If time were money, it would be important to invest wisely. That does not mean that time should be spent only on money-producing endeavors. Rather, it means that as with money (a finite resource), time must be invested in the demands and pleasures of life. How and where people spend time is as important as how and where they spend money. The box on page 215 identifies several time management ideas that work in nursing.

DEVISING A PERSONAL TIME MANAGEMENT SYSTEM

Each of us has some way of controlling our lives. Even the person who appears to be in great disarray can describe a system of "organization." Knowing how time is spent currently can be one of the most rewarding strategies of effective time management. Logging activities by fifteen or thirty-minute intervals can show what activities occur throughout the day and, in general terms, how long various activities take. This analysis can also provide insight into why someone might say, "You never have time for me." Based on goals and priorities, a manager can determine if there is

Shift Flowsheet _____

Date

Room	Name/Dx	Meds	Tx	Staff/ Patient	Nursing Priorities

FIGURE 11-3

Shift flowsheet. Data are entered in the first two columns and the last column. Expected times for medications or treatments are also entered. Specific times are planned throughout the shift to meet with staff assigned to care activities and to check on patients.

Time Management Ideas That Work in Nursing

- Chart somewhere other than in the place where you'll be most accessible.
- Ask people to put their comments in writing—don't let them catch you "on the run."
- Let the unit/office secretary know the information you need immediately.
- Conduct a conversation in the hall to help keep it short or in a separate room to keep from being interrupted.
- Be comfortable saying "No."
- When involved in a long procedure, ask someone else to cover your other responsibilities.
- Break projects into small, manageable tasks.
- Keep interruptions short—e.g., use bathrooms in patient rooms; stand during phone calls.
- Keep your manager informed of your goals.
- Be aware if one person is typically your source of interruption.
- Have a to-do list that plans for you to be done early—e.g., 1 hour early.
- In hospitals, knowing transfers come at the end of a shift, we should be prepared.
- Be positive.
- Recognize that crises and interruptions are part of the job.

an appropriate amount of time for an activity or if time needs to be reallocated.

systems

There are many systems for organizing your time. Some people use an organizer that includes appointments, to-do lists, phone numbers, and notes. Others keep a calender, telephone book, and to-do lists separately. To-do lists might consist of a piece of paper with everything to be accomplished today listed on it. To-do lists might also be small cards that can be shuffled as priorities, geography, or tasks change. The key to managing time is discipline.

It does not matter which time management system is used; what is important is to use one and use it consistently. Even the best system will only be effective if it is really used.

Knowing when the most productive time frames are can assist in major projects. When possible, it can be beneficial to control the environment, too, to avoid interruptions. As much as possible, think proactively to prevent or minimize problems. For example, doing a task before the deadline can avoid a time crunch. Providing details when delegating can avert crises by having other people know what is expected.

Two key time management strategies available to every manager that are critical to the success of a manager are managing meetings and delegating. They are discussed in the next two sections of this chapter. Even staff nurses who may not have extensive management responsibility usually have opportunities to delegate and can benefit from learning to make the most of meetings.

CHARGE NURSE KARDEX SYSTEM

Room No.	Patient Name	Age/Sex	Current Acuity

Admitting Physician / Admission date

Consulting Physician(s)
1.   6.
2.   7.
3.   8.
4.   9.
5.   10.

Current Diagnosis
Admitting Diagnosis
Invasive Procedures   Date_____
1.
2.
3.
4.
5.

Allergies

Vital signs: DNR   INTRAVENOUS FLUIDS (Site and date)
Prn Procardia?   Blue tape wrist band / Organ Donor   1.
  2.
Diet: NPO?   3.
  4.
Tube feeding: 5.

Daily Wt.   CHEMOTHERAPY
Respiratory: 1.
oxygen   2.
pulse oximeter   3.
  4.
inspirex/IPPB/HHN TX   5.

care   NARCOTIC DRIP/PCA PUMP
  1.
  2.
  3.

Cardiac: EPIDURAL DRIP
telemetry (include the box no.)   1.
rate/rhythm   2.

If DNR: Next of kin   Phone No:

CHARGE NURSE KARDEX SYSTEM

Invasive Devices: Wound Care:

Foley

Naso Gastric Tube

Supra Pubic Foley
Ileo–Conduit
Urostomy
Nephrostomy
Colostomy
Ileostomy
Jejunostomy

PEG tube

JP Drains

Abdominal Sump Drain
Penrose Drain
Chest tube(s)

Teaching Activities:

Special Care Needs:

Nursing Requirements (Other):

CHARGE NURSE KARDEX LAB SYSTEM

Pt name		Room no.	
Date to be done	Requested Lab studies and/or Xray		Abnormal Values
1.	Line one for requested admission lab/xrays		
2.			
3.			
4.			
5.			
6.			
7.			
8.			
9.			
10.			
11.			
12.			
13.			
14.			
15.			

This area for Laboratory and Xray Results:
(Replace this card when full and as necessary)

FIGURE 11-4

Charge nurse Kardex system. (Adapted with permission from a tool developed by Cooke, R., Greco, R., and Pierce, M., charge nurses, St. Mary of the Plains Hospital and Rehabilitation Center, Lubbock, TX.)

Systems for organizing time include calendars, organizers, and appointment books.

MANAGING MEETINGS

Unfocused, poorly managed meetings can waste considerable, valuable time and can frustrate busy staff members. Meetings serve a variety of purposes ranging from creating social networks to setting formal policy. They may be designed to solve problems, disseminate information, seek input, inspire the group (especially around a group project), delegate work or authority, or create/maintain a formal power base. Unless the purpose of a meeting is to socialize, the meeting is unlikely to be productive if it is not effectively managed. The box on page 218 lists several popular strategies to enhance the success of a meeting.

Planning ahead for a meeting may seem a tedious process, but overlooking this activity can result in an unsatisfactory experience. These same strategies can be used for members of a committee. For instance, a committee member could ask for an agenda in advance if one is not typically provided. A member can be sure to be on time for all meetings and be prepared to leave on time, too. If the meeting is managed poorly by an immediate superior, a committee member could volunteer to be sure the minutes and agenda are distributed. It is important to recognize that some people deliberately avoid these strategies in an attempt to control meetings in their own way. If this is the case, an individual may be ineffective in changing the behavior of the person who is skilled at running meetings poorly and who does not see the value of changing. In that case, just be certain that person is not used as a role model.

member activities

DELEGATING

Delegation is a critical strategy for a nurse manager and for most staff nurses. It is the "transfer of responsibility for the performance of an activity from one individual to another, with the former retaining accountability for the outcome" (American Nurses Association, 1994, 11). To be successful in any management position, a manager must accept that his/her work, in part, is done by others. Being willing to delegate, to empower someone to perform a task or assume an entire role on the manager's behalf includes several components. A manager must give sufficient responsibility and the concomitant authority, while requiring accountability. When delegating, the manager must

---

EXERCISE 11-4

Have you ever sat in a meeting and wondered why you were there? Perhaps you weren't clear about the purpose of the meeting, or where the meeting was headed, or even who was in charge! Analyze what irritated you about the meeting.

Managing Meetings Effectively

1. Distribute an agenda. Whenever possible, provide a written agenda to each member in advance of the meeting. If there are important related materials that participants should read or may need to refer to, those should be attached. The more advanced reading or preparation required, the earlier members should receive agendas. Different types of agendas can be used for different purposes:
   - Structured agendas—If a topic is particularly controversial, consider setting a rule that requires any negative comment to be preceded by a positive one.
   - Timed agendas—If you have experienced that a particular group drifts through the early items, consider setting a specific amount of time to be dedicated to each item. If you stick to that schedule, you can expect some people to be very uncomfortable, but discussion will stay focused.
   - Action agendas—Consider submitting the agenda with a description of the needed/desired action; for example, review proposals, approve minutes, or establish outcomes.
2. Schedule the meeting at an appropriate time. If attendance is important, carefully consider participants' schedules when scheduling the meeting. Setting, and then adhering to, a start and stop time rewards people for promptness and encourages participants to make their points quickly.
   - Keep the group's attention: Consider letting people stand if they choose or plan stretch breaks, especially if your meeting is at the end of the day, if the meeting is long, or if the discussion has been a difficult one.
   - Follow-up: It is critical to clearly state not only what needs to be done following the meeting, but also who is in charge of various tasks. Failure to note both can result in activities not being carried out or can lead to a subsequent nonproductive meeting. The manager can summarize expectations at the end of the meeting and/or distribute a memo or minutes following the meeting.
   - Consider an alternative to scheduling a meeting: If the purpose of a meeting is to share information only, consider distributing a memo or posting an announcement. If the information is sensitive or if strong reactions are likely, a meeting may be the best vehicle for sharing the information.
   - Select an appropriate setting: Select a setting where the meeting will not be readily accessible to those who pass by. When necessary, plan the seating arrangement to prevent inappropriate behaviors such as whispering or other interruptions.

Managing Meetings Effectively—cont'd

3. Use rules of order to facilitate meetings: Roberts' Rules of Order may seem overstructured for the typical meeting; however, this structure is especially helpful when diversity of opinion is likely or important. Specifically, these rules help the person chairing the meeting by setting limits on discussion and using a specific order of priorities to deal with concerns.

EXERCISE 11-5
Review a recent experience in a clinical area in which someone delegated a task to another. Was it clear to you what authority, responsibility, and accountability the receiver had? Could you differentiate between delegation and direction (that is telling someone to do specific tasks or steps)?

convey expectations. This means the person to whom work is delegated needs to know what to report and when and what decisions to make on his/her own. As Manthey (1990) notes, trust is crucial to the process of delegation. The person to whom a manager delegates must be willing to undertake the delegated activity. The "delegatee" also must understand both what is required to successfully perform the assignment and the accountability that accompanies the responsibility. That is, the other person must be able to identify that the expected performance is within his/her competence to perform. When delegation involves nursing care, a manager may delegate only tasks or implementation of care to others; as a professional, the manager remains accountable for the nursing care provided by the team. In other words, whenever care is provided by other than a registered nurse, the accountability for care remains with the manager/delegator even though others provide various aspects of care.

delegatee

With the advent of unlicensed assistive personnel (UAP), understanding delegation and the resultant supervision is critical to a nurse manager. Barter and Furmidge (1994) identify several issues related to incorporating UAPs into healthcare situations, and delegating to and supervising them. Some registered nurses in practice today have had little, if any, educational preparation for managing others and little, if any, experience in doing so, because in the past their staffs were made up largely of registered nurses. Community settings provide a special challenge, since, by virtue of the way services are delivered, direct supervision is limited. Managers in these settings must rely heavily on initial assessments of the workers, frequent written or oral communication, and regular visits with the individual UAP. Because the registered nurse is always accountable for assessment, diagnosis, planning, and evaluation, it is important that UAPs understand what elements of implementation they may carry out and why the registered nurse is responsible for analyzing data gathered.

UAPs

Various factors must be considered in delegating; several have already been cited. Education, experience, empowerment, clear expectations, and willingness are all critical to successful delegation. When the recipient of delegation is an unlicensed assistive person, the following factors identified by the American Association of Critical Care Nurses (1990) become even more important:
- Potential for harm
- Complexity of task
- Need for problem solving and innovation
- Unpredictability of outcome
- Level of interaction with patient.

Each of these factors can be rated on a scale of 0 to 3, with the expectation that the lower the score, the more likely the delegation will be successful (see Exercise 11-6).

Delegation requires a complete understanding of the position as a manager. You cannot delegate some aspect of someone else's position. Knowing what your position entails is essential. Before delegating work to others, you must know what they are capable of. Within the context of nursing care, delegation is a specific element of professional nursing covered in the *Code For Nurses* of the American Nurses Association (1976). You are ethically bound to delegate elements of care based on the qualifications of the team member to perform those tasks and the safety needs of clients.

feedback

Finally, an element sometimes overlooked in delegating is the need for feedback. This feedback should occur in both directions. The delegator needs to evaluate the implementation of the work delegated to another. Similarly, that individual should inform the delegator of findings and outcomes.

Part of the feedback needs to relate to the outcomes of delegation, which can be viewed as patient, personnel, and organizational outcomes (American Nurses' Association, 1994). Patient outcomes are frequently reviewed in terms of safety, comfort, clinical factors, and patient satisfaction. Personnel and institutional outcomes are equally important. Personnel outcomes relate to job satisfaction of all classifications and typical personnel data such as retention and performance. Institutional outcomes include costs, length of stay, and risk management data.

Delegation is a dynamic process that is influenced by numerous factors. Although the process is complex, it is critical to effective management.

CHAPTER CHECKLIST

Delegating effectively; using schedules, calendars, and other planners; and using time management principles and managing meetings are key strategies to be integrated into the nursing role to be an effective leader and manager.

- Time management refers to tools and strategies to assure that the priority goals are achieved.
- Lakein's six principles describe basic time management activities. They are:
  - List goals and set priorities.
  - Make a daily to-do list.
  - Start with the A's, not with the C's.
  - Ask: What is the best use of my time right now?
  - Handle each piece of paper only once.
  - Do it now!
- Some common obstacles to managing time effectively and achieving goals are interruptions, procrastination, and perfectionism.
  - Effective strategies for dealing with interruptions include:
    - Delaying
    - Setting an appointment
    - Screening
    - Planning and setting goals
    - Scheduling standing meetings with employees
    - Setting limits
    - Employing physical strategies (rearranging the work area, standing up when someone enters the office unexpectedly)
    - Learning to say "No."

EXERCISE 11-6

Using a clinical setting to which you have been assigned, identify what the typical work group consists of and how many patients receive care from that group. Determine how you will know about your group's work strengths. How will you assign the care of the patient group? If you have unlicensed assistive personnel on your team, how will you find what this classification of worker can do?

Create a grid of selected patients and the factors listed by the American Association of Critical Care Nurses (see p. 219). Use the following scale to rate each factor:

    0 = none
    1 = low
    2 = moderate
    3 = high

Now, evaluate whether your results are logical given what you know about the patients (that is, the low scores represent patients with more care tasks that you could delegate comfortably).

- Effective strategies for dealing with procrastination include:
    - Breaking the project into smaller, more manageable tasks
    - Defining the "leading task"
    - Creating a "five-minute plan"
    - Journaling
    - Going public with the desired goal
    - Writing reminders to help stay on target.
- When setting priorities, the most effective strategy to increase productivity is to focus on activities that are important but not urgent.
- Some effective time management tools and strategies include:
    - Time logs
    - Shift flow sheets
    - Organizers, calendars, and "to-do" lists.
- Managing meetings and delegating are two key time management strategies for every manager.
    - Key meeting management strategies include:
        - Distributing an agenda
        - Scheduling the meeting appropriately
        - Using rules of order to facilitate the meeting.
    - Key elements of successful delegation include:
        - Willingness to delegate/be delegated to
        - Giving the delegatee sufficient responsibility and authority
        - Conveying expectations clearly
        - Requiring the delegatee to be accountable.
    - Using a rating scale can help ensure that the important factors in delegation have been considered and that the delegation will be successful.

TERMS TO KNOW

- **agenda**
- **delegation**
- **flowsheet**
- **perfectionism**
- **proactive**
- **procrastination**
- **rules of order**
- **time log**
- **time management**
- **unlicensed assistive personnel**

REFERENCES

American Association of Critical Care Nurses. (1990). *Delegation of Nursing and Non-Nursing Activities in Critical Care: A Framework for Decision Making.* Irvine, CA: American Association of Critical Care Nurses.

American Nurses Association. (1976). *Code for Nurses with Interpretive Statements.* Kansas City, MO: American Nurses Publishing.

American Nurses Association. (1994). *Registered Professional Nurses and Unlicensed Assistive Personnel.* Washington, DC: American Nurses Association.

Barter, M., & Furmidge, M.L. (1994). Unlicensed assistive personnel: Issues relating to delegation and supervision. *Journal of Nursing Administration, 24*(4), 36–40.

Bliss, E.C. (1976). *Getting Things Done.* New York: Bantam.

Carter, S. (1993). Working harder and getting nowhere—No wonder you are stressed! *Nursing Administration Quarterly, 18*(1), 51–56.

Covey, S.R. (1990). *The Seven Habits of Highly Effective People: Powerful Lessons in Personal Change.* New York: Simon & Schuster.

Lakein, A. (1973). *How to Get Control of your Time and Your Life.* New York: Penguin.

Manthey, M. (1990). Trust: Essential for delegation. *Nursing Management, 21*(11), 28–31.

SUGGESTED READINGS

Bliss, E.C. (1984). *Doing it Now.* New York: Bantam.

Conger, M.M. (1994). The nursing assessment decision grid: Tool for delegation decision. *Journal of Continuing Education in Nursing, 25,* 21–27.

Josephs, R. (1992). *How to Gain an Extra Hour Every Day: More than 500 Time Saving Tips.* New York: Penguin.

Poteet, G.W. (1989). Nursing administrators and delegation. *Nursing Administration Quarterly, 13*(3), 23–32.

Chapter 11 Appendix
GOAL SETTING

Setting goals is a key to success. As you begin this exercise, keep in mind that a goal is a *specific end result.*

A. List three to five goals that include career and professional development, personal development, and family (significant others.)

_____ 1.
_____ 2.
_____ 3.
_____ 4.
_____ 5.

Now, analyze each. Is each goal area represented? Did you include *specific* information, such as time frames, activities? (Change them to goals.)

Optional: On a blank sheet of paper, list as many other goals as you can create. Do not decide if they are attainable or not, just generate ideas. Draw a blank to the left of each additional goal.

In the space to the left of each goal, record a number to reflect the goal's priority in your life now, number 1 being your first choice, 2, next, etc. Delete any goals that now appear relatively unimportant.

B. Now, complete the next section. Check one blank each for questions 1 to 4.

1. If you had to choose between career/professional development and family (significant others) goals, which would you choose?
   _____ Career/professional development goals
   _____ Family (significant others) goals

2. If you had to choose between pursuing career/professional development and personal development goals, which would you choose?
   _____ Career/professional development goals
   _____ Personal development goals

3. If you had to choose between family (significant others) and personal development goals, which would you choose?
   _____ Family (significant others) goals
   _____ Personal development goals

4. If you had to choose one life area to work on this month, which would it be?
   _____ Career/professional development
   _____ Family (significant others)
   _____ Personal development

5. List the three life areas in order of importance to you.
   _____ Most important
   _____ Less important
   _____ Least important

C. Return to your ranked goals and label each: F = Family (significant others), C = Career/professional development, and P = Personal development.

In completing this exercise, did you find a similarity or difference between the ranking of your goals and the life area of greatest importance to you? If there was a difference, reanalyze what your priorities are.

D. Next, record your highest priority for each life area in the space for goal #1 below. Then, generate a list of at least three to five activities that relate to the goal. Repeat with goal 2 and 3. Please note this section is completed using the life areas.

Career/Professional Development

Goal 1 _____

Activities

_____ a.

_____ b.

_____ c.

_____ d.

_____ e.

Family (Significant Others)

Goal 1 _____

Activities

_____ a.

_____ b.

_____ c.

_____ d.

_____ e.

Personal Development

Goal 1 _____

Activities

_____ a.

_____ b.

_____ c.

_____ d.

_____ e.

Career/Professional Development

Goal 2 _____

Activities

_____ a.

_____ b.

_____ c.

_____ d.

_____ e.

Family (Significant Others)

Goal 2 _____

Activities

_____ a.

_____ b.

_____ c.

_____ d.

_____ e.

Personal Development

Goal 2 _____

Activities

_____ a.

_____ b.

_____ c.

_____ d.

_____ e.

Career/Professional Development

Goal 3 _____

Activities

_____ a.

_____ b.

_____ c.

_____ d.

_____ e.

Family (Significant Others)

Goal 3 _____

Activities

_____ a.

_____ b.

_____ c.

_____ d.

_____ e.

Personal Development

Goal 3 _____

Activities

_____ a.

_____ b.

_____ c.

_____ d.

_____ e.

Continue with other goals in a similar manner on a blank sheet of paper.

E. Now return and prioritize each activity for each goal. Rate each by feasibility—1 for most feasible, 2 for the next, etc. Finally, consider if there is more detail you can provide for your top priority activities. If so, jot the ideas down.

You have now completed this exercise. You now know what specific activities to do in order to work toward a goal. This plan works only if you refer to it to select priorities of activities to analyze your progress.

CHAPTER 12

MANAGING INFORMATION AND TECHNOLOGY

Mary N. McAlindon, R.N., Ed.D., C.N.A.A.

PREVIEW

This chapter identifies and describes current uses of information technology for patient care that allow nurses to use the data gathered in the most effective and efficient manner. It discusses types of information technology, the nursing minimum data set, hospital and nursing information systems, knowledge technology, and future trends. Such technologies allow nurses not only to compare and contrast current patient data to previous data for the same patient, but also to compare and contrast data for other patients with the same diagnosis. The chapter concludes with a discussion of nurses' attitudes toward the new technologies and issues such as confidentiality and ethics.

OBJECTIVES

- Analyze the three aspects—data, information, and knowledge—used for patient care communication.
- Evaluate three types of computerized information technologies used in nursing.
- Evaluate three uses for biomedical technology.
- Apply the nursing minimum data set to a nursing situation.
- Compare two types of information systems used to provide patient care information.
- Analyze three types of technology for capturing data at the point of care.
- Discuss knowledge systems and their uses for patient care.
- Predict future trends in information technology useful for healthcare.
- Explore the issues of nurse ethics and patient confidentiality in information technology.

QUESTIONS TO CONSIDER

- What types of technology do you use in your daily practice?
- How do you use the data gathered in caring for patients?
- What can be done to improve the communication process while decreasing the amount of time spent in documenting care?
- Are you or your staff members reluctant to try new technologies?
- How do you and your staff approach learning new information technologies?

A Manager's Viewpoint

What do I, as a manager, need to do to manage technology? The nurses on our units spend 34 to 50 percent of their time on paperwork. They often transcribe the same data in three or four places. We decided to take a look at the manual process of documentation to see where we could be more efficient. In an effort to improve this situation, we moved the nursing section of the chart to the bedside so that we could document vital signs, observations, and medications immediately. We changed our daily assessment forms to checklists. Since we will be moving to a managed care environment, we began to develop clinical pathways for patient care. These included a daily Kardex of patient care activities that proceed to the expected patient outcome on the day of discharge. Critical events on the daily Kardex also provided a means of collecting data for quality improvement activities. We began to see that the data and information could be documented on a computer. We were asked to assist with the implementation of an information system in the clinical areas and were surprised to find that there were even more advantages to gathering data with a computer at the point of care. The most important thing that we learned is that you can't computerize a poor manual system, you just perpetuate the problems. We are hoping to improve the patient care process as we begin to use this new technology.

Hilde Farrow, B.S.N., R.N.
Nurse Manager
Intensive Care Unit
Anita Sparks, R.N.
Nurse Manager
Acute Care Unit
McLaren Regional Medical Center
Flint, Michigan

INTRODUCTION

Technology surrounds us! We find computers being used at the bank, the grocery checkout, in our cars, on our telephones, and in almost every other aspect of daily living. The purpose of all these technologies is to gather data and provide information. This allows businesses to be more efficient and effective in providing their services. **Information technology** is the use of computers to gather, aggregate, process, and communicate information; it is as useful for the business of healthcare as it is for any other business. The data gathered in the process of patient care provides information about the effectiveness of nursing care for a successful patient outcome. Is the patient better? What did we do to cause this to happen?

INFORMATION SCIENCE

information

Information is the communication or reception of knowledge. Since earliest times nurses have collected, processed, and communicated information about patients. When the personal computers or microcomputers were introduced in the 1970s, nurses began to use these electronic tools to assist with communication. Today we combine computer science and information science for managing and processing data, information, and knowledge to support the practice of nursing in the delivery of patient care.

Information science consists of three aspects of a concept generally called information. These three aspects are data, information, and knowledge. Figure 12-1 illustrates the relationship among these aspects.

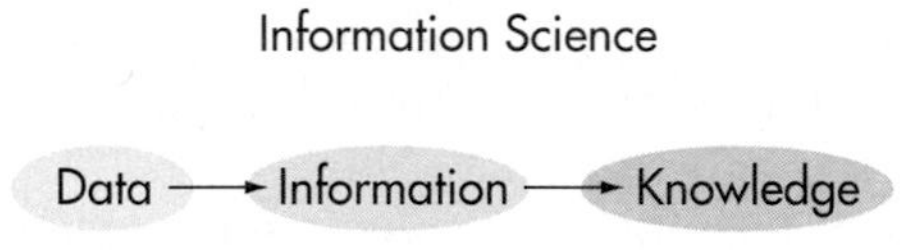

Information Science

Data ⟶ Information ⟶ Knowledge

FIGURE 12-1
Three aspects of information science.

data

Data are discrete entities that describe or measure something without interpreting it. Numbers are data; for example, the number 30, without inter-

information

pretation, means nothing. **Information** consists of interpreted, organized, or structured data. The number 30 interpreted as milliliters or as a length of time

knowledge

in minutes or hours has meaning. **Knowledge** refers to information that is combined or synthesized so that interrelationships are identified. For example, the number 30, when included in the statement that "all patients with indwelling catheters longer than 30 days developed infections" becomes knowledge, something that is known.

Data, information, and knowledge constitute the content of professional communication. Nurses deliver and manage patient care through continuous communication with patients, families, other professionals, and staff, and we study the patients' record, adding to the observations in it. We monitor instruments that provide current information about the patients. We perform tests and review the results of tests performed by others. All these examples reflect giving and receiving data, information, and knowledge.

The progression from data to information to knowledge occurs quickly in practice as data are interpreted and compared to previous information about

Using the Information Triad

Several patients in the coronary care unit had fallen at night over the last three weeks. This was very unusual, since heart patients do not usually become disoriented at night. The nurse manager became concerned about this and began to look for commonalities among the patients who had fallen. She found that they were all taking the same sleeping medication. She mentioned this at a meeting and found that several other nurse managers had noticed the same situation. Together they contacted the pharmacy who contacted the pharmaceutical representative. He found that the medication dosage had been tested on college students, and that the dose was too high for older, less healthy patients. This is an example of combining data to provide information that when aggregated and processed becomes new knowledge.

EXERCISE 12-1
Think about the data that you gather every day: the vital signs, intake and output, and the symptoms that you communicate during shift report. What data did you automatically combine or reorganize to help you make a patient care decision? Who did you report it to?
    For example: you are charting vital signs and you notice that the patient's blood pressure is lower than it was yesterday. He is also complaining of nausea and lightheadedness. You check his medications and see that he is receiving Apresoline. Based on your processing of the data that you have collected, you make a note to check the blood pressure and other symptoms again and notify the physician if the situation has not changed.

the patient to provide knowledge. Much of this value is lost however, because the data are not stored where others might retrieve and use them to synthesize new knowledge. The box above provides an example that illustrates combining and interpreting data to provide information, which, when synthesized and re-presented, provides new knowledge.

The *management component of communication* is the ability to collect, aggregate, organize and re-present information in a way that is useful. This is technology; a scientific method for achieving a practical purpose.

TYPES OF TECHNOLOGIES

As nurses we commonly use and manage three types of technologies: biomedical technology, information technology, and knowledge technology. **Biomedical technology** is evidenced in the physiologic monitoring that occurs on the critical care units, and the other electronic equipment used in the care of patients. This includes the use of ventilators to assist respirations, and computers used for diagnostic testing, drug administration, and therapeutic testing. **Information technology** is processing and using the information gathered in monitoring patient care. The nursing minimum data set provides a framework for gathering data related to patient care through the use of **nursing** and **hospital information systems. Knowledge technology** is the use of expert and decision support systems to assist nurses in making decisions about the delivery of patient care. These systems mimic the reasoning of nurse experts in making decisions related to patient care.

BIOMEDICAL TECHNOLOGY

Biomedical technology was developed in the mid-1970s to monitor the vital signs of critical care patients. It is now found in all patient care areas of the hospital and has even extended to home health and long-term-care facilities. This type of technology is used for (a) physiologic monitoring, (b) **diagnostic testing,** (c) drug administration, and (d) therapeutic treatments. The accompanying box, on page 230, lists the computer capabilities for each of these uses.

Physiologic monitoring systems measure heart rate, blood pressure, and other vital signs and include arrhythmia monitors, pressure transducers, and oxygen and carbon dioxide analyzers. Other information captured through

physiologic monitoring

Computer Capabilities for Biomedical Technology

1. Process physiologic data
2. Store patient documentation
3. Graph data
4. Regulate physiologic equipment
5. Process diagnostic equipment
6. Recognize deviations from preset ranges
7. Compare data among patients with similar diagnoses

Adapted from Saba, V., & McCormick, K. (1986). Essentials of Computers for Nurses. New York: J.B. Lippincott, p. 301.

these systems includes central venous pressure, temperature, respiratory rate, weight, blood pressure, and pulmonary artery pressure. In addition, these systems often include treatment interventions as they change oxygen or carbon dioxide levels or tidal volume after lung functions that are out of range are diagnosed by the computer.

Arrhythmia monitors and electrocardiograms (EKG) are generally used to provide continuous measurements of cardiopulmonary function. Two types of arrhythmia systems are detection surveillance and diagnostic or interpretive systems. In the detection system, the criteria for a normal EKG are programmed into the computer, which then surveys the EKG for normal and aberrant waveforms. The computer can audibly and visually alert the nurse when the preset number of aberrations has been reached. These data are stored so that the patient's history can be retrieved.

diagnostic systems   These systems can also be diagnostic. The computer, after processing the EKG, generates an analysis report. The EKG tracings may be transmitted over telephone lines from the patient's home to the physician's office or clinic. Patients with implantable pacemakers can have their cardiac activity monitored without leaving home.

Many hospitals are using oximetry to continuously monitor arterial oxygenation. This is a simple noninvasive procedure that can detect any trend in the patient's oxygenation status within six seconds. The oximeter can measure oxygenation through ear, pulse, or nasal septal oximetry. Ear oximetry measures the arterial oxygen saturation by monitoring the transmission of light waves through the vascular bed of the earlobe. If low cardiac output causes insufficient arterial perfusion in the earlobe, a pulse oximeter may be used to measure the wavelengths of light transmitted through a pulsating vascular bed such as a fingertip. As the pulsating bed expands and relaxes, the light path length changes, producing a waveform. Since the waveform is produced from arterial blood, the pulse oximeter calculates the arterial oxygen saturation for every heartbeat without interference from surrounding tissues. If the patient has reduced peripheral vascular pulsations or is taking vasoactive drugs, a nasal probe may be used. This device fits around the septal anterior ethmoidal artery to detect vascular pulsations.

Systems for diagnostic testing include blood gas analyzers, pulmonary function systems, and intracranial pressure monitors. Blood gas analyzers use arterial blood to sense and calculate arterial blood gases, saturation curves, and buffer curves from normal data. These analyzers measure the partial pressures of oxygen and carbon dioxide and the pH of the arterial blood used in the test, enter primary results as soon as they are available, communicate the results quickly, and generate trend analysis for patients throughout their hospitalization.

Pulmonary function systems automate and simplify routine lung mechanics, lung volume, and diffusion capacity measurements. They can store data, calculate results, generate a numeric report, and display volumes graphically.

Intracranial pressure monitoring predicts an increase in pressure and volume in the cerebrospinal fluid and intracranial space of head-injured patients based on changes in pressure occurring in the head. This allows for assessment and early therapy as changes occur. When the intracranial pressure exceeds a set pressure, these systems allow ventricular drainage. Remember, however, that these systems supplement rather than replace nursing observations of the patient.

Drug administration systems are often used with implantable infusion pumps that administer medications. This equipment can be programmed to deliver medication at a preestablished rate for a twenty-four-hour period. Up to six variations in medication schedules may be stored in the system. These pumps are commonly used for hormone regulation, treatment of hypertension, chronic intractable pain, diabetes, thrombosis, and cancer chemotherapy.

medication systems

Therapeutic systems may be used to regulate intake and output, regulate breathing, and assist with the care of the newborn. Intake and output systems are linked to infusion pumps that control arterial pressure, drug therapy, fluid resuscitation, and serum glucose levels. These systems calculate and regulate the intravenous drip rate.

therapeutics

Ventilators are used to deliver an adequate amount of oxygen to the patient's lungs and to control the pressure, volume, flow rate, inspiratory to expiratory time ratio, and oxygen concentration. Two types of ventilators, pressure cycled and volume cycled, have timing devices that are regulated by microprocessors. Computer-assisted ventilators are electromechanically controlled by a closed-loop feedback system to analyze and control blood volumes and alveolar gases. With these systems the volume of gas is determined by a preset inspiratory pressure. When the preset pressure is reached, the machine cycles into exhalation.

In the newborn nursery, computers monitor the heart and respiratory rates of the babies. In addition, these newborn nursery systems can regulate the tempertaure of the isolette by sensing the infant's temperature and the air of the isolette. Alarms can be set to notify the nurse when preset physiologic parameters are exceeded. Newer systems are used to monitor fetal activity before delivery; these systems monitor the EKGs of the mother and baby, pulse oximetry, blood pressure, and respirations.

The latest developments in biomedical technology include the use of implantable devices such as pacemakers, artificial organ transplants, gene therapy, and even the use of robot servants for people who are disabled. Biomedical technology has an impact on nursing care since nurses assume responsibility for monitoring the data generated by these devices and assessing their effectiveness.

Nurse managers must be aware of the latest technologies for monitoring patients' physiologic status, for diagnostic testing, for drug administration, and for therapeutic treatments. It is important to identify the data to be collected, the information that might be gained from it, and the many ways that the data might be re-presented to provide new knowledge. More importantly, nurses

EXERCISE 12-2
List the types of biomedical technology available for patient care in your organization. List ways that you presently use the information gathered by these systems. Does this information help you care for patients? Can you think of other ways to use the technology? The information? For example, patients with respiratory problems often have frequent arterial blood gases drawn to assess the effectiveness of treatment. Are there instances when the noninvasive pulse oximetry might be used? Nurses spend many hours learning to use the devices and to interpret the information gained from them. Have we come to rely on technology rather than on our own intuition?

Characteristics of Nurse-Users of Information Technology

Nurse-users of information are those registered nurses who collect data as part of their patient care activities, interpret it, and make decisions based on their interpretations. As nurses advance from novice to expert practitioner, interpretations of the data become intuitive and automatic, based on previous experience. When the information gained from previously cared-for patients is combined or synthesized so that new interrelationships are identified, nurses gain new knowledge. At this point they begin to think of other uses of data and information for improving patient care.

---

must remember that these systems are tools for our use and do not replace our responsibility for monitoring the patient. The box above describes the stages through which nurse-novices pass to become nurse-experts in the use of information technology.

INFORMATION TECHNOLOGY

computers

Information technology refers to computers and programs used to process data and information. Computers add the advantage of organizing, storing, retrieving, and communicating data with accuracy and speed. Patient care data can be entered once and stored in a central repository called a data base, then quickly and accurately retrieved many times and in many

database

combinations by patient care providers. A **database** is a collection of data elements organized and stored together. **Data processing** is the structuring, organizing, and interpreting of data into information. For example, vital signs for one patient can be entered into the computer and communicated on a graph; the vital signs of several patients can be compared to the number of doses of antibiotic given. The same vital signs can be correlated and used to show a relationship between blood pressures and hypertensive medications for male patients between the ages of 40 and 50. Nurses process data continuously, but computers do it faster and more accurately and provide a method of storage so that the data need not be remembered or written in several places on the patient record. Collecting a set of basic data from every patient care encounter makes sense because comparisons can be made among many patients, institutions, years, or countries, almost in any combination imaginable.

nursing minimum data set

The **nursing minimum data set** (NMDS) was defined to establish uniform standards for the collection of comparable essential patient data. It is based on the concept of the uniform minimum health data set (UMHDS), a minimum set of items of information with uniform definitions and categories that meets the needs of multiple data users. UMHDSs have been developed for long-term care, hospital discharge, and ambulatory care, but the hospital set is the only one in widespread use.

The NMDS was developed by Werley and Lang (1986) and represents nursing's first attempt to standardize the collection of nursing data. It follows UMHDS criteria in that (a) data items included in the set must be useful to healthcare professionals and administrators and to local, state, and federal planning, regulatory, and legislative bodies; (b) data items must be readily collectible and with reasonable accuracy; (c) data items should not duplicate data available from other sources; and (d) **confidentiality** must be protected.

The purpose of the NMDS is to (a) establish the comparability of patient care data across clinical populations, settings, geographic areas, and time; (b) describe the care of patients and families in a variety of settings; (c) provide a means to mark the trends in the care provided and the allocation of nursing resources based on health problems or nursing diagnosis; (d) stimulate nursing research through links to existing data; and (e) provide data about nursing care to influence and facilitate healthcare policy decision making. The accompanying box lists the elements of the nursing minimum data set.

The NMDS is in various stages of use across the country. A study done to determine the level of use found that both use and implementation of the NMDS are in "the stage of infancy" (Leske and Werley, 1992). The same study also indicated that the NMDS is being used as a guide to develop nursing information systems and to structure nursing documentation. Although nursing care elements are being used, the availability and use of nursing interventions and nursing outcomes are less consistently documented.

The NMDS elements of intervention and outcome are not collected so easily as the demographic and service elements, many of which are captured at patient registration or discharge. Documentation of nursing interventions and outcomes has become crucial for accreditation and for quality management activities.

Nurse managers must be aware of the existence of the NMDS and its usefulness for nursing. Even though some of the elements of information may not be easy to collect on every patient, the data set provides an excellent framework for a patient data base.

EXERCISE 12-3
Examine the elements of the NMDS. Which of them would be collected by patient registration? Which information might you collect? Using a community nursing service, determine through auditing two charts which elements are evident and which are not. For example, in an acute-care setting, you have given patient medication several times today. The nursing diagnosis was alteration in comfort due to pain. You charted that the patient stated a lessening of the pain within 30 minutes. You have documented an intervention and an outcome, two nursing care elements of the NMDS.

Elements of the Nursing Minimum Data Set

NURSING CARE ELEMENTS
1. Nursing diagnosis
2. Nursing intervention
3. Nursing outcome
4. Intensity of nursing care

PATIENT DEMOGRAPHIC ELEMENTS
5. Personal identification*
6. Date of birth*
7. Sex*
8. Race and ethnicity*
9. Residency*

SERVICE ELEMENTS
10. Unique facility or service agency number*
11. Unique health record number of the patient
12. Unique number of the principal registered nurse provider
13. Episode, admission, or encounter date*
14. Discharge or termination date*
15. Disposition of patient or client*
16. Expected payer for most of the bill

Elements comparable to those in the UMHDS.

From Werley, H.H., Devine, E.C., & Zorn, C.R. (1990). The nursing minimum data set: Issues for the profession. In McCloskey, J.C., & Grace, H.K., (eds.) Current Issues in Nursing, 3rd ed. New York: Mosby, pp. 64–70.

Information Systems

An information system uses computer hardware and software to process data into information needed to solve problems and answer questions. These systems accept patient care data, and reorganize and process them to provide information. For instance, temperatures and antibiotics, entered as separate data, may be graphed together to show a relationship between the decrease in the temperature and the doses of the antibiotic. Hospital information systems and nursing information systems can provide information to help nurses care for patients.

Hospital (Organizational) Information Systems

A **hospital information system** (HIS) is a large, integrated system that focuses on hospital functions. Other types of healthcare organizations also use information systems, and each of the systems described below could be found in such organizations. A major function of an HIS is to communicate and integrate patient care data and information and provide management support. Data are entered into the system from computer terminals located in the various departments in the hospital and stored in a central computer to be accessed by all patient care services. Nurses enter physician orders to the laboratory, pharmacy, radiology, and support services, and then are able to view the results of the orders.

system configurations

stand-alone

The nurse manager should be aware of HIS system configurations: (a) the stand-alone system, (b) the on-line interactive system, (c) the networked system, and (d) the integrated system. **Stand-alone systems** are internal to a department and automate the processes of the department. Because these systems do not communicate with each other, orders may be written as a paper requisition, and a computer in the lab processes the test. Results are then returned to the ordering department as a paper report. Statistics important to the department are also reported; the number of tests completed each month, the number done by each technician, and the revenue generated are all important information for the functioning of every department.

on-line interactive

On-line interactive systems communicate patient information throughout the hospital. Areas in the hospital are connected to the **mainframe computer** through cathode ray tubes (CRTs) or terminals (the end point of the mainframe computer). These systems are used to transmit orders to the various departments and integrate patient data in real time. When an order for electrolytes is entered it is transmitted to a computer in the laboratory that prints the order on a "pick list" for the technician. The blood is drawn and placed in a computer that will process it and send the reports to a central data base where it is available for viewing. Once the order is placed, staff can use a terminal to see if the test is pending, in process, or complete. If it has been completed, results appear on the screen. These systems save phone calls and the time it takes to write the information. They process and generate information needed to provide patient care and to document the patient care process. The entered patient care data are stored and can be retrieved at any time by anyone who has access to the system.

networks

Networked systems consist of several computers that are supported by another computer that acts as a file server. Each of the computers on the network shares a data base stored in the file server. For example, the secretaries in the nursing office are networked to a central microcomputer, the file server. The file server contains the word processing, data base, spreadsheet, and nurse staffing and scheduling programs or applications. Each secretary uses a computer to access these applications and individual work is stored in the file server. In addition, nurse managers have personal computers in their offices located throughout the hospital, but linked to the file server in the nursing office through the network. They also access these various applications, can make changes to the staffing and scheduling files, and store their work on a file server without leaving their offices. When the system provides electronic mail, anyone with a personal computer or terminal connected to the network can send instant messages to anyone else on the network. This saves time and increases the efficiency of the nurse managers.

Integrated systems are those that link one mainframe containing a central data base with terminals or personal computers in all departments in the institution. These systems contain a central data base of patient care information that is written to and accessed by all departments: laboratory, pharmacy, radiology, nursing, physical therapy, occupational therapy, and so on. The programs that link the individual departments must be able to "talk" to one another in order to exchange patient care data. For example, pharmacy needs access to certain lab results and the height, weight, and allergy information entered by nursing. This is a straightforward process if the software has been written by one computer vendor; if different systems must be linked, the process is more difficult or may even be impossible.

It is extremely important that nurse managers understand the patient care process from a data-information-knowledge perspective. In an information-intensive era, we must be aware of the data we collect, the reasons that we collect them, and the decisions that we make based upon them. The new technologies offer an opportunity to examine the way we do things and improve them rather than duplicate them. The storage of the data in a central repository accessible to all patient care providers is essential. Nurses must serve on the committtees that choose these information systems for the hospital, for nursing plays the pivotal role in establishing these data bases. The box below lists elements of the ideal hospital information system for consideration in choosing a system for an institution.

integrated systems

Elements of the Ideal Hospital Information System

1. The hardware is fail-safe.
2. The software requires minimal staff support.
3. The system is integrated wherever possible.
4. Data from the patient care process are gathered at the point of care.
5. The medical record is on-line and almost paperless and the previous medical record is available on the system.
6. The data base is complete and easy to modify.
7. Physician offices, satellites, and future external sites are interfaced to the system.
8. Data are gathered by instrumentation whenever possible so that only minimal data entry is necessary.

Adapted from McAlindon, M., Danz., S., & Theodoroff, R. (1987). Choosing the hospital information system: A nursing perspective. Journal of Nursing Administration, 17(10), 11–15.

EXERCISE 12-4
Select a hospital with which you are familiar. Does this hospital have a hospital information system (HIS)? Do you know what nursing information systems are used in this organization? Make a list of the names of these systems and the information that they provide. How do they help you in caring for patients? In making management decisions? If you have either or both systems, think about the communication of data and information between departments. Does the nursing system communicate with the HIS? If you do not have computerized systems, think about how data and information are communicated. How might a computer system help you to be more efficient?

As an example, assume that a barium enema has been ordered. Handwritten requisitions are sent to nutritional services, the pharmacy, and the radiology departments. With a computerized system, the barium enema is ordered, and the requests for dietary changes, magnesium citrate, and the barium enema itself are automatically sent to the appropriate departments. Radiology will compare its schedule openings with the patient's schedule and automatically place the date and time for the barium enema on the patient's automated Kardex.

Nursing Information Systems

Nursing information systems (NISs) are systems that use computers to process nursing data. NISs can be stand-alone systems or components of the HIS. Most are found in nursing administration and practice.

In these systems, direct patient care information is entered, stored, retrieved, processed, displayed, and communicated. The documentation of vital signs, care plans, nursing notes, and discharge plans may be incorporated for nursing documentation.

Many systems are limited to the nursing department; they do not communicate with other departmental information systems. They are often computerized versions of the paper-based systems used in hospitals that consume so much of our time. NISs may be subsystems of hospital information systems where they are a different system that is interfaced to the main system. As components of hospital information systems the patient care information entered by nurses is accessible to other patient care providers because the NIS is integrated into the HIS.

nursing administration systems

Nursing administration systems improve the effectiveness of nurse managers and administrators by providing timely and appropriate information. Figure 12-2 lists the essential components of a nursing administration information system. The key to successful administrative applications is the nurse manager's analysis and management of the volumes of information that are available to maintain effectiveness and efficiency.

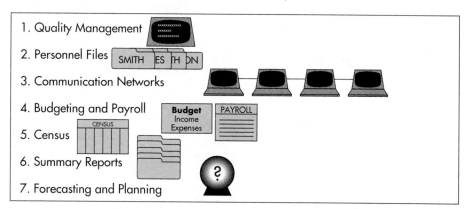

1. Quality Management
2. Personnel Files
3. Communication Networks
4. Budgeting and Payroll
5. Census
6. Summary Reports
7. Forecasting and Planning

FIGURE 12-2

Essential components of a nursing administration information system. [Adapted from Saba, V., & McCormick, K. (1986). *Essentials of Computers for Nurses.* New York: McGraw Hill, p. 165.]

quality management

Quality management, and thus the monitoring and evaluation of patient care, has become necessary for the accreditation and licensing of healthcare organizations. This can be accomplished through documentation of the patient care process. If the computerized care plan (critical path, computerized Kardex) outlines what patient care ought to occur, and nursing documentation confirms that it was done, then the computer is able to monitor and evaluate the patient outcome, an effective and efficient method for documenting quality management activities.

Beginning with the 1994 *Accreditation Manual*, the Joint Commission on Accreditation of Healthcare Organizations (JCAHO) provides standards for organizing information. The accompanying box, on page 237, details the advantages of complying with these standards; to do this, hospitals will need to

Advantages of Complying with JCAHO Standards for Information Management

1. Timely access to complete information throughout the organization.
2. Improved accuracy of data.
3. Balance of security and ease of access.
4. Use of compiled data and knowledge bases and comparative data to pursue opportunities for improvement.
5. Redesign of important information-related processes to reduce work.
6. Greater collaboration and sharing of information to enhance patient care.

Adapted from Bergman, R. (1993, June 5). JCAHO manual sets standards on information management. Hospital and Health Networks, p. 68.

gather data across departmental lines, a situation most easily accomplished by an integrated HIS.

Other data used by the computer to monitor quality are compiled from staff performance, incident reports, acuity data, and staffing and scheduling statistics. Computerized personnel files generate reminders for license renewal and track position changes to produce reports on budgeting and forecasting trends.

communication

Communication networks are used to transmit information that is entered at one terminal and received by another. These networks are usually part of the HIS and reduce the clerical functions of nursing. They can provide patient census and locations, results from tests, and lists of medications. Nursing policies and procedures may be entered onto a communication network to be accessible to everyone.

budgeting

Budgeting and payroll information is usually processed from a combination of data entered by personnel (hourly wages) and the nurse staffing and scheduling system (number of hours worked). These data, when combined with the patient census, provide valuable information for nurse managers. Hours worked should fluctuate with changes in census and acuity data. When the number of staff worked is multiplied by the hourly wage and compared to the census over a period of time, the nurse manager has the information needed to forecast staffing needs.

staffing

Summary reports can be written for any of the data entered into the computer. These are especially useful for the JCAHO accreditation process for hospitals and similar accreditation processes for home health care agencies. Incident reports, allergy and drug reaction reports, infection control reports, and utilization review reports are examples of summary reports. Forecasting and planning systems are designed to predict staffing needs, determine trends in patient care, and forecast departmental budgetary compliance.

Nurse managers must be aware of the differences between nursing information systems and hospital information systems and their limitations. Hospital information systems usually link the information needs of many departments in the organization, while nursing information systems often reflect the manual documentation systems of nursing and do not provide hospital-wide access to patient care information gathered by nursing.

community applications

Discussion has focused on information systems for acute care institutions, but many patients are cared for in community settings. The box on the next page lists types of systems used to support home health care. Community health nursing includes health promotion, maintenance, and education as well

---

Systems to Support Home Health Care

1. Client management systems
2. Personnel management systems
3. Fiscal management systems
4. Program management systems

Adapted from Saba, V., and McCormick, K. (1986). Essentials of Computers for Nurses. New York: McGraw Hill, p. 228.

---

as coordinated continuity of care. NISs are also found in community and home health programs where they are used for financial management and billing, statistical reporting, and patient care information systems. These systems are used within the agency or location, which may be the city, county, or state. Some of these systems also communicate with other agency systems in the same city or state.

Client management includes client demographics, problem lists, and information such as health status. Personnel management describes the types of client care activities performed and provides payroll information. Fiscal information systems include client charges, agency accounts, expenditures, and funding sources. Program management systems allow reporting of information from data entered through all these systems.

Nurses in community health have communicated with their offices and clients through the use of beepers and cellular phones. Day-to-day events are recorded on a Dictaphone or tape recorder and returned to the office for typing into the client record. Nurses caring for patients in the home healthcare industry have many government and insurance requirements for form completion. Computers offer a means of reducing this paperwork burden by

Nurses working in the community often use cellular phones to communicate with their offices.

allowing direct entry of data in the required format. In recent years, the portable palmtop or laptop computer has made recording of patient care information and personnel productivity possible.

These portable computers are used to download files of the patients to be seen during the day from the main data base. During each visit, the computer prompts the nurse for vital signs, assessments, diagnosis, interventions, long- and short-term goals, and medications, based on previous entries in the medical record. The nurses then enter any new data, modifications, or nursing notes directly into the portable computer. At the end of the day, patient care entries are transmitted by telephone to the host computer in the main office, which automatically updates the patient record and prepares any verbal order entry records, home visit reports, federally mandated treatment plans, productivity and quality improvement reports, and other documents for review and signature.

portable computers

The elimination of the paper trail has been partially accomplished by the placement of computer terminals at the bedside or through the use of hand-held computers. In this way, information can be entered once at the point of care and accessed over and over again. Specific applications most beneficial for documentation at the bedside are vital signs, medication administration, and intravenous fluid administration. Documentation of the patient assessment at

efficiency

 Research Perspective

Marr, P.B., Glassman, K., Kelly, J., Kovner, C., and Roberts, N. (1993). Bedside terminal and quality of nursing documentation. *Computers in Nursing, 11(4), 176–182.*

A study reported by the New York University Medical Center Nursing Department on the quality of patient care documentation before and after bedside terminal installation found no significant relationship between the presence of bedside terminals and the quality of documentation. In studying the use of terminals at the nurses station compared to terminals at the bedside, charting was found to be more timely at the patient's bedside, but the percentage of use was too low for significant benefits to be gained. The conclusion of this study was that nurses, when given a choice of entering information at the bedside or central nurses' station, chose not to use the bedside terminal.

Implications for Practice

Reasons for less charting at the bedside in favor of charting at the nurses station might include:
- nurses may need time away from the bedside where they can organize thoughts and collaborate with colleagues.
- nurses may need respite from demands on their time and an opportunity to sit down.
- the charting pathway may need to be redesigned to facilitate capture of data at the bedside.
- placement of the terminal in the patient's room was determined by available space and may have been inconvenient to use.
- the central nursing station design as the hub of staff communication and activity as well as terminal availability may not support bedside data entry.

Care facilities that wish to use bedside charting should take these reasons into consideration when designing and implementing the new charting procedure.

the bedside saves time and decreases the likelihood of forgetting to document vital information. Bedside systems that adapt to the nurse's work flow, personalize patient assessments, and simplify care planning are available. Patient care areas with bedside terminals have improved the quality of patient care by decreasing errors of omission, providing greater accuracy and completeness of documentation, reducing medication errors, providing more timely response to patient needs, and improving discharge teaching. These systems shorten or eliminate shift-to-shift communication and eliminate redundant charting of data.

There are advantages and disadvantages in the use of this technology. Bedside terminals must be suited to patient rooms. They should not have noisy fans, must be lighted to be viewed in the dark, and be either wall mounted or placed on portable stands. Research studies are being conducted to determine the usefulness of bedside technology. This chapter's "Research Perspective" (page 239) summarizes a study that points to some unanswered questions involving bedside terminals.

hand-held terminals

Hand-held technology is also used in gathering data at the point of care. These are hand-held computer terminals that have access to the central computers in the institution. Use of these terminals makes it less expensive to equip each caregiver on the shift rather than place a stationary terminal in each patient room. Hand-held terminals are available that offer documentation of care plans, medications, lab results, intake and output totals, and patient demographic information at the point of care.

Disadvantages of hand-held technology stem from their portability; they can be put down and forgotten, or dropped and broken, and are a target for theft. There must also be a convenient and adequate place to store them when they are not in use. These terminals are bulky and tiresome to carry, and the display screen is small. Users may enter selections from menus rather than entering text. For example, the appropriate numbers may be entered from a menu for vital signs, and by pressing a key on the keyboard, a menu for entering intake and output appears for data entry. Many of these terminals must be placed in a host computer so that the data can be downloaded to a central data base, a process that takes approximately fifteen minutes per patient.

wireless messaging

Wireless messaging may also change the way we work. This type of computer terminal is also hand-held and relays information as it is entered. In this way, patient care information is available as soon as it is entered in the terminal. Because nurses function in many settings with a high degree of mobility, wireless (WL) technology is especially appropriate. Nurses in hospitals are beginning to use WL technology at the bedside where data collection and graphic displays of information are real-time events. WL hand-helds are used to enter vital signs, medications, and ongoing assessments without written notes. Data are immediately transferred to a teminal located in the nurses station and then to the HIS data base.

Wireless systems are also being used by emergency medical personnel to request authorization for the treatments or drugs needed in emergency situations. Laboratories can use WL technology to transmit lab results to physicians; patients awaiting organ transplants are being provided with WL pagers so that they can be notified if a donor is found; and parents of critically ill children carry them when they are away from a phone.

A home monitoring system in use by visiting nurses uses WL technology to enter vital signs and other patient-related information. This information is transmitted to the agency so that treatment plans and bills can be generated.

Wireless technology saves cabling and other installation costs, but is limited by the power of batteries and distance. The main advantage is the ability to provide information technology to mobile healthcare professionals. Portable terminals should be light, tough, and easy to use.

Voice technology is the ability to control a computer system through voice input by the operator. It is the ability of a machine to gather, process, interpret, and execute audible signals by comparing the spoken words with a template already resident in the system. If the patterns match, recognition occurs and a previously stored command is executed by the computer. This allows untrained personnel or those whose hands are busy to work in computer-based environments without touching the computer. These systems recognize a limited number of words. Speech-dependent systems must be programmed for each user so that the system recognizes the user's voice patterns.

The management of these technologies is important. Nurse managers must make knowledgeable decisions about the type of technology to use, the education needed, and the proper care and maintenance of the equipment. Important questions to ask: What data and information do we need to gather? Where do we need to gather it? How difficult is the equipment to use? How soon will it become obsolete?

KNOWLEDGE TECHNOLOGY

Knowledge technology consists of systems that generate or process knowledge. Computers process symbols, therefore they offer a technology similar to that of the human mind, a knowledge technology. Knowledge technology combines an application of computer science and information science with nursing science to assist in the management and processing of data, information, and knowledge to support the practice of nursing and patient care.

The use of knowledge technology is called **informatics.** Nursing informatics is a specialty for nursing, recognized by the American Nurses' Association. Specialists in nursing informatics recognize that data and information are processed by nurses to make knowledgeable clinical decisions. The processing of information is complex. Information consists of data to which meaning has been attached because they have been organized into a structure that carries meaning that may result in the development of new or different information or knowledge. This new or different knowledge is then used to make decisions.

Knowledge technology relies on **expert systems.** An expert system is a computer program that mimics the inductive or deductive reasoning of a human expert. These programs process knowledge to produce decisions by means of a **knowledge base** and a software application that controls the use of the knowledge (an inference engine). To automate this process, the necessary data elements must be identified and rules for combining the data established. The same data elements are always required, and the same formula or rule is applied in the same way to the same data. The knowledge base contains the knowledge (rules, heuristics) that an expert nurse would apply to the data and information in order to solve a problem. The inference engine controls the use of the knowledge by providing the logic for its use. The box, on page 242, illustrates the use of an expert system for giving a maximum dose of morphine sulfate. The knowledge base contains eight items that are to be considered when giving the maximum dose. The inference engine controls the use of the knowledge base by applying logic that an expert nurse would use in making the decision to give the maximum dose.

informatics

expert systems

> **EXERCISE 12-5**
> Think about the data you gather as you go through the day. What data are collected directly from the patient? How do you communicate the data? Based on your answer, which point-of-care technology would you recommend for use in your setting? (For example: "I collect vital signs and intake and output on patients during the day. Sometimes the patients are in the sunroom, sometimes they are sitting in the hallway. I would like to have a portable computer to enter data as they were gathered." Or, "I travel throughout the county assessing the status of newborns. I would like to have a portable computer to enter these data.")

EXERCISE 12-6

Think about the nurses you work with every day. Are some of them newer graduates? Would an expert system help them make decisions? Can you give two examples where an expert system might do this?

For example, Mr. Jones' blood pressure has been recorded in the HIS as 100/60. Tony is about to give Mr. Jones his Apresoline. When Tony enters Mr. Jones' ID number, and the medication name, the computer warns him that Apresoline should not be given for blood pressures less than 140/90.

Expert Decision Frame for "Give Maximum Dose of Morphine Sulfate"

The Knowledge Base:
A. Severe pain
B. Painful procedure planned
C. Morphine sulfate order
D. Contraindications to morphine sulfate
E. History of allergic reaction to opiate analgesics
F. Contraindication to maximum dose of opiate analgesic
G. Time since last dose of morphine sulfate
H. Time since surgery

The Inference Engine:
Logic: Give the maximum dose of morphine sulfate
    IF:
(A or B) and (C and H < 48 hours and G > 3 hours) and not (D or E or F)
    OR:
(C and H < 48 hours and G > 4 hours) and not (D or E or F)

Adapted from Amos, L.K., & Graves, J.R. (1990). Knowledge technology: Costs, benefits, ethical considerations. In McCloskey, J.C., & Grace, H.K., eds. Current Issues in Nursing, 3rd ed. Baltimore: Mosby, pp. 592–600.

This decision frame states that IF pain is severe (A), or a painful procedure is planned (B) and there is an order for morphine sulfate (MS) (C), and the time since surgery is less than forty-eight hours (H) and the time since the last dose of MS is greater than three hours (G) and there are no contraindications to MS (D) or history of allergy (E) or contraindication to the maximum dose (F), then the "decision" would be to give the dose of MS. The rule or heuristics appearing in this logic are those that expert nurses would apply in making the decision to give pain medication. The inference engine controls the IF logic or knowledge.

benefits   One of the benefits of computerized expert systems is that they outperform non-expert human clinicians, assisting with the decision making for novices, nurses working outside their areas of expertise, and orientees. Because the systems get their information directly from patient care documentation, the computer never forgets when a patient needs pain medication or the effectiveness of the last treatment. If the expert system is used in conjunction with an HIS, the documentation of observations, care, and patient outcomes can be expected to increase significantly and improve the quality of care.

Nurse managers must be aware of the usefulness of expert systems for nursing. By helping to develop the logic used in the knowledge base through the use of critical thinking skills, changes in current practice can be made for the improvement of patient care.

FUTURE TRENDS

Because of escalating healthcare costs, insurance companies (third-party payers) and the federal government are supporting new technologies to reduce costs. Managed care, computerized patient records, and the credit-card-like devices that store health history data are technologies of the future.

Managed care is an effort by the insurance companies, the payers of healthcare, to manage healthcare costs by limiting the care provided for each diagnosis. In the hospital, this means that the number of days a patient is permitted to stay is limited, depending on the diagnosis. If the patient remains longer than the permitted days, the health insurer will not reimburse the costs of the care for the unapproved days. The concept of managed care has caused the redesign of patient care plans to clinical pathways that detail the interventions needed day by day to achieve the outcome of discharge by the final approved day.

The computerized patient record (CPR) has been mandated by the federal government, and healthcare organizations are expected to adopt this technology by the year 2000. The CPR allows for immediate and complete access to patient information for clinical decision making, outcome evaluation, and coordination of patient care resources and patient flow through the healthcare delivery system.

The computerized patient record is expected to contain a problem list, health status and functional levels, and clinician rationale for patient care decisions. It will be a "womb to tomb" record of the patient's healthcare. The CPR is necessary because of the need for better access to quality care, patient mobility, and care received from a variety of health professionals.

computerized patient record

Credit-card-like devices called **smart cards** store up to eight pages of data on a computer chip. The implementation of computer-based health information systems will lead to computer networks that will store health records across local, state, national, and international boundaries. This will help to coordinate care, improve quality of care decisions, and reduce risk, waste, and duplication of effort. Patients are mobile and consult many practitioners thereby causing their records to be fragmented. With the electronic smart card, patients and providers and notes can be brought together in any combination at any place. The box below provides examples of the kinds of data that are recorded on smart cards.

smart cards

Smart Card Information

1. Personal identifiers with a link to insurance plans
2. Emergency care information
3. Recent care encounter data including medications
4. Past care encounter summaries
5. Record locations and electronic address information to the records

Adapted from Neame, R. (1993). Making the case for healthcare smart cards. Healthcare Informatics, 10(6), 16–20.

Nurse Attitudes

The attitudes of nurses who use computers are as important as the technology itself. Nurses attitudes and anxiety toward technology and the use of computers must be explored and areas of acceptance and resistance identified in order for the nursing profession to determine the impact of computer use on the quality of patient care. Negative attitudes toward the use of computers usually lead to resistance to implementation and use of the system. There are several reasons for resistance. The first is economic, since computers are time and labor saving and thus could be associated with layoffs and unemployment.

resistance

EXERCISE 12-7
Using the self-assessment tool on pages 245 and 246 analyze your computer readiness. If time permits, use this tool in both an inpatient and community setting. Are their systems similar? Do you gather similar data? Do you aggregate data in similar ways?

The second reason is psychological, as computers can be ego-threatening. Nurses fear the loss of prestige and status because they don't know how to use computers and a loss of power because the computer contains more information than they have. A third reason is ideological barriers, such as less human contact or the depriving of personal or professional freedom. A major source of resistance involves confidentiality and perceived interference in the nurse–patient relationship.

Education and training before implementation or during orientation can alleviate the ego threat by equipping staff with the knowledge needed to maintain their status and power. User involvement is necessary during the design, implementation, and evaluation of the systems so that nurses will use the technology to provide quality care. Figure 12-3 provides a checklist of items to consider in teaching staff how to use a computer.

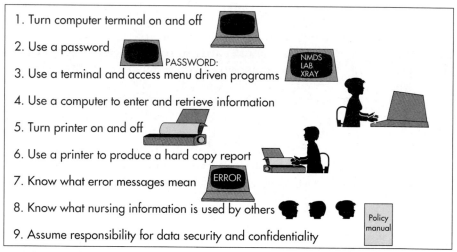

1. Turn computer terminal on and off
2. Use a password
3. Use a terminal and access menu driven programs
4. Use a computer to enter and retrieve information
5. Turn printer on and off
6. Use a printer to produce a hard copy report
7. Know what error messages mean
8. Know what nursing information is used by others
9. Assume responsibility for data security and confidentiality

FIGURE 12-3
Essential computer knowledge and skills. [Adapted from Carter, B., & Axford, R. (1993). Assessment of computer learning needs and priorities of registered nurses practicing in hospitals. *Computers in Nursing, 11*(3), 122–126.

Confidentiality

Converting the patient record to a computer generated document changes the procedures to be followed in maintaining patient confidentiality. With manually generated documents, there is only one copy of the data and caregivers access the chart on the patient care unit. With computerized data, the information may be accessed from any terminal in the medical center by persons with the proper permission.

passcodes
This makes it mandatory that system users never share the passcodes that allow them access to information in the computerized data base. Each passcode uniquely identifies a user to the system by name and title, gives approval to carry out certain functions, and provides access to data appropriate to the user. When a nurse signs onto a computer, all data and information that are entered can be traced to the passcode. Policies on the use, security, and accuracy of data must be written and enforced.

Managing Information and Technology Self-Assessment Tool

Instructions: The purpose of this tool is to lead you through the process of assessing the current state of information technology for the patient care area in which you work or learn, as well as identifying problems or areas for improvement, planning for the improvement, implementing it, and evaluating it. It's an application of the nursing process to the process for using technology for the improvement of patient care.

1. List the biomedical technologies available to you for patient care and the data that you gather from these devices:

_____
_____
_____
_____
_____

2. For each type of technology that you listed, explain what you do with the data gathered:

_____
_____
_____
_____
_____

3. Describe how you aggregate and process these data to gain information:

_____
_____
_____
_____
_____

4. Explain how you use this information to make patient care decisions:

_____
_____
_____
_____
_____

5. Think of ways to improve the manual system for gathering data and aggregating and processing it. List every idea you have—brainstorm!

_____
_____
_____
_____
_____

6. List the ways that a computerized system might eliminate steps in the manual system.

_____
_____
_____
_____
_____

Managing Information and Technology Self-Assessment Tool—cont'd

7. If you do not have any of the automated technologies for patient care (biomedical, information, knowledge), what steps might you as an individual take to get the process started?

_____
_____
_____
_____
_____

8. Think about your fellow staff members. Are they accepting of change? Would they resist computerization of the patient care process? How would you handle this?

_____
_____
_____
_____
_____

9. Name some ethical issues you might want to consider when computerizing patient care data:

_____
_____
_____
_____
_____

10. After you have installed and implemented patient care systems, how would you evaluate whether or not they have helped nurses provide patient care?

_____
_____
_____
_____
_____

11. Describe what you see as the "big picture" for healthcare computerization:

_____
_____
_____
_____
_____

12. List as many new roles for nursing in the field of nursing informatics and technology as you can think of:

_____
_____
_____
_____
_____

Ethics

Nurses must also be guided by the American Nurses Association *Code for Nurses* (1976) to prevent harm and promote the highest level of health possible. Because of the increasing ability to preserve and maintain human life via the technological interventions, questions dealing with life become complex, conceptually and ethically. Conceptually, it becomes more difficult to define extraordinary treatment and human life, because technology has changed our concepts of living and dying. The **ethics** problem becomes one of precedence, such as the dilemma of how to relieve pain without hastening death.

A frequent source of ethical dilemmas is the use of invasive technological treatment to prolong life for patients with limited or no decision-making capabilities when there are unlimited choices in determining who shall live and who shall be permitted to die. Healthcare institutions that use technology strive for efficiency and cost-effectiveness with an ethical mandate of the greatest good for the greatest number. The nursing profession holds a holistic orientation and is concerned with individual patient welfare and the impact of technological intervention as it affects the immediate and long-term quality of the patients and their families.

Nurse managers must assure the confidentiality of patient data and information by establishing policies and procedures for the collection and entering of data and the use of security measures such as passcodes. They must also be knowledgeable patient advocates in the use of technology for patient care by referring ethical questions to the organization's ethics committee.

CHAPTER CHECKLIST

Science and technology give us the means but not the ends, and nurses are the key personnel in the healthcare system to mediate the interaction among science, technology, and the patient because of their unique roles as caregivers who preserve the patients' humanity. The challenge for the profession is to continue to provide human and moral care that gives life, health, and death its meaning in a technological organization that strives for efficiency and cost-effectiveness. Nurse managers must provide leadership in managing information and technology to meet the challenge.

- Information is the communication or reception of knowledge. It consists of three aspects of the concept of information:
  - data
  - information
  - knowledge.
- Nurses commonly manage three types of information technology:
  - biomedical
  - information
  - knowledge.
- Biomedical technology includes the use of:
  - physiologic monitoring
  - diagnostic testing
  - drug administration
  - therapeutic testing to gather patient care data.

- Information technology refers to computers and programs that are used to process data and information.
- Use of the nursing minimum data set provides a framework for gathering data so that it can be retrieved and compared across time.
- Hospital and nursing information systems possess patient care data to provide information.
- Hospital information systems focus on hospital functions and may consist of:
    - stand-alone systems
    - on-line interactive systems
    - networked systems
    - integrated systems.
- Nursing information systems are used within nursing for patient care documentation and often do not communicate with other departmental information systems, although these systems may be interfaced to the hospital information system.
- Information systems for nursing administration provide information for:
    - quality improvement
    - personnel files
    - communication networks
    - budgeting and payroll
    - patient census
    - summary reports
    - forecasting and planning.
- Computer terminals to capture data at the point of care have improved communication by providing immediate access to information.
- The use of knowledge technology, which mimics the information processing of the expert nurse, is called informatics.
- The computerized patient record contains healthcare information for each individual from birth to death, allowing immediate and complete access to health information.
- Smart cards are credit-card-like devices that store up to eight pages of data. These cards and the information they provide help to coordinate care across local, state, national, and international boundaries—wherever patients may need access to healthcare.
- Confidentiality issues have become important with increased access to patient care data.

TERMS TO KNOW

- biomedical technology
- confidentiality
- data
- data processing
- database
- diagnostic testing
- ethics
- expert system
- hospital information system
- informatics
- information
- information technology
- integrated systems
- knowledge
- knowledge base
- knowledge technology
- mainframe computer
- networked systems
- nursing administration systems
- nursing information system
- nursing minimum data set
- on-line interactive systems
- physiologic monitoring systems
- smart card
- standalone systems
- technology
- therapeutic systems
- voice technology

REFERENCES

American Nurses Association (ANA) (1976). *Code for Nurses with Interpretive Statements.* Washington, DC: American Nurses Publishing.

Amos, L.K., & Graves, J.R. (1990). Knowledge technology: Costs, benefits, ethical considerations. In McCloskey, J.C., & Grace, H.K., eds. *Current Issues in Nursing,* 3rd ed. Baltimore: Mosby, pp. 592–600.

Bergman, R. (1993, June 5). JCAHO manual sets standards on information management. *Hospital and Health Networks,* p. 68.

Carter, B., & Axford, R. (1993). Assessment of computer learning needs and priorities of registered nurses practicing in hospitals. *Computers in Nursing, 11*(3), 122–126.

Leske, J.S., & Werley, H.H. (1992). Use of the nursing minimum data set. *Computers in Nursing, 10*(6), 259–263.

Marr, P., Glassman, K., Kelly, J., Kovner, C., & Roberts, N. (1993). Bedside terminals and quality of nursing documentation. *Computers in Nursing, 11*(4), 176–182.

McAlindon, M., Danz, S., & Theodoroff, R. (1987). Choosing the hospital information system: A nursing perspective. *Journal of Nursing Administration, 17*(10), 11–15.

Neame, R. (1993). Making the case for healthcare smart cards. *Healthcare Informatics, 10*(6), 16–20.

Saba, V., & McCormick, K. (1986). *Essentials of Computers for Nurses.* New York: McGraw Hill.

Werley, H.H., Devine, E.C., & Zorn, C.R. (1990). The nursing minimum data set: Issues for the profession. In McCloskey, J.C., & Grace, H.K., eds. *Current Issues in Nursing,* 3rd ed. New York: Mosby, pp. 64–70.

Werley, H., & Lang, N. (1986). *Identification of the Nursing Minimum Data Set.* New York: Springer.

SUGGESTED READINGS

Davis, M. (1993, June). Reaping the benefits of electronic medical record systems. *Health Care Financial Management*, pp. 60–66.

Gabrieli, E. (1993). Aspects of a computer-based patient record. *Journal of AHIMA, 64*(7), 70–82.

Gardner, E. (1993, April 5). Hospitals put wireless terminals to the test. *Modern Health Care*, p. 38.

Hampton, D. (1993). Implementing a managed care framework through care maps. *Journal of Nursing Administration, 23*(5), 21–27.

Hannah, K., Ball, M., & Edwards, J. (1994). *Introduction to Nursing Informatics.* New York: Springer-Verlag.

Hravenak, M., Stein, K., Dale, B., & Hazy, J. (1993). Ongoing development of the critical care information system: The collaborative approach to automating information management in the intensive care unit. *Proceedings of the Sixteenth Annual Symposium on Computer Applications in Medical Care.* New York: McGraw-Hill, pp. 3–8.

Klein, E. (1993). Automating home care. *Health Care Informatics, 10*(8), 22–28.

Lancaster, L. (1993). Nursing information systems in the year 2000. Another perspective. *Computers in Nursing, 11*(1), 3–5.

Lindeman, C. (1992). Nursing & technology: Moving into the 21st century. *Caring, 11*(9), 7–10.

Martin, C., & Baker, C. (1993). Measuring the benefits of bedside systems. *Health Care Informatics, 10*(5), 26–30.

Milholland, K., & Heller, B. (1992). Computer-based patient record: From pipe dream to reality. *Computers in Nursing, 10*(5), 191–192.

National Nursing Research Agenda. (1993). Developing knowledge for practice: Challenges and opportunities. *Nursing Informatics: Enhancing Patient Care.* Bethesda, MD: U.S. Department of Health and Human Services.

Zielstorff, R., Hudgings, C., & Grobe, S. (1993). *Next Generation Nursing Information Systems.* Washington, DC: American Nurses Publishing.

CHAPTER 13

MANAGING COSTS AND BUDGETS

Donna Westmoreland, R.N., Ph.D.

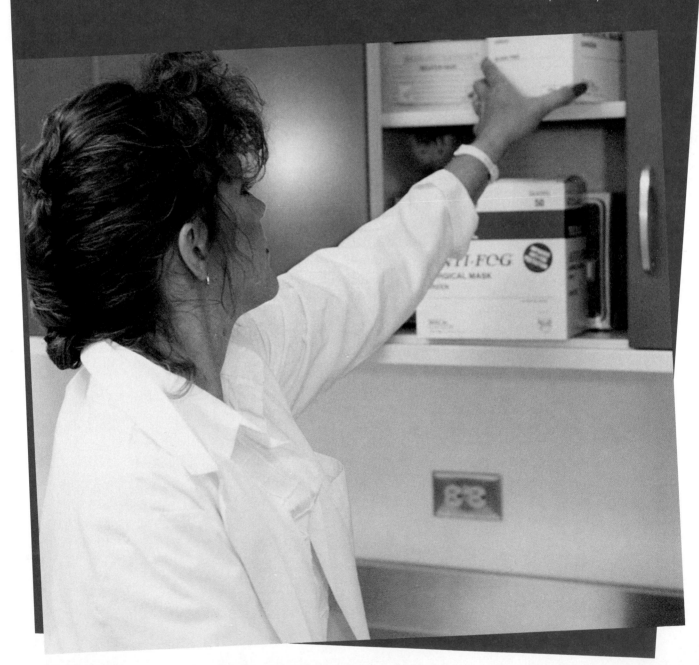

PREVIEW

This chapter focuses on methods of financing healthcare and specific strategies for managing costs and budgets in various patient care settings. It discusses the factors that escalate healthcare costs, sources of healthcare financing, reimbursement methods, cost-containment and healthcare reform strategies, and implications for nursing practice. It also explains the various types of budgets and outlines the budgeting process. An understanding of the cost and quality issues that drive changes in healthcare and the ethical implications of all financial decisions is crucial to achieving cost-conscious nursing practice.

OBJECTIVES

- Explain several major factors that are escalating the costs of healthcare.
- Compare and contrast different reimbursement methods in regard to provide incentives to control costs.
- Differentiate costs, charges, and revenue in relation to a specified unit of service, such as a visit, hospital stay, or procedure.
- Demonstrate why all healthcare organizations must make a profit.
- Give examples of cost considerations for nurses working in managed care environments.
- Discuss the purpose of and relationship among the operating, cash, and capital budgets.
- Explain the budgeting process.
- Identify variances on monthly expense reports.

QUESTIONS TO CONSIDER

- How can you stay abreast of changes in the healthcare system and what they mean for the practice of nursing?
- What are the charges for typical nursing care activities that you perform and the supplies you use?
- Who are the major payers to your organization? What is their method of payment or reimbursement?
- Does the organization recoup all of the charges? If not, what portion of the charges do they get for various patient groups?
- How is nursing reimbursed in your organization?

- How can you increase your cost-effectiveness as a nurse?
- Do the nursing practices in your organization add value for patients?

A Manager's Viewpoint

Even though some nurses don't like to think about the financial aspects of nursing, an important part of our practice today is understanding what care costs and how those costs are paid. Thinking of our practice in this way means that we must value ourselves as providers.

In the ambulatory care clinics, nurses must be familiar with the various insurance plans that reimburse us. There are numerous plans with different contract rules regarding preauthorization, types of services covered, and required vendors. For us to remain financially viable, nurses must develop and implement their plans of care with full knowledge of these reimbursement practices. Even so, the insurance plan doesn't totally drive the care. Nurses can still advocate for patients in important ways, while also working within the cost and contractual constraints.

Another important consideration for the ambulatory care clinic nurses is understanding what is required for the clinic to remain financially sound. This moves beyond thinking about costs for individual patients to thinking about income and expenses and numbers of patients needed to make a profit. With capitation we need to increase the overall patient volume and provide more comprehensive and efficient service with each visit. And we need to increase the patient volume without increasing our fixed costs, such as personnel, building, or equipment costs. To develop a plan for how we could do this, nurses collected data about room utilization patterns in one specialty clinic. Their understanding that increasing the volume might prevent staff reductions certainly increased their willingness to do this extra task. With these data, we were able to show the clinic physicians the days and times they could add new clinics or increase their volume in current clinics without hiring more nurses or support staff.

The outpatient clinic nurses also contribute to increasing patient volume, thus maintaining the financial viability of the clinics through marketing. Most of their marketing efforts consist of offering health screening services at local health fairs and staffing first-aid booths at public events.

Mary Rolf Fixley, R.N., M.P.A., Assistant Director
Ambulatory Care Services
Robin Stoupa, R.N., M.S.N., Nurse Manager
Internal Medicine Clinic
University of Nebraska Medical Center
Omaha, Nebraska

INTRODUCTION

costs

Healthcare costs in the United States continue to rise at 10 percent per year, more than twice the rate of general inflation, and consume more than 13 percent of the gross national product (GNP). In 1993, we were projected to spend $903 billion for healthcare (Burner, Waldo, and McKusick, 1992). This equals $3,380 per person and surpasses the per capita expenditures of other nations by almost 50 percent. Yet, with 37 million people uninsured and another 37 million underinsured, many Americans are going without basic healthcare. With the exception of South Africa, the United States is the only industrialized nation where healthcare is a privilege rather than a right.

health indicator

Despite our huge expenditures, the major indicators of health in the United States reveal significant problems. For example, our infant mortality rate is among the poorest of all industrialized nations with black infants dying at a higher rate than white infants. Births to teenagers are increasing, and more women and children are living in poverty, the leading cause of death in children. Breast cancer now strikes one in eight women, and violence-related injuries as well as homicides are increasing. In other words, as a nation we are not getting a high value return for our healthcare dollar.

The large portion of GNP that is spent on healthcare poses problems to the economy in other ways, too. Funds are diverted from needed social programs such as child care, housing, education, transportation, and the environment. The price of goods and services is increased, so the country's ability to compete in the international marketplace is compromised. One illustration is that up to 10 percent of the cost of a new American car goes to pay for the healthcare costs of automobile workers (Grace, 1990).

WHAT ESCALATES HEALTHCARE COSTS?

Total healthcare **costs** are a function of the **prices** and the utilization rates of healthcare services (*Costs = Price × Utilization*) (see Table 13-1). Price is the rate that healthcare providers set for the services they deliver. Utilization refers to the quantity or volume of services provided. Administrative inefficiency and unnecessary medical care were estimated to account for $200 billion of total healthcare costs in 1993. That figure does not even consider the increased costs due to overpricing of physician services and technologic procedures or fraud (Consumers Union, 1992).

billing costs

The administrative inefficiency is primarily a result of the large numbers of clerical personnel that organizations use to process reimbursement forms. Hospitals in the United States spend an average of 20 percent of their **budgets** on billing administration alone. These expenditures add to the price of healthcare services.

Several interrelated factors contribute to the overutilization of medical services. These include induced demand, the surplus of highly specialized physicians, the attitudes of consumers, and the way healthcare is financed. Increased utilization of healthcare services is also a function of changing population demographics and disease patterns.

induced demand

Induced demand refers to "the creation of medical 'need' by those who then profit from it" (Consumers Union, 1992, p. 439). It exists because physicians rather than consumers make most of the decisions regarding what healthcare services are needed and where they will be performed. In a normal

TABLE 13-1	Relationship of Price and Utilization Rates to Total Healthcare Costs			
PRICE	×	UTILIZATION RATE	= TOTAL COST	% CHANGE
$1.00		100	$100.00	0
$1.08[a]		100	$108.00	+ 8.0%
$1.08		105[b]	$113.40	+ 13.4%
$1.08		110[c]	$118.80	+ 18.8%

[a]8% increase for inflation.
[b]5% more procedures done.
[c]10% more procedures done.

marketplace, consumers and **providers** are separate and distinct, and the amount of the service demanded is mediated by its price. Generally, as the price rises the amount of the service used decreases. When the distinction between providers and consumers is blurred and when providers benefit by increased demand, higher utilization and higher prices result (Cleland, 1990). Moreover, treatment patterns, and thus costs, for similar diagnoses are highly variable among physicians, even within the same region.

This situation is further compounded by the large number of physicians choosing to practice in high-tech specialties rather than primary care (Grace, 1990). Because physicians generate demand for their services, growing numbers of specialists increase utilization of high-cost, high-tech services. And as expensive technology is purchased to support these practices, more services must be provided in order to pay for the equipment.

high-tech specialties

As a nation, our attitudes and behaviors as consumers of healthcare also contribute to rising costs (Grace, 1990). In general, we are a nation of consumers that prefer to "be fixed" when something goes wrong rather than to practice prevention. When we need "fixing," expensive, high-tech services typically are perceived as the best care. Many of us still believe that the physician knows best, so we do not seek much information related to costs and effectiveness of different healthcare options. Even when we do seek information, it is not readily available or understandable. Also, we are not used to using other less costly healthcare providers such as nurse practitioners.

attitudes and behaviors

The way healthcare is financed contributes to rising costs. When healthcare is reimbursed by third-party **payers,** consumers are somewhat insulated from personally experiencing the direct effects of high healthcare costs. We do not have a lot of incentives to consider costs when choosing among providers or using services. In addition, the various methods for reimbursing healthcare providers have implications for how they price and use services.

financing

Changing population demographics also are increasing the volume of health services needed. For example, chronic health problems increase with age, and the number of elderly Americans is increasing. By the end of the decade, there will be 36 million Americans 65 years of age or older. The fastest growing population are those aged 85 or older. Additionally, infectious diseases such as AIDS and tuberculosis, as well as the growing societal problems of homelessness, drug addiction, and violence, increase demands for health services.

demographics

HOW IS HEALTHCARE FINANCED?

funding   Healthcare is paid for primarily from three sources: government (42 percent), private insurance companies (33 percent), and individuals (20 percent) (see Figure 13-1). Three-fourths of the government funding is at the federal level. Federal programs include Medicare and health services for members of the military, veterans, Native Americans, and federal prisoners. Medicare, the largest federal program, was established in 1965 and pays for care provided to the elderly and some disabled individuals. Medicaid, a state-level program financed by federal and state funds, pays for services provided to persons who are medically indigent, blind, or disabled, and to crippled children.

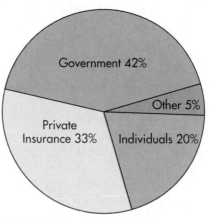

FIGURE 13-1
Sources of financing for healthcare.

Insurance is the second major source of financing for the healthcare system. Most Americans have private health insurance, which is usually provided by employers, although it can be purchased by individuals. Individuals also pay directly for health services when they do not have health insurance or when insurance does not cover the service. Often, health insurance benefits do not cover preventive care or things such as eyeglasses and nonprescription medications.

REIMBURSEMENT METHODS

Four major payment methods are used for reimbursing healthcare providers: charges, cost-based reimbursement, flat-rate reimbursement, and capitated payments (Neuman, Suver, and Zelman, 1988). These methods are summarized in the accompanying box.

Major Reimbursement Methods

• Charges
• Cost-based (retrospective)
• Flat-rate (prospective)
• Capitated

Charges consist of the cost of providing a service plus a markup for profit. Third-party payers often put limitations on what they will pay by establishing usual and customary charges. These limits are established by surveying all providers in a certain area. Usual and customary charges rise over time as providers consistently increase their prices.

charges

All allowable costs are calculated and used as the basis for payment in **cost-based reimbursement.** Each payer (government or insurance company) determines what the allowable costs are for each procedure, visit, or service. These payment schedules vary from state to state. Cost-based reimbursement is a *retrospective* payment method because the costs are determined after services are delivered. When the reimbursed costs are less than the full charge for the service, a **contractual allowance** or discount exists. Cost-based reimbursement was the predominant payment method in the 1960s and 1970s and is still used by some payers.

cost-based reimbursement

Flat-rate reimbursement is a method in which the third-party payer decides in advance what will be paid for a service or episode of care. For this reason, it is a **prospective reimbursement** method. If the costs of care are greater than the payment, the provider absorbs the loss. If the costs are less than the payment, the provider makes a profit. In 1983, Medicare implemented a prospective payment system (PPS) for hospital care that uses diagnosis-related groups (DRGs) as the basis for payment.

flat-rate reimbursement

DRGs, a classification system that groups patients into categories based on the average number of days of hospitalization for specific medical diagnoses, considers factors such as the patient's age, complications, and other illnesses. Payment includes the expected costs for diagnostic tests, various therapies, surgery, and length of stay (LOS). The cost of nursing services is not explicitly calculated. With a few exceptions, DRGs do not adequately reflect the variability of patient intensity or acuity within the DRG. This is problematic for nursing because the amount of resources (nurses and supplies) used to care for patients is directly related to the patient acuity. Thus, many nurses think that DRGs are not a good predictor of nursing care requirements.

> **EXERCISE 13-1**
> What is the contractual allowance when a hospital charges $800/day to care for a ventilator-dependent patient and an insurance company reimburses the hospital $685/day? What is the impact on hospital income (revenue) if this is the reimbursement for 2500 patient days?

In addition to Medicare, some state Medicaid programs and private insurance companies use a DRG payment system. Although DRGs are not currently used for specialty hospitals (pediatric, psychiatric, and oncology), they are a dominant force in hospital payment. The healthcare system radically changed with the implementation of PPS with DRGs as evidenced by increased patient acuity, decreased LOS in hospitals, and greater demand for home care and hospital and community-based nurses. Currently DRGs are being developed for ambulatory care and home care services.

Capitated payments are based on providing specified services to an individual over a period of time such as 1 year. Providers are paid a per person per year (or per month) fee. If the services cost more than the payment, the provider absorbs the loss. Likewise, if the services cost less than the payment, the provider makes a profit. **Capitation** is the mode of payment characteristic of health maintenance organizations (HMOs) and other managed care systems.

> **EXERCISE 13-2**
> A hospice is reimbursed $75/day by Medicare for home visits. For one particular group of patients, it costs the hospice an average of $98/day to provide care. What are the implications for the hospice? What options should the hospice nurse manager and nurses consider?

Health service researchers do not agree on the exact effects of these reimbursement methods on cost and quality. However, considering these effects is important because changes in payment systems have implications for how care is provided in healthcare organizations.

THE CHANGING HEALTHCARE ECONOMIC ENVIRONMENT

Healthcare is a major public concern, and rapid changes are occurring in order to reduce costs and to improve the health and wellness of the nation. As shown in the box below, strategies shaping the evolving healthcare delivery system include managed care, organized delivery systems, and competition based on cost and quality. These strategies affect both the pricing and utilization of health services.

Healthcare Delivery Reform Strategies

- Managed care
- Organized delivery systems
- Competition based on price, patient outcomes, and service quality

managed care

Managed care is a system of care in which a designated person determines the services that the patient uses. A major goal of managed care is to decrease unnecessary services, thereby decreasing costs. Managed care also works to ensure timely and appropriate care. HMOs are a type of managed care system in which the primary physician serves as a gatekeeper. Because HMOs are paid on a capitated basis, it is to their advantage to practice prevention and to use ambulatory care rather than more expensive hospital care. In other forms of managed care, a nonphysician case manager arranges and authorizes the services provided. Many insurance companies have used case managers for years. Nurses who work in home healthcare and in ambulatory settings often communicate with insurance company case managers in order to plan the care for specific patients.

EXERCISE 13-3
For each reimbursement method, think about the incentives for healthcare providers (individuals and organizations) regarding their practice patterns. Are there incentives to change the *quantity of services* used per patient or the *number or types of patients* served? Are there incentives to be *efficient?* List the incentives. How might each method affect overall healthcare costs? (Think in terms of effect on utilization and price.) What do you think the effect on *quality of care* might be with each payment method?

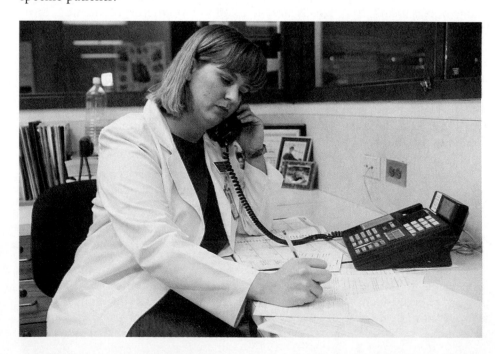

Nurses in ambulatory care settings often work directly with insurance companies to plan patient care.

Organized delivery systems (ODS) are comprised of networks of health-care organizations, providers, and payers. Typically, this means hospitals, physicians, and insurance companies. The aim of such joint ventures is to develop and market collectively a comprehensive package of healthcare services that will meet most needs of large numbers of consumers. The financial risks of the enterprise will be shared by hospitals, physicians, and payers. Although hospitals share some risk now with prospective payment, physicians have not generally shared the risk. This risk-sharing is expected to provide incentives to eliminate unnecessary services, utilize resources effectively, and improve quality of services.

organized delivery systems

Competition among healthcare providers increasingly is based on cost and quality indicators. Decision making regarding price and utilization of services is shifting from physicians and hospitals to payers. Significant contractual discounts, that is lower prices, are being demanded by payers. Scientific data that demonstrate positive health outcomes and high quality services are required. Providers who are unable to compete on the basis of price, patient outcomes, and service quality will find it difficult to survive as changes in the system proceed.

competition

WHAT DOES THIS MEAN FOR NURSING PRACTICE?

What does the changing healthcare environment mean for the practicing professional nurse? We must value ourselves as providers and think of our practice within a context of organizational viability and quality of care. To do this we must add "financial thinking" to our repertoire of nursing skills, and we must determine whether or not the services we provide add value for patients. Services that add value are of high quality, affect health outcomes positively, and minimize costs. The following sections help develop "financial thinking" skills and ways to consider how nursing practice adds value for patients through minimizing costs.

WHY IS PROFIT NECESSARY?

Private, nongovernmental healthcare organizations may be either for profit (FP) or not for profit (NFP). This refers to the tax status of the organization and designates how the profit can be used. **Profit** is the excess income left after all expenses have been paid *(Revenues − Expenses = Profit)*. FP organizations pay taxes, and their profits can be distributed to owners and managers. NFP organizations, on the other hand, do not pay taxes and must reinvest all profits in the organization.

profit/not for profit

All private healthcare organizations must make a profit in order to survive. If expenses are greater than revenues, the organization experiences a loss. If revenues equal expenses, the organization breaks even. In both cases, nothing is left over to replace facilities and equipment, expand services, or pay for inflation costs. Some healthcare organizations are able to survive in the short run without making a profit because they use interest from investments to supplement revenues. The long-term viability of any healthcare organization, however, is dependent on consistently making a profit. The box on the next page presents an example of an income statement from a neighborhood nursing center.

Nurses and nurse managers directly affect an organization's ability to make a profit. Profits can be achieved or increased by decreasing costs or increasing

EXERCISE 13-4

Obtain a copy of an itemized patient bill from a healthcare organization and review the charges. What was the source and method of payment? How much of these charges was reimbursed? How much was charged for items you regularly use in clinical care?

An Income Statement

NEIGHBORHOOD NURSING CENTER
STATEMENT OF REVENUES AND EXPENSES
FYE December 31, 1994

REVENUES		
Patient revenues	$110,700	
Grant income	60,000	
Other operating revenues	5,300	
Total	$176,000	$176,000
EXPENSES		
Salary costs	$130,500	
Supplies	14,400	
Other operating expenses (rent, utilities, administrative services, etc.)	29,900	
Total	$174,800	174,800
Excess of revenues over expenses (profit)*		$ 1,200

FYE = Fiscal Year Ending
*Loss would be shown in parentheses ( ) or brackets < >.

revenues. In tight economic times, many managers think only in terms of cutting costs. Cost-cutting measures are important, especially to keep prices down so the organization will be competitive. But ways to increase revenues also need to be explored.

COST-CONSCIOUS NURSING PRACTICE

KNOWING COSTS AND REIMBURSEMENT PRACTICES

As direct caregivers and case managers, nurses are constantly involved in determining the type and quantity of resources used for patients. This includes supplies, personnel, and time. We need to know what things cost and how they are paid for in our organization.

nursing charges

In hospitals, usually the cost of nursing care is not calculated or billed separately to patients but is part of the general per diem charge. One major problem with this method is the assumption that all patients consume the same amount of nursing care. Another problem with bundling the charges for nursing care with the room rate is that nursing as a clinical service is not perceived by management as generating revenue for the hospital. Rather, nursing is perceived predominantly as an expense to the organization.

CAPTURING ALL CHARGES IN A TIMELY FASHION

EXERCISE 13-5

How was nursing care charged on the bill you obtained? What are the implications for nursing in being perceived as an expense rather than being associated with the revenue stream?

We also help contain costs by making sure that all possible charges are captured. Several large hospitals report more than $1 million a year lost from supplies that were not charged. In hospitals, nurses must know which supplies are charged to patients and which ones are charged to the unit. Additionally, the procedures and equipment used need to be accurately documented. In ambulatory and community settings, nurses often need to keep abreast of the codes that are used to bill services. These codes change yearly, and sometimes items are bundled together under one charge and sometimes they are broken down into different charges. Turning in charges in a timely manner is also important because delayed billing negatively impacts cash flow by extending the time before an organization is paid for services provided. This is significant particularly in smaller organizations.

DISCUSSING THE COST OF CARE WITH PATIENTS

Talking with patients about the cost of care is important even though it may be uncomfortable for some of us. Discovering during a clinic visit that a patient cannot afford a specific medication or intervention is preferable to finding out several days later in a follow-up call that the patient has not taken the medication. Such information compels the clinical management team to explore optional treatment plans or to find resources to cover the costs. Talking with patients about costs is important in other ways, too. It involves the patients in the decision making and increases the likelihood that treatment plans will be followed.

MEETING PATIENT RATHER THAN PROVIDER NEEDS

Developing an awareness of how our feelings about patients' needs influence our decisions can help us better manage costs. A nurse administrator in a home health agency recently related the story of a nurse who continued to visit a patient for weeks after the patient's health problems had resolved. When questioned, the nurse said she was uncomfortable terminating the visits because the patient continued to tell her he needed her help. Later the patient revealed that he had not needed nursing care for some time, although he had continued telling the nurse he did because he thought she wanted to keep visiting him. This story illustrates how we need to make sure whose needs we are meeting with our nursing care.

EVALUATING COST-EFFECTIVENESS OF NEW TECHNOLOGIES

cost-effectiveness

The advent of new technologies is confronting us with dilemmas regarding managing costs. In the past, if a new piece of equipment was easier to use or benefited the patient in any way, we were apt to want to use it for everyone, no matter how much more it cost. Now we are forced to make decisions regarding which patients really need the new equipment and which ones will do fine with the current equipment. Essentially, we are analyzing the cost-effectiveness of the new equipment with regard to different types of patients. This is a new and sometimes difficult way to think about patient care for many of us, and at times it may not "feel fair."

PREDICTING AND USING NURSING RESOURCES EFFICIENTLY

Because healthcare organizations are service institutions, the largest part of their operating budget typically is for personnel. For hospitals in particular, nurses are the largest group of employees and often account for the majority of the personnel budget. Staffing is the major area nurse managers can impact with respect to managing costs, and supplies are the second area. To understand why this is so, it is helpful to understand the concepts of fixed and variable costs.

staffing costs

Fixed costs are costs that do not change in total as the volume of patients changes. Examples include rent, loan payments, administrative salaries, and

fixed costs

variable costs

patient classification systems

EXERCISE 13-8
A new patient visits the clinic and is given prescriptions for three medications that will cost about $120 per month. You check her chart and discover that she has Medicare and no supplemental insurance. How can you determine whether or not she has the resources to buy this medicine each month? If she cannot afford the medications, what are some options?

length of stay

EXERCISE 13-9
What data are used to determine patients' needs in different healthcare agencies? What common nursing practices should be scrutinized carefully to determine whether they are meeting patient or provider needs?

research

salaries of the minimum amount of staff needed to keep a unit open. **Variable costs** are costs that vary in direct proportion to patient volume or acuity. Examples include nursing personnel, supplies, and medications.

In hospitals and community health agencies, patient classification systems are used to help managers predict nursing care requirements (see Chapter 22). These systems differentiate among patients based on their acuity of illness, functional status, and resource needs. Some nurses do not like these systems because they feel they do not adequately reflect the essence of nursing. However, we need to remember that they are tools to help managers predict resource needs. It is not necessary to describe all nursing activities and judgments in order for a tool to be a good predictor. Misguided efforts to sabotage classification systems, in the hope that better staffing will be achieved, work primarily to keep us from developing tools to better manage our practice. Used appropriately, patient classification systems can help us evaluate changing practice patterns and patient acuity levels as well as help with budgeting processes.

In addition to managing personnel and supply costs, hospital nurse managers are being pressured to reduce patient length of stay (LOS). The patient's LOS is the most important predictor of hospital cost (Finkler and Kovner, 1993). Patients who stay extra days cost the hospital a considerable amount. Decreasing LOS also makes room for other patients, thereby potentially increasing patient volume and hospital revenues.

The diagnostic services and treatment modalities ordered by physicians also impact the cost of patient care in hospitals. According to industry consultants, it takes several years for a hospital to see reductions in costs due to changes in physician practice patterns. The most immediate reductions in costs can be achieved by managing staffing and decreasing LOS.

Hospitals strive to lower costs so they will attract new contracts and be attractive as partners in provider networks. Thus, staffing methodologies and patient care delivery models are being closely scrutinized. Work redesign, a process for changing the way we think about and structure the work of patient care, is the predominant strategy for developing systems that better utilize high-cost professionals and improve service quality and patient outcomes.

USING RESEARCH TO EVALUATE STANDARD NURSING PRACTICES

Another way nurses are restructuring their work to make sure they add value for patients is through research and quality improvement projects. For example, in the internal medicine clinics at the University of Nebraska Medical Center, nurses and physicians are developing a rule to predict which patients are at risk for orthostatic hypotension. This is significant because the mortality rates are high when orthostatic hypotension is present. Yet performing the sitting and standing blood pressure readings on all patients is costly in terms of nursing resources. After the rule has been developed and validated through research, the computerized patient record will automatically signal the nurse to take orthostatic blood pressures when needed. This chapter's "Research Perspective" illustrates cost savings from one practice alteration. The accompanying box on page 263 lists some cost-conscious strategies for nursing practice.

Strategies for Cost-Conscious Nursing Practice

1. Knowing costs and reimbursement practices
2. Capturing all possible charges in a timely fashion
3. Discussing the costs of care with patients
4. Meeting patient rather than provider needs
5. Evaluating cost-effectiveness of new technologies
6. Predicting and using nursing resources efficiently
7. Using research to evaluate standard nursing practices

BUDGETS

The basic financial document in most healthcare organizations is the budget, a detailed financial plan for carrying out the activities an organization wants to accomplish for a certain period of time. An organizational budget is a formal plan that is stated in dollar terms and includes proposed income and expenditures. The budgeting process is an ongoing activity in which plans are made and revenues and expenses are managed in order to meet or exceed the goals of the plan. The management functions of planning and control are tied together through the budgeting process.

Research Perspective

Goode, C., Titler, M., Rakel, B., Ones, D., Kleiber, C., Small, S., & Triolo, P. (1991). A meta-analysis of effects of heparin flush and saline flush: Quality and cost implications. Nursing Research, 40(6), 324–330.

The purpose of this study was to estimate the effects of heparin flush and saline flush solutions on maintaining patency, preventing phlebitis, and increasing duration of catheter placement in patients with peripheral heparin locks. Meta-analytical techniques were used to synthesize the results of seventeen existing experimental or quasi-experimental studies.

No statistical difference was found between heparin or saline flush solutions for clotting, phlebitis, or duration. Based on these data alone, the clinical use of either flush solution is equally correct. However, heparin flushes have risks not associated with saline flushes, such as anticoagulant effects and drug incompatibilities. Heparin flushes also cost more in terms of supplies, drugs, and staff time.

Because there is no difference in treatment effects and because of cost and quality of care considerations, the investigators recommend using saline flush solutions for heparin locks.

Implications for Practice

The University of Iowa Hospitals and Clinics, an 879-bed tertiary care hospital, estimated a savings of $38,000 per year in pharmacy costs alone by switching from heparin to saline flush solutions. Changing this practice nationwide was estimated to achieve a savings of $109,100,000 to $218,200,000 in yearly healthcare costs. However, this study cannot be generalized to children. Further studies are also needed to determine how often heparin locks need to be irrigated with saline.

EXERCISE 13-10

Last year a new positive pressure, needleless system for administering IV antibiotics was introduced. Because it was so easy and convenient for patients, the nurses in the home infusion company where you worked ordered them for everyone. Typically, patients get their IV antibiotics four times/day. The mini-bags and tubing for the regular procedure costs the agency $22/day. The new system costs $24/medication administration or $96/day. The agency receives the same per diem (daily) reimbursement for each patient. Discuss the financial implications for the agency if this practice is continued. Generate some optional courses of action for the nurses to consider. How should these options be evaluated?

EXERCISE 13-11

Given the definitions for fixed and variable costs, why do you think nurse managers make the greatest impact on costs through managing staffing and supplies?

A budget requires managers to plan ahead and to establish explicit program goals and expectations. Changes in medical practices, reimbursement methods, competition, technology, demographics, and regulatory factors must be forecasted in order to anticipate their effects on the organization. Planning encourages evaluation of different options and assists in more cost-effective use of resources.

TYPES OF BUDGETS

Several types of interrelated budgets are used by well-managed organizations. Major budgets that will be discussed in this chapter include the operating budget, the capital budget, and the cash budget. The way these budgets complement and support one another is depicted in Figure 13-2. Many organizations also use program, product line, or special purpose budgets. Long-range budgets are used to help managers plan for the future. Often these are referred to as strategic plans (Finkler and Kovner, 1993).

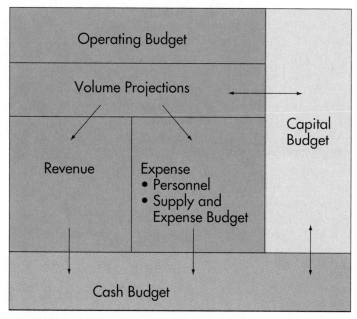

FIGURE 13-2
Interrelationships of the operating, capital, and cash budgets. [Adapted from Ward, W. (1988). *An Introduction to Healthcare Financial Management.* Owings Mills, MD: National Health Publishing.]

OPERATING BUDGET

operating budget
The **operating budget** is the financial plan for the day-to-day activities of the organization. The expected revenues and expenses generated from daily operations given a specified volume of patients is stated. Preparing and monitoring the operating budget, particularly the expense portion, is often the most time-consuming financial function of nurse managers.

expense
The expense part of the operating budget consists of a personnel budget and a supply and expense budget for each cost center. A **cost center** is an

TABLE 13-2 Work Load Calculation (Total Required Patient Care Hours)

PATIENT ACUITY LEVEL[a]	HOURS OF CARE PER PATIENT DAY (HPPD)[b]	PATIENT X DAYS[c]	= WORKLOAD[d]
1	3.0	900	2,700
2	5.2	3,100	16,120
3	8.8	4,000	35,200
4	13.0	1,600	20,800
5	19.0	400	7,600
TOTAL		10,000	82,420

[a] 1, low; 5, high.
[b] HPPD = number of hours of care on average for a given acuity level.
[c] 1 patient per 1 day = 1 patient day.
[d] Total number of hours of care needed based on acuity levels and numbers of patient days.

organizational unit for which costs can be identified and managed. The personnel budget is the largest part of the operating budget for most nursing units.

Before the personnel budget can be established, the volume of work predicted for the budget period must be calculated. A unit of service measure appropriate to the work of the unit is used. Units of service may be patient days, clinic or home visits, hours of service, admissions, deliveries, treatments, and so on. Other factors needed to calculate the work load are the patient census (including average daily census and average LOS for hospitals) and patient acuity mix. The formula for calculating the work load or the required patient care hours for inpatient units is: *Work Load Volume = Hours of Care Per Patient Day × Number of Patient Days* (see Table 13-2).

units of service

In some organizations, the work load or parts of the work load, such as patient days, are established by the financial office and given to the nurse manager. In other organizations, nurse managers forecast the volume. Even when the forecasting is centralized, nurse managers should bring to the attention of administration any factors that they know might affect the accuracy of the forecast.

The next step in preparing the personnel budget is to determine how many staff members will be needed to provide the care. (This topic is discussed in more detail in Chapter 22.) Because some people work full-time and others work part-time, **full-time equivalents** (FTEs) are used in this step rather than positions. Generally, one FTE can be equated to working 40 hours per week, 52 weeks per year, for a total of 2080 hours of work paid per year. One-half an FTE (0.5 FTE) equates to 20 hours per week. The standard for paid hours per year per FTE is different for some staffing plans and in some parts of the country, so it is important to check.

personnel

The 2080 hours paid to an FTE in a year consist of both **productive** and **nonproductive hours.** Productive hours are paid time that is worked. Nonproductive hours are paid time that is not worked, such as vacation, holiday, and sick time. Before the number of FTEs needed for the work load can be calculated, the number of productive hours per FTE is determined. This is done by adding up the total number of nonproductive hours per FTE and subtracting from total paid hours. Or payroll reports can be reviewed to

EXERCISE 13-13
Change the number of patients at each acuity level listed in the box entitled "Work Load Calculation," but keep the total number of patients the same. Recalculate the required total work load. Discuss how changes in patient acuity affect nursing resource requirements.

Productive Hours Calculation

Method 1: Add all nonproductive hours/FTE and subtract from paid hours/FTE

Example:		
	Vacation	15 days
	Holiday	7 days
	Average sick time	4 days
	Total	26 days

26×8 hrs $= 208$ nonproductive hours/FTE
$2080 - 208 = 1972$ productive hours/FTE

Method 2: Multiply paid hours/FTE by percentage of productive hours/FTE
  Example: productive hours $= 90\%$/FTE (1972 productive hour of total 2080 $= 90\%$)
  $2080 \times 0.90 = 1972$ productive hours/FTE

Total FTE Calculation

Required Patient Care Hours	÷	Productive Hours Per FTE	=	Total FTEs Needed
82,420	÷	1972	=	42 FTEs

EXERCISE 13-14
If the percentage of productive hours per FTE is 80 percent, how many worked or productive hours are there per FTE? If total patient care hours are 82,420, how many FTEs will be needed?

determine the percentage of paid hours that is productive for each FTE (see the accompanying box). Finally, the total number of FTEs needed to provide the care is calculated by dividing the total patient care hours required by the number of productive hours per FTE (see the accompanying box).

The total number of FTEs calculated by this method represents the number needed to provide care each day of the year. It does not reflect the number of positions or the number of people working each day. In fact, the number of positions may be significantly higher, particularly if many part-time nurses are employed. And on any given day, some nurses will be off, on vacation, or ill. Also, some positions that do not provide direct patient care, such as nurse managers or unit secretaries, may not be replaced during nonproductive time. Only one FTE is budgeted for any position that is not covered with other staff when the employee is off.

The next step is to prepare a daily staffing plan and to establish positions (see Chapter 22). Once the positions are established, the labor costs that make up the personnel budget can be calculated. Factors that must be addressed include straight-time hours, overtime hours, differentials and premium pay, raises, and benefits (Finkler and Kovner, 1993). Differentials and premiums are extra pay for working specific times such as evening or night shifts and holidays. Benefits usually include health and life insurance, Social Security payments, and retirement plans. Benefits often cost an additional 20 to 25 percent of a full-time employee's salary.

supply and expense   The supply and expense budget is often called the other-than-personnel services expense budget (OTPS). It includes a wide variety of items that are used in daily unit activities such as medical and office supplies, minor equipment, books and journals, orientation and training, and travel. Although different ways are used to calculate the supply and expense budget, the prior year often is used as a baseline. This baseline is adjusted for projected patient volume and specific circumstances known to affect expenses, such as predictable personnel turnover, which increases orientation and training expenses. And finally, a percentage factor is added to adjust for inflation.

The final component of the operating budget is the revenue budget. The revenue budget projects the income the organization will receive for providing patient care. Historically nurses have not been directly involved with developing the revenue budget, although this is beginning to change. In hospitals the revenue budget is established by the financial office and given to nurse managers. The anticipated revenues are calculated according to the price per patient day. Data about the volume and types of patients and reimbursement sources, that is, the **case mix** and the **payer mix,** are necessary to project revenues in any healthcare organization. Even when nurse managers do not participate in developing the revenue budget, learning about the organization's revenue base is essential.

revenue budget

CAPITAL EXPENDITURE BUDGET

The **capital expenditure budget** reflects the expenses related to the purchase of major capital items such as equipment and physical plant. A capital expenditure must have a useful life of more than 1 year and must exceed a cost level specified by the organization. The minimum cost requirement in healthcare organizations is usually anywhere from $300 to $1,000. Anything below that is considered routine operating costs.

capital expenditure budget

Capital items are kept separate from the operating budget because their high cost would make the costs of providing patient care appear too high. Each year, over the useful life of the equipment, a portion of its cost is allocated to the operating budget as an expense. Therefore, capital expenditure costs do get subtracted from revenues and in turn affect profits.

Organizations usually set aside a fixed amount of money for capital expenditures each year. The competition is stiff, so complete, well-documented justifications are needed. Justifications should include amount of use; duplication of services; safety replacement; need for space, personnel, or renovation; and impact on operational revenues and expenses.

CASH BUDGET

The cash budget is the operating plan for monthly cash receipts and disbursements. Organizational survival depends on an organization paying bills on time. Yet organizations can be making a profit and still run out of cash. In fact, a profitable trend, such as a rapidly growing census, can induce a cash shortage because of increased expenses in the short run. Major capital expenditures can also cause a temporary cash crises. Because cash is "the lifeblood of any organization" (Finkler and Kovner, 1993, p. 298), the cash budget is as important as the operating and capital budget.

cash budget

The financial officer prepares the cash budget in large organizations. Understanding the cash budget and how it is developed helps nurse managers discern when constraints on spending are necessary even though the expenditures are budgeted.

THE BUDGETING PROCESS

The steps in the **budgeting process** are similar in most healthcare organizations, although the budgeting period, budget timetable, and level of manager and employee participation vary. Budgeting is done on an annual basis and in relation to the organization's fiscal year. A fiscal year exists for financial

> **Outline of Budgeting Process**
>
> 1. Gathering information and planning
>   - Environmental assessment
>   - Mission, goals, and objectives
>   - Program priorities
>   - Financial objectives
>   - Assumptions (employee raises, inflation, volume projections)
> 2. Developing unit and departmental budgets
>   - Operating budgets
>   - Capital budgets
> 3. Developing cash budgets
> 4. Negotiating and revising
> 5. Evaluating
>   - Analysis of variance
>   - Critical performance reports
>
> *Adapted from Finkler, S., & Kovner, C. (1993). Financial Management for Nurse Managers and Executives. Philadelphia:W.B. Saunders.*

purposes and can begin at any point on the calendar. In the title of some financial reports, something like "FYE June 30, 1993," appears and means that this report is for the fiscal year ending on the date stated.

process   Major steps in the budgeting process include gathering information and planning, developing unit budgets, developing the cash budget, negotiating and revising, and using feedback to control budget results and to improve future plans (Finkler and Kovner, 1993). A timetable with specific dates for implementing the budgeting process is developed by each organization. The timetable may be anywhere from three to nine months. The widespread use of computers for budgeting is reducing the time spread for budgeting in many organizations. The box above outlines the budgeting process.

The information gathering and planning phase provides nurse managers with data essential for developing their individual budgets. This step begins *assessment* with an environmental assessment that helps the organization understand its position in relation to the entire community. The assessment includes the changing healthcare needs of the population, significant economic factors like inflation and unemployment, differences in reimbursement patterns, patient satisfaction, and so on.

Next, the organization's long-term goals and objectives are reassessed in light of the organization's mission and the environmental analysis. This helps all managers situate the budgeting process for their individual units in relation to the whole organization. At this point, programs are prioritized so that resources can be allocated to programs that best help the organization achieve its long-term goals.

objectives   Specific, measurable objectives are then established that the budgets must meet. The financial objectives might be something like limiting expenditure increases to 3 percent or making 4 percent reductions in personnel costs. Nurse managers also set operational objectives for their units that are in concert with the rest of the organization. This is where units or departments interpret what effect the changes in operational activities will have on them. For instance, what will be the impact of using case managers and care maps for selected patients? Establishing the unit level objectives is also a good place for involving staff nurses in setting the future direction of the unit.

Along with the specific organization and unit level operating objectives, managers need the organization-wide assumptions that underpin the budgeting process. Explicit assumptions regarding salary increases, inflation factors, and volume projections for the next fiscal year are essential. With this information in hand, nurse managers can develop the operating and capital budgets for their units. These are usually developed in tandem because each affects the other. For instance, the purchase of a new monitoring system will have implications for the supplies used, staffing, and staff training.

The cash budget is developed after unit and department operating and capital budgets. Then the negotiation and revision process begins in earnest. This is a complex process because changes in one budget usually require changes in others. Learning to defend and negotiate budgets is an important skill for nurse

EXERCISE 13-15
If you can interview a nurse manager, ask to review the budgeting process. Ask specifically about the budget timetable, operating objectives, and organizational assumptions. What was the level of involvement for nurse managers and nurses in each step of budget preparation? Is there a budget manual?

Statement of Operations

NEIGHBORHOOD NURSING CENTER
PROFIT AND LOSS STATEMENT
March 31, 1994

Budget	Actual	Variance	REVENUES	Budget	Actual	Variance
			Patient Revenues			
11,500	12,050	550	Routine	34,500	35,750	1,250
1,500	1,550	(50)	Contractual allowances	4,500	4,750	(250)
10,000	10,500	500	Net Patient Revenues	30,000	31,000	1,000
			Non-Patient Revenues			
5,000	5,000	0	Grant income (#138-FG)	15,000	15,000	0
500	500	0	Rent income	1,500	1,500	0
5,500	5,500	0	Net Non-patient Revenues	16,500	16,500	0
15,500	16,000	500	Net Revenues	46,500	47,500	1,000
			EXPENSES			
			Personnel services			
7,750	8,500	(750)	Managerial/professional	23,250	24,400	(1,150)
2,000	1,800	200	Clerical/technical	6,000	5,800	200
9,750	10,300	(550)	Net salaries & wages	29,250	30,200	(950)
1,200	1,400	(200)	Benefits	3,600	4,000	(400)
10,950	11,700	(750)	Net Personnel Services	32,850	34,200	(1,350)
			Other than personnel services (OTPS)			
2,500	2,500	0	Operating expenses	7,500	7,500	0
1,000	1,100	(100)	Supplies & materials	3,000	3,050	(50)
300	450	(150)	Travel expenses	900	450	450
3,800	4,050	(250)	Net OTPS	11,400	11,000	400
14,750	15,750	(1,000)	Net Expenses	44,250	45,200	50
			REVENUES OVER/UNDER			
750	250	(500)	**EXPENSES**	2,250	2,300	50

Column headers: ------Current Month-------- / --------Year-to-Date--------

EXERCISE 13-16
Review the box (page 260) entitled "An Income Statement" and identify significant budget variances for the current month. Are they favorable or unfavorable? What additional information would help you explain the variances? What are some possible causes for each variance? Are the causes you identified controllable by the nurse manager? Why or why not? Is a favorable variance on expenses always desirable? Why or why not?

managers. Nurse managers who successfully negotiate budgets are comfortable about speaking to what resources are contained in each budget category. They also know and can clearly and specifically depict what the impact of not having that resource will be on patient, nurse, or organizational outcomes. The box on the previous page shows a sample statement of operations for a neighborhood nursing center.

The final and ongoing phase of the budgeting process relates to the control function of management. Feedback is obtained regularly so that organizational activities can be adjusted to maintain efficient operations. **Variance analysis** is the major control process used. A **variance** is the difference between the projected budget and the actual performance for a particular account. For expenses, a favorable variance means that the budgeted amount was greater than the actual amount spent. Likewise, an unfavorable variance means that the budgeted amount was less than the actual amount spent.

Generally, nurse managers are expected to investigate and explain the underlying causes of variances greater than a certain percentage, such as 5 percent. After the causes are determined and if they are controllable by the nurse manager, steps are taken to prevent the variance from occurring in the future. If the causes are not controllable, then information learned from analyzing the variance is used in future budget preparations and management activities.

CHAPTER CHECKLIST

Financial thinking skills are the cornerstone of cost-conscious nursing practice and are essential for all nurses. Also, nurses must determine whether or not the services they provide add value for patients. Services that add value are of high quality, positively affect health outcomes, and minimize costs.

Understanding what constitutes profit and why organizations must make a profit to survive is basic to financial thinking. Knowing what is included in operating, capital, and cash budgets; how they interrelate, and how they are developed, monitored, and controlled is also important. And finally, considering the ethical implications of all financial decisions is imperative for cost-conscious nursing practice.

- U.S. health indicators suggest that as a nation we are not getting a high value return on our healthcare dollar.
  - Infant mortality and births to teenager rates are two critical examples.
- Total healthcare costs are a function of price and utilization of services.
  - Most use of service is physician driven because the system is not consumer driven.
  - High-tech specialties also drive up costs.
- The government and insurance companies are the major payers for healthcare services. Individuals are the third major payer.
  - Payments may be based on cost reimbursement, flat rates, or capitated payments.
- Healthcare is moving toward managed care, organized delivery systems, and competition based on cost and quality outcomes.
- All private healthcare organizations must make a profit in order to survive.

■ Nurse and nurse managers directly impact an organization's ability to make a profit.

■ Cost conscious nursing practice requires:

* knowing costs and reimbursement practices
* capturing all possible charges in a timely fashion
* discussing the costs of care with patients
* meeting patient rather than provider needs
* evaluating cost-effectiveness of new technologies
* predicting and using nursing resources efficiently
* using research to evaluate standard nursing practices.

■ Nurse managers have the most impact on costs in relation to managing personnel and supplies and decreasing patient LOS.

■ Variance analysis is the major control process in relation to budgeting.

TERMS TO KNOW

* budget
* budgeting process
* capital expenditure budget
* capitation
* case mix
* cash budget
* charges
* contractual allowance
* cost
* cost-based reimbursement
* cost center
* fixed costs
* full time equivalent
* managed care
* nonproductive hours
* operating budget
* organized delivery system
* payer mix
* payers
* price
* productive hours
* profit
* prospective reimbursement
* providers
* revenue
* unit of service
* variable costs
* variance
* variance analysis

REFERENCES

Burner, S., Waldo, D., & McKusick, D. (1992). *Health Care Financing Review, 14*(1), 1–29.

Cleland, V. (1990). *The Economics of Nursing.* Norwalk, CT: Appleton & Lange.

Consumers Union (1992, July). Wasted health care dollars: Part 1. *Consumer Reports,* pp. 435–448.

Finkler, S., & Kovner, C. (1993). *Financial Management for Nurse Managers and Executives.* Philadelphia: J.B. Saunders.

Goode, C., Titler, M., Rakel, B., Ones, D., Kleibner, C., Small, S., & Triolo, P. (1991). A meta-analysis of heparin flush and saline flush: Quality and cost implications. *Nursing Research, 40*(6), 324–330.

Grace, H. (1990). Can health care costs be contained? In McCloskey, J., & Grace, H., eds. *Current Issues in Nursing.* St. Louis: Mosby, pp. 380–386.

Neuman, B., Suver, J., & Zelman, W. (1988). *Financial Management: Concepts and Applications for Health Care Providers,* 2nd ed. Ownings Mills, MD: National Health Publishing.

SUGGESTED READINGS

Baker, M. (1992). Cost-effective management of the hospital-based hospice program. *Journal of Nursing Administration, 22*(1), 40–45.

Corley, M., & Satterwhite, B. (1993). Forecasting ambulatory clinic workload to facilitate budgeting. *Nursing Economics, 11*(2), 77–81, 114.

Eubanks, P. (1992, April 20). The new nurse manager: A linchpin in quality care and cost control. *Hospitals,* 22–29.

Finkler, S. (1992). *Budgeting Concepts for Nurse Managers,* 2nd ed. Philadelphia: W.B. Saunders.

Moss, M., & Shelver, S. (1993). Practical budgeting for the operating room administrator. *Nursing Economics, 11*(1), 7–13.

Pelfry, S. (1991). Financial techniques for evaluating equipment acquisitions. *Journal of Nursing Administration, 21*(3), 15–20.

PART FOUR

LEADING AND MANAGING PEOPLE

CHAPTER 14

TEAM BUILDING

Karren Kowalski, R.N., Ph.D., F.A.A.N.

PREVIEW

This chapter explains major concepts and presents tools with which to create and maintain a smoothly functioning team. Many areas of our lives require that we work together in a smooth and efficient manner; not the least of these is the team in the work setting. Such teams often include members with a variety of backgrounds and educational preparation. A healthcare team often includes physicians, nurses, administrators, allied health professionals, and support staff such as housekeeping and dietary. Each team member has something valuable to contribute and deserves to be treated honorably and with respect. When teams are not working, all team members must change how they interact within the team.

OBJECTIVES

- Distinguish between a group and a team.
- Identify four key concepts of teams.
- Discuss the three personal questions each team member struggles to answer.
- Apply the guidelines for acknowledgment to a situation in your clinical setting.
- Compare a setting that uses the rules of the game with your current clinical setting.
- Develop an example of a team that functions synergistically, including the results such a team would produce.

QUESTIONS TO CONSIDER

- What differentiates a team from a group?
- How does one create a team?
- What are key aspects of a well-functioning team?
- What are the key issues or questions team members want to know?
- What role do agreements or guidelines play in a well-functioning team?
- How do some teams function like well-oiled machines and achieve extraordinary results?
- What are the behaviors and attitudes that destroy teams?
- Do teams go through stages of development?

A Manager's Viewpoint

Working as a team is crucial in getting the work of the unit completed. In the neonatal intensive care unit, the medical staff and nursing staff are thrown together and expected to function smoothly and effectively. Often they are told they are a team even though they may have no understanding or preparation to function as a team. Consequently, they proceed to display several ineffective team behaviors. It's important to reinforce active participation at each meeting and to remove judgments and personal dislikes of other team members. If team members validate ineffective or destruction behavior, it guarantees future ineffectiveness in the team. There needs to be agreement among team members that each must focus on the agreed-upon outcomes and support a positive, supportive process that enables achieving the outcomes. Such team behaviors are the key to keeping the true team spirit vital and alive. This approach creates the work environment that people want.

Diane Gallagher, R.N., M.S.
Unit Leader, Neonatal ICU
Women's and Children's Hospital
Rush-Presbyterian-St. Luke's Medical Center
Chicago, Illinois

INTRODUCTION

As we experience changes such as cost cutting and downsizing within healthcare, teamwork becomes an important concept. The old adage "If we do not all hang together we will all hang separately" was never more true than now as we move through the rapidly changing times in healthcare and into the twenty-first century. In our society, where so much emphasis is placed on the individual and individual achievement, teamwork is the quintessential contradiction. In other words, with all the focus on individuals we still need individuals to work together in groups to accomplish goals. Everybody knows and understands this, particularly the rugged individuals who spend their Sundays watching football or basketball. These team sports are premier models of co-operation and competition. They are the model of **team** for business today and they represent a group of persons with their respective leader or "coach."

GROUPS AND TEAMS

group   The dictionary definition of **group** is a number of individuals assembled together or having some unifying relationship. Groups could be all the parents in an elementary school, all the members of a specific church, or all the students in a school of nursing because the members of these various groups are related in some way to one another by definition of their involvement in a certain endeavor. A team, on the other hand, is a number of persons associated together in specific work or activity. But not every group is a team and not every team is effective.

Parker (1990) says a group of people is not a team. From his perspective, a team is a group of people with a high degree of interdependence geared toward the achievement of a goal or a task. Often times we can recognize intuitively when the so-called team is not functioning effectively. We say things like, "We need to be more like a team" or "I'd like to see more team players

team   around here." Consequently, in the process of defining *team,* it is important to consider effective versus ineffective teams. Teams are groups that have defined goals, objectives, and ongoing relationships and are focused on accomplishing a task. Teams are essential in providing cost-effective high-quality healthcare. As resources are expended more prudently, patient care teams must develop clearly defined goals, use creative problem solving, and demonstrate mutual respect and support. Facilities with ineffective teams will find themselves out of business.

When a team functions effectively, there is a significant difference in the entire work atmosphere, the way in which discussions progress, the level of understanding of the team-specific goals and tasks, the willingness of members to listen, the manner in which disagreements are handled, the use of consensus, and the way in which feedback is given and received. The original work done by McGregor (1990) sheds light on some of these significant differences, which are summarized in Table 14-1.

In general, ineffective teams are often dominated by a few members, leaving others bored, resentful, or uninvolved. Leadership tends to be autocratic and rigid, and the team's communication style may be overly stiff and formal. Members tend to be uncomfortable with conflict or disagreement, avoiding and suppressing it rather than utilizing it as a catalyst for change. When criticism is offered, it may be destructive, personal, and hurtful rather than

TABLE 14-1 Attributes of Effective and Ineffective Teams

ATTRIBUTE	EFFECTIVE TEAM	INEFFECTIVE TEAM
Working environment	• Informal, comfortable, relaxed	• Indifferent, bored; tense, stiff
Discussion	• Focused • Shared by almost everyone	• Frequently unfocused • Dominated by a few
Objectives	• Well understood and accepted	• Unclear, or many personal agendas
Listening	• Respectful—encourages participation	• Judgmental—much interruption and "grandstanding"
Ability to handle conflict	• Comfortable with disagreement • Open discussion of conflicts	• Uncomfortable with disagreement • Disagreement usually suppressed, or one group aggressively dominates
Decision making	• Usually reached by consensus • Formal voting kept to a minimum • General agreement is necessary for action; dissenters are free to voice opinions	• Often occurs prematurely • Formal voting occurs frequently • Simple majority is sufficient for action; minority is expected to go along
Criticism	• Frequent, frank, relatively comfortable, constructive • Directed toward removing obstacles	• Embarrassing and tension-producing; destructive • Directed personally at others
Leadership	• Shared; shifts from time to time	• Autocratic; remains clearly with committee chairperson
Assignments	• Clearly stated • Accepted by all despite disagreements	• Unclear • Resented by dissenting members
Feelings	• Freely expressed, open for discussion	• Hidden, considered "explosive" and inappropriate for discussion
Self-regulation	• Frequent and ongoing, focused on solutions	• Infrequent, or occurs outside meetings

Adapted from McGregor, D.M. (1960). The Human Side of Enterprise. New York: McGraw-Hill.

constructive and problem-centered. Team members may begin to "stuff" their feelings of resentment or disagreement, sensing that they are "dangerous." This creates the potential for later eruptions and discord. Similarly, the team avoids examining its own inner workings, or members may wait until after

EXERCISE 14-1

Think of the last team or group of which you were a part. Think about what went on in that team or group. Specifically think about what worked for you and what didn't work. Use the "Team Assessment Questionnaire" in the accompanying box to evaluate more specifically those things that worked or did not work for you on the team in which you participated. When you have finished answering the twenty-two questions, use the scoring mechanism at the bottom to discover how well your team or group functioned in terms of roles, activities, relationships, and general environment.

Team Assessment Questionnaire

Circle the appropriate number using the scale below.
(1 = not at all; 2 = limited extent; 3 = some extent; 4 = considerable extent)

1. People are clear about goals for the group.   1 2 3 4
2. Unnecessary procedures, policies, and formality are minimized.   1 2 3 4
3. Team members feel free to develop and experiment with new ideas and approaches.   1 2 3 4
4. The allocation of rewards is perceived to be based on excellent performance.   1 2 3 4
5. Recognition and praise outweigh threats and criticism.   1 2 3 4
6. Calculated risk taking is encouraged.   1 2 3 4
7. People are clear about their responsibilities and expectations for performance.   1 2 3 4
8. People are clear about how their roles/responsibilities interrelate with those of others.   1 2 3 4
9. People perceive others in the work group to be high performers.   1 2 3 4
10. People are clear about what personal characteristics/competencies are necessary for superior performance in their jobs.   1 2 3 4
11. The team produces high-quality decisions, products, services.   1 2 3 4
12. The team is able to conduct effective meetings.   1 2 3 4
13. The team achieves its goals.   1 2 3 4
14. The team and its individual members are able to interact effectively with others outside the team.   1 2 3 4
15. The team makes decisions and produces output in a timely fashion.   1 2 3 4
16. The team members truly support each other in carrying out their respective responsibilities. 1 2 3 4
17. Team members are open in their communications with each other.   1 2 3 4
18. Team members follow through on commitments.   1 2 3 4
19. Team members trust each other.   1 2 3 4
20. All team members are equal contributors to the team process.   1 2 3 4
21. The group often evaluates how effectively it is functioning.   1 2 3 4
22. Individual members feel committed to the team.   1 2 3 4

If you'd like to score your team assessment questionnaire, enter the score you selected for each question on p. 279. Next, take the scores for each area, then calculate the average score.

Team Assessment Questionnaire—cont'd

ROLES Item/Score	ACTIVITIES Item/Score	RELATIONSHIPS Item/Score	ENVIRONMENT Item/Score
7 _____	2 _____	5 _____	1 _____
8 _____	3 _____	14 _____	2 _____
9 _____	11 _____	16 _____	3 _____
10 _____	12 _____	17 _____	4 _____
18 _____	13 _____	19 _____	5 _____
20 _____	15 _____	22 _____	6 _____
21 _____			
Total Score _____	Total Score _____	Total Score _____	Total Score _____
Average Score = _____	Average Score = _____	Average Score = _____	Average Score = _____
(Total Score ÷ by 7)	(Total Score ÷ by 6)	(Total Score ÷ by 6)	(Total Score ÷ by 6)

If the average for a column (e.g., Activities) was 3.5 it means the group is fairly productive in its activity, falling halfway between "some extent" and "considerable extent." If the average for the relationships column was 1.5 it would indicate the respondent believes that team members have not been effective in developing relationships with one another that are clearly defined, effective, or respectful of one another.

Used with permission from Dubnicki, C. (1991). Building high-performance management teams. Healthcare Forum Journal, May-June, 34, 19-24.

meetings to voice their thoughts and feelings about what went wrong and why.

In contrast, the effective team is characterized by its clarity of purpose, informality and congeniality, commitment, and high level of participation. The members' ability to listen respectfully to each other and communicate openly helps them handle disagreements in a civilized manner and work through them rather than suppress them. Through ample discussion of issues, they reach decisions by consensus. Roles and work assignments are clear, but members share the leadership role, recognizing that each person brings his or her own unique strengths to the group effort. This diversity of styles helps the team adapt to changes and challenges, as does the team's ability and willingness to assess its own strengths and weaknesses and respond to them appropriately.

KEY CONCEPTS OF TEAMS

In very rare instances, a team may produce teamwork spontaneously, like kids in a school yard at recess. However, most management teams learn about teamwork because they need and want to work together. This kind of working together requires that they observe how they are together in a group and that they unlearn ingrained self-limiting assumptions about the glory of individual effort and authority that are contrary to cooperation and teamwork. Keys to the concept of team are

- communication
- singleness of mission
- willingness to cooperate
- commitment.

COMMUNICATION

The word *team* is most frequently reserved for a very special type of working together. This working together requires communication in which the members understand how to conduct interpersonal relationships with their peers in thoughtful, supportive, and meaningful ways. It requires that team members be able to resolve conflicts among themselves and do so in ways that enhance rather than inhibit their working together. In addition, team members must be able to trust that they will receive what they need while being able to count on one another to complete tasks related to team functioning and outcomes. To communicate effectively, people must be willing to confront issues *openness* and to openly express their ideas and feelings—to use interactive skills to accomplish tasks. In nursing, constructive confrontation has not been a well-used skill. Consequently, if communication patterns are to improve, the onus is on each of us as individuals to change communication patterns. In essence, for things to change, each of us must change.

MISSION

Each and every team must have a purpose—that is a plan, aim, or intention. However, the most successful teams have a **mission**—some special work or service to which the team is 100 percent committed. The sense of mission and purpose must be clearly understood by all and agreed to by all. The more powerful and visionary the mission is, the more enrolling it will be to the team. The more energy and excitement engendered, the more motivated all members will be to do the necessary work.

WILLINGNESS TO COOPERATE

organizational structure vs. team

Just because a group of people has a regular reporting relationship within an organizational chart does not mean the members are a team. Boxes and arrows are not in anyway related to the technical and interpersonal coordination, nor the emotional investment that is required of a true team. Most of us have been involved in organizations where people could accomplish assigned tasks but were not successful in their interpersonal relationships. In essence, these employees received a salary for not getting along with a certain person or persons. Some of these employees haven't worked cooperatively for years! Organizations can no longer afford to pay people to not work together. Personal friendship or socialization is not required. Cooperation is a necessity.

COMMITMENT

commitment

Commitment is a state of being emotionally impelled and is demonstrated when there is a sense of passion and dedication to a project or event—a mission. Frequently this passion looks a little crazy. In other words, people go the extra mile because of their commitment. They do whatever it takes to accomplish the goals or see the project through to completion. An example of commitment is discussed by Charles Garfield when he talks about being a part of the team that created the lunar landing module for the first man to walk on the moon. People did all kinds of things that looked crazy, including working extended hours and shifts, calling in to see how the project was progressing, sleeping over at their workstation so as not to be separated from the project—and all because each and every individual knew they were a part of something that was much bigger than themselves. They were a part of sending a man to the moon, something that human beings had been dreaming about for thousands of years. In other words, it was a historical moment and people were intensely committed to making it happen.

Many people go through their entire lives hating every single day of work. Needless to say, most of them are not committed. Since we spend an extensive amount of time in the work setting, it is critically important to both physical and mental well-being that people enjoy what they do. If this is not the case for you, then try to find a different job or profession—one you might love. Life is too short to do something that you hate doing every single day. While you are moving into whatever you decide you love doing, commit to yourself to do your best at whatever you are now doing. Be 100 percent present wherever you are. Do the best work you are capable of doing. This honors you as a human being and it honors your co-workers and patients.

EXERCISE 14-2
The box entitled "Exploring Commitment" contains eight questions. In a quiet place, spend at least twenty minutes thinking about and writing answers to these eight questions. Pay particular notice to question 7.

Exploring Commitment

The key to finding your compelling mission/passion that will lead you to success and peak performance is to ask yourself the right questions. Your answers to these questions will tell you what you need to know about yourself. Read each question, then stop and think for a few minutes and answer each question honestly. Don't censor or edit out anything even if it seems impossible or unrealistic—allow yourself to be surprised. Let your imagination soar.

1. Am I deriving any satisfaction out of the work I am now doing?
2. If they didn't reward (praise or pay) me to do what I now do, would I still do it?
3. What is it that I really love to do?
4. What do I want to pursue with my time and energy that is worthwhile?
5. What motivates me to reach out and do my very best, to excel?
6. What is it that only I can say to the world? What needs to be done that can best be done only by me?
7. If I won $10,000,000 in the lottery tomorrow, how would I live? What would I do each day and for the rest of my life?
8. If I were to write my own obituary right now, what would be my most significant accomplishment? Is that enough?

Repeating this exercise often will give you additional insights and information about what you really want and love to do. If taken seriously, the exercise should help you to have an understanding of why you selected this profession and whether or not you have the stamina to do whatever it takes to make a contribution and to make a difference in the practice of nursing.

There are many examples of commitment, such as that of Jan Skaggs, the Vietnam veteran who was the driving force behind the building of the Vietnam War Memorial. He was a clerk in the Washington, D.C. bureaucracy who attended a veterans' meeting and decided there needed to be a memorial to those who lost their lives in Vietnam, a memorial that had all 58,000 names inscribed. He had a high school diploma and didn't even own a suit, but five years and seven million dollars later the wall was dedicated (Lopes, 1987). This is a demonstration that one does not have to have a college degree in order to be committed. Sometimes a college degree can inhibit people from accomplishing their goals, because they become diverted from a purpose, a mission, or from life goals by things like good grades and a high IQ. Rather than understanding grades and IQ as tools of measurement, they see them as an end in themselves.

It is possible to teach almost anyone the technical aspects of what needs to be done in most patient care settings. It is far more difficult to teach people to love what they do or to care about patients and their families—even the most difficult and unique patients and families.

TOOLS AND ISSUES THAT SUPPORT TEAMS

key questions

When individuals come together in a group, they spend a fair amount of their time in group process or social dynamics, which allows the group to advance toward becoming a team and getting a goal accomplished. Each person within the group struggles with three key questions that must continually be reevaluated and renegotiated. These three questions according to Weisburg (1988) are

1. Am I in or out?
2. Do I have any power or control?
3. Can I use, develop, and be appreciated for my skills and resources?

This chapter's "Literature Perspective" focuses on Weisburg's work.

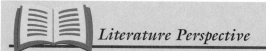 *Literature Perspective*

Weisburg, M.R. (1988). Team work: Building productive relationships. In Reddy, W.B., & Jamison, K. (eds.) Team Building: Blueprints for Productivity and Satisfaction. Alexandria, Va: NTL Institute for Applied Behavioral Sciences; San Diego, CA: University Associates, pp. 62–71.

Building productive relationships in the workplace is critical to team success. Increasing productivity requires observing team members at work and unlearning deeply ingrained, self-limiting assumptions about individual effort and authority that work against cooperation. In some respects this is an ongoing process of renewal that cannot occur without some disarray and confusion.

Implications for Practice

Every team member must deal with three key issues: (1) Am I in or out? (2) Do I have any power and control? (3) Can I use, develop, and be appreciated for my skills and resources? These issues must be addressed periodically if trust, motivation, and commitment are to be maintained in the team. Differences of opinion must be expressed constructively with honor and respect for each other.

"IN" GROUPS AND "OUT" GROUPS

Most of us want to be valued and recognized by others as a part of the group, one who "knows" or understands. Most people want to be at the core of decision making power and influence. In other words they want to be part of the "in" group, and researchers have demonstrated that those who feel "in" cooperate more, work harder and more effectively, and bring enthusiasm to the group. The more we feel not a part of the key group, the more "out" we feel, the more we withdraw, work alone, daydream, and engage in self-defeating behaviors. Often intergroup conflict results when individuals who feel they are "out" and want to be "in" create a schism or a division that prohibits the team from accomplishing its goals.

POWER AND CONTROL

Everybody wants at least some power and everybody wants to feel they are in control. When faced with changes that we are unable to influence, we feel impotent and experience a loss of self-esteem. Consequently, all of us want to feel we are in control of our immediate environment and that we have enough power and influence to get our needs met. When a situation or an event arises that we are unable to handle, we attempt to compensate for it in some way; most of these ways are not productive to smoothly functioning teams.

APPRECIATION FOR INDIVIDUAL SKILLS

It is important for all to feel as though their skills and tools and contributions are needed and valued and that they are respected for what they have to offer to the workplace/team/group. Everyone has weaknesses and there is no need to emphasize these or to spend time in ongoing correction. Rather, focus on people's strengths; acknowledge and emphasize what people do well.

contributions

Part of focusing on people's strengths is being willing to acknowledge peers, faculty, and the other significant people in one's life. In contrast, many of our role models focus on correction. Consequently, many of us spend a large portion of our time correcting others rather than appreciating people for all the wonderful things they are. It is almost as though we believe there is a finite number of available acknowledgments and we must not give out too many of them as they must be held in reserve for very important events. In addition, we do not always give acknowledgments in a way they can be received and valued. The accompanying box, page 284, can serve as a guide for giving **acknowledgment.**

To deal with the three personal issues discussed in this section, it is critically important that team members learn how to state openly what is on their minds and that they be responsive and respectful as other members of the team do the same. In other words, give and receive feedback constructively. There are essential elements that must be in place in order for people to be able to give and receive feedback in constructive ways.

GROUP AGREEMENTS

One of the most helpful tools available is to have the team come to an agreement about the ground rules concerning how they will be in relationship to one another. There are various ways that this can take place. There are even multiple kinds of guidelines or rules that can be used to set the context for how people will be. One example of a set of guidelines can be found in the box

ground rules

EXERCISE 14-3

Think about a time when you or a small group of your classmates wanted to change a class, an assignment, or the grading curve or a test. The faculty or the school administration adamantly refused. How did you feel? What was the response? Did you engage in gossip and making the faculty or the administration wrong? You may have been "right" but the sense of a loss of control or power is very uncomfortable, sometimes fear producing. Very mature behavior is required in order to maintain a positive, problem solving approach.

EXERCISE 14-4
Within the next 3 days find three opportunities to acknowledge a peer or acquaintance using the five "Guidelines for Acknowledgment" shown in the adjacent box. In addition, do at least one self-acknowledgment using the guidelines.

Guidelines for Acknowledgment

1. Acknowledgments must be specific. The specific behavior or action that is appreciated must be identified in the acknowledgment. For example, "Thank you for taking notes for me when I had to go to the dentist. You identified three key points that appeared on the test."
2. Acknowledgments must be "eye to eye" or personal. Look the person in the eye when you thank them. Do not run down the hall and say "Thanks" over your shoulder. Written appreciation also qualifies as "eye to eye."
3. Acknowledgments must be sincere, from the heart. Each of us recognizes insincerity. If you do not truly appreciate a behavior or action do not say anything. Insincerity often makes people angry or upset, thus defeating the goal.
4. Acknowledgments are more powerful when they are given in public. Most people receive pleasure from public acknowledgment and remember these occasions for a long time. For people who are shy and believe they would prefer no public acknowledgment, there is an opportunity to work on a personal growth issue with them. Public acknowledgment is an opportunity to communicate what is valued.
5. Acknowledgments need to be timely. The less time that elapses between the event and the acknowledgment, the more powerful and effective it is and the more the acknowledgment is appreciated by the recipient.

rules

on page 285. These are called "The Rules of the Game." They have gone through multiple transitions and redesign, but the basic tenets are pretty much the same. People have to agree on the goals and mission in which they are involved. In addition, they have to reach some understanding of how they will be together. Such tenets or rules as "We will speak supportively" go a long way to avoid gossip, backbiting, bickering, and misinterpreting other people. As you review these group agreements, keep in mind that a part of this process is the willingness of members of the team to be accountable for upholding the agreements and to give feedback when the agreements have been violated. When there are no rules people have implicit permission to behave in any manner they choose toward one another including angry, hurtful acting-out behavior.

TRUST

Trust is also a major issue within a group, and one of the first questions to come up in the group is who can one trust or not trust. In the early days of organizational development, McGregor (1967) defined trust in the following way:

trust

Trust means: "I know that you will not—deliberately or accidently, consciously or unconsciously—take unfair advantage of me." It means, "I can put my situation at the moment, my status and self esteem in this group, our relationship, my job, my career, even my life, in your hands with complete confidence." (p. 163)

One can see from this description how critical trust is within a team. It is also important to remember that trust is probably the most delicate aspect within relationships and is influenced far more by actions than by words. In

"Rules of the Game" for Women's and Children's Hospital, Rush-Presbyterian–St. Luke's Medical Center

These "Rules of the Game" were adapted from a San Francisco real estate broker who was the founder and president of Hawthorn-Stone. Dr. Karren Kowalski proposes that we use them, not only among ourselves, but with each new person who joins the organization, asking if we/they are willing and able to do the very best we/they can to support the rules.

1. BE WILLING TO SUPPORT RUSH'S PURPOSE, GAMES, RULES, AND GOALS
   By first asking if people will support the rules, we have their agreement that they can be held accountable for times when they violate the "rules of the game."
2. SPEAK SUPPORTIVELY
   This means no swearing; if it doesn't serve, don't say it; if it doesn't support, don't say it; don't make other people wrong; you may choose *not* to say negative things. Language either empowers or limits people in terms of achieving their potential. How we speak about a colleague, the institution, our job, the workplace, etc., does make a difference.
3. CORRECT SUPPORTIVELY
   Dr. Kowalski says, "Make corrections *without* invalidation or correct without crucifixion."
4. ACKNOWLEDGE THAT WHATEVER IS BEING COMMUNICATED IS TRUE FOR THE SPEAKER AT THAT MOMENT
   Most of the time people make comments because they truly believe them. Therefore, it is important not to judge what is being said and misinterpret it, but to listen so that we can understand what is being said. Emphasis is on active listening.
5. COMPLETE YOUR AGREEMENT
   Only make agreements that you intend to and are willing to keep. This is especially important for those who (a) procrastinate and (b) say "yes" to everything. If one must break an agreement, communicate this information ASAP.
6. IF A PROBLEM ARISES, FIRST USE THE SYSTEM FOR CORRECTIONS, THEN COMMUNICATE THE PROBLEM WITH OPTIONAL SOLUTIONS TO THE PERSON WHO CAN DO SOMETHING ABOUT THE PROBLEM
   This is another way to eliminate gossip, judgment, and self-righteousness.
7. BE EFFECTIVE AND EFFICIENT
8. OPTIMIZE EVERY EVENT—CREATE MORE WITH LESS
   Items 7 and 8 go together. Look for value in every event. Focus on what *can* be learned or done; use "lateral thinking" to create effective options.
9. HAVE THE WILLINGNESS TO WIN AND TO ALLOW OTHERS TO WIN
   "Win/lose" is a "zero sum game." Effective problem solving allows everyone to win—to get their needs met.
10. FOCUS ON WHAT WORKS
    The converse is, get beyond what's not working. Be willing to try something new. When it's broke, fix it!
11. WHEN IN DOUBT, CHECK OUT FEELINGS
    When there seem to be blocks to communication or progress, it is often related to how people are feeling. Check this out, ask the person/people in question. Get the feelings out in the open where they can be checked out, tested, responded to.
12. AGREE TO DISAGREE UNTIL REACHING CONSENSUS
    Commit to working together toward mutually agreeable solutions. This keeps things in a forward motion without judgment. It keeps things hopeful.
13. TELL THE TRUTH FROM THE POINT OF VIEW OF PERSONAL RESPONSIBILITY
    Always begin with the assumption that you are willing to assume 50 percent of the responsibility. This eliminates "you, you, you" messages and allows you to work with others toward a solution, not toward blame.

Adapted from Thurber, M., Hawthorne-Stone Real Estate, San Francisco, CA.

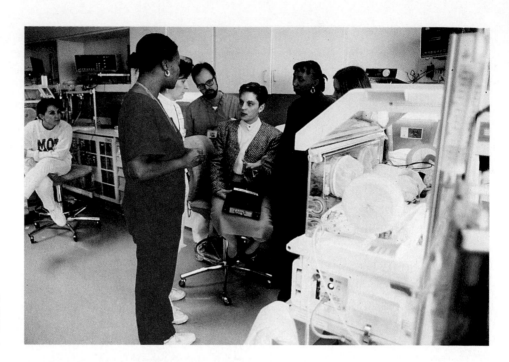

Working cooperatively, an effective team produces extraordinary results that no one team member could have achieved alone.

others words what people do is more powerful than what they say. Trust is a fragile thread that can be severed by one "act" and once destroyed, it is more difficult to reestablish than its initial creation of trust. What you do is more powerful than what you say.

CREATING SYNERGY

synergy

Teams function with varying levels of effectiveness. The interesting part of this is that effectiveness can be systematically created. Truly effective teams are ones in which people work together to produce extraordinary results that could not have been achieved by any one individual. This phenomenon is often described as **synergy.** In the physical sciences, synergy is found in metal alloys. Bronze, the first alloy, was a combination of copper and tin and was found to be much harder and stronger than either copper or tin separately. Neither could the tensile strength of bronze be predicted by merely adding the tensile strength of tin and of copper.

We see the same properties of synergy in human endeavors, for example, in the 1980 United States hockey team. Many people can remember this hockey game, in which the United States defeated the Russians. The team consisted of a bunch of kids, none of whom could establish a successful career in the National Hockey League. However, for two weeks they were the best hockey team in the world. That was because they knew how to work together to produce extraordinary results.

To consistently create synergy, one must follow some basic rules:
• Listen actively
• Be compassionate
• Tell the truth
• Be flexible
• Commit to resolution.

LISTEN ACTIVELY

Listening actively means that one is completely focused and tuned in to the individual who is speaking. It means listening without judgment. It means listening to the essence of the conversation so that you can actually repeat back to the speaker most of the speaker's intended meaning. It means being 100 percent present in the communication. It does *not* mean developing a defensive response or argument in your head while the other person is still speaking. To listen actively, a person needs to be absolutely focused on the speaker, absorbing words, posture, tone of voice, and all the clues accompanying the message, so that the intent of the communication can be received. Specific principles used in **active listening,** including examples, are found in Table 14-2.

focus

BE COMPASSIONATE

To be compassionate means to have a sympathetic consciousness of another's distress and a desire to alleviate the distress. Consequently it is inappropriate to focus time and energy on making the other person wrong, especially when your perspective differs from his or hers. It means listening from a caring perspective—one that is focused on understanding the viewpoint of the other person rather than insisting on the "rightness" of one's own point of view.

compassion

TELL THE TRUTH

To tell the truth means to speak clearly to personal points and perspectives while acknowledging that they are, merely, a personal perspective. If an observation is made about the tone or behavior of the other person that has an impact on the reception of the message, feedback can be provided in a way that does not make the speaker wrong. This is accomplished in an objective rather than subjective manner using neither a cynical nor critical tone of voice. To be effective, it is important to own—be responsible for—personal opinions and attitudes.

BE FLEXIBLE

Flexibility and openness to another person's viewpoint is critical for a team to work together well. No single person has all the right answers. It is, therefore, important to acknowledge that each person has something to contribute and needs to be heard. Flexibility reflects a willingness to hear another team member's point of view.

cooperation

COMMIT TO RESOLUTION

To commit to resolution means that one can agree to disagree with someone even when that perspective is different. Do not make the person wrong. Rather, hear his/her perspective, listen to the real message, identify differences, and creatively seek solutions to resolve the areas of differences so that there can be a common understanding and shared commitment to the issue. Both parties need to then agree that they feel heard and agree to the resolution. This differs greatly from compromise and majority vote as seen in the democratic process. When compromise exists, there is acquiescence or relinquishing of a significant portion of what was desired. This generally leaves both parties feeling negative about themselves or the agreement. Consequently, most compromises have to be reworked at some future date.

commonalities

TABLE 14-2	Active Listening

USE OF ACTIVE LISTENING	EXAMPLES
To convey interest in what the other person is saying	I see! I get it. I hear what you're saying.
To encourage the individual to expand further on his or her thinking	Yes, go on. Tell us more.
To help the individual clarify the problem in his or her own thinking	Then the problem as you see it is . . .
To get the individual to hear what he or she has said in the way it sounded to others	This is your decision, then, and the reasons are . . . If I understand you correctly, you are saying that we should . . .
To pull out the key ideas from a long statement or discussion	Your major point is . . . You feel that we should . . .
To respond to a person's feelings more than to his or her words	You feel strongly that . . . You do not believe that . . .
To summarize specific points of agreement and disagreement as a basis for further discussion	We seem to be agreed on the following points . . . But we seem to need further clarification on these points . . .
To express a consensus of group feeling	As a result of this discussion, we as a group seem to feel that . . .

Working on conflict and its resolution (Table 14-3) is time-consuming yet essential to effectively functioning teams.

Synergy cannot occur when one team member becomes a self-proclaimed expert who has the "right" answer. Synergy also cannot occur when people refuse to speak. Each team member has good ideas. These need to be shared. They are not shared, however, when someone feels uncomfortable in the team. It is a stretch to speak up and appear wrong or inadequate. The challenge each person faces is to push through discomfort levels and become a full participant in problem identification and resolution for the overall benefit of the team.

dualism   Our society tends to be dualistic in nature. **Dualism** means that most situations are viewed as right or wrong, black or white. Answers to questions are often reduced to yes or no. As a result, we sometimes forget there is a broad spectrum of possibilities. It is important to exercise creativity and explore numerous possibilities. This will allow the team to operate at its optimum level.

We have all known people who were self-proclaimed experts, to whom it was critically important that they be right and acknowledged as right, who become judgmental of others whose perspective and opinions differ from theirs. Consequently, it is important when creating a synergistic team to be able to tell the truth to these individuals and to encourage them to stretch and look at different ways of functioning. This requires good negotiation skills and conflict resolution skills, something for which few of us have been trained. If self-proclaimed experts think we are judging them, they will not hear the questions, the observations, the "truth," because the message is delivered by making them wrong rather than originating from compassion. The most valuable contribution an individual can make to an organization is a passionate commitment to the creation of synergistic teams.

THE VALUE OF TEAM BUILDING

The value of team building is to enhance functioning in any one or all of the processes identified by Dyer (1987):
- the setting of goals or priorities
- the allocation of the way work is performed
- the manner in which a group works: its processes, norms, decision making, and communications
- the relationships among the people doing the work.

When things are not going well in an organization and there are problems that need to be resolved, the first intervention people think of is "team building." Naturally, for teams (a collection of people relying upon each other) to be effective, they must function smoothly. The difficulty is that when organizations are feeling stress and facing difficulties, they generally do not have teams whose members function well together. Team building can address any one of the activities identified above, depending on the available

TABLE 14-3   Aspects of Conflict

DESTRUCTIVE	CONSTRUCTIVE
Diverts energy from more important activities and issues	Opens up issues of importance, resulting in their clarification
Destroys the morale of people or reinforces poor self-concepts	Results in the solution of problems
Polarizes groups so they increase internal cohesiveness and reduce intergroup cooperation	Increases the involvement of individuals in issues of importance to them
Deepens differences in values	Causes authentic communication to occur
Produces irresponsible and regrettable behavior such as name-calling and fighting	Serves as a release for pent-up emotion, anxiety, and stress Helps build cohesiveness among people sharing the conflict, celebrating in its settlement, and learning more about each other Helps individuals grow personally and apply what they learn to future situations

Source: Adapted from Hart, 1980, p. 6.

time and other resources. A team-building consultant can teach a team how to set goals and priorities; help a team analyze the distribution of the work load utilizing various team members' strengths; examine a team's process, norms, decision making, and communication patterns; and promote resolution of interpersonal conflicts or problems within the team.

team assessment   Regardless of which areas are problematic, appropriate assessment of the team is essential. The problems may be in priority or goal setting, allocation of the work, team decision making, or interpersonal relationships among the members. The success of the team depends on its members and its leadership.

Team building has grown out of an area of social psychology that focused on group dynamics. In the late 1950s and early 1960s group dynamics centered on an entity called training groups or "T" groups. As is often the case with new technology, some people did not have positive experiences with *"T" groups*   "T" groups and, as a result, such groups acquired a questionable reputation. The notoriety focused on the confrontational style and lack of sensitivity in sharing observations and information. People within the groups felt they were considered to be wrong about various behaviors, attitudes, and activities. As a result, distrust often predominated.

In examining group dynamics, Dyer (1987) found two major problems with "T" groups: (1) Much of the research was done with strangers who had no history with one another and could focus only on what was happening in the present. In contrast, work groups within corporations are not made up of strangers but rather of people who have a long history with each other. The "T" group trainers were not clear about what areas to explore and what areas to leave alone. (2) "T" groups were done with strangers who then dispersed and never met again. Consequently, there was safety in anonymity. In contrast, work units that continued intact after the sessions contained people who had to be responsible for interpersonal relationship issues raised in the "T" group meeting.

vulnerability   With all this heavy baggage about "T" groups, it is understandable that anxiety exists concerning the safety of being vulnerable and exposed if personal issues are revealed. That's why it is helpful for the team-building facilitator to make a thorough assessment of major issues and the willingness on the part of members to work on issues. Frequently, trainers or facilitators will interview members of the team individually to discover what the critical issues are. The kinds of questions that might be asked are found in the box entitled "Interview Questions for Team Building."

This kind of tool enables the leader of the team to understand what the issues are before going into the team-building exercise so that he or she is not surprised nor becomes defensive. It also gives the facilitator some sense of what the major issues are within the group so that he or she has a better understanding of how to work with the group.

MANAGING EMOTIONS

Probably one of the greatest fears in team-building exercises is that people will become emotional, that they will lose control of themselves or the environment or appear weakened or vulnerable. Men have a particularly difficult time with this fear but many women also want to appear in a good light and are hesitant to be open and vulnerable. When one is considering *whole person*   Bocialetti's (1988) maxim that "the whole person comes to work," the team and its leadership must define how this will be developed for them. Although many people acknowledge that we are all thinking and feeling persons, man-

Interview Questions for Team Building

1. What do you see as the problems currently facing your team?
2. What are the current strengths of your institution of work group? What are you currently doing well?
3. Does your boss do anything that prevents you from being as effective as you would like to be?
4. Does anybody else in this group do anything that prevents you from being as effective as you would like to be?
5. What would you like to accomplish at your upcoming team building session? What changes would you be willing to make that would facilitate a smoother-functioning team and accomplishment of the team goals?

agement/leadership is usually more willing to deal with the "thinking" side than the "feeling" side of individuals within the team.

Because people spend such a large percentage of their time in the work setting, it would be unrealistic to believe that they always and continually appear in an unemotional and controlled state. Human beings simply do not function that way. What is observed is people's aspirations, their achievements, their hopes, and their social consciousness; they are observed falling in love, falling in hate and anger, winning and losing, and being excited, sad, fearful, anxious, and jealous. Consequently, these "feelings" are important compo- *emotions* nents of organizational life and do much to undermine work effectiveness. Most of us know of situations where, due to an emotional disagreement, two individuals have avoided each other for years. Because of the power of emotions and the inevitability of their presence, their impact on interpersonal relationships, and because of their influence on productivity and the quality of work, emotions should be a high priority when examining the functioning of the team.

According to Bocialetti (1987), people are sensitive to what happens when emotions are revealed. When people yell or get angry or upset, and when goals, objectives, and tasks are disputed, employees see the following:

- a member intimidating and frightening others within the group
- embarrassment
- a member overstating or exaggerating one's view in order to appear right
- provocation of defensive and hostile responses
- overconcern with one's self—self-absorption
- gossip
- loss of control
- a member distracting others from "real work"
- disruption or termination of relationships within a group.

These are behaviors that destroy any hope of creating a smoothly functioning team, one that supports its members to grow and learn and provide quality patient care. On the other hand, the cost of suppressing emotions or *suppressing emotions* "feelings" include

- physical and psychological stress
- withdrawal from participation
- loss of energy and depression
- reduction of learning
- hiding of important data due to fear

- festering problems and emotions
- preventing others from being acknowledged
- decreasing motivation
- weakening the ability to receive constructive feedback
- the loss of one's influence.

These kinds of outcomes lead to the conclusion that suppressing emotions at work is neither healthy nor constructive for team members.

positive outcomes   When emotions are handled appropriately within the team, there are several positive outcomes that have impact on the work setting. One creates a sense of internal comfort with the workings of the team and the organization. When stress is lowered and kept at lower levels on the average, problems are much more easily resolved. It is similar to releasing steam slowly with a steam valve rather than having the gasket blow. Interpersonal relationships on the team are more stable and people have a sense of closer ties and collegiality if emotions are handled. There are fewer negative relationships or interactions, which results in more effective and pleasant working relationships all around.

Work group effectiveness improves when the team is functioning smoothly and emotions and "feelings" are being handled on a routine basis rather than waiting for a volcanic eruption. Problems of withdrawal, boredom, and frustration are much less likely to overwhelm the team and lead to its breakdown. The skills and tools previously discussed (e.g., speaking supportively) are the basic tools one needs to handle the emotional aspects of the team. Choosing to cope with emotional upset must be a conscious choice, one that requires practice to improve the skill.

THE ROLE OF LEADERSHIP

Teams usually have a leader. In addition, teams function within large organizations that have leaders. Without the approval and the support of the leader, team building, which can be a costly endeavor in terms of consultation fees as well as work time and resources of the team, is difficult to undertake and of questionable effectiveness. Although very strong teams may be able to educate themselves regarding some of the issues, such as establishing goals and priorities or clarifying their own team process, it is exceedingly difficult to address any kind of relationship issue among team members without a more objective outside party facilitating the process.

progressive leaders   Because leadership is such a pivotal part of smoothly functioning teams, it is illuminating to examine leaders more carefully. Truly progressive leaders understand that leadership and followership are not necessarily a set of skills; rather, these are qualities of character, a manifestation of a person's own being. On speaking specifically to leadership, we are not talking about "putting on a role." In actuality leaders realize more fully their capacity for influence, risk taking, and decision making. Leadership, and to some degree followership, is as much about character and development as it is about education. According to Peter Vaill (1989) leadership is concerned with bringing out the very best in people. For leaders who truly believe this, team building is a natural outgrowth of this value. This type of leader understands that the very best in a person is tied intimately to the individual's deepest sense of him- or herself, to one's spirit. The efforts of *spiritual aspect*   leaders must touch the spiritual aspect in themselves and others. Warren

Bennis (1989) once said that leaders simply care about more people. Consequently this caring manifests itself in doing whatever it takes to improve team functioning. This may imply involving oneself in team building with the team. The risk in such an endeavor is that the team leader is open to being vulnerable, to being judged by others, and to being wrong. However, if the leader has role modeled the "rules of the game" and has held people to account for these rules as well as holding him- or herself to account, the team-building exercise will not degenerate into judging and laying blame.

character development

If true leadership is about character development as much as anything then character development is also beneficial for "followers"—that is, members of the team. The areas of character development often addressed include communication, particularly those aspects of speaking supportively that avoid laying blame and justifying and enhance understanding the other person's message. The box on page 294 highlights an example of character development, which the chapter author relates from her own Vietnam experience.

control

Leaders understand the multiple aspects of the issue of control. They take control of their lives rather than being at the mercy of others—victims. They have clarity regarding their own control issues. They focus time and energy primarily and almost exclusively on those issues events and behaviors over which they have control. Their activities are thus primarily focused on areas relating directly to them—not on world events or other happenings over which they have neither influence nor control.

confidence

Confidence, which loosely translates as faith or belief that one will act in a correct and effective way, is a key aspect of character. Thus it follows that confidence in oneself can be closely tied to self-esteem, which is satisfaction with oneself. The greatest deterrent to self-esteem and self-confidence is fear. Fear is described by some as "false evidence appearing real" (see box at right). Susan Jeffers (1987) believes the core fear—the one that rules our lives—is one of "I can't handle it." So the core of our fears is "I can't handle it" and it is exactly the opposite of being confident or holding oneself in high esteem. Working on self-confidence requires and attitude of belief, of confidence, of I "CAN DO" whatever is required (see the box on page 294).

> ***F*** alse
> ***E*** vidence
> ***A*** ppearing
> ***R*** eal

caring

Simply caring about more people translates into a willingness to focus time and energy on members of the team. From one perspective caring is risking being with someone and sharing both suffering and joy. Healing oftentimes emerges from caring. Behaviors that demonstrate caring include giving of oneself in terms of warmth and love and particularly one's time. The second aspect of caring is truly listening to team members and hearing and understanding them. The third aspect includes being 100 percent present for them. The fourth is to honor the other person—to see their wholeness, their possibilities, their hope.

It becomes clear that leading the team is not the easiest thing to do. But neither is being an active, fully participating member of the team. Both require taking risks, including being in a relationship. Being in a team-building experience and hearing those things that have not worked for people about their interactions with peers as well as with the leader can be scary but worthwhile. It requires a focus on personal and professional growth. It requires building character.

The "Can Do" Brigade: An Army Nurse's Study in Character Development

As life events are reviewed, important or pivotal learning can be identified. One life event that significantly impacted me was the year I spent as an Army Nurse Corps officer in South Vietnam. This was the first time I remember an awareness and understanding of confidence in the face of incredible obstacles. I had spent the first ten months of my nursing career on labor and delivery at Indiana University before volunteering for a guaranteed assignment to Vietnam. I went to Fort Sam Houston for six weeks of basic training where they taught me really important things like how to salute, how to march, how many men in a battalion. No one ever asked me if I could start an IV or draw a tube of blood. This was important because Indiana University had the largest medical school class in the United States at that time and nurses did nothing that interfered with medical education. Therefore, I had never started an IV or drawn blood. When I arrived in Saigon, they put me in a sedan with another nurse and sent me up to the Third Surgical Hospital, one not unlike the one in *MASH*. We even had a Major Burns—that was not his name but it was his function. Surgical hospitals receive only battle casualties; their purpose is to stabilize and to transport.

The Third Surgical Hospital was located in the middle of the 173rd Airborne Brigade whose job it was to defend the Bein Hoi Air Base, where all the sorties in the south were flown during the war. We were stopped at the gate by an MP who stepped up and saluted very snappily. He knew that a staff car must contain either a very high ranking officer or, if it was his lucky day, females.

While I was in Vietnam, 500 American women and 500,000 American men were there. He looked in the window, saluted snappily and said "Afternoon, ma'am!" He wanted to know where we were going; he talked to us for a few minutes and assured us if there was anything he could do for us we should just give him a call. He saluted us and said, "CAN DO." I didn't understand because I didn't know that there are units with very high esprit de corps who attach snappy little sayings at the end of things like salutes, phone conversations, memos, and so forth.

The 173rd was the "CAN DO" brigade. When we got to the hospital and met the chief nurse, she took us down to the mess hall and introduced us to all the doctors and nurses. We were sitting and having coffee when the field phone rang in the kitchen and the mess sergeant yelled out, "Incoming wounded." Everybody got up and started to leave for the Preop area. I just sat there until the chief nurse said, "Come on." I said, "You don't understand, I deliver babies." She was not impressed! She took me by the arm and led me to Preop.

When we got there we discovered there weren't just a few incoming wounded, there were more than thirty and some were very seriously injured. She immediately told the sergeant to call headquarters battalion of the 173rd Airborne and tell them that the Third Surg needed blood. She turned to me and said, "Lieutenant, you are responsible for drawing fifty units of fresh whole blood." I was shocked! I had never drawn a tube of blood, but I found in the back section of "preop" a Specialist 4th class who was already setting up "saw horses" and stretchers, putting up IV poles, and hanging plastic blood sets. I started to help and soon I heard trucks out back. I opened the door and looked outside. There were two huge Army trucks and out of the back of these were jumping kids, 17, 18, 19, and 20 years old. They were covered with red mud from the bottom of their boots to the tops of their helmets. I looked at them and I looked at the clean cement floor and in an instant my mother came to me. I put my hand on my hip and said, "Where have you boys been?" One PFC stepped forward and saluted me very snappily and said, "Ma'am, we just came in this afternoon from thirty days in the field, we have been out in the rice paddies chasing the Viet Cong, we have not had a hot meal, and we've not had a shower but Sergeant Major said the Third Surg needs blood!" He saluted smartly and said, "CAN DO!" They were very clear. After thirty days of chasing and being chased by the Viet Cong, giving a unit of blood was easy. "CAN DO!" They were confident. They were kids who had looked into the face of death. At that moment, I knew if they CAN DO, I Can Do! Life requires confidence; with confidence, you can make your dreams come true!

EXERCISE 14-5

The "Gordian Knot": A Team-Building Game

Gordian knot is a term sometimes used to describe a problem that cannot be solved. However, teamwork can sometimes solve seemingly impossible problems, as this game will illustrate.

In a group of eight to ten people, form a tight circle with your shoulders touching and your hands placed in the center. Take the hand of two other people across the circle from you. The goal is to unwind the knot until the entire circle is holding hands side by side. You *may not* let go of hands to unwind the knot unless your instructor gives you special permission to do so!

Debriefing

After your group has unwound its knot, together choose one or two categories of questions from Part I of the "Team-Building Discussion" outline that follows. Discuss these questions, writing down your answers as you go so that you can report to the class later. Be sure to support your answers with examples from your group's experience with the game. Then, complete all questions in Part II.

PART I

LEADERSHIP AND BUILDING TEAMWORK

What did it feel like not to have a designated leader? _____

Who became the leader?_____

How? _____

Did the leadership process work? _____

How did you feel about it? _____

Who came up with new ideas? _____

Did the team support this process? _____

How were conflicts resolved and problems solved? _____

How did you build a sense of teamwork? _____

TEAM MEMBERSHIP

Did you feel a part of the team? _____

Why or why not? _____

Did your team have a good mix of skills and abilities? _____

Did you adapt to the needs of others or to the needs of the team?_____

Did you meet your objectives without wasting time and energy? _____

What role did you play as a team member? _____

TRUST AND OPENNESS

What was the team's level of trust and open communication? _____

Great Deal = 10   Much = 7   Some = 5   Little = 3   None = 0

What contributed to this level of trust? _____

Did you deal with issues candidly and honestly? _____

What was your level of trust? _____

What would have increased the team's level of trust and openness? _____

CONTRIBUTION TO THE TEAM-DEVELOPING RELATIONSHIPS

Did you all know and agree to the mission of the team? _____

How were decisions made?_____

Who participated in making them? _____

When did you need to make decisions? _____

Were they primarily about what to do (tasks) or how to do it (process)?_____

Did you use each other as resources?_____

Did you work well together?_____

How did your relationships develop and strengthen?_____

How do you feel about each other now? _____

CULTIVATING A FEELING OF SATISFACTION ABOUT YOUR TEAM

Do you feel proud of your team? _____

How do/did you feel rewarded by being a member of this team? _____

Did you have fun? _____

EXERCISE 14-5—cont'd

Did the challenge cease to be fun?_____

How did the team handle this?_____

Are you satisfied with your results?_____

DEVELOPING THE TEAM THROUGH RISK TAKING _____

Did you, individually or as a team, try out any new or uncomfortable communications or behavior? Give examples.

_____

Did that feel safe?_____

Did you support each other in your risk taking? _____

PART II

EVALUATE AND SHARE WITH THE REST OF THE TEAM HOW YOU FEEL YOU DID AS A PARTICIPANT

Consider the following:

Was I active or passive? _____

Did I communicate clearly?_____

Did I take risks?_____

Did I support others?_____

Did I ask for help or support from others? _____

Was my behavior typical for me?_____

How would I do it differently? _____

Give each other honest and helpful feedback on the congruency of self-perception versus the perception of other team members.

Debriefing exercise courtesy of: Walter Kowalski
                                 BreakThroughs, Inc.
                                 Englewood, CO

CHAPTER CHECKLIST

Nurse managers must help build teams. Although the manager does not have to lead the team, the manager must ensure that the group can function effectively as a team. The team members must be able to communicate with each other effectively, share a single mission, be willing to cooperate with each other, and be committed to achieving their objectives. Successful teamwork requires leadership, trust, and willingness to take risks.

- A team is a highly interdependent group of people that:
  - Has defined goals and objectives
  - Has an ongoing relationship
  - Is focused on accomplishing a task.
- Attributes of effective teams include:
  - Clarity of purpose
  - Informality
  - Participation
  - Listening
  - Civilized disagreement
  - Consensus decisions
  - Clear roles and work assignments
  - Shared leadership
  - Diversity of styles
  - Self-assessment and self-regulation.

- Each team member deals continually with three questions:
  - Am I in the "in" group or the "out" group?
  - Do I have any power or control?
  - Can I use, develop, and be appreciated for my skills and resources?
- Focusing on team members' strengths and acknowledging what they do well are two of the keys to team building.
  - To be effective, acknowledgments must be:
    - Specific
    - Personal
    - Sincere
    - Timely
    - Public.
- One of the most helpful tools for teams is a set of ground rules that govern how members will interact with each other.
- Trust is essential for successful teamwork.
- Synergy allows a team to produce results that could not have been achieved by any one individual. Creating it requires:
  - Active listening
  - Compassion
  - Honesty
  - Flexibility
  - Commitment to resolution of conflicts.
- Managing emotions is a key strategy in team building.
- Leadership is a pivotal part of a smoothly functioning team.
  - Leadership relies on personal character development as much as on education.
  - Confidence is a key aspect of the leader's character.
    - A "can do" attitude is one of the most important confidence-building strategies a leader can adopt.
- Taking a risk and experimenting with a new behavior is the most effective way to change behavior.

TERMS TO KNOW

- **acknowledgment**
- **active listening**
- **commitment**
- **constructive confrontation**
- **dualism**
- **group**
- **mission**
- **synergy**
- **team**

REFERENCES

Bennis, W. (1989). *On Becoming a Leader.* Reading, MA: Addison-Wesley.

Bocialetti, G. (1988). Teams and management of emotion. In Reddy, W.B., & Jamison, K., eds. *Team Building Blueprints for Productivity and Satisfaction.* Alexandria, VA: NTL Institute for Applied Behavioral Sciences. San Diego, CA: University Associates, pp. 62–71.

Dubnicki, C. (May-June, 1991). Building high-performance management teams. *Healthcare Forum Journal,* pp. 19-24.

Dubnicki, C. (May-June, 1991). Tuning up your team. *Healthcare Forum Journal, 34,* 25-28.

Dyer, W. (1987). *Team Building Issues and Alternatives.* Reading, MA: Addison-Wesley.

Hart, L.B. (1980). *Learning from Conflict.* Reading, MA: Addison-Wesley.

Jeffers, S. (1987). *Feel the FEAR and DO IT anyway.* Columbia, New York: Fawcett.

Lopes, S. (1987). *The Wall.* New York: Collins.

McGregor, D. (1960). *The Human Side of Enterprise.* New York: McGraw-Hill.

—(1967). *The Professional Manager.* New York: McGraw-Hill.

Parker, G.M. (1990). *Team Players and Teamwork.* San Francisco, CA: Jossey-Bass.

Vaill, P. (1989). *Managing as a Performing Art.* San Francisco, CA: Jossey-Bass.

Weisburg, M. (1988). Team work: Building productive relationships. In Reddy, W.B., & Jamison, K., eds. *Team Building Blueprints for Productivity and Satisfaction.* Alexandria, VA: NTL Institute for Applied Behavioral Sciences. San Diego, CA: University Associates, pp. 62–71.

SUGGESTED READINGS

Barr, O. (1993). Reap the benefits of a cooperative approach. *Professional Nurses,* 473–474.

Francis, D., & Young, D. (1979). *Improving Work Groups: A Practical Manual for Team Building.* San Diego, CA: University Associates.

Jeffers, S. (1992). *Dare to Connect: Reaching Out in Romance, Friendship and the Workplace:* Columbia, New York: Fawcett.

Nanus, B. (1992). *Visionary Leadership.* San Francisco, CA: Jossey-Bass.

Schmieding, N.J. (1993). Nurse empowerment through context structure and process. *Journal of Professional Nursing, 9,* 239–245.

Sibbet, D., & O'Hara-Devereaux, M. (1991). The language of teamwork. *Healthcare Forum Journal, 34,* 27–30.

CHAPTER 15

SELECTING, DEVELOPING, EMPOWERING, AND COACHING STAFF

Lori Rodriguez, R.N., C., M.A., M.SN.

PREVIEW

This chapter provides the necessary tools and information to assist new managers in the hiring and selection process. It provides a brief overview of the orientation process of new staff. Traditional and nontraditional methods for providing on-going development of staff are covered. Aspects for empowering others from creating and developing a relationship to motivation and rewards are also included. Finally, the role of the manager as a coach is explored.

OBJECTIVES

- Apply the seven steps of the interview process in a simulated interview.
- Value the manager's role in the orientation process.
- Value the role of the manager in creating a learning environment.
- Value empowerment.
- Evaluate at least five tools that can be put into place to create empowerment.
- Analyze the source of motivation.
- Value the role of the manager as coach.

QUESTIONS TO CONSIDER

- How does a manager hire and select the right people for a job?
- How does a manager develop new staff?
- Why is it important to create a learning environment?
- How does a manager coach staff?
- What are the characteristics of a great coach?
- Are staff motivated?
- How are staff empowered?

A Manager's Viewpoint

One of the key things that makes a successful department is communication. So even though you are selecting staff based on practice qualifications, communication is critical. A manager has the advantage of knowing the current staff's abilities. Therefore it's important to weigh potential new staff's contributions in context of the whole. I always do an initial interview and then, if qualified, the applicant is invited to meet with potential peers. This creates the opportunity to ask nitty-gritty questions and to have the privilege of information about me as a manager and to find out what I'm really like. This also develops the staff's ability to interview and gives them the right to select other members of the staff. My staff is empowered and I receive additional information.

I try to find workshops and resources that will help staff develop to their fullest potential. Also I "buddy" new staff with more experienced ones so they develop a sense of comfort and a sense of team. Any special interests are important to me because I can help create opportunities so that they'll do a better job.

Laurie Lott, R.N., M.S.N.
Director of Staff Development
Hendrick Medical Center
Abilene, Texas

INTRODUCTION

Imagine creating a working environment in which patient care is delivered with joy, enthusiasm, and true commitment. Imagine having a staff of super-stars who function individually as experts in their own areas of interest and function together as a harmonious and effective team. Imagine an environment where both the manager and staff communicate and grow together; where staff are participative and motivated; where accomplishment is abundantly acknowledged. This is a vision of what nursing can be and one that is worth getting up for in the morning.

The nurse manager is key in creating the work environment. It is up to the manager to hire and select the right people. The behaviors that the manager values, models, and rewards are the behaviors that will prevail in the work environment. The manager has a key role in determining how new staff will be developed and what value "learning" will have in the work environment. The nurse manager must process leadership skills and be a facilitator, coach, and cheerleader. In the rapidly changing healthcare environment the nurse manager must possess tools and methods for motivating and empowering others.

The way that people are managed in the work environment determines the way they perform and the results and outcomes that will occur. Humans are the greatest resource in the work environment, so human resource management is an essential skill.

people   Irrespective of what the business is, sales, education or healthcare, the key is *people*. And people have their own will, their own mind, and their own way of thinking. If the employees themselves are not sufficiently motivated to challenge the goals of growth and technological development, there will simply be no growth, no gain in productivity, and no technological development (Inamori, 1985).

SELECTING STAFF

Before a manager can work in great depth with staff, the staff must be interviewed, selected, and oriented. In reality, unless a whole new work entity is created, these three activities occur with only a few staff members. Much of the staff is already in place. However, the process of selecting staff is a critical part of the manager's responsibilities. Blanchard and Johnson (1981) say there are three choices: hire all winners, hire potential winners and develop them or "pray".

INTERVIEWING

Interviewing and selecting the right people is the first step and possibly the greatest point of leverage that a manager has for creating a great work environment. Organizing the interviewing process into logical steps helps managers deal with the logistics of this task in an efficient and effective way. Table 15-1 lists seven steps in the interview process.

Steps in the Interview Process

Initial preparation   In this step the manager reviews the position description and performance expectations and determines that all elements are
competencies/behaviors   up to date. It is crucial to determine what competencies and behaviors are most necessary and whether group or individual interviews best meet the

TABLE 15-1 Steps in the Interview Process
1. Initial preparation
2. Interview prework
3. Establishing rapport
4. Position summary
5. Asking questions
6. Answering questions
7. Creating closure

unit's needs. The manager also determines who needs to participate in the process. Providing photocopies of material to clarify the position for those involved in interviewing helps everyone. Position descriptions, performance expectations, and performance appraisals are some examples. The final preparation is to have the interviews scheduled.

Interview prework Prior to the interview, the manager must review the application and résumé (or curriculum vitae) of each applicant and determine any questions based on the applicant's résumé and references. The manager should look at the résumé or application (or both) and ask:

review

- Is it complete?
- Is it neat?
- Are there questions about any of the entries?
- Do applicants have work experience relevant to the specified position?

These questions individualize an interview session.

Establishing rapport Begin the interview by making the person feel comfortable and asking nonthreatening questions. Examples would be: Did you have any difficulty finding my office? Would you like a cup of coffee? The box below lists some of the factors that shape initial impressions.

Position summary Using the position description as a guideline, the manager should summarize what the position entails. This sets the framework for a mutual understanding of the specifics about the position.

mutual view

Initial Impressions

1. Is the person on time?
2. Is the person dressed neatly?
3. Does the person exhibit appropriate behavior?
4. What is the level of confidence and comfort?
5. Does the person establish eye contact?
6. Does the person appear interested in the position?
7. Does the person smile?

Interview Selection Criteria Guidelines (These criteria may be altered to fit specific organizations)

1. How do his/her answers match organization values?
   A strong work ethic
   Honesty, integrity, fairness
   Taking responsibility
   A positive attitude
   Caring and compassion
2. How does the person talk about himself/herself?
   Does he/she seem confident?
   Is he/she able to use the pronoun "I"?
   Is he/she able to talk about his/her accomplishments and honors?
   Is he/she able to recognize areas that may require training?
   Is he/she willing to look at and explore his/her own behavior?
3. Does he/she appear intelligent?
   Does he/she use an adequate vocabulary and use grammar correctly?
   Does he/she demonstrate an interest in both the micro and macro picture?
   Does he/she ask good questions?
   Does he/she bother to clarify interview questions that are not clear?
4. Does he/she seem to take the initiative?
   Does he/she open up the questions that are asked?
   Is he/she enthusiastic?
5. Is he/she achievement oriented?
   Is he/she able to relate accomplishments?
   Is he/she able to demonstrate how he/she has met goals and objectives?
6. How does he/she describe problems previously encountered?
   Does he/she describe them as problems, opportunities, disasters, pitfalls?
   Can he/she describe specific actions taken previously?
   Can he/she describe personal feelings about actions described?
7. What is his/her technical competence?
   Can he/she perform the essentials of the position?
   Does he/she know what his/her learning style is?
   Is he/she willing to learn new tasks that are not familiar?
   Is he/she willing to take a test to assess his/her skill level?
   How does he/she respond when told he/she will have a competency-based orientation?
8. How does he/she deal with change?
   What is his/her tolerance for ambiguity?
   What is his/her history of dealing with change?
   Can he/she give an example of a change he/she initiated or managed?
   Can he/she give an example of a change he/she has championed that someone else may have suggested?

interview questions

Asking questions There are three types of questions to ask in an interview. The technical question is used to determine the interviewee's skills (e.g., What have you found to be the most difficult aspects of caring for a person on the respirator?). The direct question elicits a response that will indicate values and decision-making skills (e.g., How do you feel about working with a large population of elderly patients?). The situational question is used to determine critical thinking skills (e.g., The patient is complaining of pain. You last medicated him for pain one hour ago and he is not due for more medication for at least two hours. How do you handle this?). If the preparation was thorough, the manager will be able to assess answers using criteria such as those listed in the box on page 304.

Answering questions   Providing an opportunity to ask questions is also important. The smart manager evaluates the kinds of questions asked. Do they relate only to the person or do they reflect unit goals and needs? It is important to answer honestly and to suggest specific people who might provide a different perspective if the response is a value perspective.

Creating closure   Let interviewees know when there are no more questions. Thank them for making the time to meet and let them know when and how future follow-up will occur. These are critical to a successful closure. Another way of thinking about the interview process is presented in the literature box below.

closure

SELECTION

Immediately after the interview, rating responses to the interview is critical. Weigh the importance of the questions asked and review responses to questions. Again, this chapter's "Literature Perspective" focuses on an effective selection strategy.

rating responses

Literature Perspective

Tibles, L.R. (1993). The structured interview: An effective strategy for hiring. Journal of Nursing Administration, 23(10), 42–46.

In 1990 the average cost of nursing turnover for a registered nurse was $10,000, so hiring wisely is important. One study cited indicated that unstructured interviews had a validity of only 0.14. Structured interviews' validity was found to be significantly higher.

Structured interviews require specific goals and questions that are identified before the interview. Applicants are expected to do most of the talking. Situational interviews are used to have applicants perform some aspects of the job. Behavioral interviews focus on examples of past actions.

A four-phase process is described. The first phase, planning, consists of job analysis, interview guide development, interview questions, and review of applicants' credentials. The second phase, conducting the interview, consists of setting the tone and the working phase (active solicitation of information). The third phase, the conclusion, consists of clarification of information and additional information. The final phase, evaluation, includes recording comments and conclusions, and making a decision.

Implications for Practice

Although structured interviews require more detailed work initially, they tend to result in better hiring decisions. Because a job analysis reflects what it really takes to be effective and applicants are expected to illustrate those critical behaviors, decisions are based on comprehensive information.

DEVELOPING STAFF

ORIENTATION

How are new staff systematically trained and developed to be stars? The manager should use staff development education to perform an objective competency assessment of all new personnel. Staff development intervention needs to include an assessment of interpersonal, technical, and critical thinking skills. The development of staff does not occur in a finite period of time, but needs to be considered and approached as a journey. Certain competencies required for safe performance in the job need to be mastered within a prescribed amount of time. The manager should define what the minimum competencies are. The prescribed amount of time is affected by previous experience, learning styles, level of intelligence, commitment, enthusiasm, and interest. The experienced manager, preceptor, or staff development instructor should be able to estimate the amount of time an **orientation** will take, once a competency assessment is complete.

SOCIALIZATION

An essential part of the work environment is created through the relationships that the staff and the manager have. Providing for "learning the culture" helps staff meet priorities and quality goals. The time that it takes to create a relationship with staff is time well spent. It is out of these relationships that motivation, empowerment, and coaching spring. Motivating staff means knowing who they are and what is important to them. Consider this beginning: interact with them from the best that they are. Talk about what they are doing well. Talk about what values they display in their everyday work. In other words, "look for the gold." To find the gold, ask staff what motivates and excites them. Ask them what it is about patient care that keeps them on the job. Ask them what they would like to contribute to themselves and to the rest of the staff, the unit, and the healthcare organization. Working alone with a single staff member, and using these questions works well to create a relationship. Working with a group of staff may require a different approach. Consider exercise 15-2.

Learning about staff, particularly their strengths and their interests, provides a background for involving them in projects that will challenge and develop them. Consider starting staff meetings with some sort of an exercise that will remind people who is in the room. For example, have people talk about their greatest accomplishment that week or month, something they have learned, or what new goals they have set for themselves. Frequently staff meetings begin with people trying to take action. A few minutes spent in working on relationships will assure that the right people are involved and participating in the action. Encourage relationships between staff members. Teamwork is built through relationships. Encourage staff to collaborate on patient care issues and problems and to work on projects together. Encourage communication both laterally and vertically.

The first box on page 307 is a summary for implementing a **socialization** focus at the unit level.

Ongoing Development

The value for and support of lifelong learning should be stated up front and modeled by the manager. If the staff is not constantly working at improving their skills and knowledge in rapidly changing healthcare environments they

---

assessing competency

EXERCISE 15-1
Using a list of performance expectations for a position, review the expectations and rate yourself on each expectation. The rating should be simple such as:
1 = needs development
2 = is competent
3 = a real strength
Then review the list of expectations.

---

excitement

EXERCISE 15-2
Form a group of three to four people. Ask the group to write their biographies for the future. Have them write down what they would like to accomplish professionally in the next five years. Do this for additional five-year increments. Ask them to write what they would like to have said about them at their retirement dinner.

---

lifelong learning

Techniques for Creating Relationships with Your Staff

- Interact with people from the best that they are.
- Look for the gold.
- Encourage people to take on new challenges.
- Ask them what motivates them and excites them.
- Ask them what they would like to contribute.
- Ask them to write their biography.
- Consider what they would like to be known for.
- Meet with people one on one and in groups.
- Instead of doing a project alone (even if it is an easy one) use it as an opportunity to develop and work with someone else.
- Always begin meetings with a relationship exercise; don't jump into producing results immediately.
- Encourage relationships among staff.
- Foster collaboration and communication.

EXERCISE 15-3
The next time you are involved in a group project, start the meeting with "what I bring to this project." Even if you are not the formal group leader, you can stimulate this sharing.

risk obsolescence. A staff that is constantly working on skills and incorporating new ideas and techniques is a vital and dynamic force. This type of staff can assimilate constant changes and possess the personal power to deal with the ambiguity that often accompanies change.

Many methods are available for ongoing development. Education is the traditional method but there are many other methods as well. Effective managers realize there are many other ways to develop people on the job and will make such opportunities available. The box below lists some of the more familiar methods of development.

Education consists of learning opportunities in the institution and the community. Formal programs such as academic programs and continuing education are designed to meet specific goals. Informal learning experiences, although valuable, cannot be controlled by the manager. For example, incidental learning about a new therapy may be valuable but the manager cannot assure that one person shares information with another.

education

Methods of Developing Staff

Education
Cross-training
Small projects
Start ups: introducing change in the workplace
Team-building activities
Precepting
Being mentored
Job rotation
Job enrichment

cross-training

Cross-training focuses on helping staff feel confident in another area than the usual area of assignment. Examples are pediatric oncology and adult oncology, urology and general medicine, or well-baby clinic and pregnancy clinic.

Small projects can be designed to help staff gain new skills and enrich their knowledge base. Projects could focus on new practices related to a disease entity or a new approach to patient problems. Start-ups of new services are major opportunities for developing staff. Because change requires active thinking about evolving developments, it is an ideal development activity. People's ability to solve problems and think critically are consistent elements.

Team-building activities, addressed in Chapter 14, develop common commitments and purposes. The concept of team is critical to a highly developed staff.

preceptors

Precepting allows more experienced staff to share their expertise. Benner (1984) suggests matching **preceptors** and preceptees by selecting a preceptor who is slightly more advanced on the continuum of novice to expert than the preceptee. This match allows the preceptor to recall how being less experienced felt and yet share a higher level of performance.

Being mentored is a developmental approach that relies heavily on the personal relationship between two people. That is, the relationship influences the level of learning that each participant experiences.

Job rotation is possible for some staff. This rotation might consist of moving from an inpatient setting to an outpatient setting. It also might allow for service in a role analogous to the chief of staff in medicine. Job enrichment may occur when a new or different activity and its related preparation is included in a position. The activity might be clinically focused or role focused.

Developing a culture of learning is a key strategy for nurse managers. As Peter Senge says in his book, *The Fifth Discipline,* " Learning is expanding the ability to produce the results that we truly want." The nurse manager of tomorrow must be a champion for learning.

EMPOWERING

An empowering manager is one who shares choice, control, and power. For the employee who is being empowered there is a shift of responsibility and accountability; that is, one's destiny is in one's own hands. While the employees gain choice, control, and power, they take on responsibility for everything occurring around them. Because **empowerment** shifts much decision making from the manager to the staff, it results in an empowered workforce that will be more creative and satisfied and will request and seek challenging changes in their job. The box on page 309 identifies the characteristics of an empowered work environment.

manager's role

Managers are the energizers, the connectors, and the empowerers of their teams. In essence what this means is the manager is one of the many who create the team that is focused on the patient. "We" and "us" are common words. People skills are critical because work is accomplished through groups that relate to influence, not position.

Creating Empowerment

There are specific tools designed to create empowerment in the work environment. While no tool is guaranteed to work in isolation, each tool contributes to the empowered environment. The tools must be used where there is a desired intent and a real commitment to create an empowered environ-

Characteristics of an Empowered Work Environment

- The customer is in the center.
- People work cooperatively together to do what is needed.
- Responsibility, skills, authority, and control are shared.
- Control and coordination come through continued communication and many decisions.
- Change is sometimes very quick, as new challenges come up.
- The key skill for an employee, and a manager, is the abiilty to work with others.
- There are relatively few levels of organization.
- Power comes from the ability to influence and inspire others, not from the position.
- Individuals are expected to manage themselves and are accountable to the whole; the focus is on the customer.

Used with permission from Scott and Jaffe, 1991, p. 15.

TABLE 15-2 **Tools to Create Empowerment**

TOOLS	CONTRIBUTION
Suggestion systems	Provide a way for employee input to improve work and environment
Open communication	Provides exchange of ideas, and when purposeful, creates new solution
Lunches	Provide a small reward and an opportunity to socialize as an entity
Open door policy	Assures access and a group relationship
Recognition programs	Provide reward of recognition for organizational contribution (for example, employee of the month)
Education	Contributes to knowledge and abilities to perform role
Relationship building	Creates new ways of working together
Quality improvement	Creates goal-focused efforts
Self-directed work teams	Place accountability within work group
Shared governance	Creates formal avenues for staff input
Enrichment	Provides for participation in special endeavors

magnet hospitals

ment. Table 15-2 on page 309 lists each of these tools and a general description of their contribution to environment.

Magnet hospitals reflect the qualities of empowerment. Just like a magnet attracts and retains metals, these hospitals are supportive of staff and are viewed as positive places to work. Kramer and Schmalenberg's (1988) research produced the same desired characteristics as Peters and Waterman (1982) found.

These characteristics are (a) an infusion of values of quality care, (b) nurse autonomy, (c) informal nonrigid verbal communication, (d) innovation, (e) bringing out the best in each individual, (f) value of education, (g) respect and caring for the individual, and (h) striving for excellence.

Managerial Behaviors

After reviewing the characteristics of an empowered environment and tools that can be used to create an empowered environment, what managerial behaviors are most likely to bring about an empowered environment?

Providing staff with the tools and resources they need to get the job done is a concern for a nurse manager. Being committed to staff success, even in the face of personal loss, conveys a sense of empowerment for staff. The nurse manager who challenges the status quo helps convey to staff that this is an acceptable behavior. Important, meaningful and challenging work creates confidence for staff. It also reinforces the desire to continue to develop. Staff need autonomy and authority to make decisions about tasks and resources. Decentralizing decisions may take longer but it empowers and commits the staff.

When the nurse manager acknowledges, rewards, and recognizes people for legitimate reasons, a secondary benefit is derived. The individual sees reward and the group knows sincerity is the basis. Building networks for others is possible through such activities as introducing employees to people who can make things happen. Additionally, developing one's own competence sets an example while providing personal satisfaction.

Make heroes. Heroes are people who have courage and have taken risks to accomplish something. This can be done by encouraging risk taking, by being a champion for learning and development, and by inspiring a shared vision. Sharing information with staff and encouraging collaborative problem solving again creates a sense of empowerment, the "we" approach. To achieve this, the manager must appreciate differences in others, whether it is in style, performance, or behavior. Conflicts provide learning opportunities that allow the manager to coach others as if somebody's life depended on it.

Organizational Support

"To empower people in an unaligned organization can be counterproductive" (Senge, 1990, p. 146). Certain organizational features must be present if a manager seeks empowerment. Scott and Jaffee (1991) list the organizational structures that need to be present to support empowerment. Before embarking on a one-person crusade to empower staff, a manager might want to assess which of the organizational characteristics are present (see the box on page 312). While it is possible to empower staff in an organization that does not support empowerment, it is much easier if ideas on empowerment are shared.

An empowering organization lives its vision and mission. Thus, a manager is able to see actual examples of the above factors. The less fit of the actual behaviors with the stated values, the more likely the organization will not be an empowering one. The manager needs to interpret the assessment of the organization to those who may not have the ability to do so while interpreting the needs of staff to those who can help the organization live its vision.

support for empowerment

EXERCISE 15-4

Have your staff or classmates work in groups of four. Have each group brainstorm a list of positive changes that they would like to have happen in the clinical area. Then have them determine their three top choices, based on the criteria of which ones really excite them, which ones they have complete control over (or would in a clinical setting), and what would really make a difference.

Acknowledging, rewarding, and recognizing staff members' contributions is an effective way to empower the workforce.

Why Isn't Everybody Empowered?

If empowerment is such a panacea, why aren't all managers in the business of empowering and all employees in the business of being empowered? Some managers, particularly those who do not possess self-confidence, may actually fear an empowered work force. For some people the methods of empowering others are not logical, particularly if they have learned how to manage in a patriarchal or hierarchical system; that is, cognitive dissonance may exist. These managers are comfortable working with that which is rational, quantitative, and logical; they are uncomfortable with that which is creative, qualitative, and "illogical." For some managers there is safety in adhering to the "party line," doing such things as using the common language and terminology of the organization, and fitting into the organizational culture. Being a good manager and looking good are powerful motivators in a hierarchical system. Adherence to rules is easier than having to think critically, create, and innovate. To live a personal vision on a day-to-day basis, to share choice, power, and control requires commitment, persistence, and courage.

Certainly many people have explored courage over the years and for good reason. Courage makes extraordinary things happen. Courage is the source of unimaginable results. The current environment in healthcare requires people with courage in leadership roles. The self-assessment checklist in the box on page 313 illustrates characteristics present in people who have courage. This tool can be used to determine how one envisions courage and what experience already demonstrates courage.

Empowerment of staff is difficult. It is possible that the work force does not want to be empowered. Empowerment requires accountability and responsibility. How does the manager motivate others to want to be empowered? Motivation comes from inside the individual. If there is any single formula for motivating employees it is that the manager must know staff well

"logic"

courage

> ## Organizational Characteristics
>
> **Reward systems**—Rewards are consistent with organizational values. (If risk taking and profits are important, does profit sharing exist?)
>
> **Shared values**—Commonly accepted values are well articulated and widely understood. (Can those who report to an individual and those to whom that individual reports express the same vision or mission?)
>
> **Human-capital focus**—Individual high performance (physical, emotional, and spiritual) is developed and maintained. (Are people treated as individuals or only as a classification of employees?)
>
> **Work autonomy and job flexibility**—The organization is responsive to individual life-cycle demands, provides lateral and vertical expansion of skills and contributions, and is committed to mastery of multiple skills. (How is family leave enacted? Is cross-training a formal expectation?)
>
> **Commitment to communication**—Information about vision, strategy, and direction is shared within the organization, and employee input is elicited and responded to (see Shared values, above).
>
> **Creation of a community**—People feel good about working together. (Are problems addressed openly and fairly?)
>
> **Effective stress management and career development**—People are allowed to practice self-care to avoid burnout and support to find resources to grow at work. (Is overtime highly rewarded? Is saying "no" acceptable?)
> Scott and Jaffe, 1991.

motivation   enough to know what motivates them. For one person motivation might be acknowledgment, for another it might mean being assigned to a more challenging project, and for another it might mean the agreement of a specific holiday off. The second box on page 313 lists some steps managers can use to motivate staff.

self-talk   Empowerment is a process. Hopelessness and limitations, which are human responses to great challenges, need to be recognized. Self-talk, that is, the mental tapes one runs internally, may not relate to the current work environment. Yet, it needs to be recognized and dealt with. These messages include themes related to powerlessness: not being good enough, unworthiness, not having enough energy, and not wanting to do something. Managers need to recognize these responses in staff and then help staff take action anyway. Examples of converting, or diminishing, these negative messages are found in the managerial behavior section.

Managers may reward the wrong behaviors while ignoring or even punishing correct ones (LeBoeuf, 1985). While the debate rages on over money as motivator, money cannot buy courage, commitment, or caring behavior. Great performers respond to a desire to make a difference and support others. Managers reward not only great performers but also great performance from average employees; therefore, it is important to determine the reward that works for each employee. Rewarding accomplishments can be as simple as acknowledgment, thanks, or a celebration.

EXERCISE 15-5
Do you recognize your own response or script in the examples of self-talk described on this page? Take a minute to determine what you frequently say, at least to yourself, that limits your potential.

Courage Self-Assessment Checklist

How often do you do whatever it takes to get the job done?

How often do you say what is so, even if you know the result may not be pretty?

When was the last time you declared that something was not working? (A failure)

Are you comfortable with taking 100 percent responsibility when things go wrong?

When was the last time you refused to be stopped, pursuing a new but unpopular course?

How often is your communication inauthentic because it is easier to look good or not make waves?

Are you attached to your way of being and "the way we do things here"?

Would anyone use the word *persistence* to describe you?

Are you clear on what your commitment is and do you act out of that commitment?

Are you willing to take a stand for an unpopular idea because it is part of your larger commitment?

Do you have the courage to learn from your mistakes?

Can you be as good at follow-up as you are at leadership?

Steps to Support Motivation

Determine what the employee needs

Use achievable goals

Promote a positive environment

Have a positive attitude

Encourage participation in decision making

Acknowledge, acknowledge, acknowledge

Provide honest and direct communication

Look for the gold, interact with the gold

Remove game players and nonperformers from positions crucial to success

THE MANAGER AS COACH

In an empowered environment where decision making and problem solving are delegated to staff, the manager's role as a coach becomes essential. A coach is someone who has the knowledge and expertise to get the job done for others, but instead allows others to learn, think critically, and grow. The coach knows what the desired performance is and communicates it. In some cases the staff doesn't know the desired performance and in other cases they just need to be reminded of what they already have.

The **coaching** relationship requires mutual agreement. The coach has to be   *mutual agreement*
committed to coaching and the employee has to be open to coaching. Coaches typically provide an emphasis on the fundamentals. They serve as role models for

commitment

the values and behaviors that they want to accomplish. Coaches are distinguished by their absence on the playing field. They let others do the job. Yet they are visible on the sidelines and readily accessible when problems occur. Coaching requires commitment on the part of the manager. The coach needs to be committed to the success of their staff, so committed that they give feedback on both positive and negative performance and committed enough to stand for whatever needs to be done. Coaches readily point out what has been done well. They speak stategically, reminding staff of the long-term goals and vision, especially when the staff is wrapped up in the problem of the moment. The coach makes sure that the score is being kept and that outcomes are quantified. The coach ensures that cheering is done and celebrations occur for great accomplishments.

When someone asks why, the empowering response is, "Great question, let's explore the answer together." Sometimes there is no reason, but sometimes exploring reasons and possibilities promotes communication, opens dialogue, creates new possibilities, and challenges current thinking. Brookfield (1993) states that when people act as critical thinkers they (a) identify and challenge the assumptions underlying their own or another's beliefs or behaviors; and (b) they explore and imagine options to current ways of thinking and living. A coach supports this kind of action.

critical thinking

A coach stimulates **critical thinking.** Certain techniques cultivate and promote critical thinking. For example, open-ended questions allow the learner to reflect on the reasons that an action may be taken. Such questions open dialogue. Critical incidents in nursing is a legitimate method of identifying and exploring meaningful incidents with nurses to stimulate thinking and reasoning processes. Criteria analysis is a method of examining the criteria set for judging specific events. Nurses are becoming increasingly adept at this as they explore outcomes of patient care. Critical decision simulations allow nurses to function in simulated situations. Then questions about their performance provide opportunities to explain rationale for demonstrated performance.

CHAPTER CHECKLIST

The nurse manager plays a key role in setting the tone for the work environment. The manager not only selects and hires the right people but also serves as a role model for staff members. The behaviors that the manager values, models, and rewards are the behaviors that staff will emulate. The manager also plays a key role in staff development by supporting and role modeling a commitment to lifelong learning. The nurse manager must be a facilitator, a coach, and a motivator who possesses the tools and skills to empower others.

- Interviewing and selecting staff are a manager's greatest leverage point for creating the work environment.
  - The interview process consists of seven distinct steps:
    - Preparation
    - Prework
    - Establishing rapport
    - Giving a short job summary
    - Asking questions
    - Giving the interviewee a chance to ask questions
    - Creating closure.

■ Orientation of the new employee is the first step in valuing continuous learning.
- The manager sets the tone for learning and ongoing development.
- Methods that can be used to train and develop staff include:
    - Education
    - Cross-training
    - Small projects
    - Start-ups: introducing change in the workplace
    - Team-building activities
    - Precepting
    - Being mentored
    - Job rotation
    - Job enrichment.

■ The time spent in getting to know staff is time well spent.
- Only when effective relationships are in place can managers be effective in:
    - Coaching
    - Motivating
    - Empowering
- Managers should "look for the gold" in their staff.

■ An empowered work force has choice, control, and power.
- Some managers do not want to give these up.
- Some staff do not want to take them on.

■ Creating an empowered work environment requires:
- Commitment
- Courage
- Persistence.

■ Rewards must be:
- Given in return for the desired performance
- Individualized.

■ In today's changing healthcare environment, the manager must assume the role of coach.

TERMS TO KNOW

- coaching
- critical thinking
- cross-training
- empowerment
- magnet hospital
- orientation
- preceptor
- socialization

REFERENCES

Benner, P. (1984). *From novice to expert*. Menlo Park, CA: Addison-Wesley.

Blanchard, K., & Johnson, S. (1981). *One Minute Manager*. New York: Beckley Books.

Brookfield, S. (1993). On impostership, cultural suicide, and other dangers: How nurses learn critical thinking. *The Journal of Continuing Education in Nursing, 24,* 197-205.

Inamori, K. (1985). The perfect company: Goal for productivity. Speech given at Case Western Reserve University, June 5.

Kramer, M., & Schmalenberg, C. (1988). Magnet hospitals: Part II Institutions of excellence. *Journal of Nursing Administration, 18*(2), 11–31.

LeBoeuf, M. (1985). *The Greatest Management Principle in the World: For Anyone who Needs to Get Things Done*. New York: Berkley Books.

Peters, J. J., & Waterman, R..H.. (1982). *In search of excellence*. New York: Harper & Row.

Scott, C.D., & Jaffe, D.T. (1991). *Empowerment: A Practical Guide for Success*. Menlo Park, CA: Crisp.

Tibles, L.R. (1993). The structured interview: An effective strategy for hiring. *Journal of Nursing Administration, 23*(10), 42–46.

Wilson, R.F. (1991). *Conducting Better Job Interviews*. Hauppauge, NY: Barrons.

SUGGESTED READINGS

Lombardo, M.M., & Eichinger, R.W. (1989). *Eighty-eight Assignments for Development in Place: Enhancing the Developmental Challenge of Existing Jobs.* Greensboro, NC: Center for Creative Learning.

Senge, P.M. (1990). *The Fifth Discipline: The Art and Practice of the Learning Organization.* New York: Doubleday.

Zaleznik, A. (1989). *The Managerial Mystique: Restoring Leadership in Business.* New York: Harper and Row.

CHAPTER 16

COMMUNICATING AND COLLABORATING

Elizabeth Wywialowski, R.N., C., Ed. D., C.C.R.N.

PREVIEW

This chapter discusses strategies to promote effective communication and collaboration. Many of the suggested approaches could be used to manage client care as well as to manage resources needed by others providing direct care services. This chapter emphasizes the dynamics and complexity of communication processes commonly involved in managing resources so that client care can be delivered.

OBJECTIVES

- Evaluate the components and processes involved in effective communication.
- Evaluate three examples of each of the following types of communication:
  a. behavioral
  b. verbal
  c. technological
  d. organizational.
- Differentiate intradisciplinary communication techniques from interdisciplinary communication techniques.
- Given a case study involving managerial communication needs, select techniques that could be used to communicate effectively with the intradisciplinary team on the client's behalf.
- Given a specific situation, predict client's priority needs that require interdisciplinary communication.
- Given a specific situation, describe strategies for interdisciplinary team building.
- Given a case study where the satisfaction of a client's needs requires collaboration, construct strategies that might be used to ethically advocate for the client's interests.

QUESTIONS TO CONSIDER

- When do your actions speak louder than words?
- When you have been misunderstood, how did you become aware of the missed communications? What could you have done sooner to promote effective communication?
- How do the time of day, place, and routines (i.e., the context) affect what needs to be communicated?
- Why are some communication techniques more effective for you than others?

- What ethical concepts guide your communication with members of the interdisciplinary team?
- What are characteristics of common clinical situations in which nursing input could benefit clients?

A Manager's Viewpoint

It's important to me as a nurse manager to be able to communicate and collaborate with all disciplines involved in patient care. It means continuity of patient care. It reflects how patient care is carried out for the patient, the family, and all involved. When communication and collaboration is done at the utmost level, you're going to have cost-effective care done in a timely manner, and lengths of stay can be decreased. You're going to have happier patients and happier staff.

The biggest challenge I face as a nurse manager regarding communication and collaboration is the number of people that I must communicate and collaborate with. A critical aspect of this challenge is to follow through on the communication. What I find happening on an acute medical unit is that my nursing staff knows so much about the patients. But it's getting them to communicate this information to the next shift, to the next nurse, or to the dietitian, social worker, physician, etc., that is the real challenge. Nursing staff needs to communicate its knowledge of patients in such a way that it is recorded and understood. That is, the staff needs to communicate by writing on the Kardex, in the nursing care plan, and/or a progress note. Communicating with other departments has lost its personal touch as we now do so much by E-mail.

I think the secret to effectively meeting the challenges of communication and collaboration is being visible. I think if you're a visible manager, you will have good communication. And I really firmly believe that. Be visible as much as you can possibly be visible to your staff, to all the other disciplines, and you will have good communication.

I make myself visible by staying on the unit as much as possible. For example, I have an area on the unit; it's not my office, but my staff has claimed it as my office because it's visible and I'm there a lot. Another good way is to constantly have your ears open and listening. For example, if I hear a group of physicians talking, I'm not afraid to interrupt and ask who they are discussing. Or I try to tell staff, if you see a group of physicians going into a room with a tray of some type, don't be afraid to ask, What are you doing? or Can I help you?

Being visible is the best way to communicate and collaborate. But unfortunately, being a visible manager tends to mean not getting administrative things done, so I do fall behind on paperwork because I get involved with clinical issues.

Ms. Mary Jane Hirtz, B.S.N., R.N.
Nurse Manager-Acute Medical Unit
Zablocki Veterans Affairs Medical Center
Milwaukee, Wisconsin

INTRODUCTION

Communication is a complex process. Basic communication processes form the foundation of professional communications that are used within nursing and with other disciplines. Many clinical communications really are examples of intra- and interdisciplinary communication. Being able to communicate effectively with others about client care is an expectation for nurse leaders and managers.

COMMUNICATION AND COLLABORATION CONCEPTS

feedback

The key principles of effective communication processes relate to characteristics of the basic communication and the use of feedback. That is, careful and specific attention needs to be paid to how messages are selected and transmitted in specific contexts. Feedback, a natural consequence of individual perspectives and differences in perception, needs to be analyzed to confirm the accuracy of the receiver's perceptions of the messages sent.

Principles of **collaboration** reinforce basic communication processes and involve effective communication and complex problem-solving skills. To increase the effectiveness of their communication, nurses need to practice improving their communication skills. Communicating effectively will promote self-confidence, which will more likely increase assertiveness and satisfaction with professional practice. Principles of communication appear in the accompanying box. As a dynamic process, communication is influenced by context and structure. Because communication is a means of enhancing understanding, it is important to know who the senders and receivers are.

Communication Principles

1. Communication is a means, not an end.
2. The context, or situation, affects what needs to be communicated.
3. The purpose of the communication defines who needs to send a message to whom and provides clues as to how it can best be transmitted.
4. Feedback needs to be heeded to evaluate communication effectiveness.
5. Collaborating to solve complex problems requires effective communication skills.

MAKING SENSE OUT OF WHAT NEEDS TO BE COMMUNICATED

communication as a means

Communication processes in clinical practice might be compared to transportation processes. In other words, communication is a means to an end. Various methods of transportation are used to reach different destinations or accomplish specific goals. For example, one might walk to the nearest grocery store, use public land transportation to reach a large shopping center, or schedule an international flight to attend a conference. In similar ways, different communication processes are used to meet various healthcare needs. The overall goal of professional communication is to provide quality care, in a cost-effective manner, to satisfy healthcare needs of individual clients.

A familiar illustration of the basic communication process depicts a sender, message, and receiver, and its cyclical nature (Figure 16-1). When principles of basic communication are applied in nursing practice, it often seems to the novice that something is missing, and indeed it is! What is missing relates to the individual nurse's perceptions of his/her role; expectations of other professionals; the organization's structure and corresponding expectations; and the organization's key operating policies and procedures, including standards of care and practice. The staff nurse is expected to know and adhere to established procedures, and to know when they should be adhered to and when they need to be adapted and how.

cyclical process

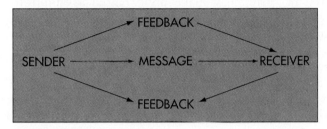

FIGURE 16-1
The basic communication process.

Modes of transportation depend on specific environmental props, for example, walkways, bicycle paths, streets, highways, or airports. Communication processes take place in various contexts or types of settings with their surrounding circumstances. Surrounding circumstances provide cues as to what needs to be communicated and what does not. Some oral communications may need to be documented for future reference for other people involved or for those who are affected by what was communicated—for example, recording a client's response to services provided, or time worked by a specific employee for personnel purposes.

contextual communication

The setting influences the complexities of communication. For example, an inpatient medical center that has well-established policies and procedures will often address a wide variety of communication needs in the course of adhering to them, such as needs involved in preparing clients for diagnostic procedures. In contrast, a nursing home, which is less likely to provide complex diagnostic services, is likely to require more communication between providers to assure that the client is adequately prepared for a specific procedure to be completed at another agency. Similarly, a healthcare agency with many major functions, such as service and education, is likely to have more complex communication needs than one that is organized primarily to provide only services. This is so because the agency's circumstances are evolving and because a variety of providers are associated with client care. Again, verbal communications often need to be documented in a timely manner for future reference by other providers involved in the client's care, since the clinical record is often used as a current accurate account of services rendered and the client's responses to them.

Each staff nurse perceives expected nursing roles and functions differently. Each nurse addresses common organizational expectations, usually by emphasizing personal strengths and recognizing limitations, while caring for each individual client according to the plan of care within the established standards of practice and care. The staff nurse formulates plans of care according to his/her perception of each client's needs and the agency's standard operating policies,

perceptions

procedures, and routines, including modification of any of them to best address priority needs. Each nurse follows agency guidelines, but proceeds slightly differently. The individual nurse decides which messages are sent and how, according to his/her individual strengths, preferences, quirks, and limitations and professional skills. Strategies for effective communication are selected on the basis of the short- and long-term goals to be met. For example, the nurse manager might use behavioral messages as a leader to influence the formation of a work group's positive approach to the complex demands placed upon them; or the nurse manager might use verbal messages when allocating staff and communicating with the central nursing staffing office to clarify staffing needs.

assumptions   Nurses, often in haste, may make unwarranted assumptions about the context of care and what the organization expects of clients and staff. Examples of unwarranted assumptions include (a) the belief that the purpose of the agency is to provide quality care, when in fact the agency's purpose (though often unwritten or unspoken) is to make a profit; (b) that all providers are acting on the same values ("see things the same way"), when in reality they frequently do not; and (c) that client care is the first priority, when in fact the organization's thrust may be to recruit physicians. These assumptions may cause communication errors and subsequent gaps in service or care. These gaps lead at best to potential conflicts; at worst, to unresolvable differences. If the nurse makes no assumptions, communication needs are unlimited, and the resulting tedious, detailed processes become boring and difficult to attend to. Consequently, communication processes become ineffective.

Nurses who communicate effectively typically are deliberate in their efforts and frequently verify the validity of their assumptions. If not, they repeat the communication process until they succeed in being understood. That is, they "check" (asking the receiver for feedback and attending to both verbal and nonverbal cues) to decipher whether the messages sent were in fact received and perceived as intended. Sometimes facial expressions or questions asked by others provide clues that a communication gap exists. For example, a client questions whether the drug dosage received was in fact what was prescribed, thus leading the nurse to discover that the prescription had been changed, or an error was made in preparing the dose.

The specific context of practice yields cues as to expectations, standard operating procedures, routines, and the messages that require repetition to assure accurate follow through. Changes in any established procedures or routines require repeated communications, often in both written and face-to-face forms, to assure accurate, detailed follow through.

BEING SENSITIVE TO COMMUNICATION STRATEGIES

The nurse sends behavioral, verbal, **technological,** and **organizational messages,** whether or not he/she is aware of them in the course of performing expected nursing functions. In using these various modalities, the nurse needs to remain sensitive to the meaning of the messages with which he/she is bombarded in the practice arena. This sensitivity makes communication more effective.

Behavioral Messages

meaning of behavior   "Actions speak louder than words." What the nurse does communicates more effectively than what the nurse says. Behaviors are often quick and seemingly automatic. The tone or inflection of the speaker's voice may convey a more obvious message than what is actually said. Frequently, these behaviors are learned and assumed to have common social or cultural meanings. However, in actuality, while some behaviors communicate common meanings, many do not; it is difficult to decipher which are which unless the receiver of the **behavioral message** confirms the accuracy of the perceived meanings with the senders.

positive behaviors

Positive behaviors (desired actions) generally communicate clearly their importance as well as what and how specific procedures need to be done. Frequently, nurses are expected to teach self-care techniques, and deliberately striving to reinforce desired behaviors and norms is a very effective strategy. Role modeling is a behavioral communication technique that can be a very effective teaching method as well (Basta, 1991).

negative behaviors

Negative behaviors (undesired actions or actions lacking desired behaviors, such as gestures or facial expressions, might convey the nurse's desire for a change in a staff member's behavior. Frequently, however, the individual might interpret a frown or grimace as disapproval; such interpretations may increase the individual's anxiety or stress in very stressful situations. Since people from different ethnic or cultural backgrounds might interpret behavior differently, it is best to use negative behaviors (verbal disapproval or nonverbal behaviors that convey disapproval of an individual's actions) *very* carefully, if at all. For example, some people might interpret prolonged eye contact to communicate interest and active listening, while others might interpret such behavior as aggression or intimidation. To determine if behaviors are being misinterpreted, the nurse seeks feedback to validate the other person's interpretation and responses. Typically, the nurse notes consistencies and inconsistencies in the individual's verbal and nonverbal responses in an effort to decipher perceptions. In a similar manner, the nurse seeks feedback from patients to check the accuracy of their perceptions.

The nurse might feel that no verbal response is a neutral communication technique conveying interest and active listening; however, a recipient of communication might interpret the lack of verbal responses as lack of interest. Again, it is essential that the sender check out the receiver's perceptions of the intended messages sent to assure that both the nurse and the other person are "on the same wavelength." This checking usually takes the form of verbal clarification, questions, or paraphrasing what was said while observing behavioral responses.

Verbal Messages

The nurse usually cannot communicate effectively with behavior alone. And again, saying what you mean is not always easy. Usually by the time the nurse has completed basic nursing courses, he/she has expended considerable effort to learn medical and scientific terminology. The nurse frequently uses these new terms in an effort to communicate accurately.

communicating accurately

On the other hand, clients usually expect to be shown common courtesies and etiquette. That is, they expect to be introduced to staff providing their care, and they expect interactions that reflect respect for their dignity and consideration of their feelings. Rude interactions, such as talking to other staff as if the client is not present, are likely to influence subsequent relationships.

Lack of fulfillment of client expectations can hinder meaningful helping relationships. Clients usually use common language that they readily understand. Cultural, educational, or social backgrounds of both nurse and client influence which terms are common and readily understood. Gearing verbal comments (choosing words wisely) to the comprehension level of the audience is critical to being an effective communicator. For example, the nurse chooses words

Actions often communicate more clearly than words.

that he/she could reasonably expect the client to understand, based on the language the client uses, questions asked, and other similar experiences that the client describes. Similar considerations need to be made when communicating with colleagues. For example, a nurse from a home health serivce may not understand the shortened communication messages of nurses working in a critical care unit. The reverse, of course, is also true.

Typically, the nurse determines the client's background during an initial admission assessment, when the nurse and client get to know each other. However, the nurse often cares for clients for whom he/she has not done admission interviews and is expected to implement their nursing care plans, including contributing to the development and reinforcement of client teaching programs. In such situations, it is especially important that the nurse evaluate at regular intervals each client's comprehension of terms used to avoid "losing" and frustrating the client. Similarly, ongoing clarification with staff is also important.

courtesy Common courtesies are requirements, not niceties. Though it almost goes without saying, effective nurse communicators avoid offensive language. Some clients and colleagues are easily offended and might give little or no negative feedback about it since they feel very vulnerable when dependent on others; so the nurse needs to be consistent in this regard. To use offensive language and expect to build a respectful and trusting working relationship is unreasonable.

Nurses, like other professional providers, need to strive continuously to improve their communication skills. To become proficient, nurse managers need to make their concerns for colleagues known in a timely manner, as well as to articulate their own feelings and responses to others in a tactful, considerate manner. Being assertive requires nurse managers to describe their own responses in specific circumstances, instead of blaming others for undesired consequences. Describing one's own responses allows the manager to help others understand the responses and subsequently change their own behaviors. In essence, the manager role models ownership of thoughts, feelings and behaviors so that others can acquire this performance, too.

Technological Messages

As the information era takes a firm grip on healthcare, nurses increasingly communicate via computers, telephones, and other electronic devices. Just as with sending messages in person or via telephone, these messages convey more than the specific words transmitted. Timeliness, organization of thought, and correct spelling and grammar are required to communicate effectively. Though the computerized technology systematizes the process, the actual messages need to be "proofed" before being transmitted. Proofreading the message prevents the receiver from needing to request clarification and the sender saves time by not needing to send another message quickly.

electronic devices

Increasingly, services provided and client responses to them are documented electronically. Since these messages have both therapeutic and legal implications, all requirements for accurate spelling and use of approved abbreviations are as critical as when manual forms of communication are used. These electronic messages are used as valid data for clinical decision making and are documented for future reference to provide a complete record. Often these electronically generated messages need to be authenticated by initials or other approved signatures.

Organizational Messages

The formal organization and culture within which the nurse practices affects communication processes and strategies. It is the formal organizational structure that conveys the nurse's clinical authority to those in the immediate work group. For example, a team leader and a primary nurse have different clinical decision-making authority because of the formal organization of the work group. Typically, the team leader has broader decision-making authority in allocating available resources than does the staff nurse providing direct care; the team leader is more likely to communicate needs and concerns to more centralized staff or to the next level of the organization. Team leaders often communicate with unit managers when policies are needed to assure implementation. With the increasing trend toward decentralizing nursing organizations, direct nursing staff tend to gain responsibilities for allocating resources for a shift-by-shift time period. Direct nursing staff usually decide what clients need, who will provide the care and how it will be done; they also may communicate vertically when special staffing, equipment, and supplies for immediate care situations are needed. Figure 16-2 on page 326 illustrates some of the vertical and horizontal communication demands of nurse managers.

organizational culture

In a somewhat similar manner, the organizational structure also typically places the staff nurse in a leadership position. The staff nurse is in a pivotal position organizationally. Each nurse's leadership characteristics influence the work group. As is so often remarked, "Who's in charge makes a big difference." Members of the work group soon learn what the staff nurse expects and whether follow-up is likely. When the nurse clearly supports the agency's purposes, clarifies expectations for client care, and follows through on evaluating

NURSING   OTHER PROFESSIONS

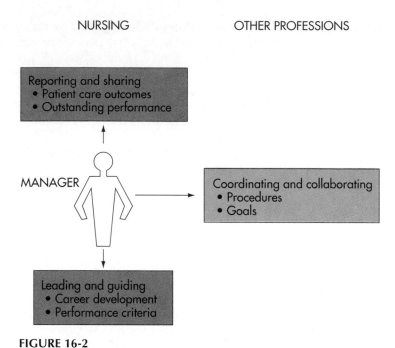

FIGURE 16-2
Managerial communication.

outcomes, the following message gets through: "Plan to get what you expect—if you don't expect high performance, you don't get it; more often than not, if you expect high performance, you get it."

The organization often expects the staff nurse to communicate with supervisory staff to obtain needed resources and administrative support, such as, adequate staffing. In a similar manner, the organization expects the staff nurse to follow established policies and procedures to achieve client care goals and to know when adjustments are needed. Experience in following and adjusting routines and procedures enables the nurse to gain valuable insight into how they might be revised to improve the quality of services provided. By participating in continuous quality improvement processes designed to provide cost-effective care, the nurse supports organizational goals. In addition, involvement in these types of activities helps the nurse keep current about organizational expectations.

In a similar way, the nurse is expected to function as a client advocate, assessing client needs and required resources, and continuing to problem solve until needs are met to each client's satisfaction. When the nurse is accountable for professional practice, the contributions of others in achieving specific and common goals becomes apparent. Effective communication precedes success, while lack of success often heralds ineffective communication.

Members of the work group are more likely to feel supported in their efforts when the organization and culture communicate that they are valued (Bice, 1990). When members of the team "know" that what they say and do makes a difference in quality care, they usually communicate concerns in a timely manner and to team leaders who they believe are likely to respond.

To build effective work groups requires that the staff nurse be committed to the agency's mission and purposes in a consistent manner. This commitment is reflected by the nurse's behavior, language, use of computerized information systems, and organizational lines of authority.

INTRADISCIPLINARY COMMUNICATION TECHNIQUES

The nurse typically works with a wide variety of nursing team members. The nursing work group, which the nurse leads and supervises, often consists of peers with dissimilar educational backgrounds and experience. In addition, the various members of the nursing team may have widely differing personal reasons for being a member of a specific work group. Some members may perceive their membership as entirely voluntary, while others feel they have no real choice in the matter.

diversity in nursing

Regardless of the individual differences in background or motivations, the nurse is expected to be reasonable and balanced in allocating work assignments to team members to provide continuity of care. To succeed, the nurse needs to accommodate a wide variety of client needs and personality differences, capitalize on individual team member talents (strengths), and minimize vulnerabilities (weaknesses) and limits (restrictions). Managing and leading a nursing group requires complex communication skills and a strong desire to perform well. An open mind and willingness to listen to others helps the novice manager adjust to this complex situation and gain experience and confidence as a nursing work group leader. Ongoing participation in various staff development programs designed to promote work group productivity helps to reinforce effective communication strategies as well as to gain insight into this complex process.

A basic communication strategy that is likely to be successful is to strive to maintain a positive perspective. When the nurse manager describes clinical decisions and corresponding plans and directs assigned nursing care in a positive manner, individual nursing team members are more likely to understand what is expected. When unforseen problem situations arise, the staff is more likely to work together to find solutions and to focus on the situation, rather than find fault. The nursing staff is also more likely to listen actively since they will have less need to feel defensive. Often concurrently, the nurse manager will encourage them to develop their talents to strengthen their work behaviors rather than avoid their vulnerabilities. Using a positive approach reduces stress related to defensiveness. In a fast-paced work environment, reducing stress is a worthy goal that promotes effective communication .

positive approach

In a manager role, the nurse needs to utilize communication and relationship principles to develop effective working relationships with the nursing team. Just as it is important to be trustworthy, dependable, respectful, and empathic with clients, it is also necessary to be so with nursing team members without biases for their organizational position or credentialing statuses. Treating team members as dignified people enables them to grow. By focusing attention on how the system might contribute to ineffectiveness rather than on individual inadequacies, team members can be influenced to communicate with each other to solve common problems. Remember, actions communicate expectations more consistently than words.

As nurses gain experience practicing within the nursing department, they develop a network of support with other nurses who provide expert advice based upon a greater knowledge, skill, or experience base. These people are excellent resources to use to develop collaborative skills.

Collaboration refers to conjoint problem solving on the client's behalf, where everyone involved interacts from a position of equal empowerment (Garcia et al., 1993). Collaboration on behalf of the profession also requires conjoint problem solving. While using the expertise of resource people, the

collaboration

EXERCISE 16-3

You are the team leader for a busy extended care unit (capacity of thirty-eight) specializing in rehabilitation of chronically disabled neurologically impaired adults. You are working with one RN, two LPNs, and four assistants. The night nurse who gave report was a "float nurse" who was unaware of the histories of the clients who needed necessitating rehabilitation programs. Consequently, desired outcomes and discharge plans for each of the clients were not made explicit. The RN is "orienting" to the unit, while the LPNs are alternating administering treatments for the entire group with personal care assignments. The assistants are assigned to provide personal care for seven to eight clients and perform other utilitarian tasks such as handling linens and equipment and stocking needed supplies.

At midday, a mandatory sexual harassment closed-television in-service education program will be televised. It will be repeated during the overlap of the day and evening shift. The LPNs and two assistants have indicated their displeasure about this mandatory program. "We have more than enough to do without having to sit and stare at a TV program that doesn't make any difference anyway."

You are expected to supervise your nursing team's work, evaluate its effectiveness in rehabilitating clients, provide for continuity of care with the next shift, and enable staff on duty to complete the day's mandatory inservice program.

Describe the communication strategies you would use to

a. inform staff of the rehabilitation efforts needed by their assigned clients;
b. maintain a positive perspective, a "can do" attitude, while providing care;
c. plan with the team to provide adequate "coverage" while meeting mandatory education requirements; and
d. update care plans and organize data collected during your shift so they are accessible to the next shift's nursing staff (care plans are computerized, while the nursing flow sheets are at the clients' bedside).

staff nurse needs to communicate client concerns clearly. Ultimately, whenever possible, the client needs to be involved in making decisions that affect him/her. However, the client or significant others are often unable to articulate their concerns or lack the assertiveness needed to resolve conflicts and satisfy healthcare needs. While advocating for the client, the nurse has many opportunities to practice assertiveness skills and to demonstrate them to clients as a teaching strategy, by modeling desired behaviors.

As the information era evolves, healthcare complexity increases, and providers are increasingly interdependent. Frequently, the expertise of more than one discipline is needed to address complex client care needs.

INTERDISCIPLINARY COMMUNICATION TECHNIQUES

Professionals possess power by virtue of their expertise. Furthermore, the history of a discipline's valuing its knowledge base contributes to how its members and the public perceive it. In other words, these values become integrated within the evolving culture. For example, both physicians and the public tend to value medical knowledge more than that of the more recently evolving disciplines, such as nursing or the behavioral sciences. Consequently, physicians often make decisions for other disciplines (and clients do not object) rather than collaborating with these other disciplines for the benefit of clients.

collaborative skills
Skills gained from collaborating within nursing can be readily transferred to interdisciplinary problem-solving situations. Every discipline has its unique purpose, goals, values, knowledge, language, and skills. The client is best served by an interdisciplinary team instead of a group of individuals striving to

meet each discipline's goals. Rather than approaching other disciplines from a "they and us" mind set, learning to work cooperatively as a team, a "we" emphasis, is essential. Each member of the team needs to value both individual contributions and the combined benefits of cooperative group efforts.

Nurses, particularily, need to value their contributions as interdisciplinary team members. Every discipline professes to address the client's needs. What is less commonly appreciated, and even more important, is the team's need to focus on the client's priority needs and to organize interdisciplinary interventions accordingly. This organizing strategy means that the discipline best able to address the client's needs receives priority in planning and accepts responsibility for providing its interventions in a timely manner. For example, social workers may receive high priority in addressing a client's social needs when those needs interfere with the client's ability to respond to therapy. They are not likely to receive priority when the client's social status is stable. In a similar manner, a client's need to participate in discharge planning or individualized health education programs is likely to take precedence over recreational or diversional therapies. The nursing perspective, which is holistic by nature and usually involves coordinating the team's efforts, is very valuable in helping the team to identify priorities, areas of progress, and gaps requiring further attention. The organization communicates its support for team work by providing comfortable meeting places and a schedule that allows the team to meet while minimizing disruptions in various scheduled therapy sessions.

focus on priorities

Staff nurses may defer clinical decisions to other disciplines and, consequently, imply lesser knowledge as professionals (Aaronson, 1989). However, staff nurses, by virtue of their generalist functions, have a broad knowledge base that is very useful in a wide variety of situations. Nurses need to share their knowledge with clients and other disciplines in a collaborative effort to find solutions to complex needs (Moulder, Staal, and Grant, 1988). Nurses also need to demonstrate confidence in their profession's knowledge base in accordance with their assessment of current client and management needs. This approach is in contrast to providing input consisting of opinions, hearsay, or statements based on past experiences. Nurses who present nursing assessments and recommendations for treatment using acceptable terminology and language are more likely to engender respect than those who do not. The nurse, like other professionals, needs to adopt a sharing attitude and an openness to learning from others. By respecting the contributions of others, the nurse is more likely to be afforded a respected position on the interdisciplinary team.

mutual problem solving

Frequently, clients communicate concerns readily to nursing staff. These concerns may reflect problems establishing healthcare priorities and values, or problems with family functions. To help clients and their families manage complex health problems, nurses need to create and maintain a climate of respect for their own professional skills, and for those of other disciplines (Baggs, 1993). Again, it is important to assess each client's situation accurately before describing individual responses to other team members. Other team members will use this information to evaluate progress and future needs of the client. Interdisciplinary discussions often involve conflict resolution and problem solving. A positive perspective helps the team to believe in their potential to succeed in often difficult and complex circumstances. With accurate information and honest discussions of the issues, suitable solutions can be identified and plans established. With repeated positive experiences in discussing

maintain respect

EXERCISE 16-4

You are attending an interdisciplinary conference held to evaluate client responses in preparation for discharge in an extended care facility. The representatives on the team include a recreational therapist, discharge planner, social worker, speech pathologist, occupational therapist, physical therapist, nurse manager, primary nurse, psychologist, pastoral counselor, and administrative assistant.

The client is a 57-year-old married mother of two adult children who is recovering from a traumatic brain injury. In addition to requiring assistance with ambulation, dressing, toileting, and personal hygiene, Mrs. T. becomes very frustrated with her expressive aphasia. She has acted out her frustrations during the last two visits with her family. She wants to go home to be with her family; her husband is employed full time, and is required to travel frequently. She is more self-sufficient than she was one month ago and selects activities that she can work on alone in her room.

a. What are Mrs. T's priority needs?

b. What disciplines will likely need to be involved in assisting Mrs. T. to progress toward meeting her priority needs?

The interdisciplinary team has difficulty finding a satisfactory conference room and a schedule to meet to regularly evaluate progress in achieving goals. Consequently, the interdisciplinary group meets infrequently, and not all disciplines are able to attend the entire discussion due to other conflicting service demands.

a. Describe your suggestions for helping this team find a comfortable meeting place and time.

b. Can temporary solutions be tried, with a specific time limit?

c. Could clients with similar needs be grouped so that the different members of the interdisciplinary team could confer on plans, thus requiring the entire team to meet less frequently?

critical issues, the team can increase the skills they need to address complex client needs.

interdisciplinary conferences

The nurse manager needs to assure that staff nurses follow through on expectations that they prepare for and attend interdisciplinary conferences. This requires allotting the staff nurse time to gather the needed information and to attend scheduled interdisciplinary conferences. In addition, staff nurses need to update plans of care as they change, so that other nursing staff members can implement the revisions. They need to communicate these plans in change of shift reports or other discussions conducted to provide continuity of care. By consistently providing accurate and reliable information, nurses establish themselves as essential interdisciplinary team members, both as client advocates and as valuable contributors to the group's efforts.

ethical client advocacy

Corcoran (1993) suggests that collaboration is a partnership between a professional and a consumer. The intent of this partnership is to empower the consumer to create personalized goals and strategies based on various factors such as lifestyle and values. Nurses, as professionals, have an ethical obligation to recognize complex needs, remain client centered (preserve the client's autonomy in decision making) and plan jointly with other disciplines to enable the client to resolve health problems. The overall goal of collaboration is to enable the client to gain knowledge and power, use decision-making authority needed to set priorities among conflicting values, and decide how limited resources will be used. Collaboration of this type is not easy, but no less necessary. It becomes less difficult as the nurse gains experience in communicating with others to solve problems and satisfy consumer health needs cooperatively.

Collaborating effectively with other disciplines requires helping clients, when necessary, to express their concerns to involved professionals. This approach requires professionals to provide the information a client needs to make decisions rather than controlling or making decisions for the client. Balancing the power in the problem-solving situation enhances communication. This requires professionals to listen actively to the client and work toward an open exchange of ideas.

In modern complex healthcare delivery systems, collaboration becomes a common nursing communication function. Just as it is critical to listen actively to clients, effective collaboration requires that the nurse learn to respect different values, knowledge bases, purposes, and functions of other disciplines. The nurse, to collaborate effectively, needs to maintain an openness to the concerns of others and a willingness to express his/her own concerns to others. Often, nurses or members of other disciplines do not perceive collaboration as necessary in meeting professional obligations to clients. By being aware of these differences in professional perspectives, the nurse can plan to express nursing concerns in a timely manner. By practicing assertiveness skills, nurses can increase satisfaction in the practice of their profession. Simultaneously, nurses increase other professionals' awareness of the potential contributions to the quality of care when collaboration occurs. With the increased emphasis on consumer satisfaction with care provided and the increased complexity of care, collaboration will grow in importance.

maintaining openness

Collaboration may make practice more satisfying. Baggs and Ryan (1990) used collaboration with physicians regarding the transfer of patients from an ICU unit to less-intensive levels of care as a measure of collaboration. They noted that nurses who perceived themselves as participants in the decision-making process with physicians about the timing of patient transfer felt more satisfied with their work. In addition, as nurses became more satisfied with their work, they were more likely to be retained in that specific agency.

As discussed in this chapter's "Research Perspective," Baggs and Ryan (1990) indicated that nurses valued and promoted collaboration in the workplace, sometimes by including it as a criterion of nursing work performance. In contrast, physicians appear to value collaboration less and are much less inclined to have their collaboration with others evaluated as a component of their practice.

value of collaboration

To exchange information in a meaningful way, in addition to common values, a common language is needed to enable the various disciplines to share knowledge with each other and to include clients and their families. As mentioned earlier in this chapter, the need to "check" others' perceptions is critical to assure that people with differing values, knowledge, and perspectives understand each other. Then it becomes possible for clients and families to express concerns, identify problems and mobilize interdisciplinary team efforts to resolve problems conjointly.

common language

Just as nurses have their own unique body of knowledge, values, and skills and use **jargon** to communicate with one another within the discipline, so does each of the other disciplines. If these differences go unrecognized, communication misses the mark and is ineffective. To understand one another on the interdisciplinary team, members need to feel comfortable asking for clarification of terminology used and explanations of goals and functions. Paraphrasing in common language until the team has worked together for awhile is usually very helpful.

Research Perspective

Baggs, J.G., & Ryan, S. (1990). ICU nurse-physician collaboration & nursing satisfaction. Nursing Economics, 8(6), 386–392.
This study was done to determine whether promoting nurse–physician collaboration, particularly in intensive care units, might be used as a strategy for increasing work satisfaction, and consequently, retention. Retention of ICU nurses would be a method of increasing cost savings.

For the purpose of this study, the researchers defined collaboration as "ICU nurses and physicians cooperatively working together, sharing responsibility for problem solving and decision making, to formulate and carry out plans for patient care" (p. 387). They hypothesized that increased collaborative practice increased job satisfaction and that increased participation in decision making with patient transfer increased nurses' satisfaction.

The sample consisted of sixty-eight registered nurses employed in a medical ICU over a six-month period. Demographic information was collected about these nurses. The collaborative practice scales (CPS) and index of work satisfaction (IWS) were used to quantify the amount of collaborative practice and the nurses' satisfaction with their work. The researchers developed a "decision about transfer" scale to grade collaboration and satisfaction at the time the decision to transfer patients was made.

The researchers did not find a significant correlation between collaborative practice and work satisfaction. Older nurses tended to report more collaboration and less satisfaction with their work. Younger nurses associated more collaboration with more satisfaction.

The researchers found a significant positive correlation between perceived participation in the decision-making process to transfer patients with more collaborative and satisfying practice. Participation in decision making was perceived as an accurate indicator of collaborative practice.

Implications for Practice

Collaborative practice is associated with participation in decision-making processes, which is related to retention. Collaboration alone does not increase general satisfaction with work. Additional educational and professional experience may promote more assertive and cooperative professional practice. Age of nurses per se does not correspond to increased collaboration and satisfaction with practice.

client involvement

Interdisciplinary team conferences are often scheduled and structured for staff convenience. It is important to include clients, allowing everyone sufficient time to express concerns and goals, and to formulate plans based on the client's informed decision making. Clients need to shape their own healthcare programs, using available interdisciplinary resources in a cost-effective manner. Collaboration requires that a common language be used to set mutually agreeable goals.

This chapter has already mentioned the need to incorporate differences in backgrounds and motivations among people. Admittedly, the goal of meeting widely varying nursing needs of clients is complex, given the differences in nursing team members' skills, strengths, and vulnerabilities. The same basic communication processes of sending and receiving messages and verifying perceptions are involved in addressing client needs that require collaborative interdisciplinary planning. The inherent need is to mobilize the work group to establish common goals, using language that everyone involved understands. Unless team members frequently check their perceptions with each other, goals are not likely to be understood, agreed upon, or met. Everyone involved needs to be actively listened to, respected for their participation, and encouraged to contribute toward needed solutions. The need for collaborators to be active listeners is just as important as being **assertive** communicators.

One dilemma that novice nurses face is that nursing students rarely have the opportunity to gain "real" experience in interdisciplinary collaboration while enrolled in formal course work (Mariano, 1989). Consequently, their lack of experience often decreases confidence. However, the novice nurse who feels confident about his/her communication skills can start with a positive attitude, an openness about communicating concerns and information, and a persistence in working toward empowering clients to reach their goals. In addition, observing how role models apply communication skills helps nurses sort out the individual, interdisciplinary, and organizational needs that are part of creative problem solving and collaborating. Talking with a mentor may also help new nurse managers develop strategies that maximize their assertiveness and build their confidence in the skills they need to empower clients.

EXERCISE 16-5

Imagine that you are one of the nursing representatives on an interdisciplinary team consisting of a community health nurse/discharge services coordinator, occupational therapist, psychiatrist, psychologist, physical therapist, recreational therapist, and social worker, speech pathologist, and vocational counselor. This interdisciplinary team works with disabled adults who frequently have dual diagnoses.

The client, Mr. A., is a 28-year-old divorced father of two school-aged children who sustained multiple injuries in a hit-and-run motor vehicle accident. He was employed as a construction worker. The client has hearing and speech deficits, deficits in self-care, right-sided hemiplegia, and needs to wear a rigid body jacket when out of bed. He is struggling with accomplishing bowel and urinary continence. He has become increasingly withdrawn, refusing to participate in his care and decisions affecting him.

a. What are Mr. A's priority needs?
b. Who on the interdisciplinary team is most important in helping Mr. A. rehabilitate himself?
c. What is the best schedule of therapies for Mr. A.?
d. What can nursing contribute to developing a plan of care and its implementation? With whom should nursing collaborate?

Discuss your strategies to find answers to these questions with a mentor in a clinical setting. When collaborating, how important is it to speak in a timely manner? How important is it to actively listen to understand the responses of other interdisciplinary team members?

CHAPTER CHECKLIST

Effective communication depends upon continual efforts to attend to the details of the basic components of the process—sender, receiver, message, and feedback. Nurse leaders and managers must be able to communicate clearly within the profession and within the broader, interdisciplinary healthcare context.

- Communication is a means of enhancing understanding; its basic principles include the following:
  - Communication is a means, not an end.
  - The purpose of communication is to determine who the sender and receiver are and how best to transmit the message.
  - Context and feedback affect communication.
  - Collaborating to solve complex problems requires effective communication skills.
- Messages are designed based on:
  - The receiver
  - The sender
  - The intent of the message.
- Assumptions interfere with effective communication.
  - Verifying the validity of assumptions is critical to effective communication.
- Behavior conveys meaning more clearly than words.
  - Positive behaviors are desired actions that clearly convey their own importance.
    - Role modeling can be an effective teaching strategy.
  - Negative behaviors are undesired actions, or actions that lack the desired behavior.
    - Negative behaviors can include gestures, facial expressions, and other forms of body language.
- Technology influences communication.
- Nurse managers must be sensitive to vertical and horizontal lines of communication.
- Factors that influence our perception of communication include:
  - Culture
  - Education
  - Experience.
- Complex healthcare demands collaboration.
- Active listening is an essential skill.
- Using a common language in interdisciplinary discussions promotes communication and team building.

TERMS TO KNOW

- assertive
- behavioral message
- collaboration
- communication
- jargon

- negative behaviors
- organizational message
- positive behaviors
- technological message

REFERENCES

Aaronson, L.S. (1989). A challenge for nursing: Re-viewing a historic competition. *Nursing Outlook, 37*(6), 274–279.

Baggs, J.G. (1993). Collaborative interdisciplinary bioethical decision making in intensive care unit. *Nursing Outlook, 41*(3), 108–112.

Baggs, J.G., & Ryan, S.A., (1990). ICU nurse-physician collaboration and nursing satisfaction. *Nursing Economics, 8*(6), 386–392.

Basta, S.M. (1991). Pressure sore prevention education with the spinal cord injured. *Rehabilitation Nursing, 16*(1), 6–8.

Bice, M. (1990, March 20). Employee orientations should stress core values. *Hospitals,* pp. 72.

Corcoran, M.A. (1993). Collaboration: An ethical approach to effective therapeutic relationships. *Topics in Geriatric Rehabilitation 9*(1), 21–29.

Garcia, M.A., Bruce, D., Niemeyer, J., & Robbins, J. (1993). Collaborative practice: A shared success. *Nursing Management, 24*(5), 72–74.

Mariano, C. (1989). The case for interdisciplinary collaboration. *Nursing Outlook, 37*(6), 285–288.

Moulder, P.A., Staal, A.M., & Grant, M. (1988). Making the interdisciplinary team approach work. *Rehabilitation Nursing 13*(6), 338–339.

SUGGESTED READINGS

Adler, M.J. (1983). *How to Speak—How to Listen*. New York: Macmillan.

Bullough, V. L. (1990). Nightingale, nursing and harassment. *Image: Journal of Nursing Scholarship, 22*(1), 4–7.

Coeling, H.V.E., & Wilcox, J.R. (1991). Professional recognition and high-quality patient care through collaboration: Two sides of the same coin. *Focus on Critical Care-AACN, 18*(3), 230–237.

Diaz, A.L., & McMillin, J.D. (1991). A definition and description of nurse abuse. *Western Journal of Nursing Research, 13*(1), 97–109.

Elgin, S.H. (1980). *The Gentle Art of Verbal Self-Defense*. Englewood Cliffs, NJ: Prentice Hall.

Evans, S.A., & Carlson, R. (1992). Nurse-physician collaboration: Solving the nursing shortage crisis. *Journal of the American College of Cardiology, 20*(7), 1669–1673.

Fagin, C.M. (1992). Collaboration between nurses and physicians no longer a choice. *Academic Medicine, 67*, 295–303.

Johnson, N.D. (1992). Collaboration—An environment for optimal outcome. *Critical Care Nursing Quarterly, 15*(3), 37–43.

Pillitteri, A. (1993). The 'doctor-nurse game': A comparison of 100 years—1888–1990. *Nursing Outlook, 41*(3), 113–116.

Reifsteck, S.W., & D'Angelo, L. (1990). Physician-nurse relationships. *Topics in Health Care Financing, 16*(3), 12–21.

CHAPTER 17

CONFLICT: THE CUTTING EDGE OF CHANGE

Mary J. Keenan, R.N., Ph.D.
Joseph B. Hurst, Ph.D., Ed.D.

PREVIEW

This chapter focuses on increasing the nurse manager's ability to deal with conflict by providing effective strategies for conflict resolution and management. To resolve conflicts, the nurse manager must be able to determine the nature of the particular conflicts, choose the most appropriate approach for each situation, and resolve the conflicts effectively. Since some conflicts are by nature unresolvable, an understanding of polarities and polarity management can also help the nurse manager recognize the upsides and downsides of an issue and capitalize on the positive.

OBJECTIVES

- Use a model of the conflict process to determine the nature and sources of hypothetical and actual conflict.
- Assess your preferred approaches to conflict and commit to new ways to be more effective in resolving future conflict.
- Determine which of the five optional approaches to conflict is the most appropriate approach in hypothetical and real situations.
- Diagram the structure and dynamics of an important polarity (unresolvable conflict) and identify ways to manage it.

QUESTIONS TO CONSIDER

- What situations, issues, and people trigger conflict for you? Why? How do you trigger conflict in others?
- How do you usually determine why people are having conflict? How do you usually react to and resolve conflict?
- What typical consequences occur from conflicts in which you are involved?
- How have you tended to handle unresolvable or recurring conflicts in the past? How could you handle them in the future?

A Manager's Viewpoint

Conflict is the most difficult challenge managers face because if not resolved effectively, it can block the organization from moving forward. Settling "turf" wars among nursing staff is probably the most disconcerting part of the job. Determining who is responsible and accountable for what is not an easy task. We often experience intrapersonal and interpersonal conflict. More simply stated, we have to embark upon a conflict resolution process that looks at who owns what and where do we go from here to make things work.

Without open, honest communication, it is an overwhelming task to confront changes in healthcare and to move a nursing unit, an entire institution, and the nursing profession forward. As leaders and managers, we must constantly be aware of the need to "read" others (really listen for others' intentions, feelings, and concerns) as well as to keep in touch with our own. We think that it is important not to get caught up in others' frustrations and emotional reactions to conflict while acknowledging the legitimacy of their concerns.

Identify the real conflict, take a breather to diffuse your anger and other feelings, and get others to feel some "ownership" of it. If this is not done, you may be left "holding the bag" or playing the role of "Mama Manager," who is supposed to resolve all conflicts and actually stifles group participation.

Mary Ann Dimmick, M.S.N., R.N.
Marsha Brown, M.S.N., R.N.
Nursing Directors
Medical College of Ohio Hospitals
Toledo, Ohio

INTRODUCTION

Much has been written and said about how to solve problems and how to resolve conflicts rationally, logically, and effectively. The trap in all this is the assumption that such rational processes lead to solutions and resolutions in all situations. For instance, Scott (1990) demonstrates this trap when she suggests:

> The basic way to use the rational-intuitive approach to managing conflict is to look on any conflict situation as a problem or potential problem to be solved. Then, you select the appropriate problem-solving techniques from a supply of possible strategies for dealing with conflict. (p. 3)

Conflict arises from a perception of incompatibility. In other words, conflict primarily stems from differences in beliefs, values, attitudes, goals, priorities, methods, information, commitments, ideas, interpretations of reality, personalities, backgrounds, needs, interests, and/or motives (Scott, 1990).

> Conflicts are more than just debates or negotiations. They represent an escalation of everyday competition and discussion into an arena of hostile or emotion-provoking encounters that strain personal or interpersonal tranquility, or both. (Scott, 1990, p. 1)

Controversy can be defined as a situation in which opinions, ideas, information, theories, and conclusions are perceived as incompatible with those of another person or group (Johnson and Johnson, 1994). Controversy, however, is very important for high-quality group decision making and individual relationships because if managed well, it can stimulate creativity, agreement, increased commitment, cohesiveness, and collaboration. Conflicts can be based upon differences in needs, values, and goals; on scarcities of particular resources; or on rivalry (Johnson and Johnson, 1994).

TYPES OF CONFLICT

Conflict occurs in all areas of our lives and in three broad categories. Conflict can be intrapersonal, interpersonal, and organizational in nature.

intrapersonal

Intrapersonal conflict occurs within a person. Questions often arise that create a conflict over priorities, ethical standards, and different ways to act. When a nurse manager decides what to do about the future (e.g., "Do I really want to study for a higher degree or start our family now?"), there are conflicts between personal and professional priorities. Some issues present a conflict over comfortably maintaining the status quo (e.g., "My relationship with the experienced nurses on the unit is so very smooth and I want it to stay that way."), or taking risks in order to make suggestions and confront people when needed (e.g., "Would telling them their technique is way out of date and suggesting new ones like I learned jeopardize my rapport with them?").

interpersonal

Interpersonal conflict occurs when we realize that everybody does not see the world exactly the same way. There are conflicts among patients, nurses, care teams, family members, physicians, and other staff. A manager may be called upon to assist two nurses in resolving a scheduling conflict, or determining whether sharing particular information would, or would not, be a violation of confidentiality. Patients resist suggestions for changing their diet, exercise, and health habits. Members of healthcare teams often have disputes over the best way to treat particular cases. Interpersonal conflict is common and can create the energy to build important relationships and teams.

Organizational conflict occurs when confronting the policies and procedures in patient care and personnel, as well as the accepted norms of behavior and communication within any organization. Some organizational conflict is related to hierarchical structure and role differentiation among employees, such as labor and management negotiations and financial administrators' and department chairs' arguments over cost cutting. Nurse managers can become enmeshed in institution-wide conflict concerning cost reductions and quality of care, advances in technology and research versus expansion of access to care, and increasing profitable services while reducing unprofitable ones.

organizational

A major source of organizational conflict stems from new systems to promote more participation and autonomy in staff nurses. The trend is to charge nurses with determining and carrying out both direct patient care and unit goals for quality patient care. Increasing autonomy in staff nurses simultaneously changes their role and relationships with nurse managers (Keenan, Hurst, and Olnhausen, 1993). As staff nurses assume more autonomy and accountability for identifying areas for quality improvement in patient care, they may desire more shared responsibility with their managers. While managers' span of control continues to increase, previously clear roles become blurred and subsequently need to be redefined for staff and managers. All such changes involve organizational conflict mixed with intrapersonal and interpersonal conflict.

THE CONFLICT PROCESS

Conflict proceeds through four stages: frustration, conceptualization, action, and outcomes (Kinney and Hurst, 1979). The ability to resolve conflicts productively depends upon understanding this process (see Figure 17-1) and upon developing creative ways to deal with conflict. Notice how the arrows in Figure 17-1 flow both ways between stages. This illustrates that moving into a subsequent stage may lead to a return to and change in a previous stage. For instance, two nurses view the conflict (conceptualize it) as a fight to control, while a third thinks it's about professional standards. A nurse manager gets them all to talk. They have expressed much frustration and mistrust. All agree that the real conflict comes from a difference in goals, which leads to less negative emotion and a much clearer understanding of all the issues.

dynamic process

FIGURE 17-1
Stages of the conflict process.

FRUSTRATION

When people or groups perceive that their goals may be blocked, they feel frustrated. This frustration may escalate into stronger emotions, such as anger and deep resignation. This frustration comes from what people believe to be true, even though there may not be a real conflict at all! For example, a nurse may perceive that a patient is uncooperative when in reality the patient has a different understanding and/or set of priorities than the nurse. At the same time, the patient may view the nurse as controlling and insensitive. When such frustrations occur, it is a cue to stop and clarify the nature of major differences.

CONCEPTUALIZATION

individual interpretation

Everyone involved develops an idea or picture of what the conflict is about. This may be an instantaneous "snapshot," or it may develop over a period of time. This concept of the conflict may be very clear in people's minds, or it may be very fuzzy. Everyone involved has an individual interpretation of what the conflict is and why it is occurring. Most often these interpretations are different and involve the person's own perspective.

unblocking

Regardless of its clarity or accuracy, however, the conceptualization forms the basis for everyone's reactions to the frustration. The way the individuals perceive and define the conflict has a great deal of influence on the creative resolution and productive outcomes to follow. For example, within the same conflict situation, some individuals may see the conflict as insubordination and become angry, while others view it as trivial bickering and withdraw. Such differences in conceptualizing the issue could block its resolution. Thus it is important for each person to clarify "the conflict as I see it" and "how it makes me feel" before all the people involved can define the conflict (create an accurate conceptualization together) and proceed to resolve their differences.

People are not likely to reach outcomes that truly resolve the conflict and satisfy them unless they have a clear understanding of the differences among them. During the conceptualization process, we can ask two very powerful questions:

1. What is the nature of our differences?
2. What are the reasons for those differences?

four aspects of conflict

People may differ on four aspects of a conflict: (1) facts, (2) goals, (3) methods to achieve goals, and (4) the values or standards used to select goals, priorities, and methods (Kinney and Hurst, 1979).

It is usually easier to provide accurate information than work out differences in values, priorities, methodology, and standards. Disagreements over facts may uncover conflicts over goals, means, and values, which may lead to the conflict expanding or even escalating out of control. Values, opinions, and beliefs are more personal, thus generating disagreements that can be threatening and adversarial. The more accurately any conflict is defined the more likely it will be resolved.

ACTION

Intentions, strategies, plans, and behavior "flow" out of the conceptualization. A pattern of interaction among the individuals involved is set in motion (e.g., "Let's work together" or "We're not getting any place this way"). As actions are taken to resolve the conflict, the way that some or all parties conceptualize the conflict may change. The important point is that people are always taking some action regarding the conflict, even if that action is avoiding it or deciding to do nothing.

There are five distinct action-oriented approaches to resolving conflict (see page 346). The longer ineffective actions continue, the more likely people will experience frustration, resistance, or even hostility. The more the actions appropriately match the nature of the conflict, the more likely it will be resolved with desirable results.

OUTCOMES

As a result of the actions taken, there are tangible and intangible consequences, or "outcomes." The conflict may be resolved with a new plan that incorporates the goals of two or more people, so no one loses. Productivity and efficiency may increase, decrease, or stay the same. Emotions may be high with anger and resistance left over, so further conflicts arise. Relationships may be strengthened, weakened, or ended. Such outcomes have very important consequences in the work setting.

Assessing the Degree of Conflict Resolution

I. Quality of decisions
    A. How creative are resulting plans?
    B. How practical and realistic are they?
    C. How well were intended goals achieved?
    D. What surprising results were achieved?
II. Quality of relationships
    A. How much understanding has been created?
    B. How willing are people to work together?
    C. How much mutual respect, empathy, concern, and cooperation has been generated?

(Adapted with permission from Hurst and Kinney, 1989)

When assessing the degree to which a conflict has been resolved, there are two general outcomes to assess: the degree to which important goals were achieved and the nature of the subsequent relationships among those involved (see the two boxes below). There are four questions you could ask about the nature of the subsequent relationships (Johnson and Johnson, 1994): (1) Are the relationships stronger and are people better able to interact? (2) Do the members like and trust each other more? (3) Are all the members satisfied with the results of the conflict? (4) Have group members become more able to resolve future conflicts with one another?

goals

relationships

Snapshot of Two Conflicts

Unproductive

Suppose I perceive a conflict between you and me because you disagree with my ideas about how to motivate others to accomplish quality improvement projects. Looking at the four steps in the process of conflict, we might find the following in an unproductive conflict:

1. **I** am **frustrated** working together on the quality improvement committee because you usually put down my ideas for change. **You** are frustrated because you perceive that I do not support your goals for improved patient care.
2. **I** see **(conceptualize)** the conflict as your ignorance of new concepts and research findings. Besides you want things pretty much your way. **You** see it as my eagerness to "shake up" people, promote myself as a leader, and increase my power.

Snapshot of Two Conflicts—cont'd

3. **My** view leads to my being forceful **(action)** with you and sharing new research studies and articles that I have found to prove my point, which confirms your judgment of me. **You** resist me with your considerations about why the new techniques will not work and by refusing to read the articles.

4. The **outcome** is that **we** have **created** a **defensive climate** and a lack of desire to work together. We have clouded the real issue and generated hostility among all of the group. The committee submits a compromise plan to which no one is committed and it then disbands. **The project essentially has failed.**

Productive

The same conflict could present itself and evolve through the same process with different outcomes.

1. **I** feel **frustrated** that we have to work on the same committee together because I believe that you tend to resist and disagree with my ideas for change. **You** seem to think that what the organization is doing now works just fine.

2. As **we talk** we realize **(conceptualize)** that we want the same thing: incentives to support quality improvement projects.

3. Our commitment to getting these incentives spurs us to identify critical areas for study. At the same time, **we decide (action)** that we need to look at new plans and research to suggest improvements and additions for our quality improvement endeavors. I say, "If you look at current and new plans, I will work on securing supporting research." We agree and others on the committee agree to do other necessary tasks.

4. The committee then prioritizes areas for study and develops a time frame **(outcomes)**. It creates an incentive program **combining the strengths** of **our** plan with some new ideas to promote internal motivation and productivity and recommends it to the personnel committee. The committee continues and the **project is successful**.

EXERCISE 17-1

Observe (or recall) a situation in which conflict is apparent. Note arguments each person/side makes and how each responds to the other's comments. What was the outcome? Was the conflict resolved? Was anything left unresolved?

Conflict Self-Assessment

Directions: Read each of the statements below. Assess yourself in terms of how frequently you tend to act that way during conflict at work. Place the number of the most appropriate response in the blank in front of each statement. Put 1 if the behavior is never typical of how you act during a conflict; 2 if it is seldom typical; 3 if it is occasionally typical; 4 if it is frequently typical; or 5 if it is very typical of how you act during conflict. Please complete all items.

_____ 1. Create new possibilities to address all important concerns.
_____ 2. Persuade others to see it and/or do it my way.
_____ 3. Work out some sort of give-and-take agreement.
_____ 4. Let other people have their way.
_____ 5. Wait and let the conflict take care of itself.

Conflict Self-Assessment—cont'd

_____ 6. Find ways that everyone can win.
_____ 7. Use whatever power I have to get what I want.
_____ 8. Find an agreeable compromise among people involved.
_____ 9. Give in so others get what they think is important.
_____10. Withdraw from the situation.
_____11. Assertively cooperate, until everyone's needs are met.
_____12. Compete until I either win or lose.
_____13. Engage in "give a little and get a little" bargaining.
_____14. Make others' needs met over my own needs.
_____15. Avoid taking any action for as long as I can.
_____16. Partner with others to find the most inclusive solution.
_____17. Put my foot down assertively for a quick solution.
_____18. Negotiate for what all sides value and can live without.
_____19. Agree to what others want to create harmony.
_____20. Keep as far away from others involved as possible.
_____21. Stick with it to get everyone's highest priorities.
_____22. Argue and debate over the best way.
_____23. Create some middle position everyone agrees to.
_____24. Put my priorities below those of other people.
_____25. Hope the issue does not come up.
_____26. Collaborate with others to achieve our goals together.
_____27. Compete with others for scarce resources.
_____28. Emphasize compromise and trade-offs.
_____29. Cool things down by letting others do it their way.
_____30. Change the subject to avoid the fighting.

Conflict Self-Assessment Scoring

Look at the numbers you placed in the blanks on the conflict assessment on the previous page. Write the number you placed in each blank on the appropriate line below. Add up your total for each column, and enter that total on the appropriate line. The greater your total for each approach, the more frequently you tend to use that approach to conflict at work. The lower the score, the less frequently you tend to use that approach to conflict at work.

Collaborating	Competing	Compromising	Accommodating	Avoiding
1.____	2.____	3.____	4.____	5.____
6.____	7.____	8.____	9.____	10.____
11.____	12.____	13.____	14.____	15.____
16.____	17.____	18.____	19.____	20.____
21.____	22.____	23.____	24.____	25.____
26.____	27.____	28.____	29.____	30.____
Total____	Total____	Total____	Total____	Total____

Throughout the rest of this section, there are descriptions of each approach and related self-assessment and commitment to action activities. Use these

EXERCISE 17-2
It's time to assess your tendencies to approach conflict. As you read and answer the thirty-item conflict survey on pp. 344–345, think of how you face and respond to conflict in professional situations. After completing the survey, tally, total, and reflect on your scores for each of the five approaches. Consider the following questions:
• Which approach(es) do you prefer? Which do you use least?
• Why do you think you tend to act that way?
• Considering the types of conflicts you tend to have, what are the strengths and weaknesses of your pattern?
As you read the rest of this section use this pattern of scores and your reflections to examine the appropriate uses of each approach, assess your use of each approach more extensively, and commit to new behaviors to increase your future effectiveness.

Conflict Self-Assessment Scoring—cont'd

totals to stimulate your thinking about how you do and could handle conflict at work. Most importantly, consider if your pattern of frequency tends to be consistent, or inconsistent, with the types of conflicts you face. That is, does your way of dealing with conflict tend to match the situations in which that approach is most useful?

Hurst, J.B. (1993). Human Resource Development Center, University of Toledo, OH. Used with permission.

MODES OF CONFLICT RESOLUTION

There are five general, distinct approaches to conflict resolution: (1) avoiding, (2) accommodating, (3) competing, (4) compromising, and (5) collaborating (Johnson and Johnson, 1994; Thomas and Killmann, 1973). These approaches can be viewed along two different continua: (1) from uncooperative to highly cooperative and (2) from unassertive to highly assertive (Thomas, 1975). (See the Conflict Self-Assessment on pages 344–346.)

continua   On the cooperative continuum actions can range from complete competition to total cooperation. Two nurses might compete for a manager position on the one extreme while teaming cooperatively to institute the expansion of their unit. On the assertiveness continuum actions range from ignoring one's own goals (highly unassertive) to doing what it takes to get what one intends (highly assertive). A nurse manager might forgo asking for time off (unassertive) at a time when the clinical manager predicts the unit will be short-staffed and overly busy (assertive).

A "teddy bear" (high cooperation and low assertiveness) and a "shark" (high assertiveness and low cooperation) were used as analogies for these two mutually exclusive approaches (Johnson and Johnson, 1994). They also used three other animals to depict the other three approaches: the wise owl (high concentration and high assertiveness) can develop ways to address both sides' concerns; the fox (in the middle of both assertiveness and cooperation) can shrewdly negotiate give and take from each side; and the turtle (low cooperation and low assertiveness) merely hides its head in its shell to avoid conflict (Johnson and Johnson, 1994).

It is unlikely that anyone would select any one approach to the exclusion of the others. In fact, as we will examine later in the section Polarity Management, people tend to move up and down or back and forth between these continua in some combined action that is appropriately assertive and cooperative, depending upon the nature of the conflict situation.

AVOIDING

unassertive/uncooperative   **Avoiding** or withdrawing (the turtle) is very unassertive and uncooperative because avoiders neither pursue their own needs, goals, and concerns immediately nor assist others to pursue theirs. The positive side of withdrawing may take the form of diplomatically side-stepping or postponing an issue until a better time or simply walking away from a "no-win" situation (see the box on page 347). The self-assessment that follows the box will help you learn to recognize your own avoidance behaviors and use them more effectively.

Positive Uses for the Avoiding Approach

1. When facing trivial and/or temporary issues, or when other far more important issues are pressing (e.g., tangential issues are only symptoms of deeper conflicts).
2. When there is no chance to obtain what one wants or needs, or when others could resolve the conflict more efficiently and effectively.
3. When the potential negative results of initiating and acting on a conflict are much greater than the benefits of its resolution.
4. When people need to "cool down," distance themselves, or gather more information, perhaps gaining a hindsight or meaningful view.

Avoidance: Self-Assessment and Commitment to Action

If you tend to use avoidance frequently then ask:
1. Do people have difficulty getting my input into and understanding my view of conflicts?
2. Do I block cooperative efforts to resolve issues?
3. Am I distancing myself from significant others?
4. Are important issues being left unidentified and unresolved?

If you do not use avoidance very often, ask yourself:
1. Do I find myself overwhelmed by a large number of conflicts and need to say "no"?
2. Do I assert myself even when things do not matter that much? Do others view me as an aggressor?
3. Do I lack a clear view of what my priorities are?
4. Do I stir up conflicts and fights for some reason?

Commitment to Action
Reflecting on my assessment of myself, what two new behaviors would increase my effective use of avoidance at work?
1.
2.

ACCOMMODATING/SMOOTHING

Like the loving teddy bear, when accommodating, people neglect their own needs, goals, and concerns (unassertive) while trying to satisfy those of others (cooperative). This approach has an element about it of being self-sacrificing, obeying orders, or serving other people. For example, sometimes we don't care where we eat, and others do. So we say, "Fine, let's eat there! I like all kinds of food, I'm really hungry, so let's go." The box on page 348 lists some appropriate uses of **accommodation.**

unassertive cooperative

Accommodators frequently feel disappointment and resentment because they "get nothing in return." This is a built-in by-product of the overuse of this approach. The self-assessment on page 348 asks you to examine your present use of accommodation and challenges you to think of new ways to use it more effectively.

Appropriate Uses of Accommodation

1. When other people's ideas and solutions appear to be better or when you have made a mistake.
2. When the issue is far more important to the other(s) than it is for you. (This is a natural, logical step to cooperation and collaboration.)
3. When you see that accommodating now "builds up some important credits" for later issues.
4. When you are outmatched and/or losing anyway; when continued competition would only damage the relationships and productivity of the group and jeopardize accomplishing major purpose(s) and maintaining credibility.
5. When preserving harmonious relationships and avoiding defensiveness and hostility are very important.
6. When letting others learn from their mistakes and/or increased responsibility is possible without severe damage (and you are able to avoid saying, "I told you so!").

Accommodation: Self-Assessment and Commitment to Action

If you use accommodation frequently, then ask yourself:
1. Do I feel that my needs, goals, concerns, and ideas, are not being attended to by others?
2. Am I depriving myself of influence, recognition, and respect?
3. When I am in charge is "discipline" lax?
4. Do I think people are using me?
Infrequent use of accommodation may result in your being viewed as unreasonable or insensitive.

If you seldom use accommodation, ask yourself:
1. Am I building goodwill with others during conflict?
2. Do I admit when I've made a mistake?
3. Do I recognize legitimate exceptions?
4. Do I know when to give in, or do I assert myself at all costs?

Commitment to Action
What two new behaviors would increase your effective use of accommodation?
1.
2.

COMPETING/COERCING

assertive/uncooperative

During competition people (and sharks) pursue their own needs and goals at the expense of others'. Sometimes people use whatever power, creativeness, or strategies are available to "win." **Competing** may also take the form of standing up for your rights, defending important principles, and contending for limited funds (see the accompanying box).

People who compete well and frequently may not be able to hear the truth, have others disagree, or be challenged, even when they are wrong. They often react by being threatened, defensive, and aggressive. Competition within work

Appropriate Uses of Competing

1. When quick, decisive action is necessary.
2. When important, unpopular action needs to be taken. When trade-offs may result in long-range, continued conflict.
3. When people are right about issues that are vital to group welfare.
4. When people have had others take advantage of their noncompetitive behavior and now feel obliged to compete.

groups can generate ill will, a win-lose stance, and "commitment to inaction" (Keenan and Hurst, 1985, p. 11). Use the self-assessment that follows to help you learn to use competing more effectively.

Competing: Self-Assessment and Commitment to Action

If you use competing frequently, ask yourself:
1. Am I surrounded by people who agree with me all the time and who avoid confronting me?
2. Are others afraid to share themselves and their needs for growth with me?
3. Am I out to win at all costs? If so, what are the costs and benefits of competing?

If you tend not to compete, ask yourself:
1. How often do I avoid taking a strong stand and then feel a sense of powerlessness?
2. Do I avoid taking a stand so that I can escape risk?
3. Am I fearful and unassertive to the point that important decisions are delayed and people suffer?

Commitment to Action
What two new behaviors would increase your use of conflict?
1.
2.

NEGOTIATING/COMPROMISING

Negotiating involves both assertiveness and cooperation on the part of everyone and requires the skills of the "fox." There is a give and take resulting in conflict resolution with people meeting their important priorities as much as possible. **Compromising** is often an exchange of concessions or creation of a middle position. This is the preferred means of conflict resolution during union negotiations, when each side is appeased to some degree. In this mode, nobody gets everything they think they need.

moderate assertive/cooperative

Negotiation and compromise are valued approaches. They are chosen when less accommodating or avoiding is appropriate (see box on page 350). Compromising is a blend of both assertive and cooperative behaviors, although it calls for less finely honed skills for each behavior than does collaboration. Negotiation is more like trading (e.g., "You can have this if I can have that."). Compromise was one of the most frequently selected behaviors used by nurse managers because it supported a balance of power between themselves and

Appropriate Uses of Compromise

1. Two powerful sides are committed strongly to perceived mutually exclusive goals.
2. Temporary solutions to complex issues need to be implemented.
3. Conflicting goals are "moderately important" and not worth a major confrontation (coercion/competing).
4. Time pressures people to expedite a workable solution.
5. When collaborating and competing fail.

Compromise supports a balance of power between self and others in the workplace.

Negotiation/Compromise Self-Assessment and Commitment to Action

If you tend to use negotiation frequently, consider:
1. Do I ignore large, important issues while trying to work out creative, practical compromises?
2. Is there a "gamesmanship" in my/our negotiations?
3. Am I sincerely committed to compromise or negotiated solutions?

If you tend to use negotiation infrequently, ask yourself:
1. Do I find it difficult to make concessions?
2. Am I often engaged in strong disagreements or do I withdraw when I see no way to get out?
3. Do I feel embarrassed, sensitive, self-conscious, or pressured to negotiate, compromise, and bargain?

Commitment to Action
What two new behaviors would increase your compromising effectiveness?
1.
2.

others in the work setting (Barton, 1991). This chapter's "Research Perspective" (page 352) describes this study. The self-assessment on page 350 will help you become more aware of your own use of negotiation and compromise and improve it.

COLLABORATING

Collaborating, the opposite of both avoiding and competing, is the position of the wise owl. It is both assertive and cooperative as people work creatively and openly to find the solution that most fully satisfies all important concerns and goals to be achieved. **Collaboration** involves analyzing situations and defining the conflict at a higher level where shared "superordinate" goals are identified and commitment to work together is generated (see box below). For example, when nurses and physicians work together, they can collaborate by replacing "Who's in charge?" with "What does the patient require?" and "Where does each of us fit into the plan?" This requires discussion about the plan (superordinate goals), how this will be accomplished, and who will make what contributions to achieving the plan.

assertive/cooperative

The same scenario fits for patients and families as well. What is their superordinate goal? Who will do what so that they can reach this goal? The stakes are high (quality patient care) as all stakeholders (e.g., patient, nurse, family, and physician) agree to work together.

Trivial issues do not require collaboration and consensus seeking. Some people favor collaboration to reduce their risk taking and to spread responsibility. Use the self-assessment on page 352 that follows to determine your own use of collaboration.

Appropriate Uses for Collaboration

1. To seek creative, integrative solutions where both sides' goals and needs are important, thus developing group commitment and a consensual decision.
2. To learn and grow through cooperative problem solving resulting in greater understanding and empathy.
3. To identify, share, and merge vastly different viewpoints.
4. To be honest about and work through difficult emotional issues interfering with morale, productivity, and growth.

At the onset of conflict, people can carefully analyze situations to identify the nature and reasons for conflict and choose an appropriate approach promoting collaboration. In other words, we can collaborate on the decision to withdraw, compete, or negotiate. For example, suppose you and I are disagreeing about the timing of procedures for patients under your care. At the point that we both agree that it's your responsibility and decision to make, we collaborate and agree. I say, "I see your point, so let's do it that way." Or we might talk and subsequently agree that you are too emotionally involved with a patient's problem and that it may be time for you to withdraw from providing the care and enlist the skills of another nurse. This discussion can result in collaborative efforts for you to withdraw. Another less desirable choice could be to compete and let the winner's position stand, e.g., "Do as I say" or "I'm in charge of this patient." The decision to compete or collaborate depends on you and the other person.

Collaboration Self-Assessment and Commitment to Action

If you tend to collaborate frequently, consider:
1. Do I spend valuable group time and energy on issues that do not warrant or deserve it?
2. Do I postpone needed action to get consensus and avoid making key decisions?
3. When I initiate collaboration, do others really respond that way? (Are there hidden agendas, unspoken hostility, and/or manipulation in the group?)

If you tend to collaborate infrequently, ask yourself:
1. Do I ignore opportunities to cooperate, risk, and creatively confront conflict?
2. Do I tend to be pessimistic, distrusting, withdrawing, and/or competitive?
3. Am I involving others in important decisions, eliciting commitment, and empowering them?

Commitment to Action
What two new behaviors would increase your collaboration effectiveness:
1.
2.

The nature of the differences, underlying reasons, importance of the issue, strength of feelings, commitment, and goals involved all have to be considered when selecting an approach to resolving conflict. Preferred and previously effective approaches can be considered, but they need to match the situation. Effective resolution may require switching to a more appropriate method.

 Research Perspective

Barton, A. (1991). *Conflict resolution by nurse managers. Nursing Management,* 22(5), 83–86.

A study of sixty-nine nurse managers used the Thomas-Kilmann Conflict Mode Instrument to determine how nurse administrators, head nurses, and assistant head nurses handled conflict. Their preferred modes of conflict resolution, in descending order, were compromise, collaboration, avoidance, accommodation, and competition. Key factors in selecting the best approach included goal importance, situation complexity, power of other parties involved, vested interests, and urgency. Assistant head nurses tended to use competition less frequently because of their liaison position and their avoidance of taking a "win/lose" stance.

Implications for Practice

The modes selected for conflict resolution by nursing personnel significantly impinge on the achievement of patient care goals. Healthcare organizations need to consider several issues: the kinds of educational programs that could increase effective conflict resolution; the relationship between preferred modes of resolution and job satisfaction; and whether new graduates and experienced nursing staff prefer different modes.

MANAGING UNRESOLVABLE CONFLICTS

Not all of the conflicts confronting people are resolvable. In fact, most of our own present problems and conflicts, especially the continuing or reappearing ones, are probably unresolvable (Johnson, 1992). Such conflicts cannot be resolved by the right amounts of money, time, resources, staff, support networks, state-of-the-art technology, diet, exercise, vacation time, teamwork, courage, training, rational thinking, and/or leadership (see box). These conflicts are inherently unresolvable (Hurst, Keenan, and Minnick, 1992; Johnson, 1992).

Many conflicts (and problems) are inherently unresolvable because they consist of two interdependent, dynamic polar opposites that require a shifting emphasis from pole to pole over time, rather than the selection of the one "best" option. Resolvable conflicts (and solvable problems) tend to be either/or choices that lead to some end. Unresolvable conflicts, or **polarities**, involve a both/and decision of when to emphasize one pole and then its opposite. For

polarities

How to Tell If A Conflict May Be Unresolvable

PROBABLY IS UNRESOLVABLE	ASK THESE QUESTIONS ABOUT THE SITUATION	PROBABLY IS RESOLVABLE
Answer is yes	Is this difficulty ongoing?	Answer is no
Answer is yes	Are there two interdependent poles?	Answer is no
Answer is yes	Does choosing one need to incorporate the other to succeed?	Answer is no
Answer is yes	Is this really a both/and decision?	Answer is no

instance, a manager's need to give clear direction to a team automatically places less emphasis on the team's deciding on the direction themselves. But sooner or later, for the team's to be successful, that manager will experience the need for the team to work on its own, setting its own direction. Johnson (1992) has identified several common polarities with which people deal continually. These include self and others, individual and team, individual and organizational responsibility, control and participatory management, specific and general communication, tasks and relationships, centralization and decentralization, and stability and change. Others you are probably confronting include "me and my department," personal life and professional life, stimulation (stress) and tranquility, conditional acceptance (love) and unconditional acceptance (love), cost and quality, management and leadership, and planning and acting.

POLARITY STRUCTURE

Polarities have six important elements (Figure 17-2) including two neutral, interdependent poles; two sets of resulting positive consequences ("upsides"), one for each pole; and two sets of associated negative consequences ("downsides"). To determine the nature of the unresolvable conflicts, one has to ask five basic questions, as shown in the box below.

upsides and downsides

By answering these basic questions an individual or team can diagram the specifics of any polarity situation. Typically, people see only half the situation—the upside of their preferred pole and the downside of its opposite—and are therefore blind to the other two quadrants—their preferred pole's downside and its opposite's upside (Johnson, 1992). This blindness, coupled with the need to be right, leads to much conflict with those who favor the opposite pole and see only the other two quadrants. Just the awareness that there are such things as polarities and diagramming important ones tends to increase collaboration and "win/win" thinking because people learn that fighting over one pole leads to experiencing its downside consequences (Hurst, Keenan, and Sipp, 1993; Johnson, 1992).

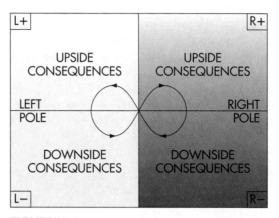

FIGURE 17-2
Generic structure and predictable flow of polarities.

POLARITY DYNAMICS

Visually, a polarity diagram consists of the two polar opposites on a horizontal axis divided into four quadrants of results by a vertical line (Hurst, Keenan and Sipp, 1993). Though simple in form, polarity diagrams clearly picture the consequences to be experienced and the nature of its historical and predictable flow.

natural flow   Notice in Figure 17-2 that polarities naturally and predictably "flow" (arrows represent a plot of changes in results) from the downside of pole L toward the upside of pole R; then into the downside of pole R; then toward the upside of the first, pole L; and finally back to the downside of L where it all began. For example, a nurse manager was confronted by an angry team because they felt as

Basic Polarity Questions

1. What neutral terms describe the two polar opposites involved?
2. What are the positive consequences of actions emphasizing the first pole?
3. What are the negative consequences of action overemphasizing that pole to the exclusion of its opposite?
4. What are the positive consequences of actions taken toward the second pole?
5. What are the negative consequences of action overemphasizing the second pole while excluding the first?

if they were being treated like children and told what to do all the time (control management's downside, L−). Working together they initiated team meetings and decision-making procedures (actions emphasizing participatory management) that resulted in more ideas, ownership of the area, and self-direction from the team and its individual members (participatory upside, R+). However, after a few months of overemphasizing participation, the team began to lose its focus and cohesiveness (participatory downside, R−) and came to the manager for direction. The manager listened and provided clarification (action emphasizing control management) and the team regained its focus and efficiency (upside of control management, L+).

Polarities have this infinite-type swing to them as represented by the shape of the flow of the arrows in Figure 17-2. Although these swings reflect quite limited or unlimited changes in consequences with vastly differing lengths of time between them, (or they may be skewed toward one goal), they will occur over time.

Wide, rapid, or very prolonged swings usually lead to disruptions in the smooth conduct of activity. When any polar opposites like change and stability are approached as separate independent problems or conflicts—as they generally are—the outcomes tend to reflect the greater amount of time and intensity of consequences in the downside "quadrants" (see Figure 17-3). Sometimes people hang onto one pole so long—usually for fear of the other pole's downside—that they either are forced to change their emphasis or do so very rapidly and extremely. This leads to a "flip" from the downside of the original pole to the downside of the new pole, with almost no experiencing of the upside on the way! (Johnson, 1992). This hanging onto one pole in order to reap the benefits of its upside and avoid its opposite's downside, is what Johnson (1992) calls, "the one pole myth," or being "stuck" (p. 156).

disruption

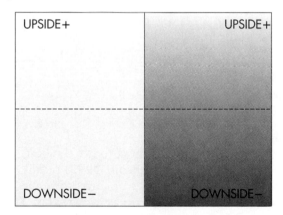

FIGURE 17-3
Polarity diagram.

The polarity diagram in Figure 17-4 was generated by a team of college students working on assertiveness ("crusading" away from the passive downside toward the assertive upside). They drew this on a chart pad by asking these questions: (L−) With what negative results of passiveness are we dissatisfied?; (R+) To what positive outcomes of assertiveness are we committed?; (R−) What negative consequences would occur from overemphasizing assertiveness (excluding any passive acceptance)?; and (L+) What are the positive consequences of being passively accepting?

flexibility   By seeing the total picture, they could take steps to make changes flexibly without overemphasizing any one pole for too long. Most importantly, they drew the results line (arrows) that best represented how this polarity usually flowed. They could see how stuck they had been, especially with almost every assertive act "feeling" negative and being resisted by others and almost every positive passive act lumped in with the negatives of "giving in." It is very important to draw such diagrams with input from as many people as possible.

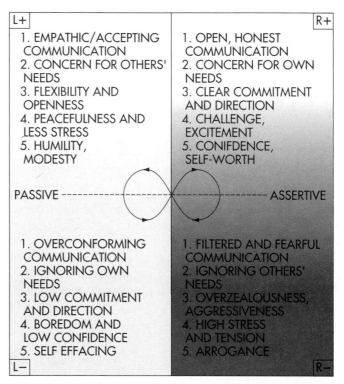

FIGURE 17-4
The passive acceptance and assertive polarity.

POLARITY MANAGEMENT

"The objective of polarity management is to get the best of both opposites while avoiding the limits of each" (Johnson, 1992, p. xii). In other words, once people determine their conflict is a polarity, they can act to maximize both poles' upsides and minimize both poles' downsides. This is called "polarity management," which requires a shifting focus from pole to pole when cues of approaching downside consequences are noted. The key to effective *sensitivity*   polarity management is to sense oncoming downside consequences, or be sensitive to feedback that there are negative consequences occurring, and take action toward the opposite pole. One nurse manager noticed that two teams had been functioning so long that individual members were complaining about being overlooked and their creativity stifled by the group. The manager scheduled a luncheon party, presented individual awards to each member, and initiated a creative suggestion box for staff to contribute individual and team ideas for improving quality and efficiency.

Polarity management involves two opposing groups that usually are in conflict. "Crusaders" are dissatisfied with the downsides of the present pole and advocate action toward its opposite. "Tradition bearers" prefer the present pole, citing its upsides, and point to the downsides of the crusaders' preferred pole as reasons to keep the emphasis where it is. Typically, the communication between crusaders and tradition bearers is argumentative, competitive, and defensive. Both sides know they are right and the other side is wrong. Polarity management alters this communication to a mood of cooperation, collaboration, and support because both sides realize that any decision to emphasize one pole results in everyone experiencing the downside of that pole, and if stuck at that pole long enough, experiencing the downsides of both poles at once! (Johnson, 1992).

crusaders and tradition bearers

There are several things a manager and an organization can do to begin managing polarities more collaboratively and effectively. Many of them are listed in the box below.

As a rule, the more skilled people are at problem solving and conflict resolution, the more likely they will mismanage polarities. This happens when

Actions for Managing a Polarity

The following list of actions exemplify steps in the management of any polarity:

- Note that the situation involves at least one continuous both/and polarity.
- Diagram in writing the polarity's poles, upsides, and downsides.
- Draw a time line (arrows representing its past, present, and predictable future flow) with dates to identify the history of this particular polarity.
- Listen carefully to people with preferences for the opposite pole. Solicit their input regularly.
- Identify key individuals and groups who are "crusading" for the new pole and "traditionally supporting" staying at the present pole. Involve them in analyzing and managing this polarity.
- State major goals and objectives in terms of maximizing the upside consequences.
- Determine what present policies, procedures, committee structures, and typical actions (a) block the effective management of this polarity (shifting from pole to pole) and (b) exemplify and/or support managing this polarity effectively. Then create new ones that would facilitate managing this polarity in the future.
- Note which people are most accurately sensitive to any changes in results toward either downside and encourage and listen to their ongoing feedback.
- Identify and create flexible ways to shift resources to either pole and to monitor results.
- Continually diagram polarities and monitor their flow.
- Value crusaders' and tradition bearers' viewpoints, their ongoing collaboration, and healthy competition between them.

people treat both/and decisions like either/or ones, thus looking for the right choice. Yet no one right choice exists, at least in the long run. To manage polarities, it is important to partner with others and shift action to what is needed next in a timely manner.

CHAPTER CHECKLIST

Conflicts may be resolvable or unresolvable, and they are common in healthcare and dealing with people. To resolve conflict, people need to identify their differences, priorities, and common goals; determine which approach to conflict is most appropriate; and act in that way to resolve it. When conflicts involve polarities, people need to analyze their structure and dynamics, identify ways to shift emphasis among opposite poles, and partner with others concerned.

- The three types of conflict are:
  - Intrapersonal
  - Interpersonal
  - Organizational.
- The conflict process flows among four stages:
  - Frustration
    - Blocked goals lead to frustration.
    - Frustration is a cue to stop and clarify differences.
  - Conceptualization
    - The way a person perceives a conflict determines how he or she reacts to the frustration.
    - Differences in conceptualizing an issue can block resolution.
  - Action
    - Intentions, strategies, plans, and behavior flow out of conceptualization.
  - Outcome (may be both tangible and intangible).
- When assessing how well a conflict has been resolved, one must consider:
  - The degree to which important goals were achieved.
  - The nature of subsequent relationships among those involved in the conflict.
- The five modes of conflict resolution are:
  - Avoiding
  - Accommodating
  - Competing
  - Compromising
  - Collaborating.
- Each mode of conflict resolution can be viewed along two different continua:
  - From uncooperative to highly cooperative
  - From unassertive to highly assertive.

■ Viewing the modes of resolution along the two continua yields a set of resulting "types":

- "Turtle" (avoiding): low cooperation/low assertiveness
- "Teddy bear" (accommodating): high cooperation/low assertiveness
- "Shark" (competing): high assertiveness/low cooperation
- "Fox" (compromising): moderately assertive/moderately cooperative
- "Wise owl" (collaborating): high cooperation/high assertiveness.

■ A conflict probably is unresolvable if:

- The difficulty is ongoing.
- There are two interdependent, polar opposite positions.
- One pole needs to incorporate the other to succeed.
- It is a "both/and" rather than "either/or" decision.

■ Polarities are unresolvable conflicts.

- Polarities have six important elements:
    - Two neutral, interdependent poles
    - Two sets of resulting positive consequences ("upsides")
    - Two sets of associated negative consequences ("downsides").
- Polarity management requires a shifting focus from one pole to the other when cues of the approaching downside consequences become evident.

TERMS TO KNOW

- **accommodating**
- **avoiding**
- **collaborating**
- **competing**
- **compromising**
- **conflict**

- **controversy**
- **interpersonal conflict**
- **intrapersonal conflict**
- **organizational conflict**
- **polarities**

REFERENCES

Barton, A. (1991). Conflict resolution by nurse managers. *Nursing Management, 22*(5), 83–86.

Hurst, J.B., & Keenan, M.J. (1986). Do you have any other ideas for improvement? *Nursing Success Today, 3*(1), 22–29.

Hurst, J.B., Keenan, M.J., & Minnick, J. (1992). Healthcare polarities: Quality and cost. *Nursing Management, 23*(9), 40–44.

Hurst, J.B., Keenan, M.J., & Sipp, R. (1993). Total quality management: A matter of quality polarity analysis and management. *The Health Care Supervisor, 11*(3), 1–11.

Hurst, J., & Kinney, M. (1989). *Empowering Self and Others.* Toledo, OH: University of Toledo.

Johnson, B. (1992). *Polarity Management: Identifying and Managing Unsolvable Problems.* Amherst, MA: HRD Press.

Johnson, D.W., & Johnson, F.P. (1994). Joining Together: Group Theory and Group Skills, 5th ed. Englewood Cliffs, NJ: Prentice-Hall.

Keenan, M.J., & Hurst, J.B. (1985). Conflict management: Problem solving through collaboration. *Nursing Success Today, 2*(12), 10–14.

Keenan, M.J., Hurst, J.B., & Olnhausen, K. (1993). Polarity management for quality care: Self direction and manager direction. *Nursing Administration Quarterly, 18*(1), 23–29.

Kinney, M., & Hurst, J. (1979). *Group Process in Education.* Lexington, MA: Ginn Custom Publishers.

Scott, G.G. (1990). *Resolving Conflict with Others and Within Yourself.* Oakland, CA: New Harbinger.

Thomas, K. (1975). Conflict and conflict management. In Dunnette, M., ed. *The Handbook of Industrial Psychology.* Chicago, IL: Rand McNally.

Thomas, K.W., & Kilmann, R.H. (1973). Thomas-Kilmann conflict mode instrument. In Pfeiffer, J.W., Heslin, R., & Jones, J.E. *Instrumentation in Human Relations Training.* San Diego, CA: University Associates, pp. 266–268.

SUGGESTED READINGS

Anderson, L. (1993). Teams, group process, success, and barriers. *Journal of Nursing Administration, 23*(9), 15–19.

Butts, B.J., & Witmer, D.M. (1992). New graduates: What does my manager expect? *Nursing Management, 22*(8), 46–48.

Curtain, L. (1993). Advanced licensure: Personal plum or public shield? *Nursing Management, 22*(8), 2.

Curtin, L. (1993). Empowerment: On eagle's wings. *Nursing Management, 24*(6), 7–9.

Dawson, R. (1993). *The Confident Decision Maker: How to Make the Right Business and Personal Decisions Every Time.* New York: William Morrow.

Flarey, D.L. (1993). The social climate of work environments. *Journal of Nursing Administration, 23*(6), 9–15.

Gollard, L.T., & Soo Hoo, W.E. (1993). Maximizing limited resources through TEAM-CARE. *Nursing Management, 14*(11), 36–43.

Hurst, J.B., & Keenan, M.J. (1986). Do you have any other ideas for improvement? *Nursing Success Today, 3*(1), 22–29.

Hurst, J., & Kinney, M. (1989). *Empowering Self and Others.* Toledo, OH: University of Toledo.

Keenan, M.J., & Hurst, J.B. (1985). Problem solving through collaboration. *Nursing Success Today, 2*(12):10–14.

Martin, K., Wimberly, D., & O'Keefe, K. (1993). Resolving conflict in a multicultural nursing department. *Nursing Management, 25*(1), 49–51.

Russo, J.E., & Shoemaker, P.J.M. *Decision Traps: Ten Barriers to Brilliant Decision-Making and How to Overcome Them.* New York: Doubleday/Currency.

CHAPTER 18
MANAGING PERFORMANCE

Cindy Whittig Roach, R.N., D.S.N.

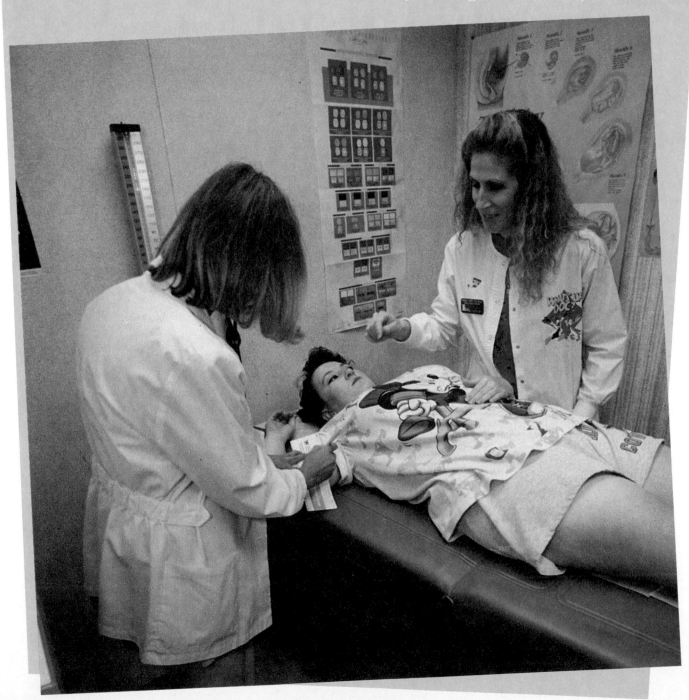

PREVIEW

This chapter illustrates various strategies surrounding performance appraisals. The basis for performance evaluation lies within the philosophy of the organization as well as the position description of the employee. **Role theory** is a useful organizing framework. Effective communication of roles and role expectations among all members can facilitate improved performance, increased worker satisfaction, and, most importantly, quality patient care. The positive outcome is consumer satisfaction!

OBJECTIVES

- Apply current philosophies of performance appraisal to a variety of situations.
- Relate concepts of role theory to performance.
- Differentiate five appraisal strategies.
- Examine specific guidelines for performance feedback.
- Distinguish key points for the appraisal interview.

QUESTIONS TO CONSIDER

- What is your role at work? At home? At school? How do you deal with conflict in these roles?
- What are some of your assumptions about performance appraisals?
- What experiences have been positive in relation to evaluative feedback?
- What type of appraisal methods are you familiar with?
- How would you improve performance appraisals?

A Manager's Viewpoint

New to the role of clinical manager and overwhelmed with paperwork, budgets, etc., I was appalled to hear that I was expected to do all of the performance appraisals for a staff of fifty-four individuals during the month of June! I barely knew all of their names. You can imagine how relieved I was to discover that the previous manager had files established on each employee and had accumulated, on a regular basis, information related to their performance, even from the last rating period! The staff had also begun the groundwork for a peer appraisal system. I reviewed the information collected on each employee and initiated the peer appraisal forms developed by the staff. I interviewed each employee to provide them feedback regarding their performance. I allowed time to clarify the position descriptions, identify training needs, and listen to the employees' future career goals. One staff nurse replied, "No one ever asked what my goals were before. Thanks!" The time and effort it required to provide a safe and positive environment was well worth the energy expended. Being prepared for each interview by reviewing all the information at hand also saved me time and embarrassment. I plan to continue this ongoing process throughout the next rating period; it was an excellent way to enhance communication between myself and all employees.

Arlene Stein, Ph.D., R.N., C.
Clinical Manager, Surgical Unit
Memorial Hospital
Colorado Springs, Colorado

INTRODUCTION

Healthcare delivery systems are businesses that are economically driven. Whether the setting is inpatient or outpatient, the emphasis is on the provision of the highest quality care at an affordable price. Professional healthcare providers must clearly understand what is expected of their performance. This can only be achieved when all members of the organization have *clearly defined roles* and overall objectives. Ambiguous roles have been proven to be more detrimental to role performance and employee satisfaction than has conflict within the role (Hardy and Conway, 1988).

Role ambiguity in the workplace creates an environment for misunderstanding and miscommunication. In this situation individuals do not have a clear understanding of what is expected of their performance or how they will be evaluated. **Role conflict,** in contrast, is easier to recognize. The employees know what is expected of them; they may not agree with it or will not meet requirements!

ROLE CONCEPTS AND THE POSITION DESCRIPTION

The acquisition of a role requires an individual to assume the personal, as well as the formal, expectations of a specified role or position. Many individuals function within multiple roles. Today's professional nurse is often a parent, spouse, and community volunteer and maintains full-time employment outside the home. There are many skills necessary for each role. There are also specified performance objectives for the *role-taker* (the individual actually performing the role) within the social context in which the role is acted out. The social context includes the physical and social environment. Acquisition of the role is time dependent; individuals apply their life experiences to each role and interpret the role within their own value system. As roles become more complex, the individual may take longer to assimilate the components of each particular role. Nursing graduates enter the profession with various levels of educational experiences as well as life experiences. The nurse manager plays an integral role in assisting these individuals in the development and acquisition of the complex role of the professional nurse. The important thing to remember is that role development evolves over time and with consideration to individual needs. Coaching is a technique that the manager can use to facilitate individual development and will be discussed later in this chapter within the context of performance appraisal.

What does all of this have to do with a position description? Everything! The **position description** provides written guidelines describing the roles and responsibilities of a specific position within the organizational context. The position description reflects functions and obligations of a specific work position. It is a contract for the individual that describes responsibilities of the work assignment as well as to whom the individual reports. The position description should reflect current practice guidelines for individuals. As paradigms of nursing delivery systems shift to the home and community, professional nurses must have a clear understanding of the performance that is expected. The nurse is also responsible for clearly understanding the position descriptions of the paraprofessionals to whom care is delegated. Clear and concise position descriptions for all employees are extremely important; they provide the basis for roles within the organization. An example of an abbreviated position description for a staff nurse in the emergency department appears in the box below:

Excerpts From A Position Description

- Responsible for the provision of direct patient care to all age groups.
- Must have current certification in advanced cardiac life support (ACLS) and pediatric advanced life support (PALS).
- Required to accurately assess and prioritize patient care needs and delegate care appropriately to parapersonnel, including LPNs and EMTs (emergency medical technicians).
- Responsible to the clinical nurse manager of the emergency department.

EXERCISE 18-1

Obtain a position description from a community nursing service and a hospital. Compare them. Analyze the general categories (for example, communication) and the specific behaviors. What competencies do you have already? How will you develop other competencies?

PERFORMANCE APPRAISALS

Providing feedback to employees regarding their performance is one of the strongest rewards that an organization can provide. **Performance appraisals** are individual evaluations of work performance. Evaluations are usually done on an annual basis but may be required after a scheduled orientation period for new employees. Ideally, evaluations are conducted on an ongoing basis, not at the conclusion of a predetermined period of time. This chapter's "Research Perspective" illustrates a positive management intervention.

feedback as reward

 Research Perspective

Goode, C.J., & Blegen, M.A. (1993). Development and evaluation of a research-based management intervention. A recognition protocol. Journal of Nursing Administration, 23(4), 61–66.

A descriptive study was conducted to identify recognition behaviors used by management and seen as important by staff nurses. Previous research has documented that positive recognition has been related to increased work satisfaction and retention. Specific interventions were identified and applied. Managers' interventions were evaluated by the staff nurses in degree of importance. Outcomes revealed increased manager sensitivity to employees regarding recognition behaviors, increased retention of nurses, and improved work satisfaction.

Implications for Practice

Timely recognition of employee performance has a positive impact on work satisfaction. Increased work satisfaction may, in turn, contribute to a positive work environment. In the end, the manager, the staff, and, most importantly, the patients and their families can benefit.

The process of providing feedback, for either above-average or below-average performance, is best received at a time closest to the incident(s) being evaluated. The actual appraisal is sometimes viewed as a negative experience. Many nurse managers perceive the appraisal as a time-consuming process of endless paperwork. Instead, the emphasis should be placed on role clarification (if necessary), evaluation of performance outcomes, and the contributions the *basis*   employee has made to the organization. Performance appraisals provide the basis for many administrative decisions including promotions, salary increases, and disciplinary actions. Appraisals should be designed so that they can be supported in court. Court decisions can be made based on the evidence, or lack of evidence presented in the evaluation instrument. Consider for example, the individual who has been fired for reasons of poor work performance. The employee must be provided written notice that performance is unsatisfactory and that notice must specify what the employee must accomplish for satisfactory performance. This simple condition can make the difference for either the employee or the employer to justify the fairness for termination.

informal   Performance appraisals can be either formal or informal. An informal appraisal might be as simple as immediately praising the individual for performance recognized. It may be conveying a compliment from a family member or patient. Some managers have a specific bulletin board for thank you notes from patients and their families. Sometimes a simple "Thank you for all your hard work today!" can be extended from the manager to the staff.

formal   The formal performance appraisal involves written documentation, according to specific organizational guidelines. In either case, the key is that the praise or corrections be made as close in time to the episode as possible.

Brief *anecdotal notes* entered into the employee's file on a regular basis are important. These anecdotal notes, when accumulated over time, provide a more accurate cumulative appraisal. The anecdotal note describes an occurrence, either favorable or unfavorable, in a brief and concise manner. The purpose is to assist the manager with information throughout an entire rating period. An example of a brief anecdotal note appears in the box below.

Example of an Anecdotal Note: Nurse "Smith"

2/14/94: Patient and family (Samuel Karruthers) stated how much they appreciated Ms. Smith's nursing care during this hospitalization. Her coordination of services and competent and caring manner decreased their anxiety and assisted them in learning what they needed to know for care in the home. She made the patient feel "special," not just another number, etc. Compliment relayed to employee.

These notes, combined with variance reporting and other means of documenting employee performance, provide a more conclusive appraisal that reflects the entire rating period.

coaching   The overall evaluative process can be enhanced if the manager employs the technique of coaching. *Coaching* is a process that involves the development of individuals within an organization. This coaching process is a personal approach in which the manager and the employee interact on a frequent and regular basis with the ultimate outcome that the employee performs at an optimum level. Coaching can be individual or may involve a team approach; when implemented in a planned and organized manner it can promote team building as well as optimum performance of the employees. Coaching is a learned behavior for the nurse manager and takes time and effort to be developed. The rewards for both the employee and the nurse manager are significant; communication is enhanced and the performance appraisal process is an active one between the employee and the manager. Coaching is a management

EXERCISE 18-2
Select a partner. Observe some behavior and prepare an anecdotal note. Ask your partner for feedback about the content.

technique that can facilitate continual employee development as well as promote team building (Haas, 1992; Orth, Wilkinson, and Benfari, 1990).

The *formal performance appraisal* usually involves some type of predetermined evaluation tool or instrument. The tool may be a simple one or may involve the integration of a variety of measuring methods. The instrument(s) should reflect the philosophy of the organization and be as objective and specific regarding the employee's performance as possible. There are numerous instruments in use along with a variety of simple to complex scoring methods for each instrument. It is important for the new employee to have a clear understanding of timing as well as the content of the appraisal tool. The following example (see box) illustrates a type of peer appraisal method in which a staff nurse could evaluate another staff nurse within the area of assessment documentation.

instrument

Peer Performance Appraisal, Staff Nurse

Area of Responsibility:
Assessment/Diagnosis: Provides continuous holistic assessment to include physical, psychosocial, spiritual, and educational needs. Directs outcome criteria so that discharge plans are timely and optimum quality care delivered.
  a. Data base (history/physical assessment) completed within 12 hours of admission.   (Score 4)
  b. Documentation reflective of continuous assessment per unit guidelines. (Example neurovascular assessment of extremity following cardiac catheterization)   (Score 3)
  c. Initiates plan of care according to critical path guidelines within 12 hours of admission.   (Score 4)
  d. Provides for safe environment.   (Score 4)

The scoring procedures for the example shown in the box can be as simple as satisfactory/unsatisfactory. A more complex scoring system including a numerical rating scheme (using a range of 1–4, with 1 meaning "rarely meets standards," to 4 meaning "always exceeds standards") appears in the box above. The results from the peer review process are then summarized and incorporated into the manager's formal performance appraisal.

PERFORMANCE APPRAISAL TOOLS

The type of appraisal tool used is not so important as *how* it is utilized. A formal written tool may have specific guidelines or a more open-ended format. General topics may be addressed in an anecdotal or "incident"-type format. The tool or evaluation form should facilitate accurate appraisal of the individual's performance as well as provide an opportunity to stimulate personal goals of the individual and goals of the organization.

There are primarily two categories of *performance appraisal tools:* structured and flexible. Table 18-1 summarizes examples of structured and flexible tools.

STRUCTURED (TRADITIONAL) METHODS
The *forced distribution scale* is a norm-referenced tool that prevents the evaluator from rating all individuals in the same manner. The evaluator is

EXERCISE 18-3
Think back to your last performance appraisal, either in the clinical situation as a professional nurse or in the role of nursing student. Did you feel you were fairly and adequately evaluated? Were the comments reflective of your current practice and made by someone who had directly observed the care that you provided? What was the environment like for the interview? Were you comfortable with the evaluator? Was feedback given, both positive and negative? How did you feel at the conclusion of the interview? Taking the time to think about the answers to these questions might provide you insight and direction before your next performance appraisal interview.

TABLE 18-1	Structured and Flexible Performance Appraisal Tools

STRUCTURED (TRADITIONAL METHOD)	FLEXIBLE (COLLABORATIVE METHOD)
Forced distribution scale Graphic rating scale	Behaviorally anchored rating scales (BARS) Management by objectives (MBO) Peer review

provided a schematic diagram (see Figure 18-1) and asked to rate the individual according to all individuals the manager evaluates. As depicted in the figure, the evaluator has indicated that the individual rated is in the top 10 percent of employees but is not the best employee. This scale also provides the employee with a brief visual picture of how this evaluator has ranked performance in reference to others. This type of scale can undermine group cohesion *rank ordering* and communication effectiveness by its very nature of rank ordering individual performance. What this scale does provide, however, is a summary of the evaluator's overall ranking methods. For example, does the evaluator rank everyone in the middle 50 percent or below? Does the evaluator rank everyone as the best? A summary of the evaluation "track record" or history can be of value for the evaluator's performance appraisal!

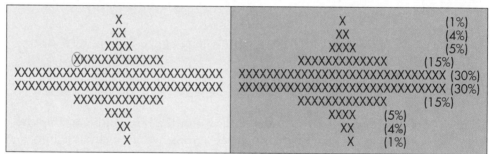

Individual Score Evaluator Summary

FIGURE 18-1
Forced distribution scale. [**X** = employee; Ⓧ = individual whom the employer is rating (Evaluation History)]

This example illustrates that this individual is considered to be in the top 10 percent of all employees evaluated. It also illustrates that this particular evaluator has an even distribution of scores for the evaluation summary of all employees. This employee should feel positive about the evaluation. In reality, however, the employee is likely to feel just the opposite. The employee can see how many other employees, above him or her on the scale, are perceived as being better. In this way the forced distribution scale can undermine morale and group cohesion.

Graphic rating scales are another example of a structured approach to evaluation. They are comprised of a numbering system that indicates low and high values for evaluating performance. The rating scale is popular because it is easy to construct and easy to use. Problems with this type of scale are that it lacks *halo/recency* specificity and promotes a **halo** or **recency effect.** The halo effect describes an evaluation based on isolated positive incident(s). The recency effect describes performance closer to the rating session as better remembered than that from previous months. For example, the employee performs in a satisfactory or less than satisfactory manner up until the month before the evaluation is due and then becomes "superemployee." The evaluation then reflects the "best" behavior rather than behavior that occurred during the majority of time in the rating period. Supervisors tend to rate people the same from one rating period to the next. Thus, there is the potential for overinflation of the evaluation if the recent performance is all that is included. Anecdotal notes compiled consistently over the entire rating period are a much more equitable method for providing an accurate summary of the employee's performance. Some managers utilize small notes with adhesive backs to place inside an employee's file to document behaviors quickly as situations warrant. An empty sheet of paper placed in the front of each file would also serve the same purpose. The electronically adept manager might also keep secured data files for the same purpose.

anecdotal notes

As you can see from the example in the box below, rating scales are relatively easy to construct and easy to complete. The problem is that they are usually comprised of generalizations, not specific behaviors, and that the rating is relatively subjective in nature. Some managers never give a "5" with the rationale that no employee "always does everything perfect" or that "no one is perfect."

Example of a Rating Scale

Criteria	Almost Never			Always Exceeds	
1. Completes nursing care in a professional and competent manner	1	2	3	4	5
2. Reliable; comes to work on time.	1	2	3	4	5
3. Provides patient teaching as appropriate.	1	2	3	4	5

FLEXIBLE (COLLABORATIVE) METHOD

The evaluation focus can also be conducted with a collaborative approach. How can the manager assist the individual to develop professionally? One method that has been used for many years is *management by objectives* (MBO). The trend now, however, is to call this method the establishment of learning goals, which are mutually established between the employee and the manager. Progress is documented throughout the rating period regarding the accomplishment of these goals. The MBO method is similar but more rigid in structure. An MBO approach requires that the employee establish clear and measurable objectives at the beginning of each rating period. These objectives are then addressed individually and in writing by both the employee and the manager during the performance appraisal interview. Learning goals are more difficult for both individuals. The approach can be simplified if it is performance based and outcome or results oriented. Then, in effect, the employee has created a "performance contract" as well having defined definite goals for future professional performance. The box on page 370 illustrates goals and accomplishments.

learning goals

Behaviorally anchored rating scales (BARS) can also be implemented as a collaborative or flexible approach. The focus is on behavior and should include employees in the development. BARS combine ratings with critical incidents

Learning Goals and Accomplishments

Learning Goals:
1. Prepare for and take certification examination.
2. Participate in shared governance committee as unit representative

Accomplishments (12 months later—summary):
1. Successfully passed certification exam!
2. Participated in monthly meetings, chaired task force for development and implementation of new delivery system. Presented inservice class to staff on several units.

criterion references

(specific examples that have occurred) or criterion references (examples usually based on standards of practice). The criteria utilized for this scale are specific to the type of nursing delivered and outcomes that are preestablished. This scale is also considered more advantageous in terms of litigation. BARS describes the employee's performance quantitatively as well as qualitatively. Staff who are involved in the development of these instruments are more likely to understand the importance of evaluation for each criteria selected, as well as to have an understanding of their performance expectations. This is another example of clarification of roles and role expectations within the organization. The primary drawback of this scale is that it is expensive to develop and time-consuming to implement; it must be specific for each specific job category or standard of practice. However, it provides the manager with concrete information regarding an employee's performance, with minimal subjective interference. The box on page 371 provides an example.

The boxed example illustrates, in part, how established nursing standards of practice, or protocols for practice, can be incorporated into the appraisal process using peer review. The data might also be used in an outcome review process as a component of continuous quality improvement program. The final result would be summarized by the manager and incorporated into the employee's performance appraisal.

peer review

Peer review is also a flexible or contemporary strategy. If the guidelines are developed collaboratively, peer review may also be considered a developmental method of evaluation. That is, employees are involved in the development and implementation process. This method has increased in popularity. Nurses tend to function in their normal patterns in the presence of peers and this can be a very solid rating method. However, it is important to obtain objective ratings based on performance, not subjective ratings based on personal friendships. This method should not be used if the manager is attempting to institute team-building strategies. The employees must trust and respect each other to willingly participate in the peer appraisal process.

SUMMARY OF APPRAISAL INSTRUMENTS

Which instrument/method of appraisal is best? The objectives of the organization determine the tool(s) used. A combination of several tools is most likely superior to any one method. The primary success of any performance appraisal lies in the skills and communication abilities of the manager. Role ambiguity and uncertainty of standards of practice and methods for evaluation are a significant contributor to decreased work satisfaction. The best-designed

Example of a Behaviorally Anchored Rating Scale

Emergency staff nurse responsibilities for patient admitted with chest pain: (ER records evaluated per protocol; minimum 10/rating period).   Met/Unmet
1. Vital signs recorded within 5 min. of admission _____
2. Cardiac monitor, IV, Lab, and EKG done within 15 min. _____
3. If sublingual nitroglycerin given, vital signs recorded every 5 min. for 30 min. _____
   a. Chest pain changes evaluated per protocol _____
   b. Post–chest pain 12-lead EKG documented _____

EXERCISE 18-4
Obtain a performance appraisal tool from the local healthcare organization where you obtained a position description. Based on the descriptions provided, how would you characterize it? Is it structured or flexible? Is it quantitatively based, qualitatively based, or both? How does the tool reflect the position description?

instrument will fail if the manager is ineffective and unable to communicate with the employee.

APPRAISAL INTERVIEW ENVIRONMENT

The appraisal instrument is not the only factor in the evaluation process. The *environment* in which the appraisal is conducted is as important as the actual interview. The interview should be conducted professionally and in a positive manner. It is an ideal time for communication between the employee and the manager. There should be no interruptions if at all possible. This time is important for clarification of employee and organizational goals. Evaluation of employee performance in an objective and non-emotional manner should be conducted. The evaluation instruments should be clearly completed and time allowed for discussion. Future goals may be established. The manager and the employee should sign the appraisal form(s) and each be provided a copy. The effectiveness of the entire appraisal method relies on the manner in which the manager uses the tools and the feedback that the employee receives. Effective communication between the manager and employees can prevent potential performance problems on a unit. Specific behaviors by the manager enhance the actual appraisal process (see the box below).

environment control

Key Behaviors for the Performance Appraisal Session

- Provide a quiet, controlled environment, without interruptions.
- Maintain a relaxed but professional atmosphere.
- Put the employee at ease; the overall objective is for the best job to be done.
- Review specific examples for both positive and negative behavior (keep an anecdotal file for each employee).
- Allow the employee to express opinions, orally and in writing.
- Write future plans and goals, training needs, etc. (a "performance contract" for the future).
- Set follow-up date as necessary to monitor improvements, if cited.
- Show the employee confidence in his/her performance.
- Be sincere and constructive in both praise and in criticism.

EXERCISE 18-5
Find a partner. Using an audio tape recorder, or a videotape recorder (preferred), conduct a performance appraisal. Seek feedback using the key behaviors in the box entitled "Key Behaviors for the Performance Appraisal Session."

Provide a quiet, controlled environment when conducting a performance appraisal.

CHAPTER CHECKLIST

Development of accurate position descriptions and tools for evaluation of employee performance are integral to role development and professional socialization. Nurse managers should utilize a variety of communication methods to include coaching techniques.

- Role theory describes how individuals perceive their position in an organization.
  - Distinction and clarity among the various positions is imperative if partnerships in quality patient care are to exist.
- The position description serves several purposes:
  - Provides written guidelines that describe roles and responsibilities.
  - Reflects the position's overall functions and obligations.
  - Serves as a contract between manager and employee.
  - Reflects current practice guidelines for the position.
- Performance appraisals are a method of providing feedback to the employee in relation to individual performance.
  - Types of structured (traditional) performance appraisals include:
    - Graphic rating scales
    - Forced distribution method.
  - Types of flexible (collaborative) performance appraisals include:
    - Behaviorally anchored rating scales (BARS)
    - Learning goals/management by objective (MBO)
    - Peer review.

- These methods may be used individually or in a combination.
    - One of the most important factors is not the method(s), but the manner in which the manager conducts the interview.
- The interview for a performance appraisal sets the tone for future performance.
    - A collaborative approach that involves the employee in goal setting and active participation in professional growth is critical.

TERMS TO KNOW

- halo or recency effect
- performance appraisal
- position description
- role ambiguity
- role conflict
- role theory

REFERENCES

Goode, C.J., & Blegen, M.A. (1993). Development and evaluation of a research-based management intervention. A recognition protocol. *Journal of Nursing Administration, 23*(4), 61–66.

Hardy, M.E., & Conway, M.E. (1988). *Role Theory: Perspectives for Health Professionals,* 2nd ed. Norwalk, CT: Appleton & Lange.

Haas, S.A. (1992). Coaching. Developing key players. *Journal of Nursing Administration, 22*(6), 54–58.

Orth, C.D., Wilkinson, H.E., & Benfari, R.C. (1990). The manager's role as coach and mentor. *Journal of Nursing Administration, 20*(9), 11–15.

SUGGESTED READINGS

Beck, S. (1990). Developing a primary nursing performance appraisal tool. *Nursing Management, 21,* 36–38.

Bednarski, D. (1992). Quality improvement through peer review. *ANNA-Journal, 19*(2), 162.

Rowe, H. (1992). How am I doing and where am I going? Individual performance review in staff appraisal. *Professional Nurse, 7*(5), 288, 290–291.

Tayler, C.M. (1992, September/October). Subordinate performance appraisal: What nurses really want in their managers. *Canadian Journal of Nursing Administration,* pp. 6–9.

Tumulty, G. (1992). Head nurse role redesign. Improving satisfaction and performance. *Journal of Nursing Administration, 22*(22), 41–47.

CHAPTER 19

MANAGING PERSONAL/ PERSONNEL PROBLEMS

Arlene P. Stein, R.N.,C., Ph.D.
Cindy Whittig Roach, R.N., D.S.N.

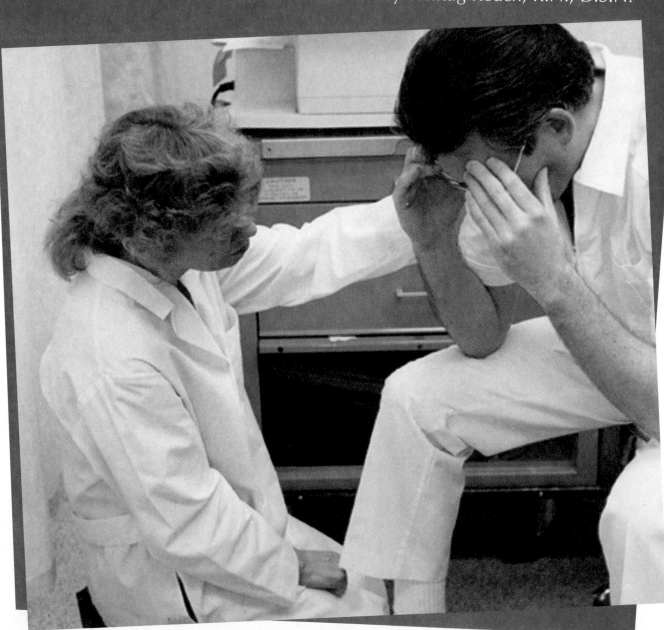

PREVIEW

The purpose of this chapter is to discuss various personal and personnel problems that a manager must face in all nursing settings. Some specific tips and tools are provided as ways to intervene, coach, correct, and document problem behaviors. Emphasis is placed on effective communication, both written and verbal.

OBJECTIVES

- Differentiate common personnel/personal problems.
- Relate role concepts to clarification of personnel problems.
- Examine strategies useful for approaching specific personnel problems.
- Prepare specific guidelines for documenting performance problems.

QUESTIONS TO CONSIDER

- How do you react when you see that an employee is absent frequently and you or others seem to have a heavier work load as a result?
- Have you ever been in a position where you were not really sure what was expected of you? How did you feel?
- What would you do if you observed clinical incompetence in a co-worker or student peer?
- What is the best approach to deal with someone you believe is chemically dependent or impaired at work?

A Manager's Viewpoint

I noticed that Sarah, a valued employee who had been on my unit for about 2 years, had been calling in sick very frequently during the last few months. Sarah always had some sick calls, but lately her calls had become more frequent. I called Sarah into my office to discuss her frequent sick calls to try to determine a cause. I told her I was sorry she was sick so often, but that regardless of the reasons causing her to be sick, I was responsible for the patient care on the unit. I pointed out the added burden her sick calls placed on her co-workers and the problems we had replacing her on a frequent basis. I reminded her of the hospital's policy—no more than five occurrences in a year, or three in a six-month period. I then pointed out that she had had four occurrences in the past eight months and said I wanted to be certain that she was aware of the established policy. She stated she was aware of this but was just "sick" often. As I explored this issue with Sarah, I found that she had some chronic sinus problems and suggested that she see a physician. She agreed to do this to find out if something could be done to prevent her frequent illnesses.

Two weeks later Sarah was again absent with a "sick" excuse. When she returned to work, I gave her a written warning stating that she was not following the established employment standard for this hospital. She then agreed to have no sick calls for the next three months. We also agreed that if she was sick she would have to provide a physician's excuse for her to return to work and that, regardless of the reason, further sick calls would cause her to lose points on her annual evaluation. I praised Sarah when she was working and told her I appreciated the effort she was making to not call in sick.

Sarah did not call in sick again until about two months later. Since this occurrence violated the agreement, I granted her a day off with pay so that she could come up with a plan describing how she was going to comply with the existing policy for absenteeism. I emphasized that she needed to decide whether or not she was going to be able to adhere to this employment standard. Sarah decided that she was unable to work a full-time schedule. Fortunately, I was able to decrease her working hours to part-time; I didn't want to lose her—she had been an excellent worker, except for the absenteeism problem. Since Sarah became part-time, she has not called in sick for the past six months. If she had decided she could not follow the standard, I would have had no choice but to terminate her employment.

Arlene P. Stein, Ph.D., R.N.,C.
Clinical Manager, Surgical Unit,
Memorial Hospital
Colorado Springs, Colorado

INTRODUCTION

In managing nursing personnel, much of the satisfaction that a manager receives comes from working with people. On the other hand, working with people presents some of the greatest challenges with which a manager must cope. Problems such as absenteeism, uncooperative or unproductive employees, clinical incompetence, employees with emotional problems, and **chemically dependent** employees are only a few of the issues that challenge a manager. If a manager wants to be successful, these problems must be dealt with in ways to minimize their effects on patient care and on staff morale. Documentation of performance problems as well as documentation for termination is discussed. Overall goals are to assist the employee in the improvement of performance, maintain the highest standards for the delivery of patient care, and provide a supportive environment in which all employees might deliver the best care and attain work satisfaction.

PERSONNEL/PERSONAL PROBLEMS

ABSENTEEISM

One of the most vexing of these problems to the nurse manager is that of **absenteeism,** because inadequate staffing adversely affects patient care both directly and indirectly. When an absent caregiver is replaced by another one who is unfamiliar with the routines, employee morale suffers, and the care may be less than established standards. Replacement personnel usually need increased supervision, which not only is costly but also decreases productivity and the quality of patient care (Martin, 1990). Indirectly, co-workers may become resentful from being forced to assume heavier work loads and/or be pressured to work extra hours. Chronic absenteeism may lead to increased staff conflicts and eventually to an increase in absenteeism among the entire staff.

morale

Absenteeism also has a deleterious effect on the financial management of a nursing unit. Replacement of absent personnel by pool personnel or overtime paid to other employees is very costly, and the cost of fringe benefits used by absent workers is very high. Managing absenteeism is important for all of the aforementioned factors. Also, as our care delivery systems become more complex and technologically oriented, the successful nurse manager must realize that technology is not a replacement for human caregivers. We cannot replace absent caregivers with machines.

financial considerations

Absenteeism cannot be totally eliminated. There are always unplanned illnesses, accidents, bad weather, sick family members, a death in the family, and even jury duty, which are legitimate reasons for missing work and cannot be controlled by management. However, most researchers believe that some portion of absenteeism is voluntary and preventable; thus, there are many attempts to identify the cause and thereby instigate a cure.

Using role theory as a framework, absenteeism can be linked to **role stress.** Lee and Eriksen (1990) state that absence from work is a way of withdrawing from an undesirable situation short of actually leaving and that many employees increase their absenteeism just prior to their resignation. If the health-care worker is experiencing some form of role stress, leading to **role strain**, it might be manifested through absenteeism. Hardy and Conway (1988) state that role strain may be reflected by (a) withdrawal from interaction, (b) re-

role stress

duced involvement with colleagues and organizations, and (c) job dissatisfaction. All of these could be manifested through absenteeism. Using this framework, management of absenteeism is based on the belief that competent role performance requires interpersonal competence. "Role competence is the ability of a person in an interdependent position, which is ongoing in time, to carry out lines of action that are task and interpersonally effective" (Hardy and Conway, 1988, p. 195). Hardy and Conway further explain that role competence is (a) learned through socialization processes, (b) necessary for adequate role performance, and (c) makes for individual and social progress. In other words, to engage successfuly in roles, people need role-specific skills but they also need interpersonal competence to guide their behaviors. Role behavior occurs in a social context rather than in isolation. Therefore, the nurse manager needs to know the existing situation, when it has changed, when it needs to be changed, and how to change it. Studies have shown an inverse relationship between job satisfaction and absenteeism, indicating that attention to enhancing nurses job satisfaction may be an effective strategy toward reducing absenteeism (Lee and Eriksen, 1990). This chapter's "Research Perspective" highlights this study.

role competence

job satisfaction

Research Perspective

Lee, J.B., & Eriksen, L.R. (1990). The effects of a policy change on three types of absence. Journal of Nursing Administration, 20(7/8), 37–40.

This descriptive study was a retrospective evaluation of absenteeism in relation to specific personnel policies. The effect of policy change on the use of absence time and excused and unexcused leave was described. Conclusions revealed a significant increase in use of sick leave with the more lenient policy in force during a specific time period. No significant changes were noted in the use of uncompensated excused or unexcused leave. The authors suggest use of positive and nonpunitive strategies for effective absenteeism control.

Implications for Practice

Increased use of sick leave could indicate that staff members are experiencing underlying problems related to stress and workload. Changes in family structure such as single parenting or caring for elders or ill children may also affect attendance adversely. The authors of this study suggest that absenteeism policy be stated clearly in a positive, nonpunitive manner.

An adaptation from Haddock's (1989) model of **nonpunitive discipline** is also useful in addressing absenteeism behavior, as the example in the next paragraph illustrates. Using absenteeism as an example, this model demonstrates how undesirable behaviors, such as absenteeism, can be successfully changed. Figure 19-1 illustrates how changing undesirable behaviors can be accomplished.

When an employee demonstrates an unacceptable level of absenteeism the manager can take the following steps to help clarify role expectations:

Step 1: Remind the employee of the employment standards of the agency. Sometimes an employee does not know, or has forgotten the existing standards, and a reminder with no threats or discipline is all that is needed.

Step 2: When the oral reminder does not result in a behavior change, put the

oral reminder of standards

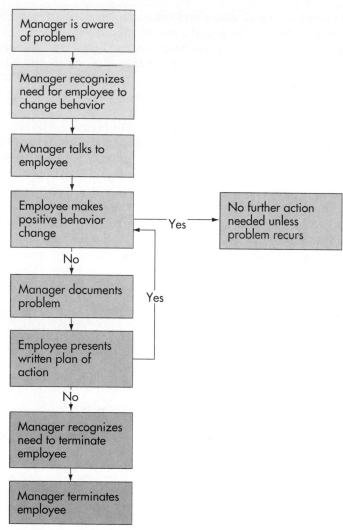

Manager is aware
of problem

↓

Manager recognizes
need for employee to
change behavior

↓

Manager talks to
employee

↓

Employee makes
positive behavior
change   → Yes →   No further action
                         needed unless
                         problem recurs

↓ No

Manager documents
problem   Yes

↓

Employee presents
written plan of
action

↓ No

Manager recognizes
need to terminate
employee

↓

Manager terminates
employee

FIGURE 19-1
Model for behavioral change.

written reminder

agreement

decision point

termination

reminder in writing for the employee. These oral and written reminders are simply statements of the problem and the goals to which both the manager and the employee agree. The employee must voluntarily agree with the manager that the behavior in question is not acceptable and must agree to change.

Step 3: If the written reminder fails, only then grant the employee a day of decision, which is a day off with pay to arrive at a decision about future action. Pay is given for this day so that it is not interpreted as punishment. The employee must return to work with a written decision as to whether or not to accept the standards for work attendance. Remember that this is a voluntary decision on the employee's part. Emphasize to the employee that it is the employee's decision to adhere to the standards.

Step 4: If the employee decides not to adhere to standards, terminate him or her. On the other hand, if the employee agrees to adhere to the standards, and in the future does not, the employee in essence has terminated employment. Keep a copy of the written agreements and also give the employee a copy (Rogers, Hutchins, and Johnson, 1990).

This model of nonpunitive discipline allows employees to free themselves from some role stress by clarification of role expectations. Employees can receive satisfaction from the realization that a problem is not inadequate performance attributed to personal faults, but rather a lack of clarification of role expectations within the organization.

UNCOOPERATIVE OR UNPRODUCTIVE EMPLOYEES

The problem of *uncooperative or unproductive* employees is another area of frustration for the nurse manager. Hersey and Blanchard (1988) identify two major dimensions of job performance—motivation and ability—that relate to this problem. The type and intensity of motivation varies among employees due to differing needs and goals that employees express. As stated in Chapter 15, the manager can best handle employees with motivation problems by attempting to determine the cause of the problem, and by trying to provide an environment that is conducive to increased motivation for the employee. If the employee is uncooperative or unproductive due to a lack of ability, education and training would be an appropriate intervention.

The manager can determine lack of ability on the part of an employee in a variety of ways. Frequent errors in judgment or techniques are often an indication of lack of knowledge, skill, or critical thinking. This illustrates the need for the nurse manager to carefully document all variances or untoward events. When the nurse manager does thorough documentation, trends may be discovered that in turn suggest a specific employee is having problems. The nurse manager can cite problem behaviors and perhaps even trends to the employee. Corrective action is easier to pursue and resolution is more effective in this manner. When the problem is determined to be due to a need for more education or training, the manager can work with the education department, or the clinical specialist for the involved unit, to help the employee improve his or her skills. Most employees are extremely cooperative in situations such as this as they want to do a good job, but sometimes don't know how. Employees may deny they need help or may be too embarrassed to ask for help. When the manager can show an employee concrete evidence of a problem area, cooperation is enhanced.

Sometimes an unproductive employee simply lacks maturity. Immaturity in an employee may not be readily apparent to the manager but may be manifested in any of the following actions: defiance, testing of workplace guidelines, passivity or hostility, or little appreciation for any management decisions. The challenge for the nurse manager is not to react in kind, but rather relate to this employee in a positive and mature manner. For example, if an employee states, "Administration is always making decisions to make our jobs harder," rather than making a hostile or defensive comment in reply, the manager could take the employee aside and say, "I notice that you seem to be angry about this new policy. Can we talk about it some more?" Immature employees either act immaturely all of the time or regress to an immature level when stressed. The nurse manager must recognize immaturity in an employee and react calmly and without anger. The manager must keep in mind that this employee may be displaying dynamics rooted in unresolved areas of personality development and that the behavior is not a personal attack on the manager. The best way to deal with this behavior is to confront the employee with the specific problem and define realistic limits of acceptable behavior with consequences for nonadherence. Generally employees comply with specific limits, but will test management in other areas. As this testing occurs, the manager must continue the same limit

assessment

maturity

EXERCISE 19-1
Review the policy manual at a local healthcare organization. Determine what constitutes excessive absenteeism. What are the consequences?

EXERCISE 19-2
A nurse comes to you, the nurse manager, and states that one of the other nurses is tying a knot in the airvent (pigtail) of nasogastric tubes. What would you do?

setting technique. Remember that the immature employee usually has problems because of a lack of self-worth, power, and self-control. Praise and affirmation are valuable tools that the manager can use to help these employees feel better about themselves.

CLINICAL INCOMPETENCE

collegial accountability

Clinical incompetence is possibly one of the most frustrating problems that the nurse manager faces, even though it may be entirely correctable. The problem may surface immediately in a new employee. At other times, clinical incompetence comes as a surprise to a nurse manager if co-workers "cover" for another employee. Some nurses are unwilling to report instances of clinical incompetence, as they do not want to feel responsible for getting one of their peers in trouble. When other employees are engaged in enabling behavior by covering for the mistakes of one of their peers, the nurse manager may be surprised to discover that the employee does not know or cannot do what is expected of him/her in the job. Sadly, the employee in question has been able to cover incompetencies by hiding behind the performance of another employee. The nurse manager must remind employees that part of professional responsibility is to maintain quality care and thus they are obligated to report instances of clinical incompetence, even when it means reporting a co-worker.

skills checklist

Most healthcare agencies use skills checklists to ascertain that their employees have and maintain essential skills for the job they're expected to do. A skills checklist is an excellent way to determine basic clinical competency (see box). "In healthcare today we must verify through a documentation system that the required standards are being met to insure competent delivery of nursing care" (Inman and Haugen, 1991, p. 238). This list typically contains a number of basic skills along with ones that are essential for safe functioning in the area of employment. The employee may be asked to do a self-assessment of the listed skills and then have performance of the skills validated by a peer or co-worker. This is a very effective method for the manager to assess the skill level of employees and to determine where additional education and training may be necessary. Additionally, if the manager discovers that an employee is unable to adequately perform a skill it is easy for the manager to check the skills list and see at what level this employee is functioning and recommend a specific plan for remediation. If in questioning the employee, or in

---

Example of a Skills Checklist

PURPOSE
1. The clinical skills inventory is a three-phase tool to enable the newly hired RN and the nurse manager to determine individual learning needs, verify competency, and plan performance goals.
2. The RN will complete the self-assessment of clinical skills during the first week of employment. The RN will use the appropriate scale to document current knowledge of clinical skills.
3. The nurse manager will document observed competency of the orientee or delegate this to a peer. All columns must be completed on the inventory level.

Example of a Skills Checklist—cont'd

4. At the end of orientation, the new RN and the manager will use the inventory to identify performance goals on the plan sheet. The skills inventory will be in a specified place on the nursing unit so that it is available to the manager and other RNs. It should be updated at appropriate intervals as specified by the manager.

SCALE FOR SELF-ASSESSMENT
1 = Unfamiliar/never done
2 = Able to perform with assistance
3 = Can perform with minimal supervision
4 = Independent performance/proficient

SCORE FOR VALIDATION OF COMPETENCY
1 = Unable to perform at present
2 = Able to perform with assistance
3 = Progressing/repeat performance necessary
4 = Able to perform independently

CLINICAL SKILLS	SELF-ASSESSMENT		COMMENT	VALIDATION			COMMENT
	SCALE	DATE		SCORE	DATE	INITIALS	
Epidural catheter care							
NG/Dobbhoff							
Insertion							
Management							
Preoperative care/teaching							
Postoperative care/teaching							

PLAN SHEET FOR SKILLS INVENTORY

Name _____
Date _____

GOALS   DATE TO BE
                                         COMPLETED

_____
_____
_____
_____
_____

Orientee's signature _____
Manager's signature _____
Date _____

Skills Inventory adapted from one used at Memorial Hospital, Colorado Springs, CO.

evaluating the employee's performance, the manager determines that there is a lack of knowledge, then formal education may be the proper course of action. In either event, the manager must establish a written contract containing a plan of action with time limits in which certain expectations must be achieved. This assures compliance on the part of the employee.

EMOTIONAL PROBLEMS

Emotional problems among nursing personnel may have an impact not only on the involved individual, but also on co-workers and ultimately on the delivery of patient care. The nurse manager must be aware that certain behaviors, such as poor judgment, increased errors, increased absenteeism, decreased productivity, and a negative attitude may be manifestations of emotional problems in employees.

Example

A nurse manager began hearing complaints from patients about a nurse named Nancy. Patients were saying that Nancy was abrupt and uncaring with them. The manager had not received any complaints about Nancy prior to this time, so she questioned Nancy about why this was occurring. Nancy reported that her mother was very ill and she was so worried about her and was so upset that she couldn't sleep and was tired all of the time. She went on to say that she was having trouble being sympathetic with complaining patients when they didn't seem to be as sick as her mother.

When a trend of these behaviors is evident, a problem that an employee is unable to handle may be the cause. The nurse manager is not and should not be a therapist, but must intercede, not only to help the individual with problems but also to maintain proper functioning of the unit. In dealing with the employee who exhibits behaviors that indicate emotional problems, the manager, after identifying the problem, should assist the individual to get professional help to cope with the problem. The manager may have to make some adjustments in the individual's work setting and schedule if this is deemed necessary and does not have a negative effect on patient care. Even though the manager is aware that an employee is experiencing emotional difficulties, the standards of care and practice cannot be compromised in the hope of "going easy" on the individual. If standards are lowered to help an individual, the effect will be deleterious to all people involved. The most important approach that the manager can take with an emotionally troubled employee is to provide support and encouragement and to assist the individual to get appropriate help. Many agencies have some kind of employee assistance program (EAP) to which the manager should refer any troubled employee. During this process, the manager must remember to check with the human resources department about any implications that may occur because of the Americans with Disabilities Act (ADA). If an employee has a documented mental illness, the employing agency may be under certain legal constraints as specified in the ADA. The nurse manager should always remember that there are many resources available to assist with personnel problems. The manager should never feel required to know all of the legal implications regarding employment policies. Rather, the manager must know that help is available and how to access it.

CHEMICAL DEPENDENCY

Chemical dependency among nursing personnel places patients and the organization at risk. The chemically dependent employee adversely affects staff morale by increasing stress on other staff members when they have to assume

professional help

EXERCISE 19-3

As a nurse manager in a community health agency, you have just had a meeting that was called by several of your staff nurses. They expressed concern regarding another nurse colleague who has come to work tearful several times during the past week. They state she frequently goes into the break room when she is in the agency and appears as if she's been crying when she comes out. She has refused to discuss her distress with her colleagues. These nurses express concern and want you to help her. What is your response? What would you do?

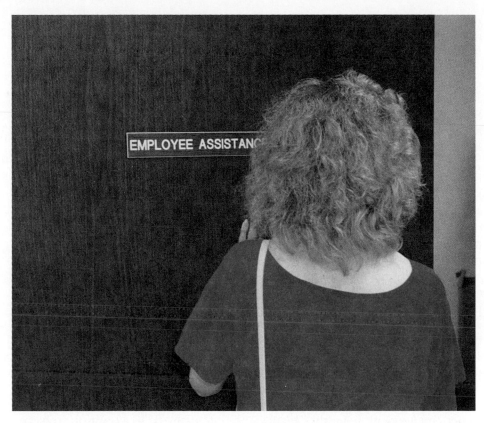

Many agencies have an Employee Assistance Program to which the manager can refer the troubled employee.

heavier work loads to cover for the chemically dependent employee who is not performing at full capacity, or who is frequently absent. As a result, patient care may be jeopardized when staff are focusing more on the problems of a co-worker than on those of the patients they are assigned to care for.

The manager is responsible for early recognition of chemical dependency and referral for treatment when appropriate. State laws vary as to the reportability of chemical dependency. As is true of all nurses, a nurse manager is responsible for upholding the Nurse Practice Act and should be familiar with the legal aspects of chemical dependency in the state in which he/she is employed. Here again, as with the employee with emotional problems, the nurse manager should be aware of ADA issues and check with the human resource department for help with how to handle the employment of a chemically dependent employee. Most states and agencies have reporting requirements regarding substance abuse. The state board of nursing is an excellent source of information for the nurse manager unfamiliar with the legal aspects of the Nurse Practice Act. All nurse managers should familiarize themselves with the Nurse Practice Act in the state in which they reside as well as the personnel policies relating to substance abuse in their employing agency. Further, they should make certain that staff are familiar with legal requirements, too.

Identification of an employee with a chemical dependency is usually difficult, especially when one of the primary symptoms is denial. The reported incidence of chemical dependency in nurses is generally less than or equal to that among non-nurses (Trinkoff, Eaton, and Anthony, 1991). Because of this, a manager is likely to encounter a chemically dependent nurse at some career point. Because so many people are affected, there is increased aware-

Nurse Practice Act

identification

behavioral change

ness of this problem, resulting in more interest in helping affected individuals rather than punishing them. In the present social climate, there is also more empathy and understanding toward them.

The primary clue that a manager should be alert for when there is a suspicion of chemical dependency is any behavioral changes in an employee. This change could be any deviation from that which the employee normally exhibits. Some specific behaviors to note might be mood swings, a change from a tidy appearance to an untidy one, an unusual interest in patients' pain control, frequent changes in jobs and shifts, or an increase in absenteeism and tardiness.

When a manager suspects an employee may be chemically dependent, the manager must intervene as patient care may be jeopardized, as described above. A manager facing a problem with an impaired nurse must be compassionate yet therapeutic. Knowing that denial may be one of the primary signs of substance abuse, the manager must focus on performance problems that the nurse is exhibiting and urge the nurse to voluntarily seek counseling or treatment.

employee assistance program

Employee assistance programs always protect the employee's privacy and are usually available free or at a minimal charge to the employee. The manager should strive to refer any troubled employee to the employee assistance program whenever possible. This removes the manager from the counseling role and helps employees get the professional help they need without fear of a breach in confidentiality. If a nurse refuses to seek help voluntarily for a substance abuse problem, the manager is responsible for following the policy established by the agency for such employees. The manager must remember that if the substance-abusing employee is terminated and not reported, the manager not only may be violating a law, but also may be enabling this employee to get employment in another agency and potentially be in a position to harm patients and co-workers.

rehabilitation

Many states have rehabilitation programs for chemically impaired nurses, so that some may return to nursing if rehabilitated. Nurse managers are sometimes asked to assist with the monitoring progress of a chemically impaired nurse. Specific guidelines are established through the rehabilitation program with the cooperation of the employee, the agency, and the manager. The manager is typically asked to provide feedback about the employee's progress to the employee as well as to the state or rehabilitation program involved. These programs vary, but, for example, a nurse who has been an admitted abuser of meperidine, may be allowed to work in a setting where this drug is never used, or the nurse may not be permitted to administer any controlled substances to patients. This, of course, puts an added burden on other staff members, but it can be a positive experience for all, as nurses face some of their professional responsibility by helping another nurse while upholding patient care. Often, as a part of their therapy, these nurses are required to openly share with other staff members what their problem is and what they are doing to control it. When handled in a positive, professional way, the nurse manager can turn a potentially destructive situation into a positive constructive one.

EXERCISE 19-4

Review your state's nurse practice act and rules and regulations. What are you required to do if you believe a nurse has a problem with chemical dependency?

DOCUMENTATION

Documentation of personnel problems is unquestionably one of the most important, but also one of the most onerous, aspects of the nurse manager's job. As much as some managers would wish, personnel problems probably will not "just go away by themselves," and so will have to be dealt with eventually. Through careful ongoing documentation of problems the manager makes the task of identifying and correcting problems much less burdensome.

Documentation cannot be left to memory! When an employee is involved in a problem occurrence, or if an employee receives a compliment or does something extremely well, a brief notation to this effect should be placed in the personnel file. This entry should include the date, time, and a brief description of the incident. It is helpful also to add a small notation as to what was done about a problem when it occurred. Along with this, the nurse manager should keep a log or summary sheet of all reported errors, unusual incidents, accidents, and any other untoward effects. These extremely important data should include the date, time, the names of involved individuals and should be tallied at monthly intervals for analysis by the manager. The few extra minutes each day that the manager spends tracking these data provides invaluable information to the manager about organizational and individual functioning. This tracking can then be used to pinpoint problem areas,

log

Documentation of Problems

- Description of incident—an objective statement of the facts related to the incident.
- Actions—statement(s) describing all actions taken by the manager when the problem was discovered.
- Plan—statement(s) describing the plan to correct and/or prevent future problems.
- Follow-up—dates and times that the plan is to be carried out, including required meeting with the employee.

Example:

Several patients reported to the nurse manager that Becky, one of the night shift RNs, was "curt" and "gruff" and seemed uncaring with them. The manager called Becky into her office and reiterated the complaints that she had received. The nurse manager was specific as to times and incidents. The manager then reminded Becky about what her expectations were relating to patient care, emphasizing the importance of a caring attitude with all patients. She discussed with Becky what the possible cause of Becky's behavior might be, such as problems at home or lack of sleep. Becky denied being curt or gruff, but agreed that some of her mannerisms might be misinterpreted. The manager suggested to Becky that perhaps she needed to be particularly aware of her body language and to soften her tone of voice. After discussing this incident and reminding Becky of the importance of caring in nursing, the manager told Becky that this behavior would not be tolerated. The manager told Becky she wanted to meet with her every Friday morning at the end of Becky's shift to discuss how the week had gone and to determine how she was interacting with the patients assigned to her. The manager also told Becky that she would be checking with patients to see what they had thought of Becky. The manager routinely asked patients about their nursing care as she made rounds, so this was not an unusual thing for her to do. These weekly meetings were to be conducted for six weeks followed by monthly meetings for a three-month period. If there was no recurrence of problems, the meetings would be discontinued after this time.

areas of excellence in individual performance, and overall organizational problem areas. The manager who keeps careful records about organizational functioning has greater control in the management of personal and personnel problems. The preceding box on page 385 describes content and format for such documentation and provides an example as an illustration.

PROGRESSIVE DISCIPLINE

When an employee's performance falls below the acceptable standard, despite corrective measures that have been taken, some form of discipline must be enacted. Most organizations use progressive discipline in a situation like this. **Progressive discipline** consists of evaluating peformance and providing feedback with steps of increasing sanctions. These sanctions progress from least severe to most severe, as described in the box below.

Steps in Progressive Discipline

1. Counsel employee regarding the problem.
2. Reprimand employee. A verbal reprimand usually precedes a written one, but some organizations issue both a verbal and written reprimand simultaneously. When the documentation is written, the employee must sign to verify that the problem was discussed. This does not mean that the employee agrees with the reprimand. It means only that the employee is aware of a written verbal reprimand that is to be placed in the employee's personnel file. The employee always receives a copy of a written reprimand.
3. Suspend employee if the problem persists. The employee will be suspended without pay for a period of time, usually several days or longer according to the agency policy. During this time the employee may realize the seriousness of the problem based on the resulting discipline.
4. Allow the employee to return to work with written stipulations regarding problem behavior.
5. Terminate employee if problem recurs.

TERMINATION

guidelines

At times, even though the manager has done everything possible to gain the cooperation of a problem employee, the problems may persist. Then, there is no choice but to terminate the employee. Since *termination* is one of the most difficult things a manager does, it is best to follow certain guidelines. First, the manager must feel secure in the fact that everything possible has been done to help the employee correct the problem behaviors. Second, the manager recognizes that if employment continues, this employee will have a deleterious effect on overall organizational functioning and, more importantly, on nursing care. Third, the employee has been made fully aware of the problem performance and all of the correct disciplinary steps have been followed. Finally, a nurse manager should check with the human resources and legal departments before proceeding to be certain termination is justifiable legally and that proper steps have been followed. It is extremely helpful to feel confident in the knowledge that all policies regarding termination have been followed prior to an actual termination meeting with the employee. It is always preferable to err on the side of caution when proceeding with termination of an employee. Remember that termination is something that the employee has caused as a result of persistent problem behaviors. Termination is not done at the whim of management; it results from failure on the part of the employee to change a problem behavior.

Example:

Linda has gone through all of the steps in the progressive discipline process as a result of her abusive behavior toward her co-workers. She returned to work and seemed to be doing well until about six weeks later when she slammed down her clipboard during report and angrily accused the charge nurse of always giving her the worst assignments. The nurse manager was present and asked Linda to come into her office. At this point, she told Linda she was relieving her of her assignment that day and asked her to go home to cool off. The manager told her that she would call her the following day about what would be done. Linda went home and the manager reviewed the incident with her boss. They both agreed that Linda's behavior not only was intolerable but also violated the terms of her probation and therefore she should be terminated. The manager called Linda the following day as she had agreed to do and asked Linda to come and meet with her. The manager and her boss met with Linda and reviewed the incidents and the disciplinary measures leading up to this one. The nurse manager asked her boss to be present at the scheduled meeting as it is a good practice to have a witness in a confrontive situation such as termination. The manager stated to Linda that she regretted it had come to this, but pointed out to her that her behavior had violated all of the agreed upon stipulations and as a result she would be terminated immediately. Linda was tearful and had numerous excuses, but the manager remained firm and merely repeated that Linda, in not fulfilling the agreement, had chosen to end her employment.

CHAPTER CHECKLIST

To obtain satisfaction from working with people, a nurse manager must be knowledgeable about personal and personnel issues that are likely to occur in the work setting. The nurse manager must be able to detect, prevent, and correct problems that affect nursing care and staff morale in a nursing agency. Proper documentation and follow-up is a key element in the successful management of all personnel issues.

- Among absenteeism's detrimental effects are these:
  - Patient care may be below standard.
  - Replacement personnel require additional supervision.
  - Absenteeism may increase among the entire staff.
  - Financial management of the unit suffers adverse effects.
- Effective strategies to reduce absenteeism include:
  - Enhancing nurses' job satisfaction.
  - Using Haddock's model of nonpunitive discipline:
    - Remind the employee of the problem orally.
    - Follow up with a written reminder if the oral one fails.
    - Grant the employee a day of decision if the written reminder fails.
    - If the employee decides not to adhere to standards, terminate.

■ Uncooperative or unproductive employees may lack motivation, ability, or maturity.

- The nurse manager can try to provide an environment that is more conducive to motivation.
- Education and training are appropriate interventions for lack of ability.
- Praise and affirmation are often the most effective strategies for an employee who lacks maturity.

■ Clinical incompetence is a highly correctable problem for nurse managers.

- Clinical incompetence may be masked by co-workers' enabling behavior.
- A skills checklist helps determine basic clinical competency and pinpoint the need for additional training and education.

■ When emotional problems are evident, the nurse manager should assist the employee in getting professional help. The nurse manager is responsible for early recognition of chemical dependency and referral for treatment when appropriate.

- The manager must:
    - Uphold the state's nurse practice act.
    - Be familiar with state laws on chemical dependency.
    - Know the healthcare organization's personnel policy on chemical dependency.
- Some warning signs of possible chemical dependency are:
    - Behavioral changes such as mood swings
    - Sudden and unusual neglect for personal appearance
    - Unusual interest in patients' pain control
    - Increased absenteeism and tardiness.

■ Documentation of problems should include:

- A description of the incident
- A description of the manager's actions
- A plan to correct/prevent future occurrences
- Dates and times of follow-ups.

■ Progressive discipline may be used when other corrective measures have failed. Steps in progressive discipline are:

- Counsel the employee regarding the problem.
- Reprimand the employee (first verbally, then in writing).
- Suspend the employee if the problem persists.
- Allow the employee to return to work, with written stipulations regarding problem behavior.
- Terminate the employee if the problem recurs.

TERMS TO KNOW

- **absenteeism**
- **chemically dependent**
- **nonpunitive discipline**

- **progressive discipline**
- **role strain**
- **role stress**

REFERENCES

Haddock, C. (1989). Transformational leadership and the employee discipline process. *Hospital Health Service Administration, 34*(2), 185–194.

Hardy, M.E., & Conway, M.E. (1988). *Role Theory: Perspectives for Health Professionals,* 2nd ed. Norwalk, CT: Appleton & Lange.

Hersey, P., & Blanchard, K. (1988). *Management of Organizational Behavior: Utilizing Human Resources,* 5th ed. Englewood Cliffs, NJ: Prentice-Hall.

Inman, L., & Haugen, C. (1991). Six criteria to evaluate skill competency documentation. *Dimensions of Critical Care Nursing, 10*(4), 238–245.

Lee, J.B., & Eriksen, L.R. (1990). The effects of a policy change on three types of absence. *Journal of Nursing Administration, 20*(7/8), 37–40.

Martin, B.J. (1990). A successful approach to absenteeism. *Nursing Management, 21*(8), 45–48.

Rogers, J., Hutchins, S., & Johnson, B. (1990). *Journal of Nursing Administration, 20*(7/8), 41–45.

Trinkoff, A., Eaton, W., & Anthony, J. (1991). The prevalence of substance abuse among registered nurses. *Nursing Research, 40*(3), 172–175.

SUGGESTED READINGS

Brooke, P. (1990). Firing for cause. *Journal of Nursing Administration, 20*(9), 45–50.

Manthey, M. (1989). Discipline without punishment. Part I. *Nursing Management, 20*(10), 19.

——— (1989). Discipline without punishment. Part II. *Nursing Management, 20*(11), 23.

McClure, M. (1990). The impaired nurse. *Journal of Professional Nursing, 6*(5), 254.

Umiker, W. (1991, October). Turning around the behavior of uncooperative employees. *Medical Laboratory Observer,* pp. 59–66.

Virden, J. (1992). Impaired nursing: The role of the nurse manager. *Pediatric Nursing, 18*(2), 137–138.

PART FIVE

MANAGING CONSUMER CARE

CHAPTER 20
CONSUMER RELATIONSHIPS

Joyce N. Faris, R.N., M.S.N.

PREVIEW

This chapter explores the changes that have altered consumer relationships with healthcare providers and looks specifically at the nurse's responsibilities to the consumer. The nurse manager sets the tone for effective staff–patient interaction. Since nurses are the healthcare providers who spend the most time with the consumer, the chapter provides concepts and strategies to assist in developing effective nurse–consumer relationships.

OBJECTIVES

- Categorize health consumers' interactions into three relationship structures.
- Interpret the results of selected changes that have influenced consumer relationships in healthcare.
- Examine the importance of a service-oriented philosophy to the quality of the nurse/consumer relationship.
- Apply the four major responsibilities of nursing, service, advocacy, teaching, and leadership to the promotion of successful nurse/consumer relationships.

QUESTIONS TO CONSIDER

- What changes have taken place that have altered the relationships between the consumers of healthcare and the providers?
- What concepts must you apply in order to provide service-oriented nursing care to consumers?
- How do you take into consideration cultural diversity and individual differences when you practice nursing?
- What is consumer advocacy and who is responsible for it?

A Manager's Viewpoint

I work in a hospital that is just starting on a "redesign" program. We have gone about redefining our process and have set the consumer as the center of everything. The consumer will drive what goes on in our hospital. We will center all activities around the consumer, including how the nursing care is delivered, the laboratory services, and all services, and it will be a "whole" concept. I think it is exciting to have the consumer as the center of focus. It's exciting to know that it's my job to facilitate the consumer's needs and wishes.

How do I make that happen? Well, I think it's basically a learning process. We are starting with redefining the roles of the nurse. I will go over each of the nursing roles and make the application from the way it has been to a service orientation. It will require going over one role at a time and applying it to the consumer. It will involve the team concept and working with care pairs. For us it will be a whole new learning process. We have a new position—**patient care associates** (PCAs), who will work with the nurses as care partners.

There is now a big learning curve to overcome. The PCA and the nurses each have new skills to learn, and while they are learning it is sometimes painful. An example is that of the PCAs learning to draw blood and being far less skillful than the lab phlebotomist, which is more painful for the consumer, but part of the learning curve. Training staff to take on new responsibilities is a step-by-step process. It sometimes requires that we learn by our mistakes or by our omissions. I go over our patient satisfaction questionnaire results with the staff and point out how we could have better served the consumer and how each staff member has to learn to be accountable. This is really hard for me because I have such high expectations for nursing care. I just want the best I can get for the patients and it's a painful process getting there.

We also need to redesign and highlight our teaching role. It is new to the staff and they do not know what it means. It has been emphasized as *strategic* in our new care concept. We've always done teaching, but more on an informal basis. We need to formalize the process and take credit for what we do. Teaching will be based on our assessment of what the patient needs and what is found on the multidisciplinary patient care rounds. We need to utilize our individualized patient assessment to get to a change in behavior.

Sharon Freeman, R.N., Charge Nurse
St. Anthony's Hospital
Provenant Health System
Denver, Colorado

INTRODUCTION

Consumer relationships refer to the multitude of encounters between the consumer (client/patient/customer) and the representatives of the healthcare system. Who are the consumers of healthcare and what do they expect from the provider? What are their likes and dislikes and how do they evaluate the care they receive?

We all are consumers of healthcare—friends, neighbors, families, people like us, and people very different from us. Consumers are diverse culturally, ethnically, socially, physically, and psychologically. Consumers have to some degree become far better connoisseurs of healthcare than in the past. They have access to a limitless amount of information regarding health. Not all of what they read, hear, or see is valid, but they are better informed now than they ever have been. They question providers regarding the care they receive or don't receive and they ask, "Why are you doing that?"

THE CONSUMER FOCUS

Consumer relationships are constantly changing and thus affect the providers of health services, hospitals, home health agencies, nursing homes, physicians, and nurses. As inpatient services stabilize and outpatient services grow, competition for patients becomes fierce. The focus has moved from the **healthcare providers** to the **healthcare consumers.** As noted in the manager's perspective, *the consumer will drive what goes on in our healthcare settings.* The healthcare processes are being redefined with the consumer as the

consumer as center   center of everything. How consumers view and value the care they receive becomes important data. In A Manager's Viewpoint at the beginning of this chapter, the charge nurse talked about reviewing the patient satisfaction questionnaire results with the staff in order to better serve the patients.

There are three distinct relationships that consumers enter into in meeting their healthcare needs. These are with the physician, the health facility, and/or insurance provider and the nurse. Changes in physician practices, in access to **service,** insurance coverage, and payment, and in nurses' roles and responsibilities are a few of the significant factors that have influenced these relationships.

PHYSICIAN/CONSUMER RELATIONSHIPS

changes   Physician/consumer relationships changed as the physician's mode of practice moved from a single, private enterprise to the multigroup practice (Winslow, 1993). The groups may even be incorporated into health maintenance organizations, managed care programs, or physician–hospital organizations. When consumers visit a group practice, they may be unable to select a specific physician. Patients no longer know, trust, and respect their physicians as they did in the past and physicians may be unfamiliar with their patients.

trust   This has resulted in insecurity and lack of trust on the part of the patient and less-individualized care on the part of the physician.

Rural consumers of healthcare have seen their local hospitals close and have had to seek care in regional health centers. They do not know the physicians from whom they are forced to seek care. This leads the consumers to be more critical and less accepting of the care delivered. They feel alienated and insecure in the unfamiliar circumstances even though they may be receiving the best medical attention.

AGENCY/CONSUMER RELATIONSHIPS

Consumers of health services are accustomed to receiving treatment and care in an inpatient setting. In many situations, this option is no longer available. Patients may be angry and frightened at the thought of being on their own or with service provided only periodically from home health agencies. When inpatient services are deemed appropriate, the specific hospital or health agency that the client must patronize most likely will be dictated by the type of insurance coverage and the insurance carrier. Managed care options require that the consumer use particular and specific health facilities or be responsible for all or a larger portion of the bill.

The insurance plans available to most people include a co-payment or a deductible clause requiring the consumer to meet a certain dollar amount before insurance will pay their 60 to 90 percent of the bill. This has had significant impact on the consumer. No longer is a trip to the emergency department an option for a sore throat at midnight. The price tag for that service is prohibitive. Consumers are seeing their options for seeking care shrinking and the costs increasing.

Walter Cronkite reported in the Public Broadcasting System's 1991 special "Children at Risk" that the situation for pregnant women and children on Medicaid is unacceptable. If you lived in Denton County, Texas in 1991 and if you were pregnant and on Medicaid, your healthcare option was to show up at an emergency department when you were ready to deliver and hope for the best. No prenatal care was available for Medicaid mothers because private physicians could not afford to care for them. The same scenario was true for children on Medicaid. Again the option available was to show up at an emergency department when the child was seriously ill and hope for the best. Preventive care was not an option in either case (Cronkite, 1991).

changes in settings

fewer options

NURSE/CONSUMER RELATIONSHIPS

Nurses are the healthcare providers who spend the most time with the consumer. This encounter is generally personal and intensely meaningful. Therefore, the nurse is in a unique position to influence and promote dramatic and effective positive consumer relationships. The nurse manager sets the tone for effective staff/patient interactions. Sharon Freeman stated in A Manager's Viewpoint, "I think it is exciting to have the consumer as the center of focus. It's exciting to know that it's my job to facilitate the consumer's needs and wishes."

Changes from hospital/nursing home care to outpatient care have particularly altered the nurse/consumer relationship. Nurses are taking leadership roles as primary providers (nurse practitioners, midwives), teachers and educators, home healthcare managers and advocates, particularly in compensation and insurance arenas. Nurses may emerge as the **gatekeepers** of the healthcare system, the liaisons between the consumer and the complex healthcare market. The nurse in the role of gatekeeper can be an influential advocate for the consumer who falls through the cracks of the complicated healthcare system. This includes those who receive no care and need it most, such as the homeless, the uninsured or underinsured, the drug user, the alcoholic, the children of poverty, the migrant worker, and the AIDS victim.

roles

Nurses are held in high regard by the consumer. The public views the nurse as knowledgeable, "one of us," worthy of respect, trustful, concerned for others, honest, caring, confidential, friendly, and hard working. Nurses, by virtue

favorable status

EXERCISE 20-1
Chart as many ways as you can think of that the nurse might carry out the four responsibilities listed to the right. Compare your chart with those of your classmates.

of this favorable status with the public, occupy positions of influence and can foster and promote successful consumer relationships in whatever healthcare setting they engage.

Four major responsibilities of nurses in promoting successful consumer relationships are developed in this chapter:

1. Service
2. Advocacy
3. Teaching
4. Leadership.

SERVICE

A service orientation responds to the needs of the customer. In A Manager's Viewpoint, it was noted that activities were centered around the patient including how nursing care and all other services were delivered so that patient care was a "whole" concept. As the box below illustrates, no matter where the services are delivered (inpatient, outpatient, home based, clinic based), the focus is the patient (**consumer focus**).

Seven Primary Dimensions of Patient-Centered Care

- **Respect for patient's values, preferences, and expressed needs,** which includes attention to quality of life, involvement in decision making, preserving a patient's dignity, and recognizing patients' needs and autonomy.

- **Coordination and integration of care,** i.e., clinical care, ancillary and support services, and "front-line" patient care.

- **Information, communication, and education,** which includes information on clinical status, progress and prognosis; information on processes of care; and information and education to facilitate autonomy, self care and health promotion.

- **Physical comfort,** which considers pain management, help with activities of daily living, and hospital environment.

- **Emotional support and alleviation of fear and anxiety,** which demands attention to anxiety over clinical status, treatment and prognosis; anxiety over the impact of the illness on self and family; and anxiety over the financial impact of the illness.

- **Involvement of family and friends,** which recognizes the need to accommodate family and friends and involve family in decision making; to support the family as caregiver and recognize family needs.

- **Transition and continuity,** which addresses patient anxieties and concerns about information on medication, treatment regimens, follow up, danger signals after leaving the hospital, recovery, health promotion, and prevention of recurrence; coordination and planning for continuing care and treatment; and access to continuity of care and assistance.

Used with permission from Gerteis M, Edgman-Levitan S, Daley J, Delbanco TL, eds. Through the Patient's Eyes: Understanding and Promoting Patient-Centered Care. San Francisco, CA: Jossey Bass, 1993.

A service orientation is different from the concept of **service lines.** In this concept all related types of services are grouped into one functional unit of management. Typical service line units are womens' services, cardiac services, orthopedics services, and oncology services.

service orientation

Most healthcare facilities are not "customer friendly," that is, they are built and organized in a manner that best serves the organization, not the consumer. They are departmentalized with each department having specialized functions. Patients are transported from department to department to receive services. They risk loss of privacy, excessive exposure, and increased discomfort during the transfer and waiting episodes. One vice president of nursing cited that on an average day a seriously ill patient in her facility would be exposed to about fifty different personnel in the course of providing treatment and care. This is *not* "service oriented." A service mentality means bringing the services of the institution to the consumer in a manner that is least disruptive. Services, when possible, should come to the consumer and should be as easy, comfortable, pleasant, and effective as possible.

focus

Providing satisfying and meaningful service is not easy. Every consumer is different and every situation is different. How things are done and how needs are met vary in each situation. Service is not a prescribed set of rules and regulations and is not a one-dimensional concept. *Service* means placing a premium on the design, development, and delivery of care. For example, a home care patient needs IV antibiotic therapy. Inserting the IV catheter is the task-oriented, production piece of the care. The service piece is taking into consideration the special needs of the patient, such as placing the needle in the left arm so he can continue to use his cane with his right arm, or using some local anesthetic before needle insertion to reduce discomfort. Several characteristics are used to differentiate a service from a product. Some of these are shown in the example in the box below.

service

EXERCISE 20-2
List the things that you think are not consumer friendly in your nursing situation. (Example: Patients admitted to healthcare facilities are asked to repeat information several times to various people in the agency such as admitting staff, nursing, and x-ray technicians.)

Differentiating Characteristics Between a Service and a Product

SERVICE	PRODUCT
• Intangible (without physical boundaries)	• Tangible (possesses physical properties)
• Unpredictable	• Predictable
• Spontaneous	• Produced and stored
• Created and consumed simultaneously	• Created/can be consumed at a later time
• Heterogeneous (no two items are alike)	• Homogeneous
• Personal, human interaction	• Impersonal

In delivering nursing care, both service and product characteristics are present. Some of the actions in nursing require very prescribed rituals—the actual physical act of production, such as insertion of a Foley catheter. In performing this act certain physical properties are apparent and the outcome predictable. At the same time, no two patients are alike, human interaction alters the situation, and unforeseen variables demand spontaneity. The amount of caring, concern, and respect for the individual are intangible characteristics that affect

tangibles

intangibles

consumer-nurse relationship

the ultimate success or failure of the physical nursing act. As nurses we provide nursing care. Quality nursing care must be clinically correct and must also be satisfying to the consumer. "Clinically correct" is the product piece and "satisfying to the consumer" is the service.

A service orientation is consumer driven, consumer focused, and places the emphasis on the quality of the nurse/patient relationship. The importance of relationships is reflected in current nursing theory in the caring philosophy. Em Bevis, a promoter of the caring philosophy states, "Caring is the moral imperative of nursing and commits us to a sense of connectedness and to community building while compelling us to act for and in behalf of those we serve." (Bevis, 1993, p. 60)

high tech
high touch

The concept of nursing as a caring service is seen in the reality of **"high tech—high touch."** High tech denotes a mechanistic perspective while high touch denotes a caring, humanistic perspective. Caring for patients can be described as challenging in an environment driven by technology. At the same time, patients are dependent upon nurses to deliver high tech care in a caring, humanistic manner (Jones and Alexander 1993). The more that high technology is used in healthcare, the more the patient wants and needs high touch—someone who is trusted and respected and who will add humanness to the experience. The quality of these human contacts becomes the measure by which the consumer forms perceptions and judgments about nursing and the health agency. Particularly in healthcare, consumers are frequently not able to judge or evaluate the quality of the medical intervention, but they always have the ability to evaluate the quality of the relationship with the person delivering the service.

Each individual nurse is responsible for quality patient care. The nurse manager is accountable for quality management. To evaluate quality, four basic nursing principles are reviewed: care and concern, thinking on one's feet, decision making, and action.

caring

Caring has been described as the essence of nursing. It denotes a special concern, interest, or feeling capable of fostering a therapeutic nurse/patient relationship. Caring is important, but it is not enough to simply care. The ability to think and take appropriate, timely action must be a part of the therapeutic process. The nurse must do the right thing right and at the right time.

EXERCISE 20-3
Make a "what-if" list of things that would enhance services to the consumers of healthcare. Example: What if nurses were referred to patients at the same time that physicians were referred to patients?

ADVOCACY

Nurses today practice in a healthcare environment dominated by unrest and insecurity. Some of these forces are shown in the box on page 399.

These forces bring about ethical and moral questions such as Who gets care?, Where do they get care?, How much care?, Who has the right to die?, Who has the right to live?, and Who makes the decisions? Differing values and beliefs, along with economic constraints and limited resources, affect decisions that are made.

consumer rights

Consumers have some basic rights that need to be protected—the right to individualized care; the right to their own values, beliefs, and cultural ways; and the right to know and participate in care decisions. Within the healthcare system remains the unresolved issue of two levels of care that is rationally based on economics, but tends to result in racial-cultural discrimination (Malone, 1993). Not only has care been on a two-tiered basis, but also minorities and women have been significantly underrepresented in health-related research.

Forces of Unrest and Insecurity in Today's Healthcare Environment

1. Increased costs
2. Shift to outpatient
3. Complex social problems (AIDS, violence)
4. Decreased accessibility
5. Aging population
6. Culturally and ethnically diverse work/consumer groups
7. Technological and genetic advances
8. Underrepresentation of women and ethnic groups in health-related research

Recent reports of studies have shown that differences do indeed exist between blacks and whites and men and women, in the type of care received and recovery rates (Whittle et al., 1993). Some cultural and racial concerns are described in this chapter's "Theory Perspective."

 Theory Perspective

Malone, B.L. (1993). Caring for culturally diverse racial groups: An administrative matter. Nursing Administration Quarterly, 17(2) 21–29.

Culturally diverse racial groups face a unique set of issues and often experience racial and cultural discrimination in the healthcare system; as this quotation from the article referenced above illustrates:

People of color who are ill are significantly different from others. If they are infants, they are three times more likely to die before the age of one year than white infants. If they are adults, ill with heart disease, cancer, diabetes, and other major illnesses, they are twice as likely to die as their white counterparts. Humorously and sarcastically in the African-American community, the differential that statistically moves people of color automatically closer to death is known as the "Black tax." In this country, it costs one to be born a person of color. It costs in decreased years of life, it costs in low average incomes; and it costs in decreased access to and receipt of healthcare services, which include nursing care.

There are very few places where people of color have less control over their lives than in healthcare settings, especially hospitals. Already weakened and notified of their mortality by the need for hospitalization, people of color view the healthcare system and those who manage it as extremely white, professionally color-blind, and unconscious to the issues of cultural and racial sensitivity. (p. 26)

Implications for Practice

This scenario has serious implications for nursing practice. High levels of cultural and racial insensitivity in a nursing staff increase the patient's risk of not receiving the necessary treatment. When a predominantly white nursing staff distances itself from culturally diverse patients, healing and caring are jeopardized. Nurse managers need to be sensitive to the ethnic and cultural makeup of their staff and attempt to hire qualified nurses from diverse backgrounds. They need to set a goal to improve cultural and racial sensitivity in the practice of nursing and role model behaviors that exhibit this sensitivity.

Who in the healthcare system is in a position to be the guardian of these rights for the consumer? The nurse is! The nurse acts as the primary person to care about anything that might happen to prevent a successful outcome for the patient and to intervene on the patient's behalf. The nurse is in the position to address the issues of cultural and racial sensitivity.

advocate

Advocacy is a multidimensional concept and has many different meanings and applications. An advocate is one who (a) defends or promotes the rights of others; (b) changes systems to meet the needs of others; (c) empowers and promotes self-determination in others; (d) promotes autonomy of diverse cultures and social groups; (e) assures respect, equality, and dignity for others; and (f) cares—cares for humanness of all.

culture shock

Nurses practice in a healthcare system that is culturally, economically and socially diverse, just as consumers are. Nurses are responsible to consumers to assist them in successfully accessing and participating in these systems. Jezewski (1993) states, "Some patients enter the healthcare system much like immigrants entering a foreign country. The results may be culture shock for such patients as they enter a system with a set of values, beliefs, behaviors and language unlike their own" (p. 80).

Nurses need to recognize the culture of their work setting and realize it differs from the culture of the consumer who enters the system. The advocate role requires the nurse to perceive value conflict and then mediate, negotiate, clarify, explain, and intervene. The nurse can advocate by being a liaison between the consumer and the system. The nurse's role is to interpret the rules and customs of the agency to the consumer. It is also to negotiate changes when the consumer and agency differ in values and beliefs. Study the example shown in the box on page 401.

cultural diversity

To provide culturally appropriate care, the nurse must possess knowledge about various culturally diverse groups. It takes time to develop cultural sensitivity and awareness. Some guidelines that are useful in learning to appreciate and value diversity are

1. Avoid stereotyping
2. Avoid making assumptions
3. Learn by observing ethnic groups in interaction
4. Adjust expectations to be culturally sensitive
5. Create a more level playing field—modify your behavior to accommodate diversity.

Powerlessness or an imbalance in power between the consumer and the system results in value decisions being forced upon the recipient of care. Consumers who lack economic means either by being uninsured or underinsured become powerless in the healthcare delivery system. They are at the mercy or will of those who control the power and the money. These consumers (described above) may be denied access to care, or if they receive access they may not receive equal care. Refer to the "Theory Perspective" to review the costs of being born of color in this country.

Less-privileged consumers have a right to healthcare and a right to know what services or care they are entitled to. The nurse must be willing to see that economic constraints do not prevent them from receiving what they need. Some advocacy for the recipients of inequality in our healthcare system is done on the here-and-now level—initiating a referral to a social agency, appealing on behalf of the consumer to the ethics committee. On a broader scale it means becoming involved professionally and politically to change the systems and policies to provide equality and access to healthcare.

EXERCISE 20-4
Using the scenario in the box on page 401, determine how the nurse working as a **culture broker** can mediate the cultural differences between the staff and the patient.

Racial and Cultural Differences

SCENARIO: A young adult African-American male, shot while running from the police, had been hospitalized for over three weeks. A psychiatric clinical nurse specialist made the following assessment:

PERSPECTIVE OF NURSING STAFF	PERSPECTIVE OF PATIENT OF COLOR
1. No one wants to take care of this patient. Avoiding him is common. His call light goes unanswered.	1. Feels isolated and forgotten. Room is at the end of the hall. Infrequently sees nurses and physicians. Has little information about his gunshot wounds and fears he's never going to walk again. He fears he will die in his room and no one will know.
2. The patient is loud, rude, and uses vulgar language.	2. Speaks loudly like he does at home and uses vulgar talk to emphasize his concerns.
3. Nursing staff suspects that sexual activity is occurring between the man and his girlfriend in the hospital.	3. Makes comments with sexual overtones and spends hours with girlfriend when she visits.
4. Nurses feel physically and sexually threatened when trying to provide care.	4. Family only comes on weekends and then in large numbers.

Summary: Stereotypes about African-American males were operational on the unit. The staff members avoided the patient due to the sexual overtones, and they withheld information regarding his condition. Overt and covert battles of will with the patient resulted in further patient isolation.

Adapted from Malone, 1993, p. 26.

Some of the keys to becoming a successful nurse advocate are (a) developing networking systems within work agencies and professional associations to assist in providing information and services to patients, (b) acquiring the knowledge needed to access systems, (c) learning what's available in the community, (d) identifying the support groups, and (e) recognizing how to refer to and engage services.

In health facilities nurses can evaluate the quality of care the consumer is receiving by comparing it to the quality indicators developed for each DRG in the quality review process. If quality review standards cite that patients with a particular bronchial condition need a chest x-ray on day two and another on day five, the underserved should receive this same level of care. In agencies using critical paths to prescribe the plan of care, patients should not be denied treatment, therapy, or tests because of ability to pay if the critical path requires specific action. Nurse managers are in a unique position to access and assure that all patients receive appropriate care. The tone set by the manager signals staff to report and document discrepancies and omissions. Nurse managers must acknowledge and respect the legal, ethical, and moral responsibilities of the staff to advocate for patients.

quality

equal access

Quality medical care and quality nursing care are not dependent on ability to pay or social acceptance. If it's good care, it's good care irrespective of the economic circumstance of the consumer. Nurses are the guardians of that right for the consumers. Nurses have historically been the champions for the poor and the underserved. It is no different today.

TEACHING

Consumers of healthcare have a right to know and a need to know how to care for their own health needs. Nurses have an obligation to teach the consumer. This obligation is mandated in the states' nurse practice acts. The Joint Commission on Accreditation of Healthcare Organizations (JCAHO) also mandates patient teaching in its family and patient education standards. The American Nurses' Association has advocated patient teaching since the publication of its Model Nurse Practice Act in 1975. Most important, the consumer is demanding to know. In A Manager's Viewpoint, teaching was emphasized as strategic.

Teaching is wonderful, fun, rewarding, and hard work. It is one of the most positive experiences nurses can have. Consumers must be knowledgeable about their health concerns, participate in caring for their health needs, and contribute to finding solutions to their health problems. Education empowers consumers

empowerment

to exercise self-determination. It allows them to have control over what happens, to make informed decisions, and to choose wisely from options. An ancient proverb says that if you give a man a fish, you feed him for a day; but if you teach a man to fish, you feed him for a lifetime. That is very powerful! Knowledge is power. Sharing knowledge means sharing power.

The changes affecting healthcare affect the way nurses teach consumers. Probably the most significant change is shorter hospital stays and more care in outpatient settings. This requires that patients be able to manage their own

technical training

healthcare in an independent setting. Hands-on, technical training is needed in many instances, such as doing a self-catheterization. For the long term, teaching prevention and health promotion will increase the consumer's quality of life. Three "P's" for a successful consumer education focus are shown in the following box.

Three "P's" for a Successful Consumer Education Focus

1. Philosophy—Patient education is an investment with a significant positive return. Money invested in teaching is money well spent. Time and energy invested is time and energy well spent.
2. Priority—Education is important. Quality nursing care always has an educational component. Informed consumers want to participate and look to nurses to teach them.
3. Performance—Clinical teaching excellence is a required skill of nurses. They must possess a variety of techniques and methods in order to meet the needs of the diverse consumers served.

Teaching can be simple or complex. In teaching elemental, task-oriented behaviors, the nurse uses basic materials, simple relationships, guides, sequencing of steps, and cause-and-effect relationships.

EXAMPLE: Teaching insulin administration

1. Material	Demonstrate the use of the equipment. Return demonstration by trainee.
2. Simple relationships	Interpret the significance of the blood sugar level to the amount and type of insulin given.
3. Guides	Illustrate by chart the rotation of injection sites.
4. Sequencing	Apply a step-by-step procedure to follow to encompass the task from start to finish.
5. Cause and effect	Explain the relationship of sterile technique to infection prevention—"If you contaminate the needle, infection can result."

As a step-by-step process, teaching can be adapted to the nursing process model shown in Figure 20-1.

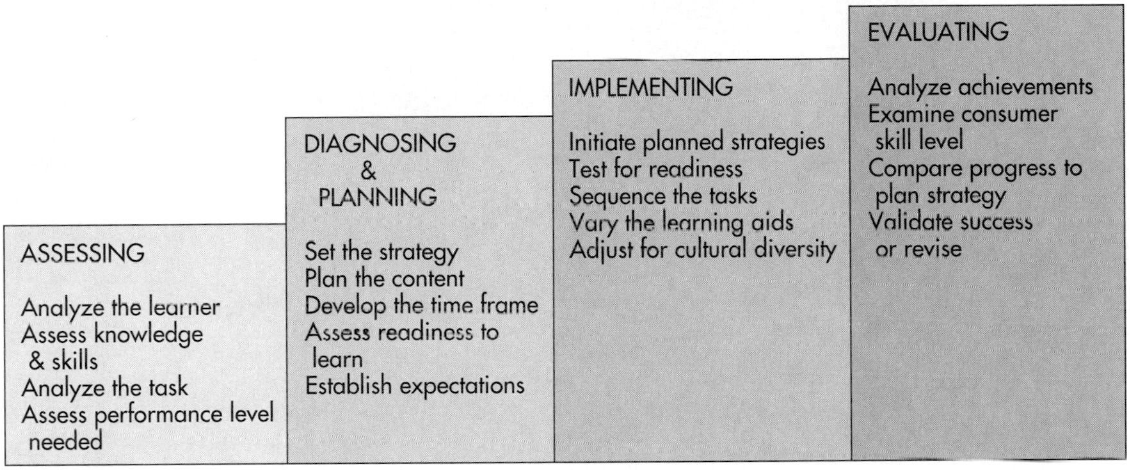

ASSESSING

Analyze the learner
Assess knowledge
 & skills
Analyze the task
Assess performance level
 needed

DIAGNOSING & PLANNING

Set the strategy
Plan the content
Develop the time frame
Assess readiness to
 learn
Establish expectations

IMPLEMENTING

Initiate planned strategies
Test for readiness
Sequence the tasks
Vary the learning aids
Adjust for cultural diversity

EVALUATING

Analyze achievements
Examine consumer
 skill level
Compare progress to
 plan strategy
Validate success
 or revise

FIGURE 20-1
Teaching model adapted to the nursing process.

The following example uses the nursing process model in teaching a patient about diabetes.

Assess	Patient is a 16-year-old, Hispanic male with no prior knowledge of diabetes or skill in drug administration. English is a second language. He needs to give his own insulin, using sterile technique, by the time he is discharged from the hospital.
Diagnose	Insulin-dependent patient needs instruction in drug administration technique at basic level.
Plan	Begin with demonstration, return demonstration of basic subcutaneous injection. Progress step by step to basic understanding of diabetes, blood sugar, and insulin dosage by the time of discharge. Home health to continue training.
Implement	Set times, twice a day, to spend one hour in instruction with patient. Begin with demonstration, return demonstration, and repeat instructions. Adjust learning materials to accommodate language barrier.
Evaluate	Patient has met minimal skill level of subcutaneous technique. He can administer insulin safely but has limited disease and cause/effect understanding. To be followed per home health with continued teaching.

As a conceptual process, teaching fits into the general systems theory model as shown in Figure 20-2. The following example uses the general systems theory model in teaching a patient with diabetes:

Successful consumer education requires excellent clinical teaching skills.

Input	Present information on the disease, the procedures to be learned, the skills necessary for successful achievement, and the cause-and-effect relationships. Have materials in Spanish at the high school reading level. Demonstrate the drug administration technique.
Throughput	Language barrier eased with materials printed in Spanish. Fears threat to macho image typical of 16-year-old male. Allow time to practice techniques demonstrated.
Output	Return demonstration successful. Give post-test to assess knowledge (in Spanish).
Feedback	Praise for successful return demonstration. Give example of sport/movie heroes with diabetes.

flexibility

Nurses need to be prepared and skilled to teach. They must be able to adapt to the learning styles of the consumer by using a variety of styles and a flexible approach in meeting the educational goals. Selected learning preferences are shown in the box below. Being knowledgeable in the subject and able to individualize the information to meet the consumer's ability to learn are critical to quality teaching (Babcock and Miller, 1994).

EXERCISE 20-5
Using one of the models presented, prepare a teaching plan based upon your actual nursing experience.

Selected Learning Preferences

- Auditory (words)
- Active (participate)
- Linear (step by step)
- Rational (reasoning)

- Visual (sight)
- Passive (contemplate)
- Circular (model, picture)
- Abstract (global)

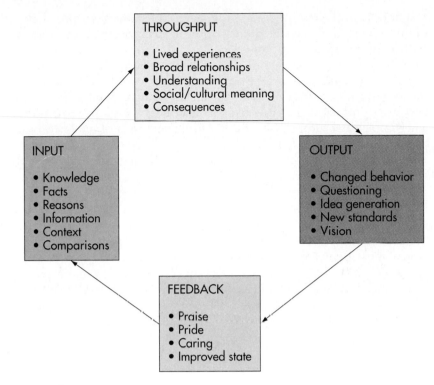

FIGURE 20-2
Teaching model adapted to general systems theory.

LEADERSHIP

Nurse managers are in a pivotal position to influence the cost and the quality of care delivered by the staff. They set the tone for the unit and the focus for the staff. They must believe in and model the consumer-based service philosophy. The one who truly believes in the need to provide service that is satisfying to the consumer knows that each and every consumer is different. What will satisfy one person will not satisfy another. To be successful as leaders in nursing requires being open, flexible, and ready to change. It requires (a) a belief that the intangibles have economic value, (b) a tolerance for ambiguity, (c) a relinquishing of direct control over every key process, (d) an appreciation that the organization is dependent on both people-related and production-related skills, and (e) a tolerance and excitement for sudden and sometimes dramatic change (Albrecht and Zemke, 1985).

Change is the modus operandi of the nursing environment no matter what the physical setting. What works today may not work six months from now. Given the rapidly changing environment, the pressure to control costs, and the advances in technology, science, and information, nurse managers need a whole new set of beliefs, behaviors, and skills. Selected examples of these are as follows:

1. Keep the consumer as the center of focus.   *consumer as center*
2. Recognize that each staff member has a unique contribution to make to the success of the unit. Accomplish this by allowing staff to be creative   *staff creativity*

and flexible in their work, asking for suggestions and new approaches to old problems, and seeking participation in decision making. Managers set the tone; staff deliver the service.

values   3. Promote dignity, worth, caring, individual contribution, and cultural diversity in the staff. Successful managers recognize individual accomplishments and support failures. They accept that human beings are not perfect at all times and that it is okay to take a risk, look foolish, and fail. They implement hiring practices that foster selection of qualified racially and culturally diverse applicants.

economics   4. Understand the economic value of service. Managers must believe that service will pay real dollar dividends to justify the cost in terms of adequate quality and quantity of staff.

outcomes   5. Evaluate patient outcomes and perceptions of care. It is imperative to ask patients about the services provided and how it felt to them, not after the fact but while they are receiving the service.

Managers must be willing to give up direct control of every process. Staff has to be given power and permission to be in control and to make decisions at the consumer-staff level of interaction. People need to be allowed to act spontaneously and at times impulsively so their "critical parent" won't jump out and stop them. Some of our greatest successes come out of spontaneous actions. Giving up control involves being willing to take a risk and a belief in the other person's ability to perform.

Leadership behaviors contributing to individual and personal excellence are (a) allowing professionals more influence over their practice, (b) giving staff opportunities to learn new and varied skills, (c) giving recognition and reward for success and support and consolation for lack of success, and (d) fostering motivation and belief in the importance of each individual and the value of his *passion*   or her contribution. The leader's role is to create within the worker a passion to do and contribute to the work effort successfully.

We do best those things that we know how to do skillfully and those things we feel passionately about. Fitting the right person to the right job is important. Maximum contribution is required from each staff member in today's healthcare agencies. Since the leader is the one who sets the standard for the success or failure of the staff's contributions, it is important to assess each staff member carefully: what is his or her skill level and commitment level, and what can be done to assist them in making a maximum contribution. Figure 20-3 is an example of a completed staff assessment tool. Nurse managers can compile similar information for members of their staff. The information can be used to form staff development plans.

When staff knows the leader is sincerely concerned about their welfare, they are better able to use their time, energy, and talents to serve the needs of the consumer. Staff that are nurtured and cared for will be better able to nurture and care for the consumer.

EXERCISE 20-6
Forming small groups, assess each member of the group using the headings shown in the staff assessment tool on page 407.

CHAPTER CHECKLIST

Times have changed and the role of the nurse manager has changed. The move into the community, home, clinic, and outpatient setting has placed a whole new perspective on how to provide quality, cost-effective nursing care. Patients must participate in their care and need service-oriented nurses to be teachers, advocates, and leaders in their behalf. Managing care delivery in these

Staff Member	Skill Level	Commitment Level	Suggested Action
(1) S. Baker, RN	High technical competence Able to teach others Learns quickly Needs improved people skills	Appears bored Does only what is assigned No enthusiasm Critical of any change	Assign challenges to utilize technical strengths Provide situations where teaching others occurs Plan: Team assign with D. Carroll
(2) D. Carroll, RN	6 mos. post basic program Learns quickly Slow with technical skills Needs technical supervision Excellent people skills	Excited about work Asks for new experiences Accepting of new ideas Volunteers to help others	Improve technical skills Provide safe & successful learning experiences Plan: Team assign with S. Baker
(3) J. Ratke, RN	Moderate technical competence Works best alone Not interested in teaching co-worker Good people skills	Restless, distracted Looking for a change Accepts new ideas Self commitment - not group oriented	Set up an independent project of her choosing (e.g. unit research idea) Provide some special technical training to ↑ skills
(4) C. Thomas, RN	High level technical skills Enjoys helping others Excellent people skills Looks for challenges	Team player Interested in welfare of group Critical of poor performers Acts as cheerleader for change	Utilize willingness and group skills to plan and present a unit activity (e.g. inservice education production, unit open house)

FIGURE 20-3
Staff assessment tool.

diverse settings requires the use of flexible and creative skills. The key is to keep the patient as the center of focus and provide cultural and racially sensitive nursing care.

- Consumer relationships in healthcare typically involve interactions between the consumer and:
  - The physician
    - Patients no longer know, trust, and respect their physicians as they did in the past.
  - The healthcare and insurance agencies
    - Insurance coverage and carriers usually dictate the services patients receive and where they receive them.
  - The nurse
    - Nurses, as the healthcare providers who spend the most time with the consumer, set the tone for effective staff–patient interactions.
- Because of their favorable status with consumers, nurses are in a unique position to promote positive consumer relationships.

- Four major responsibilities of nurses in promoting successful consumer relationships are:
  - Service
  - Advocacy
  - Teaching
  - Leadership.

■ A service orientation is consumer-driven and consumer-focused, emphasizing the quality of the nurse–patient relationship and the delivery of services in a caring atmosphere.
  - Services differ from products:
    - Services are intangible, unpredictable, created and consumed simultaneously, and personal.
    - Products are tangible, predictable, produced and stored, and impersonal.

■ The nurse can advocate by serving as a liaison between the consumer and the healthcare system.
  - Nurses can interpret the agency's rules and customs for the consumer and negotiate if conflicts arise.
  - Nurses also help secure culturally appropriate care and mediate cultural differences between staff and the patient.

■ Teaching is the sharing of information and education to help consumers become independent, self-responsible, and self-determining.
  - Nurses have an obligation to teach the consumer.
  - The three "P's" for successful consumer education are:
    - Philosophy: patient education is an investment with a significant positive return.
    - Priority: education is important.
    - Performance: clinical teaching excellence is a required skill for nurses.
  - Teaching can follow the five-step nursing process model.

■ Leadership fosters decision making at the consumer–staff level of interaction. Effective leadership strategies for the nurse manager include:
  - Keeping the central focus on the consumer.
  - Recognizing staff members' unique contributions and helping them maximize their personal excellence.
  - Promoting staff members' sense of dignity, worth, caring, and cultural diversity.
  - Understanding the economic value of service.
  - Evaluating patient outcomes and patients' perceptions of care.

TERMS TO KNOW

- advocacy
- caring
- consumer focus
- culture broker
- gatekeeper
- healthcare consumer
- healthcare provider
- high tech
- high touch
- patient care associate
- service
- service lines

REFERENCES

Albrecht, K., & Zemke, R. (1985). *Service America! Doing Business in the New Economy.* Homewood, IL: Dow Jones-Irwin.

Babcock, D.E., & Miller, M.A. (1994). *Client Education, Theory and Practice.* St. Louis, MO: Mosby.

Bevis, E. (1993). Alliance for destiny: Education and practice. *Nursing Management, 24*(4), 56–62.

Cronkite, W. (Narrator) (1991, Nov). *Children at Risk* (Film). New York: Public Broadcasting System.

Gerteis, M., Edgman-Levitan, S., Daley, J., & Delbanco, T.L. (1993). *Through the Patient's Eyes: Understanding and Promoting Patient-Centered Care.* San Francisco, CA: Jossey Bass.

Jezewski, M.A. (1993). Culture brokering as a model for advocacy. *Nursing and Health Care, 14*(2), 78–84.

Jones, D.B., & Alexander, J.W. (1993). The technology of caring: A synthesis of technology and caring for nursing administration. *Nursing Administration Quarterly, 17*(2), 11–19.

Malone, B.L. (1993). Caring for culturally diverse racial groups: An administrative matter. *Nursing Administration Quarterly, 17*(2), 21–29.

Whittle, J., Conigliaro, J., Good, C.B., & Lofgren, R.P. (1993). Racial differences in the use of invasive cardiovascular procedures in the Department of Veterans Affairs Medical System. *New England Journal of Medicine, 320*(9), 621–627.

Winslow, R. (1993, Aug. 18). Patients prefer small providers of healthcare. *The Wall Street Journal*, B1, 3.

SUGGESTED READING

Giger, J., & Davidhizar, R. (1991). *Transcultural Nursing, Assessment and Intervention.* St. Louis, MO: Mosby.

Hays, B.J. (1992). Nursing care requirements and resource consumption in home health care. *Nursing Research, 41*(3), 138–143.

Jacques, R. (1993). Untheorized dimensions of caring work: Caring as a structural practice and caring as a way of seeing. *Nursing Administration Quarterly, 17*(2), 1–10.

Jenks, J.M. (1993). The pattern of personal knowing in nurse clinical decision making. *Nursing Education, 32*(9), 399–405.

Knowles, M. (1990). *The Adult Learner: A Neglected Species,* 4th ed. Houston: Gulf.

Peters, T.J., & Waterman, R.H., Jr. (1982). *In Search of Excellence.* New York: Harper & Row.

CHAPTER 21

CARE DELIVERY SYSTEMS

Jacquelyn Komplin, R.N., M.S.N.

PREVIEW

This chapter introduces patient care delivery systems that hospitals and community-based facilities currently use: the case method, functional nursing, team nursing, primary nursing, and case management. It also discusses differentiated practice. The chapter defines and discusses each system, summarizes its benefits and disadvantages, and discusses the nurse manager's role in the system. A comparison of healthcare delivery systems concludes the chapter.

OBJECTIVES

- Specify and differentiate among five patient care delivery systems.
- Determine the nurse manager's role in each of the systems.
- Summarize the differentiated nursing practice concept.

QUESTIONS TO CONSIDER

- What system of patient care delivery would you most enjoy working in and why?
- How does your level of nursing education affect the care you provide?
- How do you think a nurse manager influences the effectiveness of the patient care delivery system?

A Manager's Viewpoint

I had many factors to consider when I was searching for a new system of patient care delivery for the medical-surgical unit I managed. The budget for full-time equivalents (FTEs) was limited and I currently had a staff mix of 60 percent RNs, 30 percent LPNs, and 10 percent nursing assistants. The nurses had different levels of competency; some had twenty years of experience and others were recent graduates. The patient acuity was important to consider because we had both high and low acuity. The last factor to consider was the unusual floor plan of the unit, with one long corridor and smaller offshoots of patient rooms.

I considered these factors when examining the traditional systems of patient care delivery, and with research I found that none of the systems met the unit needs. The staff mix wasn't appropriate for primary nursing, the functional method was totally unacceptable, and the case management system wasn't realistic yet at this hospital. The staff liked the team/modular method so we decided to make some alterations to suit our staffing and patient acuity needs.

We assigned staff in small groups, or teams, of two to three staff per group of patients. The low-acuity patients were placed in the long corridors with two to three LVNs caring for them. These LVNs received continuing education to help them become team oriented. Two RNs were "teamed" with each assistant. The RN groups were responsible for the high-acuity patients in the offshoots of the corridor. Each team was assigned two to four patients with one of the nurses, usually the one with the most experience, functioning as the charge person for the small group. In essence, there were several "charge nurses" on the unit, one per geographic region. My role changed and I became the liaison for the charge nurses and eliminated the old charge position. The mini-teams became so skilled at solving their own problems that I was rarely needed!

We also made some logistical changes, such as placing locked medication cabinets and charts at the bedside. The nurses had more total patient contact time, which increased patient and nursing satisfaction. The physicians were pleased because they found everything, including the nurse, at the bedside.

I think the biggest obstacle I had to overcome in restructuring the system of patient care delivery was the initial resistance to change. After realizing they were empowered by the new structure, the staff found more efficient methods of accomplishing everything. Of course, this change did take time to happen and I realize this system is not perfect, but it met our unit's needs. I think each manager needs to individualize a patient care delivery system to the unit's needs and consider organizational factors that could affect any change of patient care delivery.

Marlene Kimble, R.N., B.S.N., M.S.N.
Medical-Surgical Nursing Instructor
Ohlone College
Fremont, California
(formerly, Nurse Manager St. Mary's Hospital
Grand Junction, Colorado)

INTRODUCTION

A **care delivery system** is the method used to provide care to patients and clients (hereafter, the term *patients* will refer to both patients and clients). Since nursing care is viewed as a cost, it is logical for institutions to evaluate their system of providing patient care for the purpose of saving money while still providing quality care. This chapter discusses five systems of patient care delivery; case method (or total patient care), functional nursing, team nursing, primary nursing, and case management, and describes the influence that differentiated practice has on a delivery system.

Each delivery system has advantages and disadvantages and none is ideal. Some methods are conducive to large institutions while other systems may work best in community settings. Managers in any organization must examine the care delivery systems and consider the budget, staff availability, and organizational goals to determine the best system for delivery.

CASE METHOD

one to one

The **case method,** or **total patient care** method, of nursing care delivery is the oldest method of providing care to a patient. The premise of the case method is that one nurse provides total care for one patient during an eight-hour period (Figure 21-1). This method was used in the 1800s when nurses cared for the sick in their homes. Nursing students have typically used this approach at some point in providing total care to a patient. Another example is a private duty nurse who cares for one person during a specific shift.

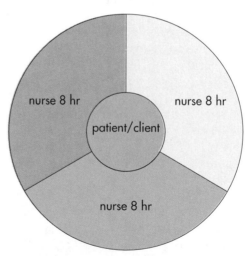

FIGURE 21-1
Case method of patient care.

ADVANTAGES AND DISADVANTAGES

consistency

In this system the patient receives consistent care during each eight-hour shift. The nurse and patient exchange mutual trust and can work together toward specific goals. Since three nurses on different shifts function independently, the patient goals are not always communicated and the patient may fail to progress toward expected outcomes (Marquis and Huston, 1992). **Expected outcomes** are the results of patient goals, achieved through medical and nursing interventions. When outcomes are not met, the amount of time required for care increases, leading to additional expense for the entire healthcare system.

The case method was necessary in the era of Florence Nightingale, when patients received total care at home. However, today, family members participate in caring for the patient, and home health visits can replace the twenty-four-hour care that is extremely costly in today's economy. Variations of the case method exist and it is possible to identify similarities after reviewing other methods of patient care delivery.

NURSE MANAGER'S ROLE

When using the case method of delivery, the manager must consider the expense of the system. The manager must weigh the expense of an RN versus LPNs and **unlicensed assistive personnel.** Unlicensed assistive personnel are staff who are not licensed as healthcare providers. They are technicians, nurse aides, and certified nursing assistants. The patient may require twenty-four-hour care; however, the manager must decide if the patient needs to have RN care or RN supervised care provided by LPNs or unlicensed personnel. To provide cost-effective care to the patients, the staff need to have adequate skills to provide total care.

unlicensed assistive personnel

The manager also needs to identify the level of education and communication skills of all staff. RNs must be educated in communicating and coordinating care as well as supervising other staff members. LPNs and unlicensed personnel also need continuing education to provide total care according to their level of practice.

FUNCTIONAL NURSING

The functional method of nursing care delivery became popular during World War II when there was a severe shortage of nurses in the United States, because many nurses went into the military to provide care to the soldiers. To provide care to patients, hospitals began to increase the number of unlicensed assistive personnel and licensed practical/vocational nurses.

Functional nursing is a method of providing patient care where each licensed and unlicensed staff member provides a specific task for a large group of patients. For example, the RN may administer all IV medications and do admissions, one LPN may provide treatments, another LPN may give all oral medication, one assistant may do all hygiene tasks, and another assistant takes all vital signs (Figure 21-2). This method is a similar to the assembly line system used by industry. A **charge nurse** coordinates care and assignments and may ultimately be the only person familiar with all needs of any patient.

task orientation

ADVANTAGES AND DISADVANTAGES

There are several advantages to this method of patient care delivery. First, each person becomes very efficient at specific tasks and a great amount of work can be done in a short time. Another advantage is that unskilled workers can be trained to perform one or two specific tasks very well, such as glucometer checks or phlebotomy. The hospital benefits financially from this system because patient care can be delivered to a large number of patients by mixing

efficiency

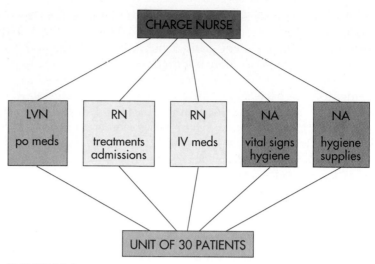

FIGURE 21-2
Functional method of nursing care delivery.

staff with a minimum number of RNs and a larger number of unlicensed assistive personnel. By decreasing the number of RNs, the hospital has fewer personnel costs.

Although financial savings may be the impetus for hospitals to choose the functional system of delivering care, the disadvantages outweigh the savings

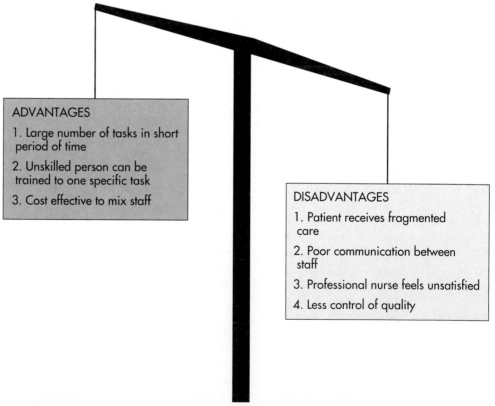

FIGURE 21-3
Advantages and disadvantages of functional nursing.

(Figure 21-3). One disadvantage is that the patients become confused with so many different care providers per shift. A patient may have as many as five different people performing different tasks for him/her during the day. These different staff members may be so busy with their assigned task that they do not have time to communicate with each other about the patient's progress. Since no one care provider sees patient care from beginning to the end, it is difficult to communicate either improvements or problems in the patient's status. This fragmented care and poor communication can lead to patient dissatisfaction and frustration.

Exercise 21-2 provides an opportunity to imagine how a patient would react to the functional method, but also to imagine how the nurse may feel. The functional method leaves the professional nurse feeling frustrated because of the task-oriented role. Nurses are educated to care for the patient holistically, and providing only a fragment of care to patient results in unmet personal and professional expectations of nursing.

NURSE MANAGER'S ROLE

In the functional nursing method, the nurse manager must be sensitive to both the institution's budgetary constraints and the responsibility for quality patient care delivery. Since staff members are responsible only for their specific task, the role of achieving patient outcomes becomes the nurse manager's responsibility. Staff members may view this system as autocratic and become discontented with the lack of input they have into patient outcomes and departmental matters.

By using good management and leadership skills, the nurse manager can improve the staff's perception of their lack of independence. The manager can rotate assignments among staff to alleviate boredom with repetition. Staff meetings should be conducted frequently. This would encourage staff to express concerns and empower them with the ability to communicate concerns about patient care and unit functions.

The functional method of patient care delivery is used mainly in extended care facilities. With the advent of severe budgetary cuts, some organizations are changing the **staff mix** to an increased proportion of unlicensed to licensed personnel. One version of a modification is the team nursing system.

TEAM NURSING

After World War II the nursing shortage continued. Many nurses who were in the military came home to marry and have children instead of returning to the work force. Since the functional method during the war received criticism, a new system of team nursing was devised to improve patient satisfaction.

In **team nursing** a team leader is responsible for coordinating a small group of licensed and unlicensed personnel to provide patient care to a small group of patients. The team leader assigns each member a patient or a specific responsibility. The members of the team report directly to the team leader who then reports to the charge nurse or unit manager (Figure 21-4). There are several teams per unit and patient assignments are made by each team leader.

ADVANTAGES AND DISADVANTAGES

Some advantages of the team method are improved patient satisfaction, organizational decision making occurring at lower levels, and cost-effectiveness

outcome issues

extended care

team leaders

EXERCISE 21-3
Think of a time when you worked with a group of four to six people to achieve a specific goal or accomplish a task (perhaps in school you were grouped together to complete a project). How did your group achieve the goal? Was one person the organizer or leader who assigned each member a component, or did you each determine what skills you possessed that would most benefit the group? Did you experience any conflict while working on this project? How did the concepts of group dynamics and leadership skills affect how your group achieved its goal? What similarities do you see between the team nursing system of providing patient care and your group involvement to achieve a goal?

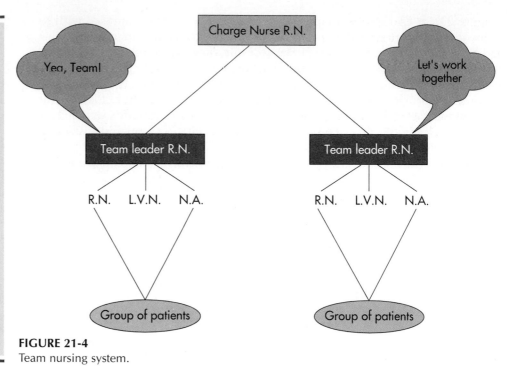

FIGURE 21-4
Team nursing system.

for the agency. Many institutions and community health areas currently use the team nursing method.

The patient is satisfied because he receives care from a small team and when he has a specific request or concern, any team member can relay the concern directly to the team leader. The team leader can either solicit solutions from the team members or notify the charge nurse if the team is unable to solve the problem. As a result, patient concerns are addressed and the patient receives care from the most qualified team member for the job.

team spirit   Each member of the team participates in the decision-making process. The team leader is responsible for facilitating a cooperative environment among team members and encouraging each member to work toward the same goals. Since decision making occurs at all levels, every member of the team feels his or her contribution is valued to have a "winning" team.

Inpatient facilities may view team nursing as a cost-effective system because it works with a high ratio of unlicensed to licensed personnel. Thus, the organization saves money by hiring fewer RNs and more unlicensed assistive personnel.

leadership skills   The team method of patient care delivery is a good system, if implemented properly; however, one major disadvantage arises if the team leader has poor leadership skills. The team leader must have excellent communication skills, delegation abilities, conflict resolution techniques, strong clinical skills, and effective decision-making abilities to provide a working "team" environment for the members. If a team environment does not exist, then team members might not assume the individual accountability necessary to provide quality patient care (Watkins, 1993). Frequently, the team leader is not prepared for this role and the team method becomes a miniature version of the functional method.

NURSE MANAGER'S ROLE

The nurse manager, charge nurse, and team leaders must have management skills to effectively implement the team nursing method of patient care delivery. The unit manager must determine which RNs are skilled and who is interested in becoming a charge nurse or team leader. A preference should be given to the baccalaureate-prepared RNs because their basic education emphasizes critical thinking and leadership concepts. The nurse manager should also provide adequate staff mix and orient team members to the team nursing system by providing continuing education about management techniques and group interaction. By addressing these factors, the manager is aiding the teams to function optimally.

education

The charge nurse functions as a liaison between the team leaders and other healthcare providers. Some charge nurses have a difficult time relinquishing authority; however, the charge nurse needs to encourage each team to solve its problems independently.

The team leader should identify the strengths of each team member. If one nurse is skilled at starting IVs she should start any new IVs. If a nursing assistant is especially successful in motivating patients to walk, assign her the patients who need to ambulate frequently. Allowing team members to provide the type of patient care they are skilled at enhances job satisfaction.

MODULAR METHOD

A modification to team nursing is the modular system of patient care delivery. The **modular method** focuses on the geographical location of patient rooms and assignment of staff members (Magargal, 1987). The unit is divided into modules, or districts, and the same team of staff members are assigned consistently to the module. Each module has a modular, or team, leader RN who assigns the patients to module staff. Each module ideally consists of one RN, one LPN, and one nursing assistant. The charge nurse expects the module leaders to be accountable for patient care but assists in problem solving when necessary. Depending on the number of staff, the charge nurse may also be a module leader. The manager, in A Manager's Viewpoint at the beginning of this chapter, addressed geographic location as a factor in choosing the team-modular method of delivery.

geography

Bennett and Hylton (1990) found increased continuity of care when staff was consistently assigned to the same module and the geographic closeness of the modular system saved nursing time. The modular system could also cost money because it requires a redesign of the work environment to allow medication carts, supplies, and charts to be located in each module. Traditional long corridors are not conducive to modular nursing.

continuity

The team nursing system originated to improve staff and patient satisfaction in the 1950s. However, RNs are educated to provide holistic care to patients and they are not able to do this in the team method of patient care delivery. In the late 1960s, the nursing care delivery methods were reevaluated and the primary nursing system evolved to provide improved autonomy for nurses.

PRIMARY NURSING

A cultural revolution occurred in the United States during the 1960s. The revolution emphasized individual rights and independence from existing societal restrictions. This revolution also influenced the nursing profession because nurses were becoming dissatisfied with their lack of autonomy. Institutions were also aware of declining quality patient care. The search for autonomy and quality care led to the primary nursing system of patient care delivery as a method to increase RN accountability for **patient outcomes.**

total care

Primary nursing is a method of patient care delivery where one RN functions autonomously as the patient's main nurse throughout the hospital stay. The **primary nurse** is responsible for twenty-four hour a day total patient care from admission through discharge. The total care involves decision making in assessing and caring for all patient needs, planning care, implementing the plan, and evaluating all goals. The primary nurse is preferably baccalaureate prepared and is held accountable for meeting **outcome criteria** and communicating with all other healthcare providers about the patient (Figure 21-5).

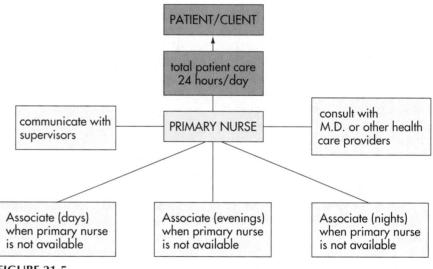

FIGURE 21-5
Primary nursing.

For example, a patient is admitted to a medical floor with pulmonary edema. His primary nurse admits him and then provides a written plan of care. When his primary nurse is not working, an associate nurse implements the plan. The **associate nurse** is any RN or LPN who provides care to the patient according to the primary nurse's specification. If the patient develops additional complications, the associate nurse notifies the primary nurse, who has twenty-four-hour responsibility. The primary nurse makes alterations in the care plan based on the associate nurse's input.

ADVANTAGES AND DISADVANTAGES

Some advantages of the primary nursing method are professional job satisfaction, quality patient care and patient satisfaction, and a decrease in the number of nonprofessional staff (Figure 21-6).

job satisfaction

RNs practicing primary nursing experience job satisfaction because they are able to utilize their education to provide holistic and autonomous care for the patient (see the "Research Perspective" on page 420). This high level of accountability for patient outcomes encourages RNs to further their knowledge and refine skills to provide optimal patient care. If the primary nurse is not mo-

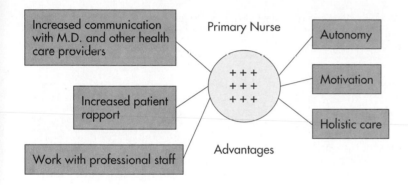

Increased communication with M.D. and other health care providers

Primary Nurse

+ + +
+ + +
+ + +

Autonomy

Motivation

Increased patient rapport

Holistic care

Work with professional staff

Advantages

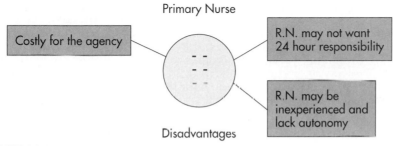

Primary Nurse

Costly for the agency

- -
- -
- -

R.N. may not want 24 hour responsibility

R.N. may be inexperienced and lack autonomy

Disadvantages

FIGURE 21-6
Advantages and disadvantages to the primary nursing system.

tivated or feels unqualified to provide holistic care, job satisfaction may decrease.

In primary nursing, patients are satisfied with the care they receive because they establish rapport with their primary nurse. Since the patient's primary nurse communicates the plan of care, the patient can move away from the sick role and begin to participate in his/her own recovery. The professional nurse is educated to provide holistic care. By considering sociocultural, psychological, and physical needs of the patient, the primary nurse can plan the most appropriate care with and for the patient.

A professional advantage to the primary nursing method is a decrease in the number of unlicensed personnel. The ideal primary nursing system requires an all RN staff. The RN can provide total care to the patient, from bed baths to patient education, even both at the same time! The unlicensed personnel are not qualified to provide this inclusive care.

A disadvantage to the primary nursing method is that the RN may not have the experience or educational background to provide total care. The agency needs to educate staff for an adequate transition from the previous role to the primary role. Additionally, the RN may not be ready or capable of twenty-four-hour responsibility of patient care. Nursing has a large number of part-time RNs who are not available to assume the primary nurse role.

With the arrival of diagnosis-related groups (DRGs), patients' hospitalization stays are shorter than in the 1970s, when primary nursing became popular. With expedited stays, it is difficult for primary nurses to adequately provide primary nursing. If the patient is admitted on Monday and discharged on

EXERCISE 21-4
Mr. Faulkner is admitted to the medical unit with exacerbated congestive heart failure. Mike Ross, R.N., B.S.N., is Mr. Faulkner's primary nurse who will provide total care to Mr. Faulkner. Mike notes this is Mr. Faulkner's third admission in six months for congestive heart failure–related symptoms. This is the first admission when Mr. Faulkner has had a primary nurse. What do you think will be different about this admission with Mike providing primary nursing to Mr. Faulkner? Do you think there will be any difference in continuity of care? How involved do you think Mr. Faulkner will be with his own care in the primary nursing system?

Research Perspective

Blegen, M. (1993). Nurses' job satisfaction: A meta-analysis of related variables. Nursing Research, 42(1), 36–40.

This study was conducted to identify the relationship between a nurse's job satisfaction and the variables associated with the satisfaction. This was a meta-analysis study that examined data from other studies on the topic of job satisfaction. Data from forty-eight studies, both published and unpublished, with 15,048 subjects from 173 different hospitals and 8 other locations, was analyzed. There were thirty different variables affecting nursing job satisfaction and this study combined and pared them down to thirteen variables. Many different statistical analysis techniques were utilized to accurately analyze the data to determine the correlation between the variables and job satisfaction.

The major significant variables were stress, commitment, communication with supervisor, autonomy, recognition, and routinization. Stress led to negative satisfaction and commitment led to positive satisfaction. Job satisfaction is present when autonomy was indicated as a variable. The greater the amount of autonomy in their work, such as in the primary nursing and nurse managed care, the greater the job satisfaction. The study also found that communication and recognition by their supervisor had a positive influence on job satisfaction.

Implications for Practice

The results are helpful in examining job satisfaction through nursing theories. There are many variables that nurse managers can examine and alter to improve job satisfaction. By increasing the nurse's autonomy, the nurse managers may actually decrease job-related stress and improve retention.

EXERCISE 21-5

Imagine you are a primary nurse at Pleasant Dreams, inpatient psychiatric facility. The patients you are assigned to are usually suicidal. How would you feel about the added responsibility for patients even when you were not at work? How would this responsibility impact your personal life? How would you make decisions?

Wednesday, the primary nurse has a difficult time meeting all patient needs before discharge if she/he is not working on Tuesday. The primary nurse must rely heavily on feedback from associates, which defeats the purpose of primary nursing.

NURSE MANAGER'S ROLE

The primary nursing system can be modified to meet patient, nursing, and budgetary demands while maintaining the positive components that spawned its conception. The nurse manager needs to determine the desire of staff to become primary nurses and then educate them accordingly. The associate nurses and all other healthcare providers need clearly defined roles. They also need to be aware of the primary nurse's role and the importance of communicating concerns directly to that nurse.

educate staff

The traditional roles of delegation and decision making have been reserved for nurse managers but must be relinquished to the autonomous primary nurse. The nurse manager should function as a role model and consultant along with the important roles of budget controller and unit quality management.

When an institution chooses the primary method, considerable research should be done to determine if the method meets the needs of the institution. The current staff mix must maximize both the current RN and LVN staff. Since it is not usually financially possible for an agency to employ only RNs, true primary nursing rarely exists. Some institutions have modified the primary

staff mix

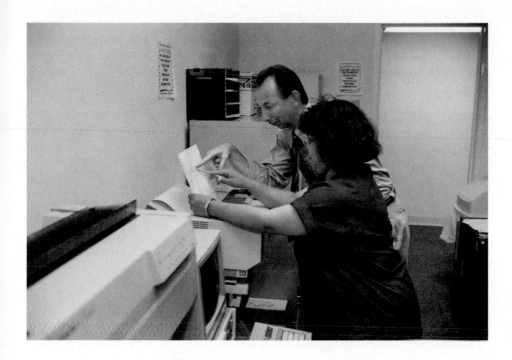

In the partnership model, the RN encourages the LPN partner's growth and the two share patient assignments.

nursing concept and implemented a partnership model to use their current staff mix.

PARTNERSHIP MODELS

In the **partnership model** (or **co-primary nursing** model) of providing patient care, an RN is paired with a nursing assistant or an LPN. The partner works with the RN consistently. When the helper is unlicensed, the RN allows the assistant to perform non-nursing functions. This frees the RN to provide semi-primary care to her assigned patients. The RN–assistant partnership is cost-effective (Manthey, 1989); however, inexperienced RNs have difficulty delegating to the assistant and it is difficult to truly partner consistently with varied shift schedules (Metcalf, 1992).

pairing

A partnership between an RN and an LPN is different. The RN's role is to encourage growth in the LPN partner and the two share the patient assignments. A study by Eriksen et al. (1992) indicated that the RN–LPN partnership model, implemented in an intensive care unit, decreased the reported level of stress experienced by the RNs and improved the quality of care provided to the patients.

Example: You are a primary nurse in a surgical intensive care unit of a small hospital. The unit you work on uses an LPN partnership to decrease the number of RNs required per shift. You and your partner are assigned four surgical patients. Mr. Jones had a lobectomy five hours ago and is on a ventilator, Mrs. Martinez had a quadruple cardiac bypass fourteen hours ago, Mr. Wong had a nephrectomy two days ago and is receiving continuous peritoneal dialysis, and Mr. Smith has a fractured pelvis and is comatose from a motor vehicle accident twenty-four hours ago. How would you distribute the staff to provide primary care to these four patients? Do you think it is possible to provide primary care in this situation? What responsibilities would you assume as the primary nurse and what could you share with the LPN?

high cost

Primary nursing can be successful in clinic, home health settings, and research centers. There are professional advantages for the RN; however, most agencies are unable to afford a true primary nursing system. A relatively new system that is cost-effective and allows the professional nurse to direct patient care is the case management system.

CASE MANAGEMENT

Case management began in 1980 at the New England Medical Center in Boston (Zander and Etheredge, 1989). This system originated because of the DRG restrictions on the length of stay patients were permitted and the amount of care allotted during the stay. The case management model of patient care delivery maintains quality care while streamlining costs.

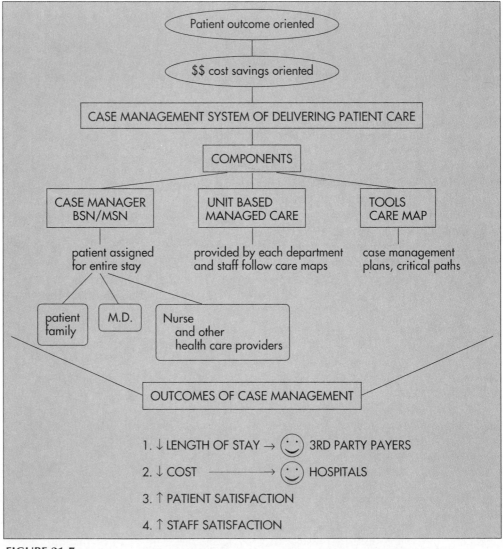

FIGURE 21-7
Diagram of the case management system.

Many hospitals have tailored the case management system to their specific needs. The original **case management method** of delivering care is based on patient outcomes and cost containment. There are three components to the case management system: a case manager, care MAPS (case management plans/critical paths), and unit-based managed care (Figure 21-7). This system can be used in hospitals, outpatient clinics, and community health settings.

three components

CASE MANAGER

The **case manager** is a baccalaureate-prepared RN, and preferably a master's-prepared clinical nurse specialist, who coordinates care for a patient from preadmission beyond discharge. The case manager must be a proficient clinician, educator, collaborator, researcher, and manager (Cronin and Maklebust, 1989). The case manager must also be especially skilled at the management roles of planning, organizing, directing, and controlling patient care.

coordination

Depending on the facility, there may be several case managers to coordinate care for all patients, or a case manager may be assigned to a specific high-risk population (see Figures 21-8 and 21-9). The case manager may be responsible to coordinate care for twenty patients. It is essential that the case manager have frequent interaction with the patient and the healthcare provider, to achieve and evaluate expected outcomes.

The case manager is assigned a patient upon admission (or preadmission) to the institution based on the case manager's specialization. The case manager then coordinates patient care until discharge. The patient will have a specific care MAP, or critical path based upon a related DRG category. The case manager will implement the plan and be responsible for monitoring patient

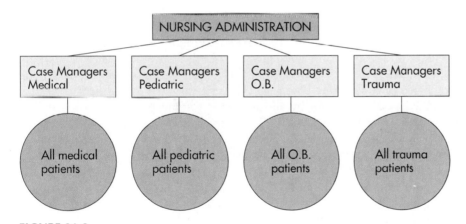

FIGURE 21-8
Case management system in which each patient is assigned to a case manager.

progress toward the desired outcome criteria. This progress is communicated to the physician, nurse, and other healthcare providers. All healthcare providers work together to decrease the patient's length of stay while addressing patient problems.

monitoring progress

Case management example: Imagine you are the case manager responsible for pediatric patients. Margo, age 3, is admitted to the ER with severe shortness of breath and a history of asthma. You introduce yourself to Margo and her mother as the case manager responsible for coordinating Margo's case throughout her hospital stay. You

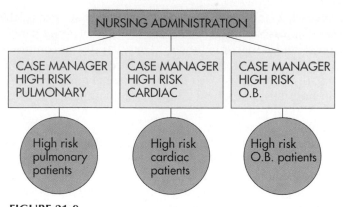

FIGURE 21-9
Hospital using case managers to manage high-risk patients.

implement the care MAP used at your hospital and plan her care with the ER nurse and physician. After two hours Margo is transferred to the pediatric ICU. The ICU nurses follow the care MAP identifying patient problems and the normal tests and treatments expected on day 1 (see box on page 425). On day three, Margo is transferred to the pediatric floor where you will coordinate her care with her mother, the nurse, and physician. The nurses follow the care MAP you initiated and discuss any variations with you. When Margo is ready for discharge on day four, you talk with her mother and arrange a follow-up phone call. You have been the pivotal person for Margo and her mother throughout this admission. Your main goal is to expedite Margo's hospitalization and prevent a readmission. If Margo is readmitted, you will be her case manager.

CARE MAPS

The tool case managers use to achieve patient outcomes is a care MAP (see the box on pages 425–426). **Care MAPs** (multidisciplinary action plans) are a combination of the nursing care plan and a critical path. The care plan component is similar to the care plans typically used except a time is indicated for each intervention of the nursing diagnosis. The **critical path** component is based on the DRG services provided by all disciplines for the patient's particular DRG classification. The box on page 427 lists the various components of a critical path.

written system   The primary reason to implement a care MAP is to provide a written system of identifying patient needs. All healthcare providers can follow the care MAP to facilitate expected outcomes. If the patient deviates from the normal plan, a variance is indicated. A **variance** is anything that occurs to alter the patient's progress through the normal critical path.

Example: If Margo (in the situation above) had abnormal ABGs on day two of the care MAP, then a variance would be indicated on the critical path and ABGs would be done the next day. An assessment to determine why she had a variance would also be indicated.

The case manager is the coordinator of care and the care MAP is a tool, when used correctly, that can decrease patient length of stay and improve insurance reimbursement (Graybeal, Gheen, and McKenna, 1993). The other component of case management is unit-based managed care.

UNIT-BASED MANAGED CARE

Unit-based managed care can also be used with the case management, primary, team, or functional methods of patient care delivery. *Managed care* is a method of organizing and delivering unit-based care to a patient with cost-saving outcomes as the main goal. These outcomes are achieved by closely monitoring and coordinating care so the patient will meet discharge criteria in a specified time frame and therefore provide savings to the patient, hospital, and third party payers. The care MAP is the tool used to achieve the positive outcomes.

Pediatric Asthma Care MAP (EXAMPLE)

CRITICAL PATH

Care Category	Day 1	Day 2	Day 3	Day 4
Consults	none	none	none	none
Tests	CBC, theophylline level, SMA 6, PPD chest x-ray, ABGs, urine dipstick, and specific gravity × 1	Theophylline level, ABGs if indicated	Theophylline level, check PPD	Theophylline level
Treatments	Pulse oximetry, postural drainage, peak exp. flow if cooperative q shift, O$_2$ therapy if indicated, IVs if indicated	Peak flow q shift, chest pt q shift	Peak flow b.i.d., chest pt q shift	Peak flow q 24 hr. consider d/c if increased peak flow
Medications	(Amount according to wt) aminophylline and/or Proventile NEB/po and or steroids	Steroids may be d/ced within 48 hours or taper over 7–10 days; assess for change to p.o. meds	Assess change to p.o. meds	Consider d/c home within 24 hours of initiation of p.o. meds
Activity	As tolerated	As tolerated	As tolerated	As tolerated
Nutrition	As tolerated	As tolerated	As tolerated	As tolerated
D/C Plan	Inquire if family used home care prior to admission; begin initial d/c plan	Initiate social work consult as indicated	Monitor progress on discharge plan, consult with MD, SW, HH care; MD to give 24 hr notice to pt and write official d/c order	Prior to d/c confirm home plan with parents, SW, and HH care

Patient Variance (Includes variances in response to treatment or special needs on admission. For example, the pt may also have an infection.)

Pediatric Asthma Care MAP—cont'd

PATIENT PROBLEMS/POTENTIAL PROBLEMS

1. Alteration in breathing patterns	Day 1	Day 2	Day 3	Day 4
	a. auscultate breath sounds for rales, wheezing, stridor, rhonchi b. assess skin and mucus membrane color and nasal flaring q 4 hr c. note agitation, anxiety d. note changes in VS or O₂ saturation e. monitor response to tx, (notify MD of HA, agitation tachycardia, resp. distress) f. chest pt q shift, position for chest expansion g. encourage p.o.fluids, assess hydration status	a. auscultate breath sounds b. assess color changes c. assess for retractions nasal flaring q 6 hr d. note changes in VS and O₂ to d/c oximeter e. chest P/T q shift f. monitor response to tx. (report to MD changes, HA, increased resp., distress, agitation, tachycardia) g. peak flow q shift h. assess pts response to activity i. encourage p.o. fluids	a. auscultate breath sounds, check color, retractions, nasal flaring q 8 hr and prn b. vital signs q 8 hr c. assess for retractions O₂ sat. determine d/c readiness d. chest P/T q shift unless contraindicated e. observe response to nebulizer treatment and check with MD f. assess response to activity g. assess clinical state, increased peak flow, tolerance of p.o. meds, theophylline level therapeutic	a. auscultate breath sounds, check color, retractions, nasal flaring q 8 hr and prn b. vital signs q 8 hr c. assess for retractions O₂ sat. determine d/c readiness d. chest P/T q shift unless contraindicated e. observe response to nebulizer treatment and check with MD f. assess response to activity g. assess clinical state, increased peak flow, tolerance of p.o. meds, theophylline level therapeutic
2. Knowledge deficit	a. orient to environment b. assess parent and child level of understanding c. familiarize with hospital protocol, i.e., IV pump, meds, tx	a. assess family and pt teaching needs for disease process and begin d/c teaching b. assess need for visiting nurse, community referrals	a. continue d/c teaching re meds tx and importance of follow up b. d/c plan with parents to minimize resp. irritants at home and in the environment	a. d/c planning b. med review c. s/s of resp distress review d. identify precipitating factors for asthma attack e. exercise regimen f. follow-up care g. when to call MD/come to ER
3. Anxiety	a. provide calm environment b. explore stressors and coping mechanisms c. assess family dynamics d. encourage parent to stay with the child	a. encourage family to state feelings, fears, and anxieties b. evaluate anxiety level and provide supportive measures prn	a. continue to encourage verbalization of concerns b. reevaluate level of anxiety	a. reevaluate level of anxiety and provide support b. reassure parents/child re knowledge of asthma

Adapted from Cohen and Cesta, (1993).

Components of a Critical Path

1. Consults
2. Tests
3. Treatment
4. Medications
5. Activities/safety/self-care
6. Nutrition
7. Discharge planning/teaching
8. Variants

If a hospital utilizes the managed care system without the case manager component, the nurse manager must coordinate care between units to ensure the care MAP is generated according to DRG guidelines. Staff must be knowledgeable about the concepts of managed patient care to meet patient needs.

ADVANTAGES AND DISADVANTAGES

The case management model decreases the average length of hospitalization, decreases readmissions, and improves patient compliance with follow-up visits (Schull, Tosch, and Wood, 1992). The case management method also has financial advantages by expediting the patient's stay using outcome-based criteria. Other advantages of this method are continuity of care and personal satisfaction for nurses and family, facilitating quality assurance parameters and collaboration with the health system (Gunderson and Kenner, 1992).

The major disadvantages of the case management method are related to inadequate staff education and financial constraints. Inadequately educated staff may be assigned as case managers. The ideal candidate for a case manager is a clinical nurse specialist. However, most hospitals use ADN nurses who may not be ready for the case manager role.

Another disadvantage to the case management system is the case managers may be assigned unmanageable case loads or assigned patients outside their area of expertise. With large case loads, the case manager cannot efficiently direct patient care, thereby eliminating the financial advantages.

NURSE MANAGER'S ROLE

The nurse manager has increased demands when leading the case management system. Quality improvement is constantly assessed to ensure the care MAP is DRG appropriate and the case managers are adequately managing their case loads. Patient satisfaction is also pertinent to evaluate for quality. If the patients are not satisfied with the system, the census may decline.

Communication among all systems must be coordinated. The case manager works with all departments, so the manager needs to assist in coordinating interdepartmental communication. The communication can be facilitated by educating all departments about the case manager's role and responsibilities. The manager must also assist in educating the staff nurses. They provide patient care according to the case manager's specifications and must know the extent of the case manager's role.

The case management system of patient care delivery is designed to move a patient from the illness state to optimal wellness in the quickest period of time.

EXERCISE 21-6
Imagine you are the nurse manager of a teen pregnancy clinic at the county health department. The RNs for the clients are case managers and each RN has a specific case load. There are many agencies the case manager must communicate with to provide comprehensive care to their clients. What departments might the case managers interact with? As the nurse manager, what are specific interventions you could implement to facilitate optimal communication between departments? How would you explain the case management system to non-nursing departments?

quality

coordination

cost savings This rapid movement saves money. The less time the patient requires health-care services, the more savings occur.

It is a concern that the art of nursing in the hospital may vanish with an increased emphasis on moving patients out rapidly to save money. The current economic climate dictates tighter controls and nursing needs to establish checks and balances to ensure that the consumer (patient) receives quality care. One way we can facilitate quality care is to consider the different abilities and education of the nurses caring for the patient.

DIFFERENTIATED NURSING PRACTICE

Differentiated nursing practice recognizes a difference in the level of education and competency of each registered nurse. This differentiation in nursing is delineated by education, job position, and clinical expertise.

The differentiation of nurses based on their education is not a new concept. Montag (1951) proposed technical and professional differentiation. The two-year associate and diploma graduate would be referred to as a "technical" nurse, and the four- to six-year-educated nurses would be the "professional" nurse. There are many factors that differentiate the two, as illustrated in the box on page 429.

Another view of differentiated practice is based on skill and competency. An institution may categorize different types of nursing practice such as manager, clinical nurse, or patient care technician (Harkness, Miller, and Hill, 1992). Nurses in these settings function in the roles they are most skilled at based on their competency to perform the job. With this view, a nurse manager with twenty years of experience is competent to be the manager without a baccalaureate degree.

clinical ladders Nursing competency and education can also determine advancement. Many organizations use clinical ladders for advancement. With a specific level attainable with certain skills or education, a nurse can advance her position and salary according to the organization's structure. Cleland, Forsey, and DeGroot (1993) stated that there should be different pay structures related to the level of education and expertise a nurse has.

NURSE MANAGER'S ROLE

Nurse managers should become aware of the need to differentiate among the skills and education of nurses. Specific jobs, such as a case manager, require additional knowledge and skills. The manager must consider all factors when hiring for these positions.

The nurse manager and the organization must also design appropriate job descriptions and evaluation tools. The job descriptions need to be specific to indicate the difference in scope of practice and salary and to be applicable to different nursing care delivery systems (Forsey, Cleland, and Miller, 1993). Performance appraisal tools should assess competency of the nurse appropriate to her expertise and education (Figure 21-10).

role model The nurse manager also has the responsibility as a role model to encourage professional growth in her staff. The manager should be educated with at least a BSN degree and should encourage staff to further their education. Educational encouragement could be in the form of financial assistance by the organization and scheduling the staff time off from work to attend classes.

Comparison of Roles of Technical and Professional Nursing in a Differentiated Nursing Practice

TECHNICAL NURSE
1. Focuses care on individual clients in structured settings.

2. Provides care to patients with well-defined nursing diagnosis.
3. Provides care in a setting where specific policies, procedures, and protocols exist as a framework for patient care.

4. Recognizes that research directs changes in nursing practice.
5. Plans and implements care in a specific work time frame.

PROFESSIONAL NURSE
1. Focuses care on individuals, families, groups, and communities in structured and unstructured settings.
2. Provides care to clients with complex problems and diagnoses.
3. Provides care where specific policies and procedures do not exist and critical thinking must be utilized to adapt to the specific situation.
4. Collects data and incorporates research into practice.
5. Plans care and assumes responsibility from admission to discharge.

Adapted from Primm (1987).

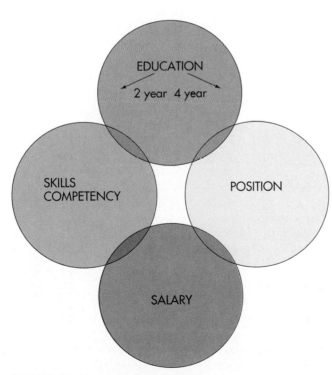

FIGURE 21-10
Components of differentiated nursing practice.

Based upon the role of the nurse in both the case management and primary nursing system it is evident that a differentiated nursing practice already exists even though the nursing profession has not made significant progress toward implementing a format differentiated nursing practice. The differentiating may exist in certain institutions or agencies but it is not accepted across the coun-

TABLE 21-1 **Comparison of Healthcare Delivery Systems***

	CASE METHOD	FUNCTIONAL	TEAM NURSING	PRIMARY	CASE MANAGEMENT
Origin date; reason designed	1800s; patients were home	1940s; shortage of nurses	1950s; move away from tasks	1960s; nurses move toward independence	1980s; DRGs and budget awareness
Clinical decision making	Done per shift	Done per shift	Shift based	Continuous, 24/hr day	Case managers, continuous 24 hour/day
Responsibility and authority	Autonomous for a small group of patients	Autonomous for large group of patients	Large group of patients	Small group of patients; very personal; great autonomy	Includes co-ordination with other departments
Work allocation	Total care to assigned patients	Specific task for all patients	Some tasks, assigned per skill patients require	Total care of own patients	Case manager can be the coordinator or provide total patient care
Professional nursing satisfaction	Yes	No	Yes	Yes	High for the case managers and the nursing staff
Major advantage	Patient receives continuous care for eight hours by one nurse	Cost-effective for a large number of patients	Cost-effective, work in small groups to provide care	Satisfied patient and nurses	Cost-effective care coordinated to achieve patient outcomes
Major disadvantage	No continuity of care	Task-oriented fragmented care	Do not always have leaders to coordinate the team	Not cost-effective to have all R/N staff	Costly to implement correctly

**Adapted from Manthey, M. (1991). Delivery systems and practice role models. Nursing Management, 22(1), 28–30.*

try in the nursing profession. This may be because of differing views about the actual difference in education or resistance to change.

COMPARISONS OF DELIVERY SYSTEMS

From the information about the different systems of healthcare delivery, it is possible to identify strengths and weaknesses of each method. There is no perfect system of delivering nursing care to patients. Table 21-1 identifies important elements of each system. A delivery system must be individualized per institution. With modification, each of these systems can be used by hospitals, outpatient clinics, and home health and community agencies.

CHAPTER CHECKLIST

The nurse manager and charge nurse roles vary with each delivery system. However, regardless of the system, both must have strong leadership/management skills for the system to work. Depending on the system, the manager has different issues to consider. But without a skilled manager, none of the patient care delivery systems would work.

- A care delivery system is the method nurses use to provide care to patients.
- There are five systems of patient care delivery, each with its advantages and disadvantages:
  - The case method focuses on total patient care for a specific time period.
    - The nurse manager must consider the expense of this system and identify all staff members' level of education and communication skills.
  - The functional method emphasizes task oriented care for a large group of patients.
    - The nurse manager is responsible for achieving patient outcomes, whereas staff members are responsible only for their specific tasks.
    - The functional method is most often used in extended care facilities.
  - The team method employs a small team whose members provide care to a small group of patients.
    - The nurse manager in this system needs strong management, critical thinking, and leadership skills.
    - The modular method is a modification of team nursing that focuses on the geographical location of patient rooms and assignments of staff members.
  - In the primary nursing method, a primary nurse provides total patient care and directs patient care from admission to discharge.
    - The nurse manager must determine staff members' desires to become primary nurses and educate them accordingly.
    - The nurse manager also functions as role model, consultant, budget controller, and unit quality manager.

EXERCISE 21-9

Reread the comments made by the manager, in A Manager's Viewpoint of this chapter. What issues did she have to evaluate to determine the most appropriate patient care delivery system for the unit? How did she choose the best system for her unit?

EXERCISE 21-10

You are now familiar with five styles of patient care delivery. Which system would be the best for the following situation?

You are a unit manager of a thirty-two-bed pediatric unit in a 400-bed teaching hospital. The acuity is very high and the census averages thirty beds per day. The current staff mix is 50 percent RN, 40 percent LVN, and 10 percent nursing assistants. The unit originally used the primary nursing system of delivering care; however, as the staff mix has changed, primary nursing has not been implemented. In analysis you find that the charge nurse is assigning patient care according to tasks.

There have been numerous studies done by your hospital's quality management department that indicate the average length of stay is four days longer than DRG requirements and 25 percent of the patients are readmitted. You and your staff have been receiving complaints from the parents that "no one ever explains anything" to them and they don't know who their child's main nurse is.

1. How would you choose a new system of patient care delivery?
2. What resources would you utilize?
3. How would you distribute the assignments and work responsibilities?
4. How would you implement the change?

- The partnership model, or co-primary nursing model, pairs an RN with a nursing assistant or LPN.
- The case management system is outcome based and is facilitated by a case manager, who directs unit-based care using a care MAP.
  - The nurse manager in this care delivery system faces increased demands and pressure to move the patient through the system as quickly as possible.
  - Managed care is a way of organizing unit-based patient care delivery with cost savings as the main goal.
- The nurse manager and charge nurse are responsible for directing patient care regardless of the delivery system. Key leadership and management concepts for directing patient care include:
  - Communication
  - Delegation
  - Promotion of autonomy
- The concept of differentiated practice emphasizes two levels of nursing practice: technical and professional.
  - Each level has specific responsibilities that depend on the nurse's educational preparation.
  - To date, few institutions have implemented the concept.

TERMS TO KNOW

- associate nurse
- care delivery system
- care MAP
- case management method
- case manager
- case method
- staff mix
- team nursing
- total patient care
- unit-based managed care
- unlicensed assistive personnel
- variance
- modular method
- outcome criteria
- partnership model
- patient outcomes
- primary nurse
- primary nursing
- charge nurse
- co-primary nursing
- critical path
- differentiated nursing practice
- expected outcomes
- functional nursing

REFERENCES

Bennett, M., & Hylton, J. (1990). Modular nursing: Partners in professional practice. *Nursing Management, 21*(3), 20–24.

Blegen, M. (1993). Nurses' job satisfaction: A meta-analysis of related variables. *Nursing Research, 42*(1), 36–40.

Cleland, V., Forsey, L., & DeGroot, H. (1993). Computer simulations of the differentiated pay structure model. *Journal of Nursing Administration, 23*(3), 53–59.

Cohen, E., & Cesta, T. (1993). *Nursing Case Management: From Concept to Evaluation.* St. Louis: Mosby.

Cronin, C., & Maklebust, J. (1989). Case managed care: Capitalizing on the CNS. *Nursing Management, 20*(3), 38–47.

Eriksen, L., Quandt, B., Teinert, D., Look, D., Loosle, R., Mackey, G., & Strout, B. (1992). A registered nurse-licensed vocational nurse partnership model for critical care nursing. *Journal of Nursing Administration, 22*(12), 28–37.

Forsey, L., Cleland, V., & Miller, B. (1993). Job descriptions for differentiated nursing practice and differentiated pay. *Journal of Nursing Administration, 23*(5), 33–39.

Graybeal, K., Gheen, M., & McKenna, B. (1993). Clinical pathway development. The Overlake model. *Nursing Management, 24*(4), 42–45.

Gunderson, L. & Kenner, C. (1992). Case management in the neonatal intensive care unit. *AACN Clinical Issues in Critical Care, 3,*(4), 769–776.

Harkness, G., Miller, J., & Hill, N. (1992). Differentiated practice: A three dimensional model. *Nursing Management, 23*(12), 26–32.

Magargal, P. (1987). Modular nursing: Nurses rediscover nursing. *Nursing Management, 18*(11), 98–104.

Manthey, M. (1989). Practice partnerships: The newest concept in care delivery. *Journal of Nursing Administration, 19*(2), 33–35.

———(1991). Delivery systems and practice role models. *Nursing Management, 22*(1), 28–30.

Marquis, B., & Huston, C. (1992). *Leadership Roles and Management Functions in Nursing.* Philadelphia: J.B. Lippincott.

Metcalf, K. (1992). The helper model: Nine ways to make it work. *Nursing Management, 23*(12), 40–43.

Montag, F. (1951). *The Education of Nursing Technicians.* New York: G.P. Putnam.

Primm, P. (1987, July-August). Differentiated practice for ADN- and BSN-prepared nurses. *Journal of Professional Nursing,* pp. 218–224.

Schull, D., Tosch, P., & Wood, M. (1992). Clinical nurse specialists as collaborative care managers. *Nursing Management, 23*(3), 30–33.

Watkins, S. (1993). Team spirit. *Nursing Times, 89*(1), 59–60.

Zander, K., & Etheredge, M. (1989). *Collaborative Care: Nursing Case Management* Chicago: American Hospital Publishing, American Hospital Association.

SUGGESTED READINGS

Barnsteiner, J., Mohan, A., & Milberger, P. (1992). Implementing managed care in a pediatric setting. *AACN Clinical Issues in Critical Care, 3*(4), 777–787.

Beyers, M., Hill, B., McClelland, M., & Wesley, M. (1992). New-wave nursing: Back to the basics? *Nursing Clinics of North America, 27*(1), 1–9.

Brchan, M., Hegge, M., & Stenvig, T. (1991). A tiger by the tail: Tackling barriers to differentiated practice. *The Journal of Continuing Education, 22*(3), 109–112.

Causer, R. (1992). Primary nursing, double benefits. *Nursing Times, 88*(1), 55–57.

DeGroot, H., Forsey, L., & Cleland, V. (1992). The nursing practice personnel data set. *Journal of Nursing Administration, 22*(3), 23–28.

Dienemann, J., & Gessner, T. (1992). Restructuring nursing care deliver systems. *Nursing Economics, 10*(4), 253–258.

Hampton, D. (1993). Implementing a managed care framework through care maps. *Journal of Nursing Administration, 23*(5), 21–27.

Katz, R. (1992). Cluster management. *AACN Clinical Issues in Critical Care Nursing, 3*(4), 743–787.

Lenz, C., & Edwards, J. (1992). Nurse managed primary care, tapping the rural community power base. *Journal of Nursing Administration, 22*(9), 57–61.

Parette, H. (1993). High-risk infant case management and assistive technology: Funding and family enabling perspectives. *Maternal-Child Nursing Journal, 21*(2), 53–63.

Petryshen, P.R., & Petryshen, P.M. (1992). The case management model: An innovative approach to the delivery of patient care. *Journal of Advanced Nursing, 17*(10), 1188–1194.

Pitts-Wilhelm, Nocolai, C., & Koerner, J. (1991). Differentiating nursing practice to improve service outcomes. *Nursing Management 22*(12), 22–25.

Sanford, M. Genrich, S., & Nowotny, M. (1992). A study to determine the difference in clinical judgment abilities between BSN and non-BSN graduates. *Journal of Nursing Education, 31*(2), 70–74.

Schank, M., & Stollenwerk, R. (1988). The leadership/management role: A differentiating factor for ADN/BSN programs? *Journal of Nursing Education, 27*(6), 253–257.

Tappan, R. (1989). *Nursing Leadership and Management: Concepts and Practice,* 2nd ed. Philadelphia: F.A. Davis.

Van Dongen, C., & Jambunathan, J. (1992). Pilot study results: The psychiatric R.N. case manager. *Journal of Psychosocial Nursing, 30*(11), 11–14.

Williams, R. (1992). Nurse case management: Working with the community. *Nursing Management, 23*(12), 33–34.

Zander, K. (1988). Nursing case management resolving the DRG paradox. *Nursing Clinics of North America, 23*(3), 503–519.

CHAPTER 22

PATIENT CLASSIFICATION, STAFFING, AND SCHEDULING

Mary Ellen Rauner, R.N., M.A.

PREVIEW

This chapter explains key concepts related to patient classification, staffing, and scheduling. It defines and discusses activity reports, the staffing budget, and the staffing matrix and identifies characteristics of various patient classification systems. Many of the issues discussed are crucial to the nurse manager's ability to monitor resource allocation, maintain appropriate delivery of service, and ensure high-quality care in all clinical settings. Nurse managers' knowledge of these issues often determines their success in the management role.

OBJECTIVES:

- Identify the key characteristics of a patient classification system.
- Calculate and project a staffing budget.
- Develop a staffing matrix and complete a time schedule.
- Analyze activity reports related to staffing and scheduling.

QUESTIONS TO CONSIDER

- How will patient classification affect staffing and scheduling?
- How do I know how many full-time equivalents are needed to staff the unit?
- What activity reports can be utilized to assess unit work-load levels?

A Manager's Viewpoint

As a manager, the issues surrounding staffing, including the budget, patient classification system (PCS), scheduling, and staffing patterns, cut right to the heart of my goal: to ensure a safe and therapeutic environment for patients. To achieve this goal effectively, you need a firm foundation and understanding of these individual variables, as well as their interrelationships—an ability to see the forest *and* the trees!

My secret strategies include:

1. *Flexibility:* Maximize your resources by cross-training your staff, knowing their capabilities, orienting staff from other units who may float voluntarily, and balancing per diem and full-time staff.

2. *Automate:* Much of the work of staffing and scheduling is grindingly repetitive, with a twist: you still have to create it anew each cycle. Computers are faster and they don't have more urgent responsibilities. (**Caveat:** Remember "Garbage in/garbage out"—put the time in up front with your scheduling program so that it knows as many of your preferences, prohibitions, etc. as possible. Enhanced templates of staffing patterns will greatly increase the usefulness of the output!)

3. *Options:* Be open to them. There is more than one way to create a schedule/staffing pattern that is cost-effective and meets the goal of providing quality patient care.

4. *Forget self-scheduling,* **unless** your staff will be responsible for a schedule that meets the unit needs, or you'll end up with a draft you can't use and disgruntled people who **thought** they were going to get what they wanted. Just let them request their paid days off and if you're lucky enough to have a computer scheduling program, let it do the rest!

5. *Optimize evaluation:* Formative evaluation to keep your staffing budget on track can be enhanced by understanding and using as many budget monitoring tools as you have available.

6. *Patient classification system:* Actively and continuously monitor your PCS to ensure unit specific accuracy and efficacy for staffing purposes.

7. *Computerize:* If you're very lucky, get help orchestrating the entire production with a computerized program that links all the above elements into a coherent (and hopefully) melodic symphony!

Kathleen White-Fletcher, M.S.N., R.N.
Nurse Manager
Obstetrics
The General Hospital Center **at Passaic**
Passaic, New Jersey

INTRODUCTION

Patient classification, staffing, and scheduling are management strategies used in the delivery of patient care. Since their inception, the scope and goals of these approaches have changed. With the advent of computerization, these systems have grown in sophistication and application.

Contemporary approaches to patient classification, staffing, and scheduling reflect sensitivity to cost containment, length of hospitalization, and improvement of patient care. With growing demands for increased fiscal responsibility and greater authority and accountabilily in patient service delivery, these systems have become vital assets to management.

PATIENT CLASSIFICATION

patient classification system

A **patient classification system** provides a method of quantitatively estimating and assessing patient needs in relation to nursing care. It is a way of determining the amount and type of care a patient requires as well as providing a means of standardizing nursing care practice.

The importance of a patient classification system cannot be underestimated. Since economic issues have become primary factors in healthcare decision making, it is essential to have a mechanism that provides input in how nursing care is delivered, assesses the amount of time required to deliver that care, identifies the cost involved, and evaluates whether the delivery of care is in the most efficient, cost-effective manner.

For cost-efficient care to be effective, a format for predictability must be established, one that considers variations in patients' needs as defined in terms of each patient's diagnosis, acuity level, and developmental stage. The ability to predict trends in the kind of care a patient will require helps in estimating the amount of time needed by the nurse to deliver that care, thereby aiding in assigning a cost factor to the services offered. Data on the actual costs of nursing services is also needed to support budgetary requirements.

One problem in accounting for the amount of time spent and the type of care delivered by nursing is generated from the general nature of the services offered. Defining nursing care through a patient classification system is one way of alleviating this difficulty.

measurement of acuity

The patient classification system can be used as a valid and reliable instrument to measure the acuity level of patients (in terms of nursing work load and number of nursing staff needed) as well as variations in nursing care. The ability to predict work load, based on the patients' conditions and mix, aids in the development of a variable staffing pattern, which helps to simplify staff allocation and scheduling. This system can also be used effectively for long-range staffing, budgeting, management planning, quality management programs, and compliance with licensing and industry standards and regulations. This chapter's "Literature Perspective" focuses on terminology issues in patient acuity classification.

Although patient classification systems offer a more reliable representation than traditional methods of identifying the nursing care needs of patients (that is, global averages—the average amount of care required per day by the "typical" patient), there are still some inherent problems. As identified by Giovannetti (1972) and Edwardson and Giovannetti (1987), the problems

Literature Perspective

McHugh, M.L., & Dwyer, V.L. (1992). Measurement issues in patient acuity classification for prediction of hours in nursing care. Nursing Administation Quarterly, 16(4), 20–31.

The study focused on clarifying and standardizing terms used with patient classification systems and in staffing decision making. A historical review of the literature definitions is provided for such concepts as patient acuity, intensity of nursing care, census, and variable staffing patterns and work load.

Factors considered vital in the actual measurement of nursing time and used in determining patient acuity classification include work sampling, standard nursing time, correlation of care points and nursing hours, and reliability and validity.

Implications for Practice

Implications for practice reflect the utility of patient classification systems to identify and measure those elements of nursing practice that affect nursing care outcomes. Since patient classification systems have the capacity to relate quantitative elements to the different types of nursing care delivered, they play an important role in decisions related to staff distribution and scheduling and use of nursing time.

associated with this system include the inadvisability of comparing a patient classification system developed in one hospital with that in another because of the difference in treatment modalities, architectural structure and design of the inpatient units, and standards and policies of the institution. Some of the factors used to weigh the categories are of a subjective nature resulting in problems of reliability; methods of validating the system and work-load indices are not transferable. In spite of these difficulties, the method of staffing by patient classification has been generally accepted by healthcare institutions across the country.

The process of classifying patients has a long history. At one time it was sufficient to classify patients by medical diagnosis. The patient was placed on a unit familiar with that diagnosis, the assumption being that staff dealing with similar diagnoses over time had the knowledge and skills as well as the resources to meet these patients' needs. However, it became apparent that there was no mechanism that actually documented patients' requirements in relation to nursing care.

Two basic types of patient classification systems evolved: prototype and factor evaluation (Giovannetti, 1979). A **prototype evaluation** is considered subjective and uses broad descriptive categories to describe the patient and the associated patient care needs. Once evaluated, the patient is then classified into the category that closely represents the patient's characteristics and level of nursing care. The **factor evaluation** system takes specific elements or critical indicators and rates the patient on each of these elements. Each of the elements or critical indicators is assigned a weight or numerical value. These values are combined to achieve an overall rating for the patient, which, when compared with a set of decision rules, identifies the appropriate care

prototype evaluation

factor evaluation

category for the patient. The factor system is referred to as "objective" because specifying particular indicators or factors associated with patient care helps to ensure objectivity by the rater. In reality, both classification systems are subject to some level of subjectivity by the rater and therefore cannot be considered truly objective. Furthermore, it is not unusual for a patient classification tool to be comprised of a combination of prototype and factor evaluations.

nursing intensity

Methods to justify variances related to resource appropriation and costs abound with increasing demand for cost-effective patient care. Nursing intensity (the amount of nursing care provided per patient day), along with various nursing interventions and staffing levels (work load), has been cited as reducing length of stay and costs associated with hospitalization.

In a study by Halloran and Kiley (1984) a nursing information system model was proposed that allocated staffing and resources using nursing diagnoses. This process was based on a nursing work load unit of analysis that calculated costs using a patient classification system for staffing. The premise for using a patient classification system rested with the fact that it was an accessible source to measure nursing work load and allocate costs as a means of costing out nursing care services from the hospital's room and board rate.

As outlined by Edwardson and Giovannetti (1987), data are extracted from the patient classification system and converted into the required hours of care used over the patient's hospitalization. The process continues with patient care hours computed into dollar costs; patients are then classified into diagnosis-related groups (DRG) categories, and nursing care costs for patients are aggregated and analyzed.

Matching the type of care a patient will need with a specific category on the patient classification instrument and then determining the amount of nursing resources needed for that patient category provides the foundation for establishing the costs of nursing services and develops a basis for charges to patients.

selecting/developing systems

At present there are multiple patient classification systems available on the market. Many are adaptable for computer use. Whether working with a classification system currently in place or assisting the department in the decision-making process of selecting or developing a patient classification, the nurse manager should remember several important points:

- Does the system designate levels of care using the appropriate critical indicators?
- Can staffing needs be projected related to the patient's level of illness?
- Do the critical indicators consider multiple aspects of nursing care?
- Can the data generated by the system be used to trend justification and resource allocation for the department/hospital?
- Will all levels of nursing be involved in monitoring the system to assure validity and reliability?
- Does the patient classification system support linkage to other systems within the organization? (Ledwitch, 1988)

Other considerations prior to the purchase, development, and implementation of a patient classification system include the understanding that while many of the aspects of nursing care are equal across all units, each institution has its own idiosyncrasies that should not be treated lightly. Many times it is the unforeseen or disregarded factor that may sacrifice the implementation and use of the entire system. Furthermore, there is no one classification system that applies to all units. A system that may have tremendous capabilities for a medical-surgical unit may fall short on its appropriateness for a postpartum unit or a home health care service. If this is a concern, it is most effective to deal with the issue prior to and during the initial implementation phase.

Since a tremendous amount of financial, technical, and personnel resources are required, organizational commitment and support is perhaps the most important consideration before purchasing or developing and implementing a patient classification system. Several decision-making options exist. One may purchase a "canned" system and, as necessary, attempt to fit it into the organization, or a patient classification system can be developed uniquely to the organization's culture and practice. Whichever decision is reached, it will require a major financial commitment on the part of the organization. Patient classification systems usually cost thousands of dollars. The hidden costs associated with the project may involve consultants with experience to assist in the development and implementation of the program. An in-house staff member must be designated with the responsibility to direct the implementation, provide instruction, assure validity and reliability, maintain upgrades, and support the staff in all phases of implementing the system. Staff participation can result in tremendous costs to the organization, but the system/program will not be successful without a major "buy-in" by this group. Whether the system is being developed in-house or purchased as a package, staff may need to participate on committees. Committee participation is important in order to develop and select tools and methodologies, define their purpose and use, identify and document expected outcomes, develop policies and procedures related to the system, and plan the implementation. The time and financial resources to train the staff must be calculated and projected. If each staff member using the system requires four hours of training, and the decision has been made that all professional nurses in the department will be trained, then the allocated hours and cost could have an impact on overall staffing, scheduling and budget.

organizational commitment

Example
300 Nurses × 4 Hours Each = 1,200 Hours of Training
1,200 Hours × $25.00/Average Hourly Rate = $30,000

The next consideration for the nurse manager is deciding when the training will occur. Can these nurses be covered during work hours or will they be required to come at another time? Decisions related to who will be trained, and on what shifts, and who will actually do the training may have impact on the staffing, scheduling patterns, and the budget.

Since patient classification systems are subject to individual judgments and biases by the reviewers, it is essential that resources be provided to support, educate, and monitor the staff to their proper use. In addition, a quality management audit should be developed to review compliance with standards and maintain accuracy of the system. This process will need to continue at least until interrater reliability and validity are established.

biases

Since patient classification systems look at various kinds of nursing activities to determine patient care requirements, it is essential that as many categories as possible be considered. Some of these appear in the box on page 442.

Some levels of correlation exist between severity of illness and the time it takes to provide care. In the case of an ICU patient who cannot perform activities of daily living and is on life support systems and on multiple

EXERCISE 22-1
Select a site that has a patient classification system. Determine the following: Is it a package purchase? Was it designed for the organization? What orientation to the system is provided for new employees?

Kinds of Nursing Activities

- Communication barriers—patients who are hearing impaired or speak a foreign language;
- Environmental issues—an assessment of the patient's physical surroundings while hospitalized, and the nursing interventions required to maintain a safe and secure environment;
- Physiologic issues—an assessment of the patient's major body systems and the associated nursing interventions required;
- Care planning, treatments, medications, and reports;
- Self-care capabilities—an assessment of the patient's ability to perform activities of daily living and the level of nursing support required;
- Psychosocial behaviors or support—an assessment of the patient/significant others' psychosocial behavior/coping mechanisms and the amount of emotional support required;
- Education—an assessment of the educational requirements of the patient/significant others relevant to the patient's condition, hospitalization, and continuing care needs; and
- Discharge planning—an assessment of the patient's need for continuing care post-discharge and the required modifications in the home environment, as well as the required referrals.

treatment modalities, there is usually no question of the relationship between the time it takes to care for this patient and the level of illness. But in the case of a newly diagnosed diabetic who is able to perform independent activities, but requires extensive teaching, the relationship may not be quite so clear. A patient classification system, however, assists in identifying indi-

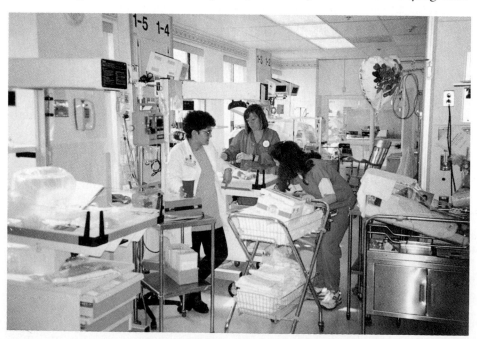

The patient's level of acuity determines how much time and how many staff members are needed to provide care as in this neonatal ICU.

vidual patient care requirements and can be instrumental in facilitating the equitable distribution of time and personnel.

Once the system has proven to be a valid and reliable measure of the nursing work load, it can be used to predict staffing requirements and assist in the decision-making processes related to staffing. Furthermore, reports generated from the patient classification system that are indicative of variances of actual staffing needs versus predicted requirements may be used to evaluate the adequacy of staffing and unit productivity.

The mechanisms related to staffing and scheduling are complex. To facilitate knowledgeable decision making and judgment, it is essential that the nurse manager be well educated in the multiple aspects of staffing and scheduling. The integration of information from clinical and financial sources allows the nurse manager to monitor resource allocation, appropriate delivery of service, and quality of care.

STAFFING

The nurse manager's role is a complex and demanding one. Of the many responsibilities and challenges that the role entails, staffing remains one of the most arduous, but crucial, in the day-to-day operation of the unit.

staffing/budgeting

It is not uncommon among new nurse managers to think of staffing as a distinct entity and process separate from the overall unit's budget. Yet the lack of proficiency in monitoring the appropriate use of personnel resources can have serious financial consequences to the organizations' bottom line.

Because the fiscal resources of the entire organization go hand-in-hand with the clinical provision allocated to individual nursing divisions, nurse managers are required to assess and evaluate multiple factors when preparing their budgets and projecting staffing needs. The variables to consider are highlighted in the following sections.

LICENSING STANDARDS AND JOINT COMMISSION REGULATIONS

An important source for guidance in projecting staffing requirements is the licensing regulations of the state department of health. **Staffing regulations** or recommendations usually relate to the minimum number of professional nurses required on a unit at a given time or to the minimum staffing in an extended care facility or prison. The nurse-to-patient staffing ratios are delineated by specialty area including, among others, adult intensive coronary care units, medical-surgical, pediatric, and neonatal intensive care units. For example, in the intensive care unit the standards recommend that the overall staffing ratio be one professional registered nurse for every three patients, with the capability of decreasing this ratio depending upon the acuity level and identified patient needs (New Jersey Department of Health, 1993).

staffing ratios

To comply with the 1994 JCAHO nursing care standards related to staffing (NC. 3.4–NC.3.4.2.4), an institution must have a mechanism to identify current patient care needs for the effective and efficient deployment of nursing staff (Joint Commission, 1993). The box on pages 444 and 445 defines each of these standards, summarizes the major points, and provides recommendations to assist in the compliance with the standards (Joint Commission, 1993).

JCAHO Standards & Implications

Standard

NC.3.4   Policies and procedures describe the mechanism used to assign nursing staff members to meet patient care needs.

NC.3.4.1   There are sufficient qualified nursing staff members to meet the nursing care needs of patients throughout the hospital.

NC.3.4.1.1.   The criteria for employment, deployment, and assignment of nursing staff members is approved by the nurse executive.

Discussion

1) Need for formal written staffing plan addressing all areas where nursing care is delivered, including consideration of:
   - nursing care needs of the patients as determined by a valid and reliable system;
   - the number and mix of nursing personnel required to meet identified patient care needs;
   - the mode of nursing care delivered;
   - the number of qualified RNs required to deliver care as well as supervise and direct the nursing care provided by other staff members
2) Involvement of nurse executive in all decision-making processes affecting quality patient care.
3) Authority of nurse executive in all areas providing nursing care as defined in the Hospital Plan for Provision of Nursing Care.

Recommendations

1) Develop formal, written staffing plan for all areas where nursing care is delivered (can be departmental rather than unit specific if individual unit/department matrix or pattern is identified).
2) Plan must reference all four factors cited above.
3) Develop policy statement regarding nurse executive's approval of staffing plan.

Standard

NC.3.4.2.2   The staffing schedules are reviewed and adjusted as necessary to meet defined patient needs and unusual occurrences.

Discussion

1) Need for policies and procedures defining staffing process, including staffing assignments, adjustments, reassignments.
2) JCAHO reviews schedules to verify adequate staffing.
3) Need for mechanisms to determine validity and interrater reliability of the patient classification system.
4) Staff perceives that needs are met and must "buy in" to the classification tool/mechanism.
5) Need for annual evaluation of staffing plan, at least as part of budget process, when patient population changes or when the need is identified through any other process.
6) Policy statement.

Recommendations

1) Unit-specific operational definitions (generated by staff).
2) Staff perception of staffing questionnaire = validity (*).
   (*) Tool considered valid when scheduled Nursing Care Hours are plus or minus 2 of nurse's assessment of Patient Care Hours (perception of need).
3) Policies and procedures to ensure interrater reliability: audits on a regular basis, and PRN when interrater agreement is out of range (< 90%), or when Hours Per Patient Day (HPPD) is 40% above or below budgeted HPPD.
4) Defined mechanism for annual review and results of most current annual review.

Standard
NC.3.4.2.3 Appropriate and sufficient support resources are available to allow nursing staff members to meet the nursing care needs of patients and their significant others.

Discussion

1) Need to ascertain adequate support services to ensure that nursing staff members have sufficient time to provide nursing care to patients, and do not perform non-nursing duties.

Recommendations

1) Place statement regarding commitment of resources in Hospital Plan for Provision of Nursing Care.

Standard
NC.3.4.2.4 Staffing levels are adequate to support participation of nursing staff members, as assigned, in committee meetings and in educational and quality assessment and improvement activities.

Discussion

1) Staff members scheduled to participate in committee activities to improve and facilitate patient care.

Recommendations

1) Provide adequate staffing levels to support nursing staff member's participation in committee activities.

Used with permission of the Joint Commission on Accreditation of Healthcare Organizations (1993), 1994 Accreditation Manual for Hospitals, Volume I: Standards, p. 144, Oakbrook Terrace, IL: JCAHO.

EXERCISE 22-2
Review an organization's policy and procedures for assigning nursing staff. Review a specific unit's staffing plan. Note if any changes were made. Is the actual schedule reflective of the plan? Are committee meetings, educational times, and quality management activities noted on the weekly schedules? Are they noted on anyone's assessment for the day?

THE WORK LOAD OF THE UNIT

Institution-wide reports are generated that describe the *activity level* of each unit. Although the particular format of these reports may vary among institutions, the information that they contain is commonly used to account for:

- the number of admissions for the day,
- the overall number of available patient beds,
- the number of occupied beds for that period,
- the number of patient days for the unit, and
- occupancy levels presented as both month and year-to-date.

Additional statistical data include average length of stay, census, transfers, and discharge information. Statistical work-load reports assist the nurse

statistical reports

manager in the decision-making process related to the allocation and use of available resources, e.g., budget, staff, supplies, and equipment.

PERCENTAGE OF OCCUPANCY

occupancy

Another way of assessing a unit's activity level is by the **percentage of occupancy,** which is calculated by dividing the patient census by the number of beds actually occupied. For example, if a unit has 38 beds and 37 of those beds are occupied, the average occupancy is $37 \div 38 = .974$ or 97.4 percent. Table 22-1 is an example of a typical occupancy report.

EXERCISE 22-3
The next time you are in the clinical area, assume that the census is typical for the unit. Calculate the occupancy percentage.

TABLE 22-1 Typical Occupancy Report

| | OCCUPANCY | | |
AVAILABLE BEDS	FOR DAY	MONTH-TO-DATE	YEAR-TO-DATE
38	97.4%	95.5%	95.5%
38	86.8%	82.7%	82.7%
42	90.5%	92.9%	92.9%
42	88.1%	79.3%	79.3%
0	0.0%	0.0%	0.0%
32	75.0%	63.8%	63.8%
32	87.5%	73.2%	73.2%
Total: 224	**99.1%**	**88.1%**	**88.1%**

EXERCISE 22-4
If a 40-bed unit with an 85% occupancy has an average daily census of 34 and each of those 34 beds are occupied by 1 patient for 30 days, what is the equivalent in patient days? If this same unit experiences 10 discharges a day equating to 300 discharges in 30 days, what is the **average length of stay** for that unit?

resource use indicator

If, on average, the 38-bed unit, referred to above, is occupied 97 percent of the time, resources, staffing, supplies, equipment, and dollars need to be budgeted to meet the requirements of the unit at that level of occupancy.

It is essential that the person responsible for staffing the unit knows the average percentage of occupancy. As in most organizations, the dollars allocated for personnel and clinical resources are based on the average of the previous year's activity levels.

AVERAGE LENGTH OF STAY

The major index of an institution's ability to meet its financial obligations in this changing healthcare environment is the patient's length of stay. The amount of time a patient is hospitalized is also a good indicator and predictor of resource use.

To calculate the **average length of stay,** the nurse manager divides the number of patient days in a given time period by the number of discharges in that same time period. A **patient day** is considered as one patient occupying a bed for one day.

Example
One patient occupying one bed for 30 days of a month is equivalent to 30 patient days (1 patient $\times$ 1 bed $\times$ 30 days = 30 patient days).

STAFFING BUDGET

A major expenditure related to the operation of a unit is the staffing budget. When calculating/projecting the staffing budget, the nurse manager identifies the **full-time equivalents** (FTE) needed to run the unit and the related positions and costs. Staffing projections are done in full-time equivalents. A full-time equivalent is an employee who works full-time, 40 hours per week. This is calculated to 80 hours per pay period or 2080 hours per year. For example:

full-time equivalent

1.0 FTE =
40 Hours per week =
80 Hours per pay period (a 2-week period) =
2,080 Hours per year
(40 Hours/Week × 52 Weeks/Year = 2,080 Hours/Year
8 Hours/Day × 5 Days/Week = 40 Hours/Week).

The 2,080 hours of a full-time equivalent includes all paid time. This includes **productive** as well as **nonproductive time.** Productive time is the time the employee actually works. Benefit time, also referred to as nonproductive time, includes paid time off, vacation, holiday, sick, personal, and education time. Although the organization pays an FTE for 2,080 hours, that employee does not actually work those hours. This is a concept that nurse managers sometimes fail to consider when preparing and calculating their staffing and scheduling.

productive/nonproductive time

Example
An employee's benefit time can include:
- Holiday time   equivalent to   56 Hours (7 Days)
- Vacation time   equivalent to   160 Hours (20 Days)
- Sick time   equivalent to   96 Hours (12 Days)
- Personal time   equivalent to   48 Hours (6 Days)
- Funeral time   equivalent to   24 Hours (3 Days)
- Education time   equivalent to   16 Hours (2 Days)

                              Total: 400 Hours

This nurse is available to work only 1,680 hours per year (2,080 hours − 400 hours = 1,680 hours.)

Benefit time is not the same for all employees. Therefore, the paid nonproductive time is calculated based on the skill category or designation of the employee. Whereas an FTE always equals 40 hours of work per week, a full-time employee may not always equate to a 1.0 FTE. Flexible scheduling and shifts that evolved during the 1980s have produced the phenomenon of a 36-hour work week with paid time equivalent to 40 hours. For example, in a program of Work 36: Pay 40 an employee will be available to work three 12-hour days per week, which equates to 36 hours/week or 1,872 hours/year. However, this employee will be paid as if he/she actually worked for 40 hours/week or 2,080/year.

Thirty-six hours will be paid productive time and four hours will be paid nonproductive time. This four hours of paid nonproductive time per week equals 208 hours per year of time the employee is not available to work. In addition, the employee (nurse) will receive vacation time, holiday time, sick time, personal time, and education time throughout the year in some quantity.

Example
Four paid nonproductive hours/week = 4 hours/week × 52 weeks = 208 hours

Additional Paid Nonproductive Time
- Vacation time   equivalent to   160 Hours
- Holiday time   equivalent to   56 Hours
- Sick time   equivalent to   96 Hours
- Personal time   equivalent to   48 Hours

> **EXERCISE 22-5**
> Select a community health organization. Review the benefits policy. Calculate how many FTEs need to be employed to assure the presence of one registered nurse each day of operation.

- Education time   equivalent to   24 Hours
- Funeral time   equivalent to   36 Hours
                              Total: 420 Hours

2,080 Hours − 208 Hours = 1,872 Hours available to work *before* paid nonproductive time. 1,872 Hours − 420 Hours/paid nonproductive time = 1,452 hours of actual paid productive time (this time represents the *actual* hours the employee will work for the organization).

This employee, although paid for 2,080 hours, is only available to work a total of 1,452 hours per year.

A unit that functions twenty-four hours per day, seven days per week, must be staffed to meet that need. Since the calculations confirm that there are paid nonproductive hours that must be covered, so must regular days off. An eight-hour employee will work five days per week, but the unit will operate and require staffing for seven days per week. Each eight-hour workday of a full-time employee's time is considered to be 20% of that FTEs time.

Example

Monday	=	20% or 0.2 FTE
Tuesday	=	20% or 0.2 FTE
Wednesday	=	20% or 0.2 FTE
Thursday	=	20% or 0.2 FTE
Friday	=	20% or 0.2 FTE
Total	**=**	**100% or 1.0 FTE**

Saturday and Sunday also each equate to 0.2 or 20% of an FTE. This calculates to an additional 40% of time that requires coverage. Since the 1.0 FTE is not always available to work the weekend, additional coverage must be calculated and provided.

Example

1.0 FTE + 0.4 FTE = 1.4 FTEs required to cover 7 days/week. (0.4 FTE represents the additional 40% of time that needs to be covered.)

paid nonproductive time

In addition, the paid nonproductive time that the employee is not available to work will also need to be covered. To calculate the paid nonproductive time factor, the number of paid nonproductive hours are divided by the paid productive hours. An example will help illustrate this point.

Example

A full-time employee working five eight-hour shifts per week is entitled to 400 hours of paid nonproductive time per year. This employee is available to work only 1,680 hours per year, or 80.76% of the time (1,680 ÷ 2,080 = 80.76%).

To provide staffing on a unit, an additional calculation using the paid nonproductive time must be completed.

Example   1.0 FTE + 0.40 (days off) + 0.19* = 1.6 FTEs.

*Percentage of paid nonproductive time: difference between paid productive time and total paid time.

2,080 Hours = 100%	(Total paid time)
− 1,680 Hours = 80.76%	(Total hours available to work before paid, nonproductive time)
400 Hours = 19.26%	(Total paid, nonproductive time or benefit time)

For every 1 FTE, 1.6 FTEs will need to be hired to cover the unit seven days per week, 365 days per year.

variable cost

Staffing is considered a *variable cost*. As the census and patient care needs fluctuate, so should staffing. Staffing and the patterns that result are considered to have a direct correlation. As the patient census increases, so does the unit's work load, thereby requiring additional personnel. As the census decreases, the work load is reduced, having the concomitant effect on staffing requirements.

Justification is needed if staffing and census are not reflective of this type of direct patterning. Reasons may include changes in patient care needs that necessitate adjustments in the nurse/patient ratio (the number of nurses required to care for a certain number of patients).

STAFFING PATTERN/MATRIX

Since staffing and census are both considered variable resource factors, a question that is usually asked by nurse managers is: How many FTEs are needed to meet the work-load demands of the unit?

work-load demands

Since the work load and services delivered vary from unit to unit, several methods may be used to estimate the total number of FTEs needed and skill mix required.

One of the easiest ways of accomplishing this task is to develop a **staffing matrix/pattern.** A staffing matrix is a plan that outlines the number of individuals and job classifications needed by unit, per shift, per day. This is accomplished by assessing the current daily staffing patterns and asking the question: Does the current staffing meet the patient care needs of the unit?

staffing matrix

Daily staffing patterns are developed based on historical data that relate to the patient population being served. If there is a shift or change in that patient population on a particular unit, the staffing pattern or matrix may require adjustments.

The staffing matrix may change by day and by shift, depending on the services provided. For example, if a hospital performs cardiac surgery Monday through Friday, and those patients are cared for on a one-to-one basis,the required staffing will be reflected in the staffing pattern Monday through Saturday until 3:00 P.M. However, it will not be reflected from 3:00 P.M. Saturday to 7:00 A.M. on Monday. If the demand for cardiac surgery on Saturday and Sunday increases, the staffing pattern will change to meet the identified change in patient care requirements.

Another method that may be used to arrive at the FTEs is to calculate the number of hours to be staffed. For example: An outpatient endoscopy unit that operates from 7:00 A.M. to 3:00 P.M., Monday through Friday, 52 weeks per year will require staffing for 2,080 hours. If the unit is closed on the holidays observed by the organization, those hours may be deducted from the total.

Example
7 Holidays/Year × 8 Hours/Day = 56 Hours that the unit is closed for holidays.
2,080 Total Hours/Year − 56 Holiday Hours = 2,024 Hours that the unit is in operation and requires staff.

If the available productive hours for each employee working in this unit is 1,680 hours, the actual number of staff to be hired to cover the 2,024 hours per year is approximately 1.2 FTEs.

Example
2,024 Hours of Operation ÷ 1,680 Hours/FTE = 1.204

$$\frac{\text{Desired}}{\text{Available}} \quad = \quad \frac{2,024}{1,680} \quad = \quad 1.204$$

The nurse manager then determines the categories of staff needed to cover these hours of operation. If there are two endoscopy rooms that are used simultaneously, and one nurse is required to be in each room during a procedure, the nurse manager's staffing would be:

2 RN FTEs × 1.2   =   2.4 RN FTEs to cover both rooms during the hours of operation

This same method is completed for each category of staff required to adequately meet the needs of the unit.

Endoscopy Unit Staffing

2 RNs × 1.2	=	2.4 FTE RNs
1 Secretary × 1.2	=	1.2 FTE Secretaries
1 Endo Tech × 1.2	=	1.2 FTE Endo Techs

Total: 4.8 FTEs + Nurse Manager

This endoscopy unit requires a total of 4.8 FTEs plus the nurse manager to cover the two rooms and meet the standards of patient care and staffing requirements.

Projected patient days and the **patient care standard** or hours of patient care per patient day may also be used to calculate FTEs. A medical-surgical unit that has 12,000 patient days per year providing 5 hours of patient care per patient day will require 60,000 productive hours for patient care.

Example

12,000 Patient Days × 5 Hours per Patient Day = 60,000 Productive Hours.

If, on the average, each FTE is available to work 1,680 productive hours, this unit will require 35.7 FTEs.

Example

60,000 Hours ÷ 1,680 = 35.7 FTEs.

division of resources

Once the total number of FTEs has been calculated, the total FTEs are divided among all shifts. This *division of resources* is usually calculated in percentages and is related to work load and activity. Historically, the majority of staff was placed on the day shift and the remaining numbers were divided between the remaining two shifts.

Example

50% allocated to 7:00 A.M.–3:00 P.M.
30% allocated to 3:00 P.M.–11:00 P.M.
20% allocated to 11:00 P.M.–7:00 A.M.

If the activity and work load has shifted to later in the day, the staffing resources would be divided in a different manner:

Example

45% allocated to 7:00 A.M.–3:00 P.M.
35% allocated to 3:00 P.M.–11:00 P.M.
20% allocated to 11:00 P.M.–7:00 A.M.

If the work load is evenly distributed throughout the twenty-four hour period, as in a *critical care unit,* the division may be:

Example

33 ⅓% allocated to 7:00 A.M.–3:00 P.M.
33 ⅓% allocated to 3:00 P.M.–11:00 P.M.
33 ⅓% allocated to 11:00 P.M.–7:00 A.M.

For a medical-surgical unit with a total budget of 35 FTEs, the staffing allocation for each shift, assuming the historical approach is used, would be:

50% allocated to 7:00 A.M.–3:00 P.M.	=	17.50 FTEs
30% allocated to 3:00 P.M.–11:00 P.M.	=	10.50 FTEs
20% allocated to 11:00 P.M.–7:00 A.M.	=	7.00 FTEs

staffing mix

After deciding the *percentage allocation* of the total staff, the nurse manager then projects what the *staffing mix* will be for the unit on each shift. The nurse manager utilizing historical, current, and projected data of the unit determines the number of RNs, LPNs, unlicensed assistive personnel, and unit secretaries to be placed on each shift. Using the example of the medical-surgical unit, the nurse manager would create the following staffing pattern:

<u>Total FTEs = 17.50</u>   <u>7:00 A.M.–3:00 P.M. (Day Shift)</u>
8.00 RN
1.58 LPN
4.65 UAP
<u>1.55 US</u>
15.78 TOTAL

<u>Total FTEs = 10.50</u>   <u>3:00 P.M.–11:00 P.M. (Evening Shift)</u>
4.77 RN
1.58 LPN
3.10 UAP
<u>1.55 US</u>
11.00 TOTAL

<u>Total FTEs = 7.00</u>   <u>11:00 P.M.–7:00 A.M. (Night Shift)</u>
3.49 RN
1.58 LPN
<u>1.55 UAP</u>
6.62 TOTAL

Total FTEs = 35.0   Total FTEs = 33.40

The total staffing pattern initially established accounts for 35.0 FTEs. There is still 1.60 FTE (35.0 FTEs − 33.40 FTEs) available for the nurse manager to use on whatever shift requires the additional resources. Although the proposed staffing pattern does not exactly equal the original number of personnel, it is still considered within the total FTE allocation and provides reasonable coverage for the unit.

If the nurse manager decides to have five RNs on the 7:00 A.M. to 3:00 P.M. shift each day, she/he must calculate the total coverage required for seven days/week as well as the coverage required for the paid nonproductive time. As referred in a previous example (Staffing Budget section) the paid nonproductive time factor equates to 1.6 FTE (1.59 rounded to the nearest whole number). The nurse manager then takes the 1.6 FTE and multiplies it by the chosen number of FTEs in that category/skill mix. As noted in this example, 1.0 FTE + 0.4 (days off) + 0.19 (paid nonproductive time) = 1.59 FTEs × 5 RNs = 7.95 RN FTEs. After these calculations have been completed, the nurse manager needs to allocate 8.0 FTE (rounded to the nearest whole number) RN positions to the 7:00 A.M.–3:00 P.M. shift to provide five RNs on duty each day. This step is then completed for each category of staff to meet the projected staffing patterns.

SCHEDULING

TIME SCHEDULE

The next issue facing the manager is to take the FTEs that were allocated to each shift and prepare the time schedule. At this point, the manager is faced with variables that need serious consideration when preparing the actual staffing schedule. Some of these factors appear in the box on page 452.

The nurse manager also needs to be aware of any rules or regulations that dictate minimum staffing requirements or recommended nurse–patient ratios. Labor contracts that stipulate the terms and conditions of employment also require careful consideration when preparing the schedule. A variable that is difficult to project is illness, either short- or long-term, and a leave of absence. The nurse manager must be aware of labor laws and personnel policies regarding these issues. For instance, a personnel policy may require that the positions of employees on sick leave remain open for a minimum period of time before they can be filled.

minimum staffing requirements

Variables That Affect Staffing Schedules

- Each FTE or portion of an FTE position carries certain obligations. For example, in one institution, all full-time equivalent nurses work every other weekend, but a 0.6-FTE nurse is required to work only one weekend per month.
- There is either no shift rotation or only personnel employed less than five years are required to rotate to other shifts.
- Each employee may be required to work 25 out of 26 weekends per year, therefore they may be allowed a weekend off with no replacement or weekend "make-up." This situation is allowed as long as that weekend is attached to a day off.
- There will be requests from staff members for specific days off, which may include holidays, personal days, vacation, and days to attend school and educational programs.
- The nurse manager may need to consider staff participation in committees, when the personnel may be off the unit for long periods of time.

Nursing Unit_____ Unit Staffing Schedule Date _____ to _____

PROPOSED STAFFING 7am - 3pm

NAME	S	M	T	W	T	F	S	S	M	T	W	T	F	S	S	M	T	W	T	F	S	S	M	T	W	T	F	S
RN #1 1.0 FTE	X	7	7	7	7	X	7																					
RN #2 1.0 FTE	7	X	7	7	7	7	X																					
RN #3 1.0 FTE	X	7	7	7	X	7	7																					
RN #4 1.0 FTE	7	7	X	7	7	7	X																					
RN #5 1.0 FTE	X	7	7	7	7	X	7																					
RN #6 1.0 FTE	7	7	PD	7	7	7	X																					
RN #7 1.0 FTE	X	7	7	H	V	X	7																					
RN #8 1.0 FTE	7	X	7	Conf	7	7	X																					
TOTAL RN	4	6	6	6	6	5	5																					
LPN #1 1.0 FTE	7	X	7	7	7	7	X																					
LPN #2 .6 FTE	X	7	X	X	X	ED	7																					
TOTAL LPN	1	1	1	1	1	1	1																					
UAP #1 1.0 FTE	7	X	7	7	PD	7	X																					
UAP #2 1.0 FTE	X	7	7	V	7	X	7																					
UAP #3 1.0 FTE	7	7	Conf	X	7	7	X																					
UAP #4 1.0 FTE	X	7	7	7	X	7	7																					
UAP #5 .8 FTE	7	X	X	7	7	X	7																					
TOTAL NA	3	3	3	3	3	3	3																					

Nurse Manager _____ Coordinator_____

FIGURE 22-1

Example of a completed time schedule. (V = vacation day request; ED = education day request; Conf = conference day request; PD = personal day request; H = holiday request; X = off; 7 = on duty at 7 A.M.)

Taking all these issues under consideration, the nurse manager sets out on the quest of preparing the staffing schedule, always keeping in mind the goal of delivering safe, effective, quality patient care. Using the previous example again of the medical-surgical unit, a completed time schedule is presented in Figure 22-1. This schedule indicates that the projected staffing goals for this unit are met on all but one day, Sunday. However, on Monday, Tuesday, Wednesday, and Thursday, the unit's goal is exceeded. Since nurse managers are responsible for achieving appropriate staffing levels, they may need to negotiate with one of the RNs who has Sunday off to come to work and take another day off during the week, preferably on a day when the staffing goal has been surpassed. Another approach may be for the nurse manager to reevaluate the number of 1.0 FTEs allocated to the staffing pattern. Perhaps it would be more beneficial to the needs of the unit to convert a full-time employee position to a part-time one. Options include two 0.5-FTE positions, or an 0.8-FTE and a 0.2-FTE, or a 0.6-FTE and a 0.4-FTE position. As the schedules for the unit are developed, this same process may be used by the nurse manager for all categories of personnel.

FLEXIBLE STAFFING

Numerous flexible staffing/scheduling options have been developed. One such arrangement, the weekend incentive program, allows employees to work only weekends, receiving monetary incentives with minimal weekends off and fulfilling a holiday work commitment only if the holiday falls on a weekend. Another popular innovation is the twelve-hour shift plan. Some twelve-hour shift programs offer a "work 36 hours, pay for 36 hours," while others provide the added incentive of work 36 hours and pay for 40 hours. In addition, a ten-hour shift plan allows nurses to work 40 hours in four days with three days off each week. Night shift programs also abound, attracting staff with a "work four shifts, pay for five" option. These programs may appear to offer the best of all worlds. While in and of themselves, these staffing arrangements appear harmless, they may contain hidden caveats not apparent at first.

Primarily, these incentive/flexible staffing programs attract employees to the organization, which in turn is able to fulfill staffing needs on shifts that are considered less desirable to work (that is, nights, weekends) or more difficult to attract staff. But do these programs really meet the needs of the unit, and what is the cost to the organization? Nurse managers need to assess their units and their hours of operation and patient populations to be confident about a particular staffing/scheduling option. A twelve-hour shift alternative may be requested by the staff. If the unit currently uses eight-hour shifts, what impact will a twelve-hour staffing plan have on the staff and the unit? Are all staff on the unit going to be required to work twelve hours or will some be allowed to remain at eight hours? If all staff on the unit are required to switch to twelve hours, are positions available on another unit or area for staff who cannot make the change? With a twelve-hour shift schedule, will the FTE weekend, holiday, personal day commitment, and hours alter? How will the nurse manager schedule with a combination of eight- and twelve-hour shifts? Look closely at the weekend commitment. An example might be an FTE working eight hours per day, five days per week, who is required to work every other weekend, usually two weekends per month. When this same FTE employee changes to a twelve hours per day, three days per week schedule, the weekend commitment is altered to every third weekend or usually one weekend per month. This unit has now reduced its available coverage by nine weekends per year and unless these days do not require coverage, an increase in personnel resources will be needed to staff the hours required by the nine weekends.

The financial impact of special incentive programs on the department's staffing budget can be staggering. A weekend incentive program of "work 24

financial impact

EXERCISE 22-6
Copy Figure 22-1. Assume the following policies are present; complete the staffing schedule for the month.
Weekends: Every other weekend off
Holiday: (The second Monday of the schedule is a holiday) Time and one-half for working a holiday Equivalent must be taken in same schedule period
Committees: Two one-hour meetings scheduled for all RNs in weeks 2 and 3
Education: RN #4 and RN #8 to attend conference last Friday of month

hours, pay for 36 hours" equates to 24 hours of paid productive time and 12 hours of paid nonproductive time for each weekend.

Example

24 Hours at $25.00/Hour	=	$600
12 Hours at $25.00/Hour	=	$300
Total: 36 hours	=	**$900 Per Staff Nurse**

Further, the additional twelve hours of paid, nonproductive time may need to be covered as well. In this instance the organization may need to double the projection for nonproductive time.

overtime
Overtime related to special staffing incentive programs may harbor additional hidden costs. The twelve hour shift employee who works 36 hours but is paid for 40 hours may receive overtime after 40 hours if all time paid is considered time worked. Overtime for this employee really occurs beginning with the 37th hour that the employee works. This occurs because the four hours of paid nonproductive time each week is considered as time worked. This same scenario may be true for various incentive programs and the impact on FTEs and dollars is of utmost importance to the nurse manager.

A nurse manager may be adequately budgeting FTEs related to activity, acuity, and history, but a change in compensation protocols may indicate that rather than paying for 35 FTEs the unit is now actually allocating dollars for 40 FTEs (even though the staffing has not changed). Although the nurse manager may not have additional resources to use to provide patient care or to increase the productivity of the unit, the financial report indicates that the costs equivalent to five more FTEs than were originally budgeted are now being paid by that unit. It is the responsibility of the nurse manager to be aware of the contrast in the FTE allocation and to be able to justify all staffing variances.

THE SCHEDULE

Schedules are usually prepared in blocks of time. To provide management and staff with enough time to plan, there is usually a mechanism in place within the organization or nursing department for the staff to employ in requesting days off and to know when the schedule will be posted. Staffing schedules may be prepared by a centralized staffing coordinator or by the individual unit. There are pros and cons related to each method.

staffing schedules
One benefit to centralized staffing is that the coordinator is usually aware of the abilities, qualifications, and availability of supplemental personnel. In many organizations the centralized staffing coordinator is also aware of the budget and number of shifts allocated to supplemental staffing agencies. On the other hand, a disadvantage to centralized staffing is the limited knowledge related to specific patient care needs, activities, and resource allocation for individual units. Usually a combination of both mechanisms meets the needs of the majority of staff involved.

The staffing schedule for a four- to six-week period is prepared by the nurse manager of each unit and submitted to a centralized staffing coordinator for review. The centralized staffing coordinator cross-references the established approved staffing pattern with the one submitted. To assure a coordinated effort in achieving the established staffing pattern, any variance in the pattern is brought to the attention of the appropriate nurse manager.

The centralized staffing coordinator has control of the supplemental staffing, whether it is float, per diem, or agency personnel. These personnel are used on an as-needed basis throughout the department and are best allocated by the centralized staffing coordinator who takes the bigger picture into consideration when facilitating the overall staffing of the department.

Float staff are personnel trained to work in a variety of patient care settings throughout the hospital. The per diem staff also work on an as-needed basis or a few days per month and may or may not be assigned to a regular unit. Float and per diem staff are employed by the hospital and paid at a higher hourly rate than a full-time or part-time employee. This rate is usually less than overtime because these employees do not accrue benefits or paid time off (paid nonproductive time). Float and per diem staff are used to supplement regular staffing before overtime costs are incurred. Agency personnel are contracted through an outside staffing service and are used in various areas to fill temporary staffing needs.

float/per diem staff

The JCAHO standards require that all nursing staff, regardless of their employment criteria or status, are competent to fulfill the duties and responsibilities of their position. Competency levels may be ascertained through the implementation and use of generic and unit-specific performance skills lists. Generic skills are those that can be carried out by the majority of personnel who deliver care and perform skills in a variety of clinical settings. Unit specific skills are activities that relate to a more defined patient population.

Another important consideration when the nurse manager is preparing the schedule is given not only to the staffing pattern and availability of staff, but also to the qualifications needed for each day. A patient care unit requires and demands various duties and responsibilities of each individual staff member. One may be responsible to take charge. This nurse usually has seniority, education, and experience in caring for the patient population on the unit, is current in technical skills, and has experience in the charge nurse role. This unit may also be required to care for patients on cardiac monitors. Ideally, the nurse manager would want all nurses on duty to have that ability; however, a nurse orientee has been assigned to the unit and has not had the opportunity to attend staff development education to acquire this skill. The nurse manager must then determine how best to achieve the desired staffing. The decision may be that as long as the charge nurse and the other three nurses on the unit can interpret readings from the monitor, there may be sufficient coverage and resources available to the staff nurse who is unable to use the equipment. Another approach may be not to assign cardiac monitored patients to this nurse. Of further consideration for the nurse manager is that although everyone may have received education and training in an area, for example the charge nurse role, certain nurses perform the duties and responsibilities of that role more expertly than others. On a busy day or a day when the nurse manager may be out of the building, the appropriate decision may be to schedule and assign the most experienced charge nurse on duty.

qualifications

On a weekly basis, staffing sheets are used to make daily shift-to-shift revisions that may occur related to census, acuity, sick calls, and emergencies. These daily staffing sheets are reviewed by the nurse manager to assess attendance of staff and unplanned variances. Once the schedule is posted and the staff arrives on duty, the daily assignment is completed. The actual assignment of the staff may be accomplished by the nurse manager or delegated to the charge nurse. When completing this task, two major factors are considered: the needs of the patients and the qualifications of the staff. The combining of staff to patients occurs every shift, every day, on hundreds of nursing units around the world. Determining the skills and qualifications of the staff has historically

staffing sheets

been the responsibility of the organization. These standards for practice are evaluated annually or semiannually and are reflected in the staff's performance evaluations.

A large amount of time spent preparing the staffing schedule has been alleviated by computerized programming. Currently there are several computerized staffing and scheduling packages on the market. These systems, though expensive, have the ability to save countless hours for the nurse manager and centralized staffing coordinator, streamline record keeping, and generate staffing justification and utilization reports.

computerized staffing systems

These computerized staffing systems have the ability to retain multiple variables about each employee, in every category entered, and develop a schedule. Once a pattern by an employee has been developed and programmed into the computer, the system can generate a schedule in a matter of minutes. This is far more expedient and productive than the most experienced nurse manager can be.

CHAPTER CHECKLIST

Patient classification, staffing, and scheduling are essential components of a nurse manager's duties and responsibilities. The nurse manager's skill and knowledge base related to these issues often govern his or her success in the management role. The nurse manager is also responsible for making informed choices related to resource allocation and for understanding the impact of those choices on the unit.

▪ Patient classification systems allow the nurse manager to:

- Identify the nursing care requirements of patients on the unit
- Facilitate the equitable distribution of nursing resources
- Ensure the effective and efficient delivery of high-quality patient care
- Predict staffing requirements for the unit
- Facilitate decision making related to staffing
- Assess unit productivity.

▪ According to Ledwitch (1986), questions to ask about patient classification systems include:

- Does the system designate levels of care utilizing the appropriate critical indicators?
- Can staffing needs be projected related to the patient's level of illness?
- Do the critical indicators consider multiple aspects of nursing care?
- Can the data generated by the system be used to justify and track trends in resource allocation for the department and the hospital?
- Will all levels of nursing be involved in monitoring the system to ensure validity and reliability?
- Does the patient classification system support linkage to other systems within the organization?

▪ Patient classification systems should take into account as many different types of nursing activities as possible, including:

- Assessment of communication barriers (hearing impairment, foreign language, etc.)
- Assessment of environmental issues (physical surroundings, patient safety needs)
- Physiologic assessment
- Care planning, treatments, medications, and reports
- Assessment of self-care capabilities
- Assessment of psychosocial behaviors or support
- Educational assessment
- Discharge planning.

■ When projecting staffing requirements, the nurse manager must be familiar with state department of health licensing standards and the JCAHO nursing care standards related to staffing.

■ Activity reports describe the unit's work load, occupancy, patient days, and average length of stay.

■ When calculating and projecting the staffing budget, the nurse manager must identify:

- The work load of the unit
- The full-time equivalents (FTEs) needed
- Associated positions and costs.

■ The staffing matrix is a plan that outlines the number of individuals and job classifications needed by unit, per shift, per day.

■ Flexible staffing/scheduling options include:

- Weekend incentive programs
- Ten- or twelve-hour shift plans
- Night shift programs.

■ Staffing schedules may be prepared by a centralized staffing coordinator or by the individual unit.

■ Computerized staffing and scheduling programs are also available.

TERMS TO KNOW

- **average length of stay**
- **factor evaluation**
- **full-time equivalent (FTE)**
- **nonproductive time**
- **patient care standard**
- **patient classification system**

- **patient day**
- **percentage of occupancy**
- **productive time**
- **prototype evaluation**
- **staffing matrix/pattern**
- **staffing regulations**

REFERENCES

Edwardson, S., & Giovannetti, P. (1987). A review of cost accounting methods for nursing services. *Nursing Economics, 5*(3), 107–117.

Giovannetti, P. (1972, May). *Measurement of Patient's Requirements for Nursing Services.* Paper presented to the National Institute of Health Conference, Virginia.

——— (1979, February). Understanding patient classification system. *Journal of Nursing Administration, 9,* 4–9.

Halloran, E., & Kiley, M. (1984). Case mix management. *Nursing Management, 15*(2), 39–45.

Joint Commission. (1993). *1994 Accreditation Manual for Hospitals Volume I: Standards.* Oakbrook Terrace, IL: Joint Commission.

Ledwitch, L. (1988). Expanded utilization of the patient classification system. In Scherubel, J.C. & Shaffer, F.A., eds. *Patient and Purse Strings II.* New York: National League for Nursing, pp. 150.

McHugh, M.L., & Dwyer, V.L. (1992). Measurement issues in patient acuity classification for prediction of hours in nursing care. *Nursing Administration Quarterly, 16*(4), 20–31.

New Jersey Department of Health. (1993). *Licensing Standards for Hospitals.* Trenton, NJ: New Jersey State Department of Health Division of Health Facilities Educational Licensing, CN 367.

SUGGESTED READINGS

Cockerill, R., O'Brien-Pallas, L., Bolley, H., & Pink, G. (1993). Measuring nursing workload for case costing. *Nursing Economics, 11*(6), 342–349.

Finkler, S. (1992). *Budgeting Concepts for Nurse Managers.* Philadelphia: W.B. Saunders.

Finnigan, S., Abel, M., Dobler, T., Hudson, L., & Terry, B. (1993). Automated patient acuity: Linking nursing systems and quality measurement with patient outcomes. *Journal of Nursing Administration, 23*(5), 62–71.

Fraser, L. (1984). *Contemporary Staffing Techniques in Nursing.* East Norwalk, CT: Appleton-Century-Crofts.

Kahl, K., Ivancin, L., & Fuhrmann, M. (1991). Automated nursing documentation system provides a favorable return on investments. *Journal of Nursing Administration, 21*(11), 44–45.

Prescot, P. (1991). Nursing intensity: Needed today for more than staffing. *Nursing Economics, 9*(6), 409–414.

St. Morris, K. (1992). Criteria for selection of an automated "intelligent" scheduling system. *Nursing Administration Quarterly, 16*(4), 70–77.

Simpson, R. (1992). *Technology: Nursing the System.* Atlanta, GA: HBO & Company.

Stevens, B. (1985). *The Nurse as Executive.* Rockville, MD: Aspen.

Stevens, B., & Mallard, C. (1989). *Essentials of Nursing Management: Concepts and Context of Practice.* Rockville, MD: Aspen.

Strasen, L. (1987). *Key Business Skills for Nurse Managers.* Philadelphia: J.B. Lippincott.

Van Slyck, A. (1991). A system approach to the management of nursing services, Part I–Part VII. *Nursing Management, 22*(3,4,5,6,7,9).

PART SIX

MANAGING PERSONAL RESOURCES

CHAPTER 23
ROLE TRANSITION

Jennifer Jackson Gray, R.N., M.S.N.

PREVIEW

This chapter provides information about role transition, the process of moving from a clinically focused position to a supervisory position with increased responsibility. A basic overview of management roles illustrates the complexity of managing work done by others and provides a foundation for understanding role transition. The exercises offer opportunities to recognize one's own expectations, resources, and management potential.

OBJECTIVES

- Construct a non-nursing role using Responsibilities, Opportunities, Lines of communication, Expectations, and Support (ROLES).
- Analyze specific examples of Mintzberg's managerial roles in the daily activities of a nurse manager.
- Hypothesize the phases of role transition using comparisons to the phases in developing an intimate relationship.
- Compare the strategies used during a previous role transition: strengthening internal resources, negotiating a role, growing with mentors, or learning necessary skills.

QUESTIONS TO CONSIDER

- What do I need to know about a management position before accepting it?
- How can I quickly make the transition from clinical nurse to nurse manager?

A Manager's Viewpoint

I learned about the management role from observing other people. I knew what the staff nurses on the floor expected of the supervisor and was willing to take on the responsibility. I wanted to be able to have more say in what went on and to help the nurses on the floor because I understood their perspective. The downside of the new role was that I missed the patient care, yet in my new role I have found an expanded role in the area of patient teaching.

My nursing education did not prepare me for the managerial decisions I have to make. If I am going to stay in management, I need additional education on the business side.

My transition into management was made easier because other nursing managers and the director of nursing were supportive. We have a nurse managers' meeting and a nursing quality assurance meeting. In those meetings, there has been an environment where the attitude has been helpful. When I presented my material, I was able to take risks and express myself. The other managers have suggested other people I could contact to get information pertinent to management in my unique clinical setting. They have made suggestions and shared materials that they had that they thought would be helpful.

Gayla Bruner, R.N., B.S.N.
Nurse Manager of the Family Practice Residency Clinic
Formerly Night Supervisor
Charlton Methodist Hospital
Dallas, Texas

INTRODUCTION

Changing from a staff nurse to a nurse manager involves transforming one's professional identity. The staff nurse directly performs tasks related to the care of patients. As a doer, the staff nurse has individual responsibility and accountability for the work that is accomplished. The nurse manager is a generalist, orchestrating diverse tasks and getting work done through others. The transformation requires "learning what it means to be a manager, developing interpersonal judgment, gaining self-knowledge, and coping with stress and emotion" (Hill, 1992, p. 6).

Knowing what to expect during the transformation can reduce the stress of accepting and transitioning into a new role. Following an overview of managerial roles, this chapter describes the process of role transition with an emphasis on strategies that can be used to ease the transition.

TYPES OF ROLES

change agent

Accepting a management position dictates accepting several roles, ones that involve complex activities. The role of change agent involves identifying a potential solution to a problem, developing a plan, and working with others to implement the solution. To describe and yet simplify this complexity, Henry Mintzberg (1975) categorized management roles as being either interpersonal, informational, or decisional. A noted management researcher, Mintzberg studied managers and executives and identified ten management roles that he placed in these three categories (see box on page 463).

interpersonal
figurehead

Interpersonal management roles express the manager's formal authority through basic interpersonal relationships (Mintzberg, 1975). In the *figurehead* role, the nurse manager greets new employees during orientation or writes a manufacturer to obtain free samples of a new product that the nurses want to try. Activities in the figurehead role involve little decision making but are essential to the smooth operation of the work group. The *leader* role involves motivating employees and reconciling individual needs with the needs of the organization. As part of this role, the nurse manager evaluates employee performance and rewards or disciplines as necessary. The *liaison* role involves the manager making contacts outside the vertical chain of command. These contacts with peers in other departments provide the manager with information about the organization and opportunities to discuss common concerns.

leader

liaison

informational

The manager is the nerve center of the organizational unit. Pieces of information are the electrical impulses along the nerves that pass through the nerve center. Consequently, **informational management roles** consume 40 percent of a manager's time (Mintzberg, 1975). The *monitor* role involves scanning the environment for information that will impact the people or the work of the organization. Since the most current information is verbal, the manager uses the interpersonal contacts of the leader and liaison roles to collect this information. For example, a nurse manager, attending a workshop, learns about a new computer system for home health agencies. Deciding with whom to share the information is the function of the *disseminator* role. The nurse manager drops by the office of the home health department manager to leave a brochure about the new computer system. As a disseminator of information, the manager can influence peers, those being supervised, and even upper level executives.

dissemination

Mintzberg's Managerial Roles

INTERPERSONAL
- Figurehead
- Leader
- Liaison

INFORMATIONAL
- Monitor
- Disseminator
- Spokesperson

DECISIONAL
- Entrepreneur
- Disturbance handler
- Resource allocator
- Negotiator

From Mintzberg, H. (1975). The manager's job: Folklore and fact. Harvard Business Review, 53(4), 49–61.

EXERCISE 23-1
Read the position description of a nurse manager. What are the responsibilities of the person in this position in their role as a *figurehead?* Repeat the question for each of Mintzberg's roles.

spokesperson

The last informational role, the *spokesperson* role, is seen as the manager shares information on behalf of others. The manager must inform those at higher levels of management about the needs and concerns of the group being managed. As a spokesperson, the manager also presents the views of the group to those outside the group. For example, the nurse manager presents the nurses' concerns about time required to enter a nursing assessment on the computer to the information systems manager.

decision maker

Information is not an end unto itself; information is the basic input for decision making. **Decisional management roles** make up Mintzberg's third category of managerial roles. In the *entrepreneur* role, the manager uses information to improve the unit. New ideas are implemented and changes are made in this role. While the entrepreneur proactively makes changes, the *disturbance handler* responds to unexpected situations. The manager decides how, when, and where to respond to resolve the disturbance or problem.

entrepreneur

disturbance handler

A third decisional role, *resource allocator,* involves the responsibility of deciding who will get what, including the manager's time. Resources of people and funds are allocated in the context of overlapping decisions. The nurse manager who allocates funds to one project is by that decision not allocating funds to a competing project. These difficult decisions imply the need for the last of Mintzberg's roles— *negotiator.* The manager has information and the authority to commit resources, two conditions necessary to negotiating. The manager weighs competing values and priorities to find a solution that will be best for all parties concerned.

resource allocator

negotiator

Considering so many different roles can be overwhelming to a new manager! Since learning about the roles of a manager is an essential first step in role transition, another approach to the complexity of managerial roles is the acronym "ROLES," in which each letter represents a component common to all roles.

"ROLES": THE ABCs OF UNDERSTANDING ROLES

R   "R" stands for *responsibilities*. What are the specified duties in the position description for the management position? What tasks are to be completed? What decisions are made by the person in this position? The answers to these questions may vary depending on the respondent. Each position has specific tasks for which the position holder is responsible.

O   "O" stands for *opportunities*, which are untapped aspects of the position. In the employment interview the nurse executive may have said that the previous manager did not encourage the staff nurses to participate in continuing education. Or while touring the unit, a manager observes that the report room is lacking in amenities. Maybe there is a new method of delivering patient care appropriate for the unit. These possibilities represent opportunities for a manager to have impact on organizational and unit goals.

"ROLES" Acronym

Responsibilities
Opportunities
Lines of communication
Expectations
Support

L   "L" represents *lines of communication*. Roles involve relationships with other people. Some of these people are above the manager on the organizational chart; others are below. Still others are peers. Roles incorporate patterns of structured interactions between the manager and people in these groups. The nurse manager receives and sends messages. Being a skillful listener can be more important than being skillful in sending messages. These two-way communications require the languages of emotion and logic (Covey, 1990). Skill is required to effectively communicate both the content and the intent of the message; skill can only be developed through practice. Chapter 16 describes techniques of effective communication that are extremely important to a new manager.

E   "E" stands for *expectations*. Staff nurses have specific expectations of their manager, particularly wanting the manager to be a facilitator and a leader. The nursing executive or administrator will likely have expectations about how managers spend their time on the job—even about how much time they spend at work. Nurse executives' expectations evolve from their perspective of the manager's accountability and duties. (Nurse managers report a sense of being in the middle—a sense of being different from the staff and also different from the administration (Westmoreland, 1993). This chapter's "Research Perspective" describes the three roles identified from this study.

There are also personal expectations related to performance as a manager. Hill (1992) found that new managers had expectations of power and control that were "inconsistent with the workload, pace, and dependence on others that they encountered" (p. 52). The process of role transition unfolds as a new manager identifies the expectations from each source, recognizes their similarities and differences, and develops the management roles, incorporating personal expectations.

EXERCISE 23-2
Observe communication on a clinical unit. Diagram lines to represent what you see.

"S" stands for *support*, which is closely tied to expectations about performance. The manager's role is shaped to some degree by the support and services others provide. For example, if the staffing office calls nurses to replace those who call in sick, the role as a resource allocator will not include those shift-by-shift phone calls. If the accounting department provides a detailed analysis of the unit's expenditures, the manager may spend less time as a disturbance handler justifying the unit's operating budget to nursing administration. Each role has some support available. What is important is to evaluate whether the position provides supports in areas where a manager may lack knowledge or skill.

Research Perspective

Westmoreland, D. (1993). Nurse managers' perspective of their work: Connection and relationship. *Journal of Nursing Administration, 23(1),* 60–64.

This qualitative study described what nurse managers experience and interpret as meaningful in the performance of their roles. Field notes and transcripts of semi-structured interviews with nine managers were analyzed for themes. Three perspectives of nurse manager identity were described by the subjects.

The "nurse self" role perspective involved giving patient care as a means of connection with oneself and others. Nurse managers reported using patient care as a grounding or focusing technique to remind themselves of why they were nurses.

Stress was associated with the second role perspective of "nurse manager-self." A significant source of stress was the feeling of not fitting in with staff and also being different from the hospital and nursing administrators.

The "career self" perspective yielded personal growth and satisfaction over time. Relationships with family and friends, personal needs, and perceived opportunities were found to be more important in making career decisions than were career goals. Work was seen as important, but not more important than relationships.

Implications For Practice

The themes of the nurse managers' perspectives were connection and relationships. Active engagement in the realities of giving patient care may provide a foundation for commitment to *nursing* management. Supportive work environments provide opportunities for personal development and satisfaction. Sharing stories and experiences with other nurse managers was identified as a empowering strategy to support the managers' goal of providing high-quality patient care on their units.

EXERCISE 23-3
Assume you are seeking a management position. When considering this position, write down the information related to each of the letters in ROLES. Writing the information down may help you organize your thoughts so that you can make the best decision. Complete the "Roles Assessment" exercise found in the box on pages 466 and 467 for your potential management position.

ROLE TRANSITION

Unlearning old roles while learning new roles requires an identity adjustment over time. The persons involved must invest themselves in the process. In this way, **role transition** can be compared to relationships. The process of developing an intimate relationship with another person provides a familiar framework for considering role transition. Relationships typically move through the phases of dating, commitment, honeymoon, disillusionment, resolution, and maturity.

ROLES Assessment

Answer these questions for a position in management that you are considering.

RESPONSIBILITIES

1. From the position description, what are the responsibilities?

2. For what decisions are you responsible?

3. Consider information about the management position that you learned during the interview (this may be role played). Also consider the responsibilities of managers you have observed. Are there other responsibilities to add to your list?

OPPORTUNITIES

4. What would you like to do differently from the previous manager?

5. How could your strengths or expertise benefit the people or nursing unit you would manage?

6. Dream a little (or a lot). If a person who had been a patient on the unit was describing the nursing care to another potential patient, what would you want the first patient to say? Describe the unit as you want it to be known.

ROLES Assessment—cont'd

LINES OF COMMUNICATION

7. Draw yourself in the middle of the space provided. Now fill in the people above you and below you with whom you would communicate. Draw lines from you to each person or group. On the line, identify the form of communication. For example, if you communicate with the director of nursing through a weekly report, write on the line, "Written report."

EXPECTATIONS

8. This may be the most difficult part to assess. List in short sentences or phrases the expectations each person or group may have for you in relation to your management position.

SELF   FAMILY

ADMINISTRATION   IMMEDIATE SUPERVISOR

PEOPLE YOU WILL MANAGE

Now compare the lists. Place a star next to those expectations that are held by more than one person or group. For example, you want to handle the budget of the unit efficiently, an expectation shared with nursing administration. Circle those items that could cause conflicts. Read the strategies section in the chapter for ideas on how to resolve these conflicts.

SUPPORT

9. What people do you know in the organization who could provide information that you will need to do your job?

10. What departments provide services that you could access for assistance?

Save your responses to these questions to review in three months. You may be surprised how your own perception of your ROLES may change over time.

dating   During the dating phase, the interested persons spend structured time together. Both parties present their best characteristics and dedicate a lot of energy to developing the relationship. While both parties present their best characteristics, both are also alert to clues that the other party cannot meet their expectations.

When you are interviewing for a management position, it is like dating. An interview involves touring the unit, visiting with people, and attempting to make a good impression. The potential employer is also attempting to make a favorable impression. Questions are asked about the role of the manager, and the potential manager mentally evaluates whether the described role matches personal expectations about management. Both of these examples represent the phase "role preview."

commitment   Through the dating process, two people decide that they want to spend the rest of their lives together and commit to the relationship. Sometimes one or both of the people decide that they do *not* want to establish a long-term relationship. In a similar way, following the role preview of the interview process, both parties may agree to establish a relationship as employee and employer. Or one or more of the parties may decide not to establish the relationship. In dating, the public decision to leave other similar relationships and establish this new relationship represents a formal commitment. In role transition, the formal commitment of the employment contract implies acceptance of the management role, or "role acceptance."

honeymoon   In new relationships, a time of dating and commitment is usually followed by a honeymoon. More than a trip to a vacation spot, the honeymoon has become synonymous with excitement, happiness, and confidence. In a new position in management, people also experience a honeymoon phase. The employer is excited that the new manager is available. The staff is happy to have a leader, especially if staff members had input into the hiring decision. The new manager is happy, excited, and, most of all, confident in exploring the new roles involved in the management position.

disillusionment   Maybe it is a gradual process or maybe there is a particular event as the turning point. Either way, the honeymoon is over and disillusionment about the relationship occurs. For example, one person makes an expensive purchase without consulting the partner. An argument is followed by a period of painful silence. Similarly, the honeymoon phase in a new position can be followed by a period of disillusionment.

resolution   **Role discrepancy,** a gap between role expectations and role performance, causes discomfort and frustration. Role discrepancy can be resolved by either dissolving the relationship or by changing expectations and performance. The importance of the relationship and the perceived differences between performance and expectations, the basis of role discrepancy, must be considered in light of personal values. When the relationship is valued and the differences are seen as correctable, the decision is made to stay in the relationship. This decision requires the couple or the manager to develop the role.

Choosing to change either role expectations or role performance or both is the process of **role development.** In an intimate relationship, open communication can clarify expectations. Negotiation may result in reasonable expectations. Certain behaviors may be changed to improve role performance. For example, one person in the relationship learns to call home to let the other know about the possibility of being late.

To reduce role discrepancy in a new management position, the same open communication and negotiation needs to occur. Expectations need to be clarified and stipulated by both parties. New managers evaluate management styles and techniques to determine which ones best fit them and the situation. The personal management style evolves as the individuals develop the management roles in their own unique ways. If role discrepancy can be reduced and the role developed to be satisfactory to both parties, the new manager can focus on developing the roles of the position and proceed to the phase of **role internalization.**

Role internalization occurs in relationships as they mature. No longer do the persons in the relationship consciously consider their roles. They have learned the behaviors that maintain and nurture the relationship. The behaviors become second nature. The energy spent on establishing and developing the relationship can be redirected toward achieving mutual goals. In the same way, managers who have been in management positions for several years have internalized their roles. Most of the time they do not consciously consider their roles. Managers know they have reached the stage of role internalization when they focus on accomplishing mutual goals instead of contemplating whether their role performance matches their role expectations. Managers who have internalized their roles have developed their own unique personal style of management. Table 23-1 on page 470 summarizes the comparison between the phases of developing an intimate relationship and the phases of role transition to a nurse manager.

The phases of role transition can vary in length and intensity. Hill (1992) believes that transition into a management role takes at least one year. With changes in organizational structure, it is possible to experience role transition without changing positions. Being the manager of a traditionally governed unit is very different from being the "manager" of a self-governed unit. Role transition is to be expected any time there are major changes in position descriptions.

STRATEGIES TO PROMOTE ROLE TRANSITION

Becoming a manager requires a transformation—a profound change in identity. Such a transformation invokes stress as the manager unlearns old roles and learns the management role. Several strategies can be helpful in easing the strain and quickening the process of role transition (see box).

Strategies to Promote Role Transition
• Strengthen internal resources
• Negotiate the role
• Grow with a mentor
• Develop management knowledge and skills

INTERNAL RESOURCES

A key strategy in promoting role transition is to recognize, utilize, and strengthen the internal resources of commitment, character, and self-respect. Commitment arises out of the need to manage—a strong psychological need to influence the performance of others. Miner (1975) maintains that the need

maturity

> **EXERCISE 23-4**
> Think about a difficult time you have experienced while developing a relationship. Maybe you chose a best friend who had different goals for the relationship. Maybe you had to work through a conflict about roles in the relationship. What did you learn from the difficult time? How could what you learn apply to the process of role transition?

> **EXERCISE 23-5**
> List reasons for being a nurse manager. What goals can be reached as a manager that cannot be reached as a staff nurse? How strong is your need to manage?

need to manage

TABLE 23-1   Comparison of Phases in Developing an Intimate Relationship and in Undergoing Role Transition as a Nurse Manager

PHASE IN DEVELOPING AN INTIMATE RELATIONSHIP	PHASE IN ROLE TRANSITION AS A NURSE MANAGER	CHARACTERISTICS OF PHASE
Dating	Role preview	Presentation of best characteristics to make favorable impression; both parties evaluate each other to determine likelihood of the other being able to fulfill one's expectations
Commitment to relationship	Role acceptance	Public announcement of mutual decision to initiate contract
Honeymoon	Role exploration	Experience of excitement, confidence, and mutual appreciation
Disillusionment	Role discrepancy	Awareness of difference between role expectations and role performance; reconsideration of whether to continue with contract
Resolution	Role development	Negotiation of role expectations; adjustment of role performance to approximate expectations and to find own unique style
Maturation of relationship	Role internalization	Performance of role congruent with own beliefs and individual style; achievement of mutual goals

to manage is crucial to management success. Without the need to manage, no one is likely to maintain the commitment necessary to get high performance from others. Being a manager is not for everyone. Consider whether personal goals and professional fulfillment can best be achieved through management. One's own commitment to the challenges of managing can provide the desire to persevere during the process of role transition.

character   Another internal resource is character. Character is the essence of the person—the values, beliefs, and habits of a person. Centering one's character on correct principles creates power to realize dreams (Covey, 1990). Persons whose characters are based on principles continue to be educated by their experiences and are service oriented. Principle-centered people believe in others, creating a climate that promotes growth and opportunity. A manager with a principle-centered character can be trusted.

energy   Managers need energy and stamina (Hill, 1992) and principle-centered character provides positive energy and synergy (Covey, 1990). While life is seen as an adventure, people with principle-centered character lead balanced lives, taking time for self-renewal. Living a life congruent with ethical principles guides the individual and sets an example for others. The nurse manager with character can rely on tested life principles during the transition to management.

Closely related to character is another internal resource—self-respect. Self-respect allows managers to weather the difficult times when there may be little external recognition. Always remember that a person's value does not depend upon the quality or quickness of the adjustment to the management role. Knowing what you believe in is especially important during a transition period. Writing down short statements of belief or self-affirmations and posting this information may be helpful as a visual reminder.

self-respect

ROLE NEGOTIATION

A strategy that is helpful during conflicting role expectations is **role negotiation.** The ROLES assessment (see box) may have identified areas of significant conflict. Writing the expectations down provides the first step in resolving areas of conflict. It is important to review the expectations listed to determine if they are realistic. Unrealistic expectations strongly held by others may require diplomatic reeducation so their expectations can become more realistic.

The priority of different role expectations may also require role negotiation with the nursing administrator. Ask for input as to which expectations have the highest priorities. Explain personal and family expectations and clearly state the priority that meeting those expectations have. The process may have to be repeated several times before agreement on the expectations related to roles and the priority of each expectation is found. Rewriting the unrealistic expectations to be achievable can reduce three common sources of role strain—ambiguity, overload, and conflict.

EXERCISE 23-6
Identify one area of conflict between your personal expectations and your immediate supervisor's (clinical instructor) expectations. Decide how you would like your supervisor to respond to you when you discuss this area of conflict. Write out the desired response. Now consider how you can present your viewpoint to elicit this response.

MENTORS

In Greek mythology, Mentor was the name of a character who advised and counseled (Parsloe, 1992). The word **mentor** refers to an older, more experienced adult who helps a younger adult navigate the world. The mentor serves as a role model and supports, guides, and counsels the young adult (Kram, 1985).

Functions of a Mentor	
CAREER FUNCTIONS	Sponsorship
	Exposure/Protection
	Coaching
	Challenging Assignments
PSYCHOSOCIAL FUNCTIONS	Role modeling
	Mutual positive regard
	Counseling
	Social interaction

Adapted from Kram, K.E. (1985). Mentoring at Work: Developmental Relationships in Organizational Life. Glenview, IL: Scott, Foresman, p. 23.

Mentors can be a tremendous source of guidance and support for staff nurses and managers, serving both career functions and psychosocial functions. Career functions are possible because the mentor has sufficient professional experience and organizational authority to facilitate the career of the "mentee." Psychosocial functions are possible because of an interpersonal relationship based on mutual trust (Kram, 1985).

sponsorship

Sponsorship involves volunteering or nominating the mentee for additional responsibilities. A mentor can be a sponsor by creating opportunities for individual achievement. The mentor may suggest the mentee be appointed to a key nursing committee or volunteered for a special assignment. Sponsorship leads to exposure or opportunities for the mentee to build a reputation of competence. With exposure, the mentor provides protection by absorbing negative feedback, sharing responsibility for controversial decisions, and teaching the unwritten rules. These unwritten rules about "how things are done around here" may be more important to job success than the written rules.

exposure/protection

coaches

Coaches provide information about how to improve performance, including feedback on current performance. Coaching requires frequent contact and willingness on the part of the mentee to accept feedback. Challenging assignments are given to the mentee that will stretch the limits of knowledge and skill. The mentor helps the mentee learn the technical and management skills necessary to accomplish the task, such as which numbers on the budget printout are added to get the total expenditures.

challenging assignments

The interpersonal relationship between the mentor and the mentee involves mutual positive regard. Because the mentee respects the career accomplishments of the mentor, the mentee identifies with the mentor's example. This role modeling is both conscious and unconscious. The mentee with character and self-respect will evaluate the behaviors of the mentor and select those behaviors worthy of being emulated.

role modeling

counseling

Counseling, as another psychosocial function of the mentor, allows the mentee to explore personal concerns. Confidentiality is a prerequisite to this sharing of personal information. Since the opinion of the mentor is respected, the mentor may provide guidance to the mentee. The best mentors can provide guidance, while recognizing that the mentee may choose to disregard the advice.

Being mentored is a learning process. A mentee may have to develop an openness to receiving support and guidance. A mentee can identify potential mentors by noting whose names are frequently mentioned in favorable terms and developing a broad network of contacts (Kaponya, 1990). Invest time and energy in getting to know more about the potential mentors. Admiration for a mentor and a recognition of the mentor's commitment to self-success can provide an environment of trust in which a mentor–mentee relationship begins. Both persons develop positive expectations of the relationship and both take the initiative to nurture the new relationship. As more of the mentor functions are experienced, the bond between the mentor and mentee grows stronger.

social interaction

mutual positive regard

Relationships between mentors and mentees vary due to individual characteristics and to the career phase of each. During early phases of a career, a nurse manager is concerned about competence and a mentor can provide valuable coaching. As the nurse manager develops, sponsorship by a mentor can prepare the manager for a promotion. A mentor nearing the end of the work career can find fulfillment in sharing knowledge with new managers and at the same time benefit from the counsel of a recently retired colleague.

MANAGEMENT EDUCATION

Much of the learning to be a manager is learned through personal experience (Hill, 1992). Yet management performance can be hindered by a specific knowledge deficit. For example, the manager may lack business skills or knowledge about legal aspects of supervision. Most healthcare organizations have little or no management orientation. Instead of depending on others for management development, a manager should identify areas where competence will require new information and actively pursue acquiring this information through educational programs, workshops, books, and professional journals. While the majority of nurse managers have no education beyond their basic nursing preparation (Dienemann and Shaffer, 1993), graduate education in nursing administration and business is a valuable professional investment.

Reading professional books and journals and attending conferences are effective management education strategies.

FROM ROLE TRANSITION TO ROLE TRIUMPH

Developing an intimate relationship can be a difficult process but the majority of people still value relationships enough to make the effort. Making the transition and transformation into a management role is also worth the effort. Leading lives of integrity and commitment, nurse managers set examples, bringing out the best in staff nurses and thereby multiplying their influence on quality patient care. The self-assessment on page 474 is designed to determine readiness for management.

Self-Assessment

Respond to each item using the scale. Add up your score.
1 = strongly disagree
2 = disagree
3 = unsure
4 = agree
5 = strongly agree
1. I am responsible for my own professional development.
2. I feel confident about my ability to learn the skills I need to be an effective manager.
3. I am able to balance multiple priorities and activities.
4. I have a strong psychological desire to influence others.
5. I can develop a personal network of support.
   There is no magical score that indicates your readiness for management. A person who is unsure in every category will score 15. A score of 20 or above indicates that you are confident that you could master the management role. If you currently have a mentor, ask that person to respond to each item to analyze your abilities. Compare those responses with your own. Do you have a realistic view of yourself?

CHAPTER CHECKLIST

Role transition is a process that takes time and energy—two scarce resources for nurse managers. Knowing what to expect and how to facilitate the process can speed role transition and minimize the expenditure of energy as the nurse manager negotiates new roles.

- Responsibilities, opportunities, expectations, lines of communication, and support are aspects common to all roles. When considering a management role, gather information about each of these aspects.
- Mintzberg describes managerial roles as being either interpersonal, informational, or decisional.
  - The interpersonal roles are figurehead, leader, and liaison.
  - Monitor, disseminator, and spokesperson are the roles where the emphasis is on collecting and sharing information.
  - Information is needed to make decisions in the management roles of entrepreneur, resource allocator, disturbance handler, and negotiator.
- Role transition is a process of unlearning old roles and learning new roles.
  - The phases of role transition are as follows:
    - role preview
    - role acceptance
    - role exploration
    - role discrepancy
    - role development
    - role internalization.

- The phase of role preview is similar to dating in that both parties present their best characteristics in order to make a favorable impression.
- Commitment to a relationship is analogous to role acceptance, a public announcement of a mutual decision to initiate a contract.
- Role exploration compares to the honeymoon phase of an intimate relationship.
- Role discrepancy has its roots in the disillusionment experienced when role expectations do not match role performance.
- Role development is a time of resolution, when role expectations are negotiated and performance is adjusted to approximate expectations.
- A maturing relationship is similar to role internalization; during role internalization, the performance of the role is congruent with one's own beliefs.

■ Commitment, character, and self-respect are internal resources that can facilitate the process of role transition.

■ Role negotiation involves communicating with your supervisor to come to an agreement as to role expectations.

■ Mentors can provide career and psychosocial functions enhancing the career development of the manager.

■ Educational programs provide information needed by nurses to fulfill management roles.

TERMS TO KNOW

- decisional management roles
- informational management roles
- interpersonal management roles
- mentor
- role development
- role discrepancy
- role internalization
- role negotiation
- role transition

REFERENCES

Covey, S.R. (1990). *Principle-Centered Leadership*. New York: Simon and Schuster.

Dienemann, J., & Shaffer, C. (1993). Nurse manager characteristics and skills: Curriculum implications. *NursingConnections, 6*(2), 15–23.

Hill, L.A. (1992). *Becoming a Manager: Mastering a New Identity*. New York: Penguin.

Kaponya, P. (1990). *How to Survive the First 90 Days at a New Company*. Hawthorne, NJ: Career Press.

Kram, K.E. (1985). *Mentoring at Work: Developmental Relationships in Organizational Life*. Glenview, IL: Scott, Foresman.

Miner, J.B. (1975). *The Challenge of Managing*. Philadelphia: W.B. Saunders.

Mintzberg, H. (1975). The manager's job: Folklore and fact. *Harvard Business Review, 53*(4), 49–61.

Parsloe, E. (1992). *Coaching, Mentoring, and Assessing*. London: Kogan Page.

Westmoreland, D. (1993). Nurse managers' perspectives of their work: Connection and relationship. *Journal of Nursing Administration, 23*(1), 60–64.

SUGGESTED READINGS

Armstrong, M. (1988). *How to be an Even Better Manager.* New York: Nichols.

Bethel, S. M. (1990). *Making a Difference: Twelve Qualities that Make You a Leader.* New York: Berkley.

Bridges, F.J. (1993). *So You Want to be a Manager?* Decatur, GA: Educational Services for Management Books.

Cicarelli, J. (1993). The secret of management. *Management Review, 82*(8), 40.

Darling, L.W. (1985). What to do about toxic mentors. *Journal of Nursing Administration, 15*(5), 43–44.

Darling, L.W., & McGrath, L. (1983). Minimizing the promotion trauma. *Journal of Nursing Administration, 13*(9), 14–19.

Gibbs, S., & Megginson, D. (1993). Inside corporate mentoring schemes: A new agenda of concerns. *Personnel Review, 22*(1), 40–54.

Graen, G.B. (1989). *Unwritten Rules for your Career: The 15 Secrets for Fast-Track Success.* New York: John Wiley.

Holloran, S.D. (1993). Mentoring: The experiences of nursing service executives. *Journal of Nursing Administration,* 23(2), 49–54.

Holton, B., & Holton, C. (1992). *The Manager's Short Course.* New York: John Wiley.

Kriegel, R.J., & Patler, L. (1991). *If it Ain't Broke . . . Break it!* New York: Warner Books.

McCormack, M.M. (1984). *What They Don't Teach You in Harvard Business School.* New York: Bantam.

Pendola, C.J. (1993). A professional manager's view of the art of management. *The CPA Journal, 63*(1), 69–70.

Popper, M., & Lipshitz, R. (1992). Coaching on leadership. *Leadership and Organizational Development Journal, 13*(7), 15–18.

Waitley, D. (1987). *Being the Best.* Nashville, TN: Oliver Nelson.

CHAPTER 24

POWER, POLITICS, AND INFLUENCE

Karen Kelly Schutzenhofer, R.N., Ed.D., C.N.A.A.

PREVIEW

This chapter describes how power and politics influence the roles of leaders and managers. It focuses on contemporary concepts of power, empowerment, types of power exercised by nurses, key factors in developing a powerful image, and personal and organizational strategies for exercising power. Having the opportunity to relate to politics in the workplace is critical for effective leadership and management.

OBJECTIVES

- Apply the concept of power to leadership and management in nursing.
- Employ different types of power in the exercise of nursing leadership.
- Develop a power image for effective nursing leadership.
- Choose appropriate strategies for exercising power to influence the politics of the work setting, professional organizations, and legislatures.

QUESTIONS TO CONSIDER

- What kind of image does the phrase "a powerful nurse" conjure up in your mind?
- Do you ever think of yourself as a powerful nurse?
- What factors, persons, and events have influenced your development as a nurse?
- What kinds of behaviors do you observe in people that tell you whether they are powerful? Which of these behaviors do you consider socially desirable? Which are undesirable?
- What are your own powerful behaviors?
- What are your beliefs and values about power and politics in organizations?

A Manager's Viewpoint

Why is it important for nurses to exercise power? I can't manage effectively unless nurses exercise power! Nurses must be able to make decisions and function independently to get the work done. I can't provide total supervision to every nurse at every moment, nor would I want to! Exercising one's professional judgment is the exercise of power. I expect every nurse to be able to make decisions, to think about what might happen next, to use his or her expertise.

I think the manager's role is primarily to provide guidance and support. If nurses exercise professional judgment, power, then I only need to provide that guidance. I don't have to provide constant supervision; that shouldn't be the manager's role if you are working with a group of professionals. I can't think of a more frustrating experience than trying to manage a group of nurses who view themselves as powerless.

The exercise of power allows people to be creative and innovative. They are free to think, to resolve old problems with new ideas. They empower one another, thus enabling one another to be more creative and innovative. Powerful people are highly self-confident. They don't have to worry constantly about the "what-ifs" that haunt powerless people. They recognize that they are not infallible; they assume responsibility for their own mistakes, learn from them and move on.

I want powerful nurses to work for me and with me. They energize you as a manager, and they empower one another and the patients and families for whom they care.

Ann Fingerhood, M.H.A., R.N.
Staffing Office Manager
St. Louis, Missouri

INTRODUCTION

The profession of nursing was born in the United States at a time when women had limited legal rights (for example, most were prohibited from voting and many could not own property). Women were viewed as neither powerful nor political; in the late nineteenth century, *feminine* and *powerful* were practically contradictory terms. In the twentieth century, as the status and role of women have changed in contemporary American society, so have the status and role of nurses. As the economic and social power of women has evolved, so has the power of nurses.

HISTORY

history

Power was once considered almost a taboo in nursing. In the profession's earliest years, the exercise of power was considered inappropriate, unladylike, and unprofessional. Many decisions about nursing education and practice were often made by persons outside of nursing (Ashley, 1976). Nurses began to exercise their collective power with the rise of nursing leaders like Lillian Wald, Isabel Stewart, Annie Goodrich, Lavinia Dock, M. Adelaide Nutting, and Isabel Hampton Robb, and the development of organizations that evolved into the American Nurses Association and the National League for Nursing.

Many social, technological, scientific, and economic trends have shaped nursing, nurses, and our ability to exercise power over the last century. As we move toward the next century, nurses must be skilled and confident in exercising power to ensure the continuing development of the profession. However, even in the contemporary profession of nursing, there are nurses who see themselves as powerless and oppressed, who demonstrate aspects of oppressed group behavior. Like many politically and economically oppressed people, some nurses still persist in engaging in intragroup conflicts (e.g., "infighting") and they distance themselves from other nurses (e.g., the failure of many nurses to join professional organizations) (Roberts, 1983). Hence, nurses have a continued need to expand their understanding of the concept of power and to develop their skills in exercising power. Avoiding involvement in the politics of nursing, either in the workplace or in the profession at large, limits the power of the individual nurse and the profession as a collective whole.

politics

Some nurses are still uncomfortable about politics, treating "politics" as if it is a "dirty" word. Politics can be defined in many ways (e.g., the science of government, the process of allocation of scarce resources, or a process of formal human interactions). **Politics** is simply a process of human interaction within organizations. Politics permeates all organizations, including workplaces, legislatures, professions, and even families. Young children often learn that one parent is more likely than the other to give permission for special activities and more likely to buy toys and other desired items. They quickly learn to ask permission or ask for a desired item from that parent before asking the other. This is an unwritten political rule in many families.

Political activism is a powerful form of professional involvement. Kalisch and Kalisch (1982) describe four levels of political participation or activism:

apathetics, who engage in little or no political activity, may not even be registered to vote, and, if registered, they are unlikely to vote;

spectators, who vote, may wear a political button or display a political bumper sticker, and engage in political discussions with family and friends;

transitionals, who attend meetings and rallies and other political events, lobby their legislators, and contribute to political campaigns and political actions committees (PACs); and

gladiators, who work in political campaigns of candidates, solicit campaign funds, become active within a political party, or run for political office. (pp. 315–316)

These same levels of political activism can be applied to professional involvement in nursing:

apathetics, who belong to no professional organizations, serve on no committees in the workplace; if assigned to such a committee, they fail to do the work of the committee;

spectators, who pay dues to one or more professional organizations, but rarely, if ever, attend meetings or serve on committees; or they serve on committees in the workplace occasionally and, perhaps, reluctantly; they read an occasional article on national issues and trends in nursing and discuss these with colleagues;

transitionals, who are actively involved in local professional organizations and may attend state and national conventions of these organizations; they read extensively about trends and issues in nursing and knowledgeably discuss these with colleagues; they assume leadership roles on committees and task forces in the workplace and in professional organizations; and

gladiators, who serve in leadership roles in professional organizations on the state and national level.

Not surprisingly, nurses who are active participants in the politics of the profession of nursing tend also to be involved in legislative politics because of the close interaction of the two forms of political activism.

political activism

FOCUS ON POWER

Power comes from the Latin word *potere,* to be able. Simply defined, **power** is the ability to influence others in the effort to achieve goals. Nurses have sometimes viewed power as if it were something immoral, corrupting, and totally contradictory to the caring nature of nursing. However, the above definition demonstrates the essential nature of power to nursing. When providing health teaching to patients and their families, the nurse's goal is to provide needed information and to change behavior to promote optimum health. That is the exercise of power in nursing practice. Nurses regularly influence patients in an effort to improve their health status as an essential element of nursing practice. Changing a colleague's behavior by instructing her about a new policy being implemented on the nursing unit is another example of how a nurse can exercise power.

Social scientists have studied the use and abuse of power in human organizations. They have analyzed and categorized the sources and applications of power in human experience. Hersey, Blanchard, and Natemeyer (1979) offer one formulation on the bases of social power. They identified seven bases of power, which are most easily understood as sources or types of social power (see the box on page 482). These types of power are not mutually exclusive. They are frequently used in concert to exert influence on individuals or groups.

Nurses use all of these types of power frequently in both clinical practice and management. Nurses who teach parents about the care of their newborn use *expert* and *information* power by virtue of the information they share with par-

power

types of power

EXERCISE 24-1
Recall a recent opportunity you had to observe the work of an expert nurse. Think about that nurse's interactions with patients, family members, nursing colleagues, and other professionals. What kinds of power did you observe this nurse exercise? What did the nurse do that suggested to you "this is a powerful person?"

Types of Social Power

Coercive power: based on fear, coercion, and the ability to punish. Parents are viewed as powerful by children because of their ability to punish inappropriate behavior.

Reward power: based on the ability to grant rewards and favors. Parents are viewed as powerful by children also because of their ability to reward appropriate behavior.

Expert power: results from the knowledge and skills one possesses that are needed by others. A professor is viewed as the expert within the classroom and as a relatively powerful person.

Legitimate power: possessed by virtue of one's position with an organization or status within a group. The President of the United States is viewed around the world as powerful person as a result of election to this office.

Referent power: results from one's followers' desire to identify with a powerful person. Teenagers may dress like their favorite rock stars in order to copy an aspect of the performers' behavior.

Information power: stems from one's possession of selected information that is needed by others. A student who seems to grasp the day's math assignment easily may be sought out by classmates for assistance with their homework.

Connection power: gained by association with people who are perceived as powerful. Some people go to political conventions and meetings just to be seen with people they perceive as politically powerful.

ents; they also exercise *legitimate* power because they are registered nurses and, thus, are accorded a certain status by society. New graduates are employed on probationary status until they successfully meet and demonstrate the initial clinical competencies of a position. They may view the nurse manager as exercising both *coercive* and *reward* power related to their evaluation for continued employment. Nursing faculty and skilled clinicians often serve as role models to nursing students. The faculty and clinicians exercise *referent* power as students emulate their behavior. Examples of *connection* power are evident at any kind of social gathering in the workplace. People of high status (e.g., vice presidents or directors) within an organization may be sought out for conversation by managers who want to move up the organizational hierarchy.

These types of power describe the potential for power. Having a high status position in an organization immediately provides stature, but power depends on the ability to accomplish goals within that position. While we frequently hear that "knowledge is power," power is derived from what we do with that knowledge (Curtin, 1989). Sharing knowledge expands one's power and, in turn, empowers our colleagues by giving them information or skills that they need to take action in a situation.

EMPOWERMENT

empowerment

Empowerment is a term that has come into common usage in nursing in recent years. It has been used extensively in the nursing literature related to administration and management; it is also highly relevant to the domain of clinical practice. **Empowerment** is the process by which we facilitate the participation of others in decision making and taking action within an environment where there is an equitable distribution of power. Empowerment is power sharing and a form of feminine-feminist leadership (Mason, Backer, and Georges, 1991). This concept of empowerment is consistent with the contemporary view of leadership, a paradigm that is exemplified by behaviors characteristic of nurses: facilitator, coach, teacher, and collaborator. These leadership skills are an essential component of professional nursing practice, whether a nurse is a clinician, an educator, a researcher, or an administrator/manager. Nursing leaders, whether in the employment setting or in professional organizations, exercise power in making professional judgments as they do their daily work.

Empowerment is the process by which power is shared with colleagues and patients as part of the nurse's exercise of power. This is in sharp contrast to traditional conceptualizations of power, a patriarchal model of power, which relies on coercion, hierarchy, authority, control, and force. Empowerment, by embracing a feminist conceptualization of power, emphasizes cooperation as a vital element for the exercise of power (Wheeler and Chinn, 1989). Nurses have too often viewed power as a finite quantity: "If I give you some of my power, I will have less." Empowerment emphasizes the notion that power grows when shared. Nurses who view power as finite will avoid cooperation with their colleagues and refuse to share their expertise. Nurses who conceptualize power as infinite are strong collaborators who gain satisfaction by helping their colleagues expand their expertise and their power base.

cooperation

The empowerment of nurses makes truly professional practice possible, the kind of professional practice that is satisfying to both managers and clinicians. Empowered clinicians are essential for effective nursing management, just as empowered managers set the stage for excellence in clinical practice. Encouraging a reticent colleague to be an active participant in committee meetings serves to empower that nurse. Guiding a novice nurse in exercising professional judgment empowers both the manager and the novice clinician. Coaching a patient on how to be more assertive with a physician who is reluctant to answer the patient's questions is another form of empowerment. Teaching a newly diagnosed diabetic patient and the family about diabetic care is an exercise both of the nurse's expert and legitimate power and of the empowerment of the patient and family.

professional practice

EXERCISE 24-2
Think about a recent clinical experience when you empowered a patient. What did you do for and/or with the patient (and family) that was empowering? How did you feel about your own actions in this situation? How did the patient respond?

STRATEGIES FOR DEVELOPING A POWERFUL IMAGE

As Margaret Thatcher, former prime minister of Great Britain, said, "Being powerful is like being a lady. If you have to tell people you are, you aren't."

The most basic power strategy is the development of a powerful image. Lady Thatcher's statement emphasizes the importance of this powerful image. If nurses think they are powerful, others will view them as powerful; if they view themselves as powerless, so will others. A sense of self-confidence is a strong foundation in developing one's "power image," and it is essential for successful political efforts in the workplace or within the profession. Such self-confidence is simply the belief that one has the power to make things happen (Grainger, 1990). Several key factors contribute to one's power image:

self-confidence

- Self-image: thinking of one's self as powerful and effective;
- Grooming and dress: well-groomed hair and face, and clothing and appearance are neat, clean, and appropriate to the situation;
- Good manners: treating people with courtesy and respect;

- Body language: good posture, gestures that avoid too much drama, good eye contact, confident movement; and
- Speech: a firm, confident voice, good grammar and diction, an appropriate vocabulary and good communication skills.

Strategies for Developing a Powerful Image

- Self-image
- Grooming and dress
- Speech
- Body language
- Belief in power as a positive force
- Belief in value of nursing to society
- Career commitment
- Continuing professional education

attitudes and beliefs

Attitudes and beliefs are another important aspect of a powerful image; they reflect one's values. Believing that power is a positive force in nursing is essential to one's powerful image. It is also important to believe firmly in nursing's value to society and the centrality of nursing's contribution to the healthcare delivery system. Powerful nurses do not allow the phrase "I'm just a nurse" in their vocabulary. Behavior reflects one's pride in the profession of nursing. This not only increases a nurse's own power, but also helps to empower nursing colleagues.

career commitment

Make a commitment to nursing as a career. Nursing is a profession; professions offer careers, not just a series of positions. For a long time, nursing marketed itself to recruits as the perfect preparation for marriage and family. Even some contemporary job advertisements hint at romance as an outcome of employment at the agency featured. Some people still view nurses only as members of an occupation who drop in and out of employment, not as members of a profession with a long-term career commitment. Having a career commitment does not preclude leaving employment temporarily for family, education, or other demands. Having a career commitment implies that a nurse views himself or herself first and foremost as a member of the discipline of nursing with an obligation to make a contribution to the profession. Status as an employee of a particular hospital, home health agency, long-term-care facility, or other healthcare agency is secondary to the person's status as a member of the profession of nursing.

continued development

Value continuing education in nursing. Valuing education is one of the hallmarks of a profession. The continuing development of one's professional skills and knowledge is an empowering experience, preparing the nurse to make decisions with the support of an expanding body of knowledge. Seminars, workshops, and conferences offer opportunities for continued professional growth and empowerment. Returning to school for higher degrees is also a powerful growth experience and reflects commitment to the profession of nursing. An additional advantage of participating in educational experiences is that it creates opportunities for networking, a strategy that will be discussed later in this chapter.

Professional grooming and dress are basic strategies for developing a powerful image.

PERSONAL POWER STRATEGIES

Developing a collection of power strategies, or power tools, is an important aspect of personal empowerment. These strategies should be used in situations that demand the exercise of leadership. Such strategies are techniques for building a professional power base and for developing political skills within an organization (see the box on page 486). They also indicate to others that one is a powerful nurse and a leader. This box identifies additional personal power strategies beyond those discussed in this section.

COMMUNICATION SKILLS

The most basic tool is effective verbal communication skills, which help define a power image. These are the same communication skills nurses learn to ensure effective interaction with patients and families. Listening skills are essential management skills. Just as the clinician listens to the patient to collect assessment data, the manager uses listening skills to assess and evaluate. Managers who are good listeners develop reputations for being fair and consistent. Listening to recurring themes related to minor issues of staff dissatisfaction in informal conversations may enable the manager to take action before a staff crisis occurs.

Verbal and nonverbal skills are important personal power strategies; the ability to assess these messages is a critical power strategy. Experts in communication estimate that 90 percent of the messages we communicate to others are nonverbal. When nonverbal and verbal messages conflict, the nonverbal

verbal

nonverbal

message is more powerful. The basic lessons on the power of nonverbal communication most nurses learn in an introductory psychiatric course are relevant in all nursing arenas!

Additional Personal Power Strategies

- Be honest.
- Always be courteous; it makes other people feel good!
- Smile whenever appropriate; it puts people at ease.
- Accept responsibility for your own mistakes and learn from them.
- Be a risk taker.
- Win and lose gracefully.
- Learn to be comfortable with conflict and ambiguity; they are both normal states of the human condition.
- Give credit to others where credit is due.
- Develop the ability to take constructive criticism gracefully; learn to let destructive criticism "roll off your back."
- Use business cards when introducing yourself to new contacts and collect the business cards of those you meet when networking.

NETWORKING

network

Networking is an important power strategy and political skill. A **network** is a system of contacts that are developed, nurtured, and maintained as sources of information, advice, and moral support (Schutzenhofer, 1992). Networking supports the empowerment of participants through interaction and the refinement of their interpersonal skills. Most nurses have relatively limited networks within the organizations where they are employed. The tend to have lunch or coffee with those people with whom they work most closely. One strategy to expand a workplace network is to have lunch or coffee with someone from another department, including managers from non-nursing departments, at least two or three times a month.

professional organizations

Active participation in nursing organizations is the most effective method of establishing a professional network outside one's place of employment. Participation in professional organizations can propel a nurse into the politics of nursing. State and district nurses associations offer an excellent opportunity to develop a network that includes nurses from a variety of clinical and functional areas. Membership in specialty organizations, especially organizations for nurse managers and executives, provide the opportunity to network with nurses with similar expertise and interests. Additionally, membership in civic, volunteer, and special interest groups and participation in educational programs (for example, formal academic programs and conferences) also provide networking opportunities.

The successful networker identifies a core of networking partners who are particularly skilled, insightful, and eager to support the development of colleagues. These partners need to be nurtured. Send them articles on topics of interest to them. Call them to keep in touch if face-to-face contact is sporadic or infrequent. Never argue the merit of advice given by a networking partner;

Research Perspective

Holloran, S.D. (1993). Mentoring: The experience of nursing service executives. Journal of Nursing Administration, 23(2), 49–54.

This study examined the impact of mentoring on nurse executives. The concept of mentoring has become very popular in the nursing literature in recent years, yet little research has been done to measure the impact of mentoring. The sample consisted of 393 female nurse executives from teaching hospitals that are members of the American Hospital Association. A questionnaire of twenty-eight forced-choice items and four critical incident questions was returned by 274 of the nruse executives. Over 70 percent of these executives had experienced mentoring. The respondents reported a variety of positive experiences/mentor behaviors. The five most commonly reported were the following: showed confidence in me; encouraged independent decision making; inspired me; demonstrated behaviors I tried to imitate; and provided opportunities for me to demonstrate what I could do (p. 50). The critical incidents reported in the study revealed four common themes: encouragement and recognition of mentee's potential, provision of opportunities and responsibilities to encouarge development; inspiring role model; and assistance with career opportunities (pp. 51–52). The misuse of power was also evident in some mentoring relationships. Three common themes of this misuse of the mentor's power were overpossessive behavior, rejection, and oppression (p. 52). The mentoring relationship provided these nurse executives with the benefits of instilling self-confidence (power of belief); learning the use of power; developing expertise in organizational, business, and management skills; and others. The mentored executives viewed their experiences as critical to their career development and advancement.

Implications for Practice

These relationships were not just casual work relationships. They were intense relationships in which the mentor made a commitment to the development of the novice executive. The respondents emphasized the powerful impact these mentoring relationships had on their careers.

consider its value later. Be reasonable in making requests for help or information; ask for only one thing at a time and be specific about what is wanted. Most importantly, be prepared to reciprocate with networking partners (Schutzenhofer, in press).

MENTORING

In recent years mentoring has become a driving force in nursing. Mentors are competent, experienced professionals who develop a relationship with a novice for the purpose of providing advice, support, information, and feedback in order to encourage the development of the individual (Huston and Marquis, 1988). Mentoring has been an important element in the career development of men in business, academia, and selected professions. Mentoring has become a significant power strategy for women in general and for nurses in particular during the last twenty years. Mentoring provides novices with expanded access to information, power, and career opportunities. Mentors have historically been a critical asset to novices trying to negotiate workplace and professional politics. This chapter's "Research Perspective" describes the impact of mentoring on nurse executives.

mentors

EXERCISE 24-4
You encounter an old friend in a restaurant. You greet one another warmly, each stating how good it is to see the other. Yet your friend visibly backs away when you extend your arms to embrace. What is your immediate reaction? Despite the warm words of greeting, do you question your old friend's sincerity because of the strong nonverbal message regarding physical contact? Consider other situations you have experienced recently when words and actions contradict one another. Which message, the verbal or the nonverbal, did you accept as the person's "real" communication to you? Practice with a friend: pretend you are greeting a visitor to your home, a colleague, or a patient. In the first trial, state your greeting warmly, extend your hand to shake the other person's hand, smile, and make eye contact. In the second trial, use the same words of greeting, but use an angry tone of voice, avoid eye contact, and fold your arms across your chest while moving one step back from the other person. Observe the physical actions and listen carefully, especially to the tone of voice. Repeat the exercise, switching roles. Discuss your response to these interactions.

long-term goals

expertise

Mentoring is an empowering experience for both mentors and novices. The process of seeking out mentors is an exercise in growth for novices or proteges. Mentors frequently come from one's professional networks. Some mentors select their proteges; sometimes the reverse is true. Novices may attract mentors by implementing these strategies:
- Demonstrate one's developing expertise.
- Develop a sensitivity to the attention of powerful people within the organization.
- Volunteer to serve on committees and do good work.
- Openly discuss one's professional goals and desire to grow.
- Ask experienced and talented people within one's network for advice and help (Black, 1989).

Novices learn new skills from influential mentors, gain in self-confidence, and may eventually serve as mentors to the next generation of novices. Mentors gain stature within their peer groups, extend their scope of influence through relationships with novices, refine their professional skills, and gain self-confidence through the satisfaction gained in observing the development of novices.

GOAL SETTING

Goal setting is another power strategy. Every nurse knows about setting goals. Students learn to devise patient care goals or patient outcomes as part of the care planning process. Nurses may be expected to write annual goals for performance reviews at work. Even a project at home, for example, painting rooms, may necessitate setting goals, like painting a room each day of one's vacation. Goals help one to know if what was planned was actually accomplished. Likewise, a successful nursing career needs goals to define what one wants to achieve as a nurse. Without such goals, one can wander endlessly through a series of jobs without a real sense of satisfaction. As the Cheshire Cat told Alice during her trip through Wonderland: Any road will take you there if you don't know where you are going.

Well-defined, long-term goals may be hard to formulate early in a career. For example, few new graduates know specifically that they want to be chief nurse executives, deans, managers, or researchers. Yet, eventually some will choose those career paths. However, developing such a vision early in a career is an important personal power strategy. Once this career vision is developed, one must create opportunities to move toward that vision. Such planning is empowering; it puts the nurse in charge, rather than letting a career unfold by chance. Having this sense of vision is consistent with the commitment to a career in nursing that is part of developing a power image. This vision is always subject to change as new opportunities are experienced, and new interests, knowledge, and skills are gained. Education and work experiences are tools for achieving the vision of one's career.

DEVELOPING EXPERTISE

As noted earlier in this chapter, expertise is one of the bases of power. Developing expertise in nursing is an important power strategy. Expertise must not be limited to clinical knowledge. Leadership and communication skills, for example, are essential to the effective exercise of power in a range of nursing roles. Education and practice provide the means for developing such expertise in any of the domains of nursing: clinical practice, education, research, and management. Developing expertise expands one's power among nursing colleagues, other professional colleagues, and patients. A high level of expertise can make one nearly indispensable within an organization. This is a very powerful position to have within any organization, whether it is the workplace or a professional association. A high level of expertise can also lead to a high level of visibility within an organization.

HIGH VISIBILITY

This strategy of high visibility within an organization also requires volunteering to serve as a member or the chairperson of committees and task forces. High visibility can be nurtured by attending the open meetings of committees and other groups of which one is not a member in the workplace, professional associations, or the community. Review the agendas of such meetings if they are circulated ahead of the meeting. Use opportunities both before and after meetings to share one's expertise, providing valuable information and ideas to members and leaders of such groups. Share this expertise at open meetings when appropriate. Speak up confidently, but have something relevant to say. Be concise and precise; members of the committee will ask for more information if they need it.

committees

EXERCISE 24-5

Almost everyone has attended a class, meeting, or workshop with a "know-it-all." These group members are capable of commenting on everything at great length without saying anything of substance (for example, Cliff, the postal worker on the television show "Cheers.") These self-appointed experts tend to create great tension within a group: members begin to shift in their seats, give one another frustrated looks, and may eventually lose interest in the topic at hand. In a highly effective group with strong leadership, someone may intervene to end the speaker's soliloquy. No matter how this situation is resolved, the unfortunate speaker at least suffers a loss of respect from members of the group. Compare this unfortunate scenario to another kind of experience you may have had. A member of the group, or perhaps a nonmember who is simply sitting in on the meeting, offers a comment or piece of information that energizes the group and propels them toward more effective action. This individual gains the respect of those in attendance by virtue of this valued contribution. Compare your reactions to these two types of experiences. How do you feel? Are you embarrassed by or for the first kind of speaker? Why? Compare your interactions with both kinds of speakers after these kinds of events. Do you handle these situations differently? Why?

EXERCISING POWER AND INFLUENCE IN THE WORKPLACE AND OTHER ORGANIZATIONS

To use influence effectively in any organization, understanding how the system works and developing organizational strategies are critical. Developing *organizational savvy* includes identifying the real decision makers and those persons who have a high level of influence with the decision makers. Recognize the informal leaders within any organization. In the workplace, an influential senior staff nurse may have more decision-making power than the nurse manager on significant aspects of the nursing unit's operations. Secretaries of chief nurse executives (CNE), for example, are usually very powerful people, although they are not always recognized as such. The CNE's secretary has a great deal of control over information, making decisions about who gets to meet with the nurse executive and when, screening incoming and outgoing mail, letting the CNE know when a letter or memo needs

savvy

immediate attention, or placing another memo on the bottom of the stack of mail for review at a later time.

COLLEGIALITY AND COLLABORATION

unity

Nursing does not exist in a vacuum, nor do nurses work in isolation from one another, other professionals, and support personnel. Nurses function within a wide range of organizations, such as schools, hospitals, community health organizations, government agencies, professional associations, and universities. Nursing's historic lack of unity on important issues, such as basic educational preparation for entry into professional practice, has weakened our power base and political clout in the healthcare and educational systems (Huston and Marquis, 1988). Developing a sense of unity requires each nurse to act collaboratively and collegially in the workplace and in other organizations (e.g., professional associations). Collegiality demands that nurses value the accomplishments of nursing colleagues and express a sincere interest in the efforts of colleagues. Turning to nursing colleagues for advice and support empowers them and expands one's own power base at the same time. Unity of purpose does not contradict diversity of thought. It is important for colleagues to agree that disagreement based on differences of ideas, not on the basis of personalities, is healthy for professional growth (Vance, 1985). One does not have to be a friend to everyone who is a colleague. Collegiality demands mutual respect, not friendship.

collegiality

volunteerism

Collaboration and collegiality require that nurses work collectively to ensure that the voice of nursing is heard in the workplace. Volunteer to serve on committees and task forces in the workplace, not only within the nursing department but also on organization-wide committees. Get involved in the politics of the organization. If the organization uses shared governance or continuous quality improvement models, get involved in these councils, committees, task forces, and work groups to share your energy, ideas, and expertise. Many organizations have instituted joint practice committees that bring together nurses and physicians to improve the quality of interdisciplinary collaboration and, in turn, the quality of patient care. Become an active, productive member of such groups.

AN EMPOWERING ATTITUDE

social status

Demonstrate a positive and professional attitude about being a nurse to nursing colleagues, patients, and their families and other colleagues in the workplace. This attitude is very contagious and can empower colleagues. A power image is an important aspect of demonstrating this positive professional attitude. The current trend of nurses to identify themselves by first name only may decrease one's power image in the eyes of physicians, patients, and others. When physicians are always addressed as "Dr." but are free to address others by their first names, a notable difference in social status is apparent, limiting the collegial relationship between physician and nurse (Campbell-Heider and Hart, 1993). The use of first names among colleagues is not inappropriate, so long as everyone is playing by the same rules. Managers may want to enhance the empowerment of their staffs by encouraging them to introduce themselves as "Dr.," "Ms.," or "Mr." Arriving at work, appointments, or meetings on time; looking neat and appropriately attired for the work setting or other professional situation; and speaking positively about one's work are examples of how easy it is to demonstrate a positive professional attitude.

DEVELOPING COALITIONS

The exercise of power is often directed at creating change. While an individual can often be effective at exercising power and creating change, in many situations creating change within most organizations requires collective action. Coalition building is a very effective political strategy for collective action. **Coalitions** are groups of individuals or organizations that join together temporarily around a common goal. This goal often focuses on an effort to effect change. The networking between organizations that results in coalition building requires members of one group to reach out to members of other groups. This often occurs at the leadership level and may come through formal mechanisms, such as letters that identify an issue or problem, a shared interest, around which a coalition could be built. For example, a state nurses' association may invite the leaders of organizations interested in child health (for example, organizations of pediatric nurses, public health nurses and physicians, elementary school teachers, and day-care providers) to discuss collaborative support for a legislative initiative to improve access to immunization programs in urban and rural areas. Informal mechanisms may also lead to coalition building. For example, members of a practice council at a small hospital are developing a parent education program to increase awareness about immunizations in the community served by the hospital. Public health nurses in the community are developing a similar program. A nurse who serves on the practice council mentions this effort to a friend who is a public health nurse. They both go back to their own work groups, informing their colleagues about the other group's work. A coalition of the two groups of nurses creates a very effective community education program by working collaboratively and collectively. The coalition of over sixty nursing and healthcare organizations that joined together to support "Nursing's Agenda for HealthCare Reform" offers a vivid example of such collective action (American Nurses Association, 1991).

Enlisting the support of others who share the same goal or interest often results in greater success in effecting change and exercising power in the workplace and within other organizations. Expanding networks in the workplace, as suggested earlier in this chapter, facilitates creating a coalition by developing a pool of candidates for coalition building before they are needed. Invite people with common goals to lunch or coffee. Discuss this shared interest and gain the commitment of the individual. Meet over lunch or coffee with members of the committee or task force that is working on this issue. Share ideas on how to create the desired change most effectively.

Coalition building is an important skill for involvement in legislative politics. Nursing organizations frequently use coalition building when dealing with state legislatures and Congress. Changes in nurse practice acts to expand opportunities for advanced nursing practice have been accomplished in many states through coalition building. Such changes are often opposed by state medical societies or the state agencies that license physicians. Efforts by a single nursing organization (for example, a state nurses association or a nurse practitioners organization), representing a limited nursing constituency, often lack the clout to overcome opposition by the unified voice of the official voice of the state's physicians. However, the unified effort of a coalition of nursing organizations, other healthcare organizations, and consumer groups can be very powerful in effecting change through legislation (see the boxes on pages 492 and 493).

coalitions

EXERCISE 24-6
How do you routinely introduce yourself to patients, families, physicians, and other colleagues? A powerful and positive approach involves making eye contact with each individual, shaking hands, and introducing yourself by saying, "I'm Ann Jones (Dan Jones), a registered nurse (or nursing student)." If you do not currently use this technique, try it out. Note any difference in the responses of people whom you meet using this technique in comparison with your usual approach.

legislative politics

> **Colorado Nurses Act Powerfully in the Workplace and With the Legislature**
>
> A group of public employee nurses in Colorado were threatened with pay cuts by the state legislature while their agencies were experiencing a vacancy rate of 17.5 percent and a 37.5 percent turnover rate. Legislators indicated that nurses were overpaid. Data on local nurses' salaries demonstrated that public employee nurses were paid significantly less than nurses in the private sector. The nurses hired a part-time lobbyist and lobbied legislators, the governor, and the public. When these efforts were unsuccessful, a large number of the nurses affected by the proposed pay cuts threatened to resign, since they could not strike as public employees. They took a major risk by tendering their resignations. However, in the end their risk taking paid off for them. The governor invoked his emergency powers to grant the nurses a 7.5 percent raise and other improvements (Meyer, 1992).

NEGOTIATING

negotiating

Negotiating, or bargaining, is another important skill for organizational power and political activity. It is a process of making trade-offs. Children are natural negotiators. Often they will initially ask their parents for more than what they are willing to accept in the way of privileges, toys, or activities. The logic is simple to children: ask for more than is reasonable and negotiate down to what you really want! Negotiating often works the same way within organizations. People will sometimes ask for more than what they want and be willing to accept less. In other situations, both sides will enter a negotiation asking for radically different things, but each may be willing to settle for a position that differs significantly from their original positions. In the simplest forms of bargaining, each participant has something that the other party values, for example, goods, services, or information. At the "bargaining table," each party presents an opening position and the process moves on until they

mutual agreement

reach a mutually agreeable result or until one or both parties walk away from the unsuccessful process.

Bargaining in the workplace may take many forms. Individuals may negotiate with a supervisor for a more desirable work schedule or with a peer to effect a schedule change so the nurse can attend an out-of-town conference. A nurse manager may sit at the bargaining table with the department director during budget planning to expand training hours for the nursing unit in the next year's budget. A group of nurses may bargain with nursing and hospital administration over wages, staffing levels, other working conditions, and the

collective bargaining

conditions and policies that govern clinical practice. This is called "collective bargaining," a specific type of negotiating that is regulated by both state and federal labor laws and that usually involves representation by a state nurses' association or a nursing or non-nursing labor union.

Successful negotiators are well informed about not only their own positions, but also those of the opposing side. Successful negotiators must be able to discuss the pros and cons of both positions. They are able to assist the other party in recognizing the costs versus the benefits of each position. These same skills are also essential to exercising power effectively with the arenas of professional and legislative politics.

Coalitions Create New Opportunities For Advanced Practice Nurses

In the 1993 legislative term, advanced practice nurses (APNs) made significant gains in both Kansas and Missouri. In Kansas, a coalition created by the Kansas State Nurses Association gained the support of physicians, organizations of APNs, and representatives of the American Association of Retired Persons to overcome the opposition of the Insurance Association and Kansas State Blue Cross/Blue Shield for legislation that provides direct reimbursement to APNs in urban areas. Legislation passed in 1990 already mandated direct reimbursement to APNs in rural areas by third-party payers (e.g., insurance companies, Medicare, and Medicaid) (Sebastian, 1993).

In Missouri, a coalition of nursing organizations, including the Missouri Nurses Association and the Missouri Organization of Nurse Executives, the state medical society, consumer groups, and the state hospital association, worked to perfect legislation to sanction collaborative practice between APNs and physicians, granted limited prescriptive privileges to APNs, and expanded school-based healthcare services by school nurses (Fulwinder, 1993).

EXERCISE 24-7
Consider a situation in which you engaged in bargaining or negotiating. Have you ever bought a car? Negotiating the price of the car is a great American tradition. Few people enter into the purchase of a car intending to pay the sticker price. Most sticker prices are set by the manufacturer at a level that gives the dealer room to negotiate the price down. Have you ever negotiated a schedule change at work/school? What was the trade-off you made in the process? How far did the other person move from his/her original position? What factors led to your success or failure in this negotiation?

CHAPTER CHECKLIST

Power was once a taboo issue in nursing. The exercise of power in nursing conflicted sharply with the historic feminine stereotypes that surrounded nursing. The evolving social and political status of women has also opened nursing to the exercise of power. Power is essential to the effective implementation of both the clinical and managerial roles of nurses.

- Contemporary concepts of power focus on power as influence and a force for collaboration rather than coercion, an infinite quality rather than a finite quantity.
  - Empowerment is a feminine-feminist process of power sharing and leadership.
  - Contemporary views of leadership in social systems are consistent with the concept of empowerment.
- Seven types of power exercised by nurses include:
  - coercive
  - reward
  - expert
  - legitimate
  - referent
  - information
  - connection.
- Key factors in developing a powerful image include:
  - self-confidence
  - body language
  - self-image
  - career commitment
  - grooming and dress
  - speech

- attitudes, beliefs, and values
- continuing professional education.

■ Key personal and organizational strategies for exercising power include:

- communication skills
- career goal setting
- high visibility
- a sense of unity
- coalition building
- networking
- expertise
- organizational savvy
- collaboration and collegiality
- negotiation skills
- mentoring
- an empowering attitude.

TERMS TO KNOW

- coalitions
- empowerment
- negotiating
- network
- politics
- power

REFERENCES

American Nurses' Association. (1991). *Nursing's Agenda for Health Care Reform* (PR-3 25M, revised). Kansas City, MO: American Nurses' Association.

Ashley, J.A. (1976). *Hospitals, Paternalism, and the Role of the Nurse.* New York: Teachers' College Press.

Black, K.S. (1989, September). Why it pays to have a mentor. *Working Mother,* pp. 33–34, 36.

Campbell-Heider, N., & Hart, C.A. (1993). Updating the nurses's bedside manner. *Image: Journal of Nursing Scholarship, 25,* 133–139.

Curtin, L.L. (1989). Powers: The traps of trappings. *Nursing Management, 20*(6), 7–8.

Fulwinder, K. (1993, September). First Lady praises Missouri legislation. *The American Nurse,* p. 10.

Grainger, R.D. (1990). Self-confidence: A feeling you can create. *American Journal of Nursing, 90*(10), 12.

Hersey, P., Blanchard, K., & Natemeyer, W. (1979). Situational leadership, perception and impact of power. *Group and Organizational Studies, 4,* 418–428.

Holloran, S.D. (1993). Mentoring: The experience of nursing service executives. *Journal of Nursing Administration, 23*(2), 49–54.

Huston, C.J., & Marquis, B. (1988). Ten attitudes and behaviors to overcome powerlessness. *Nursing Connections, 1*(2), 39–47.

Kalisch, B.J., & Kalisch, P.A. (1982). *Politics of Nursing.* Philadelphia: J.B. Lippincott.

Mason, D.J., Backer, B.A., & Georges, C.A. (1991). Toward a feminist model for the political empowerment of nurses. *Image: Journal of Nursing Scholarship, 23,* 72–77.

Meyer, C. (1992). Nursing on the political front. *American Journal of Nursing, 92*(10), 56–60, 63–64.

Roberts, S.J. (1983). Oppressed group behavior: Implications for nursing. *Advances in Nursing Sciences, 5,* 21–30.

Schutzenhofer, K.K. (1992). Essential for the year 2000. *Nursing Connections, 5*(1), 15–26.

——— (In press). Networking and professionalism. In Strader, M., Decker, P.J., eds. *Role Transition to Patient Care Management.* Norwalk, CT: Appleton & Lange.

Sebastian, L. (1993, September). Kansas nurses gain reimbursement in urban areas. *The American Nurse,* p. 10.

Vance, C.N. (1985). Political influence: Building effective interpersonal skills. In Mason, D.J., & Talbott, S.W., eds. *Political Action Handbook for Nurses: Changing the Workplace, Government, and Organizations, and Community.* Menlo Park, CA: Addison-Wesley, pp. 165–180.

Wheeler, C.E., & Chinn, P.L. (1989). *Peace and Power: A Handbook of Feminist Process,* 2nd ed. New York: National League for Nursing.

SUGGESTED READINGS

Ashley, J.A. (1980). Power in structured misogyny: Implications for the politics of care. *Advances in Nursing Science, 2,* 3–22.

Borman, J., & Biordi, D. (1992). Female nurse executive: Finally, at an advantage? *Journal of Nursing Administration, 22*(9), 37–41.

Costello-Nikitas, D.M., & Mason, D.J. (1992). Power and politics in health care organizations. In Decker, P.J., & Sullivan, E.J., eds. *Nursing Administration: A Micro/Macro Approach for Effective Nurse Executives.* Norwalk, CT: Appleton & Lange, pp. 45–67.

del Bueno, D. (1986). Power and policy in organizations. *Nursing Outlook, 34,* 124–128.

Fisher, R., Ury, W., & Patton, B. (1991). *Getting to Yes: Negotiating Agreement Without Giving In,* 2nd ed. New York: Penguin.

Flaherty, M.J. (1991). Global empowerment in nursing: Personal, professional, and environmental. *AORN Journal, 54,* 1200–1210.

Goldwater, M., & Zusy, M.J.L. (1990). *Prescription for Nurses: Effective Political Action.* St. Louis: C.V. Mosby.

Gorman, S., & Clark, N. (1986). Power and effective nursing practice. *Nursing Outlook, 34,* 129–134.

Hoelzel, C.B. (1989). Using structural power sources to increase influence. *Journal of Nursing Administration, 9*(11), 10–15.

Kalisch, B.J., & Kalisch, P.A. (1982). *Politics of Nursing.* Philadelphia: J.B. Lippincott.

Kippenbrock, T.A. (1992). Power at meetings: Strategies to move people. *Nursing Economics, 10,* 282–286.

Manthey, M. (1992). Leadership: A shifting paradigm. *Nurse Educator, 17*(5), 5, 14.

——— (1992). Power: Grace under pressure. *Nursing Management, 23*(4), 22–26.

Mason, D.J., & Talbott, S.W., eds. (1985). *Political Action Handbook for Nurses: Changing the Workplace, Government, and Organizations, and Community.* Menlo Park, CA: Addison-Wesley.

Pike, A.W. (1991). Moral outrage and moral discourse in nurse-physician collaboration. *Journal of Professional Nursing, 7,* 351–363.

Schorr, T., & Zimmerman, A., eds. (1988). *Making Choices, Taking Chances: Nurse Leaders Tell Their Stories.* St. Louis: C.V. Mosby.

Schutzenhofer, K.K., Shelley, S.R., & Pontious, S.L. (1992). Communication systems. In Decker, P.J., & Sullivan, E.J., eds. *Nursing Administration: A Micro/Macro Approach for Effective Nurse Executives.* Norwalk, CT: Appleton & Lange, pp. 185–206.

Wieczorek, R.R., ed. (1985). *Power, Politics, and Policy in Nursing.* New York: Springer.

Wolf, G.A. (1989). The effective use of influence. *Journal of Nursing Administration, 19*(11), 8–9.

CHAPTER 25

STRESS MANAGEMENT: THE BALANCING ACT

Nancy Beardslee, R.N., Ed. D.

PREVIEW

This chapter discusses causes of stress for the nurse manager and explains the reaction to stress, which helps illustrate the significance of mismanaged stress. Stress management includes using cognitive and psychosocial activities to decrease stress or enhance one's ability to handle stress. This chapter offers strategies that managers and staff members can use to cope with stress. Strong stress management skills are a vital component in managing and leading.

OBJECTIVES

- Define the term *stress*.
- Explore four causes of stress in nursing.
- Analyze selected strategies to decrease stress.
- Analyze the manager's role in helping staff to manage stress.

QUESTIONS TO CONSIDER

- What types of activities cause stress for you?
- How do you usually handle stress?
- What are new methods you can practice to handle stress better?
- If you have suggested a stress management strategy to someone else, how did you convey this help?

A Manager's Viewpoint

If I can't deal with stress then I lose my ability to lead and manage my units. I'm very aware that if I don't keep my stress under control that I may end up leaving my position.

I realize that a certain amount of stress is good; it keeps me on my toes. However, if the stress starts to build up and becomes overwhelming then my decision-making ability goes down. I'm unable to see things clearly and problems can just grow until we're at a crisis point.

What causes me the most stress is when the staff doesn't communicate in a professional manner with other health professionals. For example, they may have a treatment plan for one of the clients based on their assessment of and relationship with the patient. However, another health professional may come in and leave directions for a completely different approach that the nurse doesn't feel will be appropriate. I try to role model effective communication skills. I either talk with the nurse privately, or in a group I present the problem and present other ways to negotiate.

Another source of stress for nurses today is the economic threat of being dismissed. Managed care has meant a decrease in the number of available staff so that the patient-staff ratio is increasing dramatically. Staff are afraid to complain and ask for more help because they could be laid off. The insecurity of not knowing if you will keep your position is very stressful.

The two most important strategies for me to reduce my stress level are exercise and a support network. Although I work long hours I make it a priority to stop at the YMCA on the way home from work three times a week. I am less stressed when I exercise on a regular basis and I know I am more productive. And having a support network is wonderful. I have friends and colleagues who let me vent my frustrations and offer suggestions. I also work very hard at separating my work and home life. Unless there is a crisis I don't talk about all the little things that go on at work. I plan some fun activities and look forward to vacations a great deal. Just planning a vacation reduces stress. I find I'm much better at work if I haven't worried all night about work problems.

Laurie Izzo, R.N.
Charge Nurse
Mount Auburn Hospital
Boston, Massachusetts

INTRODUCTION

When nurses discuss being "stressed at work," they may mean many different things by the term *stress*. For one nurse, working with a new employee is "stressful," and for another nurse working with one half the usual number of staff is stressful. There are degrees and individual interpretations that give different responses to the term *stress*. The nurse manager is in the challenging role of balancing her personal and work stress in addition to the staff's stress.

STRESS

Edwards (1988) defines **stress** in the workplace as any characteristic of the job environment that poses a threat to the individual—either excessive demands or insufficient supplies to meet the needs. The individual appraises the situation as harmful, threatening, or challenging. There can be **external demands** from many sources such as the workplace, environment, economy, technology, and family. The sources of **internal demands** are also important to consider such as family, personal needs, health status, and self-esteem. Stress comes about when these demands tax or exceed the adaptive resources of an individual (Monat and Lazarus, 1991).

eustress A normal amount of stress is involved in everyday living and all people experience stress. **Eustress** is a term for the stress that enhances life. This term refers to the challenges that excite people to engage in activities and feel vitalized. However, when the stressors exceed resources, we experience the detrimental aspects of stress that are prevalent today. The term **burnout** means stress can no longer be handled and the behavior becomes dysfunctional. Maslach (1982) defines burnout as the loss of human caring. This can occur when nurses have expended all their energy and have no resources left to call upon. When the stressor exceeds resources there will be detrimental effects to the nurse or client or both unless the environment is changed or the nurse changes his/her reaction to it.

general adaptation syndrome Selye (1991) found that reactions to stress follow a pattern of flight or fight, which he named the **general adaptation syndrome.** Selye's theory simply stated is that there are three main components: alarm, resistance, and exhaustion or adaptation. When faced with a stressor, the first reaction is an increase in adrenalin and a resultant warning to all the body systems to be on the alert for danger. This happens in different degrees of response depending on the individual and occurs whether the demand is a positive one or negative one. For example, a promotion may be a positive stress but a nurse may still respond with various emotional, cognitive, and physical reactions such as **anxiety,** cognitive dissonance, or gastric pain. Perceived stress levels (reactions) vary from one person to another and depend on an individual's personal factors such as heredity, habits, personality, past experiences, illness, and previous coping mechanisms used (Marriner-Tomey, 1992).

Other theorists (Lazarus and Folkman, 1991) have studied job stress in a multidisciplinary approach. A combination of these approaches is demonstrated in Figure 25-1. This model presents the stages concept of Selye integrated with the range of individual reactions.

coping At stage 5 certain positive or negative coping mechanisms occur, such as exercise, cognitive self-talk and networking, alcohol abuse, or denial. **Coping** is

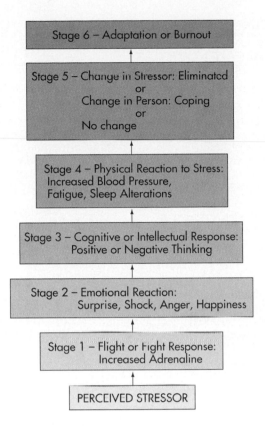

FIGURE 25-1
The stress diagram. [Based on Selye, H. (1991). History and present status of the stress concept. In Monat, A., & Lazarus, R., eds. *Stress and Coping: An Anthology.* New York: Columbia University Press, pp. 21–36.]

the immediate response of a person to a threatening situation (Lazarus and Folkman, 1991). Coping is described as dealing with problems or situations in a purposeful manner to promote well-being. One of the most effective coping strategies is social support. Belle (1991) discusses the positive role of support in times of stress. This chapter's "Research Perspective" discusses collegial support as a main factor in decreasing stress. The desired effect is that activities to decrease stress will be successful so that resolution or decrease of the stressors will occur (stage 6) and burnout will be avoided.

Responses to stress are sometimes categorized as either effective or ineffective depending on the results. Ineffective coping strategies that may work in the short-term process of alleviating stress are such things as drugs, alcohol, withdrawal, and denial (Kozier, Erb, and Blais, 1992). Effective coping strategies are ones that will bring a resolution of the problem causing the stress or change the reaction of the stress (adaptation). Confrontation, problem solving, and communicating are given as examples of effective coping strategies. In the healthcare system there may not be the opportunity for changing a situation, that is, a disease condition already exists or abuse has already occurred.

effective coping

CAUSES OF STRESS

Why are there reports of stress among nurses? We need to examine two major factors—the environment and the nurse. Exercise 25-1 assists in exploring personal causes and reactions to stress. Being aware of what

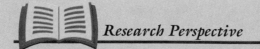

Research Perspective

Chapman, J. (1993). Collegial support linked to reduction of job stress. Nursing Management, 24(5), 52–54.

The relationship between nurses' perceptions of collegial support and job stressors was studied. Five hundred staff nurses working in acute care settings were mailed a questionnaire, Staff Nurse Survey, which contained the collegial communication and nursing stress scale. Two hundred nurses returned the surveys. The Survey of Collegial Communication was adapted to be appropriate for staff nurses. There were forty questions related to eight components:
1. confidence and trust
2. team efforts toward goal achievement
3. open communications
4. mutual help
5. mutual support
6. creativity
7. freedom from threat
8. friendliness and enjoyment.

The nursing stress scale measures the frequency and major sources of stress staff nurses' experience. There were seven major sources of stressors:
1. death and dying
2. conflict with physicians
3. inadequate preparation
4. lack of support
5. conflict with other nurses
6. workload
7. uncertainty concerning treatment.

The results indicated that as staff nurses perceive a decrease in their level of collegial support, they perceive an increase in the frequency of job stressors. Co-worker support was more than twice as important as other sources of support. Nurses over the age of 50 had the highest support scores and the lowest frequency of stressors. The Survey of Collegial Support results indicate that nurses need time to participate in group discussions concerning their work and work-related problems. Efforts must be made to either eliminate the stressors or assist nurses in coping.

Implications for Practice

Support from co-workers is important for nurses to give quality care to patients. There is a need to develop support through group communication activities with a stable group. Rotating staff through shifts by groups would help in providing a group support network. Nurses can help each other face stress better. With increased stress related to cost containment there needs to be efforts to assist nurses in meeting the demands of their work.

causes stress and how one reacts is the first step in learning to balance stress more effectively.

environment   The environment in which nurses work and the nature of the work that nurses do are very stressful. Studies have shown that the strongest symptoms of dysfunctional stress were associated with those occupations in which the worker had the greatest responsibility for the well-being of others, in other words the people-caring professions (Atkinson, 1985; Maslach, 1982). Caring for acutely ill people demands a great deal of accountability. Benner and Wrubel (1988) found that caring causes stress; but not being able to do what needs to be done is the major stressor. There are decreasing resources in healthcare, such as cost containment, that cause frustration. For example, the work load has increased and staffing has not.

EXERCISE 25-1

Identify what stress you experience and how you usually manage it. Create and complete the following log at the end of every workday for one week. Review the log and note what situations (people, technology, value conflict, etc.) were the most frequent. Also identify how you most frequently react to stress: physically, mentally, and emotionally/spiritually. *Keeping this diary for a week is helpful to determine what causes you stress at work and in learning about your reactions.*

DATE	SITUATION	YOUR RESPONSE	ACTION	EVALUATION

The environment in which nurses work today is constantly changing. Although change may be uncomfortable in itself, the rapid changes in technology, payment systems, skills needed, and consumer demands all exacerbate the effects of change. Nurses need to continually learn new skills, and this adds to the pressure of caregiving. The constant demand to learn and practice increased technological skills does not allow time for expertise to develop. As a result, the nurse has a lowered self-esteem.

change

Healthcare organizations are constantly changing in response to financial and political pressures, and nurses are responsible for implementing the changes that they may not have had any role in designing. Downsizing, combining units, and new organizational frameworks means that staff is constantly required to make adjustments with little time for preparation. This constant influx of change causes insecurity for nurse managers and staff. Assisting staff in handling these pressures while defending the changes places the manager in a difficult role.

Consumers of healthcare are also demanding different skills from nurses. Although nurses may want to concentrate on preventive health and educational programs because they know they are more cost-effective, consumers may not opt for this choice. There is demand for high-tech care and the use of healthcare to fix the self-inflicted problems caused by such products as tobacco, drugs, and alcohol. This demand can cause internal conflict within the nurses as they struggle to meet the consumers' needs. People are much more willing to risk the need for high-technology treatment than to change lifestyles. Another problem is that the public has some information about healthcare but does not have the in-depth knowledge to make truly informed decisions. For example, the family may want everything to be done for a client so that they feel comfortable knowing that the client has the best care. However, they may not realize that the "everything" may be painful, unnecessary, and expensive.

consumer demands

A significant source of stress for nurses is dealing with clients who do not share the same values in healthcare. Societal problems including AIDS, violence, and family disintegration are also evident in the nursing arena. These complex issues strain the resources of the health industry, and as the direct care providers nurses are intimately involved in helping people cope with these issues.

nurse's role
The second major factor that causes stress is the role of the nurse. Nursing is still primarily a female profession and the women who enter nursing are attracted to the caregiving and nurturing role. They tend to take these personal attributes and apply them to the professional arena. They may care for their clients, care for their colleagues, care for their supervisors, and care for their families. This does not leave much time or energy to care for themselves. Their own well-being is at the end of their "to-do" list. Nurses today have multiple roles they are trying to fulfill and caring for people is exhausting and draining.

Woodhouse (1993) discusses the many demands on the role of the nurse that cause strain. Physicians may see the role of the nurse as the technical caregiver and communicate this to the nurse. As one nurse states:

> I questioned the doctor's order and he told me that the role of the nurse was to do exactly what the doctor ordered. I explained that the medication that he ordered was contraindicated in the PDR for a breast-feeding mother. He stated that I was to give the medication on his order and he would later check the medication sheet to make sure I had administered the medication. After teaching the patient about the side effects, the patient refused the medication and I charted this. The physician and I have a truce relationship at this point.

long-term stress
When stress is not balanced there may be physiological and psychological manifestations of long-term stress. The long-term physical results of poorly managed stress are chronic health conditions such as hypertension, increased heart rate and blood pressure, muscle tension, and mental lassitude. The psychological manifestations include anxiety, anger, and cognitive impairment. Excessive anxiety often has destructive effects. Anxiety is an arousal state that is a reaction to stress as the individual attempts to identify and define the problems (Kozier, Erb, and Blais, 1992).

The nurse manager's primary role, a potentially stress-filled one, is to lead, but sometimes the role becomes that of a "buffer" between the causes of stress and the staff nurses' reaction or that of a coach who helps the nurse use his/her own abilities to cope with stress. A Manager's Viewpoint at the beginning of this chapter provides insight into the balancing act the manager performs.

EXERCISE 25-2
Using Table 25-1, assess your own signs of overstress.

SIGNS OF OVERSTRESS

Factors that affect a nurse's reactions are individual and based on either inborn or learned behaviors. The same stressor may result in very different reactions. For example, one nurse may perceive an acutely ill patient as a challenge that will test skills and enhance confidence. Another nurse may perceive the same patient as a catastrophic event and may feel a lack of self-confidence in handling the situation.

Nurses may be able to cope by denying their feelings and reactions to stress; eventually chronic stress will exact a toll on the body, mind, or spirit. It is important for nurses to be able to assess when they may be feeling the overload of stress and perhaps be in danger of burnout. The nurse manager can also detect signs in the staff and be able to determine when the stress is becoming an overload. Thus, steps can be taken to assist nurses in better handling the stress and/or to change the environment to decrease stress. Table 25-1 divides the signs of stress into physical, mental, and emotional/spiritual components.

These signs are termed "overstress" because they are a result of prolonged exposure to stress and usually not just a one-time experience. It is also important to realize that stress may be originating from personal living problems or from a combination of work and living problems.

TABLE 25-1 Signs of Overstress in Individuals		
PHYSICAL	**MENTAL**	**SPIRITUAL/EMOTIONAL**
Physical signs of ill health: a. increased flu, colds, accidents b. change in sleeping habits c. fatigue Chronic signs of decreased ability to manage stress: a. headaches b. hypertension c. backaches d. gastrointestinal problems Use of unhealthy coping activities: a. increased use of drugs and alcohol b. increased weight	Dread going to work everyday Rigid thinking and a desire to go by the rules in all cases; being unable to tolerate any changes Being forgetful and anxious about work to be done; errors and incidents more frequent Returning home exhausted and unable to participate in enjoyable activities Confusion about duties and roles	Sense of being a failure; disappointed in work performance Anger and resentment towards clients, colleagues and managers; overall irritable attitude Lack of positive feelings toward others Cynicism toward clients, blaming them for their problems Excessive worry; insecurity; lowered self-esteem Increased family and friend conflicts

IMPORTANCE OF BALANCING STRESS

The repercussions of stress not being balanced are detrimental to the individual, patient, and healthcare organization. Blegen (1993) found that stress was the most important variable related to job satisfaction for nurses. The higher the level of stress the lower the level of job satisfaction. Dissatisfaction with work can lead to a decrease in work performance, and eventually the person may leave the profession.

job satisfaction

Client care may be affected by stress in the workplace. Grant (1993) describes how nurses preoccupied with work stress can experience disruption in vital thought processes during critical decision-making times and the client suffers the results. There are more medication, treatment, and recording errors when stress is uncontrolled.

Greenberger et al. (1989) cite the relationship of stress to organizational problems. Stress leads to high turnover and increased absenteeism. It is estimated that stress causes the health industry $150 billion yearly secondary to increased sick days, outpatient tests for employees, substance abuse, hospitalizations, and orientations. The box on page 506 lists some of the signs that may be indicative that stress may be emanating from the workplace and not the individual.

EXERCISE 25-3
Copy the box entitled "Signs of Overstress in an Organization." Take this to the clinical area the next time you are there. Are any of the signs present? What is your view about the item(s) you perceived as present?

Signs of Overstress in an Organization

1. Turnover rate of nursing staff increasing.
2. Absenteeism above normal without identifiable cause (e.g., flu).
3. Increased errors and incident reports.
4. Complaints of poor care from clients, physicians, and managers.
5. Increased costs incurred by benefits department.
6. Problems with productivity.
7. Trouble in group dynamics; blaming others, unwillingness to help, withdrawal from other staff.

There are effective methods to decrease the stress or change the reaction to stress. By identifying specific causes for individuals and then developing appropriate coping strategies, these individuals might remain in nursing.

STRATEGIES FOR COPING WITH STRESS

Ideally stresses could be reduced to an acceptable level where people could function at their best and not feel unwell. Examining the environment to determine what can be changed is the first step, and the second step is to help with better coping strategies. Together managers and staff can address these concerns.

environmental stressors

If environmental stressors can be identified, decisions need to be made to assess if they can be changed. If there is an extreme amount of turnover and nurses that remain feel the stress of constantly working understaffed or orienting new staff, there is a need to identify specific causes for the turnovers. High turnover rates lead to higher turnover rates (Grant, 1993). The problem may lie with management policies, personality conflicts, high patient acuity, or other factors. Individual nurses need to look closely at the environment to see if causes of high stress are present and if they can be altered. Does there seem to be any effort on the part of administration to meet the needs of the staff? An environment where no effort is being made to meet employees' needs may not be where that nurse should continue working. A complete change in units or institutions can sometimes be the best and easiest choice. Before taking this approach, a nurse must evaluate prospective situations and weigh various benefits and liabilities before making a decision.

High turnover rates increase the turnover rate and cause increased stress levels for staff. The nurse manager is on the frontline in assessing stress levels on the unit and developing ways to modify or buffer the stress. In building a team, the most important first step may be to reduce stress levels. As in the example presented in A Manager's Viewpoint, the manager needs to be a role model and keep his/her stress levels under control. Table 25-2 on page 508 lists different strategies that may be used individually or in a group situation.

EXERCISE 25-4
Analyze your own physical, mental, and emotional/spiritual response to stress. Do you rely on only one strategy? If so, you need to consider other options.

PHYSICAL STRATEGIES

The physical strategies are focused in diffusing the tensed muscles, increased heart rate, and other physical agitation signs that are a result of stress. The first strategy involves acceptance of physical limitations. There is only so much an individual can accomplish in a given time. Grant (1993) points out the dangers in overwork and understaffing. There needs to be

acceptance of physical limitations

Eating well is an important physical strategy for stress management.

a realistic appraisal of what can be accomplished. Jacobson and McGrath (1983) state that nurses may believe that (a) their self-worth depends on receiving approval and love from others, (b) the notion that anything short of perfection is failure, and (c) the perception of nursing is selfless service to others. These beliefs need to be addressed, and role modeling by the manager of working toward realistic goals is important. Home responsibilities need to be shared and renegotiated from time to time. If the family does not share household duties, then an alternative is to hire help in the home.

The next strategy involves nutrition. Jacobson and McGrath (1983) relate that nurses overeat as a method to reduce stress but in actuality this increases stress because of the consequences. Eating a diet high in carbohydrates, low in caffeine, and low in sugar is the important first step.

nutrition

Exercise has been shown to be a most effective stress reducer. Selye (1991) suggests that physical activity is an excellent way to relieve the pressure on the mind and to equalize the wear and tear throughout the body. But the activity needs to be enjoyable (Kozier, Erb, and Blais, 1992). In the late 1980s there was emphasis on a target heart rate, efficiency, and effectiveness. However, people who were involved in activities that they did not enjoy soon dropped out of all exercise. Today there is encouragement to be involved in activities that are enjoyable, such as hiking, walking, birdwatching and so forth. These may not be the most efficient activities, but if there is enjoyment people may do them more often and thus achieve the same benefits.

exercise

Considering nurses' needs, including physical, and making them a priority is an important strategy for the nurse manager to incorporate. There are nurses who will continually work overtime to make heros of themselves; this needs to be discouraged. Other methods involve making sure that staff members nurture themselves and take time for breaks and lunch. Managers would not expect clients to be able to perform their best without meals but some staff members may feel that they don't have a right to ask for a break. Refreshed

TABLE 25-2	Stress Management Strategies

PHYSICAL	MENTAL	EMOTIONAL/SPIRITUAL
Acceptance of physical limitations	Learn to say no!	Use meditation
Nutrition: high carbohydrate, low caffeine, low sugar	Use cognitive restructuring and self-talk.	Seek solace in prayer
	Imagery	Seek professional counseling
Exercise: enjoyable activity three times a week for 30 minutes	Develop hobbies or activities	Participate in support groups
	Plan vacations	Participate in networking
Make your physical health a priority	Learn about the system and how problems are handled	Communicate feelings
Nurture self by taking time for breaks and lunch		Identify and acquire a mentor
Sleep: quantity and quality	Learn communication, conflict resolution, and time management skills	Ask for feedback and clarification
Relaxation: meditation, massage, yoga, biofeedback	Take continuing education courses	

nurses are better able to provide high-quality care to their clients with less stress to the nurse (Jones, 1983).

lack of quality sleep

Insufficient or poor-quality sleep is a result and cause of stress. Gowell and Boverlie (1992) suggest that shift assignment and rotation schedules are factors in stress and job satisfaction. There are principles to be observed in staffing that can assist staff members in meeting their individual needs. Attempting not to schedule a staff member for a day shift immediately following an evening shift can prevent tiredness, decreased productivity, and increased stress levels.

relaxation

The final physical strategy is relaxation. Humphrey (1988) discusses the use of meditation and biofeedback for lowering stress levels by quieting the mind through concentration. Other relaxation techniques, such as massage, music, and yoga, are refreshing and revitalizing. They can be done in a room near the unit before or after work.

MENTAL STRATEGIES

The mental strategies are based on learning new skills and considering different viewpoints. Learning to say no, setting reasonable goals at work and

EXERCISE 25-5   RELAXATION RESPONSE

This exercise can be used in the middle of a working day, or last thing at night, or at any time you feel tense or anxious.

1. Find a place away from interruption for 10 minutes.
2. Loosen tight clothes; lie on the floor, a mat, a towel, or a couch, if possible. Close your eyes, and let your body go slack.
3. Starting from the top of your body, work steadily through all your muscles, tightening and then relaxing them.
4. Lift up your head and pull it forward as far as you can then let it fall back gently.
5. Continuing downward, press your shoulders down hard then slowly relax them.
6. Open your fingers wide, stretch your arms out to your side and hold them as tight and hard as you can. Then slowly let them go.
7. With your arms lying at your side, tighten your abdominal muscles as hard as you can, then relax them.
8. Lift your buttocks, tightening them as they go, and then gently let them fall back. Relax the buttocks and spine muscles, thinking consciously of the areas you are working on.
9. Do a mental check to make sure other muscles have not tightened up. Put your heels together and stretch your legs and toes as far as you can, then slowly relax them.
10. Turn on your side and lie that way for two to three minutes. Sit up slowly and think how you are feeling and try to keep that feeling as you go back to your activities.

Adapted from Wilson, J. (1990). Woman, Your Body, Your Health. New York: Harcourt Brace Jovanovich.

at home, giving yourself recognition for accomplishments, and cognitive restructuring are all measures to raise and maintain a healthy self-esteem. Mental set can influence stress levels; there is a need to put problems in perspective.

The Relaxation Response (Exercise 25-5) provides a way to regain a sense of proportion and clarity in decision making. Self-talk can be useful in learning how to reframe thoughts, from thinking about being a terrible person to this is not the end of the world, or it is unreasonable to expect that everything can be accomplished (Grant, 1993).

imagery

Mental activities that include imagery are helpful, such as planning a vacation and developing hobbies or activities that can take the mind away from work problems. An activity or hobby involving an actual product can be very rewarding. As mentioned in A Manager's Viewpoint, just planning a vacation reduces stress. Imagining a different activity or environment provides a release from stress.

learning

Another mental activity is learning new activities and skills. It is important to learn about the organizational system and how problems are handled. For example, some nurses are required to use new computer programs but are not given time or training to do so. This needs to be changed so that nurses can be more efficient in their work and not feel the resultant frustration from "crashing" computers inadvertently. Learning communication, conflict resolution, and time management skills is important in today's world. Nurses need to have experiences that provide practice in these skills. Continuing education is a lifeline for learning new client care skills, for practicing the skills, and for acquiring increased knowledge that provides for a sense of security in performing one's job.

EMOTIONAL/SPIRITUAL STRATEGIES

Emotional and spiritual supportive strategies can come from formal and informal directions. The formal aspects concern organized religion, professional counseling, or value clarification workshops. Seeking sustenance from spiritual supports is valuable for the caregiver (Hodges et al., 1988). Meditation and prayer can be very effective.

counseling

Professional counseling can be useful when stress is building to burnout levels. Feelings of exhaustion and deep depression may signal a need for counseling. There is no longer a stigma to receiving emotional support through counseling, and short-term focused therapy is more prevalent today.

Galbraith et al. (1992) discuss the use of support groups to handle stress in settings away from the hospital. Support groups and networking can build confidence, mutual help, mutual support, and friendships, and it can be enjoyable. Group meetings away from the hospital enable staff members to see their colleagues in a different light. Galbraith et al. describe the use of overnight retreats for the staff to foster a collegial atmosphere, where ideas can be exchanged, former clients remembered, and the life and work of caregivers celebrated. This is useful in decreasing stress and increasing work enjoyment. The "Research Perspective" presented earlier in this chapter supports the use of this strategy to reduce strain.

communication

Another valuable strategy that seems simple, but is underused, is communicating feelings to others so that they can support you. Lazarus and Folkman (1991) emphasize the importance of collegial support but that people are afraid to share their problems and concerns because they may not be thought of as achievers. It can help to identify a mentor who can provide direction, focus, and experience in surviving as a nurse.

Asking for feedback and clarification often proves helpful in allaying fears of poor performance. Nurses are extremely critical of themselves and sometimes a "reality" check as to performance can provide reassurance and decrease stress (Jacobson and McGrath, 1983).

> **EXERCISE 25-6**
> Ask yourself these questions when faced with a stressor:
> Does this problem have any real significance?
> Will this be important in 10 minutes, 10 hours, 10 days, 10 years?
> What is the real problem?
> What can I realistically do about it?

> **EXERCISE 25-7**
> Identify from the list of strategies in Table 25-2 on page 508 one strategy from each area that you would like to keep track of for one week. Record if you used it, how often, when and where, and evaluate how effective the strategy was in decreasing stress. You may wish to write it on a small card to carry with you. Based on your weekly review you can determine if you want to continue to use it or try another strategy.
>
> | STRESS REDUCERS | WHEN | WHERE | HOW OFTEN | EVALUATE HOW EFFECTIVE |
> |---|---|---|---|---|
> | 1. Physical
2. Mental
3. Emotional/Spiritual | | | | |

ORGANIZATIONAL STRATEGIES TO REDUCE STRESS

Nurse managers are in the position to suggest strategies that can be undertaken by individuals, units, and others. The box on page 512 lists several strategies that can be used in the healthcare system.

supportiveness

Supportiveness refers to the emotional assistance given to fellow nurses. Aurelio (1993) notes that nurses continually try to help each other cope with

Networking builds confidence, mutual support, friendliness, and enjoyment.

stress. One example is a nurse staying with another nurse who is sitting with a dying client. Another example is staying late to finish chores rather than leaving them for the next shift. Rather than assigning blame, when mistakes occur, a manager can provide a supportive attitude that encourages the staff to learn from mistakes and to increase mutual cooperation.

Employee assistance programs are useful for reducing stress among employees and supervisors (Woodhouse, 1993). It is important that the staff knows about this resource and that there is not a stigma attached to utilizing this form of support.

employee assistance program

Formal discussion groups and consultations are additional ways to help staff verbalize anxiety and seek help and advice from colleagues (Aurelio, 1993). Expert consultants in psychology or stress management can be brought in to assist the staff in identifying causes, solutions, and effective strategies to decrease stress. An unbiased observer can provide direction for the group.

formal discussion group

professional consultations

Schumacher and Larson (1993) discuss the need for rites and rituals to share achievement and provide a sense of stability and community. Different units have different personalities and celebrating the personalities is important in fostering group cohesiveness. When units are changed or combined with other units it is important to retain some of the traditions of each unit as a way to help staff cope with change. Defining and redefining values and the vision of the organization as it changes can be valuable. Providing time for reflection and understanding of the issues is important to prepare staff for changes.

rites and rituals

Specific classes in time management, prioritization, and formal stress management programs are also helpful. Grant (1993) promotes the use of formal meetings to communicate to staff and receive feedback on changes or problems that occur. Formal stress management programs have physical and emotional health components. The physical program may include health appraisals and counseling, weight loss, stop-smoking groups, and partial payment of fees

time management

problems that occur

Organizational Strategies to Alleviate Stress

1. Supportiveness
2. Employee assistance program
3. Formal discussion groups
4. Professional consultations
5. Rites and rituals
6. Time management classes
7. Formal stress management programs
8. Humor

for exercise clubs. Formal education programs that are based on staff needs can decrease the pressures.

humor   Hagaseth (1988) outlines the benefits of humor in the workplace. Humor workshops can be offered so that all employees can utilize this stress-reducing technique.

The nurse manager is also an advocate and spokesperson for staff to upper levels of management. Grant (1993) suggests that the manager assess and determine the financial projections of stress on staff. Presenting data to administration on the costs of turnover, orientation, illness, and absences can give administration an understanding of the costs of stress. Jones (1992) found that the average cost to replace a nurse is $12,147. It makes more sense to retain the nurses that are employed and to try to help them with their needs concerning stressors than to have fewer staff and add to stress.

CHAPTER CHECKLIST

Balancing stress means caring for your emotional, physical, and mental needs. Stress is inherent in the nursing profession, and nurses can adapt and cope with the stress in the healthcare field by learning effective ways to care for themselves. By assessing and reducing specific stressors nurses will manage to thrive on the challenges. Increasing skills in coping with stress is a vital component in management and leadership. A nurse manager who can role model and support her staff in times of stress is a beacon of light.

- Stress management includes using cognitive and psychosocial activities to decrease the stress or enhance the ability to handle stress.
- Signs of overstress need to be heeded to prevent burnout or chronic health problems.
- Strategies to reduce stress include:
  - Physical
    - acceptance of physical limitations
    - nutrition
    - exercise
    - physical health
    - breaks
    - relaxation.
  - Mental
    - saying no
    - using self talk
    - using imagery
    - developing hobbies
    - continuing education.
  - Emotional
    - using meditation and prayer
    - seeking counseling
    - communicating feelings
    - using mentors
    - clarifying roles.

TERMS TO KNOW

- anxiety
- biofeedback
- burnout
- cognitive restructuring
- coping
- eustress
- external demands
- general adaptation syndrome (GAS)
- internal demands
- stress

REFERENCES

Atkinson, H. (1985). *Women and Fatigue*. New York: G.P. Putnam.

Aurelio, J. (1993). An organizational culture that optimizes stress: Acceptable stress in nursing. *Nursing Administration Quarterly, 18*(1), 1–10.

Belle, D. (1991). Gender difference in the social moderators of stress. In Monat, A., & Lazarus, R., eds. *Stress and Coping: An Anthology*. New York: Columbia University Press.

Benner, P., & Wrubel, J. (1988). Caring. *American Journal of Nursing, 88*(8), 1073–1075.

Blegen, M. (1993). Nurses' job satisfaction: a meta-analysis of related variables. *Nursing Research, 42*(1), 36–41.

Chapman, J. (1993). Collegial support linked to reduction of job stress. *Nursing Management, 24*(5), 52–54.

Edwards. J. (1988). The determinants and consequences of coping with stress. In Cooper, C., & Payne, R., eds. *Causes, Coping and Consequences of Stress at Work*. St. Louis: John Wiley.

Galbraith, L., Kaiser, S., Mahoney, D., Moore-Harris, L., Polman, L., Ross, L., Vaugh, G., & Willenvrink, D. (1992). Overnight retreat as a way to cope with stress. *Pediatric Nursing, 18*(4), 372–373.

Gowell, Y., & Boverlie, P. (1992). Stress and satisfaction as a result of shift and number of hours worked. *Nursing Administration Quarterly*, 14–18.

Grant, P. (1993). Manage nurse stress and increase potential at the bedside. *Nursing Administration Quarterly, 18*(1), 16–22.

Greenberger, D., Strasser, S., Cummings, L., & Dunham, R. (1989). The impact of personal control on performance and satisfaction. *Organizational Behavior and Human Decision Making Processes, 43*, 29–51.

Hagaseth, C. (1988). *A Laughing Place: The Art and Psychology of Positive Humor in Love and Adversity*. Fort Collins, CO: Berwick.

Hodges, H., Jutras, M., Riddle, L., Wagner, K., & Webb, D. (1988). *Nursing from Education to Practice*. San Mateo, CA: Appleton & Lange.

Humphrey, J. (1988). *Stress in the Nursing Profession*. Springfield, IL: Charles C. Thomas.

Jacobson, S., & McGrath, H. (1983). *Nurses under Stress*. New York: John Wiley.

Jones, C. (1992). Calculating and updating nursing turnover costs. *Nursing Economics, 10*(1), 39–45.

Jones, M. (1983). Contributions of nursing service administration to stress reduction. In Jacobson, S., & McGrath, H., eds. *Nurses Under Stress*. New York: John Wiley, pp. 269–282.

Kozier, B., Erb, G., & Blais, K. (1992). *Concepts and Issues in Nursing Practice*. New York: Addison-Wesley Nursing.

Lazarus, R., & Folkman, S. (1991). The concept of coping. In Monat, A., & Lazarus, R., eds. *Stress and Coping: An Anthology*. New York: Columbia University Press.

Marriner-Tomey, A. (1992). *Guide to Nursing Management.* St. Louis: Mosby–Year Book.

Maslach, C. (1982). *Burnout—The Cost of Caring.* Englewood Cliffs, NJ: Prentice Hall.

Monat, A., & Lazarus, R., eds. (1991). *Stress and Coping: An Anthology.* New York: Columbia University Press.

Schumacher, L., & Larson, K. (1993). Thriving and striving on the turbulence of rural health care. *Nursing Administration Quarterly, 18*(1), 11–15.

Selye, H. (1991). History and present status of the stress concept. In Monat, A., & Lazarus, R., eds. *Stress and Coping: An Anthology.* New York: Columbia University Press, pp. 21–36.

Wilson, J. (1990). *Woman, Your Body, Your Health.* New York: Harcourt Brace Jovanovich.

Woodhouse, P. (1993). The aspects of humor in dealing with stress. *Nursing Administration Quarterly, 18*(1), 80–89.

SUGGESTED READINGS

Benner, P. & Wrubel, J. (1988). Caring. *American Journal of Nursing, 88* (8), 1073–1075.

Blegen, M. (1993). Nurses' job satisfaction: a meta-analysis of related variables. *Nursing Research, 42* (1), 36–41.

Grant, P. (1993). Manage nurse stress and increase potential at the bedside. *Nursing Administration Quarterly, 18* (1), 16–22.

Humphrey, J. (1988). *Stress in the nursing profession.* Springfield, ILL: Charles C. Thomas Publishers.

Monat, A. & Lazarus, R., eds. (1991). *Stress and coping: An anthology.* New York: Columbia University Press.

CHAPTER 26

CAREER MANAGEMENT: PUTTING YOURSELF IN CHARGE

Patricia S. Yoder Wise, R.N., C., Ed.D., C.N.A.A., F.A.A.N.

PREVIEW

This chapter focuses on career development, identifying career styles and describing the importance of continuing education and certification to professional development. Linking career goals with specific strategies provides a way to enhance career success. Attending to professional expectations before beginning a career can further develop successful outcomes. The appendix to this chapter contains tools to use in preparing a curriculum vitae, résumé, and cover letter, as well as a checklist for interviewing.

OBJECTIVES

- Differentiate career styles and how they influence career options.
- Analyze person/position fit.
- Evaluate the relevance of curriculum vitae and resumes as entrees to interviews.
- Use critical elements of curriculum vitae and résumés to develop each.
- Analyze critical elements in an interview.
- Compare and contrast different types of professional learning opportunities.
- Value professional expectations.

QUESTIONS TO CONSIDER

- What clinical nursing experience thus far was most stimulating and challenging? Why?
- What excites you about nursing? What excites you about leadership and management options?
- What do you want to be doing in five years? (Describe as much as possible about your desirable future.)

A Manager's Viewpoint

My career has spanned several years. I'd say it was a typical spiral career. I advanced in the hospital and returned to graduate school. While completing my master's in nursing, I continued in management, left hospital nursing for a private business in nursing personnel, and then returned to a director's position in a large hospital system.

As I've moved along in my career, I thought it was important to gain academic and continuing education and to be certified in nursing administration. Being able to share what I know, and constantly learn about nursing and its role within healthcare, I am consistently impressed with how rich our heritage as a profession is. The research that has shaped today's practice was designed by a relatively few nurses. Today, I expect all professional nurses to be avid translators of the current research and I expect some to design studies based on problems we encounter in delivering nursing care.

Personally, I believe I am most fortunate to be among the nurses who have held elective office at the local and state level in the nurses' association. In addition to the value I derive from being able to share my leadership, I find that I am very well informed about all of the major issues facing nursing because I have access to the leadership of the other states and the national level. This kind of opportunity is one that influences my career and helps me help others in their career development. I truly believe you have to stay in control of your career because there are limitless possibilities!

Sarah Moody, R.N., M.S., C.N.A.A.
Patient Care Administrator
Presbyterian Hospitals of Dallas
Dallas, Texas

INTRODUCTION

Although it is important to take advantage of opportunities as they develop during a career, it is also important to make decisions about what you want to do in nursing and how you can go about doing it. Because nursing extends across the lifespan and is not institutionally based (that is, not defined by the institution but rather by state law), the options for careers in nursing are vast. Some options build primarily on experience, others build primarily on educational background, and still others require a mix of education and experience. In general, you can assume that you must continue to learn and to develop your expertise. How you reach a career goal, however, depends on what goal you set.

CAREER MANAGEMENT

career

A **career** can be defined as progress throughout a person's professional life. Some people, including professional nurses, have a series of positions with no connection among them. Others can have divergent positions that are connected in some way.

EXAMPLE

Nurse A moves between hospitals each time one of the hospitals offers a major new benefit or opens a new unit. Nurse A also has worked in a few community settings and served on a cruise ship one summer. When asked about career patterns, Nurse A says, "I've capitalized on any opportunity that has come along. I really want to work in long-term care; but there don't seem to be openings to fit my needs."

Nurse B also moves between hospitals providing the positions always relate to care of newborns. This nurse has worked in entry positions and nurse manager positions. The clinical areas have ranged from labor and delivery to pediatrics and neonatal intensive care units. Nurse B belongs to the state nurses' association and the Association of Women's Health, Obstetrics, and Neonatal Nurses (AWOHNN). In addition to volunteering as a professional resource person at a local day-care center, nurse B has attended many professional conferences about newborns and recently applied to a graduate program to become a pediatric nurse practitioner. When asked about career patterns, nurse B states, "Well, I've sort of been all over the map; but I know that each time I've changed jobs, I've had opportunities to work in a different phase of pediatric nursing."

There are several ways to develop a career. Basing career decisions on goals is a useful beginning. Chapter 11 provided the opportunity to develop goals according to the three life areas of family/significant others, career/professional development, and personal development. (If you have completed the goal-setting exercise in the appendix to Chapter 11, refer to pages 223–225 to review your career and professional development goals. If you have not completed that exercise, return there before proceeding.)

career styles

Some of the most notable work about careers has been conducted by Friss (1989), who identifies four career styles. The box on page 519 summarizes the key points related to each style. One career pathway is not better than another; rather, each is different. For example, the types of positions sought differ. Steady state and linear are the traditional career styles. The first remains at a plateau positionally and becomes increasingly competent; the second moves up the hierarchy of the organization. The entrepreneurial and transient style is one that has fostered many nurses' creative bent. This style allows for a great deal of flexibility and, in a time of rapid changes in healthcare, can permit creative solutions to traditional problems. Finally, the spiral style is one seen in situations where nurses move in and out of active practice and in situations where nurses move in and out of subcareer foci, such as general pediatrics and neonatal nursing.

The motivations and resultant management implications vary among the styles. Providing the same structure, feedback, and guidance for all would not

---

Career Styles

STEADY STATE
  Example: staff nurses
  Description: constancy in position with increasing professional skill
  Motivation and characteristics: increasing expertise
                                      high professional identity
                                      obligation to serve
                                      maintenance of standards
                                      autonomy in performance of care
                                      preference for action
                                      personal accountability
                                      the work itself
                                      stability
  Managerial implications: hold work in high esteem
                              decentralize
                              utilize and recognize abilities
                              provide feedback about client outcomes
                              reward competence and tenure
                              provide continuing education
                              provide permanent assignment

LINEAR
  Example: director of a nursing service
  Description: hierarchical orientation with steady climb
  Motivation and characteristics: requisite authority and power
                                      had a challenging first job
                                      guided by internalized norms
                                      money
                                      recognition
                                      opportunities for self-development
  Management implications: provide management development
                              reward and value both education and
                                  competence
                              modify management selection and development
                                  systems
                              provide decreasing supervision

ENTREPRENEURIAL AND TRANSIENT
  Example: nurses in private practice; temporary assignment
  Description: desire to create new service; meeting own priorities
  Motivation and characteristics: limited organizational commitment
                                      opportunists
                                      novelty/creativity
                                      other people
                                      achievement

Career Styles—cont'd.

Managerial implications:	use flexibility to organization's benefit
	avoid burdening them with organizational and practice decisions
	provide immediate feedback

SPIRAL
Example: nurse who returns after raising a family
Description: rational, independent responsibility for shaping career

Motivation and characteristics:	novelty
	prestige
	intense period of employment followed by nonemployment or a different employment
	care for others and provide sustenance
	seeks opportunities for self-development
	typically well paid, service oriented
	recognition
Managerial implications:	configure specific job that needs doing
	be flexible about terms and length of commitment
	find challenging initial assignment
	negotiate
	encourage creativity

Adapted from Friss, 1989.

capitalize on varying career styles. Similarly, nurses who choose a less traditional path (one that is not steady state or linear) may need to describe how they see their careers and how they have managed them to others. Sometimes because of a personal need or geographic location, a particular approach to a career in nursing may need to be modified.

person/position fit   To achieve a good person/position fit, there are several strategies that can be employed to elicit appropriate information before selecting a position. A good fit is built on strong similar goals and tolerable or growth-producing differences. Figure 26-1 suggests that the whole of any work situation is composed of two elements interacting in an environment with other elements. That whole is symbolized by the blending of a person's talents with the position's expectations to create a productive whole.

MARKETING STRATEGIES

Irrespective of career style, core career development strategies are important. Selecting professional peers and mentors to share your development is important. Even the steady-state nurse needs to develop a curriculum vitae or résumé that can document continued development of expertise. Interviewing, a two-way process, is also an important strategy to control.

peers & mentors   Few nurses have achieved a significant nursing career without assistance from peers and mentors. Heeding the "naysayers" can dampen career

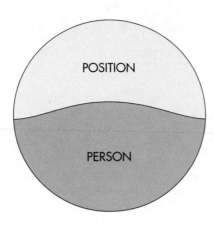

GOAL: A FIT

FIGURE 26-1
Person/position fit.

prospects. It is important to have a few well-chosen peers and mentors who can respond openly with various perspectives to help with career decisions. For example, a nurse who seeks a career as a manager should obtain information from a peer or mentor about managerial qualities (see this chapter's "Research Perspective") and potential positions. Such a person could also provide honest appraisals of an individual's career development, suggest specific strategies to enhance development, and help with meeting the leaders in an organization.

A **curriculum vitae** (CV) is a listing of professional life activities. It is designed to be all-inclusive, but not detailed. The reverse is true of a résumé. A **résumé** is a summary of professional abilities and facts. It is designed for specific opportunities to illustrate a fit of a person with a position. For the steady-state nurse, a résumé could be used to reflect increasing skills and abilities; for others, a résumé can create specific messages about an individual's unique experiences, education, and abilities. In other words, a CV or résumé opens doors.

CV

résumé

The exercise "Writing to Sell Yourself" (found in the appendix to this chapter) is designed to help create a system for developing and maintaining professional data and create both a curriculum vitae and résumé.

A cover letter conveys the quality of experience when paired with a CV. Because a CV is merely a set of facts, it conveys little quality. A cover letter serves to describe specific assets or qualities you have. When seeking a position, you can make several key points about yourself and how you fit the position. When providing your CV or résumé for career advancement purposes, you can highlight specific qualities that enhance your potential to be seen as the right choice.

cover letter

Assuming you are using these strategies to secure a new position, the next logical step is seeking an interview. Interviewing is a two-way proposition; the interviewee should be gathering as much information as the interviewer is. Both should be making judgments throughout the process so that if a position is offered, the interviewee will be prepared to accept, decline, or explore further. Interviews may take place with one or more individuals and may include a range of activities. To be at ease, the interviewee should wear comfortable, but pro-

interview

EXERCISE 26-2
Using part II of the appendix to this chapter, "The Cover Letter," write a letter that highlights information from at least two of your fact cards.

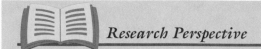

Research Perspective

Pedersen, A. (1993). Qualities of the excellent head nurse. *Journal of Nursing Administration, 8(1)*, 40–50.

Head nurses (nurse managers) link nurses and patients with quality care and with the larger organization. This qualitative research focused on sixteen nurses—five managers and eleven staff—who were asked to describe an excellent head nurse. Nurses were solicited to participate, and the actual participants were randomly selected from the volunteers. A semistructured interview guide was used; and the interviews were audiotaped. 178 qualities were identified and sorted into the following seven broad categories.

1. Management behaviors ($n = 65$)—conflict resolution (fair and open), problem solving, political abilities, power, skilled negotiation, visibility and accessibility, responsiveness.
2. Relationship-oriented behavior ($n = 26$)—supportive, caring, sensitive, empathic, understanding, listening; provide reward and recognition.
3. Temperament ($n = 42$)—authentic, genuine, reliable, honest, sincere, positive energy level, balanced.
4. Credibility ($n = 21$)—education, experience, good knowledge base, good resource.
5. Forward thinking ($n = 8$)—courageous, activist, challenger, change agent, creator, innovator, risk taker, facilitator.
6. Professionalism ($n = 22$)—good appearance, appropriate behavior, respectful, posture, high standards and expectations, collegial.
7. Advocacy ($n = $ unspecified)—advocate for nurse and nursing, protector, defender.

This study first reported data from staff and managers and reported on the role of the advocate.

Implications for Practice

This study suggests that nurse managers play a critical role in the overall structure of the healthcare organization. In addition to developing skills in specific management behaviors such as those listed above, personal qualities such as temperament are also essential in helping a manager perform well.

EXERCISE 26-3
Select a partner and role play an interview. The potential employer role should include questions and scenarios about common conflicts and challenges seen in clinical settings. The interviewee role should include responses from experiences and concerns.

fessional, clothing. Try rehearsing specific questions to ask and points to make. Be prepared to cite challenges and dilemmas you faced and what you did and why, because these types of questions may be posed to you. The appendix to this chapter includes three tools designed to be used in preparing for an interview: "Checklist for Interviewing," "Questions to Ask/to be Asked," and "Interview Topics and Questions of Concern." One other tool, "The Successful Thank You," is included to illustrate an additional opportunity to market yourself.

The interrelationship of these strategies allows people to emphasize specialization or diversity. Each strategy leads to the next so that the potential for attaining a preferred position is enhanced. As careers progress, factors other than the specific nursing school or in-school activities take precedence in influencing career development and how an individual is seen by others. Thus, updating a CV or résumé is important. Keeping a passion alive must be evident.

Interviewing is a two-way proposition in which both participants gather as much information as possible.

CONTINUING LEARNING

Learning occurs in various ways. It can occur in a conversation with colleagues, by reading an article in the general literature, or sometimes in an "ah hah" experience that provides sudden enlightenment. Although nurses could share these experiences with others, the continued learning that the profession, healthcare employers, boards of nursing, and professional associations are most concerned with is formal study—graduate education and continuing education.

A graduate degree opens numerous career opportunities and leads to new levels or areas of expertise. A graduate education may focus on a clinical area, a functional area, or a combination of both. Admission to graduate programs typically requires taking a test (frequently the Graduate Record Examination [GRE]), having an above-average grade point average (GPA), and graduating from a professionally accredited school of nursing.

graduate education

Graduate education consists of both master's- and doctorate-level study. In some employment situations or career specialties, graduate education is required. For example, the Joint Commission on Accreditation of Healthcare Organizations (1992) now requires graduate preparation of the nurse in charge of the nursing division in a hospital. Expectations for nurse practitioner preparation are centered on graduate-level preparation as opposed to the earlier certificate programs. As healthcare becomes more complex, it would be fairly easy to argue that persons licensed as individual practitioners, such as nurses, would need more education to continue to meet the healthcare system's demands.

Deciding to pursue graduation education may be very simple. Some applicants to baccalaureate programs already have a specific career focus in mind and the required graduate preparation is a given. New graduates are sometimes encouraged (or even required) to gain experience prior to seeking a master's or doctorate. While experience enriches previous learning, it may not be relevant to specific graduate programs such as those entailing a major career redirection. Working while attending a graduate program may be difficult. The box below lists some factors to consider in selecting a graduate program.

Factors to Consider in Selecting a Graduate Program

Accreditation	• Does the program have National League for Nursing accreditation? (Master's level) • Is the institution regionally accredited? (for example, North Central Association of Colleges and Schools)
Clinical/functional role	• How closely do the descriptions of clinical/functional courses of study meet career goals?
Credits	• How many graduate credits are minimally required to complete the degree? • How many are devoted to gaining experience? • How many relate to classroom experiences?
Thesis/research	• Is a thesis required? • If not, what opportunities exist for research development? • What support is available for graduate students?
Faculty	• What credentials do faculty hold? • Are they in leadership positions in the state/nation? • What is their reputation?
Current research	• What are the current research strengths of the institution?
Flexibility	• Is flexibility present in scheduling, progress through the program?
Admission	• What is required? • Is the GRE used? • What is the minimum undergraduate GPA expected? • Is experience required? What kind? How much?
Costs	• What are the total projected costs? • What financial aid is available?

If you are geographically bound, your fields of study may be limited. If you are not and you know what general area you want to pursue, consider the following illustration:

EXAMPLE

You know you want to work with the elderly. Your library subscribes to *The Journal of Gerontological Nursing* and *Geriatric Nursing*. Pull the most recent year's issues of both. Scan the masthead (the page with the editors, board members, etc.). Where are these individuals affiliated? Now scan the articles. Are there some that are particularly intriguing? Where are the authors affiliated? Finally, look back over your lists. Are there any places emerging as where the leaders in the field may be? You now have a good starting place.

Current listings of graduate programs accredited by the National League for Nursing are found annually in the June issue of *Nursing and Health Care.*

Continuing education also contributes to professional growth. **Continuing education** is defined as "those learning activities intended to build upon the educational and experiential bases of the professional nurse for the enhancement of practice, education, administration, research, or theory development to the end of improving the health of the public" (American Nurses Credentialing Center, 1991, p. 76).

Numerous opportunities for continuing education exist at local, state, regional, and national levels. Selecting which opportunities to pursue may be a difficult choice. The box below lists several factors to consider in selecting any offering; but depending on your particular goal, certain factors may be more influential than others. For example, if cost is a major factor, length and speaker may be less influential factors.

continuing education

EXERCISE 26-6
Even though you are not an organization, you still develop strategic plans for yourself. Imagine you have decided to earn a master's degree in nursing. This is a long-term or strategic plan. What values do you have that influence your plan? Are your interests in primary care, administration, or education? What is your target date for completion of the master's program? What are other factors that would interfere with your strategic plan? Do you have specific short-term goals, or operational plans, that must be attained first? Even though you are not an organization you do use the same type of planning method. Do you see the similarities?

Factors to Consider in Selecting a Continuing Education Course

Accreditation/Approval	• Is the course accredited/approved? If so, by whom? • Is that recognition accepted by a certification entity, by the board of nursing (if continuing education is required for reregistration of licensure)?
Credit	• Is the amount of credit appropriate in terms of the expected outcomes?
Course title	• Does it suggest the type of learner to be involved? (e.g., advanced) • Does it reflect the expected outcomes?
Speaker(s)	• Is the instructor known as an expert in the field? • Is the instructor experienced in the field?
Objectives	• Are the objectives logical and attainable? • Do they reflect knowledge, skills, or attitudes, or a combination of these? • Do they fit a learner's needs?
Content	• Is the content reflective of the objectives? • Is the content at an appropriate level?
Audience	• Is the audience designed as a general or target one? (e.g., all RNs or experienced nurses in state health positions)
Cost	• Is it equitable with what similar nursing conferences cost? • Is travel required? • What is the actual direct expense for an individual to attend? Is it affordable?
Length	• Is the total time frame logical in terms of objectives, personal needs, and time away from work? • Does the time frame permit breaks from intense learning?
Provider	• Does the provider have an established reputation?

In addition to increasing your knowledge base, continuing education opportunities provide professional networking opportunities, contribute to meeting certification and licensure requirements, and document additional pursuits in maintaining or developing clinical expertise. Sponsors of continuing education include employers, professional associations, schools of nursing, and private entrepreneurial groups.

Both types of continued learning, graduate education and continuing education, are valuable to your professional development, and both can contribute to a specific area of career development—certification.

CERTIFICATION

clinical/functional

In 1989, Styles identified at least forty-five different types of certification. These include clinical areas such as cancer as well as functional areas such as administration. Many of these include an expectation for participation in continuing education, as reported annually in the January-February issue of *The Journal of Continuing Education in Nursing* (Yoder Wise, 1994). **Certification** is the designation of special knowledge beyond basic **licensure.** It is an expectation in some employment settings for career advancement; in the field of advanced practice nursing, it is viewed as an expectation of practice. Further, in some states certification in advance practice is the avenue to designation by the state as an advanced practitioner and to reimbursement and practice privileges of advanced practice. Certification may range from testing and continuing education to documented time in practice in the specialty area plus testing and continuing education.

recertification

Recertification is a process of continued recognition of competence within a defined practice area. As an example, the American Nurses Credentialing Center (ANCC) provides for recertification every five years. The ANCC provides two certification examinations in nursing administration: one is basic (CNA), the other is advanced (CNAA). Nurses certified through this process initially provide a variety of information and sit for a licensure examination. Effective in 1998, all generalist examinations will require a baccalaureate in nursing for initial certification. During each subsequent five-year period, nurses complete a stipulated practice requirement and choose either to retake the examination or to document participation in appropriate continuing education activities.

Certification plays an important part in the advancement of a career. In some fields more than one examination exists; in some there is an examination in the broad field and numerous options for very defined subspecialties; and in other fields no examination exists. If certification does exist, however, the current trend is to expect commensurate recognition in the workplace if career advancement is anticipated.

PROFESSIONAL EXPECTATIONS

Being a professional holds both privileges and obligations. The legal privileges and expectations are codified in the state nursing practice acts, rules, and regulations. Because licensure is designed to provide the baseline, that is, the minimum expectation, it does not identify or obligate any practitioner to function in a professional manner as defined by the profession itself. For example, no practice act identifies membership in a professional association as an expectation. Nor is there an expectation for community service or scholarship. Yet, the profession, through various professional organizations, holds the expectation that nurses will belong to professional associations and provide leadership in improving communities. How to incorporate these activities in a busy, committed life can at times seem difficult. The key is to use a concept known as **reintegration** (Langford, 1990), which refers to the process of returning to a whole of nursing. It designates an incorporation of four role aspects into the role of professional nursing: education, scholarship, service, and practice. For example, the nurse who is expert in geriatrics nursing might provide guest lectures at a nearby university in problems related to aging (education). This same nurse might help explain the latest research related to dementia, a common concern of institutionalized elderly, to the staff of a nursing facility (scholarship). Additionally, this nurse might provide community blood pressure screenings at a senior citizens center and belong to the Gerontological Nurses' Association (service). This individual might also be certified as a gerontological nurse through the American Nurses Credentialing Center as an example of expertise in a specialized area of practice (practice). Thus, each of the four elements of reintegration capitalizes on all other areas to contribute to this nurse's expertise in caring for the elderly. Figure 26-2 reflects the reintegration model. Each element could stand alone as a major role; instead the synthesis of these functional elements in an area of expertise contributes to the totality of professional competence.

reintegration

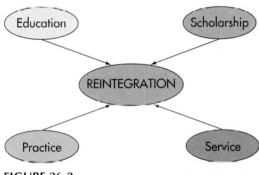

FIGURE 26-2
Reintegrated nursing.

Belonging to a **professional association** not only demonstrates professional leadership but also provides numerous opportunities to meet the other leaders, participate in policy formation, continue specialized education, and shape the future of the profession. To learn more about an association, it is probably useful to write to the national association and ask for information. Each April in the *American Journal of Nursing* all state boards of nursing and professional associations are listed, including addresses and telephone numbers. Requesting information should provide insight into both direct and indirect benefits. For example, a direct benefit may be receiving a publication or attending a meeting at reduced, or no, cost. An indirect benefit is knowing that your association actively lobbies on behalf of professional nurses.

association membership

Depending upon the type of career you want to have, it might be very important to belong to a specific association because it is synonymous with leadership in the field. In nursing, in general, the American Academy of Nursing and Sigma Theta Tau are such entities. Determining a logical level of involvement in an association at the local, state, regional, or national level is important. When a bright, articulate, committed member is discovered, that individual is frequently asked to meet other expectations of the association's work. Once again, knowing what is important in professional goals can help you decide what level of involvement is desirable and acceptable.

obligations and privileges

Because the public places its trust in any licensed profession, there are numerous other obligations and privileges to being a professional. Some are exciting, for instance providing testimony related to healthcare concerns. Others are troublesome, for instance reporting a colleague to the state nursing board for incompetent practice. These are opportunities to improve the profession and the resultant care the general public can expect.

CAREER POTENTIAL

Traditionally, nursing has been seen by the public as hospital based. Yet there are numerous other nursing careers, such as teacher, administrator, manager, clinical specialist, researcher, organizational executive, entrepreneur, and practitioner. Additionally, the number of clinical specialties continues to increase. Some have been a part of nursing for a long time and are experiencing major growth and recognition because of financial impact on healthcare. These include such foci as occupational health, school health, public health, and visiting nurse services. Concomitantly, the traditional hospital careers are simultaneously focusing and expanding. Nurses with these focused, expert skills need to be able to function with more than one clinical population. This ability to increase expertise and flexibility will continue to be in demand. Positioning within the profession to achieve this flexibility and expertise requires career commitment, continuous self-development, a passion for nursing, and a strong foundation as a leader.

CHAPTER CHECKLIST

It is important for nurse managers to make decisions about career goals and career development. Managing a career requires a set of planned strategies designed to lead systematically toward the desired goal. The use of each strategy should be geared toward finding a good person/position fit. Continued learning, whether via graduate education or continuing education, is a crucial component of success as a nurse manager.

- Career styles contribute to the diversity of the nursing profession and reflect different ways of achieving success.
  - The four career styles are:
    - Steady state: characterized by constancy with increasing professional skill.
    - Linear: a hierarchical orientation with a steady climb.
    - Entrepreneurial/transient: creates new services and meets personal priorities.
    - Spiral: rational, independent responsibility for shaping the career.
- Certain career control strategies are effective with every career style:
  - Selecting professional peers and mentors to help shape professional development.
  - Interviewing at its best is a two-way interaction that enables both

people to determine whether there is a good person/position fit.

- Designing personal/professional documents that open doors for further action include:
  - The curriculum vitae (a listing of facts).
  - The résumé (a sampling of the most relevant facts, with details).

■ Both graduate education and continuing education contribute to a nurse's ability to provide competent care.

- Graduate education (master's- or doctorate-level study) may focus on:
  - A clinical area
  - A functional area
  - A combination of both.

- Factors to consider in selecting a graduate program include:
  - Accreditation
  - Clinical/functional role
  - Credits
  - Thesis/research requirements
    Faculty
  - Current research
  - Flexibility
  - Admission policy
  - Cost.

- Continuing education opportunities exist at local, state, regional, and national levels.

■ Certification is the designation of special knowledge beyond the basic licensure and is a requirement in some employment settings. Being a professional carries additional obligations and privileges to ensure that the nurse remains competent, advances the profession, and improves healthcare.

TERMS TO KNOW

- career
- certification
- continuing education
- curriculum vitae
- licensure
- professional association
- reintegration
- résumé

REFERENCES

American Nurses Credentialing Center. (1991). *Manual for Accreditation as a Provider of Continuing Education in Nursing*. Kansas City, MO: ANCC.

Friss, L. (1989). *Strategic Management of Nurses: A Policy Oriented Approach*. Owings Mills, MD: AUPHA Press.

Joint Commission on Accreditation of Healthcare Organizations. (1992). *Accreditation Manual for Hospitals*. Chicago: The Commission.

Langford, T.L. (1990). *Managing and Being Managed: Preparation for Reintegrated Professional Nursing Practice*. Lubbock, TX: Landover Publishing.

Pedersen, A. (1993). Qualities of the excellent head nurse. *Journal of Nursing Administration, 8*(1), 40–50.

Styles, M.M. (1989). *On Specialization in Nursing: Toward a New Endowment*. Kansas City, MO: American Nurses Foundation.

Yoder Wise, P.S. (1994). Annual CE survey: State and association/certifying boards CE requirements. *The Journal of Continuing Education in Nursing, 25*, 5–8.

SUGGESTED READINGS

Bolles, R.N. (1993). *What Color is Your Parachute?: A Practical Manual for Job Hunters and Career-Changers*. Berkeley: Ten Speed Press.

Bronstein, E., & Hisrich, R.D. (1983). *The MBA Career: Moving on the Fast Track to Success*. Woodbury, N.Y.: Barrons Educational Series.

Dadich, K.A. (1992). Questions I should ask and answer: A student handbook for interviewing. *Healthcare Trends and Transitions, 3*(3), 26–31.

———(1992). Your cover letter. *Healthcare Trends and Transitions, 3*(2), 22–24.

———(1992). Your resume. *Healthcare Trends and Transitions, 3*(2), 20–21, 96.

Fry, R.W. (1989). *Your First Resume*, 2nd ed. Hawthorne, NJ: Career Press.

Chapter 26 Appendix

MARKETING YOURSELF AS A COMPETENT PROFESSIONAL*

THE CURRICULUM VITAE AND THE RÉSUMÉ: WRITING TO SELL YOURSELF

OBJECTIVES

Using this material, you will be able to:

- compile a curriculum vitae
- write a professional résumé
- access professional data in an organized manner

Things you will need: index cards, file box, pencil, scratch paper, (or computer disk) typing paper, and typewriter (or access to a professional service) or computer.

Time to allocate: Depending upon your unique background, this assignment varies considerably. It is not necessary to set aside a block of time in the data collection stage; but it may be useful to do so in the data assembly stage for the résumé.

Although there are numerous ways to record professional data, the fact remains that most nurses do not do so in a systematic manner. Therefore, when asked a question, it is often difficult to recall the information needed. The goal of this exercise is to develop a systematic plan that you can use throughout your professional career so that developing a curriculum vitae (CV) or a résumé will be relatively easy.

Curriculum vitae (note there is no singular form of the word *vitae*) means one's life story. It need not include personal facts, but it should include *all* professional facts. A résumé (the word is French, meaning summary) is a summary

---

of one's professional abilities and facts. It is designed to match a certain job or type of job.

DATA COLLECTION

The first step is to collect all previous professional information about yourself. If you are fairly new in the profession, it would help to analyze anything special you did in school, e.g., electives, offices held, or special assignments or awards. If you have an employment history, you can start with your nursing positions. Keep in mind, also, that you should include other relevant information. For example, serving as a volunteer in a day-care center may augment a brief professional history; serving on voluntary health association committees or boards may be useful to secure a position related to the group's focus.

It may be most useful to start where you are and think back. If you have limited "thinking back" to do, you are in great shape for starting a systematic plan. If, however, you have been practicing nursing for a long time, you may have some difficulty. In fact, some information may be irretrievable—do not dwell on that aspect, just record as much as you can.

At the end of this first step, you will have a series of index cards (or entries in your computer) with one data element on each card or a comparable computer data set. The areas in the box on page 532, however, should be considered, even if you currently have nothing to record under these topics. Create topic cards (divider cards) and place a fact card for each different experience, committee, article, activity, etc. behind the appropriate topic card. The "checklist" in the box on page 536 will help you keep track of your data and assemble it attractively.

index cards

DATA ASSEMBLY
Curriculum Vitae

The hard part is over. To develop a curriculum vitae (CV), simply select a logical flow of information and assemble the CV. Information should be in a chronological order. Most recent first (reverse chronological) draws attention to your latest contributions and is a better presentation of your information than a regular chronological sequence. You need to include your name, credentials, degrees, address, and phone number; this set of information should be distinct so you are easy to contact. Using the information facts by category, assemble a CV that reflects all professional involvement. A sample CV appears on page 533. A CV must be typed and appear organized. Therefore, since you are providing facts only, it is helpful to have subheadings:

sequence

Education

Name of Institution/Location	Dates Attended	Degree	Year
•			
•			
•			

Experience

Name of Institution/Location	Dates of Service	Title of Position
•		
•		
•		

Develop a curriculum vitae (typed). Be sure to have the curriculum vitae error-free and on quality bond paper.

Data Collection

Topics — *Facts Needed*

1. Education — Years of attendance, year of graduation, name of school, location, name of degree (diploma) received, special recognition—e.g., two concurrent degrees, minor or with honors.

2. Continuing education — Dates attended, places, topics and any special outcomes, type and amount of credit earned during the last few years.

3. Experience — Dates of employment, title of position, name of employing agency, location and phone number, name of chief executive officer, chief nursing officer, immediate supervisor, salary range, typical duties (role description).

4. Community/institutional service — Dates of service, name of committee/task force and the parent organization (e.g., name of hospital or district nurses association), your role on the committee (e.g., chairperson or member), general description of the committee's functions, any unique accomplishments.

5. Publications — Articles: author(s) name(s), year of publication, title, journal, volume, issue pages.
Books: author(s) name(s), year of publication, title, city, publisher.
If appropriate, description of item (e.g., internal policy manual, first article on quality assurance in a rural hospital, or letter to the editor). Be sure to note your contribution if the project was a group effort, and keeping the sequence of authorship straight is important.

6. Honors — Date, description of award, special factors related to the award (e.g., competitive, community-wide, national, etc.)

7. Speeches/presentations — Date, place, title of speech made, name of sponsoring group and nature of the presentation (e.g., keynote), your honorarium.

8. Workshops/conferences — Date, place, title of conference conducted, name of sponsoring group, nature of the presentation, brief description of the effort, your honorarium.

9. Certification — Date, certifying body, area of certification.

Résumé

To "sell" yourself to someone, you need to provide more than the facts; and the information needs to be brief and to the point. Thus, the résumé is the best choice for selling your abilities to a potential employer. A résumé focuses on a particular position's expectations or an individual's special abilities. A sample résumé appears on page 535.

There are basically two ways to develop a résumé—conventional and functional.

- The *conventional* approach provides:
  NAME
  ADDRESS
  PHONE NUMBER

  CAREER SUMMARY (optional)

  TITLE OF POSITION
      Name of employer (compression of experiences may be necessary to keep the résumé brief)
      Inclusive dates
      Responsibilities and achievements

conventional résumé

Sample Curriculum Vitae

SALLY JONES, R.N., B.S.N.
4370 South Sunset Drive
Troy, Texas 79430
(806) 555-2736

EDUCATION

Institution	Degree	Year
The Ohio State University Columbus, Ohio	6 Grad. Credits	1993
Texas Tech University Health Sciences Center Lubbock, Texas	Bachelor of Science in Nursing	1989

EXPERIENCE

Institution	Position	Dates
Childrens' Hospital Columbus, Ohio	Staff Nurse, Adolescents	2/93–present
Health Services Hospital Troy, Texas	3-11 Charge Nurse Maternal Child Division	7/90–12/92
Llano Estacado Hospital Troy, Texas	Staff Nurse Maternal Child Division	6/89–6/90

HONORS

Sigma Theta Tau, Inc., inducted into Iota Mu Chapter, 1987.

MEMBERSHIPS/OFFICES/COMMITTEES

Member	District 18 Program Committee	1989–90
Member	American Nurses' Association– Texas Nurses' Association	1989–present
Secretary	Evening Shift Staff Council, Llano Estacado Hospital	1989
President	Texas Nursing Students' Association, TTUHSC Chapter	1988–89
Member	Sigma Theta Tau, Inc.	1987–present
Member	Texas Nursing Students' Association	1985–89

PRESENTATIONS/PUBLICATIONS

Letter to the Editor, *Southwest Airlines,* p. 45	February, 1988
Testimony to the legislature of the State of Texas on diabetes education	January 13, 1987

MISCELLANEOUS

Recipient of the C.W. Smith Scholarship	1988–89

functional résumé

OTHER CATEGORIES OF *SPECIAL* MEANING FROM FACT CARDS
- The *functional* approach provides:

NAME

ADDRESS

PHONE NUMBER

CAREER SUMMARY

FUNCTION (e.g., neonatal nursing)
   Paragraph description of activities and for whom

NEW FUNCTION (e.g., management)
   Same

NEW FUNCTION
   Same

EDUCATION

OTHER CATEGORIES OF *SPECIAL* MEANING

Keep in mind that a résumé should be brief—a one- or two-page summary is best. The "other categories of *special* meaning" should relate to the specific career goal you have or position you seek. Sometimes a career goal is included on the résumé; other times it is described in a cover letter. A functional approach is best if you are planning a sharp departure from present positions. The focus is on what you've done, not when.

Develop a résumé (typed). Be sure to have the résumé error-free and on quality bond.

THE COVER LETTER

Using the information in this section, you will be able to write a cover letter that is brief and that contains the essential information.

Things you will need:
- Your curriculum vitae or résumé, scratch paper, pencil, (or computer disk) typing paper and typewriter (or access to a professional service) or computer.

Time to allocate:
- Approximately 10 to 20 minutes.

length

The cover letter can be a vital source of information and the opportunity to assure yourself of an interview. It is a brief (generally no more than one page) statement that says why you are writing, why you "fit" the organization and a specific position (or type[s] of position[s]), and how you will follow up (e.g., write or call).

purpose

Numerous positions may be advertised by a major organization simultaneously. Thus, it is crucial to state immediately why you are writing. If a particular advertisement or referral does not include the name of the key nursing contact, you should obtain this information and send your letter to that person (even if you are sending a copy to the personnel office). (Note: This assumes the position you are seeking is in the purview of the nursing division.)

Once you have stated your reason for writing, i.e., referencing a particular position or type(s) of position(s), you should address the issue of "why you." That is, why should someone take time to read your attached résumé or curriculum vitae? This statement should reflect what you know about the

Sample Résumé (Conventional)

SALLY JONES, R.N., B.S.N.
4370 South Sunset Drive
Troy, Texas 79430
(806) 555-2736

CAREER SUMMARY: Maternal child health is the general focus of my career with a specialty in adolescent care. In addition to taking elective credit in this area in my undergraduate program and to completing 6 credits as a special student at the graduate level, I have worked in general maternal child service areas since graduating with my Bachelor of Science in Nursing.

EXPERIENCE:

STAFF NURSE Childrens' Hospital Columbus, Ohio February, 1993–	While pursuing graduate education, I am working part-time on an adolescent unit that includes acutely ill and unstable chronically ill patients.

CHARGE NURSE
Health Services
  Hospital
Troy, Texas
July, 1990–
  December, 1992
	As 3-11 charge nurse in a 50-bed postpartum unit, I assigned between 18 and 25 staff nurses per shift. I had responsibility for orientation to the unit on evenings. During this time, I designed a reporting format for change of shift report.

STAFF NURSE
Llano Estacado
  Hospital
Troy, Texas
June, 1989–
  June, 1990
	As primary nurse typically caring for six normal newborns or two critically ill newborns, I refined skills in this specialty. Additionally, I helped institute standardized care plans with individual modifications and designed a plan for overflow to the normal newborn area.

HONORS:	Member of Sigma Theta Tau, Inc., 1987–present. Recipient of C.W. Smith Scholarship, 1988–89.

Both of these honors were based on the fact that I carried a 3.9 GPA while working 20 hours a week as a nursing assistant. I also was selected to present testimony on behalf of the Texas Nursing Students' Association to the legislature regarding diabetes education.

PROFESSIONAL COMMITMENTS: As a student, I joined the Texas Nursing Students' Association and served as president of my local chapter for a year. Upon graduation, I joined the Texas Nurses' Association and served on the program committee of the local district. As a result of serving as secretary of the evening shift staff council at Llano Estacado, I joined AWOHNN, the Association of Women's Health, Obstetrics, and Neonatal Nurses.

EDUCATION: After completing my B.S.N. at Texas Tech University Health Sciences Center in 1989, I enrolled in six graduate credits at Ohio State University. These courses focus on management and computer science.

Checklist for Constructing a Curriculum Vitae/Résumé/Qualifications Brief

DATA COLLECTION
_____1. Index cards for information development (computer).
_____2. Information assembled in categorical manner.

DATA ASSEMBLY
_____ 1. Discrete categories are used.
_____ 2. Assembly addresses *specific* position (or cover letter for CV).
_____ 3. Current name, address, and telephone number are prominent.
_____ 4. Career summary (if used) (or cover letter for CV) is prominent.
_____ 5. Key points about positions are evident.
_____ 6. A logical flow is evident.
_____ 7. Grammar, spelling, and syntax are correct.
_____ 8. Writing style is direct, but not terse, and positive.
_____ 9. Action verbs are evident.
_____10. If writing in full sentences, third person and passive voice are avoided, i.e., write in the active voice.
_____11. "Canned" résumé language is avoided—e.g., "distinguished" and "all phases of . . ."
_____12. Emphasis is on competence (cover letter for CV).
_____13. Specific examples of key competencies are cited (cover letter for CV).
_____14. The format is consistent throughout.

APPEARANCE AND FORMAT
_____1. There are no typos.
_____2. The product is "clean"—e.g., no smudges, no discrepant margins.
_____3. It is readable—e.g., layout design is pleasing: white space, capitalization, etc.
_____4. The paper is *high*-quality bond.
_____5. The type is businesslike (no script).
_____6. Emphasis is evident—e.g., centering, bold print, and underlining.
_____7. It is only one or two pages in length (not applicable for a CV).

OVERVIEW
_____1. It is attractive, interesting, quick-reading, and competence-based.
_____2. The package *sells you*.
_____3. You are pleased to have it precede you.
_____4. Additional items are enclosed or they are assembled for personal handling at an interview.
_____5. If you were receiving this CV or résumé, would *you* want to interview this person?

"fit" organization and how you will fit in. This point may take the form of comparable experience, or diverse experiences that will blend in in a unique way, or how your education program prepared you to work in such a place. Reference to the enclosed résumé or curriculum vitae is appropriate. Examples of competencies can be included to clarify your strengths.

The closing comment should convey optimism—that is, you anticipate being interviewed. If you want to *assure* yourself of having an additional opportunity to sell yourself, you should indicate when you will follow up with a phone call.

The letter should include your name as it appears on your résumé or curriculum vitae, and your address and telephone number. It is especially helpful to designate both daytime and evening telephone numbers. Quality bond paper reflects the image you wish to portray. A printed letterhead can be used, but it is not necessary. If you have a business card, you can enclose it, paper-clipped to the letter and résumé or curriculum vitae. Only blue or black ink or ballpoint pens should be used.

If you already know the person, it may be easy to use first names in conversation. Using the appropriate title and last name is generally more acceptable for written communication. A personal note, using the person's first name, can be handwritten on an enclosed note or at the bottom of the letter.

THE INTERVIEW

The box below provides key activities to help you prepare for an interview. The box on page 538 presents questions you may want to ask (questions 25 and 26), questions that will be asked of you (questions 4 and 19) and questions that can serve either the interviewer or interviewee when modified. For example, question 6 can be reworded to ask, "Why should I work for you?"; question 9 can be something each of you wants to know about the other.

Checklist for Interviewing

1. Check interviewing guides, such as *What Color is Your Parachute?*
2. Check out the new organization
   a. Read, call, network, visit
   b. Obtain statistics, facts, etc.
   c. Learn the buzz words
   d. Ask about new directions
3. Recheck your résumé or vitae for
   a. emphasis
   b. new information
4. Practice using "action" words
5. Decide about
   a. appearance
   b. key points
      1) to make
      2) to learn
   c. format for quick check (for example a file card with key points)
6. Arrive on time and alone
7. Make a memorable entrance:
   1. make eye contact, 2. shake hands, 3. smile, 4. say "Hello, I'm . . ."
8. Position yourself with the interviewer
9. Keep in mind your key points
10. Appear interested—project confidence, energy, and ability
11. Accentuate the positive!
12. Answer questions directly, or know when not to
13. Ask for more information
14. Say only positive things about your present employer
15. Thank interviewer, at the time and later
16. Write thank you
17. Let interviewer know your decision
18. Put commitments in writing

Questions to Ask/To be Asked

1. What kinds of experiences did you have in your _____ program? [new graduates]
2. Why did you select that type of program? [new graduate]
3. Tell me what your strengths are.
4. What can you contribute to *this* position? *This* organization?
5. Tell me what you believe to be a major ethical dilemma. What would you do in such a situation?
6. Why should I hire you?
7. What do you expect to get from this position?
8. What do you expect to be doing in 3 years?
9. What do you do best?
10. What would people who report to you say was your best ability? Your worst?
11. What do you like best about your present (last) job? Least?
12. How do you reach decisions in relation to your job?
13. What have you done for your professional development?
14. What do you like to do to relax?
*15. How did you prepare for this interview?
16. How does this position fit with your goals?
*17. What criteria are you using to evaluate and choose a position?
*18. What are some adjectives that describe you?
*19. How do you handle criticism?
20. What is your philosophy of nursing care?
21. Describe how you interact with physicians. Nurses. Assistive personnel.
22. Have you ever reported anyone for improper care? How did you feel about it?
23. How would your peers describe you—as a leader?
 as a member of the profession?
 as a manager?
 as a nurse?
 as a follower?
24. Picture this situation: (a typical one). How would you respond?
25. What percentage of registered nurses belong to the state nurses' association? to the specialty association in your clinical field?
26. Who chairs your peer review committee? Quality committee?

From Bronstein, E., & Hisrich, R.D. (1983). The MBA Career: Moving on the Fast Track to Success. Woodbury, NY: Barrons Educational Series.

INTERVIEW TOPICS AND QUESTIONS OF CONCERN

During interviews, employers should ask all applicants for a given position the same questions. In addition to providing comparable information as the basis for a decision, the applicant's expectation for equal treatment is upheld. Only questions related to the position and its description are legitimate. Employers should not ask other questions (see box on page 539) and applicants should express appropriate concern if asked such inappropriate questions.

If the interviewer asked an inappropriate question, the applicant can choose not to answer the direct question by addressing the content area. For exam-

Sample of Inappropriate Questions

1. How old are you?
2. What does your husband (wife) do?
3. Who takes care of your children?
4. Are you working "just to help out?"
5. Do you have any handicaps?
6. Where were you born?
7. What are the names of all organizations to which you belong?
8. What is your religious preference?

ple, if asked about your spouse's employment, you might say, "I believe what you are asking is how long I will be able to be in this position. Let me assure you that I intend to be here for at least 2 years."

Each of the content areas in the box may be acceptable, but the question as phrased is inappropriate. The following examples are ways to verify/secure the information as an employer, in a manner that is both appropriate and legal.

1. Do you know that this position requires someone at least 21 years old?
2. This position requires that no one in your immediate family be in the healthcare field or own interest/shares in any healthcare facility. Does this pose a problem for you?
3. Attendance is important. Are you able to meet this expectation?
4. What are your short-term and long-term goals?
5. Is there anything that would prevent you from performing this work as described?
6. This position requires U.S. citizenship. May I assume you meet this criterion?
7. What professional organizations do you belong to?
8. As you have read in our philosophy, you are aware that we subscribe to a Christian philosophy. Do you understand that all employees are expected to promote the philosophy?

The key to assuring a fair interviewing process is being prepared ahead of time and knowing what can be asked legitimately and what a reasonable answer is.

THE SUCCESSFUL THANK YOU

This may be the last chance you have to sell yourself. As a result, careful thought should be given to what you need to say in your "thank-you" letter.

Use the full inside address (name, title, division/department, organization's name and address). This action conveys accuracy and detail. The greeting should use the title the interviewer prefers (ask the personnel office/secretary). It should read: "Dear Mr./Ms./Dr./Miss/Mrs. (last name):". The lead sentence should recall the interview date and purpose so the reader can place you. If you discussed more than one position, list your preference first or follow it with "as well as other positions."

The body of the letter should focus on some key point the interviewer defined as crucial and your abilities to focus on that point. Use "action" words in describing your "fit" in this organization.

Your closing should reference specific time frames if necessary, for example, when you are available. Be sure to sign your full name above a typed name with credentials including degrees.

Proof the letter for layout, typographical errors, spelling, and content. Mail it promptly. The interviewer should receive it within a week of the interview if it is to be most effective.

GLOSSARY

Absenteeism The rate at which an individual misses work on an unplanned basis. *(Chapter 19)*

Acceptance The second phase of the change process when the change is willingly used. *(Chapter 5)*

Accommodating An unassertive, cooperative approach to conflict in which the individual neglects own personal needs, goals, and concerns in favor of satisfying those of others. *(Chapter 17)*

Acculturation The process of becoming familiar and comfortable with and able to function within a different culture or environment, while retaining one's own cultural identity (Simons et al., 1993). *(Chapter 8)*

Acknowledgment Recognition that an employee is valued and respected for what he or she has to offer to the workplace, team, or group; acknowledgments may be verbal or written, public or private. *(Chapter 14)*

Active listening Focusing completely on the speaker and listening without judgment to the essence of the conversation; an active listener should be able to repeat accurately at least 95 percent of the speaker's intended meaning. *(Chapter 14)*

Advocacy Multidimensional concept that refers to acting on or in behalf of another who is unable to act for him/herself. *(Chapter 20)*

Agenda A written list of items to be covered in a meeting and the related materials that meeting participants should read beforehand or bring along. Types of agendas include structured agendas, timed agendas, and action agendas. *(Chapter 11)*

Anxiety An arousal state that is a reaction to stress as the individual attempts to identify and define the problem (Kozier et al., 1992). *(Chapter 25)*

Apparent agency Doctrine whereby a principal becomes accountable for the actions of his/her agent; created when a person holds himself/herself out as acting in behalf of the principal; also known as apparent authority. *(Chapter 3)*

Arbitration Process by which an impartial person, chosen by the parties to a dispute, attempts to resolve the dispute. *(Chapter 3)*

Assertive Communicating one's own responses to specific circumstances, instead of blaming others for undesired consequences. *(Chapter 16)*

Associate nurse A licensed nurse in the primary nursing system who provides care to the patient according to the primary nurse's specification while the primary nurse is not working. *(Chapter 21)*

Autonomy Personal freedom and the right to choose what will happen to one's own person. *(Chapter 3)*

Average length of stay The number of patient days in a specific time period divided by the number of discharges in that same time period. *(Chapter 22)*

Avoiding An unassertive, uncooperative approach to conflict in which the avoider neither pursues his/her own needs, goals, and concerns nor helps others to do so. *(Chapter 17)*

Awareness The first phase of the change process when the need for change or innovation emerges. *(Chapter 5)*

Barrier A factor in the change situation that prevents or slows down the achievement of the change goal. *(Chapter 5)*

Behavioral message The meaning that is communicated by a person's actions and behaviors, which may differ from the person's verbal message. *(Chapter 16)*

Beneficence Principle that states that the actions one takes should promote good. *(Chapter 3)*

Biofeedback A stress-reduction strategy wherein an individual learns, via systematic training and practice, to exert conscious control over unconscious or involuntary body processes (such as heart rate or blood pressure). *(Chapter 25)*

Biomedical technology The use of machines and implantable devices to provide physiologic monitoring, diagnostic testing, drug administration, and therapeutic treatments in patient care. *(Chapter 12)*

Budget A detailed financial plan, stated in dollars, for carrying out the activities an organization wants to accomplish in a specific period of time. *(Chapter 13)*

Budgeting process An ongoing activity of planning and managing revenues and expenses in order to meet the goals of the organization. *(Chapter 13)*

Bureaucratic organization	Characterized by formality, low autonomy, a hierarchy of authority, an environment of rules, division of labor, specialization, centralization, and control. *(Chapter 9)*
Burnout	A type of reaction to stress; a syndrome manifested by emotional exhaustion, depersonalization, and reduced personal accomplishment. *(Chapter 25)*
Capital expenditure budget	A plan for purchasing major capital items, such as equipment or physical plant, with a useful life greater than one year and exceeding a minimum cost set by the organization. *(Chapter 13)*
Capitation	A reimbursement method where healthcare providers are paid a per person per year (or per month) fee for providing specified services over a period of time. *(Chapter 13)*
Care delivery system	A method nurses use to provide care to patients and clients. *(Chapter 21)*
Care MAP	An abbreviation for care multidisciplinary action plan, which combines a nursing care plan with a critical path. The purpose is to expedite patient care by improving expected outcome during a designated day. *(Chapter 21)*
Career	Progressive achievement throughout a person's professional life. *(Chapter 26)*
Caring	Behaviors and attitudes that denote special concern, interest, and/or feeling. *(Chapter 20)*
Case management method	A method of delivering patient care based on patient outcomes and cost containment. Components of case management are a case manager, critical paths, and unit-based managed care. *(Chapter 21)*
Case manager	A baccalaureate or master's prepared clinical nurse who coordinates patient care from preadmission to and through discharge. *(Chapter 21)*
Case method	A method of care delivery in which one nurse provides total care for one patient during an entire eight-hour period or shift. *(Chapter 21)*
Case mix	The volume and type of patients served by a healthcare provider. *(Chapter 13)*
Cash budget	A plan for an organizations's cash receipts and disbursements. *(Chapter 13)*
Certification	Designation of special knowledge beyond basic licensure. *(Chapter 26)*

Change	Something new or different from what existed prior to a change or innovation. *(Chapter 5)*
Change agent	An individual or group whose purpose is to create and lead a change process. *(Chapter 5)*
Change goal	The desired end product of a deliberate or unanticipated change. *(Chapter 5)*
Change process	An ongoing group of means/activities actively used to move toward the change goal. *(Chapter 5)*
Change situation	The conditions and circumstances composing the place within which change implementation occurs. *(Chapter 5)*
Charge nurse	A registered nurse responsible for delegating and coordinating patient care and staff on a specific unit. A resource person for all staff, usually one charge nurse each shift. *(Chapter 21)*
Charges	The cost of providing a service plus a markup for profit. *(Chapter 13)*
Chemically dependent	A psychophysiological state in which an individual requires a substance such as drugs or alcohol to prevent the onset of symptoms of abstinence. *(Chapter 19)*
Coaching	The strategy a manager uses to help others learn, think critically, and grow through communications about performance. *(Chapter 15)*
Coalitions	Groups of individuals or organizations that join together temporarily around a common goal. This goal often focuses on an effort to effect change. *(Chapter 24)*
Cognitive restructing	A mental stress–reduction strategy in which the individual learns to reframe his or her thought processes in order to alleviate stress (e.g., substituting positive self-talk for negative thoughts about oneself). *(Chapter 25)*
Collaboration	Conjoint, interdisciplinary problem solving from an equal power base on the client's behalf. *(Chapter 16)* Also, an assertive, cooperative approach to conflict in which the individual is able to work creatively and openly with others to find the solution that best achieves all important goals. *(Chapter 17)*
Collective bargaining	Mechanism for settling labor disputes by negotiation between the employer and representatives of the employees. *(Chapter 3)*

Commitment A state of being emotionally impelled—feeling passionate about and dedicated to a project or event. *(Chapter 14)*

Common law System of jurisprudence that is derived from principles rather than rules and regulations and consists of comprehensive principles based on justice, reason, and common sense. *(Chapter 3)*

Communication A goal-directed process of sending messages and analyzing feedback until the goal is met. *(Chapter 16)*

Competing An assertive, uncooperative approach to conflict in which the individual pursues his or her own needs at the expense of others'. *(Chapter 17)*

Compromising A moderately assertive, cooperative approach to conflict in which the individual's ability to negotiate and willingness to "give and take" results in conflict resolution and fulfillment of important priorities for all involved. *(Chapter 17)*

Confidentiality Right of privacy to the medical record of a patient/client. *(Chapter 3)* Also, a respect for the privacy of information and the ethical use of information for its original purpose. *(Chapter 12)*

Conflict A perceived difference among people and a four-stage process including frustration, conceptualization, action, and outcomes. *(Chapter 17)*

Consent A voluntary action by which one agrees to allow someone else to do something; may be oral, written, or implied based upon the circumstances. *(Chapter 3)*

Consolidated systems A group of healthcare organizations that are united based on common characteristics of ownership, regional location, or mutual performance objectives for the purpose of optimizing utilization of their resources in achieving their missions. *(Chapter 7)*

Constructive confrontation A means by which group or team members can deal with issues by openly expressing their ideas and feelings, thereby using interactive skills to accomplish tasks and improve outcomes. *(Chapter 14)*

Consumer focus Centering of action or attention on the participant or user as a whole. *(Chapter 20)*

Continuing education Those learning activities intended to build upon the educational and experiential bases of the professional nurse for the enhancement of practice, education, administration, research, or theory development to the end of improving the health of the public (ANCC, 1991, p. 76) *(Chapter 26)*

Continuous quality improvement (CQI)	A management process that advocates agency-wide planning and implementation of a program designed to improve the quality of care (Wilson, 1992, pp. 182–183). *(Chapter 4)* Also, an ongoing process that involves a multidisciplinary team for planning/problem solving. Similar to quality improvement but emphasizes the continuous nature of the process. *(Chapter 10)*
Contractual allowance	A discount from full charges. *(Chapter 13)*
Controversy	A situation in which opinions, ideas, information, theories, and conclusions are perceived as incompatible with those of another person or group (Johnson and Johnson, 1984). *(Chapter 17)*
Coping	The immediate response of a person to a threatening situation. *(Chapter 25)*
Co-primary nursing	See *partnership model*. *(Chapter 21)*
Corporate health alliance	Business or industrial organization that enrolls all corporation employees in a health plan with which it has negotiated to provide a comprehensive benefit package. *(Chapter 7)*
Cost	The amount spent on something; the national healthcare costs are a function of the price and utilization of healthcare services; a healthcare provider's costs are the expenses involved in providing a good or service. *(Chapter 13)*
Cost-based reimbursement	A retrospective payment method where all allowable costs are used as the basis for payment. *(Chapter 13)*
Cost center	An organizational unit for which costs can be identified and managed. *(Chapter 13)*
Creativity	Conceptualizing new and innovative approaches to solving problems or making decisions. *(Chapter 6)*
Critical path	A component of a care MAP that is specific to diagnosis-related group reimbursement. The purpose is to ensure patients are discharged before insurance reimbursement is eliminated. *(Chapter 21)*
Critical thinking	A composite of knowledge, attitudes, and skills; intellectually disciplined process. *(Chapter 6)* Also, the ability to assess a situation by asking open-ended questions about the facts and assumptions that underlie it, and to use one's own judgment and problem-solving ability in deciding how to deal with it. *(Chapter 15)*

Cross-culturalism Involving or mediating between two cultures, one's own and that of another (Simons et al., 1993). *(Chapter 8)*

Cross-training A method of developing staff and building their confidence that involves assigning them to areas other than the one in which they usually work, to gain expertise. *(Chapter 15)*

Cultural diversity A vast range of cultural differences related to institutional, ethnic, gender, religious, or other variables that convey a set of beliefs or values that have become factors needing attention in living and working together. Often applied to an organization that seeks to deal with the interface of people who are different from each other (Simons et al., 1993). *(Chapter 8)*

Cultural sensitivity The capacity to feel, convey, or react to ideas, habits, attitudes, customs, or traditions that help to create standards for a group of people to coexist. *(Chapter 8)*

Culture A way of life. It is developed and communicated by a group of people, consciously or unconsciously, to subsequent generations. It consists of ideas, habits, attitudes, customs, and traditions that help to create standards for a group of people to coexist. It makes a group of people unique (Simons et al., 1993). *(Chapter 8)*

Culture broker One who interprets, mediates, and/or negotiates cultural or racial differences between people. *(Chapter 20)*

Curriculum vitae A listing of professional life activities. *(Chapter 26)*

Data Discrete entities that describe or measure something without interpretation. *(Chapter 12)*

Data base A collection of data elements organized and stored together. *(Chapter 12)*

Data processing Structuring, organizing, and interpreting of data into information. *(Chapter 12)*

Decision making Purposeful and goal-directed effort utilizing a systematic process to choose among options. *(Chapter 6)*

Decisional management roles Roles in which the manager plays a pivotal part in decision making. Examples include entrepreneur, disturbance handler, resource allocator, and negotiator (Mintzberg, 1975). *(Chapter 23)*

Defendant The party against whom a suit is brought; in a criminal action, the person accused of committing a crime. *(Chapter 3)*

Delegation Empowering someone to perform a task or assume an entire role on one's behalf, and to be accountable for the outcome. *(Chapter 11)*

Demographics A study of human population (size, growth, distribution, statistics). *(Chapter 4)*

Deontological theory From the Greek for "duty," derived norms and rules from the duties that human beings owe to one another by virtue of commitments made and roles assumed; has sometimes been subdivided into situational ethical theory. *(Chapter 3)*

Descriptive/ behavioral model A problem-solving/decision-making approach used when not all options or consequences are known; as uncertainty exists, options that are acceptable are chosen. *(Chapter 6)*

Diagnostic testing Systems that provide ongoing information for the establishment of diagnoses from data such as blood gases, pulmonary functions, intracranial pressure, and drug levels. *(Chapter 12)*

Differentiated nursing practice Recognizing a difference in the level of education and competency of each registered nurse. The differentiation is based on education, job position, and clinical expertise. *(Chapter 21)*

Dualism An "either/or" way of conceptualizing reality in terms of two opposing sides or parts (right or wrong, yes or no), limiting the broad spectrum of possibilities that exist between. *(Chapter 14)*

Emancipated minor Persons under the age of adulthood who are no longer under the control and regulation of their parents and who may give valid consent for medical procedures; examples include married teens, underaged parents, and teens in the armed services. *(Chapter 3)*

Empowerment A sharing of power and control with the expectation that people are responsible for themselves. *(Chapter 15)* Also, the process by which we facilitate the participation of others in decision making and taking within an environment where there is an equitable distribution of power. *(Chapter 24)*

Ethics Science relating to moral actions and moral values; rules of conduct recognized in respect to a particular class of human actions. *(Chapter 3)* Also, a branch of morthat examines human behavior. *(Chapter 12)*

Ethnocentrism   Using the culture of one's own group as a standard for the judgement of others, or thinking of it as superior to other cultures that are merely different (Simons et al., 1993). *(Chapter 8)*

Eustress   Positive sense of well-being evoked when confronted with a situation. *(Chapter 25)*

Expected outcomes   The result of patient goals that are achieved through a combination of medical and nursing interventions with patient participation. *(Chapter 21)*

Expenses   Costs of goods and services provided. *(Chapter 13)*

Expert system   A program that mimics the inductive and deductive reasoning of a human expert. *(Chapter 12)*

Expert witness   Person testifying who has special knowledge about a given subject or occupation; knowledge of an expert witness must generally be such that it is not normally possessed by the average person; contrasts with lay witness. *(Chapter 3)*

External demands   Stressors that are outside the individual, such as workplace, environment, economy, technology, and family. *(Chapter 25)*

Facilitator   A factor in the change situation that promotes the achievement of the change goal. *(Chapter 5)*

Factor evaluation   A patient classification system that incorporates specific elements or critical indicators and rates patients on each of these elements. Each indicator is assigned a weight or numerical value. *(Chapter 22)*

Fee for service system   A system in which patients have the option of consulting any healthcare provider, subject to reasonable requirements that may include utilization review and prior approval for certain services, but does not include a requirement to seek approval through a gatekeeper. *(Chapter 7)*

Fidelity   Keeping one's promises or commitments. *(Chapter 3)*

Fit   The possession of characteristics that are suitable to the work that is to be carried out and the technologies by which the work is to be accomplished. *(Chapter 9)*

Five-why technique   Asking the question "Why?" at least five times to attempt to get at the root of a problem. *(Chapter 10)*

Fixed costs   Costs that do not change in total as the volume of patients changes. *(Chapter 13)*

Flat organization   Characterized by decentralization of decision making to the level of personnel carrying out the work. *(Chapter 9)*

Flat-rate reimbursement   A method in which a third-party payer decides in advance what will be paid for a particular service. *(Chapter 13)*

Flowsheet   A tool for planning the workday that summarizes information a manager typically needs to know about assigned patients, organizing both the time flow and overall care. *(Chapter 11)*

Foreseeability   Concept that certain events may reasonably be expected to cause specific consequences; third element of negligence/malpractice. *(Chapter 3)*

For-profit   Financial gains are distributed to stockholders. *(Chapter 7)*

Full-time equivalent (FTE)   An employee who works full time, 40 hours per week, 2,080 hours per year. *(Chapters 13 and 22)*

Functional nursing   A method of providing patient care where a mix of licensed and unlicensed personnel each provide a specific task for a large group of patients. *(Chapter 21)*

Gatekeeper   Position or role that serves as a liaison between the consumer and the system being used (healthcare system). *(Chapter 20)*

General adaptation syndrome (GAS)   Hans Selye's concept describing the individual's three-part response to stress, which consists of alarm, resistance, and exhaustion or adaptation. *(Chapter 25)*

Group   An assemblage of individuals who share some unifying relationship (such as their mutual involvement in a certain endeavor). (A group may or may not also be a *team*.) *(Chapter 14)*

Halo or recency effect   Performance is based on one positive incident or the most recent performance. *(Chapter 18)*

Healthcare consumer   One who consumes or uses products and/or services from the healthcare industry. *(Chapter 20)*

Healthcare provider   One who provides and/or delivers products and services from the healthcare industry. *(Chapter 20)*

Hierarchy   A body of persons organized in a pyramidal fashion according to authority for decision making with those with greatest decision-making authority at the top and those with least authority at the bottom. *(Chapter 9)*

High tech	Mechanistic perspective that relates to the use of technology in the diagnosis and treatment of disease. *(Chapter 20)*
High touch	Caring, humanistic perspective that relates to the use of human skills in the care and treatment of patients. *(Chapter 20)*
Hospital information system	A large integrated computer system that focuses on hospital processes. *(Chapter 12)*
Hybrid organization	Possessing characteristics from several types of organizational structures. *(Chapter 9)*
Indemnification	Obligation resting on one person to make good any loss or damages another has incurred because of the first person's actions or non-actions; refers to the total shifting of the economic loss to the party chiefly responsible for that loss. *(Chapter 3)*
Independent contractor	One who makes an agreement with another to perform a service or piece of work and retains in himself/herself control of the means, method, and manner of producing the result to be accomplished; sometimes called an independent practitioner. *(Chapter 3)*
Informatics	The use of knowledge technology. *(Chapter 12)*
Information	Communication or reception of knowledge, consisting of interpreted, organized, or structured data. *(Chapter 12)*
Information technology	The use of computer hardware and software to process data into information to solve problems. *(Chapter 12)*
Informational management roles	Roles in which the manager serves as the nerve center of the organizational unit. Examples include monitor, disseminator, and spokesperson (Mintzberg, 1975). *(Chapter 23)*
Informed consent	Voluntary permission given only after full notice as to what consent is being given for; person must be appraised of the nature, risks, benefits, optional therapies, and potential complications of a medical procedure before true and valid consent is obtained. *(Chapter 3)*
Innovation	A new idea or approach that initially may be seen as not fulfilling a niche or function. *(Chapter 5)*
Innovator	An individual or group who has developed a new idea whose efficacy may not be recognized initially. *(Chapter 5)*

Integrated systems	Computer systems that link one mainframe containing a central data base with terminals or personal computers in all departments in the organization. *(Chapter 12)*
Integration	The third phase of the change process when the change is integrated into work processes. *(Chapter 5)*
Internal demands	Stressors that are within the individual, such as personal needs, health status, and self-esteem. *(Chapter 25)*
Interpersonal conflict	Conflict that occurs between or among people. *(Chapter 17)*
Interpersonal management roles	Roles that express the manager's formal authority through basic interpersonal relationships. Examples include figure-head, leader, and liaison (Mintzberg, 1975). *(Chapter 23)*
Intrapersonal conflict	Conflict that occurs within the individual. *(Chapter 17)*
Intrapreneur	An individual or group within an organization who develops a novel idea for implementation on the basis of benefit to the organization. *(Chapter 5)*
Jargon	Terminology that is used among and understood by the members of one discipline but that may not be understood or shared by members of other disciplines; careless use of jargon can lead to unclear communication. *(Chapter 16)*
Jurisprudence	Study of the structure of the legal system; sometimes used synonymously with the "law." *(Chapter 3)*
Justice	Concerns the issue that persons should be treated equally and fairly. *(Chapter 3)*
Knowledge	Information that is combined or synthesized so that inter-relationships are identified. *(Chapter 12)*
Knowledge base	The structure of an expert system that contains the rules the expert nurse would apply to make a decision. *(Chapter 12)*
Knowledge technology	A system that generates or processes knowledge. *(Chapter 12)*
Labor union	Association of workers that exists for the purpose of bargaining, either in whole or in part, on behalf of the workers with management about the terms of employment. *(Chapter 3)*

Law	Sum total of rules and regulations by which a society is governed; rules and regulations established and enforced by authority or custom within a given community, state, or nation. *(Chapter 3)*
Lay witness	Person who testifies to what he or she has seen, heard, or otherwise observed; contrasts with *expert witness*. *(Chapter 3)*
Leader	A pace setter, forerunner. *(Chapter 2)*
Leadership	The personal traits necessary to establish a vision for patient care consistent with the mission and purpose of an organization, assess the current condition of status of the patient or organization, and enter into relationships with others (patients, families, or peers) to motivate and inspire these individuals to achieve the desired outcome. *(Chapter 1)*
Liability	Refers to one's responsibility for his/her actions or inactions. *(Chapter 3)*
Liable	To be responsible for; to be obligated in law. *(Chapter 3)*
Licensure	A right granted that gives the licensee permission to do something that he/she could not legally do absent such permission. *(Chapter 3)* Also, the minimum form of credentialing, providing baseline expectations for those in a particular field without identifying or obligating the practitioner to function in a professional manner as defined by the profession itself. *(Chapter 26)*
Magnet hospitals	Hospitals that attract and support committed staff members and that are viewed as desirable, positive places to work. *(Chapter 15)*
Mainframe computer	The largest, fastest computer that can collect, store, and process large amounts of data. *(Chapter 12)*
Malpractice	Failure of a professional person to act in accordance with the prevalent professional standards or failure to foresee potential consequences that a professional person, having the necessary skills and expertise to act in a professional manner, should foresee. *(Chapter 3)*
Managed care	Care purchased through a public or private healthcare organization whose goal is to promote quality healthcare outcomes for its clients at the lowest cost possible through planning, directing, and coordinating care delivered by healthcare organizations that it may own, have contractual agreements with, or have authority over by virtue of the fact that it reimburses the organization for services

	provided its clients. *(Chapter 7)* Also, a system of care in which a designated person determines the services the patient uses. *(Chapter 13)*
Management	The activities needed to plan, organize, motivate, and control the human and material resources needed to achieve outcomes consistent with the organization's mission and purpose. *(Chapter 1)*
Marketing	The "analysis, planning, implementation, and control of carefully formulated programs designed to bring about voluntary exchanges of values with target markets for the purpose of achieving organizational objectives" (Harvey, 1990, pp. 186–187). *(Chapter 4)*
Matrix organization	A multiple command system that emphasizes coordination of a person designated as responsible for a given output or product and a person designated as responsible for administrative functions necessary to produce the output. *(Chapter 9)*
Mentor	An experienced professional who sponsors, coaches, and supports a typically younger professional, promoting the career development of the younger professional. *(Chapter 23)*
Mission	A statement of duties or function and identification of the population for whom the duties or functions will be carried out, a statement of purpose that defines the reason for the existence of an organization. *(Chapter 9)* Also, the plan, aim, or intention of a team. *(Chapter 14)*
Modular method	A system of patient care delivery that uses team nursing but focuses on the geographical location of patient rooms for assignment of staff. *(Chapter 21)*
Multiculturalism	The existence within one society of diverse groups who maintain their unique cultural identity while accepting and participating in the larger society's legal and political system (Simons et al., 1993). *(Chapter 8)*
Negligence	Failure to exercise the degree of care that a person of ordinary prudence, based upon the reasonable person standard, would exercise under the same or similar circumstances; also known as ordinary negligence. *(Chapter 3)*
Negotiating	A process of making trade-offs. *(Chapter 24)*
Network	A group of interconnected or cooperating points of service that together provide a full range of health services. *(Chapter 7)* Also, a system of contacts who are developed, nurtured, and maintained as source for information, advice, and moral support (Schutzenhofer, 1992). *(Chapter 24)*

Networked systems Several computers that are supported by another computer that acts as a file server. *(Chapter 12)*

Non-maleficence Ethical principle that states that one should do no harm. *(Chapter 3)*

Nonproductive hours Paid time that is not worked, such as vacation, holiday, and sick time. *(Chapter 13)*

Nonproductive time Also referred to as benefit time and includes time off, vacation, holiday, sick, personal, and education time. *(Chapter 22)*

Nonpunitive discipline A four-step process beginning with a friendly reminder of standards and ending with the employee realizing that he/she is not committed to the organization and therefore is terminated. *(Chapter 19)*

Normative/ prescriptive model An analytical approach to finding the ideal option or solution, used when options and consequences are known. *(Chapter 6)*

Not for profit Financial gains are reinvested in the organization. *(Chapter 7)*

Nurse manager An individual responsible for an ascribed population of patients/clients found in a variety of healthcare settings. *(Chapter 2)*

Nurse practice act Statutory enforcement that defines the practice of nursing and gives guidance with scope of practice issues; passed on a state-by-state basis. *(Chapter 3)*

Nursing administration systems Computer systems that process data for quality management activities, personnel files, communication networks, budgeting and payroll, summary reports, and forecasting and trending. *(Chapter 12)*

Nursing information systems Computer systems that manage the information required for the practice of nursing. *(Chapter 12)*

Nursing minimum data set A minimum set of items of information designed to standardize the collection of nursing data. *(Chapter 12)*

On-line interactive systems Computer systems that communicate patient information throughout the hospital by way of on-line terminals. *(Chapter 12)*

Operating budget The financial plan, that is the revenues and expenses, for the day-to-day activities of the organization; it includes the volume and revenue budget, supply and expense budget, and personnel budget. *(Chapter 13)*

Optimizing decision   Selecting the most ideal solution or option to achieve goals. *(Chapter 6)*

Orientation   The initial development of new employees to make them "job-ready." *(Chapter 15)*

Organizational chart   A map of the organization's structure that defines authority, responsibility, and accountability for work through diagramming positions, departments, functions, and their relationships. Units of the organization are indicated and connected to each other by solid lines, which indicate the chain of command, and broken lines, which indicate a supportive but non–decision-making relationship. *(Chapter 9)*

Organizational structure   A framework that divides work within an organization and delineates points of authority, responsibility, accountability and non–decision-making support. *(Chapter 9)*

Organizational conflict   Conflict that occurs when a person confronts an organization's policies and procedures for patient care and personnel and its accepted norms of behavior and communication. *(Chapter 17)*

Organizational message   Implicit messages communicated by the organization's formal structure that convey the nurse's clinical authority to those in the work group (e.g., a work group's formal organization determines the different levels of authority of the team leader and the primary nurse). *(Chapter 16)*

Organized delivery system   Networks of healthcare organizations, providers, and payers who provide a comprehensive package of healthcare services at a competitive price. *(Chapter 13)*

Outcome criteria   See *expected outcomes*. *(Chapter 2)*

Partnership model   A system of providing patient care when an RN is paired with an LPN or an unlicensed assistive person to provide total care to a few patients. *(Chapter 21)*

Paternalism   Principle that allows one to make decisions for another; often called parentalism. *(Chapter 3)*

Patient care associate   Non-licensed healthcare worker who assists in the care of patients and/or tasks of the work unit. *(Chapter 20)*

Patient care standard   The hours of patient care per patient day. *(Chapter 22)* Also the criteria statements related to quality of patient care.

Patient classification system   A method of quantitatively estimating and assessing patient needs in relation to nursing care. *(Chapter 22)*

Patient day   One patient occupying a bed for one day. *(Chapter 22)*

Patient outcomes   See *expected outcomes*. *(Chapter 21)*

Patterns of   Varying responses of individuals and groups to acceptance
behavior   of change or innovation. *(Chapter 5)*

Payer mix   The volume and type of reimbursement sources for a
                       healthcare provider. *(Chapter 13)*

Payers   Sources of healthcare financing or payment for health ser-
                       vices; includes government, private insurance, and individ-
                       uals (self-pay). *(Chapter 13)*

Peer review   A process whereby a group of practicing nurses evaluates
                       the quality of another's performance. *(Chapter 4)*

Percentage of   The patient census divided by the number of beds actually
occupancy   occupied. *(Chapter 22)*

Perfectionism   The tendency to never finish anything because it isn't
                       quite perfect. *(Chapter 11)*

Performance   A method by which employees are evaluated for their per-
appraisal   formance, based on a specific position description and fur-
                       ther defined by specific standards of practice. *(Chapter 18)*

Personal liability Serves to make each person responsible at law for his/her
                       own actions. *(Chapter 3)*

Personal motives   Those intangible driving factors that direct and initiate be-
                       haviors, consistent with each person's values and beliefs
                       and through which the meaning and purpose of personal
                       and professional life dimensions are enriched. *(Chapter 1)*

Philosophy   A statement of beliefs and values concerning the con-
                       sumer for whom services are provided, that nature of the
                       work being carried out, and the workers performing the
                       work. *(Chapter 9)*

Physiologic   Computer systems used to measure heart rate, blood pres-
monitoring   sure, and other vital signs through the use of arrhythmia
systems   monitors, pressure transducers, and oxygen and carbon
                       dioxide analyzers. *(Chapter 12)*

Plaintiff   Party bringing a civil lawsuit seeking damages or other re-
                       lief; usually synonymous with the injured patient or
                       his/her representative. *(Chapter 3)*

Point-of-service   An interconnected or free-standing unit that provides a
                       specific healthcare service such as home care, rehabilita-
                       tion care, emergency care, etc. *(Chapter 7)*

Polarities	Situations involving two interdependent opposites between which a shifting of emphasis naturally occurs. *(Chapter 17)*
Politics	A process of human interaction within organizations. *(Chapter 24)*
Position description	A general overall description of the duties and responsibilities of the employee. *(Chapter 18)*
Positive behaviors	Desired actions; positive behaviors clearly convey their own importance and often concern specific skills and how to execute them. *(Chapter 16)*
Power	The ability to influence others in the effort to achieve goals. *(Chapter 24)*
Preceptor	An experienced staff member who is paired with a less experienced preceptee in order to share expertise and serve as a role model. *(Chapter 15)*
Price	The rate that healthcare providers set to charge for their services and products. *(Chapter 13)*
Primary care	Points of entry into the healthcare system, such as health maintenance, health promotion, and disease prevention activities. *(Chapter 7)*
Primary nurse	A nurse responsible for 24 hours a day total patient care from admission to and through discharge. *(Chapter 21)*
Primary nursing	A method of patient care delivery where one RN functions autonomously as the patient's main nurse throughout the hospital stay. *(Chapter 21)*
Privacy	The right to protection against unreasonable and unwarranted interference with one's solitude; the right of an individual to be left alone. *(Chapter 3)*
Private	Owned and operated by an individual citizen or group of citizens. *(Chapter 7)*
Proactive	Acting on one's own behalf (rather than being *reactive*—acting in response to external events, forces, or people). *(Chapter 11)*
Problem solving	Utilizing a systematic process to solve a problem. *(Chapter 6)*
Procrastination	The tendency to put off to another time something that is important. *(Chapter 11)*

Product line   Referred to also as service line where a manager is ac-
                         countable for efficiency and productivity. *(Chapter 4)*

Productive hours   Paid time that is worked. *(Chapter 13)*

Productive time   Time an employee actually works. *(Chapter 22)*

Professional   An alliance of practitioners within a profession that pro-
association   vides opportunities for its members to meet leaders in the
                         field, hone their own leadership skills, participate in policy
                         formation, continue specialized education, and shape the
                         future of the profession. *(Chapter 26)*

Profit   An excess of revenues over expenses. *(Chapter 13)*

Program   Organizational structure whereby care is organized ac-
management   cording to patient needs. Each program is separate for pa-
                         tient planning, budgeting, and service delivery.
                         (Chapter 4)

Progressive   A step-by-step process of increasing disciplinary measures,
discipline   usually beginning with an oral warning, followed by a
                         written warning, suspension, and termination, if necessary.
                         (Chapter 19)

Prospective   A method of payment where the third-party payer decides
reimbursement   in advance the flat rate that will be paid for a service or
                         episode of care. *(Chapter 13)*

Prototype   A patient classification system that is subjective and uses
evaluation   broad categories to describe patients and their care
                         requirements. *(Chapter 22)*

Providers   Individuals or organizations that dispense healthcare to
                         people. *(Chapter 13)*

Public   Supported by government organization funds and oper-
                         ated by the government for the purposes of providing
                         services to a specifically designated segment of the popula-
                         tion or a specific service to the public. *(Chapter 7)*

Quality   Periodic evaluation of healthcare services by examining
assurance (QA)   factors such as policies, procedures, job descriptions, client
                         care, and client outcomes. The evaluation is conducted af-
                         ter the completion of services and compared to accepted
                         standards to identify problems/errors. *(Chapter 10)*

Quality control   On-going process of monitoring completed products and
                         services to detect and correct deviations. Processes and
                         products are compared to previously established norms
                         and specifications. *(Chapter 10)*

Quality improvement (QI)	Multidisciplinary planning/problem-solving process that uses a systematic approach. Analysis and evaluation of services to prevent errors and achieve customer satisfaction. *(Chapter 10)*
Quality management (QM)	Management philosophy similar to TQM but with the belief that *total* quality is never achieved. Focus on quality is built into the product or service from the initial planning stage through the implementation phase. Emphasizes teamwork, customer satisfaction, and avoiding errors. *(Chapter 10)*
Recency effect	See *halo effect. (Chapter 18)*
Reengineering	The radical redesign of a company's processes, organization, and culture with a focus on process orientation and a rethinking of end-to-end activities that create value for customers and an abandoning of the most basic notions on which organizations have been founded, the division of labor, the need for elaborate controls, and the managerial hierarchy. *(Chapter 9)*
Regional healthcare alliance	An organization, either a private or government agency, that enrolls all eligible persons in a specific geographic area into a health plan with which it has negotiated to provide a comprehensive benefit package. *(Chapter 7)*
Reintegration	A concept that focuses on a return to the whole of nursing, incorporating all aspects of the professional nurse's role: education, scholarship, practice, and service. *(Chapter 26)*
Reporting statutes	Laws that mandate healthcare providers or their employees to give certain information to the proper state or federal agencies. *(Chapter 3)*
Respect for others	The highest ethical principle, respect for others acknowledges the right of individuals to make decisions and to live by those decisions. *(Chapter 3)*
Respondeat superior	A doctrine by which the employer is given accountability and responsibility for an employee's negligent actions incurred during the course and scope of employment. *(Chapter 3)*
Résumé	A summary of professional abilities and facts designed for specific opportunities. *(Chapter 26)*
Revenue	Money earned by an organization for providing goods or services. *(Chapter 13)*

Risk management	Process of developing and implementing strategies that will minimize the adverse effects of accidental losses on an organization. This includes preventing client injury, minimizing financial loss after a problem/error occurs, and preserving agency reputation. *(Chapter 10)*
Role	A function performed within a particular organization or process. *(Chapter 2)*
Role ambiguity	Lack of clarity or definition in the expectations regarding a specific role. *(Chapter 18)*
Role conflict	Lack of congruence between employee expectations/evaluations and those of the organization/management. *(Chapter 18)*
Role development	The choice to change either one's role expectations or role performance, or both. *(Chapter 23)*
Role discrepancy	The gap between a person's role expectations and actual role performance, often a source of discomfort and frustration. *(Chapter 23)*
Role internalization	The stage at which a person has learned the behaviors that maintain the role so thoroughly that the person performs them without consciously considering them; energy once spent on establishing these behaviors can now be redirected toward other goals. *(Chapter 23)*
Role negotiation	Resolving conflicting expectations about personal management performance through communication. *(Chapter 23)*
Role strain	A subjective condition that may be manifested by increased frustration, heightened emotional awareness, or emotional fragility to situations. *(Chapter 19)*
Role stress	A situation in which the employee may feel that obligations are unclear, difficult, or conflicting. *(Chapter 19)*
Role theory	A framework used to understand how individuals perform within organizations. *(Chapter 18)*
Role transition	The process of unlearning an old role and learning a new role. Transforming one's identity from being an individual contributor as a staff nurse to being a leader as a nurse manager. *(Chapter 23)*
Rules of order	A meeting management strategy (typically *Roberts' Rules of Order*) in which a set of rules is used to help the meeting's chairperson set limits on discussion and follow a specific order of priorities to deal with concerns. *(Chapter 11)*

Satisficing decision	Selecting an option that is acceptable, but not necessarily the best option. (*satisfy* + *suffice* = "satisfice") *(Chapter 6)*
Scope of practice	Refers to legally permissible boundaries of practice for a health professional; the allowable boundaries are defined by statute, rule, or a combination of statute and rule. *(Chapter 3)*
Secondary care	A point of service of the healthcare system that is focused on providing services that prevent complications of disease conditions (such as an acute care facility). *(Chapter 7)*
Service	Multidimensional concept that places a premium on the design, development, and delivery of consumer-focused needs. *(Chapter 20)*
Service lines	Grouping of related types of services into one functional management unit. *(Chapter 20)*
Shared governance	Empowerment of staff in regard to accountability, direction, and self-determination (Perry and Code, 1991, p. 27). *(Chapter 4)* Also, a system that places responsibility for patient care with the caregiver. Structure is constructed from the center of the work rather than from the hierarchical periphery. Authority is based in functional processes of patient care, education, quality, and peer governance, which guide organizational design. Designs range from centralized committees to interactive planning models. Synonyms—self-governance, professional practice models. *(Chapter 9)*
Situational theory	A leadership approach based on the leader's self-understanding, understanding of the group affected by the situation, and comprehension of the situation itself. This approach to leadership suggests that no one leadership style is appropriate to all circumstances faced by the leader in a changing environment. *(Chapter 1)*
Smart card	Credit-card–like devices that contain the equivalent of eight pages of health history data. *(Chapter 12)*
Socialization	An opportunity to "learn the culture" of an organization and create an effective team. *(Chapter 15)*
Staff mix	A combination of RNs, LPNs, and unlicensed personnel providing care to a group of patients. *(Chapter 21)*
Staffing matrix/pattern	A plan that outlines the number of individuals and job classification needed by unit, per shift, per day. *(Chapter 22)*

Staffing regulations	The minimum number of professional nurses required on a unit at a given time. *(Chapter 22)*
Stand-alone systems	Computer systems that are internal to the department and automate the functions of the department. *(Chapter 12)*
Standard of care	Level or degree of quality considered adequate by a given profession; skills and learning commonly possessed by members of a profession; also written at minimum level. *(Chapter 3)*
Statutes	Rules and regulations created by elected legislative bodies; also known as statutory laws. *(Chapter 3)*
Strategic planning	A process designed to achieve goals in dynamic, competitive environments through the allocation of resources (Andrews, 1990, p. 103). *(Chapter 4)*
Strategy	A specific method or approach designed to achieve a specific purpose. *(Chapter 5)*
Stress	Demand on an individual that taxes or exceeds the person's ability to meet it. *(Chapter 25)*
Subculture	A group with distinct, discernible, and consistent cultural traits existing within and participating in a larger cultural grouping (Simons et al., 1993). *(Chapter 8)*
Synergy	A phenomenon in which teamwork produces extraordinary results that could not have been achieved by any one individual. *(Chapter 14)*
Teaching institutions	Academic health centers that provide education programs for preparing healthcare professionals or an affiliated agency that provides a clinical portion of the educational program. *(Chapter 7)*
Team	A group of highly interdependent people who have defined goals, objectives, and ongoing relationships and who are geared toward the achievement of a goal or task. *(Chapter 14)*
Team nursing	A method of nursing in which a leader is responsible for coordinating a small group of licensed and unlicensed personnel to provide care to a small group of patients. *(Chapter 21)*
Technological messages	Messages communicated via telephones, fax machines, computers, and other electronic devices; their effectiveness is influenced by factors such as timeliness, organization, and correct spelling and grammar. *(Chapter 16)*

Technology	A method, process, or system for providing services. *(Chapter 9)* Also, a scientific method of achieving a practical purpose. *(Chapter 12)*
Teleological theory	From the Greek for "end," derived norms or rules for conduct based upon the consequences of one's actions; often referred to as utilitarianism. *(Chapter 3)*
Tertiary care	A point of service of the healthcare system that is focused on rehabilitation and long-term care. *(Chapter 7)*
Testimony	The statements of a witness given under oath. *(Chapter 3)*
Theory X	A set of propositions that describes the management role as directing, motivating, and modifying workers' behavior based on the premise that all workers are passive in their desire to achieve organizational success over their own personal needs. *(Chapter 1)*
Theory Y	A set of propositions that describes the management role as enabling, supporting, and fostering workers in an environment where workers willingly contribute to organizational success and therefore enhance their own self-worth and personal goals. *(Chapter 1)*
Therapeutic systems	Computer systems used for such activities as to regulate intake based on output, regulate breathing, and assist with the care of the newborn. *(Chapter 12)*
Third-party payers	Private and public agencies that contract to pay under defined conditions for specified health services based on payment of specific sums of money and/or the fulfillment of specified conditions such as earnings at or below a specified income level in the case of medicaid. *(Chapter 7)*
Time log	A time management tool consisting of a grid on which work-related activities and the amount of time spent on each are recorded for a given time period (e.g., a week); analysis of the time log helps in estimating time required for particular activities. *(Chapter 11)*
Time management	Personal and professional management tools and strategies used to assure that investment in activities leads toward achievement of priority goals. *(Chapter 11)*
Total patient care	See *case method*. *(Chapter 21)*

Total quality management (TQM)	An organizational philosophy that ascribes to and supports continuous customer/client satisfaction. *(Chapter 2)* Also, a philosophy similar to quality management but emphasizes involvement from the total organization to strive to prevent all errors from occurring. Focuses on teamwork building, obtaining customer satisfaction, and planning to prevent errors. *(Chapter 10)*
TQM	See *total quality management (TQM)*.
Trait	A characteristic, quality, or attribute. *(Chapter 2)*
Transculturalism	Being grounded in one's own culture but having the culture-general and culture-specific skills to be able to live, interact, and work effectively in a multicultural environment (Simons et al., 1993). *(Chapter 8)*
Transformational leadership	A type of leadership that encourages subordinates to mesh their own interests into group interests for goal attainment. *(Chapter 2)*
Triangulation	Process of utilizing multiple data sources and data collection techniques to obtain information about a problem/solution. Includes qualitative as well as quantitative data. *(Chapter 10)*
Unit-based managed care	A method of organizing and delivering patient care with cost saving outcomes. *(Chapter 21)*
Unit of service	A measure of the work being produced by the organization, such as patient days, patient or home visits, procedures, etc. *(Chapter 13)*
Unlicensed assistive personnel	Healthcare workers who are not licensed and who are prepared to provide certain elements of care under the supervision of a registered nurse (e.g., technicians, nurse aides, or certified nursing assistants). *(Chapters 11 and 21)*
Values	The beliefs that are used when an individual is faced with decision making and that dominate over other values when conflict occurs. *(Chapter 1)* Also, personal beliefs about the truths and worth of thoughts, objects, or behaviors; motives and attitudes and the relationship of these motives and attitudes to the good of the individual. *(Chapter 3)*
Variable costs	Costs that vary in direct proportion to patient volume and acuity. *(Chapter 13)*

Variance The difference between the projected budget and the actual performance. *(Chapter 13)* Also, a component of a care MAP where patient deviation from expected outcomes are documented. *(Chapter 21)*

Variance analysis Process of identifying a variance and determining its cause. *(Chapter 13)*

Veracity Truth-telling. *(Chapter 3)*

Vicarious liability Imputation of accountability upon one person or entity for the actions of another person; substituted liability or imputed liability. *(Chapter 3)*

Voice technology The ability to control a computer system through voice input by the user. *(Chapter 12)*

REFERENCES

American Nurses Credentialing Center (ANCC). (1991). *Manual for Accreditation as a Provider of Continuing Education in Nursing.* Kansas City, MO: ANCC.

Andrews, M. (1990). Strategic planning: Preparing for the twenty-first century. *Journal of Professional Nursing, 6*(2), 103–112.

Harvey, J. (1990). Integrating marketing into health care organizations. In Dienemann, J. *Nursing Administration: Strategic Perspectives and Applications.* Norwalk, CT: Appleton & Lange.

Johnson, D.W., & Johnson, F.P. (1994). *Joining Together: Group Theory and Group Skills,* 5th ed. Englewood Cliffs, NJ: Prentice-Hall.

Kozier, B., Erb, G., & Blais, K. (1992). *Concepts and Issues in Nursing Practice.* New York: Addison-Wesley Nursing.

Mintzberg, H. (1975). The manager's job: Folklore and fact. *Harvard Business Review, 53*(4), 49–61.

Perry, F., & Code, S. (1991). Shared governance: A Canadian experience. *Canadian Journal of Nursing Administration, 4*(2), 27–28, 30.

Schutzenhofer, K.K., Shelley, S.R., & Pontious, S.L. (1992). Communication systems. In Decker, P.J., & Sullivan, E.J., eds. *Nursing Administration: A Micro/Macro Approach for Effective Nurse Executives.* Norwalk, CT: Appleton & Lange, pp. 185–206.

Simons, G., Vazquez, C., & Harris, P.R. (1993). *Transcultural Leadership: Empowering the Diverse Workforce.* Houston, TX: Gulf Publishing.

Wilson, S. (1992). Market research techniques. A synopsis for CE providers. *Journal of Continuing Education in Nursing, 23*(4), 182–183.

INDEX

PHOTO CREDITS*

Cover photos, Patrick Watson, photographer.
Chapter 1 [internal], p. 5, © Patrick Watson, photographer.
Chapter 7 [opener], p. 130 (top), © Patrick Watson, photographer; [opener] p. 130 (bottom), courtesy of Gretchen Halstead, The Baptist Home, Rhinebeck, NY; [internal] p. 137, © Patrick Watson, photographer.
Chapter 8 [opener], p. 150, © Patrick Watson, photographer.
Chapter 10 [internal], p. 194, © Patrick Watson, photographer.
Chapter 12 [opener], p. 226, courtesy of Corometrics Medical Systems, Wallingford, CT.
Chapter 14 [internal], p. 286, © 1994, Linda Bartlett.
Chapter 16 [internal], p. 324, © Patrick Watson, photographer.
Chapter 20 [internal], p. 404, © Jim Flanigan 1994 for MEDSURG Nursing (R) at U. of Pa.
Chapter 22 [internal], p. 442, Patrick Watson, photographer (from *Whaley & Wong's Essentials of Pediatric Nursing,* ed. 4, 1994, The C.V. Mosby Company).
Chapter 25 [internal], p. 507, © Patrick Watson, photographer.

*All other photos not listed specifically above are courtesy of Patrick Watson, photographer.